A HISTORY OF
ENGLISH VERSIFICATION

BY

JAKOB SCHIPPER, Ph.D.

PROFESSOR OF ENGLISH PHILOLOGY IN THE UNIVERSITY OF VIENNA
MEMBER OF THE KAISERLICHE AKADEMIE DER WISSENSCHAFTEN, VIENNA
HON. D.LITT. OXON. ; HON. LITT.D. CANTAB.
HON. I.L.D. EDINBURGH AND ABERDEEN
HONORARY MEMBER OF THE MODERN LANGUAGE ASSOCIATION OF AMERICA

OXFORD
AT THE CLARENDON PRESS
1910

HENRY FROWDE, M.A.
PUBLISHER TO THE UNIVERSITY OF OXFORD
LONDON, EDINBURGH, NEW YORK
TORONTO AND MELBOURNE

PRINTED IN ENGLAND.

PREFACE

It is now more than twenty years since a reviewer of the author's *Englische Metrik*, in three volumes, expressed the opinion that 'an English translation of it would do a service to English philology'. At that time, however, it seemed doubtful whether such a voluminous work, which probably would have interested only a comparatively small circle of English scholars, would have found a market. Even in Germany, although the work was favourably reviewed, and although at the time when it appeared great interest was felt in metrical research, the sale was comparatively slow.

Much livelier, on the other hand, was the demand for an abridged edition of it which appeared under the title *Grundriss der englischen Metrik* (Wien, 1895). It was therefore found possible, several years after its publication, to make arrangements with the Delegates of the Clarendon Press for an English edition of this smaller book. Unfortunately, however, the printing of the manuscript, which was submitted to the supervision of the late Professor York Powell, was delayed, first by the illness and the untimely death of that eminent scholar, and afterwards by other circumstances which it is not necessary to mention here.

On the whole the English text of the present volume is a close rendering of the German book, except in the first few chapters, which have been somewhat more fully worked out.   It may also be mentioned that one or two modern English poets who seemed to be unduly neglected in the German book have received a larger share of attention in the English edition.   Some errors of the original work have, of course, also been corrected here.

The treatment of the subject in this handbook is the same as in the author's larger work.   The systematic arrangement of the different kinds of verse in Book I, and of the varieties of stanzas in Book II, will enable the reader easily to find the appropriate place for any new forms of verse or stanza that may come in his way, and will also facilitate the use of the large German work, to which frequent references are given, for the benefit of those students who may desire more detailed information.

From the Preface to the German edition of the present work some remarks on the accents, chiefly in Part II of Book I, may be repeated here in order to prevent misunderstanding.

These accents on particular syllables in equal-measured rhythms are merely meant to facilitate the scansion of the verse according to the author's view of its rhythmical movement, and to enable the student to apprehend more readily the precise meaning of the descriptions.   They are by no means intended to dictate a schematic scansion to the reader, as it is obvious that the finer shades of the rhythm cannot be indicated by such a mode of accentuation.   The safer and easier way undoubtedly would have been to put no accents at all; but this would have been less convenient for the reader, to whose own judgement it may be left in every case to be guided by the accents just so far as he may think proper.

In making this statement, however, I may be allowed to mention that none of the English friends who kindly assisted me in revising my manuscript has found fault with my system of accentuation.

My sincerest thanks for their kind help and advice are due to Dr. Francis J. Curtis, now Professor of English Philology in the Mercantile Academy at Frankfort on the Main, and in a still higher degree to Dr. James Morison, of Shotover Cottage, Headington Quarry, Oxford, Examiner in Sanskrit and German, both of them formerly Lectors of English in the University of Vienna. I am under equally great obligations to Dr. Henry Bradley, to whose care the final revision of the MS. was entrusted by the Delegates of the Clarendon Press, and who also had the great kindness to superintend the printing of it. To him I am indebted for several useful suggestions regarding the typographical arrangement, and still more for his valuable help in regard to the style of the book. To the Delegates and the Secretary of the Clarendon Press I feel greatly obliged not only for undertaking the publication, but also for the patient consideration they have shown me during the slow progress of this work.

J. SCHIPPER.

VIENNA, *Feb.* 6, 1910.

CONTENTS

BOOK I.   THE LINE

PART I.   THE NATIVE METRE

CHAPTER I

GENERAL INTRODUCTION TO THE SCIENCE OF METRE
AND THE STRUCTURE OF VERSE

		PAGE
§ 1.	Uses of the study of English metre	1
2.	Object of the science of metre	1
3.	Definition of rhythm	2
4.	Distinction between prose and poetry	3
5.	Phonetic qualities of syllables	4
6.	Definition and use of the word *accent*	4
7.	Classification of accent	5
8.	Marks indicating position of accent	8
9.	Principles of versification and their terms	9
10.	Rhyme; its twofold purpose	11
11.	End-rhyme, or full-rhyme	12
12.	Vocalic assonance	12
13.	Alliteration	13

CHAPTER II

THE ALLITERATIVE VERSE IN OLD ENGLISH

		PAGE
§ 14.	General remarks	15
15.	Theories on the metrical form of the alliterative line . .	15
16.	The four-beat theory	16
17.	The two-beat theory	19
18.	Accentuation of Old English	24
19.	The secondary accent	28
20.	Division and metrical value of syllables	29
21.	Structure of the whole alliterative line	30
22.	The structure of the hemistich in the normal alliterative line .	31
23.	Number of unaccented syllables of the thesis . . .	33
24.	Order of the verse-members in the hemistich . . .	35

ANALYSIS OF THE VERSE TYPES.

I. *Hemistichs of four members.*

		PAGE
25.	Type A, with sub-types A 1–3	36
26.	Type B, with sub-types B 1, 2	41

CONTENTS

§ 27. Type C, with sub-types C 1-3 42
28. Type D, with sub-types D 1-4 42
29. Type E, with sub-types E 1, 2 43

II. *Hemistichs of five members.*

30. Type A*, with sub-types A* 1, 2; Type B*; Type C*; Type D*,
   with sub-types D* 1-3 44
31. Principles adopted in classification 45
32. Combination of hemistichs by means of alliteration . . . 45

PRINCIPLES OF ALLITERATION.

33. Quality of the alliteration 46
34. Position of the alliterative words 48
35. Alliteration in relation to the parts of speech and to the order
   of words 50
36. Arrangement and relationship of verse and sentence . . . 54

THE LENGTHENED VERSE.

37. The lengthened line; alliteration 55
38. The origin and structure of the lengthened verse . . . 57
39. Examples of commonly occurring forms of the lengthened
   hemistich 59

FORMATION OF STANZAS AND RHYME.

40. Classification and examples 62

CHAPTER III

THE FURTHER DEVELOPMENT OF THE FREER FORM OF THE ALLITERATIVE LINE IN LATE OLD ENGLISH AND EARLY MIDDLE ENGLISH

A. TRANSITIONAL FORMS.

§ 41. Increasing frequency of rhyme 64
42. Combination of alliteration and rhyme 65

B. THE 'PROVERBS OF ALFRED' AND LAYAMON'S 'BRUT'.

43. Development of the progressive form of the alliterative line . 67
44. Nature and origin of the four-beat short-lined metre . . 69
45. Number of stresses 72
46. Analysis of verse-types 74
47. Extended types 75
48. Verse-forms rhythmically equivalent 78

C. THE PROGRESSIVE FORM OF THE ALLITERATIVE LINE, RHYMED THROUGHOUT. 'KING HORN.'

49. Further development of the Layamon-verse 79
50. The metre of *King Horn* and its affinity to the alliterative line 82
51. Characteristics of *King Horn* and Layamon compared . . 84

CONTENTS

CHAPTER IV

THE ALLITERATIVE LINE IN ITS CONSERVATIVE FORM DURING THE FOURTEENTH AND FIFTEENTH CENTURIES

A. THE ALLITERATIVE VERSE WITHOUT RHYME.

§ 52. Homilies and lives of the saints in rhythmical prose. Poems in regular alliterative verse 85
53. Use and treatment of words in alliterative verse . . . 87
54. Examples of alliteration 88
55. Comparison of Middle and Old English alliterative verse . 90
56. The versification of *Piers Plowman* 93
57. Modification of forms in the North of England and in the Midlands 95

B. THE ALLITERATIVE LINE COMBINED WITH RHYME.

58. Growing influence of verse formed on foreign models . . 97
59. Lyrical stanzas: four-beat and two-beat lines . . . 97
60. Forms of structure and versification 99
61. Narrative verse 101
62. Relation between rhyme and alliteration 102
63. Features of alliterative-rhyming lines 105
64. Structures of the *cauda* 105
65. Two-beat lines in tail-rhyme stanzas 106
66. Rhyming alliterative lines in Mystery Plays 108
67. Alliteration in Moralities and Interludes 109
68. Four-beat scansion of Bale's verses 110
69. Examples of the presence or absence of anacrusis in the two hemistichs 110
70. Entire tail-rhyme stanzas 113
71. Irregular tail-rhyme stanzas: Skeltonic verse 114

C. REVIVAL OF THE FOUR-BEAT ALLITERATIVE VERSE IN THE MODERN ENGLISH PERIOD.

72. Examples from Gascoigne, Wyatt, Spenser, &c. . . . 117
73. Attempted modern revival of the old four-beat alliterative line without rhyme 119
74. Examples of the development of the four-beat alliterative line in reversed chronological order 120
75. Summing-up of the evidence 124

PART II. FOREIGN METRES

DIVISION I. THE FOREIGN METRES IN GENERAL

CHAPTER V

INTRODUCTION

§ 76. Influence of French and Low Latin metres 126
77. The different kinds of line 127
78. The breaking up of long lines 128

§ 79. Heroic verse; tail-rhyme staves 131
80. Different kinds of caesura 131
81. Causes of variation in the structure of metres of equal measures 133

CHAPTER VI

VERSE-RHYTHM

§ 82. Lines with and without diaeresis 135
83. Effect of diaeresis on modulation 136
84. Suppression of the anacrusis 137
85. Level stress, or 'hovering accent' 138
86. Absence of thesis in the interior of a line 139
87. Lengthening of a word by introduction of unaccented extra
    syllable 141
88. Inversion of rhythm 141
89. Disyllabic or polysyllabic thesis 143
90. Epic caesura 145
91. Double or feminine endings 146
92. Enjambement, or run-on line 147
93. Rhyme-breaking 148
94. Alliteration 149

CHAPTER VII

THE METRICAL TREATMENT OF SYLLABLES

§ 95. General remarks on formative and inflexional syllables . . 151
96. Treatment of the unaccented e of words of three and four
    syllables in Middle English 152
97. Special remarks on individual inflexional endings . . . 154
98. Treatment of -en in Middle and Modern English . . . 155
99. The comparative and superlative endings -er, -est . . . 156
100. The ending -est 157
101. The endings -eth, -es ('s) 158
102. The ending -ed ('d, t) 158
103. The ending -ed (-od, -ud) of the 1st and 3rd pers. sing. pret. and
     plur. pret. of weak verbs 159
104. The final -e in Middle English poetry 160
105. Examples of the arbitrary use of final -e 161
106. The final -e in later poetry of the North 162
107. Formative endings of Romanic origin 163
108. Contraction of words ordinarily pronounced in full . . . 165
109. Amalgamation of two syllables for metrical purposes . . 166
110. Examples of slurring or contraction 167
111. Other examples of contraction; apocopation . . . 168
112. Lengthening of words for metrical purposes 169

CHAPTER VIII
WORD-ACCENT

§113. General remarks 171

I. WORD-ACCENT IN MIDDLE ENGLISH.
A. Germanic words.

114. Alleged difference in degree of stress among inflexional endings containing *e* 172
115. Accent in trisyllables and compounds 174
116. Pronunciation of parathetic compounds 175
117. Rhythmical treatment of trisyllables and words of four syllables 175

B. Romanic words.

118. Disyllabic words 177
119. Trisyllabic words 178
120. Words of four and five syllables 179

II. WORD-ACCENT IN MODERN ENGLISH.

121. Romanic accentuation still continued 180
122. Disyllabic words 181
123. Trisyllabic and polysyllabic words 181
124. Parathetic compounds 182

DIVISION II. VERSE-FORMS COMMON TO THE MIDDLE AND
MODERN ENGLISH PERIODS

CHAPTER IX

LINES OF EIGHT FEET, FOUR FEET, TWO FEET, AND ONE FOOT

§125. The eight-foot line and its resolution into four-foot lines . 183
126. Examples of the four-foot line 183
127. Treatment of the caesura in four-foot verse . . . 185
128. Treatment of four-foot verse in North English and Scottish
  writings 186
129. Its treatment in the Midlands and the South . . . 187
130. Combinations of four-foot and three-foot verse in Middle English 188
131-2. Freer variety of this metre in Modern English . . 188
133. Two-foot verse 190
134. One-foot verse 191

CHAPTER X

THE SEPTENARY, THE ALEXANDRINE, AND THE THREE-FOOT LINE

§135. The septenary 192
136. Irregularity of structure of the septenary rhyming line as shown
  in the *Moral Ode* 193
137. Regularity of the rhymeless septenary verse of the *Ormulum* . 193

CONTENTS

§138. The septenary with a masculine ending 194
139. The septenary as employed in early lyrical poems and ballads 195
140. Use of the septenary in Modern English 196
141-4. Intermixture of septenaries, alexandrines, and four-beat lines 197
145, 146. Origin of the 'Poulter's Measure' 202
147. The alexandrine: its first use 204
148. Structure of the alexandrine in Mysteries and Moral Plays . 205
149. The alexandrine in Modern English 205
150. The three-foot line 206

CHAPTER XI

THE RHYMED FIVE-FOOT VERSE

§151. Rhymed five-foot verse in Middle English 209
152. Sixteen types of five-foot verse 210
153. Earliest specimens of this metre 212
154. Chaucer's five-foot verse; treatment of the caesura . . 213
155. Masculine and feminine endings; rhythmic licences . . 214
156. Gower's five-foot verse; its decline. 215
157. Rhymed five-foot verse in Modern English . . . 216
158. Its use in narrative poetry and by Shakespeare . . 217
159. The heroic verse of Dryden, Pope, and later writers . . 218

DIVISION III. VERSE-FORMS OCCURRING IN MODERN ENGLISH POETRY ONLY

CHAPTER XII

BLANK VERSE

§160. The beginnings of Modern English poetry 219
161. Blank verse first adopted by the Earl of Surrey . . . 219
162. Characteristics of Surrey's blank verse 221
163. Further development of this metre in the drama . . . 222
164. The blank verse of Shakespeare 223
165. Rhymed and unrhymed lines in Shakespeare's plays . . 224
166. Numerical proportion of masculine and feminine endings . 225
167. Numerical proportion of 'weak' and 'light' endings . . 225
168. Proportion of unstopt or 'run-on' and 'end-stopt' lines . 226
169. Shakespeare's use of the full syllabic forms of -est, -es, -eth, -ed 227
170. Other rhythmical characteristics of Shakespeare's plays . . 228
171. Alexandrines and other metres occurring in combination with blank verse in Shakespeare 230
172. Example of the metrical differences between the earlier and later periods of Shakespeare's work 232
173. The blank verse of Ben Jonson 233
174. The blank verse of Fletcher 234
175. Characteristics of Beaumont's style and versification . . 235
176. The blank verse of Massinger 236
177. The blank verse of Milton 237
178. The dramatic blank verse of the Restoration . . . 239
179. Blank verse of the eighteenth century 240
180. Blank verse of the nineteenth century 240

CHAPTER XIII

TROCHAIC METRES

§181. General remarks ; the eight-foot trochaic line 242
182. The seven-foot trochaic line 243
183. The six-foot trochaic line 244
184. The five-foot trochaic line 245
185. The four-foot trochaic line 246
186. The three-foot trochaic line 246
187. The two-foot trochaic line 247
188. The one-foot trochaic line 247

CHAPTER XIV

IAMBIC-ANAPAESTIC AND TROCHAIC-DACTYLIC METRES

§189. General remarks 249

I. Iambic-anapaestic Metres.

190. Eight-foot iambic-anapaestic verse 250
191. Seven-foot iambic-anapaestic verse 250
192. Six-foot iambic-anapaestic verse 251
193. Five-foot iambic-anapaestic verse 251
194. Four-foot iambic-anapaestic verse 252
195. Three-foot iambic-anapaestic verse 253
196. Two-foot iambic-anapaestic verse 253
197. One-foot iambic-anapaestic verse 254

II. Trochaic-dactylic Metres.

198. Eight-foot trochaic-dactylic verse 254
199. Seven-foot trochaic-dactylic verse 255
200. Six-foot trochaic-dactylic verse 255
201. Five-foot trochaic-dactylic verse 256
202. Four-foot trochaic-dactylic verse 256
203. Three-foot trochaic-dactylic verse 257
204. Two-foot dactylic or trochaic-dactylic verse 257
205. One-foot dactylic verse 258

CHAPTER XV

NON-STROPHIC, ANISOMETRICAL COMBINATIONS OF RHYMED VERSE

§206. Varieties of this metre ; Poulter's measure 259
207-8. Other anisometrical combinations 260

CHAPTER XVI

IMITATIONS OF CLASSICAL FORMS OF VERSE AND STANZA

§209. The English hexameter 262
210. Structure of the hexameter 263

§211. Elegiac verse; the minor Asclepiad; the six-foot iambic line; Phaleuciac verse; Hendecasyllabics; rhymed Choriambics . 264
212. Classical stanzas:—the Sapphic metre; the Alcaic metre; Anacreontic stanzas 266
213. Other imitations of classical verses and stanzas without rhyme. 267

BOOK II
THE STRUCTURE OF STANZAS

PART I

CHAPTER I. DEFINITIONS

STANZA, RHYME, VARIETIES OF RHYME

§214. Structure of the stanza 270
215. Influence of lyrical forms of Provence and of Northern France on Middle English poetry 271
216. Classification of rhyme according to the number of the rhyming syllables : (1) the monosyllabic or masculine rhyme; (2) the disyllabic or feminine rhyme ; (3) the trisyllabic, triple, or tumbling rhyme 272
217. Classification according to the quality of the rhyming syllables : (1) the rich rhyme ; (2) the identical rhyme; (3) the broken rhyme ; (4) the double rhyme ; (5) the extended rhyme ; (6) the unaccented rhyme 273
218. Classification according to the position of the rhyming syllables : (1) the sectional rhyme; (2) the inverse rhyme; (3) the Leonine rhyme or middle rhyme ; (4) the interlaced rhyme ; (5) the intermittent rhyme; (6) the enclosing rhyme ; (7) the tail-rhyme 276
219. Imperfect or 'eye-rhymes' 278

CHAPTER II

THE RHYME AS A STRUCTURAL ELEMENT OF THE STANZA

§220. Formation of the stanza in Middle English and Romanic poetry 279
221. Rhyme-linking or 'concatenation' in Middle English . . 280
222. The refrain or burthen; the wheel and the bob-wheel . 280
223. Divisible and indivisible stanzas 281
224. Bipartite equal-membered stanzas 282
225. Bipartite unequal-membered stanzas 282
226. Tripartite stanzas 283
227. Specimens illustrating tripartition 284
228. The envoi 286
229. Real envois and concluding stanzas. 286

PART II. STANZAS COMMON TO MIDDLE AND MODERN ENGLISH, AND OTHERS FORMED ON THE ANALOGY OF THESE

CHAPTER III

BIPARTITE EQUAL-MEMBERED STANZAS

I. ISOMETRICAL STANZAS.

§230. Two-line stanzas 288
231. Four-line stanzas, consisting of couplets 288
232. The double stanza (eight lines of the same structure) . . 289
233. Stanzas of four isometrical lines with intermittent rhyme . . 290
234. Stanzas of eight lines resulting from this stanza by doubling . 290
235. Stanzas developed from long-lined couplets by inserted rhyme 291
236. Stanzas of eight lines resulting from the four-lined, cross-rhyming stanza and by other modes of doubling . . 292
237. Other examples of doubling four-lined stanzas . . . 293
238. Six-lined isometrical stanzas 294
239. Modifications of the six-lined stanza ; twelve-lined and sixteen-lined stanzas 295

II. ANISOMETRICAL STANZAS.

240. Chief species of the tail-rhyme stanza 296
241. Enlargement of this stanza to twelve lines . . . 297
242. Further development of the tail-rhyme stanza . . . 298
243. Variant forms of enlarged eight and ten-lined tail-rhyme stanzas 298
244. Tail-rhyme stanzas with principal verses shorter than tail-verses 299
245. Other varieties of the tail-rhyme stanza 300
246. Stanzas modelled on the tail-rhyme stanza . . . 300
247. Stanzas formed of two septenary verses 301
248. Analogical developments from this type 302
249. Eight-lined (doubled) forms of the different four-lined stanzas . 302
250. Other stanzas of similar structure 303

CHAPTER IV

ONE-RHYMED INDIVISIBLE AND BIPARTITE UNEQUAL-MEMBERED STANZAS

I. ONE-RHYMED AND INDIVISIBLE STANZAS.

§251. Three-lined stanzas of one rhyme 305
252. Four-lined stanzas of one rhyme 306
253. Other stanzas connected with the above 307

II. BIPARTITE UNEQUAL-MEMBERED ISOMETRICAL STANZAS.

254. Four-lined stanzas 308
255. Five-lined stanzas 308
256. Four-lined stanzas of one rhyme extended by the addition of a couplet 310

III. Bipartite Unequal-membered Anisometrical Stanzas.

§257-8. Four-lined stanzas; Poulter's measure and other stanzas . 311
  259. Five-lined stanzas 314
  260. Shortened tail-rhyme stanzas 316
  261. Six-lined stanzas 317
  262. Seven-lined stanzas 319
  263. Eight-, nine-, and ten-lined stanzas 320
  264. The bob-wheel stanzas in the Middle English period . 321
  265. Bob-wheel stanzas of four-stressed rhyming verses . . 322
  266. Modern English bob-wheel stanzas 323

CHAPTER V

TRIPARTITE STANZAS

I. Isometrical Stanzas.

§267. Six-lined stanzas 326
  268. Seven-lined stanzas; the Rhyme Royal stanza . . 327
  269. Eight-lined stanzas 329
  270. Nine-lined stanzas 330
  271. Ten-lined stanzas 331
  272. Eleven-, twelve-, and thirteen-lined stanzas . . . 332

II. Anisometrical Stanzas.

273-4. Six-lined stanzas 333
  275. Seven-lined stanzas 335
276-8. Eight-lined stanzas 337
  279. Nine-lined stanzas 339
280-1. Ten-lined stanzas 341
  282. Eleven-lined stanzas 343
  283. Twelve-lined stanzas 344
  284. Thirteen-lined stanzas 345
  285. Fourteen-lined stanzas 346
  286. Stanzas of fifteen to twenty lines 347

PART III. MODERN STANZAS AND METRES OF FIXED FORM ORIGINATING UNDER THE INFLUENCE OF THE RENASCENCE, OR INTRODUCED LATER

CHAPTER VI

STANZAS OF THREE AND MORE PARTS CONSISTING OF UNEQUAL PARTS ONLY

§287. Introductory remark . . . . . , . . 348
  288. Six-lined stanzas 349
  289. Seven-lined stanzas 351

§290-2. Eight-lined stanzas; the Italian *ottava rima* . . . 352
293. Nine-lined stanzas 355
294. Ten-lined stanzas 355
295. Eleven-lined stanzas 356
296. Twelve-lined stanzas 356

CHAPTER VII

THE SPENSERIAN STANZA AND THE FORMS DERIVED FROM IT

§297. First used in the *Faerie Queene* 358
298-300. Imitations and analogous forms 359

CHAPTER VIII

THE EPITHALAMIUM STANZA AND OTHER ODIC STANZAS

§301. The Epithalamium stanza 363
302. Imitations of the Epithalamium stanza 365
303-5. Pindaric Odes, regular and irregular 366

CHAPTER IX

THE SONNET

§306. Origin of the English sonnet 371
307. The Italian sonnet 371
308. Structure of the Italian form illustrated by Watts-Dunton . 373
309. The first English sonnet-writers, Surrey and Wyatt . . 373
310. Surrey's transformation of the Italian sonnet, and the form adopted by Shakespeare 374
311. Another form used by Spenser in *Amoretti* . . . 375
312. The form adopted by Milton 375
313. Revival of sonnet writing in the latter half of the eighteenth century 376
314. The sonnets of Wordsworth 377
315. The sonnet in the nineteenth century 379

CHAPTER X

OTHER ITALIAN AND FRENCH POETICAL FORMS OF A FIXED CHARACTER

316-7. The madrigal 380
318-9. The terza-rima 381
320-1. The sextain 383
322. The virelay 385
323. The roundel 385
324. The rondeau 387
325. The triolet 388
326. The villanelle 388
327. The ballade 389
328. The Chant Royal 390

LIST OF EDITIONS REFERRED TO

The quotations of Old English poetry are taken from Grein-Wülker, *Bibliothek der Angelsächsischen Poesie*, Strassburg, 1883-94. For the Middle English poets the editions used have been specified in the text. Most of the poets of the Modern English period down to the eighteenth century are quoted from the collection of R. Anderson, *The Works of the British Poets*, Edinburgh, 1795 (15 vols.), which is cited (under the title *Poets*) by volume and page. The remaining Modern English poets are quoted (except when some other edition is specified) from the editions mentioned in the following list.

Arnold, Matthew. *Poetical Works*. London, Macmillan & Co., 1890. 8vo.

Beaumont, Francis, and **Fletcher**, John. *Dramatick Works*. London, 1778. 10 vols. 8vo.

Bowles, W. L. *Sonnets and other Poems*. London, 1802-3. 2 vols. 8vo.

Browning, Elizabeth Barrett. *Poetical Works*. London, Chapman & Hall, 1866. 5 vols. 8vo.

Browning, Robert. *Poetical Works*. London, Smith, Elder & Co., 1868. 6 vols. 8vo.

Bulwer Lytton, Sir E. (afterwards Lord Lytton). *The Lost Tales of Miletus*. London, John Murray, 1866. 8vo.

Burns, Robert. *Complete Works*, ed. Alexander Smith. London, Macmillan & Co., 1870. (Globe Edition.)

Byron, Lord. *Poetical Works*. London, H. Frowde, 1896. 8vo. (Oxford Edition.)

Campbell, Thomas. *Poetical Works*, ed. W. A. Hill. London, G. Bell & Sons, 1875.

Coleridge, Samuel Taylor. *Poems*, ed. Derwent and Sara Coleridge. London, E. Moxon & Co., 1863.

Cowper, William. *Poetical Works*, ed. W. Benham. London, Macmillan & Co., 1870. (Globe Edition.)

Dryden, John. *Comedies, Tragedies, and Operas*. London, 1701. fol.

—— —— *Poetical Works*, ed. W. D. Christie. London, Macmillan & Co., 1870. (Globe Edition.)

Fletcher, John. See Beaumont.

Goldsmith, Oliver. *Miscellaneous Works,* ed. Prof. Masson. London, Macmillan & Co., 1871. 8vo. (Globe Edition.)

Gorboduc, or *Ferrex and Porrex, a Tragedy,* by Thomas Norton and Thomas Sackville, ed. L. Toulmin Smith. *(Englische Sprach- und Litteraturdenkmale des* 16., 17. *und* 18. *Jahrhunderts,* herausgegeben von K. Vollmöller, I.)   Heilbronn, Gebr. Henninger, 1883. 8vo.

Hemans, Felicia. *The Works of Mrs. Hemans, with a Memoir of her life by her sister.* Edinburgh, W. Blackwood & Sons, 1839. 7 vols.

Herbert, George. *Works,* ed. R. A. Willmott. London, G. Routledge & Co., 1854. 8vo.

Hood, Thomas. *Poetical Works,* ed. Thornton Hunt. London, Routledge, Warne, and Routledge, 1860. 8vo.

Hymns, Ancient and Modern, for Use in the Services of the Church. Revised and Enlarged Edition. London, n.d.

Jonson, Ben. Chiefly cited from the edition in *Poets* iv. 532–618 (see the note prefixed to this list) ; less frequently (after Wilke, *Metr. Unters. zu B. J.,* Halle, 1884) from the folio edition, London, 1816 (vol. i), or from the edition by Barry Cornwall, London, 1842. A few of the references are to the edition of F. Cunningham, London, J. C. Hotten, n.d. (3 vols.)

Keats, John. *Poetical Works.* London, F. Warne & Co. (Chandos Classics.)

Longfellow, Henry Wadsworth. *Poetical Works.* Edinburgh, W. P. Nimmo. 8vo. (Crown Edition.)

Lytton. See Bulwer Lytton.

Marlowe, Christopher. *Works,* ed. A. Dyce. London, 1850. 3 vols. 8vo.

—— — *Works,* ed. F. Cunningham. London, F. Warne & Co., 1870. 8vo.

Massinger, Philip. *Plays,* ed. F. Cunningham. London, F. Warne & Co., 1870. 8vo.

Milton, John. *Poetical Works,* ed. D. Masson. London, Macmillan & Co., 1874. 3 vols. 8vo.

—— — *English Poems,* ed. R. C. Browne. Second Edition. Oxford, Clarendon Press, 1872. 3 vols. 8vo.

Moore, Thomas. *Poetical Works.* London, Longmans, 1867. 8vo.

Morris, William. *Love is Enough.* Third Edition. London, Ellis & White, 1873. 8vo.

Norton, Thomas. See *Gorboduc.*

Percy, Thomas. *Reliques of Ancient Poetry.* London, H. Washbourne, 1847. 3 vols. 8vo.

Poe, Edgar Allan. *Poetical Works.* London, Sampson Low, Son & Co., 1858. 8vo.

Pope, Alexander. *Poetical Works,* ed. A. W. Ward. London, Macmillan & Co., 1870. 8vo. (Globe Edition.)

Rossetti, Dante Gabriel. *Poems.* London, F. S. Ellis, 1870.

Sackville, Thomas, and **Norton,** Thomas. See *Gorboduc.*

Scott, Sir Walter. *Poetical Works,* ed. F. T. Palgrave. London, Macmillan & Co., 1869. 8vo. (Globe Edition.)

Shakespeare, William. *Works,* ed. W. G. Clark and W. Aldis Wright. London and Cambridge, Macmillan & Co., 1866. 8vo. (Globe Edition.)

Shelley, Percy Bysshe. *Poetical Works.* London, Chatto & Windus, 1873-1875. 3 vols. 8vo. (Golden Library.)

Sidney, Sir Philip. *Arcadia.* London, 1633. fol.

—— — — *Complete Poems,* ed. A. B. Grosart. 1873. 2 vols.

Southey, Robert. *Poetical Works.* London, Longman, Orme, Brown, Green & Longmans, 1837. 10 vols. 8vo.

Spenser, Edmund. *Complete Works,* ed. R. Morris. London, Macmillan & Co., 1869. 8vo. (Globe Edition.)

Surrey, Henry Howard, Earl of. *Poems.* London, Bell & Daldy. 8vo. (Aldine Edition.)

Swinburne, Algernon Charles. *Poems and Ballads.* Third Edition. London, J. C. Hotten, 1868. 8vo.

—— — — *Poems and Ballads, Second Series.* Fourth Edition. London, Chatto & Windus, 1884. 8vo.

—— — — *A Century of Roundels.* London, Chatto & Windus, 1883. 8vo.

—— — — *A Midsummer Holiday and other Poems.* London, Chatto & Windus, 1884. 8vo.

Tennyson, Alfred. *Works.* London, Kegan Paul & Co., 1880. 8vo.

Thackeray, William Makepeace. *Ballads and The Rose and the Ring.* London, Smith, Elder & Co., 1879. 8vo.

Tusser, Thomas. *Fiue Hundred Pointes of Good Husbandrie,* ed. W. Payne and S. J. Herrtage, English Dialect Soc., 1878.

Wordsworth, William. *Poetical Works,* ed. W. Knight. Edinburgh, W. Paterson, 1886. 8 vols. 8vo.

Wyatt, Sir Thomas. *Poetical Works.* London, Bell & Daldy. (Aldine Edition.) The references marked N. are to vol. ii. of *The Works of Surrey and Wyatt,* ed. Nott, London, 1815. 2 vols. 4to.

ERRATA

P. 268. In the references to Bulwer, *for* p. 227 *read* p. 147; *for* p. 217 *read* p. 140; *for* p. 71 *read* p. 45; *for* p. 115 *read* p. 73.

P. 315, l. 14. *For* p. 123 *read* p. 78.

P. 340, l. 34. *For* p. 273 *read* p. 72.

P. 353, l. 15. *For* 89 *read* 5.

P. 381, l. 12. *For* ii. 137–40 *read Poetical Works*, London, 1891, pp. 330–32.

BOOK I. THE LINE

PART I. THE NATIVE METRE

CHAPTER I

GENERAL INTRODUCTION TO THE SCIENCE OF METRE AND THE STRUCTURE OF VERSE

§ 1. The study of English Metre is an integral part of English Philology. It is indispensable to the investigator of the history of the language, since it supplies sometimes the only (or at all events the surest) means of restoring the older pronunciation of word-stems, and of inflexional terminations. In many cases, indeed, the very existence of such terminations can be proved only by the ascertained requirements of metre. As an aid to the study of English literature in its aesthetic aspects the science of metre is no less important. It exhibits the gradual development of the artistic forms of poetical composition, explains the conditions under which they took their rise, and by formulating the laws of their structure affords valuable help in the textual criticism of poems which have been transmitted in a corrupt or imperfect condition.

§ 2. The object of the science of metre is to describe and analyse the various rhythmical forms of speech that are characteristic of poetry in contradistinction to prose.

Poetry is one of the fine arts, and the fine arts admit of a division into Plastic and Rhythmic ; the Plastic arts comprehending Sculpture, Architecture, and Painting, the Rhythmic arts, on the other hand, comprehending Dancing, Music, and Poetry. The chief points of difference between these classes are as follows. In the first place, the productions of the Plastic arts can be enjoyed by the beholder directly on their completion by the artist without the interposition of any help, while those of the Rhythmic arts demand, after the original creative artist has done his work, the services of a second or executive artist, who is usually termed the performer, in order that these productions may be fully enjoyed by the spectator or hearer. A piece of

B

music requires a singer or player, a pantomime a dancer, and poetry a reciter or actor. In early times the function of executive artist was commonly discharged by the creative artist himself. In the second place, the Plastic arts have no concern with the relations of time; a work of painting or sculpture presents to the beholder an unchanging object or represents a single moment of action. The Rhythmic arts, on the other hand, are, in their very essence, connected with temporal succession. Dancing implies a succession of movements of the human body, Music a succession of inarticulate sounds, Poetry a succession of articulate sounds or words and syllables. The Plastic arts, therefore, may be called the arts of space and rest, and the Rhythmic arts the arts of time and movement. In this definition, it must be remembered, the intrinsic quality of the movements in each of these rhythmical arts is left out of account; in the case of poetry, for instance, it does not take into consideration the choice and position of the words, nor the thought expressed by them; it is restricted to the external characteristic which these arts have in common.

§ 3. This common characteristic, however, requires to be defined somewhat more precisely. It is not merely succession of movements, but succession of different kinds of movement in a definite and recurring order. In the dance, the measure, or succession and alternation of quick and slow movements in regular and fixed order, is the essential point. This is also the foundation of music and poetry. But another elementary principle enters into these two arts. They are not founded, as dancing is, upon mere silent movements, but on movements of audible sounds, whether inarticulate, as in music, or articulate, as in poetry. These sounds are not all on a level in respect of their audibility, but vary in intensity: broadly speaking, they may be said to be either loud or soft. There is, it is true, something analogous to this in the movements of the dance; the steps differ in degree of intensity or force. Dancing indeed may be looked upon as the typical form and source of all rhythmic movement. Scherer brings this point out very well.[1] He says: 'Rhythm is produced by regular movements of the body. Walking becomes dancing by a definite relation of the steps to one another—of long and short in time or fast and slow in motion. A regular rhythm has never been reached by races among which irregular jumping, instead of walking,

[1] *Zur Geschichte der deutschen Sprache*, zweite Ausgabe, p. 624, Berlin, 1868.

has been the original form of the dance. Each pair of steps forms a unity, and a repetition begins with the third step. This unity is the bar or measure. The physical difference between the comparative strength of the right foot and the weakness of the left foot is the origin of the distinction between elevation and depression, i. e. between relatively loud and soft, the "good" and the "bad" part of the measure.'

Westphal [1] gives a similar explanation: 'That the stamp of the foot or the clap of the hands in beating time coincides with the strong part of the measure, and the raising of the foot or hand coincides with the weak part of it, originates, without doubt, in the ancient orchestic.' At the strong part of the bar the dancer puts his foot to the ground and raises it at the weak part. This is the meaning and original Greek usage of the terms 'arsis' and 'thesis', which are nowadays used in an exactly opposite sense. *Arsis* in its ancient signification meant the raising of the foot or hand, to indicate the weak part of the measure; *thesis* was the putting down of the foot, or the stamp, to mark the strong part of the measure. Now, however, it is almost the universal custom to use *arsis* to indicate the syllable uttered with a raised or loud voice, and *thesis* to indicate the syllable uttered with lower or soft voice. From the practice of beating time the term *ictus* is also borrowed; it is commonly used to designate the increase of voice which occurs at the strong, or so-called rhythmical accent.

All rhythm therefore in our dancing, poetry, and music, comes to us from ancient times, and is of the same nature in these three arts: it is regular order in the succession of different kinds of motion.

§ 4. The distinction between prose and poetry in their external aspects may be stated thus: in prose the words follow each other in an order determined entirely, or almost entirely, by the sense, while in poetry the order is largely determined by fixed and regular rhythmic schemes.

Even in prose a certain influence of rhythmical order may be sometimes observable, and where this is marked we have what is called rhythmical or artistic prose. But in such prose the rhythmic order must be so loosely constructed that it does not at once obtrude itself on the ear, or recur regularly as it does in poetry. Wherever we have intelligible words following each other in groups marked by a rhythmical order which is at once recognizable as intentionally chosen with a view to symmetry,

[1] *Metrik der Griechen*, 1ᵃ, 500.

there we may be said to have poetry, at least on its formal side. Poetical rhythm may accordingly be defined as a special symmetry, easily recognizable as such, in the succession of syllables of differing phonetic quality, which convey a sense, and are so arranged as to be uttered in divisions of time which are symmetrical in their relation to one another.

§ 5. At this point we have to note that there are two kinds of phonetic difference between syllables, either of which may serve as a foundation for rhythm. In the first place, syllables differ in respect of their *quantity*; they are either ' long' or ' short', according to the length of time required to pronounce them. In the second place, they differ in respect of the greater or less degree of force or stress with which they are uttered; or, as it is commonly expressed, in respect of their *accent*.

All the poetic rhythms of the Indogermanic or Aryan languages are based on one or other of these phonetic qualities of syllables, one group observing mainly the quantitative, and the other the accentual principle. Sanskrit, Greek, and Roman poetry is regulated by the principle of the quantity of the syllable, while the Teutonic nations follow the principle of stress or accent.[1] With the Greeks, Romans, and Hindoos the natural quantity of the syllables is made the basis of the rhythmic measures, the rhythmical ictus being fixed without regard to the word-accent. Among the Teutonic nations, on the other hand, the rhythmical ictus coincides normally with the word-accent, and the order in which long and short syllables succeed each other is (with certain exceptions in the early stages of the language) left to be determined by the poet's sense of harmony or euphony.

§ 6. Before going further it will be well to define exactly the meaning of the word *accent*, and to give an account of its different uses. Accent is generally defined as ' the stronger emphasis put on a syllable, the stress laid on it ', or, as Sweet[2] puts it, ' the comparative force with which the separate syllables of a sound-group are pronounced.' According to Brücke[3] it is produced by increasing the pressure of the breath. The stronger the pressure with which the air passes from the lungs through the glottis, the louder will be the tone of voice, the

---

[1] It should be remarked that in Sanskrit, as in the classical languages, that prominence of one of the syllables of a word, which is denoted by the term ' accent', was originally marked by pitch or elevation of tone, and that in the Teutonic languages the word-accent is one of stress or emphasis.   [2] *Handbook of Phonetics*, § 263.
[3] *Die physiologischen Grundlagen der neuhochdeutschen Verskunst*, 1871, p. 2.

louder will be the sound of the consonants which the stream
of air produces in the cavity of the mouth. This increase of
tone and sound is what is called 'accent'. Brücke seems to
use tone and sound as almost synonymous, but in metric we
must distinguish between them. Sound (*sonus*) is the more
general, tone (τόνος) the more specific expression. Sound, in
this general sense, may have a stronger or weaker tone. This
strengthening of the tone is usually, not invariably, accompanied by a rise in the pitch of the voice, just as the weakening
of the tone is accompanied by a lowering of the pitch. In
the Teutonic languages these variations of stress or accent
serve to bring into prominence the relative importance logically
of the various syllables of which words are composed. As
an almost invariable rule, the accent falls in these languages
on the root-syllable, which determines the sense of the word,
and not on the formative elements which modify that sense.
This accent is an expiratory or stress accent.

It must be noted that we cannot, using the term in this
sense, speak of the accent of a monosyllabic word when isolated,
but only of its sound; nor can we use the word *accent* with
reference to two or more syllables in juxtaposition, when they
are all uttered with precisely the same force of voice. The
term is significant only in relation to a *variation* in the audible
stress with which the different syllables of a word or a sentence
are spoken. This variation of stress affects monosyllables only
in connected speech, where they receive an accentuation relative
to the other words of the sentence. An absolute uniformity
of stress in a sentence is unnatural, though the amount of
variation in stress differs greatly in different languages. 'The
distinctions of stress in some languages are less marked than
in others. Thus in French the syllables are all pronounced
with a nearly uniform stress, the strong syllables rising only
a little above the general level, its occurrence being also uncertain and fluctuating. This makes Frenchmen unable without
systematic training to master the accentuation of foreign
languages.'[1] English and the other Teutonic languages, on
the other hand, show a marked tendency to alternate weak
and strong stress.

§ 7. With regard to the function which it discharges in
connected speech, we may classify accent or stress under four
different categories. First comes what may be called the
syntactical accent, which marks the logical importance of a

[1] Sweet, *Handbook of Phonetics*, Oxford, 1877, p. 92.

word in relation to other words of the sentence. In a sentence like 'the birds are singing', the substantive 'birds' has, as denoting the subject of the sentence, the strongest accent; next in logical or syntactical importance comes the word 'singing', denoting an activity of the subject, and this has a comparatively strong accent; the auxiliary 'are' being a word of minor importance is uttered with very little force of voice; the article 'the', being the least emphatic or significant, is uttered accordingly with the slightest perceptible stress of all.

Secondly, we have the rhetorical accent, or as it might be called, the subjective accent, inasmuch as it depends upon the emphasis which the speaker wishes to give to that particular word of the sentence which he desires to bring prominently before the hearer. Thus in the sentence, 'you have done this,' the rhetorical accent may fall on any of the four words which the speaker desires to bring into prominence, e. g. '*yóu* (and no one else) have done this,' or 'you *háve* done this (though you deny it), or you have *dóne* this' (you have not left it undone), or, finally, 'you have done *thís*' (and not what you were told). This kind of accent could also be termed the emphatic accent.

Thirdly, we have the rhythmical accent, which properly speaking belongs to poetry only, and often gives a word or syllable an amount of stress which it would not naturally have in prose, as, for instance, in the following line of *Hamlet* (III. iii. 27)—

> *My lord, he's going to his mother's closet,*

the unimportant word 'to' receives a stronger accent, due to the influence of the rhythm, than it would have in prose. Similarly in the following line of Chaucer's *Troilus and Cryseide*, l. 1816—

> *For thóusandés his hóndes máden dýe,*

the inflexional syllable *es* was certainly not ordinarily pronounced with so much stress as it must have here under the influence of the accent as determined by the rhythm of the line. Or again the word 'writyng', in the following couplet of Chaucer's *Canterbury Tales* (Prol. 325–6)—

> *Therto he couthe endite and make a thing,*
> *Ther couthe no wight pynche at his writyng,*

was certainly not pronounced in ordinary speech with the same stress on the last syllable as is here demanded both by the rhythm and rhyme.

As a rule, however, the rhythmical accent in English coincides with the fourth kind of accent, the etymological or word-accent, which we now have to deal with, and in greater detail.

Just as the different words of a sentence are pronounced, as we have seen, with varying degrees of stress, so similarly the different syllables of a single word are uttered with a varying intensity of the force of the breath. One of the syllables of the individual word is always marked off from the rest by a greater force of tone, and these others are again differentiated from each other by subordinate gradations of intensity of utterance, which may sometimes be so weak as to lead to a certain amount of indistinctness, especially in English. In the Teutonic languages, the root-syllable, as the most important element of the word, and that which conveys the meaning, always bears the chief accent, the other syllables bearing accents which are subordinate to this chief accent. As the etymology of a word is always closely associated with the form of the root-syllable, this syllabic accent may be called the etymological accent. It naturally happens that this syllabic accent coincides very often with the syntactical accent, as the syntactical stress must be laid on the syllable which has the etymological accent.

The degrees of stress on the various syllables may be as many in number as the number of the syllables of the word in question. It is sufficient, however, for purposes of metre and historical grammar, to distinguish only four degrees of accent in polysyllabic words. These four degrees of syllabic and etymological accent are as follows: 1. the chief accent (*Hochton, Hauptton*); 2. the subsidiary accent (*Tiefton, Nebenton*); 3. the absence of accent, or the unaccented degree (*Tonlosigkeit*); 4. the mute degree, or absence of sound (*Stummheit*). These last three varieties of accent arise from the nature of the Teutonic accent, which is, it must always be remembered, a stress-accent in which the volume of breath is expended mainly on the first or chief syllable. The full meaning of these terms can most easily be explained and understood by means of examples chosen either from English or German, whose accentual basis is essentially the same. In the word, *wonderful*, the first syllable has the chief accent (1), the last has the subsidiary accent (2), and the middle syllable is unaccented (3). The fourth or mute degree may be seen in such a word as *wondrous*, shortened from *wonderous*. This fuller form may still be used, for metrical purposes, as a trisyllable in which the first syllable has the chief accent, the last the subsidiary accent, and the middle syllable is unaccented, though audible. The usual pronunciation is, however, in agreement with the usual spelling, disyllabic, and is *wondrous*; in other words, the vowel *e* which originally formed the middle syllable, has been dropped altogether in speech as in writing. From the point of view of the accent, it has passed from the unaccented state to the state of muteness; but may be restored to the unaccented, though audible, state, wherever emphasis or metre requires the full syllable. We have the line: 'And it grew wondrous cold,' for which we might have 'The cold grew wonderous'. In other cases the vowel is retained in writing but is often dropped in colloquial pronunciation, or for metrical convenience. Thus, in Shakespeare, we find sometimes the full form—

> *why the sepulchre*
> *Has oped his ponderous and marble jaws.*
>
> Hamlet, i. iv. 50.

and sometimes the curtailed form—

> *To draw with idle spiders' strings*
> *Most ponderous and substantial things.*
>
> Measure for Measure, iii. ii. 290.

This passing of an unaccented syllable into complete muteness is very frequent in English, as compared with other cognate languages. It has led, in the historical development of the language, to a gradual weakening, and finally, in many instances, to a total loss of the inflexional endings. Very frequently, an inflexional vowel that has become mute is retained in the current spelling; thus in the verbal forms *gives*, *lives*, the *e* of the termination, though no longer pronounced, is still retained in writing. Sometimes, in poetical texts, it is omitted, but its position is indicated by an apostrophe, as in the spellings *robb'd*, *belov'd*. In many words, on the other hand, the silent vowel has ceased to be written, as in *grown*, *sworn*, of which the original forms were *growen*, *sworen*.

§ 8. Written marks to indicate the position of the accent were employed in early German poetry as early as the first half of the ninth century, when they were introduced, it is supposed, by Hrabanus Maurus of Fulda and his pupil Otfrid. The similar marks that are found in certain Early English MSS., as the *Ormulum*, are usually signs of vowel-quantity. They may possibly have sometimes been intended to denote stress, but their use for this purpose is so irregular and uncertain that they give little help towards determining the varying degrees of accent in words during the earliest stages of the language. For this purpose we must look for other and less ambiguous means, and these are found (in the case of Old English words and forms) first, in the alliteration, secondly, in comparison with related words of the other Teutonic languages, and, thirdly, in the development in the later stages of English itself. After the Norman Conquest, the introduction of rhyme, and of new forms of metre imitated from the French and mediaeval Latin poetry, affords further help in investigating the different degrees of syllabic accent in Middle English words. None of these means, however, can be considered as yielding results of absolute certainty, chiefly because during this period the accentuation of the language was passing through a stage of transition or compromise between the radically different principles which characterize the Romanic and Teutonic families of languages. This will be explained more fully in a subsequent chapter.

Notwithstanding this period of fluctuation the fundamental law of accentuation remained unaltered, namely, that the chief accent falls on the root of the word, which is in most cases the first syllable. For purposes of notation the acute (´) will be used in this work to denote the chief accent, the grave (`) the subsidiary accent of the single word; to indicate the rhythmical or metrical accent the acute alone will be sufficient.

§ 9. In English poetry, as in the poetry of the other Teutonic nations, the rhythmical accent coincides normally with the syllabic or etymological accent, and this, therefore, determines and regulates the rhythm. In the oldest form of Teutonic poetry, the original alliterative line, the rhythm is indicated by a definite number of strongly accented syllables, accompanied by a less definite number of syllables which do not bear the same emphatic stress. This principle of versification prevails not only in Old English and Old and Middle High German poetry, but also, to a certain extent, in the period of Middle English, where, in the same manner, the number of beats or accented syllables indicates the number of 'feet' or metrical units, and a single strongly accented syllable can by itself constitute a 'foot'. This practice is a feature which distinguishes early English and German poetry, not only from the classical poetry, in which a foot or measure must consist of at least two syllables, but also from that of the Romanic, modern German, and modern English languages, which has been influenced by classical example, and in which, accordingly, a foot must contain one accented and at least one unaccented syllable following one another in a regular order. The classical terms 'foot' and 'measure' have, in their strict sense, relation to the quantity of the syllables, and can therefore be applied to the modern metres only by analogy. In poetry which is based on the principle of accent or stress, the proper term is *bar* (in German *Takt*). The general resemblances between modern accentual and ancient quantitative metres are, however, so strong, that it is hardly desirable to discontinue the application of old and generally understood technical terms of the classical versification to modern metres, provided the fundamental distinction between quantity and accent is always borne in mind.

Setting aside for the present the old Teutonic alliterative line, in which a 'bar' might permissibly consist of a single syllable, we may retain the names of the feet of the classical quantitative versification for the 'bars' of modern versification, using them in modified senses. A group consisting of one unaccented followed by an accented syllable may be called an *iambus*; one accented followed by an unaccented syllable a *trochee*; two unaccented syllables followed by an accented syllable an *anapaest*; one accented syllable followed by two unaccented syllables a *dactyl*. These four measures might also be described according to the length of the intervals separating the accents, and according as the rhythm is *ascending* (passing from an unaccented to an accented syllable) or *descending* (passing from an accented to an unaccented syllable). We should then have the terms, (1) *ascending disyllabic* (iambus), (2) *descending disyllabic* (trochee), (3) *ascending trisyllabic* (anapaest), and (4) *descending trisyllabic* (dactyl).[1] But we may agree with Prof. Mayor that 'it is certainly more convenient to speak of iambic than of ascending disyllabic'.[2] It is, however, only in the case of these four feet or measures that it is desirable to adhere to the terminology of the ancient metres, and as a matter of fact iambus, trochee, anapaest, and dactyl are the only names of classical feet that are commonly recognized in English prosody.[3] As to the employment in the treatment of English metre of less familiar technical terms derived from classical prosody, we agree with Prof. Mayor, when he says: 'I can sympathize with Mr. Ellis in his objection to the classicists who would force upon us such terms as *choriambic* and *proceleusmatic* to explain the rhythm of Milton. I do not

---

[1] Cf. *Transactions of the Philological Society*, 1875-6, London, 1877, pp. 397 ff.; *Chapters on English Metre*, by Prof. J. B. Mayor, 2nd ed., pp. 5 ff.   [2] *Transact.*, p. 398.

[3] They are used by Puttenham, *The Arte of English Poesy*, 1589, Arber's reprint, p. 141.

deny that the effect of his rhythm might sometimes be represented by such terms ; but if we seriously adopt them to explain his metre, we are attempting an impossibility, to express in technical language the infinite variety of measured sound which a genius like Milton could draw out of the little five-stringed instrument on which he chose to play.' The use of these and other classical terms is justifiable only when we have to deal with professed imitations of ancient forms of verse in English.

Whatever names may be chosen to denote the metrical forms, the *measure* or *foot* always remains the unity which is the basis of all modern metrical systems, and of all investigation into metre. For a line or verse is built up by the succession of a limited number of feet or measures, equal or unequal. With regard to the limit of the number of feet permissible in a line or verse, no fixed rule can be laid down. In no case must a line contain more feet than the ear may without difficulty apprehend as a rhythmic whole ; or, if the number of feet is too great for this, the line must be divided by a *pause* or *break* (caesura) into two or more parts which we may then call rhythmical *sections*. This break is a characteristic mark of the typical Old English alliterative line, which is made up of two rhythmical sections. The structure of this verse was at one time obscured through the practice of printing each of these sections by itself as a short line ; but Grimm's example is now universally followed, and the two sections are printed as parts of one long line.[1] Before entering into a detailed consideration of the alliterative long line, it will be needful to make a few general remarks on rhyme and its different species.

§ 10. Modern metre is not only differentiated from metre of the classical languages by the principle of *accent* as opposed to *quantity* ; it has added a new metrical principle foreign to the ancient systems. This principle is Rhyme. Instances of what looks like rhyme are found in the classical poets from Homer onwards, but they are sporadic, and are probably due to accident.[2]

Rhyme was not in use as an accessory to metre in Latin till the quantitative principle had given way to the accentual principle in the later hymns of the Church, and it has passed thence into all European systems of metre.

In our poetry it serves a twofold purpose : it is used either simply as an ornament, or as a tie to connect single lines into

---

[1] J. Grimm's ed. of *Andreas and Elene*, 1840, pp. lv ff.
[2] Cf. Lehrs, *de Aristarchi studiis Homericis*, 1865, p. 475.

the larger metrical unity of stanza or stave, by the recurrence of similar sounds at various intervals.

In its widest sense rhyme is an agreement or consonance of sounds in syllables or words, and falls into several subdivisions, according to the extent and position of this agreement. As to its position, this consonance may occur in the beginning of a syllable or word, or in the middle, or in both middle and end at the same time. As to its extent, it may comprehend one or two or more syllables. Out of these various possibilities of likeness or consonance there arise three chief kinds of rhyme in this wide sense, alliteration, assonance, and end-rhyme, or rhyme simply in the more limited and usual acceptation of the word.

§ 11. This last, end-rhyme, or full-rhyme, or rhyme proper, consists in a perfect agreement or consonance of syllables or words except in their initial sounds, which as a rule are different. Generally speaking, the agreement of sounds falls on the last accented syllable of a word, or on the last accented syllable and a following unaccented syllable or syllables. End-rhyme or full-rhyme seems to have arisen independently and without historical connexion in several nations, but as far as our present purpose goes we may confine ourselves to its development in Europe among the nations of Romanic speech at the beginning of the Middle Ages. Its adoption into all modern literature is due to the extensive use made of it in the hymns of the Church. Full-rhyme or end-rhyme therefore is a characteristic of modern European poetry, and though it cannot be denied that unrhymed verse, or blank verse, is much used in English poetry, the fact remains that this metre is an exotic product of the Renaissance, and has never become thoroughly popular. Its use is limited to certain kinds of poetic composition, whereas rhyme prevails over the wider part of the realm of modern poetry.

§ 12. The second kind of rhyme (taking the word in its broader sense), namely, vocalic assonance, is of minor importance in the treatment of English metre. It consists in a similarity between the vowel-sounds only of different words; the surrounding consonants do not count. The following groups of words are assonant together: *give, thick, fish, win ; sell, step, net ; thorn, storm, horse.* This kind of rhyme was very popular among the Romanic nations, and among them alone. Its first beginnings are found in the Latin ecclesiastical hymns, and these soon developed into real or full-rhyme.[1] It

---

[1] Cf. J. Huemer, *Untersuchungen über die ältesten lateinisch-christlichen Rhythmen*, Vienna, 1879, p. 60.

passed thence into Provençal, Old French, and Spanish poetry, and has continued in use in the last named. It is very rarely found in English verse, it has in fact never been used deliberately, as far as we know, except in certain recent experiments in metre. Where it does seem to occur it is safest to look upon it as imperfect rhyme only. Instances are found in the Early English metrical romances, Lives of Saints, and popular ballad poetry, where the technique of the metre is not of a high order ; examples such as *flete, wepe ; brake, gate ; slepe, ymete* from *King Horn* might be looked on as assonances, but were probably intended for real rhymes. The consistent use of the full-rhyme being difficult, the poets, in such instances as these, contented themselves with the simpler harmony between the vowels alone, which represents a transition stage between the older rhymeless alliterative verse, and the newer Romanic metres with real and complete rhyme. Another possible form of assonance, in which the consonants alone agree while the vowels may differ, might be called *consonantal assonance* as distinguished from *vocalic assonance*, or assonance simply. This form of assonance is not found in English poetry, though it is employed in Celtic and Icelandic metres.[1]

§ 13. The third species of rhyme, to use the word still in its widest sense, is known as alliteration (German *Stabreim* or *Anreim*). It is common to all Teutonic nations, and is found fully developed in the oldest poetical monuments of Old Norse, Old High German, Old Saxon, and Old English. Even in classical poetry, especially in the remains of archaic Latin, it is not unfrequently met with, but serves only as a means for giving to combinations of words a rhetorical emphasis, and is not a formal principle of the metre bound by strict rules, as it is in Teutonic poetry. Alliteration consists in a consonance or agreement of the sounds at the beginning of a word or syllable, as in *love* and *liking, house* and *home, woe* and *weal.* The alliteration of vowels and diphthongs has this peculiarity that the agreement need not be exact as in 'apt alliteration's artful aid', but can exist, at least in the oldest stages of the language, between all vowels indiscriminately. Thus in the oldest English not only were *ellen* and *ende, ǽnig* and *ǽr, ēac* and *ēage* alliterations, but *ēage* and *īdel, ǽnig* and *ellen, eallum* and *œðelingum* were employed in the strictest forms of verse as words which perfectly alliterated with each other.

[1] In the Icelandic terminology this is *skothending*, Möbius, *Háttatal*, ii, p. 2.

This apparent confusion of vowel-sounds so different in their quantity and quality is probably to be explained by the fact that originally in English, as now in German, all the vowels were preceded by a ' glottal catch ' which is the real alliterating sound.[1] The harmony or consonance of the unlike vowels is hardly perceptible in Modern English and does not count as alliteration.

The most general law of the normal alliterative line is that three or at least two of the four strongly accented syllables which occur in every long line (two in each section) must begin with an alliterative letter, for example, in the following Old English lines :

> *wereda* **w***uldorcining* | *wordum hērigen.* Gen. 2.

> m*ōdum* l*uſien* | *he is* m*ægna spēd.* Gen. 3.

> **æ***sc biŏ o**ferhēah* | **e***ldum dȳre.* Run. 26.

> *on* **a***ndsware* | *and on* **e***lne strong.* Gū. 264.

or in early Modern English :

> *For* m*yschefe will* m*ayster us* | *yf* m*easure us forsake.*
> Skelton, Magnif. 156.

> *How sodenly* **w***orldly* | **w***elth doth dekay.* ib. 1518.

> *I am your* **e***ldest son* | **E***sau by name.* Dodsl. Coll. ii. 249.

The history of the primitive alliterative line follows very different lines of development in the various Teutonic nations. In Old High German, after a period in which the strict laws of the verse were largely neglected, it was abandoned in favour of rhyme by Otfrid (circa 868). In Old English it kept its place as the only form of verse for all classes of poetical composition, and continued in use, even after the introduction of Romanic forms of metre, during the Middle English period, and did not totally die out till the beginning of the seventeenth century. The partial revival of it is due to the increased interest in Old English studies, but has been confined largely to translations. As an occasional rhetorical or stylistic ornament of both rhymed and unrhymed verse, alliteration has always been made use of by English poets.

---

[1] Cf. Sievers, *Altgermanische Metrik*, § 18. 2.

CHAPTER II

THE ALLITERATIVE VERSE IN OLD ENGLISH

§ 14. General remarks. It is highly probable that alliteration was the earliest kind of poetic form employed by the English people. There is no trace in the extant monuments of the language of any more primitive or simpler system. A predilection for alliteration existed even in prose, as in the names of heroes and families like Scyld and Sceaf, Hengist and Horsa, Finn and Folcwald, pairs that alliterate in the same way as the family names of other Teutonic nations: the names of the three sons of Mannus, Ingo, Isto, Irmino, conform to this type.[1] The earliest monuments of Old English poetry, as the fragmentary hymn of Cædmon in the More MS. (Cambridge) and the inscription on the Ruthwell Cross, are composed in the long alliterative line. The great body of Old English verse is in this metre, the only exceptions being the 'Rhyming Poem' (in the *Exeter Book*),[2] and a few other late pieces, in which alliteration and rhyme are combined. This Old English poetry, therefore, together with the Old Norse and Old Saxon remains (the *Heliand* with 5,985 lines, and the recently discovered fragment of the Old Saxon *Genesis*, edited by Zangemeister and Braune, 1894, with 335 lines), affords ample and trustworthy material for determining the laws of the alliterative verse as used by the Teutonic nations. In comparison with these the remains of Old High German alliterative verse are both scanty and lax in structure.

§ 15. Theories on the metrical form of the alliterative line. Notwithstanding their comparative scantiness, the Old High German fragments (*Hildebrandslied, Wessobrunner Gebet, Muspilli* and two magical formulae, with a total of some 110 lines) formed the basis of the earliest theories of the laws of the accentuation and general character of the original alliterative line. They were assumed to have preserved the features of the

---

[1] Tacitus, *Germania*, cap. 2.   [2] Grein-Wülker, iii. 1, p. 156.

primitive metre, and conclusions were drawn from them as to the typical form of the verse. When examined closely, the Old High German remains (and this is true also of the longer monuments in Old Saxon) are found to differ widely from Old Norse and Old English verse in one respect. While the general and dominating features of the line remain the same, the Old High German and Old Saxon lines are much longer than the Old Norse or Old English lines. In Old Norse or Old English the half line frequently contains no more than four syllables, in marked contrast to Old High German and Old Saxon, where the half line or section is considerably longer.

The first attempt at a theory of the metrical structure of the alliterative line was made by Lachmann. He based his theory on the form of verse created by Otfrid, in imitation of Latin models, which consists of a long line of eight accents, separated by leonine rhyme into two sections each of four accents alternately strong and weak.[1] The laws of the rhyming and strophic verse of Otfrid were applied by Lachmann to the purely alliterative verses of the Old High German *Hildebrandslied*, and this system of scanning was further applied by his followers to the alliterative verse of Old English, the true nature of which was long misunderstood on the Continent. In England itself a sounder view of the native alliterative verse was propounded by Bishop Percy as early as 1765, in his *Essay on the Metre of Pierce Plowman* published along with his well-known *Reliques of Ancient English Poetry*, not to speak of the earlier writings of G. Gascoigne (1575) and James VI (1585). But the number and authority of some of Lachmann's followers are such that some detailed account of their theories must be given.[2]

§ 16. The four-beat theory of the alliterative verse, based on the assumption that each of the two sections must have had four accented syllables to bring out a regular rhythm, was applied by Lachmann himself only to the Old High German *Hildebrandslied*,[3] while on the other hand he recognized a freer variety with two chief accents only in each section, for the Old Norse, Old Saxon, and Old English. The four-beat theory was further applied to the Old High German *Muspilli* by

---

[1] The influence of the Latin system on Otfrid is clear from his own words, I. i. 21.

[2] For a review of recent metrical theories see Sievers, *Altgermanische Metrik*, 1893, pp. 2-17, and his article on metre in Paul's *Grundriss*, ii. 2.

[3] Cf. Lachmann, 'Über althochdeutsche Betonung und Verskunst,' *Schriften*, ii. 358 ff., and 'Über das Hildebrandslied', *ib.*, ii. 407 ff.

Bartsch,[1] and to the rest of the smaller relics of Old High German verse by Müllenhoff.[2] The next step was to bring the Old Saxon *Heliand* and the Old English *Beowulf* under this system of scansion; and this was taken by M. Heyne in 1866 and 1867. But the metre of *Beowulf* does not differ from that of the other alliterative poems in Old English, and these in their turn were claimed for the four-beat theory by Schubert,[3] but with this important modification, made before by Bartsch, that side by side with the usual four-beat sections there were also to be found sections of three beats only. One obvious difficulty in applying the theory of four strongly marked beats to the Old English half-lines or hemistichs is this, that in Old English these hemistichs consist in very many cases of not more than four syllables altogether, each one of which would on this theory have an accent to itself. To meet these cases E. Jessen[4] started the theory that in certain cases pauses had to be substituted for 'beats not realized'. A further modification of the four-beat doctrine was introduced by Amelung,[5] who maintained that in the metre of the *Heliand* each hemistich had two primary or chief accents and two secondary or subordinate accents. In order to bring the verse under this scansion he assumes that certain syllables admitted of being lengthened. He further regarded the *Heliand* verse as a metre regulated by strict time, and not as a measure intended for free recitation and depending only on the number of accented syllables.

A few other more recent attempts at solving the problem must be mentioned before we pass on to explain and discuss Sievers's system in the next paragraph. The views of Prof. Möller of Copenhagen[6] have found an adherent in Lawrence, from whose book[7] we may quote the following summary of Möller's theory. According to Prof. Möller the hemistich consists theoretically of two measures (*Takte*), each of four *morae* $\acute{\times} \times \grave{\times} \times$ (a *mora*, $\times$, being the time required for one short syllable), and therefore the whole verse of four measures, thus:

$$\acute{\times} \times \grave{\times} \times \mid \acute{\times} \times \grave{\times} \times \parallel \acute{\times} \times \grave{\times} \times \mid \acute{\times} \times \grave{\times} \times \parallel.$$

[1] *Germania*, iii, p. 7.

[2] *Zeitschrift für deutsches Altertum*, i, p. 318, and *de Carmine Wessofontano*, 1861, p. 10.

[3] *De Anglo-Saxonum arte metrica*, 1871.

[4] 'Grundzüge der altgermanischen Metrik,' *Zeitschrift für deutsche Philologie*, ii. 114 ff.   [5] *Ibid.*, iii. 280 ff.

[6] *Zur althochdeutschen Alliterationspoesie*, Kiel and Leipzig.

[7] John Lawrence, *Chapters on Alliterative Verse*, London, 1893; reviewed by K. Luick, *Anglia*, Beiblatt iv, pp. 193, 201.

Where, in a verse, the *morae* are not filled by actual syllables, their time must be occupied by rests (represented by r*) in reciting, by holding on the note in singing.[1] A long syllable, —, is equivalent to two *morae*. Thus v. 208 of *Beowulf*

$$\textit{súnd-wùdu . sôhtè . sécg . wísàde.}$$

would be symbolically represented as follows:

$$\smile \dot{x} \; x \, | \, \smile \dot{x} \, r \, \| \, \smile rr \, | \, \smile \dot{x} \; x \, .$$

According to this system the pause at *secg* will be twice as long as that at *sôhte*, whilst at *wudu* there will be no real pause and the point will merely indicate the end of the measure.

Others reverted to the view of Bartsch and Schubert that there could be hemistichs with only three accents alongside of the hemistichs with the normal number of four. Among these may be mentioned H. Hirt,[2] whose view is that three beats to a hemistich is the normal number, four being less usual, the long line having thus mostly six beats, against the eight of Lachmann's theory; K. Fuhr,[3] who holds that every hemistich, whether it stands first or second in the verse, has four beats if the last syllable is unaccented (*klingend*; in that case the final unaccented syllable receives a secondary rhythmical accent, for example, *féond máncýnnès*) and has three beats if it is accented (*stumpf*, for example, *fýrst fórð gewât*, or *múrnénde môd*, &c.); and B. ten Brink,[4] who calls the hemistichs with four beats full or 'complete' (e.g. *hýràn scôldè*), but admits hemistichs with three beats only, calling them 'incomplete' from the want of a secondary accent (e.g. *twélf wíntra tíd, hâm gesôhte*, &c.). The four-beat theory was reverted to by M. Kaluza, who endeavours to reconcile it with the results of Sievers and others.[5] A somewhat similar view is taken by R. Kögel.[6]

---

[1] Möller's own notation; Lawrence's sign for the rest is a small point, and his sign for the end of a section is a thick point.

[2] *Untersuchungen zur westgermanischen Verskunst* I, Leipzig, 1889; 'Zur Metrik des alts. und althochd. Alliterationsverses,' *Germania*, xxxvi. 139 ff., 279 ff.; 'Der altdeutsche Reimvers und sein Verhältnis zur Alliterationspoesie,' *Zeitschrift für deutsches Altertum*, xxxviii. 304 ff.

[3] *Die Metrik des westgermanischen Alliterationsverses*, Marburg, 1892.

[4] Paul's *Grundriss der germanischen Philologie*, ed. 1, ii. i. 518.

[5] *Der altenglische Vers* : I. *Kritik der bisherigen Theorien*, 1894; II. *Die Metrik des Beowulfliedes*, 1894; III. *Die Metrik der sog. Caedmonischen Dichtungen*, &c., 1895. This last part is by F. Graz. These are reviewed by K. Luick, *Anglia*, Beiblatt iv. 294; M. Trautmann, ib., iv. 131; vi. 1–4; Saran, *Zeitschrift für deutsche Philologie*, xxvii. 539.

[6] *Geschichte der deutschen Litteratur*, 1894, i. 228, and *Ergänzungsheft zu Band I, Die altsächsische Genesis*, 1895, p. 28 ff.

Trautmann[1] takes Amelung's view that certain words and syllables must be lengthened in order to get the four accented syllables necessary for each hemistich. Thus, according to Trautmann's scansion,

sprécað fǽgeré befóran

would run x́ x | x́ x | x́ x | ꭒ x, and

ónd þú him mǽte sýlest

would also have the formula x́ x | x́ x | x́ x | ꭒ x,

ond being protracted to two units. Another instance of this lengthening would, on this theory, occur in the final syllable of the word *radores* in the hemistich *únder rádorès rýne*, while in a section like *gúð-rinc monig*, or *of fold-grǽfe*, the words *rinc* and *of* would be extended to two, and *gúð* and *fold* would each be extended to four units, in order to fit in with the scansion x́ x | x́ x | x́ x | ꭒ x. Most of the partisans of the four-beat theory for the hemistich agree in making two of these beats primary, and two secondary; Trautmann, however, does not seem to recognize any such difference in the force of the four accents. All the supporters of the four-beat theory have this in common, that the rhythm of the verse is assumed to be based on time (*taktierend*), but in other respects differ widely from each other; Hirt, for example, in his last discussion of the subject,[2] claiming that his own view is fundamentally different from that of Kaluza, which again he looks on as at variance with those of Möller and Heusler.

§ 17. **The two-beat theory**, on the other hand, is that each of the two hemistichs of the alliterative line need have only two accented syllables. In England this view was taken by two sixteenth-century writers on verse, George Gascoigne[3] who quotes the line,

No wight in this world, that wealth can attain,

giving as the accentual scheme ＼ ／ ＼ ＼ ／ ＼ ／ ＼ ＼ ／ ; and by King James VI, whose example is—

Fetching fude for to feid it fast furth of the Farie.[4]

---

[1] 'Zur Kenntniss des germanischen Verses, vornehmlich des altenglischen,' in *Anglia*, Beiblatt v. 87 ff.   [2] *Z.f.d. A.*, xxxviii. 304.

[3] *Certayne notes of Instruction concerning the making of verse or ryme in English*, 1575; Arber's reprint, London, 1868, p. 34.

[4] *Ane Schort Treatise, conteining some Revlis and Cautelis to be obseruit and eschewit in Scottis poesie*, 1585, pp. 63 ff. of Arber's reprint. The scheme would be ＼ ＼ ／ ＼ ＼ ／ ＼ ＼ ／ ＼ ＼ ／ ＼ ／ .

In 1765, Percy, in his *Essay on Pierce Plowman's Visions*, pointed out 'that the author of this poem will not be found to have invented any new mode of versification, as some have supposed, but only to have retained that of the old Saxon and Gothick poets, which was probably never wholly laid aside, but occasionally used at different intervals'. After quoting[1] two Old Norse, he gives two Old English verses :—

> *Sceop þa and scyrede   scyppend ure* (Gen. 65),
> *ham and heahsetl   heofena rices* (ib. 33);

he continues : 'Now if we examine the versification of Pierce Plowman's Visions' (from which he quotes the beginning—

> *In a somer season | when softe was the sonne*
> *I schop me into a schroud | a scheep as I were, &c.*)

'we shall find it constructed exactly by these rules', which are, in his own words, 'that every distich [i. e. complete long line] should contain at least three words beginning with the same letter or sound; two of these correspondent sounds might be placed either in the first or second line of the distich, and one in the other, but all three were not regularly to be crowded into one line.' He then goes on to quote further specimens of alliterative verse from *Pierce the Ploughman's Crede, The Sege of Jerusalem, The Chevalere Assigne, Death and Liffe* and *Scottish Fielde*, which latter ends with a rhyming couplet :

> *And his ancestors of old time | have yearded theire longe*
> *Before William conquerour | this cuntry did inhabitt.*
> *Jesus bring them to blisse | that brought us forth of bale,*
> *That hath hearkened me heare | or heard my tale.*

Taken as a whole his dissertation on the history of alliterative verse is remarkably correct, and his final remarks are note-worthy :

Thus we have traced the alliterative measure so low as the sixteenth century. It is remarkable that all such poets as used this kind of metre, retained along with it many peculiar Saxon idioms, particularly such as were appropriated to poetry : *this deserves the attention of those who are desirous to recover the laws of the ancient Saxon poesy, usually given up as inexplicable :* I am of opinion that they will find what they seek in the metre of Pierce Plowman. About the beginning of the sixteenth century this kind of versification began to change its form ; the author of *Scottish Field*, we see, concludes his poem with a couplet of rhymes ; this was an innovation[2] that did but prepare the way for the general admission of that

---

[1] From Hickes's *Antiq. Literat. Septentrional.*, tom. i, p. 217.
[2] It is now well known that this innovation was introduced much earlier.

more modish ornament. When rhyme began to be superadded, all the niceties of alliteration were at first retained with it: the song of Little John Nobody exhibits this union very closely. . . . To proceed ; the old uncouth verse of the ancient writers would no longer go down without the more fashionable ornament of rhyme, and therefore rhyme was superadded. This correspondence of final sounds engrossing the whole attention of the poet and fully satisfying the reader, the internal imbellishment of allitera-tion was no longer studied, and thus was this kind of metre at length swallowed up and lost in our common burlesque alexandrine, now never used but in songs and pieces of low humour, as in the following ballad ; and that well-known doggrel :

> ' A cobler there was and he lived in a stall '.

Now it is clear that this verse is of exactly the same structure as the verses quoted by Gascoigne :

> *No wight in this world that wealth can attayne,*
> *Únléss hè bèléue, thàt áll ìs bùt vaýne,*

where the scheme of accents is Gascoigne's own, showing that he read them as verses of four accents in all, two in each hemistich. They show the same rhythmical structure as the ' tumbling ' or alliterative line given by James VI[1] (1585):

> *Fetching fude for to feid it fast furth of the Farie,*

and described by him as having ' twa [feit, i. e. syllables] short, and ane lang throuch all the lyne ', in other words with four accented syllables in the verse.

Percy detected very acutely that the Middle English alliterative line stood in close connexion with the Old English alliterative line, and suggested as highly probable that the metre of *Pierce Plowman* would give a key to the rhythm of that older form of verse, which would have to be read with two accented syllables in the hemistich, and therefore four in the whole line.

Had this essay of Percy's been known to Lachmann's followers, many of the forced attempts at reconciling the Old English verse with a scheme that involved a fixed number of syllables in the line would not have been made. Lachmann himself, it must be remembered, admitted the two-beat scansion for Old Norse, Old Saxon, and Old English. Meanwhile other investi-gators were at work on independent lines. In 1844 A. Schmeller, the editor of the *Heliand*, formulated the law that, in the Teutonic languages, it is the force with which the different syllables are uttered that regulates the rhythm of the verse, and not the

---

[1] From Alexander Montgomery, *The Flyting*, &c., l. 476.

number or length of the syllables (which are of minor importance), and established the fact that this alliterative verse was not meant to be sung but to be recited.[1] He does not enter into the details of the rhythm of the verse, except by pointing out the two-beat cadence of each section. Somewhat later, W. Wackernagel[2] declared himself in favour of the two-beat theory for all Teutonic alliterative verse. In every hemistich of the verse there are according to Wackernagel two syllables with a grammatical or logical emphasis, and consequently a strong accent, the number of less strongly accented syllables not being fixed. The two-beat theory was again ably supported by F. Vetter[3] and by K. Hildebrand, who approached the subject by a study of the Old Norse alliterative verse,[4] and by M. Rieger in his instructive essay on Old Saxon and Old English versification.[5] In this essay Rieger pointed out the rules prevailing in the poetry of those two closely related Teutonic nations, dealt with the distribution and quality of the alliteration, the relation of the alliteration to the noun, adjective, and verb, and to the order of words, with the caesura and the close of the verse, and, finally, with the question of the accented syllables and the limits of the use of unaccented syllables.[6] Other scholars, as Horn, Ries, and Sievers, contributed further elucidations of the details of this metre on the basis of Rieger's researches.[7]

Next to Rieger's short essay the most important contribution made to the accurate and scientific study of alliterative verse was that made by Sievers in his article on the rhythm of the Germanic alliterative verse.[8] In this he shows, to use his own words, 'that a statistical classification of groups of words with

[1] 'Über den Versbau der alliterierenden Poesie, besonders der Altsachsen,' *Bay. Akademie der Wissenschaften, philos.-histor. Classe*, iv. 1, p. 207 ff.

[2] *Litteraturgeschichte*, p. 45 ff., second ed., p. 57.

[3] *Über die germanische Alliterationspoesie*, Vienna, 1872, and *Zum Muspilli*, &c., Vienna, 1872.

[4] 'Über die Vertheilung der Edda,' *Zeitschr. für deutsche Phil.*, Ergänzungsband, p. 74.

[5] *Die Alt- und Angelsächsische Verskunst*, Halle, 1876, reprinted from *Z.f.d. Ph.*, vol. vii.

[6] The author's larger work on English Metre was indebted in paragraphs 28–33 to Rieger's essay; succeeding paragraphs (34–39) of the same work exhibited in detail the further development or rather decay of the Old English alliterative line.

[7] C. R. Horn, *Paul und Braune's Beiträge*, v. 164; J. Ries, *Quellen und Forschungen*, xli. 112; E. Sievers, *Zeitschr. f. deutsche Phil.*, xix. 43.

[8] *Paul und Braune's Beiträge*, x, 1885, pp. 209–314 and 491–545.

their natural accentuation in both sections of the alliterative line makes it clear that this metre, in spite of its variety, is not so irregular as to the unaccented syllables at the beginning or in the middle of the verse as has been commonly thought, but that it has a range of a limited number of definite forms which may be all reduced to five primary types.' These five types or chief variations in the relative position of the accented and unaccented syllables are, as Sievers points out, of such a nature and so arbitrarily combined in the verse, that they cannot possibly be regarded as symmetrical feet of a line evenly measured and counted by the number of syllables. 'The fundamental principle, therefore, of the structure of the alliterative line, as we find it in historical times, is that of a free change of rhythm which can only be understood if the verse was meant to be recited, not to be sung.' [1] Soon after the publication of Sievers's essay on the rhythm of the Germanic verse, the first part of which contained a complete classification of all the forms of the line occurring in *Beowulf*, other scholars applied his method and confirmed his results by examining in detail the other important Old English texts ; Luick dealt with *Judith*,[2] Frucht with the poems of Cynewulf,[3] and Cremer with *Andreas*, &c.[4] Sievers himself, after contributing to the pages of Paul's *Grundriss der germanischen Philologie* a concise account of his theories and results, expounded them in greater detail in his work on Old Germanic Metre [5] in which he emphasizes the fact that his five-type theory cannot properly be called a theory at all, but is simply an expression of the rules of the alliterative verse obtained by a statistical method of observation. In spite of the criticisms of his opponents, Möller, Heusler, Hirt, Fuhr, and others, he maintained his former views. In principle these views are in conformity with the manner of reading or scanning the alliterative verse explained by English writers on the subject from the sixteenth century downwards, though their terminology naturally is not the same as Sievers's. We may, therefore, accept them on the whole as sound.

It would be out of place here to enter into the question

---

[1] Sievers, Paul's *Grundriss*, ii. 1, p. 863, or ii. 2, p. 4, second ed.
[2] *Paul und Braune's Beiträge*, xi. 470.
[3] Ph. Frucht, *Metrisches und Sprachliches zu Cynewulfs Elene, Juliana und Crist*, Greifswald, 1887.
[4] M. Cremer, *Metrische und sprachliche Untersuchung der altengl. Gedichte Andreas, Gûðlâc, Phoenix*, Bonn, 1888.
[5] *Altgermanische Metrik*, Halle, 1893.

of prehistoric forms of Teutonic poetry. It will be enough to say that in Sievers's opinion a primitive form of this poetry was composed in strophes or stanzas, intended to be sung and not merely to be recited; that at a very early period this sung strophic poetry gave way to a recited stichic form suitable to epic narrations; and that his five-type forms are the result of this development. As all the attempts to show that certain Old English poems were originally composed in strophic form [1] have proved failures, we may confidently assent to Sievers's conclusion that the alliterative lines (as a rule) followed one upon another in unbroken succession, and that in historic times they were not composed in even and symmetrical measures (*taktierend*), and were not meant to be sung to fixed tunes.

The impossibility of assuming such symmetrical measures for the Old English poetry is evident from the mere fact that the end of the line does not as a rule coincide with the end of the sentence, as would certainly be the case had the lines been arranged in staves or stanzas meant for singing. The structure of the alliterative line obeys only the requirements of free recitation and is built up of two hemistichs which have a rhythmical likeness to one another resulting from the presence in each of two accented syllables, but which need not have, and as a matter of fact very rarely have, complete identity of rhythm, because the number and situation of the unaccented syllables may vary greatly in the two sections.

§ 18. **Accentuation of Old English.** As the versification of Old English is based on the natural accentuation of the language, it will be necessary to state the laws of this accentuation before giving an account of the five types to which the structure of the hemistich has been reduced.

In simple polysyllables the chief or primary accent, in this work marked by an acute (′), is as a rule on the root-syllable, and the inflexional and other elements of the word have a less marked accent varying from a secondary accent, here marked by a grave (‵), to the weakest grade of accent, which is generally left unmarked : thus *wúldor, héofon, wítig, wúnode, ǽðelingas,* &c.

In the alliterative line, as a general rule, only syllables with the chief accent carry either the alliterating sounds or the four rhythmical accents of the verse. All other syllables, even those

---

[1] Mainly by H. Möller, *Das Volksepos in der ursprünglichen strophischen Form*, Kiel, 1883.

with secondary accent, count ordinarily as the 'theses' (*Sen-kungen*) of the verse[1]:

> síndon þā béarwas   blĕdum gehóngene
> wlítigum wæstmum: þǣr nō wániað ó
> hálge under héofonum   hóltes frǣtwe.   Phoenix 71–73.

In compound words (certain combinations with unaccented prefixes excepted) the first element of the compound (which modifies or determines the meaning of the second element) has the primary accent, the second element having only a secondary accent, e. g. *wúldor-cýning*, *héah-sèll*, *sóð-fæst*.[2] If therefore the compound has, as is mostly the case, only one alliterative sound, that alliteration must necessarily fall on the first part of the compound:

> wítig wúldorcyning   wórlde and héofona.   Dan. 427.

Sometimes it happens that in hemistichs of no great length the second part of the compound carries one of the two rhythmical accents of the hemistich, e. g.

> on héah-sétle   héofones wáldend.   Cri. 555.

and in a particular form of alliteration[3] it may even contain one of the alliterating sounds, as in the verse:

> hwæt! we Gárdéna   in géardágum.   Beow. 1.

The less strongly accented derivational and inflexional suffixes, though they are not allowed to alliterate, may occasionally have the rhythmical accent, on condition that they immediately follow upon a long accented syllable, e. g.

> mid Wýlfíngum,   þā hine Wára cýn.   Beow. 461.

> ne méahte ic æt hílde   mid Hrúntínge.   ib. 1659.

The rhythmical value of syllables with a secondary accent will be considered more fully later on.

These general rules for the accent of compound words formed of noun + noun or adjective + noun require modification for the cases where a prefix (adverb or preposition) stands in close juxtaposition with a verb or noun. The preposition standing before and depending on a noun coalesces so closely

---

[1] Besides the unaccented syllables of polysyllabic words, many monosyllables, such as prepositions, pronouns, &c., are unstressed, and occur only in the theses.

[2] This rule applies to modern English also, as in words like *birth-right*.

[3] If this cross alliteration is intentional. See Sievers, *Altger. Metrik*, p. 41.

with it that the two words express a single notion, the noun having the chief accent, e. g. *onwég*, *āwég* (away), *ætsómne* (together), *ofdúne* (down), *toníhte* (to-night), *onmíddum* (amid); examples in verse are:

> *gebād* **wíntra** **wórn**   *ǣr he on***wég** *hwúrfe.* Beow. 264.

> *síd* **ætsómne** *þā ge***súndrod** *wǽs.* Gen. 162.

But while the prepositional prefix thus does not carry the alliteration owing to its want of accent, some of the adverbs used in composition are accented, others are unaccented, and others again may be treated either way. When the adverbial prefix originally stood by itself side by side with the verb, and may in certain cases still be disjoined from it, it has then the primary accent, because it is felt as a modifying element of the compound. When, however, the prefix and the verb have become so intimately united as to express one single notion, the verb takes the accent and the prefix is treated as proclitic, and there is a third class of these compounds which are used indifferently with accent on the prefix or on the verb.

Some of the commonest prefixes used in alliteration are [1]: *and, æfter, eft, ed, fore, forð, from, hider, in, hin, mid, mis, niðer, ongēan, or, up, út, efne,* as in compounds like *ándswarian, íngong, ǽfterweard,* &c. :

> *on* **ánds**wáre   *and on* **éln**e stróng. Gū. 264.

> **éð**elīc **íng**ong   **éal** *wæs ge***búnd**en. Cri. 308.

> *and* **éac** *þāra* **ýf**ela   **órsorh** *wúnað.* Met. vii. 43.

> **úpl**ang gestód   *wið* **I**'*sra***hélum.** Ex. 303.

Prefixes which do not take the alliteration are: *ā, ge, for, geond, oð,* e. g.

> **āh**ōn and **āh**ébban   *on* **héahne** **béam.** Jul. 228.

> *hǽfde þā ge***fóhten**   **fórem**ǣrne blǽd. Jud. 122.

> **brónde** for**bǽrnan**   *ne on* **bǽl** *hládan.* Beow. 2126.

The following fluctuate: *æt, an, bī* (*big*), *bi* (*be*), *of, ofer, on, tō, under, þurh, wið, wiðer, ymb.* These are generally accented and alliterate, if compounded with substantives or adjectives, but are not accented and do not alliterate if compounded with

---

[1] See Koch, *Historische Grammatik der englischen Sprache*, Weimar, 1863, i. 156.

verbs or other particles,[1] e. g. *óferhēah*, *óferhȳd*, but *ofercúman*, *oferbídan*. The following lines will illustrate this :

(*a*) prefixes which alliterate :

þára þe þurh óferhȳd úp ástígeð. Dan. 495.

átol is þín ónsēon hábbað we éalle swá. Satan 61.

ýmbe-síttendra ǽnig þára. Beow. 2734.

(*b*) prefixes which do not alliterate :

oðð̄æt he þā bȳsgu oferbíden hæfde. Gū. 518.

ne wíllað ēow ondrǣdan déade féðan. Exod. 266.

sýmbel ymbsǣton sǣgrunde néah. Beow. 564.[2]

When prepositions precede other prepositions or adverbs in composition, the accent rests on that part of the whole compound which is felt to be the most important. Such compounds fall into three classes : (i) if a preposition or adverb is preceded by the prepositions *be, on, tō, þurh, wið*, these latter are not accented, since they only slightly modify the sense of the following adverb. Compounds of this kind are : *beǽftan, befóran, begéondan, behíndan, beínnan, benéoðan, búfan, bútan, onúfan, onúppan, tofóran, wiðínnan, wiðútan, undernéoðan*.[3] Only the second part of the compound is allowed to alliterate in these words :

he féara súm befóran géngde. Beow. 1412.

ne þe behíndan lǣt þonne þu héonan cýrre. Cri. 155.

Most of these words do not seem to occur in the poetry. (ii) In compounds of *þ̄ær* + preposition the preposition is accented and takes the alliteration :

swā he þ̄æorínne ándlangne dǣg. Beow. 2115.

þe þ̄æorón síndon éce drýhten. Hy. iv. 3.

(iii) *weard*, as in *æfterweard, foreweard, hindanweard, niðerweard, ufeweard*, &c., is not accented :

hwít híndanweard and se háls grêne. Ph. 298.

níoðoweard and úfeweard and þæt nebb líxeð. ib. 299.

féðe-géstum flét ínnanweard. Beow. 1977.

---

[1] Compare Streitberg, *Urgermanische Grammatik*, 1900, § 143, p. 167, or Wilmanns, *Deutsche Grammatik*, 1897, i, p. 407, § 349.

[2] For exceptions to these rules see *Englische Metrik*, i, pp. 43, 45.

[3] Koch adds *wiðæftan, wiðfóran, wiðnéoðan*.

§ **19. The secondary accent.** The secondary or subordinate accent is of as great importance as the chief or primary
accent in determining the rhythmical character of the alliterative
line. It is found in the following classes of words:

(i) In all compounds of noun + noun, or adjective + noun, or
adjective + adjective, the second element of the compound has
the subordinate accent, e.g. *hēah-sètl*, *gúð-rínc*, *hríng-nèt*, *sóð-fæst*.
Syllables with this secondary accent are necessary in certain
cases as links between the arsis and thesis, as in forms like
þégn Hróðgàres ($\acute{-}\,|\,\acute{-}\,\grave{\times}\,\times$) or *fýrst fórð gewàt* ($\acute{-}\,|\,\acute{-}\,\times\,\grave{\times}$).
(ii) In proper names like *Hróðgàr*, *Béowùlf*, *Hýgelàc*, this
secondary accent may sometimes count as one of the four chief
metrical accents of the line, as in

    b**é**ornas on b**l**áncum   þǣr wæs B**é**owúlfes.   Beow. 857.

contrasted with

    éorl Béowùlfes   **é**alde láfe.   Beow. 797.

(iii) When the second element has ceased to be felt as a distinct
part of the compound, and is little more than a suffix, it loses
the secondary accent altogether; as *hláford*, *ǽghwylc*, *ínwit*, and
the large class of words compounded with *-líc* and *sum*.

    þæt he H**é**ardréde   h**l**áford wǽre.   Beow. 2375.

    l**ú**fsum and l**í**ðe   l**é**ofum monnum.   Cri. 914.

(iv) In words of three syllables, the second syllable when long
and following a long root-syllable with the chief accent, has,
especially in the early stage of Old English, a well-marked
secondary accent: thus, *ǽrèsta*, *óðèrra*, *sémnìnga*, *éhlènde*; the
third syllable in words of the form *ǽðelìnga* gets the same
secondary accent. This secondary accent can count as one of
the four rhythmic accents of the line, e.g.

    þā ǽrèstan ǽlda cýnnes.   Gū. 948.

    s**í**gefolca sw**é**g oð þæt sémnínga.   Beow. 644.

Words of this class, not compounded, are comparatively rare,
but compounds with secondary accent are frequent.

These second syllables with a marked secondary accent in
the best examples of Old English verse mostly form by themselves a member of the verse, i. e. are not treated as simple theses
as in certain compositions of later date, e. g.

        dýgelra gescéafta.   Creat. 18.

        ágenne bróðor.   Metr. ix. 28.

(v) After a long root-syllable of a trisyllabic word a short second syllable (whether its vowel was originally short or long) may bear one of the chief accents of the line, e. g. *bōcère, bíscòpe* :

þǣr bíscéopas and bōcéras.   An. 607.

or may stand in the thesis and be unaccented, as

gódes bísceope þā sprǣc gúðcýning.   Gen. 2123.

This shows that in common speech these syllables had only a slight secondary accent.

(vi) Final syllables (whether long or short) are as a rule not accented even though a long root-syllable precede them.

§ 20. **Division and metrical value of syllables.** Some other points must be noticed with reference to the division and metrical value of the syllables of some classes of words.

The formative element *i* in the present stem of the second class of weak verbs always counts as a syllable when it follows a long root-syllable, thus *fund-i-an, fund-i-ende* not *fund-yan*, &c. In verbs with a short root-syllable it is metrically indifferent whether this *i* is treated as forming a syllable by itself or coalescing as a consonant with the following vowel, so that we may divide either *ner-i-an,* or *ner-yan*; in verbs of the first and third class the consonantal pronunciation was according to Sievers probably the usual one, hence *neryan* (*nerian*), *lifyan* (*lifǥan*), but for verbs of the second class the syllable remained vocalic, thus *polian.*[1]

In foreign names like *Assyria, Eusebius,* the *i* is generally treated as a vowel, but in longer words possibly as a consonant, as *Macedonya* (*Macedonia*). As to the epenthetic vowels developed from a *w,* the question whether we are to pronounce *gearowe* or *gearwe, bealowes* or *bealwes* cannot be decided by metre. Syllabic *l, m, n* (*ļ, m̨, ņ*) following a short root-vowel lose their syllabic character, thus *sètl, hrǣgl, swèfn* are monosyllables, but *er* coming from original *r* as in *wæter, leger* may be either consonantal or vocalic. After a long root-syllable vocalic pronunciation is the rule, but occasionally words of this kind, as *túngl, bósm, tācn,* are used as monosyllables, and the *l, m,* and *n* are consonants. Hiatus is allowed; but in many cases elision of an unaccented syllable takes place, though no fixed rule can be laid down owing to the fluctuating number of unaccented syllables permissible in the hemistich or whole line.

---

[1] Sievers, *Beiträge,* x. 225, and *Angelsächsische Grammatik*³, §§ 410, 411, 415.

In some cases the metre requires us to expunge vowels which have crept into the texts by the carelessness of copyists, e. g. we must write *éðles* instead of *éðeles*, *éngles* instead of *éngeles*, *déofles* instead of *déofeles*, and in other cases we must restore the older and fuller forms such as *óðerra* for *óðrā*, *eówere* for *eówre*.[1] The resolution of long syllables with the chief accent in the arsis, and of long syllables with the secondary accent in the thesis, affects very greatly the number of syllables in the line. Instead of the one long syllable which as a rule bears one of the four chief accents of the verse, we not unfrequently meet with a short accented syllable plus an unaccented syllable either long or short ($\cup \times$). This is what is termed the resolution of an accented syllable. A word accordingly like *fároðe* with one short accented syllable and two unaccented syllables has the same rhythmical value as *fóron* with one long accented and one unaccented syllable, or a combination like *se þe wæs* is rhythmically equivalent to *sécg wæs*.

§ 21. We now come to **the structure of the whole allite-rative line.** The regular alliterative line or verse is made up of two hemistichs or sections. These two sections are separated from each other by a pause or break, but united by means of allitera-tion so that they form a rhythmical unity. Each hemistich must have two syllables which predominate over the rest in virtue of their logical and syntactical importance and have on this account a stronger stress. These stressed syllables, four in number for the whole line, count as the rhythmical accents of the verse. The force given to these accented syllables is more marked when they carry at the same time the alliteration, which happens at least once in each hemistich, frequently twice in the first and once in the second hemistich, and in a number of instances twice in both hemistichs. The effect of the emphasis given to these four words or syllables by the syntax, etymology, rhythm, and sometimes alliteration, is that the other words and syllables may for metrical purposes be looked upon as in comparison unaccented, even though they may have a main or secondary word-accent.

In certain cases, in consequence of the particular structure of the hemistich, there is found a rhythmical secondary accent, generally coinciding with an etymological secondary accent, or with a monosyllable, or with the root-syllable of a disyllabic

---

[1] For details on these points and on the question of the treatment of forms in which vowel contraction is exhibited in the MSS. see Sievers, *Altgermanische Metrik*, §§ 74–77, and *Beiträge*, x. 475 ff.

word.   Sievers looks on these syllables as having in the rhythm of the verse the nature of a minor arsis (*Nebenhebung*); they rather belong to the class of syllables standing in thesis but with a slight degree of accent (*tieftonige Senkung*).

The two sections of the alliterative line rarely exhibit a strict symmetry as to the number of the unaccented syllables and their position with regard to the accented syllables.   In the great majority of cases their similarity consists merely in their having each two accented syllables, their divergence in other respects being very considerable.   It is to be noted that certain combinations of accented and unaccented syllable occur with more frequency in one hemistich than in the other, or are even limited to one of the two hemistichs only.

Besides the ordinary or normal alliterative line with four accents, there exists in Old English and in other West-Germanic poetry a variety of the alliterative line called the *lengthened line* (*Schwellvers* or *Streckvers*).   In this line each hemistich has three accented syllables, the unaccented syllables standing in the same relation to the accented ones as they do in the normal two-beat hemistich.

§ 22. **The structure of the hemistich in the normal alliterative line.**   The normal hemistich consists of four, seldom of five members [1] (*Glieder*), two of which are strongly accented (arses), the others unaccented or less strongly accented (theses). Each arsis is formed, as a rule, of a long accented syllable ($\_$), but the second part of a compound, and (less frequently) the second syllable with a secondary accent of a trisyllabic or disyllabic word, is allowed to stand as an arsis.   By resolution a long accented syllable may be replaced by two short syllables, the first of which is accented.   This is denoted by the symbol $\cup \times$. The less strongly accented members of the hemistich fall into two classes according as they are unaccented or have the secondary accent.   This division depends ultimately on the logical or etymological importance of the syllables.   Unaccented syllables (marked in Sievers's notation by $\times$) whether long or short by etymology, are mostly inflexional endings, formative elements, or proclitic and enclitic words.

Secondarily accented verse-members, mostly monosyllabic and long (denoted by $\dot{\times}$, and occasionally, when short, by $\cup$), are root-syllables in the second part of compounds, long second syllables of trisyllabic words whose root-syllable is long, and

other syllables where in ordinary speech the presence of a
secondary accent is unmistakable. The rhythmical value of
these syllables with secondary accent is not always the same.
When they stand in a foot or measure of two members and are
preceded by an accented syllable they count as simply unaccented, and the foot is practically identical with the normal
type represented by the notation _⌣ × (as in the hemistich *wísra
wórda*), but these half-accented syllables may be called *heavy*
theses, and the feet which contain them may be denoted by the
formula _⌣ ×̀, as in *wísfæst wórdum* (_⌣ ×̀ | _⌣ ×). A hemistich
like the last is called by Sievers strengthened (*gesteigert*), or if it
has two heavy unaccented syllables in both feet, doubly
strengthened, as in the section *gúðrìnc góldwlànc* (_⌣ ×̀ | _⌣ ×̀).
In these examples the occurrence of a heavy unaccented syllable
is permissible but not necessary; but in feet or measures of
three members they are obligatory, being required as an inter-
mediate degree between the arsis and thesis, or strongly accented
and unaccented member, as in *þégn Hróðgàres* (_⌣ | _⌣ ×̀ ×), or
fýrst fórð gewàt (_⌣ | _⌣ × ×̀), or *héalærna mæst* (_⌣ ×̀ × | _⌣).
In these cases Sievers gives the verse-member with this secondary accent the character of a subordinate arsis, or beat
(*Nebenhebung*). But it is better, in view of the strongly marked
two-beat swing of the hemistich, to look on such members with
a secondary accent as having only the rhythmical value of
unaccented syllables, and to call them *theses* with a slight accent.
The two-beat rhythm of the hemistich is its main characteristic,
for though the two beats are not always of exactly equal force [1]
they are always prominently distinguished from the unaccented
members of the hemistich, the rhythm of which would be
marred by the introduction of an additional beat however
slightly marked.

Cases in which the two chief beats of the hemistich are not of
exactly the same force occur when two accented syllables, either
both with chief accent or one with chief and the other with
secondary accent, stand in immediate juxtaposition, not separated
by an unaccented syllable. The second of these two accented
syllables may be a short syllable with chief accent, instead of
a long syllable as is the rule. But in either case, whether
long or short, this second beat following at once on the first
beat is usually uttered with somewhat less force than the first, as
can be seen from examples like *gebún hæfdon*, Beow. 117; *tó*

---

[1] Sievers, *Altgerm. Metrik*, § 9, 3. 4.

hắm fáran, 121 ; *mid ǽrdǽge*, 126. The second beat rarely predominates over the first. The cause of this variation in the force of the two beats is to be sought in the laws of the syntactical accent.

In other respects verse-members with a secondary accent obey the same laws as those with a primary accent. They usually consist of one long syllable, but if a member which has the arsis immediately precedes, a short syllable with a secondary accent may be substituted. Resolution of such verse members is rare, which shows that they are more closely related to the thesis than to the arsis of the hemistich. One unaccented syllable is sufficient to form the thesis (x), but the thesis may also have two or more unaccented syllables (x x, x x x ..), their number increasing in proportion to their shortness and the ease with which they can be pronounced, provided always that no secondary accent intervenes. All of these unaccented syllables are reckoned together as one thesis, as against the accented syllable or arsis. The single components of such a longer thesis may exhibit a certain gradation of force when compared with one another, but this degree of force must never equal the force with which the arsis is pronounced, though we sometimes find that, owing to the varying character of the syntactical or sentence accent, a monosyllable which in one case stands in the thesis, may in another connexion bear the secondary or even the primary accent.

§ **23.** The number of the unaccented syllables of the thesis was formerly believed to depend entirely on the choice of the individual poet.[1] Sievers first put this matter in its right light by the statistics of the metre.[2] He showed that the hemistich of the Old English alliterative line is similar to the Old Norse four-syllable verse, and is as a rule of a trochaic rhythm ($\angle$ x $\angle$ x). The proof of this is that in *Beowulf*, for instance, there are 592 hemistichs of the type $\angle$ x | $\angle$ x (as *hýran scólde*, 10), and that in the same text there are 238 of the type $\angle$ x x | $\angle$ x (as *góde gewýrcean*, 20 ; *héold þenden lífde*, 57), making 830 hemistichs with trochaic or dactylic rhythm, as against eleven hemistichs of similar structure but with an unaccented syllable at the beginning, x | $\angle$ x (x) | $\angle$ x, and even four or five of these eleven are of doubtful correctness. From these figures it seems almost beyond doubt that in the

---

[1] See, for example, Rieger, *Alt- und Angelsächsische Verskunst*, p. 62.
[2] *Paul-Braune's Beiträge*, x, p. 209.

type $\underline{\prime}\times(\times)|\underline{\prime}\times$ the licence of letting the hemistich begin with an unaccented syllable before the first accented syllable was, generally speaking, avoided. On the other hand, when the first accented syllable is short with only one unaccented syllable as thesis ($\cup\times$), we find this initial unaccented syllable to be the rule, as *genúmen hǽfdon* Beow. 3167 ($\times|\cup\times|\underline{\prime}\times$), of which form there are 130 examples, while, as Rieger noticed, $\cup\times|\underline{\prime}\times$ is rare, as in *cýning mǽnan* Beow. 3173. It is perhaps still more remarkable that while the form $\underline{\prime}\times\times|\underline{\prime}\times$ occurs some 238 times, a verse of the form $\times|\cup\times\times|\underline{\prime}\times$ is never found at all. The numerical proportion of the form $\underline{\prime}\times|\underline{\prime}\times$ (592 cases) to $\underline{\prime}\times\times|\underline{\prime}\times$ (238 cases) is roughly 5 to 2, and that of $\times|\cup\times|\underline{\prime}\times$ (130 cases) to $\times|\cup\times\times|\underline{\prime}\times$ (no cases) is 130 to nothing. The quantity of the second arsis is, as bearing on the prefixing of unaccented syllables to the hemistich, much less important than the quantity of the first arsis. Hemistichs of the type $\underline{\prime}\times|\cup\times$ occur 34 times, and in 29 cases the last unaccented syllable is a full word, either a monosyllable or a part of a compound. The same type, with an initial unaccented syllable $\times|\underline{\prime}\times|\cup\times$ also occurs 34 times, but then the last syllable is quite unaccented. The proportion of the form $\underline{\prime}\times|\underline{\prime}\times$ to the form $\times|\underline{\prime}\times|\underline{\prime}\times$ is 592 to 11, and that of the form $\underline{\prime}\times|\cup\times$ to $\times|\underline{\prime}\times|\cup\times$ is 34 to 34, a noticeable difference.

Further, it was formerly supposed that the number of unaccented syllables following the accented syllable was indifferent. This is not the case. The form $\underline{\prime}\times\times|\underline{\prime}\times$ is found 238 times, and the form $\underline{\prime}\times|\underline{\prime}\times\times$ only 22 times. Many of the examples of the latter form are doubtful, but even counting all these the proportion of the two forms is 11 to 1.

If the two accented syllables are not separated by an unaccented syllable, that is to say, if the two beats are in immediate juxtaposition, then either two unaccented syllables must stand after the second arsis, thus $\underline{\prime}|\underline{\prime}\times\times$ (a form that occurs 120 times in *Beowulf*), or an unaccented syllable must precede the first arsis and one unaccented syllable must follow the second arsis, thus $\times\underline{\prime}|\underline{\prime}\times$ (127 times in *Beowulf*), or with the second arsis short $\times\underline{\prime}|\cup\times$ (257 times); the form $\underline{\prime}|\underline{\prime}\times$ does not occur.

From these statistics it results that hemistichs of the form $\underline{\prime}\times|\underline{\prime}\times$ are met with about 17 times to one occurrence of the form $\underline{\prime}\times|\cup\times$, and that on the other hand, the form $\times\underline{\prime}|\cup\times$ is about twice as frequent as $\times\underline{\prime}|\underline{\prime}\times$.

§ 24. The order of the verse-members in the hemistich.
Every hemistich consists of two feet or measures, each containing an accented syllable. Usually these two feet or measures
together contain four verse members, seldom five. In the
hemistich of four members, which first falls to be considered,
the measures may consist of two members each (2 + 2), or one
may contain one member and the other three (1 + 3 or 3 + 1).
A measure of one member has a single accented syllable only
(´); a measure of two members has an accented and an unaccented syllable, which may stand either in the order ´× or
×´; a measure of three members has one accented and two
unaccented syllables, one of which has a secondary accent, and
the order may be either ´x̀ × or ´× x̀. Measures of two
members may be grouped in three different ways so as to form
a hemistich: i. ´×|´× (descending rhythm); ii. ×´|×´
(ascending); iii. ×´|´× (ascending-descending)[1]; i. and ii.
are symmetrical, iii. is unsymmetrical, but as the number of
members in the feet of these three types (2 + 2 members) is
the same, we may call them, as Sievers does, types with equal
feet (*gleichfüssige Typen*), while the others (1 + 3 members or
3 + 1 members) may be called types with unequal feet or
measures.

The normal hemistich, then, which consists of four verse-
members, will fall, according to the relative position of these
measures or feet, into the following five chief types:

a. Types with equal feet (2 + 2 members)

1. A. ´×|´× double descending.
2. B. ×´|×´ double ascending.
3. C. ×´|´× ascending-descending.

b. Types with unequal feet

4. D. $\left\{ \begin{array}{l} ´|´\grave{x}\ × \\ ´|´×\ \grave{x} \end{array} \right\}$ (1 + 3 members).

5. E. $\left\{ \begin{array}{l} ´\grave{x}\ ×\ |´ \\ ´×\ \grave{x}\ |´ \end{array} \right\}$ (3 + 1 members).

Theoretically type E might be looked on as a type with equal
feet, if divided thus, ´×|×´, but by far the greatest number of
instances of this type show at the beginning of the hemistich
one trisyllabic word which forbids such a division of feet, as

---

[1] For the type ´ × ×|´ see below, § 29, and Sievers, *Paul-Braune's Beiträge*, x, p. 262.

wéorčmýndum þáh, Beow. 8.[1] Types like × × $\angle$ — and ×̇ × $\angle\angle$, which we might expect to find, do not occur in Old English poetry. In addition to these ordinary four-membered hemistichs there are others lengthened by the addition of one syllable, which may be unaccented, or have the secondary accent. These extended forms (*erweiterte Formen*)[2] may be composed either of 2 + 3 members or of 3 + 2 members. These extended hemistichs must be carefully distinguished from the hemistichs which have one or more unaccented syllables *before* the first accented syllable, in types A, D, and E; such a prefix of one or more syllables is called an *anacrusis* (Auftakt).[3]

The simple five types of the hemistich admit of variation: i. by extension (as above); ii. by resolution ($\smile$× for $\angle$) and shortening of the long accented syllable ($\smile$); iii. by strengthening of thesis by means of a secondary accent (*Steigerung*); iv. by increase in the number of unaccented syllables forming the thesis; also (less frequently) v. by variation in the position of the alliteration, and vi. by the admission of anacruses; the varieties produced by the last-mentioned means are not sub-types but parallel forms to those without anacruses.

In describing and analysing the different combinations which arise out of these means of variation, and especially the peculiar forms of the sub-types, the arrangement and nomenclature of Sievers will be followed.[4]

Analysis of the verse types.

I. *Hemistichs of four members.*

§ 25. **Type A** has three sub-types, A 1, A 2, A 3.

The sub-type **A 1** ($\angle$ × | $\angle$ ×) is the normal form with alliteration of the first arsis in each hemistich, or with alliteration of both arses in the first hemistich and one in the second, and with syllables in the thesis which are unaccented according to the usual practice of the language; examples are, *þéodnes*

---

[1] Sievers, *Paul-Braune's Beiträge*, x, p. 262.

[2] As Sievers calls them, *Altgerm. Metrik*, § 13. 2; they are marked A*, B*, &c.

[3] The notation of Sievers for hemistichs with anacrusis (*auftaktige Verse*) is aA, aD, aE, &c.

[4] Sievers, *Altgermanische Metrik*, pp. 33 ff.

þégnas An. 3, *hýran scólde* Beow. 106, *gómban gýldan* Beow. 11. This is the commonest of all the types; it occurs in Beowulf, according to Sievers, 471 times in the first and 575 times in the second hemistich, and with the like frequency in the other poems.

The simplest modification of this type arises from the resolution of one or two long accented syllables. Examples of resolution of the first arsis are very numerous, *cýninga wúldor* El. 5, *scéaðena préatum* Beow. 4, *séofon niht swúncon* Beow. 517,[1] *níðer gewíteð* Beow. 1361. Examples of the resolution of the second arsis are less numerous, as *wúldor cýninge* El. 291, *éllen frémedon* Beow. 3, *Scýldes éaferan* Beow. 19, *óft gefrémede* Beow. 165; resolution of both in the same hemistich is rare, but is found, as *gúmena géogoðe* An. 1617, *mǽgenes Déniga* Beow. 155, *gúmum ǽtgǽdere* Beow. 1321.

The chief type is further modified by making the thesis after the first arsis disyllabic (rarely trisyllabic); the formula is then ⌣ x x | − x. This modification is frequent, as *ríhta gehwýlces* El. 910, *góde gewýrcean* Beow. 20, *swéordum ǽswébban* An. 72, *súnnan ond mónan* Beow. 94, *fólce tō frófre* Beow. 14, *wéox under wólcnum* Beow. 8.

Resolution of the arsis may be combined with this disyllabic thesis, as (in the first arsis) *wérum on þām wónge* An. 22, *éotenas ond ýlfe* Beow. 112, or (in the second arsis) *hálig of héofenum* An. 89, *hélpe gefrémede* Beow. 551, or (in both) *dúguðe ond géoguðe* Beow. 160, *hǽleð under héofenum* Beow. 52.

The first thesis rarely exceeds two syllables; a thesis of three syllables is occasionally found, as *sǽgde se þe cúðe* Beow. 90, *hwílum hie gehéton* Beow. 175, and this can be combined with resolution of the first arsis, as *swéotulra ond gesýnra* An. 565, *bítere ond gebólgne* Beow. 1431; or with resolution of the second arsis, as *útan ymbe ǽðelne* An. 873, *wíge under wǽtere* Beow. 1657; or with resolution of both, as *réceda under róderum* Beow. 310. Examples of thesis of four syllables are (in the first thesis) *séalde þām þe hē wólde* Beow. 3056, *sécge ic þē tō sóðe* Beow. 591. A thesis with five syllables is still less common, as *lǽddon hine þā of lýfte* Gū. 398, *stópon þā tō þǽre stówe* El. 716.

The cases in which the second thesis has two syllables are rare and to some extent doubtful, as *wúndor scéawian* Beow. 841 and 3033.[2]

---

[1] It must be remembered that *ea, eo*, &c., are diphthongs, and have not the value of two vowels.

[2] Sievers, *Paul-Braune's Beiträge*, x, p. 233.

The anacrusis before the type $\angle \times (\times) | \angle \times$ is also of rare occurrence: examples are *swā sǣ bebúgeð* Beow. 1224, or, with resolution of the first arsis, *swā wǣter bebúgeð* Beow. 93. Most of the instances occur in the first hemistich; in this position the anacrusis may be polysyllabic (extending sometimes to four syllables), sometimes with resolution of the arsis, or with polysyllabic thesis. Examples: *forcóm æt cámpe* An. 1327, *gewāt æt wíge* Beow. 2630; with resolution, *ābóden in búrgum* An. 78; *genéred wið níðe* Beow. 828; disyllabic anacrusis *ic wæs éndesǣta* Beow. 241; with resolution, *þǣr wæs hǽleða hléahtor* Beow. 612; trisyllabic anacrusis, *oððe him Óngenþéowes* Beow. 2475; four-syllable anacrusis, *þæt we him þā gúðgeatwa* Beow. 2637; monosyllabic anacrusis with disyllabic thesis, as in *mǣgðe gehwǣre* Beow. 25, *āblénded in búrgum* An. 78; disyllabic anacrusis with disyllabic thesis, *ge æt hám ge on hérge* Beow. 1249; trisyllabic anacrusis with disyllabic thesis, *þú scealt þā fóre geféran* An. 216; monosyllabic anacrusis with trisyllabic thesis, *gemúnde þā sē góda* Beow. 759; monosyllabic anacrusis with resolution of first arsis and trisyllabic thesis, *ne mágon hie ond ne móton* An. 1217; with resolution of second arsis, *gewāt him þā tō wároðe* Beow. 234; disyllabic anacrusis, *ne geféah he þǣre fǣhðe* Beow. 109; combined with thesis of four syllables, *ofslóh þā æt þǣre sǽcce* Beow. 1666.

The sub-type A 2 is type A with strengthened thesis (i. e. a thesis with secondary accent) and with alliteration on the first arsis only. This sub-type has several varieties:

(i) **A 2 a**, with the *first* thesis strengthened $(\angle \dot{\times} | \angle \times)$; frequent in the second hemistich. The second arsis may be either long or short $(\angle \dot{\times} | \angle \times$, or $\angle \dot{\times} | \cup \times)$. We denote $\angle \dot{\times} | \angle \times$ by A 2 a l and $\angle \dot{\times} | \cup \times$ by A 2 a sh, or, for brevity, A 2 l, A 2 sh. Examples of A 2 l are, *gódspèl ǽrest* An. 12, *wísfǽst wórdum* Beow. 626, *hríngnèt bǣron* Beow. 1890; with resolution of the first arsis, *médusèld búan* Beow. 3066; with resolution of the second arsis, *gársècg hlýnede* An. 238, *hórdbùrh hǽleða* Beow. 467; with resolution of both, *fréoðobùrh fǽgere* Beow. 522; with resolution of the strengthened thesis, *súndwùdu sóhte* Beow. 208; resolution of the first arsis and thesis, *mǣgenwùdu múndum* Beow. 236; resolution of the first thesis and the second arsis, *gúðsèaro gúmena* Beow. 328.

Examples of A 2 sh are numerous, as *wǣrfǽst cýning* An. 416, *gúðrìnc mónig* Beow. 839, *þréanỳd þólað* Beow. 284; it is exceptional to find the second arsis short when the thesis which precedes has no secondary accent, as *Hréðel cýning* Beow.

2436, *Hrúnting náma* Beow. 1458, *ǽðeling bóren* Beow. 2431 ;
with resolution of the first arsis, *séaronèt séowað* An. 64, *snótor
cèorl mónig* Beow. 909, *sígeròf cyning* Beow. 619, *mágodrìht
micel* Beow. 67, &c. Most of the hemistichs which fall under
this head have double alliteration.

(ii) A 2 *b*, with the *second* thesis strengthened ($\perp \times | \perp \dot{\times}$).
Most of the cases of this type occur in the first hemistich ;
when they occur in the second hemistich the measure $\perp \dot{\times}$ is
usually a proper name, not a real compound. Examples :
Gréndles gúðcrǽft Beow. 127, *lèofa Béowùlf* Beow. 855 ; with
resolution of the first arsis, *gámol ond gúðrèow* Beow. 58 ; with
resolution of the second arsis, *béorna béaducrǽft* An. 219 ; with
resolution of both, *séfa swā séarogrìm* Beow. 595 ; with resolution of the strengthened thesis, *lönd ond lèodbȳrig* Beow. 2472 ;
with resolution of both the second arsis and thesis *mǽg ond
mágopègn* Beow. 408.[1]

This type may still further be varied by a first thesis of two or
more syllables, *út on þæt íglànd* An. 15, *fólc oððe frèobùrh* Beow.
694, *réste hine þā rúmhèort* Beow. 1800 ; by resolution of the
first arsis, *glídon ofer gársècg* Beow. 515, of the second, *lád
ofer lágustrèam* An. 423, *sýmbel on sélefùl* Beow. 620 ; by resolution of the thesis with secondary accent, *éahtodon éorlscìpe*
Beow. 3173 ; the anacrusis is rarely found, as *gesáwon séledrèam*
Beow. 2253, and double alliteration (in the first hemistich) is
the rule in this form of type A.

(iii) A 2 *ab*, with both theses strengthened $\perp \dot{\times} | \perp \dot{\times}$, *bánhùs
blódfàg* An. 1407, *gúðrìnc góldwlànc* Beow. 1882, *ǽnlìc ánsȳn*
Beow. 251 ; with resolution of first arsis, *wlítesèon wrǽðlìc* Beow.
1651, and of the second arsis, *glèawmòd góde lèof* An. 1581,
gúðswèord géatolìc Beow. 2155, and of both first and second
arsis, *héorowèarh héfelìc* Beow. 1268 ; with resolution of the first
(strengthened) thesis, *nýdwràcu nìðgrìm* Beow. 193 ; with resolution of both the first arsis and the first thesis, *býrelàde brȳd
gèong* Gū. 842 ; with resolution of the second strengthened thesis,
égeslìc éorðdràca Beow. 2826 ; with resolution of the first and
second thesis, *fȳrdsèaru fúslìcu* Beow. 232. This form of the
type has also as a rule double alliteration.

The sub-type A 3 is type A with alliteration on the second
arsis only and is limited almost entirely to the first hemistich.
A strengthened thesis occurs only after the second arsis ; this
sub-type might therefore be designated A 3 *b*.

---

[1] Here *n* counts as a syllable, see Sievers, *Angelsächsische Gram.*, § 141,
and *Altgerm. Metrik*, § 79.

Verses falling under this head, with their alliteration always on the last syllable but one, or (in the case of resolution) on the last syllable but two, are distinguished by the frequent occurrence of polysyllabic theses extending to five syllables, in marked contrast to types A 1 and A 2 where theses of one or two syllables are the rule, longer theses the exception. In A 3, however, shorter theses are met with along with the usual resolutions : a monosyllabic thesis in *hwǽr se þéoden* El. 563, *éow hēt sécgan* Beow. 391 ; with resolution of first arsis, *wúton nū éfstan* Beow. 3102 ; with resolution of the second arsis, *þús me fǽder mīn* El. 528, *íc þæt hógode* Beow. 633 ; with disyllabic thesis, *héht þā on úhtan* El. 105, *hǽfde se góda* Beow. 205 ; with resolution of the first arsis, *þánon he gesóhte* Beow. 463 ; with resolution of the second arsis, *wéarð him on Héorote* Beow. 1331 ; with strengthened second thesis, *éart þū sē Béowùlf* Beow. 506 ; with trisyllabic thesis, *gíf þē þæt gelímpe* El. 441, *fúndon þā on sánde* Beow. 3034 ; with resolution of the first arsis, *hwǽðere mē gesǽlde* Beow. 574, of the second arsis, *sýððan ic for dúgeðum* Beow. 2502 ; with strengthened second thesis, *nó hē þone gífstòl* Beow. 168 ; with thesis of four syllables, *swýlce hī mē gebléndon* Cri. 1438, *hábbað wē tō þǽm mǽran* Beow. 270 ; with resolution of the first arsis, *útan ūs tō þǽre hýðe* Cri. 865 ; with resolution of the first and second arsis, *þóne þe him on swéofote* Beow. 2296 ; with strengthened second thesis, *nó þý ǽr þone héaðorìnc* Beow. 2466 ; with thesis of five syllables, *sýððan hē hine to gúðe* Beow. 1473 ; with thesis of six syllables, *hýrde ic þæt hē þone héalsbèah* Beow. 2173. These forms are also varied by monosyllabic anacrusis combined with monosyllabic thesis, *þe éow of wérgðe* El. 295, *þæt híne on ýlde* Beow. 22 ; with strengthened second thesis, *þæt híne séo brímwỳlf* Beow. 1600; with disyllabic thesis, *ne þéarft þū swā swíðe* El. 940, *gesprǽc þā sē góda* Beow. 676 ; the same with resolution of the first arsis, *gewítan him þā góngan* Cri. 533 ; disyllabic anacrusis and disyllabic thesis, *ne gefrǽgn ic þā mǽgðe* Beow. 1012 ; with resolution of the second arsis, *geséah hē in récede* Beow. 728 ; with strengthened second thesis, *ge swýlce séo hérepàd* Beow. 2259 ; monosyllabic anacrusis with trisyllabic thesis, *on hwýlcum þāra béama* El.851 ; with four-syllable thesis, *gewíteð þonne on sealman* Beow. 2461 ; with resolution of the first arsis, *ne mágon hī þonne gehýnan* Cri. 1525 ; with resolution of the second arsis, *gesáwon þā æfter wǽtere* Beow. 1426. The last measure may be shortened exceptionally to $\acute{\cup} \times$, as *wǽs mīn fǽder* Beow. 262.

On the whole type A seems to occur more frequently in the

first than in the second hemistich; in Beowulf out of the 6366
hemistichs of which the poem consists, 2819 fall under this type,
and of these 1701 are first and 1118 second hemistichs.[1]

§ 26. **The chief type B,** $\times \stackrel{\angle}{} | \times \stackrel{\angle}{}$, has apart from resolu-
tions only one form. But as the second thesis may consist of
either one or two syllables, we may distinguish between two sub-
types, B 1 (with monosyllabic second thesis) and B 2 (with disyllabic
second thesis). The commonest variation of the type occurs in
the first thesis, which may be polysyllabic.

(i) The simplest form, sub-type B 1, $\times \stackrel{\angle}{} | \times \stackrel{\angle}{}$, is not very
common; according to Sievers there are only 59 instances in
the whole of Beowulf, as *ond Hálga tíl* Beow. 61, *þām hálig gód*
An. 14; with resolution of the first arsis *in séle þām héan* Beow.
714, and of the second arsis, *þurh rúmne séfan* Beow. 278, and
of both, *ǽr súmeres cýme* El. 1228. Hemistichs of this type, on
the other hand, with a disyllabic first thesis are not uncommon,
sýððan fúrðum wéox Beow. 914, *him þā Scýld gewát* Beow. 26;
with resolution of the first arsis, *under Héorotes hróf* Beow. 403;
with resolution of the second, *þæt séo céaster híder* An. 207, and
of both, *æfter hæleða hrýre* Beow. 2053; a trisyllabic first thesis
is also common, *þēah þe hē átres drýnc* An. 53, *oð þæt him éft
onwóc* Beow. 56, *sē þe on hánda bǽr* Beow. 495; with resolution
of the first arsis, *forðan híe mægenes cræft* Beow. 418; of the
second arsis, *ond hū þý príddan dæge* El. 185; of both, *þæt hē þā
géoguðe wíle* Beow. 1182; with first thesis of four syllables, *ne
hýrde ic síð ne ǽr* El. 240, *swylce híe æt Fínnes hám* Beow. 1157;
with first thesis of five syllables (rare) *síððan hē hire fólmum hrán*
Beow. 723, and with resolution of second arsis *þonne hý him
þurh mínne nóman* Cri. 1351.

(ii) The sub-type B 2, or B with disyllabic second thesis, is
rarely found when the first thesis has only one syllable, *þe drýhtnes
bibód* Cri. 1159, *þū wást gif hit is* Beow. 272, *þām wífe þā wórd*
Beow. 640; with resolution of the first arsis, *þurh dároða gedrép*
An. 1446, and of the second, *þurh níhta genípu* Gū. 321; it is
commoner with a disyllabic first thesis, *þā of wéalle geséah* Beow.
229, *hē þæs frófre gebád* Beow. 76; with resolution of the first
arsis, *mid his hæleða gedríht* Beow. 663, *ofer wároða gewéorp*
An. 306; with trisyllabic first thesis, *þonne hē ǽr oððe síð* El. 74,
wes þū ūs lárena gód Beow. 269; with resolution of the first
arsis, *þēah hē þǽr mónige geséah* Beow. 1614, and of the second
arsis, *þæt nǽfre Gréndel swā féla* Beow. 592; with first thesis of

---

[1] See the statistics in Sievers, *Paul-Braune's Beiträge*, x, p. 290.

four and five syllables, *hwæðre hē in brēostum þā gít* An. 51, *þæs þe hire sē wílla gelámp* Beow. 627.

Verses with trisyllabic second thesis are extremely rare and doubtful.[1] It should be noticed that, in this second type too, the thesis seldom consists of a second part of a compound, as *hine fýrwìt bræc* Beow. 232, the exceptions are proper names, as *nū ic Bēowùlf þéc* Beow. 947, *ne wearð Héremòd swá* Beow. 1710.

Type B, according to Sievers, occurs 1014 times in Beowulf, of which 293 are in the first hemistich and 721 in the second.

§ 27. **The Type C** has three sub-types: (i) C 1, the normal type $\times\!\perp\!\mid\!\perp\!\times$, without resolution, as *oft Scýld Scéfing* Beow. 4, *gebún hǽfdon* 117. Here too the first thesis may consist of two, three, four, or five syllables, *þæt hīe ǽghwýlcne* An. 26, *þone gód sénde* Beow. 13, *ofer hrónráde* Beow. 10, *ǣr hē onwég hwúrfe* Beow. 264, *mid þǣre wǽlfýlle* Beow. 125, *þe ic him tó séce* El. 319, *þāra þe mid Bēowúlfe* Beow. 1052, *oð þæt hine sémnínga* An. 821, *þāra þe hē him míd hǽfde* Beow. 1625, *swylce hīe ofer sǽ cómon*, An. 247. (ii) C 2 is the normal type C with resolution of the first arsis, and is of such frequent occurrence that it may be looked on as a special type, *on hérefélda* An. 10, *forscrífen hǽfde* Beow. 106, *in wórold wócun* Beow. 60; a less common form is that with resolution of the first and second arsis, *tō brímes fároðe* Beow. 28, *swā féla fýrena* Beow. 164; sometimes with resolution of the second arsis only, *tō sǣs fároðe* An. 236 and 1660, *for fréan égesan* An. 457, but not in Beowulf. The first thesis may have two, three, or four syllables, *þā wið góde wúnnon* Beow. 113, *ofer lágustrǣte*; with two resolutions, *ic þæs wíne Déniga* Beow. 350, *hū sē mága frémede* An. 639, *þæt him his wínemágas* Beow. 65, *ne hīe húru wínedríhten* Beow. 863. (iii) C 3 is type C with short second arsis, $\times\!\perp\!\mid\!\smile\!\times$, and is pretty common, *in géardágum* Beow. 1, *of féorwégum* Beow. 37; the first thesis may have from two to five syllables, *þæt wæs gód cýning* Beow. 11, *þæt hīe in béorséle* Beow. 482, *sē þe hine déað nímeð* Beow. 441, *ne meaht þū þæs síðfǣtes* An. 211, *þonne hē on þæt sínc stáráð* Beow. 1486. Resolution seems to be avoided, though it occurs here and there, *of hlíðes nósan* Beow. 1892, *on þǣm méðelstéde* Beow. 1083. Thesis with secondary accent is not found. The number of hemistichs of type C in Beowulf is, according to Sievers, 564.

§ 28. **The type D** always ends with a disyllabic thesis, of which the first is generally the second syllable of a compound

---

[1] Sievers, *Paul-Braune's Beiträge*, x. 241 and 294.

and has the secondary accent. There are four sub-types.
(i) D 1 is the normal form, $\acute- \mid \acute- \grave\times \times$, as *hélm ǽlwìhta* An. 118,
féond máncỳnnes Beow. 164, *wígwéorðùnga* Beow. 176, *wéard*
Scýldìnga Beow. 95, *lándbúèndum* Beow. 95, *hríng gýldènne,*
Beow. 2810, *hóf mǫ́dìgra* Beow. 312, *fréan úsèrne* Beow. 3003.
The chief variations arise from resolution of the first arsis, *cýning*
ǽlmìhtig El. 145, *fǽder álwàlda* Beow. 316, *mérelìðènde* Beow.
255, *flótan éowèrne* Beow. 294, *cýning ǽnìgne* Beow. 1851, or of
the second arsis, *héan hýgegèomor* An. 1089, *mǽg Hígelàces*
Beow. 738 and 759; resolution of first and second arsis, *hláden*
hérewǽdum Beow. 1898, *néfan Hérerìces* Beow. 2207. Hemistichs like *wiht unhǽlo* Beow. 120, which have compounds with
un, may be read *wíht únhǽlo* according to type D 2, or *wíht*
unhǽlo according to type A, $\acute- \times \mid \acute- \times$ (Sievers, *Paul-Braune's*
Beiträge, x. 251, and Kluge in *Paul's Grundriss*, i², p. 1051).
(ii) D 2 is the same form, but with the thesis short and with
secondary accent, $\acute- \mid \acute- \smile \times$, *béorht blǽdgìfa* An. 84, *léof lánd-*
frùma Beow. 31, *stréam út þònan* Beow. 2546, *rǽd éahtèdon*
Beow. 172 ; with resolution of the first arsis, *mǽgen sámnòde*
El. 55, *mága Héalfdènes* Beow. 189; with resolution of the
second arsis, *hórd ópenìan* Beow. 3057, the only example.
(iii) D 3 is the normal type, but with short second arsis
(rare), $\acute- \mid \smile \grave\times \times$, *éorðcýnìnga* El. 1174; with resolution of the
first arsis, *rádorcýnìnges* El. 624.   (iv) D 4 has the form
$\acute- \mid \acute- \times \grave\times$, and is closely allied to the type E ($\acute- \grave\times \times \mid \acute-$),
as it has the secondary accent on the last syllable of the thesis
(Sievers, *Paul-Braune's Beiträge*, x. 256), *bréost ínnanwèard*
An. 649, *hólm úp æthǽr* Beow. 519, *fýrst fórð gewàt* ib. 210;
varied by resolution of the first arsis, *géaro gúðe fràm* An. 234,
flóta fámighèals Beow. 218, *súnu déað fornàm* Beow. 2120; by
resolution of the second arsis, *wlánc Wédera lèod* 341, and of
both first and second arsis, *wlítig wéoruda hèap* An. 872; and
resolution of the last thesis with secondary accent, *wóp úp āhàfen*
Beow. 128, *wúnað wíntra fèla* Ph. 580. Certain hemistichs
which may belong to this sub-type admit of an alternative accentuation, and may belong to the following type; for example,
scop hwílum sang Beow. 496 may be read $\acute- \mid \acute- \times \grave\times$, or as E
$\acute- \grave\times \times \mid \acute-$, so *werod eall ārās* Beow. 652.

§ 29. The type E has two sub-types, distinguished by the
position of the syllable bearing the secondary accent; this syllable
is generally the second syllable of a compound or the heavy
middle syllable of a trisyllabic word with a long root-syllable.
E 1 has the form $\acute- \grave\times \times \mid \acute-$, the syllable with secondary

accent standing first in the thesis, *mŏdsòrge wǽg* El. 61, *wéorð-*
mỳndum þắh Beow. 8, *Sứðdènà fólc* Beow. 463, *ĕhìènde wǽs*
Beow. 159, *hǽðènra hýht* Beow. 179, *ǽnìgne þónc* Cri. 1498,
wórdhòrd onléac Beow. 259, *úplàng ăstŏd* Beow. 760, *scŏp hwìlum*
sáng Beow. 496 (cf. above, § 29); varied by resolution of the
first arsis, *héofonrìces weárd* El. 445, *Scédelàndum ín* Beow. 19,
wlítebèorhtne wáng Beow. 93, *lífigènde cwŏm* Beow. 1974,
ǽðelìnges wéox El. 12, *médofùl ǽtbǽr* Beow. 625, *dúguð èall ārắs*
Beow. 1791; resolution of the second arsis is rare, *tìrèadge hǽleð*
An. 2 (the MS. reading *ēadige* must be corrected to *ēadge*, see
Sievers, *Beiträge*, x. 459 on these middle vowels after long root-
syllable), *hélþègnes héte* Beow. 142; resolution of both is rare,
sélewèard ăsélèd Beow. 668, *wínedrỳhten frǽgen* An. 921; resolution of the accented thesis, *glédègesa grím* Beow. 2651.

E 2 has the last syllable of the thesis with secondary accent,
and is very rare, $-\times\dot\times|\;-$, *mórðorbèd strěd* Beow. 2437; with
resolution of last arsis, *gĕomorgìdd wrécen* An. 1550, *bǽron ùt*
hrǽðe An. 1223.

II. *Hemistichs of five members.*

§ **30.** Hemistichs of five members (extended) occur much more
rarely than the normal types of four members. The extended
types are denoted by the letters A*, B*, C*, &c.

Type A* has two sub-types distinguished by the position of
the syllable with the secondary accent.

(i) A* 1, $-\dot\times\times|-\times$ occurs chiefly in the first hemistich,
gŏdbèarn on gálgan El. 719; with resolution of first arsis,
gĕolorànd tŏ gúðe Beow. 438; with thesis of two unaccented
syllables following on the secondary accent, *glǽdmòd on gesìhðe*
Cri. 911, *fǽstrǽdne geþŏht* Beow. 611; with final thesis
strengthened by secondary accent, *gắstlìcne gŏddrèam* Gū. 602,
gámolfèax ond gúðròf Beow. 609.

(ii) A* 2 $-\times\dot\times|-\times$ may possibly occur in *mǎðð umfǽt*
mǽre Beow. 2405, *wúldorlèan wéorca* Cri. 1080; with resolution
of the thesis with secondary accent, *mórðorbèalo mága* Beow. 1079.
Possibly, however, the syllables *um* in *mǎððum* and *or* in *wuldor*
and *morðor* are to be written *m* and *r*, so that the scansion of
the hemistich would be A 2 $-\;-|-\times$ and $-\;\smile\times|-\times.$[1]

Type B* $\dot\times\times-|\times-$ does not seem to occur in O.E. poetry,
though it does in Old Norse.

---

[1] Sievers, *Altgerm. Metrik*, § 85, 2, Anm. 3.

Type C* in the forms $\dot\times\ \times\!\stackrel{\_}{\ }|\stackrel{\_}{\ }\times$, $\dot\times\ \times\cup\times\,|\stackrel{\_}{\ }\times$, $\times\ \times\!\stackrel{\_}{\ }|\cup\times$ are also not found in O.E.

Type D* on the other hand does occur, but almost exclusively in the first hemistich. It has three sub-types: (i) D* 1 $\stackrel{\_}{\ }\times\,|\stackrel{\_}{\ }\times\ \times$, *síde sǽnæssas* Beow. 223, *áldres órwéna* Beow. 1002; with resolution of the first arsis, *æðeling ánhȳdig* Beow. 2668; more commonly with resolution of the second arsis, *mǽton mérestrǽta* Beow. 514; with resolution of both, *lócene léoðosȳrcan* Beow. 1506. (ii) D* 2 $\stackrel{\_}{\ }\times\,|\stackrel{\_}{\ }\cup\times$, *mǽre méarcstàpa* Beow. 103, *éaldor Éastdéna* Beow. 392; with resolution of the first arsis, *æðele órdfrùma* Beow. 263; with resolution of the second arsis, *módges mérefàran* Beow. 502, *Béowulf máðelòde* Beow. 505, &c. (iii) D* 3 $\stackrel{\_}{\ }\times\,|\cup\dot\times\ \times$ is not found. (iv) D* 4 $\stackrel{\_}{\ }\times\,|\stackrel{\_}{\ }\times\ \dot\times$ is rare, *grétte Géata léod* Beow. 625, *þrȳðlíc þégna héap* Beow. 400; with resolution of first arsis, *éaforan éllorsíð* Beow. 2452; with resolution of the second, *ȳðde éotena cȳn* Beow. 421; with resolution of the secondarily accented syllable, *wín of wúndorfàtum* Beow. 1163; this type is varied by anacrusis, *ongínneð géomormòd* Beow. 2045, and by anacrusis together with disyllabic thesis in the second foot, *oferswám þá stoleða bigòng* Beow. 2368.

Type E* does not occur in O.E. poetry.[1]

§ 31. To assign the different hemistichs of a poem to these various types we have to follow as a regulating principle the natural word accent and syntactical accent of each sentence. In some cases the similarity or relation with one another of the types renders it a matter of difficulty to determine exactly to what particular type a hemistich may belong. Systematic investigations as to the principles which govern the combinations of the five types in pairs to form the long line have not yet been made. From such observations as have been made it would appear that by preference hemistichs of different rhythmical structure (ascending and descending) were combined with a view to avoid a monotonous likeness between the two halves of the verse.[2]

---

[1] Cf. Sievers, *Altgermanische Metrik*, § 15, 3 c, and § 116. 9.

[2] See Max Cremer, *Metrische und sprachliche Untersuchungen der altenglischen Gedichte Andreas, Gūðlāc, Phoenix*, &c., 1888, pp. 31 ff.; Sievers, *Altgermanische Metrik*, § 86; and chiefly Eduard Sokoll, 'Zur Technik des altgermanischen Alliterationsverses,' in *Beiträge zur neueren Philologie*, Vienna, 1902, pp. 351-65.

§ **32.** The combination of two hemistichs so as to form a long line is effected by means of alliteration, one at least of the two fully accented syllables being the bearer of an alliterative sound. In no case is an unaccented syllable or even a syllable with a secondary accent allowed to take part in the alliteration. This fact, that secondarily accented syllables are debarred from alliterating, is another proof that it is better to look on them as belonging to the thesis rather than to the arsis of the verse.

The Principles of Alliteration.

§ **33. Quality of the Alliteration.** It is an all but invariable rule that the correspondence of sounds must be exact and not merely approximate. A *g* must alliterate to a *g*, not to a *c*, a *d* to a *d*, not to a *t*, and so on. There is, however, one remarkable exception, namely, that no distinction is made between the guttural *c* (as in *cūðe*) and the palatal *c* (as in *cēosan*), nor between the guttural *g* (as in *god*) and the palatal *g* (as in *gierede*), not even when the latter represents Germanic *j* (as in *geong, gēar*). With exceptions hereafter to be noted, a consonant followed by a vowel may alliterate with itself followed by another consonant: thus *cūðe* alliterates not only with words like *cyning*, but with words like *cræft, cwellan*; and *hūs* alliterates not only with *heofon* but with *hlēapan, hnǣgan*, &c. The fact that different vowels, as *ī*, *ū*, and *æ* in *īsig ond ūtfūs æðelinges fær* Beow. 33, alliterate together is only an apparent exception to the strictness of the rule, as it is really the glottal catch or *spiritus lenis*[1] before all vowels which alliterates here. Wherever a vowel seems to alliterate with an *h* we are justified in assuming a corruption of the text, as in *oretmecgas æfter hæleðum frægn* Beow. 332, where Grein improves both sense and metre by substituting *æðelum* for *hæleðum*; other examples are Beow. 499 1542, 2095, 2930. In some cases where foreign names beginning with *h* occur we occasionally find instances of this inexact alliteration, as *Hólofernus únlyfigendes* Jud. 180 and 7, 21, 46, contrasted with *Hólofernus hógedon āninga* 250; in later works as in Ælfric's *Metrical Homilies* we find alliteration of *h* with a vowel not only in foreign names but with native words, as

---

[1] But on this last expression see Sievers, *Phonetik*[1], § 359.

and he ǽfre his fýrde þam hǽlende betǽhte.

Ælfr. Judges[1] 417.

and *h* before consonants (viz. *r, l, w*) is disregarded as

and hē hig āhrédde of þām réðan þéowte.   Ælfr. Judges 16.

on hwám his stréngð wæs and his wúndorlíce míht. ibid. 306.

It is important to observe that the combinations *st, sc, sp* are not allowed to alliterate with each other or with words beginning with *s* not followed by a consonant, but *st* can alliterate only with *st, sc* only with *sc, sp* only with *sp*; thus *spere* and *scyld, stillan* and *springan, sǽ* and *styrman* do not count as alliterations. The invariable practice is seen in the following lines:—

hēt stréamfare stíllan, stórmas réstan. An. 1578.

he scéaf þā mid þam scýlde, þæt se scéatt tóbǽrst and þæt spére spréngde, þæt hit spráng ongéan.

Byrhtnoth 136–7.

In later times this rule was not so strictly observed. The metrical Psalms alliterate *sc* with *s* and *sw* with *s*, as

hi hine him sámnuncga scéarpum strélum. Ps. lxiii. 4.

on þíne þā swíðran, ond þe ne scéaðeð ǽnig. Ps. xc. 7.

but *sp* and *st* do not alliterate with each other or with *s*. In Ælfric all these combinations of consonants alliterate indifferently with each other or with *s* + another consonant or with simple *s*, as in

wið þām þe héo beswíce Sámson þone stróngan.

Ælfr. Judges 308.

Sometimes in Ælfric the alliterating letter does not stand at the beginning of the word,

and hē hæfde héora gewéald ealles twéntig géara. ibid. 85.

and the alliteration may even fall on an unaccented particle as in

frám his geléafan and his ǽ forsāwon. ibid. 51.

For a full account of Ælfric's alliteration the reader may be referred to an interesting essay by Dr. Arthur Brandeis, *Die Alliteration in Aelfric's metrischen Homilien,* 1897 (Programm der Staatsrealschule im VII. Bezirk in Wien).

[1] Edited by Grein in *Anglia*, ii. 141 ff.

§ **34. Position of the alliterative words.** Out of the four accented syllables of the line two at least, and commonly three, must begin with an alliterative sound, and this alliteration still further increases the stress which these syllables have in virtue of their syntactical and rhythmical accent.

The position of these alliterative sounds in the line may vary in the same way as their number. The general laws which govern the position of the alliteration are the following:—(i) One alliterating sound *must*, and two *may* occur in the first hemistich; (ii) In the second hemistich the alliterating sound (called the head-stave [1]) must fall on the first of the two accented syllables of that hemistich, and the second accented syllable in the second hemistich does not take part in the alliteration at all; (iii) When there are three alliterating sounds in the whole line two of them must be in the first hemistich and only one in the second. Examples of lines with three alliterating sounds:

séolfa he gesétte súnnan ond mónan. Sat. 4.

úfan ond útan him wæs ǽghwǽr wá. Sat. 342.

Lines with only two alliterative sounds, the first of which may coincide with either of the accented syllables of the first hemistich (the second of course coinciding with the first accented syllable of the second hemistich) are very common:

héafod éalra héahgescéafta. Gen. 4.

hí hýne þá ætbǽron to brímes fároðe. Beow. 28.

If the first hemistich contains only one alliterative sound this alliteration generally falls on the more emphatic of the two accented syllables of the hemistich which is usually the first, as

on flódes ǽht féor gewítan. Beow. 42.

In the type A the single alliteration of the first hemistich not unfrequently falls on the second accented syllable, such cases being distinguished, as A 3

þá wæs on búrgum Béowulf Scýldinga. Beow. 53.

In types C and D the single alliteration of the first section must always fall on the first accented syllable which in these types is more emphatic than the second. In types B and E

---

[1] The Old Norse hǫfuðstafr, Germ. *Hauptstab*. The alliterations in the first hemistich are called in Old Norse stuðlar (sing. stuðill) 'supporters', Germ. *Stollen* or *Stützen*.

alliteration on the second arsis would bring the alliteration too near to the end of the hemistich, and is therefore rare.

Double alliteration in the first hemistich occurs in all of the five types, and chiefly when the two accented syllables have equally strong accents. It is, therefore, least common in C $\times \perp \mid \perp \times$ where the first arsis predominates over the second, and is most frequent in the strengthened hemistichs, in D, E, A 2, and in the five-membered D* types, where it is the rule.[1]

A third form of alliteration, though much less important and frequent than these two, occurs when the second accented syllable of the second hemistich shares in alliteration, in addition to the first accented syllable. There are then two different pairs of alliterative sounds distributed alternately between the two hemistichs. The commonest form of this double alliteration of the whole line is represented by the formula a b | a b, as

hwæt! we **G**árd**é**na   in g**é**ard**á**gum.   Beow. 1.

Scýldes **é**aferan   **Sc**édelandum ín.   Beow. 19.

híldew**ǽ**pnum   ond h**é**aðow**ǽ**dum.   Beow. 39 ;

less commonly by the formula a b | b a :

þā w**ǽ**ron m**ó**nige   þe his m**ǽ**g wríðon.   Beow. 2982.

hwílum for d**ú**guðe   d**ó**htor **H**róðg**á**res.   Beow. 2020 ;

verses corresponding to the formula a a | b b are not found in early poetry. No doubt certain instances of this double alliteration may be accidental, but others seem intentional.

The foregoing rules as to alliteration are strictly observed in the early and classic poetry, but in later times certain licences crept in. Three of these may be noticed. (i) The second accented syllable of the second hemistich is allowed to carry the alliteration instead of the first accented syllable,

l**á**stas l**é**gde   oðð**ǽ**t hē gel**ǽ**dde.   Gen. 2536.

(ii) Both accented syllables of the second hemistich alliterate with one accented syllable of the first hemistich,[2]

me s**é**ndon tő þē   s**ǽ**men sn**é**lle.   Byrhtnoth 29.

---

[1] Sievers, *Altgerm. Metrik*, § 20.

[2] This is not very common in poetry of the more regular metrical structure, but is found in Ælfric's lines, in which we find hemistichs without any alliterating letter, and others where the alliteration is continued in the following line; two-thirds, however, of his lines are formed quite correctly.

(iii) The four accented syllables of the line all alliterate together,

Gódwine ond Gódwíg gúðe ne gýmdon. Byrhtn. 192.

In the majority of cases the same alliterative letter is not employed in two successive lines, but we find cases like

þā tōbrǽd Sámson bégen his éarmas
þæt þā rǽpas tobúrston þe he mid gebúnden wæs.
Ælf. Judges 269;

and earlier in Andreas 70, 197, 372, 796, 815, 1087, &c., or in Beowulf 403, 489, 644, 799, 865, 898, &c.

And even three lines in succession, as

swýlce he āfédde of fíxum twám
ond of fíf hláfum fíra cýnnes
fíf púsendo; fédan sǽton. An. 589 ff.

This usage, which in Middle English became very popular, is noticeably frequent in the poem of Judith, probably with a view to emphasis. Many examples of such pairs of verses are to be found collected by Dr. A. Brandeis from Ælfric.

The unaccented words may begin with the same letter as the accented words which bear the alliteration proper,[1] as

ne hīe huru héofona hélm hérian ne cúðon. Beow. 182,

or one of the unaccented words may begin with the same letter as an accented word which does not alliterate, as

þæt fram hám gefrǽgn Hígelāces þégn. Beow. 194;

this of course has nothing to do with alliteration, though in later times it was often mistaken for it.

Verses without any alliteration at all, as

he hélpeð þearfan swýlce éac wǽdlan. Ps. lxxi. 13,

occur only in late OE. poetry like Ælfric's Homilies, and when rhyme was beginning to creep in.

§ 35. **Alliteration in relation to the parts of speech and to the order of words.** Both alliteration and the whole structure of the alliterative line depend in the first place on the natural or etymological accent of the single words, and next on the syntactical accent which these words bear in their

___

[1] Snorri, the Icelandic metrician, permits this in the case of certain monosyllabic words, but looks on it as a licence (*leyfi en eigi rétt setning*, Háttatal, p. 596).

relation to one another in the sentence. Just as only the accented syllable of a single word can take part in the alliteration, so only can those words take part in it which are marked out in the sentence as important and therefore strongly accented.

The relative degree of stress is influenced at times by the rhetorical accent, but generally speaking we find a certain gradation of accent among the accented words depending on their intrinsic and not on their rhetorical importance in building up the sentence.

Two general principles may be laid down : (1) If the syntactical value of the two accented syllables of the hemistich is not equal, then the word which has the stronger accent of the two is chosen to alliterate. In the second hemistich it is always the first accented word (the 'head stave'), in the first hemistich it is generally the first accented word, though the second accented word may alliterate as well. (2) If the two accented syllables of the section are equal in syntactical value, then the first alliterates, and when double alliteration is allowed the second may also alliterate.

The various grammatical classes of words are treated in regard to the alliteration in the following way :—

Nouns, including adjectives and the infinitives and participles of verbs, have the strongest accent of all words in the sentence. A noun therefore takes precedence over the other parts of speech among which it occurs and has the alliteration, as

ně in þā céastre becúman méahte. An. 931.

híre þā Ádam andswárode. Gen. 827.

If two nouns occur in the same hemistich it is always the first which alliterates,

húsa sélest. Wæs séo hwíl micel. Beow. 146.

lánge hwíle. Him wæs líffréa. Beow. 16.

géongum ond éaldum, swylc him gód séalde. Beow. 72.

The only exceptions are when a special rhetorical emphasis is given to the second word.

When a noun and two adjectives or two nouns and an adjective occur in the same hemistich, one of these is always subordinated to the other, and the two together are treated as a combination. In such cases, where there is double alliteration in the hemistich, the position of the alliterating words may be either *a a x*, or *a x a*, the subordinate element (*x*) standing either in the last or the second place in the hemistich,

> béorht béacen Gódes brímu swáðredon.   Beow. 570.

> twélf wintra tíd   tórn gepólode.   Beow. 147.

In the case of single alliteration, it is always the first of the nouns or adjectives which alliterates.

The verb (excluding the infinitive and participles) is usually less strongly accented than the noun. It may therefore precede or follow the noun or adjective without alliteration, either in the arsis or thesis, as

> lét se héarda   Hígelaces pégn.   Beow. 2977.

> him pā Scýld gewāt   tō gescép-hwíle.   Beow. 26.

> gewāt pā twélfa súm   tórne gebólhen.   Beow. 2401.

On the other hand, when a hemistich consists only of one noun and one verb, the verb may alliterate, as

> gódne gegýrwan   cwæð hē gúð-cýning.   Beow. 199.

> hwétton hígerófne   hǽl scéawedon.   Beow. 204.

When a substantive and an adjective are closely combined, a verb in the same hemistich may alliterate, as

> býreð blódig wæl,   býrgean pénceð.   Beow. 448.

> séofon niht swúncon;   hē pē æt súnde oferflát.   Beow. 517.

In formulas consisting of noun+verb the noun predominates over the verb and takes the alliteration, as

> wérodes wísa   wórdhord onléac.   Beow. 259.

But if the verb is emphatic it may alliterate though there is a noun in the same hemistich; this occurs chiefly in the second hemistich, as

> ond be héalse genám;   hrúron him téaras.   Beow. 1872.

> grýrelícne gíst.   Gýrede hine Béowulf.   ib. 1441,

but a few instances are found in the first hemistich, as

> gemúnde pā se góda   mǽg Hígeláces.   Beow. 758.

When one of two verbs in the hemistich is subordinate to the other the verb in the subordinate clause alliterates, having a stronger accent than the verb in the main clause,

> mýnte þæt hē gedǽlde   ǽr þon dǽg cwóme.   Beow. 731.

If the two verbs are co-ordinate the first alliterates,

> wórolde lífes: wýrce sē þe móte.   Beow. 1387;

in the first hemistich both verbs commonly alliterate,

> séomade ond sýrede   sínnìhte héold.   Beow. 161.

The adverb. Adverbs of degree like *micle, swīðe, ful,* &c., are commonly found in the thesis, and even if they stand in the arsis they usually do not alliterate, as

> óftor mícle   þonne on ǽnne síð.   Beow. 1580.

When adverbs of this kind have a special rhetorical emphasis they may of course alliterate, as

> éfne swā mícle   swā bið mǽgða crǽft.   Beow. 1284.
> ac hē is snél and swíft   and swíðe léoht.   Phoen. 317.

Adverbs which modify the meaning of the word which they precede alliterate, as

> ǽscholt úfan grǽg: wæs sē írenþréat.   Beow. 330.

Adverbial prepositions preceding the verb also alliterate,

> hēt þā úp béran   ǽðelìnga gestréon.   Beow. 1920,

but not when they follow the verb,

> Géat wæs glǽdmōd,   géong sòna tó.   Beow. 1785.

Adverbs derived from nouns are more strongly accented than the verb which they modify and therefore alliterate,

> álégdon þā tōmíddes   mǽrne þéoden.   Beow. 3141.

Pronouns (and pronominal adjectives like *monig, eall, fela*) are usually enclitic, and precede or follow the noun without alliterating, as

> manigu óðru gescéaft   éfnswìðe hím.   Metr. xi. 44.
> ealne míddangéard   ōð mérestréamas.   Dan. 503.
> fela ic mónna gefrǽgn   mǽgðum wéaldan.   Wid. 10.

With a special rhetorical accent they may alliterate even if they precede the noun,

on þǽm dǽge þýsses lífes. Beow. 197.

The pronoun *self* and the pronouns compounded with the prefix *ǽ* (*ǽghwā, ǽghwylc*, &c.) are usually accented, and alliterate if they form the first arsis of the hemistich, as

sélran gesốhte þǽm be him selfa déah. Beow. 1840.

hǽfde ǽghwæðer énde geférd. Beow. 2845.

Prepositions, conjunctions, and particles are not as a rule accented, but prepositions if followed by an enclitic pronoun take the accent and alliterate, as

éaldum éarne and ǽfter þón. Phoen. 238.

nis únder mé ǽnig óðer. Riddle xli. 86.

Whether words of these classes, standing in the first arsis of the first hemistich along with another alliterating word, were intended also to alliterate is somewhat uncertain, but it is probable that they were so, as in

mid þȳ mǽstan mǽgenþrýmme cýmeð. Crist 1009.

These laws of accentuation are strictly observed only in the older poetry; by the end of the tenth century, in Byrhtnoth, the Metres of Boethius and the Psalms, they are frequently neglected.

§ 36. **Arrangement and relationship of verse and sentence.** The following rules hold good in general for the distribution of the sentence or parts of the sentence between the hemistichs of the verse. Two distinct pauses occur in every alliterative line, one (commonly called the caesura) between the first and second hemistichs, the other at the end of the line, and these pauses are determined by the syntactical construction; that is to say, they coincide with the end of a clause or lesser member of the sentence. The hemistich must contain such parts of the sentence as belong closely together; and such coherent parts, as, for example, a pronoun and noun to which it refers or adverb with adjective, must not be separated from one another by the caesura, unless the pronoun or adverb is placed in the second arsis of the hemistich, as

wýrd æfter þissum wórdgeméarcum. Gen. 2355.

gif ge willað mínre míhte geléfan. Sat. 251.

In Beowulf this separation of closely connected words is

permitted only if the word standing in the arsis alliterates at the same time. Longer parts of a sentence may be separated both by the caesura and the pause at the end of the line. The syntactical connexion between the parts of a sentence thus broken up makes the unity of the parts clear, and when the division occurs in the caesura between the two halves of the verse, the alliteration common to both hemistichs serves further to emphasize this unity.

The single alliterative lines are connected with one another by the prevailing usage of ending the sentence not at the end of the completed line, but at the end of the first hemistich or in the middle of the line, and of beginning a new sentence with the second hemistich. The great variety of expression, and the predilection for paraphrase by means of synonyms which is so characteristic of OE. poetry, contribute to make such breaks in the line easy. Whatever may be the explanation, it is certainly the fact that in the OE. poetry the metrical and syntactical members do sometimes coincide, but at other times overlap in a way which does not admit of being reduced to rule.[1]

The Lengthened Verse.

§ 37. Besides the normal four-beat line (with two beats to each hemistich) there is in OE. and Old Saxon another variety, the **lengthened line** (*Schwellvers*) with three beats in each hemistich.[2] These verses occur in almost all OE. poems, either isolated or more commonly in groups, and occasionally we find lines with one hemistich of two beats and the second hemistich of three, like.

> *gástes dúgeðum þǽra þe mid gáres órde.*   Gen. 1522,

and *Jud.* 96, *Crist* 1461, &c., or with a lengthened hemistich of three beats and a normal hemistich of two beats, like

> *bǽron brándas on brýne blácan fýres.*   Dan. 246,

and *Sat.* 605, *Gnom. Ex.* 200, &c.

In the *Psalms* and in Cynewulf's *Juliana* they are wanting entirely, in Cynewulf's *Elene* out of 1321 verses there are only fourteen lengthened whole lines, and three lengthened hemistichs.

---

[1] The subject of the preceding paragraphs was first investigated by M. Rieger in his essay *Alt- und Angelsächsische Verskunst*, p. 18, where many details will be found.

[2] Cf. Sievers in *Paul-Braune's Beiträge*, xii. 455; K. Luick, *ib.*, xiii. 389, xv. 441; F. Kaufmann, *ib.*, xv. 360; Sievers, in *Paul's Grundriss*, pp. 891 ff., and in *Altgermanische Metrik*, §§ 88–96.

Examples of groups of these lengthened verses will be found in
Gen. 44–46, 1015–1019, 2167–2169, 2854–2858; *Exodus*
569–573, *Dan.* 59–106, 203–205, 226–228, 238–246, 262–
271, 435–438, 441, 448, 452–458; *Judith* 2–12, 16–21, 30–34,
54–61, 63–68, 88–99, 272–274, 289–291, 338–349; *Satan* 202,
232, 237, 605, *Crist* 621, 889, 922, 1050, 1382–1386, &c., and
in many of the smaller poems.[1]

Lengthened verses of a looser type occur in *Salomon and
Saturn*, and *Genesis* B ; they have unusually long theses of four
or five unaccented syllables after the first accented syllable, as

> ǽnne hǽfde hē swā swíðne gewórhtne.   Gen. 252,

or have equally long anacruses before the first accented
syllable, as

> þæt wē him on þām lánde láð gefrémedon.   Gen. 392.[2]

It is not always possible to draw a sharp distinction between
regular lines with somewhat long first theses and lengthened lines.
The general tone and rhythm of the passage in question help to
determine whether we have the normal or the lengthened line
before us.   The lengthened line occurs in places where the sense
demands a solemn and slow rhythm, in other cases where the
movement of the passage is quicker we may assume a normal
four-beat line with a long anacrusis, or a polysyllabic thesis in
the middle of the hemistich.   What distinguishes clearly undoubted examples of the lengthened verse is that in each hemistich
we find three beats and three feet of equal and independent
value.   But, as in the usual two-beat hemistich of the normal
line, both beats need not be equally strong, so in the three-beat
hemistich the three beats do not always stand on the same
footing as regards stress, nor does the position of the stronger
beat require to be always the same in the two hemistichs.
The beats which are accompanied by alliteration are, generally
speaking, stronger than those without alliteration.   In the
employment of alliteration and in the structure of the hemistich
the lengthened line is closely allied to the normal line.

Alliteration. 1. The first hemistich has commonly two
alliterative sounds, which fall as a rule on the first and second
beats :

> gesēoð sórga mǽste.   Crist 1209;

---

[1] In *Paul-Braune's Beiträge*, xii, pp. 454, 455, Sievers gives a list of
the undoubted regular lengthened verses occurring in OE. poetry.

[2] Sievers discusses the lengthened verses of these poems in *Beiträge*, xii.
479.

more rarely on the second and third beats, as in

wǽron hyra rǽdas ríce.   Dan. 497 ;

sometimes on the first and third beats, as

líf hēr mén forléosað.   Rhyming Poem 56.

Now and then we find hemistichs with three alliterations :

dól bið sē þe him dríhten ne ondrǽdeð.   Seafarer 106,
þý sceal on þéode geþéon.   Gnom. Ex. 50 ;

and others with one alliteration only, in which case the alliteration falls more rarely on the first beat, as

cýning sceal ríce héaldan   céastra béoð féorran gesýne.
Gnom. Ex. 1,

than on the second, as

þæt sē wǽre míhta wáldend   sē þe híe of þām mírce genérede.
Dan. 448.

2. In the second hemistich the chief alliterative sound, the
head-stave, generally falls on the second accented syllable, as in
the last example, and only exceptionally on the first accented
syllable, as

Stýran sceal mon stróngum môde.   Stórm oft hólm gebríngeð.
Gnom. Ex. 51.

§ 38. The origin and structure of the lengthened verse.

It is clear from the comparative infrequency and the special use
to which it is put that the lengthened line must be looked upon
as originating in some way from the normal four-beat line.
Two explanations of its development have been given. The
first, which is Sievers's original view,[1] is that a foot or measure
with the form $\perp \ldots$ (i.e. one accented syllable plus several
unaccented ones) was prefixed to one of the five normal types;
hence $\perp \times$ prefixed to A would give the form $\perp \times \mid \perp \times \perp \times$, and
$- \times$ prefixed to B would give $\perp \times \mid \times \perp \times \perp$. The other explanation, given by Luick,[2] is that the lengthened hemistich is due to
a blending of several types of the normal kind in this way.
The hemistich starts with the beginning of one of the normal
types A, B, C, then with the second accented syllable another type

---

[1] *Beiträge*, xii. 458.   [2] *Beiträge*, xiii. 388, xv. 445.

is begun and continued, as if the poet found the original beginning inadequate to express his emotion.

The manner in which the blending of two normal types
results in new lengthened types of three beats will be seen in the
following illustrations :

$$
\begin{array}{rl}
A & \acute{}\times\acute{}\times \\
+\,C & \times\,\acute{}\,\acute{}\times \\
\text{gives A C} & \acute{}\times\acute{}\,\acute{}\times\;;
\end{array}
$$

$$
\begin{array}{rl}
A & \acute{}\times\acute{}\times \\
+\,D & \acute{}\,\acute{}\grave{\times}\times \\
\text{gives A D} & -\times\acute{}\,\acute{}\grave{\times}\times\;;
\end{array}
$$

$$
\begin{array}{rl}
B & \times\acute{}\times\acute{} \\
+\,C & \times\,\acute{}\,\acute{}\times \\
\text{gives B C} & \times\acute{}\times\acute{}\,\acute{}\times\;;
\end{array}
$$

$$
\begin{array}{rl}
B & \times\acute{}\times\acute{} \\
+\,A & \acute{}\times\acute{}\times \\
\text{gives B A} & \times\acute{}\times\acute{}\times\acute{}\times\;;
\end{array}
$$

$$
\begin{array}{rl}
C & \times\,\acute{}\,\acute{}\times \\
+\,A & \acute{}\times\acute{}\times \\
\text{gives C A} & \times\,\acute{}\,\acute{}\times\acute{}\times\;;
\end{array}
$$

$$
\begin{array}{rl}
A & \acute{}\times\acute{}\times \\
+\,A & \acute{}\times\acute{}\times \\
\text{gives A A} & \acute{}\times\acute{}\times\acute{}\times\;.
\end{array}
$$

As Prof. Sievers himself[1] has accepted this theory (or, at
least, has recognized it as a convenient method of exhibiting
the structural varieties of the lengthened line), we shall adopt it
here.

Of the fifteen different possible combinations of the original
types, some do not actually occur, but with the sub-types to be
taken into consideration we get no less than eighteen different
types of the regular lengthened whole line, and these again admit
of variations by means of resolution of accented syllables, polysyllabic theses, &c.

Only the most commonly occurring forms of the lengthened
hemistich will be given here ; for the others the reader may be
referred to Sievers.[2]

[1] *Altgermanische Metrik*, § 94. 3.   [2] *Altgermanische Metrik*, § 95.

§ 39. By far the most common type is **A A** (some 525 examples),

$$\acute{\times} \ldots \acute{\times} . \acute{\times},$$

as in

wéaxan wítebrógan. (*Hǽfden hīe* wróhtgetéme). Gen. 45;

or with resolution of the first accented syllable in the first hemistich,

súnu mid swéordes écge. Gen. 2857,

and in the second hemistich,

féla bið fýrwet-géornra. Gnom. Ex. 102;

with resolution of the second accented syllable in the second hemistich,

þǽr þū þólades síððan. Crist 1410;

or of each of the three accented syllables in the second hemistich,

hýre þæs fǽder on róderum. Jud. 5.

The chief variation of this type arises from the prolongation of the first thesis, which may run from one to six syllables. At the same time the usual resolutions may be introduced, as in the following examples: Ordinary type, $\acute{\times} \times \times \| \acute{\times} \| \acute{\times} | \acute{\times}$, very common,

grímme wið gód gesómnod. Gen. 46;

with resolution of the first accented syllable,

réced ofer réadum gólde. Gen. 2404;

with resolution of the last two accented syllables,

snúde þā snóteran ídese. Jud. 55;

type with trisyllabic thesis, $\acute{\times} \times \times \times \| \acute{\times} | \acute{\times}$,

méda syndon mícla þína. Gen. 2167;

with resolution of the first accented syllable,

wíton hyra hýht mid drýhten. Gū. 61;

thesis of four to six syllables, $(\acute{\times} \times \ldots \ldots \| \acute{\times} | \acute{\times})$,

ǽleð hȳ mid þȳ éaldan líge. Crist 1547,

síððan hē hæfde his gást onsénded. Cross 49,

bétre him wǽre þæt hē bróðor áhte. Gnom. Ex. 175.

Less frequently the second foot has two unaccented syllables, and in that case the first foot has either one or sometimes two unaccented syllables, thus

(i) $\acute{}\times \| \acute{}\times \times | \acute{}\times$, or (ii) $\acute{}\times \times \| \acute{}\times \times | \acute{}\times$,

as   (i) *swá þū A'bele wúrde.* Gen. 1019;

with resolution of the first arsis,

                  sígor and sóðne geléafan. Jud. 89.

      (ii) *rínca tō rúne gegángan.* Jud. 54.

Type A 2 A, $\acute{}\times \grave{}\times \acute{}\times$, which is type A A with secondary accent on the first thesis, occurs, according to Sievers, some twenty times, and always in the first hemistich. Examples are,

                 wǽrfæst wíllan mínes. Gen. 2168;

with resolution of the last arsis,

                 þéarlmòd þéoden gúmena. Jud. 66;

with disyllabic second thesis,

                 fréobèarn fǽðmum beþéahte. Gen. 2867.

Type A* A, $\acute{}.\grave{}\times \times | \acute{}\times . | \acute{}\times$, which is A A strengthened and with disyllabic first thesis, is nearly as common as A 2 A, and is always in the first hemistich, as for example,

        árlèas of éarde þínum. Gen. 1019,
        béalofùl his béddes néosan. Jud. 63;

with trisyllabic first thesis,

      hréohmòd wæs sē hǽðena þéoden. Dan. 242.

Type A B, $\acute{}\times \ldots \acute{}\times . \acute{}$, some thirty instances equally distributed between the first and second hemistichs. Examples are,

        éorðan ýðum þéaht. Riddle xvii. 3,
        wǽsceð his wárig hrǽgl. Gnom. Ex. 99.

Type A C, $\acute{}\times \ldots \acute{}\acute{}\times$, about twenty-nine instances, of which more than the half occur in the first hemistich, as

        hríncg þæs héan lándes. Gen. 2854,
        wlítige tō wóruldnýtte. Gen. 1016.

Type A D, $\acute{}\times . . \acute{}\acute{}\grave{}\times \times$, is rarer, occurring about twelve times, apparently only in the first hemistich, as béalde býrnwíggènde. Jud. 17,

Júdas hire ongén þíngòde. El. 609.

Type A E, _⏑ × . . _⏑ × × . _⏑, somewhat more common than
the last, and in both hemistichs, as

swéord and swátigne hélm. Jud. 338,

ségde him únlýtel spéll. Gen. 2405.

Type B A, × . _⏑ × . . . _⏑ × . _⏑ ×, about 120 instances, has
as its simplest form, × _⏑ × _⏑ × _⏑ ×, as

álséton líges gánga. Dan. 263;

with disyllabic thesis after the first arsis, × _⏑ × × _⏑ × _⏑ ×, as

áwýrged tō wídan áldre. Gen. 1015;

with trisyllabic thesis, × _⏑ × × × _⏑ × _⏑ ×, as

hý twégen sceolon téfle ymbsíttan. Gnom. Ex. 182;

the initial thesis or anacrusis is rarely disyllabic.

Type B B, × . _⏑ × . . . _⏑ × . _⏑, about nine times and mostly
in the first hemistichs, as

gebídan þæs hē gebédan ne még. Gnom. Ex. 105;

with resolution of two of the accented syllables,

ofercúmen bið hē ér hē ácwéle. Gnom. Ex. 114.

Type B C, × . . _⏑ × . . . _⏑ _⏑ ×, nearly as common as the last
and nearly always in the first hemistich, as

and náhte bealdféondum. Dan. 454,

begóten of þæs gúman sídan. Cross 49.

Type B D, × . _⏑ × . . _⏑ _⏑ × ×, about sixteen times, and in
either hemistich, as

on bordan únswéslìcne. Jud. 65,

alédon hīe þér límwérìgne. Cross 63.

Type C A, × _⏑ _⏑ × . _⏑ ×, with some fifteen examples, of
which eight are in the first hemistich, as

geséoð sórga méste. Crist 1209,

tō cwále cníhta féorum. Dan. 226.

Type C C, × . . . . _⏑ _⏑ ⌣ ×, occurs only nine times, of which
six are in the second hemistich, as

þæt wæs gód élmíhtig. Cross 396;

with resolution of the first accented syllable,

> *ne sē brýne béotmǽcgum.*   Dan. 265,
>
> *þē þæt wéorc stáðoláde.*   And. 800.

Other combinations are given by Sievers, *Altgermanische Metrik*, § 95, but these occur so rarely or are so doubtful that they need not be mentioned here. A few lengthened hemistichs have four beats, as

> *engel in þone ófn ínnan becwóm.*   Dan. 238,

and others in Sievers's *Altgermanische Metrik*, § 96.

Formation of Stanzas and Rhyme.

§ 40. OE. poetry is mainly narrative, and does not run into any kind of recurring stanza or strophe, but is entirely stichic. Traces of an arrangement of lines so as to form a stanza are found in Dēor, the Runic Poem, the Psalms and Hymns, the so-called First Riddle, and in the Gnomic verses of the Exeter Book, which may be compared to the Old French ' tirades '.[1]

On the other hand, end-rhyme of the two hemistichs, combined with alliteration, is not very uncommon, though in most cases it seems only an incidental ornament, as

> *fýlle gefǽgon ; fǽgere geþǽgon.*   Beow. 1014.
>
> *wórd-gyd wrécan   ond ymb wér sprécan.*   Beow. 3172.

In the Rhyming Poem of the Exeter Book we have eighty-seven lines in which the first and second hemistichs rhyme throughout, and in some passages of other poems, noticeably in the *Elene*, vv. 114–115, and vv. 1237–1251, in which Cynewulf speaks in his own person, or Crist 591–595, And. 869–871, 890, Gūthl. 801, Phoen. 15–16, 54–55; assonance is found not unfrequently alongside of perfect rhyme, as in Gūthl. 802, Phoen. 53. These places are sufficient to prove a systematic and deliberate use of rhyme, which serves to accentuate the lyrical tone of the passages.

Monosyllabic rhymes such as *nān : tān* (Rhym. Poem 78), *rād : gebǽd* (ib. 16), *onláh : onwráh* (ib. 1) are called masculine, and disyllabic rhymes like *wóngum : góngum* (ib. 7), *géngdon : méngdon* (ib. 11), or trisyllabic *hlýnede : dýnede* (ib. 28), *swínsade : mínsade* (ib. 29), *bífade : hlífade* (ib. 30), are called feminine.

According to their position in the hemistich, rhymes fall into

---

[1] See Sievers, *Altgerm. Metrik*, § 97.

two classes (*a*) interior rhymes like *hónd rónd gefèng* Beow.
2609, *stíðmòd gestód* Beow. 2567, in compounds *wórd-hòrd
ontéac* Beow. 259, in co-ordinate formulae like *þā wæs sǽl and
mǽl* Beow. 1008, *wórdum and bórdum* El. 24, *grund ond sund*
And. 747, and as so-called grammatical rhymes *lāð wið lāðum*
Beow. 440, *béarn æfter béarne*, Gen. 1070 ; (*b*) sectional rhymes
joining the two halves of one line, as

    sécgas mec sǽgon   *sýmbel ne ālǽgon*.   Rhym. P. 5 ;

not unfrequently, very often in the Rhyming Poem, two, three,
four or more alliterative lines are connected in this fashion.

    The OE. end rhymes are either (*a*) complete rhymes as
hond : rond, gefǽgon : geþǽgon, or (*b*) assonances, in which only
the vowels correspond, as *wæf : læs* El. 1238 ; *wrāðum : ārum*
Crist. 595 ; *lúfodon : wúnedon* And. 870 ; that the assonances
are not accidental is clear from the fact that they occur alongside of perfect rhymes.[1]

---

[1] For other subdivisions of rhyme see Sievers, *Altgerm. Metrik*, §§ 99–102,
with the treatises on the subject, and Bk. II, sect. ii, ch. 1 of this work.

CHAPTER III

THE FURTHER DEVELOPMENT OF THE FREER FORM OF THE ALLITERATIVE LINE IN LATE OLD ENGLISH AND EARLY MIDDLE ENGLISH

A. Transitional Forms.

§ 41. **Increasing frequency of Rhyme.** The alliterative line was, as we have seen, the only kind of verse known in English poetry down to the end of the Old English period. In the eleventh century, however, the strict conventions which governed the use of alliteration began to be relaxed and, at the same time, end-rhyme began to invade the alliterative line, and by this means it was resolved in the course of time into two separate lines. The process by which this came about is of great importance in enabling us to follow the further development of English versification. It has two varieties :—

1. Systematic combination of end-rhyme and alliteration.
2. Unintentional or accidental combination of rhyme and alliteration.

The former—the intentional combination of rhyme with alliteration—never became popular in Old English ; indeed, the few examples previously quoted are all that have been preserved. In these examples the hemistichs of each line conform to the ancient rules with regard to their rhythmic and alliterative structure, but are more uniform in type than was usual in the older poetry, and are more closely paired together by the use of final rhyme, which occurs in all its three varieties, monosyllabic, disyllabic, and trisyllabic.

> *wúniende wǽr wílbec biscǽr.*
> *scéalcas wǽron scéarpe, scýl wæs héarpe,*
> *hlúde hlýnede ; hléoðor dýnede.* Rhyming Poem 26–28.

The rhythm of the verse is mostly descending, Type A being the prevalent form, while Types D and E occur more rarely. The Types B and C, however, are also found. Possibly this kind of verse was formed on the model of certain Mediaeval Latin rhymed verses, or, somewhat more probably, on that of the Old Norse 'runhenda', as this poetic form may have been made known in England by the Old Norse poet, Egil Skalla-grimsson, who in the tenth century had lived in England and twice stayed at the court of King Æðelstan.

§ **42.** Of greater interest than this systematic combination of alliteration and rhyme is the irregular and more or less unintentional occurrence of rhyme which in the eleventh century is found frequently in the native metre.

Isolated instances of rhyme or assonance may be met with even in the oldest Old English poems. For certain standing expressions linked by such a similarity of sound, mostly causing interior rhyme (i. e. rhyme within a hemistich), were admitted now and then in alliterative poetry, e. g.

siþþan ic hónd and rónd | hébban míhte. Beow. 656.

sǽla and mǽla ; | þat is sóð métod. ib. 1611.

In other cases such rhymes are to be found at the end of two hemistichs,

Hróðgār máðelode, | hílt scéawode. Beow. 1687.

Wýrmum bewúnden, | wítum gebúnden. Judith 115.

Examples of this kind occur not unfrequently in several early OE. poems, but their number increases decidedly in the course of time from *Beowulf, Andreas, Judith,* up to *Byrhtnoth* and *Be Dōmes dæge.*

From the two last-mentioned poems, still written in pure alliterative verse, a few examples of rhyming-alliterative verses, or of simply rhymed verses occurring accidentally among the normal alliterative lines, may also be quoted here :

Býrhtnōð máðelode, | bórd háfenode. Byrhtn. 42.

ǽfre embe stúnde | he séalde sume wúnde. ib. 271.

þǽr þā wǽterbúrnan | swégdon and úrnon. Dom. 3.

innon þam gemónge | on ǽnlicum wónge. ib. 6.

nū þū scealt gréotan, | téaras géotan. ib. 82.

Thus it may be taken for granted that end-rhyme would have come into use in England, even if Norman-French poetry had never been introduced, although it is certainly not to be denied that it only became popular in England owing to French influence.

But can this influence explain the gradually increasing use

of end-rhyme in some OE. poems written shortly before the Norman Conquest (as e. g. *Byrhtnoth*, *Be Dōmes dæge*, the poetical passage in the *Saxon Chronicle* of the year 1036), or are we to attribute it to the influence of mediaeval hymn poetry, or, lastly, to the lingering influence of the above-mentioned Old Norse ' runhenda ' ? It is not easy to give a decided answer to these questions.

In any case it would appear that towards the end of the Old English period combined Mediaeval Latin and French influence on English metre became of considerable importance on account of the constantly growing intercourse between the British isles and the continent. This may be seen in the more frequent use of rhyme, as indeed was only to be expected in consequence of the increasing popularity of Norman-French and Mediaeval-Latin poetry in England and the reception of Norman-French words into the language.

This combination of alliteration and rhyme, however, only becomes conspicuous to a considerable extent for the first time in the above-mentioned passage of the *Saxon Chronicle*, and in another passage of the year 1087.[1]

The chief difference between these verses and those of the *Rhyming Poem* is this, that the former have not such a symmetrical structure as the latter, and that rhyme and alliteration are not combined in all of them, but that regular alliterative lines, rhyming-alliterative lines, and lines with rhyme only occur promiscuously, as e. g. in the following lines (4–7) of the above-mentioned passage of the *Chronicle* of the year 1036 :

> súme hī man bénde, | súme hī man blénde,
> súme man hámelode | and súme héanlīce hǽttode ;
> ne wearþ dréorlīcre dǽd | gedón on þisan éarde,
> siððan Déne cómon | and hēr frýð nǽmon.

The verses of the year 1087 of the *Saxon Chronicle* have a similar but on the whole less rhythmical structure. In some of the lines the hemistichs are neither joined by alliteration, nor by end-rhyme, but merely by the two-beat rhythm of each of them ; cf. ll. 1–5 :

> *Castelas he let wyrcean | and earme men swiðe swencean.*
> *Se cyng wes swa swiðe stearc | and benam of his under-þeoddan*

---

[1] Some less important examples, of which the metrical character is not quite clear, are mentioned by Luick, Paul's *Grundriss*, ed. 2, II. ii. p. 144.

manig marc goldes | and ma hundred punda seolfres ;
þat he nam be wihte | and mid mycelan unrihte
of his landleode | for litelre neode.[1]

On the other hand, the poetical piece of the *Saxon Chronicle* on Eadweard of the year 1065 is written in perfectly regular alliterative lines.

These two ways of treating the old alliterative line which occur in the latter part of the *Saxon Chronicle*, and which we will call the progressive and the conservative treatment, indicate the course which this metre was to take in its further development. Out of the long alliterative line, separated by the caesura into two hemistichs, again connected by rhyme, there sprang into existence a short rhyming couplet. This was by no means identical with the three-beat couplet evolved from two rhyming hemistichs of a line on the model of the French Alexandrine, nor with the short four-beat couplets modelled on the French *vers octosyllabe*, but had points of similarity enough to both, especially to the former one, to be easily used in conjunction with them, as several Early English poems show.

The conservative treatment of the old alliterative line, which probably at no time was altogether discontinued, was revived in the thirteenth and especially in the fourteenth and fifteenth centuries, when it degenerated again in the same way as the progressive line had done several centuries before.

B. The ' Proverbs of Alfred ' and Layamon's ' Brut '.

§ 43. The first subject which we have to consider here is the further development of the progressive form of the alliterative line, the representatives of which [2] are closely connected in their rhythmic form with the two specimens of the poetical parts of the *Saxon Chronicle* quoted above. From *Alfred's Proverbs* we take No. xv (ll. 247–66) :

þus queþ Alured :
Ne schal-tu néuere þi wíf | by hire wlýte chéose,   247–8
for néuer none þinge | þat heo tó þe brýngeþ ;
ac leorne hire cúste, | heo cúþeþ hí wel sóne ;

---

[1] In this passage and for the future we refrain from indicating the quantity of the vowels. The rhythmic accentuation is omitted, as being very uncertain in this passage.

[2] Viz. the so-called *Proverbs of King Alfred* (ed. by R. Morris, E. E. T. S., vol. XLIX), and Layamon's *Brut*, ed. by Sir Frederic Madden, London, 1847, 2 vols.

for móny mon for áyhte | *úvele iáuhteþ,*
and ófte mon of fáyre | *frákele ichéoseþ.*   255-6
Wó is him þat úvel wìf | *brýngeþ to his cótlỳf;*
só is him alýve | *þat úvele ywýueþ.*
For hé schal uppen éorþe | *dréori i-wúrþe.*
Mónymon síngeþ | *þat wíf hom brýngeþ*
Wíste he hwat he bróuhte | *wépen he mýhte.*   265-6

The metre of Layamon's *Brut* may be illustrated by the following passage (ll. 13841-13882):

þa ánswerede þe óðer | *þat was þe áldeste bróðer*
'*Lust me nú, lauerd kíng* | *and ích þe wullen cúðen*
what cníhtes we béoð, | *and whanene we icúmen séoð.*
Ich hátte Héngest, | *Hórs is mi bróðer;*
we beoð of A'lemáinne, | *áðelest alre lónde;*   13849-50
of þat ílken ǽnde | *þe A'ngles is iháten.*
Béoð in ure lónde | *sélcùðe tìðènde:*
vmbe fífìène ʒér | *þat fólc is isómned,*
al ure lédene fólc, | *and heore lóten wérpeð;*
uppen þán þe hit fáleð, | *he scal uáren of lónde;*   13859-60
bilǽuen scullen þa fíue, | *þa séxte scal fórð-lìðe*
út of þan léode | *to úncùðe lónde;*
ne beo he ná swa léof mon | *vórð he scal lìðen.*
For þer is fólc swiðe múchel, | *mǽre þene heo wálden;*
ba wíf fareð mid chílde | *swa þe déor wílde;*   13869-70
ǽueralche ʒére | *heo béreð chíld þère.*
þát beoð an us féole | *þat we fǽren scólden;*
ne míhte we bilǽue | *for líue ne for dǽðe,*
ne for náuer nane þínge, | *for þan fólc-kìnge.*
þús we uerden þére | *and for þí beoð nu hére,*   13879-80
to séchen vnder lúfte | *lónd and godne láuerd.*

These extracts illustrate only the general metrical character of the two literary monuments, the versification of which in many passages considerably deviates from the type here exhibited. It frequently shows a still more arbitrary mixture of the different kinds of verse, or a decided preference for some of them over the others. But the examples given will suffice to show that here, as in the two passages from the *Saxon Chronicle* quoted above, we have four different kinds of verse distinguished by the different use of rhyme and alliteration, viz.:

1. Regular alliterative lines, which are very numerous, and at least in the first half of Layamon's *Brut*, possibly throughout

the poem, form the bulk, e. g. *Prov.* xv. 247–8, Layamon, 13847–8, 13851–2, 13855–6, 13859–60, 13867–8, 13881–2, or

Búte if he béo | in bóke iléred.   Prov. iii. 65–6.

þat his blód and his bráin | bá weoren todáscte.   Lay. 1468–9.

2. Rhyme (or assonance) and alliteration combined; equally numerous, e. g. *Prov.* xv. 253–4, Lay. 13841–2, 13845–6, 13869–70, &c., or

Þat þe chíriche habbe grýþ | and the chéorl beo in frýþ.
                                    Prov. v. 93.

his sédes to sówen, | his médes to mówen.   ib. 95.

biuóren wende Héngest, | and Hórs him alre hǽndest.
                                    Lay. 13973–4.

Heo cómen into hálle | hǽndeliche álle.   ib. 13981–2.

3. Verses with rhyme (or assonance) only, without alliteration, also not unfrequent, e. g. *Prov.* xv. 249–50 ff., or Lay. 13853–4, &c.

And his plóuh beo idrýue | to ure álre bihóue.   Prov. v. 97–8.

þe póure and þe ríche | démen ilýche.   ib. iv. 80–1.

On Itálȝe heo comen to lónde, | þer Róme nou on stóndeþ.
                                    Lay. 106–7.

fele ȝér under súnnan | nas ȝet Róme biwónnen.   ib. 108–9.

4. Four-beat verses without either rhyme or alliteration, occurring comparatively rarely, and in most cases probably to be attributed to corruption of the text.   Examples :

he may béon on élde | wénliche lórþeu.   Prov. vi. 101–2.

we habbeð séoue þúsund | of góde cníhten.   Lay. 365–6.

It is certain that these four different forms of verse cannot have been felt by the poets themselves as rhythmically unlike ; their rhythmic movement must have been apprehended as essentially one and the same.

§ 44. **Nature and origin of this metre.   Theories of Trautmann and Luick.**   We need not here discuss the theory of Prof. Trautmann, who endeavours to show that the hemistichs of Layamon's verse were composed in imitation of the four-beat short-lined metre in which the Old High German poet Otfrid had written his religious poem *Krist*, a form which, according to Trautmann and his followers, had been frequently employed in late Old English and early Middle

English poetry. References to the criticisms of this hypothesis, by the present writer and others, are given by G. Körting in his *Encyklopädie der Englischen Philologie*, p. 388, and by K. Luick in Paul's *Grundriss der Germanischen Philologie*, ed. 2, II. ii. 152. The author of this book, in his larger work on the subject (*Englische Metrik*, i. §§ 67–73), has shown, as English and German scholars had done before him, that Layamon's verse has its roots in the Old English alliterative line. Twelve years after the publication of that work this theory received further confirmation at the hands of Prof. Luick, who has shown in Paul's *Grundriss* (l.c.) that the five types of the Old English alliterative line, discovered by Prof. Sievers, reappear (although in a modified form) in the lines of Layamon's *Brut*. But we are unable wholly to agree with Prof. Luick's view on the origin and nature of this metre.

In order to explain the origin of Layamon's verse he starts from the hypothesis of Prof. Sievers[1] that the Old Germanic alliterative verse, as historically known, which was intended to be *recited*, and therefore not restricted to uniformity of rhythm, originated from a primitive Old Germanic verse meant to be sung, and therefore characterized by rhythmic regularity. According to Prof. Luick this primitive metre, although not represented by any extant example in Old English, had never quite died out, and forms the basis of the metre of Layamon and his predecessors in early Middle English. For this ingenious hypothesis, however, no real evidence exists. On the contrary, the fact that the beginnings of the peculiar kind of metre used by Layamon can be traced back to purely alliterative Old English poems, where they occur amongst regular alliterative lines, and therefore undoubtedly must be of the same rhythmical structure, seems to be decisive against Prof. Luick's theory.

For the same reason it is impossible to follow Prof. Luick in regarding Layamon's line as having an even-beat rhythm, and containing not only two primary accents, but two secondary accents as well. A further strong objection to this view is to be found in the circumstance, that in the early part of Layamon's *Brut*, although rhyme already occurs not unfrequently, alliterative lines decidedly predominate; in the passage consisting of forty long lines (ll. 106–185, quoted in our *Altenglische Metrik*, pp. 152-3), we have thirty-three regular alliterative lines and only five rhymed lines, two of which are alliterative at the same time.

[1] Paul's *Grundriss*, ed. 2, II. ii. p. 10, and *Altgermanische Metrik*, p. 139.

Even in the middle portion of Layamon's *Chronicle*, where the poet, as Prof. Luick thinks, must have attained to a certain skill in handling his metre, alliterative lines are in some passages quite as numerous as rhymed ones. In the passage quoted above (p. 68), for example, which consists of twenty-one long lines, eleven of them are alliterative and ten are rhymed. On the other hand, in the continuation of this passage (quoted *Altengl. Metrik*, p. 156), containing twenty-nine long lines, the reverse is the case, the number of alliterative lines being only seven, and that of rhymed and assonant lines twenty-two in all; of the latter, however, eleven are alliterative at the same time.

While then it might be admissible to speak of progressive neglect of alliteration and of increasing predilection for end-rhyme on the part of the poet, as he advances with his work, it is not in accordance with the facts to assert that 'alliteration had ceased to play its former part, and had been reduced to the level of a mere ornament of the verse'. On the contrary, in the first part of the *Chronicle* alliteration is the predominant form, and, as the work advances, it is still used to a considerable extent as a means to connect the two hemistichs or short lines so as to form one long line. The strict laws formerly observed in the use of alliteration, it is true, are not unfrequently disregarded, chiefly with respect to the head-stave, which often falls on the fourth accented syllable of the long line; and other licences (first occurring in Ælfric's *Metrical Homilies*) may be met with. Nevertheless both *Alfred's Proverbs* and Layamon's *Brut* (as is sufficiently shown by the many specimens quoted in our *Altenglische Metrik*, pp. 150 ff.), contain a great number of perfectly regular alliterative lines. The fact that, in the second half of Layamon's *Chronicle*, end-rhyme is used more and more frequently as a means to connect the two hemistichs, is with much more probability to be explained by the continual occupation of the poet with the Norman-French original poem, and by the increasing influence which its short octosyllabic couplets must naturally have exercised upon his own rhythms, than by a supposed intention of the poet to write in 'primitive Germanic four-beat song-metre', the very existence of which is hypothetical. Furthermore, the fact that in some (not all or even most) of the passages, where end-rhyme is used almost exclusively, e. g. in the passage quoted above (ll. 13883–940), an even-beat rhythm is distinctly noticeable, can be explained quite naturally by the influence of the Norman-French original, the even-measured verses of which the poet was translating.

But even supposing that Layamon *intended* to use the primitive Germanic four-beat song-metre in his translation of Wace's *Chronicle*, although it certainly was not intended for singing, what can have been his reason for composing the first half of his work, and a very considerable portion of the rest, in a rhythmical form which only to a small extent shows the peculiarities of a rhyming even-beat metre, whereas the main part of it consists of the native unevenly stressed alliterative verse? It is quite incorrect to say that the author in the course of his work not unfrequently fell back into the alliterative verse. The fact is just the opposite: the author started by using the native alliterative verse to which he was accustomed, and gradually came to adopt the rhymed verse of the Norman-French chronicle which he was translating, without, however, entirely giving up the former metre. Alliteration and end-rhyme, which he used sometimes separately and sometimes in combination, were evidently looked upon by Layamon as equally legitimate means for connecting his hemistichs or short lines.

§ 45. **Number of stresses.** Quite as unfounded as the assertion that Layamon's verse is of an even-beat nature is the other assertion that it contains two primary and two secondary accents, and that the second of these secondary accents in verses with disyllabic endings may fall on a syllable which by its etymology ought to have no accent.

This statement is refuted by the treatment of rhyme in Layamon's *Brut* and in some earlier poems of a similar form or containing the same kind of verse.

Not only in the *Brut*, but also in several Old English and earlier Middle English poems, we meet both with regular rhymes and with simple assonances and other still more imperfect correspondences in sound intended to serve as rhymes.

Examples of actual rhyme in the *Brut* are the monosyllabic pairs: *seon : beon* 13837–8, *king : þing* 13883–4, *cniht : riht* 13887–8; besides inexact rhymes like *mon : anān* 13605–6, 13615–16, *mon : dōn* 13665–6, 13677–8 ,*wīn : in* 14349–50, 14998–9, *chin : wīn* 14994–5; disyllabic rhymes: *icúmen : gúmen* 13787–8, *góde : flóde* 13791–2, *sóhten : róhten* 13803–4, *óðer : bróðer* 13841–2, *childe : wilde* 13870–1, *þére : hére* 13871–2, *hálle : álle* 13981–2. We see no reason to accent these last-mentioned rhymes differently from similar rhymes occurring in Old English poems, as e. g. *wédde : aspédde* Andr. 1633, *wúnne : blúnne* ib. 1382, *bewúnden : gebúnden* Jud. 115, *stúnde : wúnde* Byrhtn. 271, &c.

Examples of the more numerous group formed by assonances are *tō : idōn* 13801–2, *lond : gold* 13959–60, *strong : lond* 13969–70, and disyllabic assonances like *cníhten : kínges* 13793–4, *wólden : londe* 13821–2, &c.

These are strictly parallel with instances like *wǽf : lǽs* El. 1238, *onlāg : hād* ib. 1246, or like *wrāðum : ārum* Crist 595, *lýre : cýme* Phoen. 53, *rǽdde : tǽhte* By. 18, *flánes : genáme* ib. 71, *hléorum : téarum* Be Dōmes dæge 28, &c., and must, in our opinion, be metrically interpreted in exactly the same way. That is to say, the root-syllable must, not only in real assonances like *cníhten : kínges*, *lónde : strónge*, but also in consonances like *Péohtes : cníhtes*, *mónnen : ínnen*, be looked upon as the chief part of the rhyme, and the flexional endings, whether rhyming correctly or incorrectly, must be regarded as forming only an unessential, unaccented, indistinctly heard part of the rhyme, just as they admittedly do in the similar Old English assonances quoted above.

Now, as it is inconsistent with the two-beat rhythm of the hemistich in Old English verse, to attribute a secondary accent to those endings, although they were in some cases more distinctly pronounced than the Middle English endings, it is impossible to suppose that the Middle English endings bore a secondary accent. A further objection is that although the syllables which, according to Luick's theory, are supposed to bear a secondary accent are of course usually preceded by a long root-syllable, it not unfrequently happens that a disyllabic word with long root-syllable rhymes with one having a short root-syllable, in which case the ending is not suited to bear a secondary accent at all, e. g. *flúzen : únnifōge* 14043–4, *to-fóren : gréten* 14071–2, *sǽres : wólde* 14215–16, *fáreð : iuéren* 14335–6, *icúmen : þréoien* 14337–8, *lágen* (= *laws*) *: lónde* 14339–40, *húnden : láuien* 14480–1, *scóme : sōne* 14604–5, *cúmen : hálden* 14612–13, *scípe : bróhte* 14862–3, *fáder : unrǽdes* 14832–3, *fáder : rǽdes* 14910–11, *fóten : biscópen* 14821–2, *iwíten : scipen* 14251–2, *wíten : wenden* 15060–1, *gúme : bisíden* 15224–5, *fréondscìpe : séoluen* 15226–7, *wúde : wéien-lǽten* 15508–9, *ibóren : béarne* 15670–1, *bizáte : wéorlde-rìche* 15732–3, *scáðe : fólke* 15784–5, *biswíken* (pret. pl.) *: cráften* 29016–17, *azíuen : zélden* 29052–3, *biuóren : fúsen* 29114–15, *súne : þéode* 29175–6, *idríuen : kínerìchen* 29177–18, *grúpen* (pret. pl.) *: múzen* 29279–80, *stúden* (= *places*) *: bérnen* 29285–6, &c.

The only cases in which a secondary accent seems to be required for an unaccented final syllable are such rhymes as the

following :—*hâlì : forþí* 13915–16 (cf. *Altengl. Metrik*, p. 160) ;
men : cômèn 13997–8 (MS. B : *men : here*), *men : dédèn* 13975–6,
isómned wés : lóndès 25390–1, and so forth.[1] But rhymes of this
kind are in comparison to the ordinary disyllabic or feminine
endings so very rare (occurring, for the most part, in lines which
admit of a purely alliterative scansion, or which have come down
to us in an incorrect state), that they have no bearing on the
general rhythmic accentuation of those final syllables, or on
the rhythmic character of Layamon's verses in general (cf.
p. 78, end of § 47).

§ **46. Analysis of verse-types.** In turning now to a closer
examination of the rhythmic structure of the metre in Layamon's
Brut and in the somewhat earlier *Proverbs of Alfred*, we are
glad to find ourselves more nearly than hitherto (though still
not altogether) in agreement with the views of Prof. Luick.

It is no small merit of his to have shown for the first time
that the five types of rhythmic forms pointed out by Sievers as
existing in the alliterative line are met with also in each of the
four forms of verse of Layamon's *Brut* and of the *Proverbs*.
And here it is of interest to note that not only are the normal
types of frequent occurrence (chiefly in the *Proverbs*), but the
extended types also, especially in Layamon's *Brut*, are met with
even more frequently.

On account of our limited space only a few examples of each
of the five types can be given in this handbook.

Instead of quoting hemistichs or isolated short lines as
examples of each of the single types A, B, C, D, E, we prefer
always to cite two connected short lines, and to designate the
rhythmic character of the long line thus originating by the types
of the two hemistichs, as follows: A+A, A*+B, B*+C,
C*+E, &c., where A*, B*, C* signify the extended types, to
be discussed more fully below, and A, B, C, &c., the normal
types. This mode of treatment is necessary in order that our
examples may adequately represent the structure of the verse.
The short lines are always connected—either by alliteration, by
rhyme (or assonance), or by both combined, or sometimes
merely by identity of rhythm—into pairs. These pairs of short
lines are regarded by Luick as even-measured couplets, while
we regard them as alliterative long lines; but on either view
each of them forms a coherent unity. We believe that an
examination of the couplet or long line as an undivided whole

[1] On the nature of these rhymes, cf. § 53 and the author's paper, 'Metrische
Randglossen,' in *Englische Studien*, x. 192 ff., chiefly pp. 199–200.

will show unmistakably that the assumption of the even-measured character of Layamon's verse is erroneous, or at least that it applies only in certain cases, when the metre is strongly influenced by Romanic principles of versification. The examples are for the most part the same as those which Prof. Luick has quoted,[1] but we have in all cases added the complementary hemistichs, which are generally of somewhat greater length:

A +A: *Ich hátte Héngest,* | *Hórs is my bróðer.* Lay. 13847–8.

A* +A: *and ích þe wulle ræchen* | *déorne rúnen.* ib. 14079–80.

B +A: *þær þa sæxisce mén* | *þæ sæ isóhten.* ib. 14738–9.

B(E?)+A: *hw hi héore líf* | *léde schólde.* Prov. i. 15–16.

A +B: *lónges lýves,* | *ac him lýeþ þe wrénch.* ib. x. 161–2.

B* +A: *vmbe fíftene ʒér* | *þat fólc is isómned.* Lay. 13855–6.

B +C: *and eoure léofue gódd* | *þe ʒe tó lúteð.* ib. 13891–2.

B +C: *ne wurð þu néver so wód,* | *ne so wýn-drúnke.* Prov. xi. 269–70.

A +C: *mi gást hine iwárðeð* | *and wírð stílle.* Lay. 17136–7.

C +C: *for þat wéorc stóndeð* | *inne Írlónde.* ib. 17176–7.

A* +D: *kómen to þan kínge* | *wíl-tíþende.* ib. 17089–90.

D +A*: *vólc únimete* | *of móni ane lónde.* ib. 16188–9.

E +E: *fíf þusend mén* | *wúrcheð þer ón.* ib. 15816–17.

B* +E: *þæt he héfde to iwíten* | *séouen hundred scípen.* ib. 15102–3.

D +*A: *for nys no wrt uéxynde* | *a wúde ne a wélde.* Prov. x. 168–9.

A* +D: *þat óuer mvwe þas féye* | *fúrþ ýp-holde.* ib. 170–1.

It is easy to observe that it is only when two identical types, like A+A, C+C, E+E, are combined, that an even-beat rhythm (to some extent at least) can be recognized; in all the other combinations this character is entirely absent.

§ 47. **Extended types.** We now turn to the more numerous class of such couplets or long lines which in both their component hemistichs exhibit extended variations of the five types, resulting from anacrusis or from the insertion of unstressed syllables in the interior of the line. These verses, it is true, are somewhat more homogeneous, and have a certain resemblance to an even-beat rhythm in consequence of the greater number of un-

---

[1] In Paul's *Grundriss*, ed. 2, II. ii. pp. 145–7.

accented syllables, one of which (rarely two or more) may, under the influence of the even-beat metre of the Norman-French original, have been meant by the poet to be read with a somewhat stronger accentuation. We are convinced, however, that in feminine endings, in so far as these are formed, which is usually the case, by the unaccented endings -e, -en, -es, eþ, &c., these final syllables never, or at most only in isolated cases, which do not affect the general character of the rhythm, have a stronger accent or, as Prof. Luick thinks, form a secondary arsis. As little do we admit the likelihood of such a rhythmic accentuation of these syllables when they occur in the middle of the line, generally of such lines as belong to the normal types mentioned above.

It is convenient, however, to adopt Luick's formulas for these common forms of Layamon's verse, with this necessary modification, that we discard the secondary accent attributed by him to the last syllable of the types A, C, D, accepting only his types B and E without any change. We therefore regard the normally constructed short lines of Layamon's metre—so far as they are not purely alliterative lines of two accents, but coupled together by rhyme or assonance, or by alliteration and rhyme combined—as belonging to one or other of the following two classes: (1) lines with four accents and masculine or monosyllabic endings (types B and E); and (2) lines of three accents and feminine or disyllabic endings (types A, C, D). In this classification those unaccented syllables which receive a secondary stress are, for the sake of brevity, treated as full stresses—which, indeed, they actually came to be in the later development of the metre, and possibly to some extent even in Layamon's own verse.

Assuming the correctness of this view, the chief types of Layamon's verse may be expressed by the following formulas, in which the bracketed theses are to be considered optional:

Type A: (×)´(×)x̓ ×´×. Type B:(×)x̓ ×´(×)x̓ ×´.
Type C: (×)x̓ ×´´×. Type D: (×)´×´x̓ ×.
Type E: ×´(×)x̓ × x̓ ×´.

As these types may be varied by resolutions in the same way as the primary types, there arise various additional formulas such as the following:

A: (×)⌣×(×)x̓ ×´×. B: (×)x̓ ×´(×)x̓ ×⌣×.
C: (×)x̓ ×⌣×´×, &c.

Other variations may be effected by disyllabic or even polysyllabic theses in the beginning ('anacruses') or in the middle of the verse instead of monosyllabic theses.

Apart from these another frequently occurring variation of type C must be mentioned which corresponds to the formula $(\times)\times\ \times\underline{\angle}\times\underline{\angle}\times$, and may be designated (with Professors Paul and Luick) as type C^a, because the position of its accented syllables points to type C, while on the other hand it bears a certain resemblance to type A.

The following examples, many of which have been quoted before by Luick, may serve to illustrate these types of short lines or rather hemistichs and their combination in couplets or long lines, in which a normal hemistich is often followed by a lengthened one and vice versa:

A* + A*: *Stróng hit ìs to rówe | ayèyn þe sée þat flóweþ.* Prov.
x. 145–6.

A* + A*: *And swá heo gùnnen wénden | fórð tò þan kínge.*
Lay. 1381–12.

A* + A*: *ne míhte wè bilǽue | for líue nè for dǽþe.* ib. 13875–6.

B + A*: *ùmbe fíftène ȝér | þat fólc ìs isómned.* ib. 13855–6.

A* + C*: *ǽveràlche ȝére | heo bèreð chíld þére.* ib. 13871–2.

B* + B*: *þèr com **H**éngest, þèr com **H**órs, | þèr com míni mòn ful óht.* ib. 14009–10.

B* + B*: *ànd þe clérek ànd þe knýht, | he schùlle démen èuelyche ríht.* Prov. iv. 78–9.

C^a + C*: *þèr þes cníhtes cómen | bifòren þan fólc-kínge.*
Lay. 13817–18.

C* + A*: *ȝìf heo gríð sóhten, | and of his fréondscipe ròhten?*
ib. 13803–4.

C* + C^a: *hìt beoð tíðénde | ìnne Sǽxe lónde.* ib. 14325–6.

A* + C*: *for he wólde wìð þan kìnge | hòlden rúnínge.*
ib. 14069–70.

A* + D*: *heo sǽden tò þan kínge | nèowe tíðènden.* ib. 13996–7.

A* + D*: *and míd him bròuhte hére | an húndred rídæren.*
ib. 15088–9.

E* + B*: *Hǽngest wès þan kìnge léof | ànd him Líndesàȝe géf.*
ib. 14049–50.

Types with resolutions:

A* + A*: *and þús pìne dúȝeþe | stílle hè fordémeð.* ib. 14123–4.

A* + B*: *Wóden hèhde þa hǽhste làȝe | an ùre ǽldèrne dǽȝen.*
ib. 13921–2.

The first hemistich of the last line offers a specimen of a variation of the ordinary types with feminine endings (chiefly of A, C, and C^a), designated by Prof. Luick as A$_1$, C$_1$, C$^a_1$, and showing the peculiarity that instead of the ending $\angle$ × somewhat fuller forms occur, consisting either of two separate words or of a compound word, and thus corresponding either to the formula $\angle$ $\dot{\times}$, or, if there are three syllables, to the formula $\angle$ × $\dot{\times}$, or in case of a resolution (as in the above example) to the formula $\angle$ × $\cup$ ×. We differ from Prof. Luick, however, in admitting also endings corresponding to the formula $\cup$ $\dot{\times}$ ×.

As a rule, if not always, such forms of verse are occasioned by the requirements of rhyme. This is not the case, it is true, in the following purely alliterative line:

A$_1$*+A*: *þe kíng sòne úp stòd | and sétte hine bì him séoluen.*
                                                  Lay. 14073–4.

but in other verses it is so, e. g. :

B*+A$_1$*: *Ah of éou ich wùlle iwíten | þurh sóðen éouwer
                                            wùrðscìpen.* ib. 13835–6.

and similarly (not corresponding to $\angle$ × $\dot{\times}$, as Prof. Luick thinks):

A$_1$*+B*: *bìdden us to fúltúme | þàt is Críst gòdes súne.*
                                                  ib. 14618–19.

but the formula $\angle$ × $\dot{\times}$ is represented by the following verses:

A$_1$*+A$_1$*: *þe þúnre heo ʒìven þúnresdæi | forþí þat hèo heom
                                            helpen mæi.* ib. 13929–30.

A$_1$*+A$_1$*: *þe éorl ànd þe éþelỳng | ibúreþ ùnder gódne kìng.*
                                                  Prov. iv. 74–5.

C$_1$*+C$^a_1$*: *nès þer nán crístindòm, | þèr þe kíng þat máide nòm.*
                                                  Lay. 14387–8.

In the last but one of these examples this accentuation is corroborated in the Jesus College MS. by the written accent on the word *gódne*, whereby not only the rhyme *-lyng : king* is shown to be an unaccented one, but at the same time the two-beat rhythm of the hemistich is proved as well as that of the preceding hemistich. Moreover, the alliteration in all these examples is a further proof of the two-beat character of their rhythm.

§ 48. It was owing to the use of these two more strongly accented syllables in each verse which predominate over the other syllables, whether with secondary accents or unaccented, that the poets, who wrote in this metre, found it possible to regard the different kinds of verse they employed as rhythmically equivalent. These were as, follows: (1) purely alliterative lines with hemistichs of two stresses, (2) extended lines of this kind with secondary accents in the middle of the hemistich, (3) rhyming-alliterative or merely rhyming lines with a feminine ending and a secondary accent in the middle of the verse, or with a masculine ending and two secondary accents, one on the last syllable, as is also the case with the corresponding verses mentioned under the second heading. These two last-mentioned verse-forms are very similar to two popular metres formed on the model of Romanic metres. The former of them—the hemistich with three stresses (one of which is secondary) and feminine ending, together with the much rarer variety that has a masculine ending—resembles the sections of the Alexandrine ; and the hemistich with a masculine ending (more rarely a feminine) and four stresses (two of which have secondary accents only) is similar to the short four-beat couplet, and also to the first section of the Septenary line (the second section being similar to the former three-beat group). It is, therefore, not to be wondered at that this metre of Layamon in its different forms (that of the purely alliterative line included) is in several Middle English poems, chiefly in *The Bestiary*, employed concurrently (both in separate passages and in the same passage) with the above-mentioned foreign metres formed on Romanic or mediaeval-Latin models. By this fact the influence of the Romanic versification on the origin and development of this form of the native verse gains increased probability.[1]

The limits of our space do not permit of further discussion of this peculiar metre, which, as presented in the extant examples, appears rather as in process of development than as a finished product, and of which a complete understanding can be attained only by elaborate statistical investigation.

C. The progressive form of the alliterative line, rhymed throughout. 'King Horn.'

§ 49. **The further development of the Layamon-verse** is very simple and such as might naturally be expected from its previous history.

The use of final rhyme becomes constant, and consequently

---

[1] Cf. our remarks in Book I, Part II, on the Septenary Verse in combination with other metres.

alliteration, although remnants of it still are noticeable even in short lines connected together, becomes more and more scarce.[1]

The unaccented syllables are interposed between the accented ones with greater regularity; and among the unaccented syllables the one (or, in some sub-species of the verse, more than one) which is relatively stronger than the rest receives full metrical stress, or at least nearly approaches the fully-stressed syllables in rhythmical value.

This form of the metre is represented by a short poem[2] consisting of only twelve lines, belonging to the first half of the thirteenth century, and by the well-known poem *King Horn*[3] (1530 lines) which belongs to the middle of the same century.

The prevailing rhythmical form of this poem is exemplified by the following verses, which for the sake of convenience we print here, not in the form of couplets (as the editors, quite justifiably, have done), but in that of long lines as they are written in the Harleian MS.:

Hórn þu àrt wel kéne | and þát is wèl iséne.   91–2.

Þe sé bigàn to flówe | and Hórn chìld to rówe.   117–18.

This form occurs in more than 1300 out of the 1530 short lines of which the poem consists. It is evident that the rhythm of these lines is nearly the same as in the following taken from earlier poems:

ǽfre embe stúnde | he séalde sume wúnde.   Byrhtn. 271.

ínnon þǽm gemónge | on ǽnlicum wónge.   Dom. 6.

súme hi man bénde | súme hi man blénde.   Chron. 1036. 4.

þát he nam be wíhte | and mid mýcelan unríhte.   ib. 1087. 4.

wiþ póuere and wiþ ríche | wiþ álle monne ilýche.   Prov. 375–6.

ne míhte we bilǽve | for líve ne for dǽþe.   Lay. 13875–6.

If those syllables which have the strongest accent in the unaccented parts of these verses are uttered a little more loudly than was usual in the alliterative line the rhythm becomes exactly the same as in the corresponding verses of King Horn, where the three-beat rhythm already has become the rule.

This rule, however, is by no means without exceptions, and even the old two-beat rhythm (which may have been the original

[1] Cf. Wissmann, *King Horn*, pp. 59–62, and *Metrik*, i, pp. 189–90.
[2] *Signs of Death* in *Old Engl. Misc.* (E. E. T. S.), p. 101.
[3] Cf. Hall's edition (Clar. Press, 1901), pp. xlv–l, where our views on the origin and structure of the metre are adopted.

rhythm) is, in the oldest form of the poem, sometimes clearly perceptible, rarely, it is true, in both hemistichs, as e.g. in the following line :

Hi slóȝen and fúȝten | þe níȝt and þe úȝten. 1375–6,

but somewhat oftener in one of them, as in the following :

Hi wénden to wisse | of hère líf to mísse. 121–2.

So schàl þi náme sprínge | from kínge to kínge. 211–12.

In Hórnes ilíke | þú schalt hùre beswíke. 289–90.

Hi rúnge þe bélle | þe wédlak fòr to felle. 1253–4.

Of this type of verse a great many examples are of course to be met with in the earlier alliterative poems :

wúldres wédde | wítum āspédde. An. 1633.

wýrmum bewúnden, | wítum gebúnden. Jud. 115.

rǻd and rǽdde | ríncum tǽhte. Byrhtn. 18.

on míddan gehǽge | éal swā ic sécge. Dom. 4.

þat lónd to léden | mid láweliche déden. Prov. 75–6.

þe póure ànd þe ríche | démen ilíche. ib. 80–1.

bivóren þan kínge | fáirest àlre þínge. Lay. 14303–4.

The third type (three beats with masculine ending), which is of rarer occurrence, is represented by the following lines :

Þú art grèt and stróng, | fáir and èuene lóng. 93–4.

Þu schàlt be dúbbed kníght | are còme séue níȝt. 447–8.

Léue at hìre he nám | and into hálle cám. 585–6.

As corresponding lines of earlier poems may be quoted :

éarn ǽses gèorn, | wæs on éorþan cýrm. Byrhtn. 107.

þat þe chírche hàbbe grýð | and þe chéorl bèo in frýð. Prov. 93–4.

lóuerd kìng wæs hǽil! | for þine kíme ìch æm vǽin.

Lay. 14309–10.

The fourth type (four beats with masculine ending), which occurs somewhat oftener, has the following form :

Ófte hàdde Hòrn beo wó, | ac nèure wúrs þan hìm was þó. 115–16.

Þe stúard wàs in hèrte wó, | fòr he núste whàt to dó. 275–6.

The corresponding rhythm of the earlier poems occurs in verses like:

and his geféran he fordráf, | *and sume míslice of slóh.* Chr. 1036. 2.

þe éorl ànd þe éþelíng | *ibúreþ ùnder gódne kìng.* Prov. 74–5.

and sélde wùrþ he blýþe and glèd | *þe món þat ìs his wíves quèd.*

ib. 304–5.

þe þúnre heo ʒìven þúnres dèi, | *forþí þat hèo heom hélpen mèi.*

Lay. 13931–2.

The fifth type (four beats with feminine endings) is represented by the following verses:

To déþe hè hem álle bròʒte, | *his fáder dèþ wel dére hi bòʒte.* 883–4.

Tomóreʒe bè þe fíʒtìnge, | *whàne þe líʒt of dáye springe.* 817–18.

As corresponding verses of earlier poems we quote:

súme hi man wiþ féo **s**éalde, | **s**úme hrēowlūce ācwéalde.

Chron. 1036. 3.

and sóltes bòlt is sóne iscòte, | *forþí ich hòlde híne for dòte.*

Prov. 421–2.

in þèere sè heo fùnden utláwen, | *þa kénneste þa wèoren ò þon dáwen.*

Lay. 1283–4.

The circumstance that these different types of verse occur in different poems promiscuously makes it evident that they must all have been developed from one original rhythmical form. It is clear that this fundamental type can only be found in the old two-beat alliterative hemistich, the more so as this kind of verse is the very metre in which the earlier poems *Byrhtnoth* and *Be Dōmes Dæge* for the greatest part are written, and which is exemplified in about a third part of the poetical piece of the *Saxon Chronicle* of 1036 and a fifth part of the later piece of 1087, and again very frequently in *Alfred's Proverbs* and in Layamon's *Brut,* and which still can be traced as the original rhythm of *King Horn.*

§ 50. The evidence of the metre of this poem, showing its affinity to the alliterative line and its historical origin from it, is so cogent that it is unnecessary to discuss the theories of Prof. Trautmann and the late Dr. Wissmann, both of whom, although from different points of view, agree in ascribing a four-beat rhythm to this metre.[1]

[1] See Paul's *Grundriss,* ed. 2, II. ii. p. 156.

The frequent use again in this poem of the types of line occurring in Layamon's *Brut*, as pointed out by Prof. Luick (l. c.), puts the close connexion of the metre of *King Horn* with that form of the alliterative line beyond doubt. We cannot, however, in conformity with the view we have taken of Layamon's verse, agree with Prof. Luick in assigning a secondary accent to the last syllable of the feminine ending of the ordinary three-beat verse, in which the greater part of *King Horn* is written. Prof. Luick himself does not insist upon that particular point so strongly for this poem as he did for the earlier poems written in a similar metre.

The following examples serve to show that the same extended types of line which were found to be the commonest in Layamon's *Brut* (cp. p. 77) recur as the most usual types also in this poem:

A + C : *Álle bèon he blíþe | þat tò my sóng lýþe!* 1–2.

A + A : *A sáng ihc schàl ȝou sínge | of Múrrȳ þè kínge.* 2–3.

A + A : *He fónd bì þe strónde, | aríued òn his lónde,* 35–6.

B + C : *Àll þe dáy and àl þe níȝt, | tìl hit spráng dái líȝt.*
  123–4.

B + B : *Fàirer nis nón þàne he wás, | hè was bríȝt sò þe glás.*
  13–14.

C + C : *Bì þe sé síde, | ase hè was, wóned (⌣ ×) ríde.* 33–4.

C + A : *Of þìne méstére, | of wúde and òf rivére.* 229–30.

D + A : *Schípes fíftène | with sárazìn[e]s kéne.* 37–8.

C + A : *Þe chìld him ánswérde, | sóne so hè hit hérde.* 199–200.

B + E : *Hè was whít sò þe flúr, | róse-rèd was hìs colúr.* 15–16.

In most cases we see that identical or similar types of verse are connected here so as to form a couplet (printed by us as one long line). Even where this is not so, however, the two chief accents in each short line serve to make all the different forms and types of verse occurring in this poem sound homogeneous. This admits of a ready explanation, as the poem, in which no stanzaic arrangement can be detected, although styled a 'song' (line 2), was certainly never meant to be sung to a regular tune. On the contrary, it was undoubtedly recited like the 'Song' of Beowulf—probably not without a proper musical accompaniment—by the minstrels.

At all events the treatment of the words with regard to their rhythmic use in this poem does not deviate from that of Layamon.

§ 51. The two poems are of the same period, and in both the etymological and syntactical accentuation of natural speech forms the basis of the rhythmic accentuation. Monosyllabic words and the accented syllables of polysyllabic words having a strong syntactical accent are placed in the arsis; unaccented inflectional syllables as a rule form the theses of a verse; second parts of compounds and fully sounding derivative syllables are commonly used for theses with a somewhat stronger accent, and may, if placed in the arsis, even bear the alliteration, or, if they are less strongly accented, the rhyme:

Þèr þas cníhtes cómen | bìfòren þan fólc-kínge. Lay. 13818–19.
Ah of éou ich wùlle iwíten | þurh sóðen èouwer wúrðscìpen.

ib. 13835–6.

A mórȝe bò þe dáy gan sprìnge, | þe kíng him ròd an húntìnge.

Horn 645–6.

He wàs þe faíréste, | ànd of wít þe béste. ib. 173–4.

Unaccented inflexional syllables as a rule stand in the thesis of a verse. Only in exceptional cases, which admit of a different explanation (see above, pp. 74 and 76), they may bear the rhythmical accent if the rhyme demands it.

That a thesis in Layamon's *Brut* and in *Alfred's Proverbs* may be disyllabic or even trisyllabic both in the beginning and the middle of a line is evident from the many examples quoted above.

In *King Horn*, where the division of the original long lines into two short ones has been carried out completely, and where the rhythm of the verse has consequently become more regular, the thesis, if not wanting entirely, as usually the case in the types C, D, E, is generally monosyllabic. But, as the following examples, *faírer ne mìȝte* 8, *þe paíns còme to lònde* 58, *þanne schólde withùten óþe* 347, will show, disyllabic theses do also occur, both after the first and second arsis, and in the beginning of the line.

CHAPTER IV

THE ALLITERATIVE LINE IN ITS CONSERVATIVE FORM DURING THE FOURTEENTH AND FIF-TEENTH CENTURIES

A. The alliterative verse without rhyme.

§ 52. The progressive or free form of the alliterative line came to an end as early as the middle of the thirteenth century, when it broke up into short rhyming couplets. The stricter form was for nearly three centuries longer a very popular metre in English poetry, especially in the North-Western and Northern districts of England and in the adjacent lowlands of Scotland. The first traces, however, of its existence after the Norman Conquest are to be found in the South of England, where some poetical homilies and lives of saints were written at the end of the twelfth and in the beginning of the thirteenth century which are of the same character, both as to their subjects and to their metre, as the poetical paraphrases and homilies written by Ælfric. These poems are *Hali Meidenhad* (a poetical homily), the legends of *St. Marharete, St. Juliana,* and *St. Katherine.* These poems have been edited for the Early English Text Society, Nos. 18, 13, 51, 80; the first three by Cockayne as prose-texts, the last by Dr. Einenkel, who printed it in short couplets regarded by him as having the same four-beat rhythm (Otfrid's metre) which he and his teacher, Prof. Traut-mann, suppose to exist in Layamon and *King Horn.*[1] The Homilies have no rhymes.

The form of these homilies and legends occasionally exhibits real alliterative lines, but for the most part is nothing but rhyth-mical prose, altogether too irregular to call for an investigation

---

[1] This view has been combated by the author. The stages of the dis-cussion are to be found in articles by Einenkel, *Anglia,* v. Anz. 47; Traut-mann, *ibid.* 118; Einenkel's edition of *St. Katherine,* E. E. T. S. 80; the author's 'Metrische Randglossen', *Engl. Studien,* ix. 184; *ibid.* 368; and *Anglia,* viii. Anz. 246. According to our opinion Otfrid's verse was never imitated in England, nor was it known at all in Old or Middle English times.

here. Some remarks on passages written in a form more or less resembling alliterative verse may be found in our *Englische Metrik*, vol. i, § 94.

It is quite out of the question to suppose these Southern works, with their very irregular use of alliteration and metre, to have had any influence on the metrical form of the very numerous alliterative poems written in the fourteenth and fifteenth centuries in the Midland and Northern districts of England. It is, however, not at all likely that alliterative poetry should have sprung up there without any medium of tradition, and that it should have returned to the strict forms of the Old English models. Nor can we assume that it was handed down by means of oral tradition only on the part of the minstrels from Old English times down to the fourteenth century. The channel of tradition of the genuine alliterative line must be sought for in documents which for the most part have been lost.

A few small remnants, however, have been preserved, viz. a charm in a MS. of the twelfth century (cf. Zupitza, *Zeitschrift für deutsches Altertum*, xxxi. 49), a short poem, entitled 'Ten Abuses', belonging to the same period (E. E. T. S. 49, p. 184), a prophecy of five lines contained in the chronicle of Benedict of Peterborough (*Rerum Britannicarum Scriptores*, 49, ii. 139), finally a prophecy ascribed to Thomas of Erceldoune (E. E. T. S., vol. 61, xviii, *Thom. of Erc.*, ed. by A. Brandl, p. 26). But these pieces, treated by Prof. Luick in Paul's *Grundriss*, ed. 2, II. ii, p. 160, are either too short or are too uncertain in text to admit of our making definite conclusions from them.

But from the middle of the fourteenth century onward we have a large number of poems composed in regular alliterative verse, e. g. *King Alisaunder* (Als.) and *William of Palerne* (W.), both in E. E. T. S., Extra-Ser. No. 1; *Joseph of Arimathie* (J.A.), E. E.T. S. 44; *Sir Gawain and the Green Knight* (Gr.), E.E.T. S. 4; *Piers Plowman* (P. P.), by W. Langland, E. E. T. S., Nos. 17, 28, 30, 38, 54; *Pierce the Plowman's Crede* (P. P. Cr.), E.E.T.S. 30; *Richard the Redeles* (R. R.), E. E. T. S. 54; *The Crowned King* (Cr. K.), ibid.; *The Destruction of Troy*, E. E. T. S. 39, 56; *Morte Arthure*, E. E. T. S. 8; *Cleanness* and *Patience*, E. E. T. S. 1; *The Chevalere Assigne*, E. E. T. S., Extra-Ser. 6; and others of the end of the fifteenth and the beginning of the sixteenth centuries: see Prof. W. W. Skeat's list in 'Bishop Percy's Folio MS.', London, 1867 (ed. Furnivall and Hales), vol. iii, p. xi, and many recent publications of the Early English Text Society.

On the **structure of this metre** the opinions of scholars differ a good deal less than on that of the progressive or free form of the alliterative line. Yet there are a few adherents of the four-beat theory who apply it to the alliterative line of this epoch, amongst others Rosenthal ('Die alliterierende englische Langzeile im 14. Jahrhundert,' *Anglia*, i. 414 ff.). The two-beat theory, on the other hand, has been upheld also for this form of the alliterative line by Prof. W. W. Skeat, *Essay on Alliterative Poetry*, Percy Folio MS. 1867 (ed. Furnivall and Hales), by the present writer in *Englische Metrik*, i, pp. 195–212, and by Prof. Luick, *Anglia*, xi, pp. 392–443 and 553–618, and subsequently in Paul's *Grundriss*, ed. 2, II. ii, pp. 161–3.

§ 53. **The use and treatment of the words in the verse** is on the whole the same as in the Old English period. The chief divergence is, that in this period of the language the difference between long and short syllables was lost, in consequence of the lengthening of short vowels in open syllables which had taken place in the interval, and that consequently the substitution of a short accented syllable and an unaccented one for a long accented syllable (the so-called resolution) was no longer admissible. Otherwise syllables with a primary accent, syllables with a secondary accent, and unaccented syllables are treated just as in the Old English poetry. Accented syllables are as a rule placed in the arsis, as are also second parts of compounds. Other syllables with secondary accent (derivative and inflectional syllables) are only in exceptional cases placed in the arsis of a verse.

It is of special interest, however, to notice that words of Romanic origin which in the course of time had been introduced into the language are in many cases accented according to Germanic usage. Words of which the last syllable was accented in French have in their Middle-English form the chief accent thrown on a preceding, frequently on the first, syllable, and in consequence of this the originally fully accented syllable in trisyllabic words receives the secondary accent and is treated in the rhythm of the verse in the same way as syllables with a secondary accent in English words. The laws, too, which in Old English affect the subordination and position of the parts of speech in their relationship to the rhythm of the verse and to the alliteration, remain, generally speaking, in force. It is remarkable that ' if an attributive adjective is joined to a substantive, and a verb to a prepositional adverb, the first part of these groups of words still has the chief accent ' (Luick). The relationship, on the other hand, of verse and sentence is changed. While in Old English poetry run-on-lines were very popular and new sentences therefore frequently began in the middle of a line, after the caesura, we find that in Middle English, as a rule, the end of the sentence coincides with the end of the line. Hence every line forms a unity by itself, and the chief pause falls at the end, not, as was frequently the case in Old English times, after the caesura.

§ 54. **Alliteration.** On the whole, the same laws regarding the position of the alliterative sounds are still in force as before; it is indeed remarkable that they are sometimes even more strictly observed. In the *Destruction of Troy*, e.g. triple alliteration according to the formula *a a a x* is employed throughout.

*Now of **T**róy forto **t**élle | is myn ent**é**nt euyn,*
*Of the **st**óure and þe **st**rýfe, | when it di**st**róyet wás.* Prol. 27–8.

Alongside of this order of alliteration we find in most of the other poems the other schemes of alliteration popular in Old English times, e.g. *a x a x, x a a x, a b a b, a b b a*:

*In þe **f**órmest yére, | that he **f**írst réigned.* Als. 40.

*Þénne gonne I **m**éeten | a **m**érvelous svévene.* P. P. Prol. 11.

*I had **m**índe on my **s**lépe | by **m**éting of **s**wéuen.* Als. 969.

*And **f**ónd as þe **m**éssageres | hade **m**únged be**f**óre.* W. 4847.

Irregularities, however, in the position of the alliteration are frequently met with, e. g. parallel alliteration : *a a, b b*:

*What þis **m**óuntein be**m**éneþ | and þis **d**érke **d**ále.*
                                                    P. P. i. 1;

or the chief alliterative sound (the 'head-stave') may be placed in the last accented syllable (*a a x a*) :

*'Now be **C**ríst,' quod the **k**íng, | '3if I míhte **ch**ácche.*
                                                    ib. ii. 167 ;

or it may be wanting entirely, especially in *William of Palerne* :

*Sche **k**ólled it ful **k**índly | and áskes is náme.* W. 69 ;

and there are even found a certain number of verses without any alliteration at all in *Joseph of Arimathie*:

Whan Jóseph hérde þer-of, | he bád hem not demáy3en. J. A. 31.

In such cases it may sometimes be noticed that a line which has no internal alliteration is linked by alliteration with a preceding or with a following line, in the same way as was to be observed already in the last century of the Old English period (cf. p. 50):

Bot on the Crístynmes dáye, | whene they were álle sémblyde,
That cómliche cónquerour | cómmaundez hym selvyne.

> Morte Arth. 70–1.

Again an excess of alliteration is found, which happens in different ways, either by admitting four alliterative sounds in one line (*a a a a*) as was sometimes done even in Old English:

In a sómer séson | when sófte was þe sónne. P. P. Prol. 1 ;

or by retaining the same alliterative sound in several consecutive lines, e. g. :

þenne was Cónscience iclépet | to cómen and apéeren
tofore the kýng and his cóunsel, | clérkes and óþure.
knéolynge Cónscience | to the kýng lóutede. ib. iii. 109–11 ;

or, finally, by allowing the somewhat more strongly accented syllables of the theses to participate in the alliteration :

and was a bíg bold bárn | and bréme of his áge. W. 18.

By the increasing use of this kind of alliteration it ultimately degenerated so much that the real nature of it was completely forgotten. This is evident from the general advice which King James VI gives in his *Revlis and Cavtelis to be observit and eschewit in Scottis Poesie* (Arber's Reprint, p. 63):

> Let all your verse be *Literall*, sa far as may be, quhatsumeuer kynde they be of, but speciallie *Tumbling* verse [evidently the alliterative line] for flyting. Be *Literall* I meane, that the maist pairt of your lyne sall rynne vpon a letter, as this tumbling lyne rynnis vpon F.
>> *Fetching fude for to feid it fast furth of the Farie.*[1]

He then gives a description of this kind of verse which makes it evident that he looked upon 'tumbling verse' as a rhythm of two beats in each hemistich or four beats in the full line, for he says :

> ȝe man observe that thir Tumbling verse flowis not on that fassoun as vtheris dois. For all vtheris keipis the reule quhilk I gave before, to wit

---

[1] This line is inaccurately quoted by King James from the poet Alexander Montgomerie, who lived at his court. It should read as follows :—
Syne fetcht food for to feid it, | foorth fra the Pharie. Flyting 476.

the first fute short the secound lang and sa furth. Quhair as thir hes twa short and ane lang throuch all the lyne quhen they keip ordour, albeit the maist pairt of thame be out of ordour and keipis na kynde nor reule of Flowing and for that cause are callit Tumbling verse.

King James VI was a contemporary of the last poets who wrote in alliterative lines in the North and therefore undoubtedly had heard such poems read by reciters who had kept up the true tradition of their scansion. We have here then the very best proof we can desire not only of the four-beat rhythm of the line, but also of the fact that unaccented words, although they may alliterate intentionally, as they do often in poems of the fifteenth century, or unintentionally, as earlier, do not get a full accent in consequence of the alliteration, as some scholars have thought, but remain unaccented.[1]

As to the quality of the alliteration the same laws on the whole still prevail as in Old English poetry, but are less strictly observed. Thus frequently voiced and unvoiced sounds alliterate together, and the aspiration is neglected; *f* alliterates with *v*, *v* with *w*, *w* with *wh*, *s* with *sh* or with combinations of *s* and other consonants, *g* with *k*, *h* with *ch*:

hértes and híndes | and óþer bestes mánye.   W. 389.

of fálsnesse and fásting | and vóuwes ibróken.   P. P. Prol. 68.

þat he wíst wíterly | it was the vóis of a childe.   W. 40.

to acórde wiþ þe kíng | and gráunte his wílle.   ib. 3657.

I sáyle now in þe sée | as schíp boute mást.   ib. 567.

such chástite withouten chárite | worþ cláymed in hélle!

P. P. i. 168.

On the other hand, sometimes (as e. g. in the *Alisaunder* fragments) greater strictness may be noticed in regard to alliteration of vowels, as only the same vowels[2] are allowed to alliterate:

wiþ þé érldam of Énuye | éuer forto láste.   P. P. ii. 63.

Later on, in the fifteenth century, vocalic alliteration in general falls into disuse more and more.

§ 55. **Comparison of Middle English and Old English alliterative verse.** With regard to the rhythmic structure of the verse the Middle English alliterative line is not very different

---

[1] Cf. the writer's paper 'Zur Zweihebungstheorie der alliterierenden Halbzeile' in *Englische Studien* v. 488–93.

[2] Cf. *Chapters on Alliterative Verse* by John Lawrence, D.Litt. London : H. Frowde. 1893. 8⁰ (chapter iii).

from the corresponding Old English metre. Two beats in each hemistich are, of course, the rule, and it has been shown by Dr. K. Luick, in a very valuable paper on the English alliterative line in the fourteenth, fifteenth, and sixteenth centuries,[1] that all the different types which Prof. Sievers has discovered for the two sections of the Old English alliterative line occur here again, but with certain modifications.

The modifications which the five chief types have undergone originated in the tendency to simplify their many varieties exactly in the same way as the Old English inflexional forms of the language were simplified and generalized in the Middle English period.

Only three of the five old types, viz. those with an even number of members (A, B, C), are preserved in the second section of the verse, and those not in their original forms. They show further a certain tendency to assimilate to each other.

In types B and C the variations with disyllabic anacrusis occurred most frequently, as was also the case in type A, and verses of this kind now become predominant. Furthermore, in the Old English alliterative line, endings consisting of an accented and an unaccented syllable (feminine endings) prevailed ; and type B was the only one of the symmetrical types ending with an accented syllable. In Middle English the use of feminine endings goes so far that the original type B has disappeared altogether and given place to a new type with an unaccented last syllable corresponding to the form $\times \times \overset{\angle}{} \times \overset{\angle}{} \times$.

Prof. Luick very properly calls this type B C, holding that it originated from the variations $\times \times \overset{\angle}{} \times \overset{\smile}{\cup} \times$ and $\times \times \overset{\smile}{\cup} \times \overset{\angle}{} \times$ of the old types B and C in consequence of the lengthening of the originally short accented syllable. Verse-ends with two unaccented syllables, which might have arisen in the same way from $\overset{\angle}{} \times = \overset{\smile}{\cup} \times \times$, did not become popular; and verse-ends with one unaccented syllable predominated. Lastly, an important feature of the later verse-technique deserves notice, that a monosyllabic anacrusis (an initial unaccented syllable) is generally allowed in types where it was not permitted in the Old English alliterative line. The consequence of these changes is that the rhythm of the verse which was in Old English a descending rhythm, becomes in Middle English ascending, and is brought into line with the rhythm of the contemporary even-beat metres.

[1] ' Die englische Stabreimzeile im 14., 15., 16. Jahrhundert ' (*Anglia*, xi. 392-443, 553-618).

This is the state of development presented by the Middle
English alliterative line in one of the earliest poems of this
group, viz. in the fragments of *King Alisaunder*, the versification
of which, as a rule, is very correct.

Here the three types only which we have mentioned occur in
the second hemistich.

Type A is most common, corresponding to the formula
(×) $\stackrel{\prime}{-}$ × × $\stackrel{\prime}{-}$ × :

> lórdes and óoþer 1, déedes of ármes 5, kíd in his tíme 11, térme
> of his lífe 16,

or with anacrusis:

> or stérne was hólden 10, and sóne beráfter 25.

More than two unaccented syllables may occur *after* the first
accented syllable.   These two peculiarities seldom occur together
in one and the same second hemistich (though frequently in the
first hemistich); but there are some examples:

> is túrned too him álse 165, and príkeden abóute 382, hee
> fáred òn in háste 79;

in this last example with a secondary accent on the word òn, as
also in the verse: þe méssengères þei cámme 1126.

Type C, (×) × × $\stackrel{\prime}{-}$ $\stackrel{\prime}{-}$ × :

> was þe mán hóten 13, þat his kíth ásketh 65, as a kíng
> shólde 17, withoute míscháunce 1179.

Type B C, (×) × × $\stackrel{\prime}{-}$ × $\stackrel{\prime}{-}$ × :

> or it týme wére 30, in his fáders life 46, of þis méry tále 45,
> þat þei no cómme þáre 507.

The same types occur in the first hemistich; but type C
disappears almost entirely, and in the other two the last
syllable not unfrequently is accented, especially if a considerable number of unaccented syllables occur in the middle of
the hemistich; such verses may be looked upon as remnants
of types B and E:

> þo was cróuned kíng 28, hee made a uéry uów 281, and
> wédded þat wíght 225, þe bérn couth þerbý 632, &c.

Type D also seems to occur sometimes:

> móuth méete pertò 184, what déath drý[e] thou shàlt 1067.

Besides these types the first hemistich has, as in Old English times, some forms of its own. The succession of syllables $\acute{-} \times \times \acute{-} \times$ (type A) is extended either by several unaccented syllables before the first accented one (polysyllabic anacrusis) or by the insertion of a secondary accent between the two main accented syllables, or after the second accented syllable, with a considerable number of medial unaccented syllables.

(*a*) *That ever* stéede *be*stróde 10,

    Hee brought his ménne to þe bórowe 259.

(*b*) *And* chéued fòrthe *with þe* chílde 78,

    Þe cómpanìe *was* cárefull 359.

(*c*) α. Glísiande *as* góldwìre 180,

    Þei craked *þe* cournales 295.

   β. *Hue* lóued *so* lécherìe 35,

    And Phílip *þe* férse kìng 276.

   γ. Stónes stírred *þei* þò 293,

    Þe fólke *too* fáre *with* hìm 158.

The examples under (*a*) show the tendency noticeable already in the first hemistich of the Old English alliterative line to admit anacrusis. The examples under (*b*) and (*c*) may be looked upon as extended forms of types E and D.

§ **56.** Several poems of somewhat later date deviate more frequently from these types than the *Alisaunder* fragments, chiefly in the following points :

The end of the hemistich sometimes consists of an accented syllable instead of an unaccented one; the thesis is sometimes monosyllabic instead of polysyllabic, especially in A, or the anacrusis may be polysyllabic instead of monosyllabic. Secondary accents are introduced more frequently into the second hemistich also, but by poets whose technique is careful they are admitted only between the two accented syllables. Owing to these licences, and to the introduction of polysyllabic theses, the rhythm of the verse sometimes becomes very heavy.

Belonging to this group are *William of Palerne, Joseph of Arimathie*, both belonging to the middle of the fourteenth century, the three editions of William Langland's *Vision concerning Piers Plowman*, of somewhat later date, and a few minor poems. The *Romance of the Chevelere Assigne*, written in the East Midland district, at the end of the fourteenth century, and the works of the Gawain-poet, viz. *Sir Gawain and the Green Knight, Cleanness, Patience,* and the *Legend of St. Erkenwald* (Horstmann, *Altengl. Legenden*, 1881, p. 265), form the transition to another group of poems belonging to the North of England, but differing somewhat from the preceding with regard to their metre.

The most important amongst these is Langland's great work, but it is at the same time most unequal in respect to its versification. In many passages, especially in the beginning of the several Passus, as they are called, the flow of the verses is very regular; in other passages the theses are frequently of such great length, and the arsis stands out so indistinctly, that the rhythm of the verse can only be made out with difficulty. Some examples taken from the B-text (c. 1377) may serve to illustrate this:

Extended second hemistich (Type A):

To bóres and to bróckes | þat bréketh adówn myne hégges.
vi. 31.

And so I trówe tréwly | by þat men télleth of chárite.
xv. 158.

Ac ʒut in mány mo máneres | mén offènden þe hóligòste.
xvii. 280.

Extended first hemistich (Type A):

Léue him nòuʒt, for he is lécherous | and líkerous of tónge.
vi. 268.

Láboreres þat haue no lánde | to lýue on but her hándes.
ib. 309.

' Now, by þe péril of my soúle!' quod Pieres, | 'I shal apéyre ʒou álle!'
vi. 173.

Such verses obviously contain only two beats in each hemistich, although at the same time some of the syllables forming the thesis may have a somewhat stronger accent than others. For as a rule such extended verses are succeeded by a normal line, clearly bringing out again the general four-beat rhythm, as is the case with the line (A + A) following immediately upon the last-mentioned example:

And hóuped after húnger | þat hérd hym atte fírste. vi. 174.

Type A is in *Piers Plowman* the usual one, but the types C and B C frequently occur. In the following examples we have type C in the second hemistich:

And hadden léue to lýe | al here lýf áfter. Prol. 49.
I seigh sómme that séiden | þei had ysóuȝt séyntes. ib. 50 ;

in the first hemistich it occurs rarely :

Ac on a Máy mórnynge | on Máluerne húlles. ib. 5.

Type B C is frequently to be met with in both hemistichs ;
e. g. in the first :

In a sómer séson, | whan sóft was the sónne. ib. 1.
And as I láy and léned | and lóked in þe wáteres. ib. 9 ;

in the second :

Bídders and béggeres | fast abóute ȝéde. ib. 40.
Wénten to Wálsyngham, | and here wénches áfter. ib. 54.

Masculine endings, however (originating from the dropping
of the final *-e* in the last words of the types A and C, as e. g. in
and drédful of síght Prol. 16, *crístened þe kýnge* xv. 437, *as þe
kýng híght* iii. 9), occur very rarely here. They are, on the
other hand, characteristic forms in another group of alliterative
poems.

§ 57. These belong to the **North of England** and the
adjacent parts of the Midlands.

In these districts the final *e* had by this time become silent,
or was in the course of becoming so. Thus many verses of
West-Midland poems were shortened in the North by omitting
the final *-e*, and then these forms were imitated there. Hence
the middle of the line was much less modified than the end
of it.

Types A, C, B C, therefore, occur not only in the ordinary
forms with unaccented syllables at the end, but also, although
more rarely, with accented ones, viz. corresponding to the
schemes :

$$A_1, (\times)\overset{\angle}{-} \times \times \overset{\angle}{-}, \quad C_1, (\times) \times \times \overset{\angle}{-} \overset{\angle}{-}, \quad BC_1, (\times) \times \times \overset{\angle}{-} \times \overset{\angle}{-}.$$

These forms of the hemistich first occur in the *Destruction
of Troy*, a poem written in a West-Midland dialect very like
to the Northern dialect, and in the North-English poems,
Morte Arthure and *The Wars of Alexander* (E. E. T. S.,
Extra-Ser. 47). Examples of these types (taken from the
first-mentioned poem) are : of type A_1 in the second hemistich,
for lérning of ús 32, *þat ónest were áy* 48 ; with a polysyllabic
thesis, *and lympit of the sóthe* 36 ; with a secondary accent,

with c**lé**ne m**è**n *of* w**í**t 790; without anacrusis,[1] l**é**mond *as* g**ó**ld
459, b**lé**ssid *were* Í 473; in the first hemistich, with disyllabic
anacrusis, þ*at ben* d**ré**p*it with* d**é**th 9, þ*at with the* G**ré**kys *was*
gr**é**t 40; without anacrusis, B**ý**g *y-noghe vnto* b**é**d 397, T**rý**ed
men þ*at were* t**á**ken 258, &c.; examples for C_1 (only occurring
in the second hemistich), þ*at he* f**ó**re *with* 44, *into your* l**o**nd
h**ó**me 611, *ye have* s**á**id *well* 1122, þ*at ho* b**ó**rne w**á**s 1388, *of
my* c**ó**rs h**á**s 1865; examples for B C_1, in the second hemistich
(of rare occurrence), *when it* de**st**r**ó**yet w**á**s 28, *and to* s**ó**row
br**ó**ght 1497, þ*ere* þe c**í**tie w**á**s 1534.

The same modification of types took place later in other parts
of the Midlands, as appears from two works of the early sixteenth
century, *Scottish Field* and *Death and Life* (Bishop Percy's
Folio MS., edited by Furnivall and Hales, i. 199 and iii. 49).
The last North-English or rather Scottish poem, on the other
hand, written in alliterative lines without rhyme, Dunbar's well-
known Satire, *The twa mariit wemen and the wedo*, has, apart
from the normal types occurring in the North-English poems,
many variants, chiefly in the first hemistich, which are characterized by lengthy unaccented parts both at the beginning
of the line, before the second arsis, and after it; frequently
too syllables forming the thesis have a secondary accent and
even take part in the alliteration, as e.g. in the following
examples:

ӡ*aip and* ӡ**í**ng, *in the* ӡ**ó**k | *ane* ӡ**é**ir *for to* dr**á**w. 79.

Is b**à**ir *of* b**lí**s *and* b**á**ilfull, | *and greit* b**á**rrat w**í**rkis. 51.

Sometimes the second hemistich participates in this cumulation
of alliterating words, which not unfrequently extends over several,
even as many as six or seven consecutive lines:

He gr**á**ythit *me in* g**á**y silk | *and* g**ú**dlie arr**á**yis,

In g**ó**wnis *of in*gr**á**nit *clayth* | *and greit* g**ó**ldin chén**ӡ**eis. 365–6.

This explains how King James VI came to formulate the
metrical rule mentioned above (p. 89) from the misuse of
alliteration by the last poets who used the alliterative line, or
the alliterative rhyming line to be discussed in the next paragraph, which shares the same peculiarity.

---

[1] Prof. Luick, in his longer treatise on the subject (*Anglia*, xi. 404), distinguishes between two forms of this type with anacrusis ($\times \perp \times \times \perp$) and
without ($\perp \times \times \perp$), which he calls A_1 and A_2, a distinction he has rightly
now abandoned (Paul's *Grundriss*, ed. 2, II. ii. p. 165).

B. The alliterative line combined with rhyme.

§ 58. In spite of the great popularity which the regular alliterative line enjoyed down to the beginning of the Modern English period, numerous and important rivals had arisen in the meantime, viz. the many even-beat rhymed kinds of verse formed on foreign models; and these soon began to influence the alliterative line. The first mark of this influence was that end-rhyme and strophic formation was forced upon many alliterative poems. In a further stage the alliterative line was compelled to accommodate its free rhythm of four accents bit by bit to that of the even-beat metres, especially to the closely-related four-foot iambic line, and thus to transform itself into a more or less regular iambic-anapaestic metre. The alliterative line, on the other hand, exercised a counter influence on the newer forms of verse, inasmuch as alliteration, which was formerly peculiar to native versification, took possession in course of time to a considerable extent of the even-beat metres, especially of the four-foot iambic verse. But by this reciprocal influence of the two forms of verse the blending of the four-beat alliterative line with that of four equal measures and the ultimate predominance of the even-beat metres was brought about more easily and naturally.

Alliterative-rhymed lines, the connexion of which into stanzas or staves will be treated of in the second part of this work under the heading of the ' Bob-wheel-stanza', were used during the Middle English period alike in lyric, epic, and dramatic poetry.

§ 59. Lyrical stanzas. The earliest stanzas written in alliterative rhyming lines were lyrical.

We must distinguish between isometric and anisometric stanza forms. In the former the whole stanza consists of four-beat alliterative lines, commonly rhyming according to a very simple scheme (either *a a a a* or *a b a b*). In the latter four-beat long lines as a rule are combined with isolated lines of one measure only and with several of two measures to form the stanza. The two-beat verses frequently have a somewhat lengthened structure (to be discussed further on sections on the epic stanzas), in consequence of which many of them having theses with secondary accents can be read either as even-beat verses of three measures or as three-beat verses on the model of those in *King Horn*. The four-beat alliterative lines, on the other hand, are mostly of more regular structure, the distances between the first and second arsis not being so unequal and the theses as a rule being disyllabic. The anacrusis too in these verses admits of a somewhat free treatment. The difference, however, between the first and second hemistich is less conspicuous than it was in those forms of the Middle English alliterative line before mentioned. Alliteration, on the other hand, is abundantly used.

The main rhythmic character of the verse is again indicated here by the frequent occurrence of the types A and A_1. The types B C, B C_1, C, C_1, however, likewise occur pretty often, and the two last types present serious obstacles to the assumption that the lines of these poems were ever recited with an even beat. But how exactly these poems were recited or to what sort of musical accompaniment can hardly be definitely decided in the absence of external evidence.

The first verses of a West-Midland poem of the end of the thirteenth century (Wright's *Political Songs*, p. 149) may serve as a specimen:

> Ich herde mén vpo móld | máke muche món,
> Hou hé beþ iténed | of here tílýnge:
> Góde ʒeres and córn | bóþe beþ agón,
> Ne képeþ here no sáwe | ne no sóng sýnge.

The second hemistichs in ll. 2 and 4 belong to type C. In other poems also, with lines of more regular rhythm (chiefly type A), this type may be met with now and then, e. g. in a poem published in Wright's *Specimens of Lyric Poetry*, p. 25, especially in the second hemistich, e. g. haueþ þis mái mére, line 9, and þe gýlófre, line 40, þat þe bór béde, line 44.

It is not difficult to distinguish such rhymed four-beat alliterative lines from those of four measures which have fairly regular alliteration, for the long line of the native metre always has a somewhat looser fabric, not the even-beat rhythmic cadence peculiar to the iambic verse of four measures, and, secondly, it always has a caesura after the first hemistich, whereas the even-beat verse of four measures may either lack distinct caesura or the caesura may occur in other places in the verse as well as after the second arsis. This will be evident by comparing the following four-beat verses of the last stanza of a poem in Wright's *Spec. of Lyr. Poetry*, p. 31:

> Ríchard, | róte of résoun rýght,
> rýkeníng of rým ant rón,
> Of máidnes méke þóu hast mýht,
> on mólde y hólde þe múrgest món;

with the following first four-beat alliterative lines of another
poem (ibid. p. 25):

> *Ichot a bûrde in a bóure, | ase béryl so brýght,*
> *Ase sáphir in sélver | sémly on sýht,*
> *Ase iáspe þe géntil, | þat lémeþ wiþ lýht,*
> *Ase gérnet in gólde, | and rúby wel rýht.*

In similar lines are written several other poems, as **M**on
in þe **m**one (ibid. p. 110); *Of ríbaudz y rýme* (Wright's *Pol.
Songs*, p. 237); and five songs by Laurence Minot (nos. ii, v,
ix, x, xi), written in the middle of the fourteenth century.

§ **60**. In other poems the four-beat long lines used in the
main part of the stanza are followed by shorter lines forming
the cauda, which in part are of a variable rhythmic cadence
either of three beats (or three measures) or of two beats, as e.g.
in the well-known poem in Percy's *Reliques*, ii, p. 1.[1] The
first stanza may be quoted here:

> *Sítteþ alle stílle | and hérkneþ to mé:*
> *Þe kýng of Alemáigne, | bi mi léauté,*
> *Prítti þousent póund | áskede hé*
> *Forte máke þe pées | in þé countré,*
> *Ant só he dùde móre.*
> *Ríchard,*
> *þah þou be éuer tríchard,*
> *Trícchen shàlt þou néuer mòre.*

In the following stanzas of this poem the four-beat rhythm,
although rarely marked by regular alliteration, is (in the main
part or 'frons') still more distinctly recognizable, in spite of
several rhythmically incorrect lines.

Second hemistichs of the type C_1 are not infrequent, e. g.
opon swývýng 9, *sire Édwárd* 46, *o þy lýárd* 47. Lines 5 and 7
are of a two-beat rhythm, l. 8 probably as well (cf. our scansion).

There is a decided similarity in regard to structure and versification between this stanza and that of a poem in Wright's
Pol. Songs, p. 153, although the long lines are divided in
the middle by interlaced rhyme. This may be illustrated by
its second stanza:

---

[1] Also printed in Ritson's *Ancient Songs*, i, p. 12; Wright's *Pol. Songs*,
p. 69; Mätzner's *Altenglische Sprachproben*, i, p. 152; Böddeker's *Altenglische Dichtungen, Pol. Lieder*, no. i.

Nou haþ **prúde** *þe* **prís** | *in éuervche* **pláwe**,
By mony **wýmmon** *onwís* | *y* **súgge** *mi* **sáwe**.
For ʒef a **lády** **lýue** *is* | **léid** *after* **láwe**,
Vch a **strúmpet** *þat þer is* | *such* **dráhtes** *wol* **dráwe**.
   In prúde
   Vch a **scréwe** *wol hire* **shrúde**,
   Þoh he **nábbe** *nout a* **smók** | *hire* **fóule** *ers to* **húde**.

There is no line here corresponding to l. 5 of the preceding
poem. Otherwise, however, the *cauda* of this poem is of a
similar structure to that of the preceding one, at least in this
and possibly in the following stanzas, whereas the last line of
the first stanza has a two-beat rhythm, and in the others the last
lines probably are to be scanned with three beats. The second
line of the *cauda* of the first stanza of this poem belongs to
type C. Another poem (Wright's *Polit. Songs*, p. 155; Böddeker, *P. L.* no. iv) shows a very artificial form of stanza, either
corresponding to the formula $a\, a_4\, b_2\, c\, c_4\, b_2\, d\, d_4\, b_2\, e\, e_4\, b_2\, ff\, g\, g\, g\, f_2$
(if we look upon the verses as four-beat and two-beat lines, which
the poet probably intended), or corresponding to the formula
$a\, a_4\, b_3\, c\, c_4\, b_3\, d\, d_4\, b_3\, e\, e_4\, b_3\, ff\, g\, g\, g\, f_2$ (if we look upon the *frons* as
consisting of ordinary tail-rhyme-stanza lines of four and three
even-beat measures).

The four- and two-beat cadence of the verses comes out
still more clearly in the stanzas of another poem (Wright's *Pol.
Songs*, p. 187; Ritson, *Anc. Songs*, i. 51; Böddeker, *P. L.* no. v),
the rhymes of which follow the scheme $a\, a\, a_4\, b_2\, c\, c\, c_4\, b_2$ (extended
tail-rhyme-stanzas). Some of its long lines, it is true, admit
of being read as even-beat verses of three measures, e. g. *and
béo huere chéuentéyn* 20, *and móni anóþer swéyn* 24; but the true
scansion in all probability is *and béo huere chéuentèyn* (or *chè-
uentéyn*): *ant móni anòþer swéyn*, in conformity with the
scansion of the following lines *to cóme to parís : þourh þe flóur
de lís* 52–6, or *wiþ éorl and wiþ knýht : with húem forte fýht*
124–8.

As a first step to the epic forms of stanza to be considered
in the next paragraph a poem of the early fourteenth century
(Wright's *Pol. Songs*, p. 212; Ritson, *Anc. Songs*, p. 28; Böddeker, *P. L.* no. vi) may be quoted:

Lýstneþ, **Lórdinges**, | *a newe* **sóng** *ichulle* **bigýnne**
Of þe **tráytours** *of* **Scótland**, | *þat* **táke** *beþ wyþ* **gýnne**.
Món *þat* **loveþ** **fálsnesse**, | *and nule* **néuer** **blýnne**,
Sóre *may him* **dréde** | *þe* **lýf** *þat he is* **ýnne**,

> *Ich vnderstónde:*
> *Selde wes he glád,*
> *Þat néuer nes asád*
> *Of nýþe ant of ónde.*

The fifth line has one arsis only (as appears more clearly from that in the second stanza: *wiþ Lóue*), thus corresponding to the above-mentioned poems (pp. 99, 100); the other lines of the *cauda* have two stresses.

Prof. Luick[1] looks upon the long lines of this poem and of several others (e. g. Wright's *Pol. Songs*, pp. 69 and 187) as doubled native verses of the progressive or Layamon form, but rhyming only as long lines. This can hardly be, as the rhythmic structure of these verses does not differ from that of the other poems quoted above, which belong, according to Prof. Luick himself, to the class of the normal, lyric rhyming-alliterative lines.

§ 61. **Narrative verse.** Alliterative-rhyming verses occur in their purest form in narrative poetry, especially in a number of poems composed during the fourteenth and fifteenth centuries in stanzas of thirteen lines, and republished recently in a collective edition by the Scottish Text Society in vol. 27 under the title *Scottish Alliterative Poems* (ed. by F. J. Amours, Edinburgh, 1892). The poems contained in this collection are *Golagras and Gawane* (also in *Anglia*, ii. 395), *The Book of the Howlat* by Holland, *Rauf Coilȝear* (also in E. E. T. S., Extr.-Ser. vol. xxxix), *The Awntyrs off Arthure at the Terne Wathelyne*, *The Pistill of Susan* (also in *Anglia*, i. 93). Douglas's *Prologue* to the Eighth Book of his translation of the *Aeneid* (although written in the beginning of the sixteenth century) likewise belongs to this group, as do also the poems of John Audelay, composed in Shropshire in the fifteenth century (Percy Soc. xiv, p. 10 ff.), and a poem *Of Sayne John the Euaungelist* (E. E. T. S. 26, p. 87) written in stanzas of fourteen lines in the North of England. The stanzas of all these poems—generally speaking —consist of two unequal parts, the *frons* written in alliterative lines, rhyming according to the formula *a b a b a b a b*, and the *cauda* which contains five or six lines, the first of which may either be a long line as in the *frons*, or, as in *The Pistill of Susan*, a short one-beat one, with four two-beat sectional verses following. Only in the last-mentioned poem does the *cauda* consist of six two-beat sectional verses.

[1] Paul's *Grundriss*, ed. 2, II. ii, p. 158.

The rhythm of this alliterative-rhyming metre may first be illustrated by the opening lines of *Golagras and Gawane*:

I.

In the týme of Árthur, | as tréw men me táld,
The king túrnit on ane týde | tówart Túskàne,
Hym to séik our the séy, | that sáiklese wes sáld,
The sýre that sèndis all séill, | súthly to sáne;
With bánrentes, bárounis, | and bérnis full báld,
Bìggast of báne and blúde | bréd in Brítàne.
Thei wálit out wérryouris | with wápinnis to wáld,
The gàyest grúmys on grúnd, | with géir that myght gáne;
Dúkis and dígne lòrdis, | dóuchty and déir,
Sémbillit to his súmmòvne,
Rénkis of grete rénòvne,
Cùmly kíngis with cróvne
Of góld that wes cléir.

II.

Thus the róyale can remóve, | with his Róund Tábill,
Of all ríches maist ríke, | in ríall arráy.
Wes neuer fúndun on fóld, | but fénʒeing or fábill,
Ane fàyrar flóure on ane féild | of frésche men, in fáy; &c.

Lines like the four last quoted illustrate the normal structure of the rhyming-alliterative verse, especially the relationship of rhyme and alliteration to each other in monosyllabic and disyllabic words. It will be seen that the rhyming syllable, as a rule the root-syllable, or at least the accented syllable of the word, at the same time carries the fourth accent of the line, and in consequence the fourth alliterative sound. In all other respects the rhymed-alliterative verse is structurally similar to that without rhyme, and it is therefore evident that rhyme exercises no decisive influence on the rhythm of the verse. In this comparatively pure form—if we do not take into account the secondary accents occurring in the first hemistichs of the stanza in the later poem— are written the great majority of the lines in the earliest of poems mentioned above, viz. *The Awntyrs off Arthure.*

§ **62.** The relation, however, between rhyme and alliteration and consequently the relation of the rhythmic accentuation of the words to their natural accentuation is less clear in the first stanza quoted above. The following verses rhyming together may serve to elucidate this:

Than schir **G**áwyne *the* **g**áy, | **g**úde *and* **g**ráciùs . . .
Jóly *and* **g**éntill, | *and full* **ch**éuailrús. Gol. 389, 391.
Ouer heor **h**édes *gon* **h**ýng
Þe **w**ínce *and þe* **w**éderlỳng. Susan, 101–2 ;

or the verses *Gol.* 648, 650, 654 :

Thus **é**ndit *the* **á**uynantis | *with* **m**ékil **h**ónòur ;
Thair **b**ódeis *wes* **b**éryit | **b**áith *in ane* **h**òur,
Ane **ú**thir *heght* **É**dmond, | *that* **p**róuit **p**áramòur.

In the first couplet the last syllable of the word *gráciùs*, although bearing only a secondary accent and forming the last thesis of the verse, rhymes with the last syllable of the word **ch**éuailrús, which likewise in ordinary speech has a secondary accent, but here is the bearer of the fourth metrical accent of the verse. In the second couplet the syllable *lyng* of the word *wéderlỳng*, which has a secondary accent and forms part of the thesis, rhymes with the word *hyng* which has the rhythmical accent. In the last group of verses the last syllable of the words *paramour, honour* having secondary accents rhymes with the word *hour*, the bearer of the last rhythmical accent. Similar rhymes occur even in Modern English poetry, e. g. in the works of Thomas Moore : *Váin were its mélodỳ, Róse, without thée* or *Whát would the Róse bè Únsung by thée ?* [1]

It also frequently happens that all the rhyming syllables, which have a secondary accent and occur in the thesis of a verse, belong to trisyllabic words, while the accented syllables in the arsis, whether alliterating or not, do not take part in the rhyme, e. g.:

Þou brak **g**ódes *Com*á*undement*,
To **sl**é *such an* **Í**nnocent
With **é**ny *fals* **j**úggement. Susan, 321–3.

Similar unaccented rhymes are also met with in disyllabic words :

' *In* **f**áith,' *said Schir* **R**ólland,
' *That is* **f**úll *euill* **w**ýn *land*
To **h**áue *quhill thow ar* **l**éuand.' Rauf Coilȝear, 917–19.

Other rhymes of the same kind are *sémbland : léuand, conséntand : endúrand*, Gol. 428 ff., &c.

In all such cases the natural accentuation of the words is not interfered with by the rhythm of the verse.

---

[1] Cf. *Metrik*, ii. 146 ; and Luick, *Anglia*, xii. 450, 451.

The kind of irregular rhyme most frequently occurring, however, is that which is formed by the unaccented syllable of a disyllabic word (the first syllable of which alliterates and bears
the last arsis of the verse) rhyming with a monosyllabic word
which likewise bears the fourth rhythmical accent of another
alliterative line (or the second of a short line forming part of
the cauda) and takes part in the alliteration as well, as e. g. in
the rhymes *Túskane : sane : Brítane : gane* and *súmmovne : ré-
novne : crovne* of the above-mentioned stanza of the poem
Golagras and Gawane.

It is not likely that a complete shifting of accent in favour of
the rhyming syllable ever took place, as the first syllables of the
words usually take part in the alliteration, and therefore have
a strongly marked accent.   Sometimes, it is true, in the poems
of this epoch, unaccented syllables do participate in the alliteration, and in the case of the words *Tuskane, Britane, summovne,
renovne* their Romance origin would explain the accent on the
last syllable; but these words, both as to their position and as
to their treatment in the line, are exactly on a par with the
Germanic rhyme-words in ll. 870–2:

*For he wes býrsit and béft, | and bráithly blédand ...
And wáld that he nane hárm hynt | with hárt and with hánd.*

In both cases we thus have ' accented-unaccented rhymes ' (cf.
Chapter I in Book II), which probably were uttered in oral
recitation with a certain level stress.   This is probable for several
reasons.   First it is to be borne in mind that Germanic words
in even-beat rhythms of earlier and contemporary poems were
used in the same way, e. g.:

*Quhen thái of Lórne has séne the kíng
Set ín hymsélff sa grét helpíng.*   Barbour, Bruce, iii. 147–8.

*And bád thame wénd intó Scotlánd
And sét a sége with stálward hánd.*   ib. iv. 79–80.

Only in these cases the rhythmical accent supersedes the word
accent which has to accommodate itself to the former, while
in the uneven-beat rhythm of the four-beat alliterative line the
word-accent still predominates.   In the even-beat lines, therefore,
the rhythmical accent rests on the last syllable of a disyllabic
rhyme-word, but in the alliterative lines it rests on the penultimate.
In the case of words of Romance origin, however, which
during this period of the language could be used either with
Germanic or with Romanic accentuation, the displacement of the

word-accent by the rhythmic accent in non-alliterative words
may in these cases have been somewhat more extensive; cf. e. g.
rhymes like *rage : curáge : suáge* Gol. 826–8; *day : gay : journáy*
ib. 787–9; *assáill : mettáill : battáil* R. Coilȝear, 826–8, &c.
(but *ȝone bérne in the báttale* Gol. 806).

As a rule, however, for these too the same level-stress accentuation must be assumed as for the rhyme-words of the first
stanza of *Golagras* quoted above (p. 102).

§ 63. This is all the more probable because, in these alliterative-rhyming poems, there are many sectional verses corresponding to the old types C and C_1, these answering best the
combined requirements of alliteration and of end-rhyme, for
which frequently one and the same Germanic or Romanic word
had to suffice in the second hemistich, as e. g. in the following
sectional verses rhyming together :— *What is þi góod réde : for his*
kníȝthéde : (*by* **crósse** *and by* **créde**) Awnt. of Arth. 93–7; (*and*
bláke *to þe* **bóne**): *as a* **wómáne** ib. 105–7; *enclósed with a*
crówne : *of the* **trésóne** ib. 287–91; *of ane fáir* **wéll** : **téirfull** *to*
téll : *with ane* **cástéll** : **kéne** *and* **crúéll**, or, as Prof. Luick scans,
kéne and cruéll (but l. 92 *crúel and* **kéne**) Gol. 40–6; *at the*
mýddáy : (**wént** *thai thar* **wáy**) Howl. 665–7. &c.

Also in the even-beat metres the influence of this type is still
perceptible; cf. rhymes like

> Súmwhat óf his clóþíng
> Fór þe lóue of héuene kýng.
>
> Rob. Mannyng, Handl. Sinne, 5703–4.

which are of frequent occurrence.

For the rest both in these alliterative-rhyming poems and in
the poems with alliteration only the types A and A_1, B C and
B C_1 are frequent. These alliterative-rhyming lines have
this feature in common with the pure alliterative lines, that
the first hemistich differs materially from the second in having
often an anacrusis of several syllables (initial theses) and
somewhat lengthened theses in the middle of the line, and in
permitting such theses with only a secondary accent to take
part in the alliteration. All this tends to give a somewhat
heavy rhythmic cadence to the whole line.

§ 64. The same difference is perceptible, as Prof. Luick was
the first to show (*Anglia*, xii, pp. 438 ff.), in the single two-beat
lines of the *cauda*, the three first (ll. 10–12 of the whole stanza)
having the looser structure of the extended first hemistichs of
the long lines, while the last two-beat line (line 13 of the whole

stanza) has the normal structure (commonly type A, A₁, as e. g. *Birnand* th*rétty and* th*ré* Gol. 247; *Of gôld that wes cléir* ib. 1) of second sections of the long line, as is evident. from the first stanza of *Golagras and Gawane* quoted above (p. 102). In this concluding line, however, other types of verse peculiar to the second hemistich of long lines may also be met with, as e. g. C, C₁, B C, B C₁, e. g.: *For thi mánhéde* Awnt. of Arth. 350; *Withoutin distánce* Gol. 1362; *As I am tréw knight* Gol. 169; *Couth na léid sáy* ib. 920; *In ony ríche réime* ib. 1258, *Quhen he wes líghtit dóun* ib. 130.

In other poems the group of short lines rhyming according to the scheme *a a a b* and forming part of the *cauda* is preceded neither by a long alliterative line nor by a one-beat half section of it (as in *Susan*), but by a complete two-beat sectional verse, which then, in the same way as the last verse rhyming with it, corresponds in its structure to that of the second hemistich of the long line; as e. g. in *The Tournament of Tottenham* (Ritson's *Ancient Songs*, i. 85–94), rhyming on the scheme *A A A A b c c c b* (the capitals signifying the long lines), and in *The Ballad of Kynd Kittok*, possibly by W. Dunbar (Laing, ii. 35, 36; Small, i. 52, 53; Schipper, 70).

In *Sayne John the Euaungelist* the 'cauda' has the structure of a complete tail-rhyme-stanza, the order of rhymes of the whole stanza being *A B A B A B A B c c d c c d*.

§ 65. In connexion with this it is particularly interesting to note that such two-beat sections of the alliterative line are also used by themselves for whole poems written in tail-rhyme-stanzas (as was first shown by Prof. Luick, *Anglia*, xii, pp. 440 ff.); cf. e. g. the translation of the *Disticha Catonis* (E. E. T. S. 68), the two first stanzas of which may be quoted here :

> *If þóu be made wíttenèsse,*
> *For to sáy þat sóþ ìs,*
>   *Sáue þine honóur,*
> *Als míkil, as þou may fra bláme,*
> *Lame þi fréndis sháme,*
>   *And sáue fra dishonóur.*

> *For-sóþ flípers,*
> *And alle fáls fláters*
>   *I réde, sone, þou flé ;*
> *For þen sálle na gode mán,*
> *Þat any góde lare cán,*
>   *Þár-fore blame þé.*

In the same stanza *The Feest* (Hazlitt, *Remains*, iii. 93) is written.

Still more frequently such lines were used for extended tail-rhyme-stanzas rhyming on the scheme *a a a b c c c b d d d b e e e b*, as e. g. in a poem, *The Enemies of Mankind*, of the beginning of the fourteenth century, published by Kölbing (*Engl. Studien*, ix. 440 ff.).

The first stanza runs as follows:

> Þe sìker sópe who so séys,
> Wiþ dìol dréye we our dáys
> And wàlk máni wil wáys
>   As wándrand wíȝtes.
> Al our gámes ous agás,
> So mani ténes on tás
> Þurch fónding of fele fás,
>   Þat fást wiþ ous fíȝtes.
> Our flèsche is fóuled wiþ þe fénd;
> Þer we fínde a fals frénde:
> Þei þai héuen vp her hénde,
>   Þai no hóld nouȝt her híȝtes.
> Þis er þré, þat er þrá,
> Ȝete þe férþ is our fá,
> Dèþ, þat dérieþ ous swá
>   And díolely ous díȝtes.

Here, again, the difference between the lines on the pattern of the first hemistich of the long line, which form the body of the stanza (*a a a, b b b, c c c, d d d*), and those on the pattern of the second hemistich used as tail-rhyme lines (*b, b, b, b*) is plainly recognizable.

The same is the case in other poems written in this form of stanza, as e. g. in the Metrical Romances, *Sir Perceval*, *Sir Degrevant* (Halliwell, *Thornton Romances*, Camden Society, 1844, pp. 1, 177) and others; cf. Luick, *Anglia*, xii, pp. 440 ff., and Paul's *Grundriss*, ii a, p. 1016. But in these later works, one of the latest of which probably is the poem *The Droichis Part of the Play*, possibly by Dunbar (Laing, ii. 37; Small, ii. 314; Schipper, 190), the two-beat lines are frequently intermingled and blended with even-beat lines, which from the beginning of the fifth stanza onward completely take the place of the two-beat lines in the last-mentioned poem. Likewise in the 'Bob-wheel-staves', i. e. stanzas of the structure of those sixteenth-century stanzas quoted above (§§ 60, 61), the *cauda*, as is expressly stated by King James VI in his *Revlis and Cavtelis*, is written in even-beat lines of four and three measures, though the main part of the stanza (the *frons*) is composed in four-beat rhyming-alliterative lines (cf. Luick, *Anglia*, xii, p. 444).

§ 66. In the contemporary **Dramatic Poetry** this mixture of four-beat (or two-beat) alliterative lines with lines of even measures is still more frequent, and may be used either strophically or otherwise.

In the first place, we must note that in the earlier collections of Mystery Plays (*Towneley Mysteries, York Plays*, and *Ludus Coventriae*) the rhyming alliterative long line, popular, as we have seen, in lyric and in narrative poetry, is also used in the same or cognate forms of stanzas.

But the form of verse in these Mysteries, owing to the loss of regular alliteration, cannot with propriety be described as the four-beat alliterative long line, but only as the four-beat long line. In many instances, however, the remnants of alliteration decidedly point to the four-beat character of this rhythm, as e. g. in the following stanza of the *Towneley Mysteries* (p. 140):

> Moste mýghty Máhòwne | méng you with mýrthe,
> Both of búrgh and of tówne | by féllys and by fýrthe ;
> Both kýng with crówne | and bárons of bírthe,
> That rádly wylle równe, | many gréatt gríthe
> > Shalle be hápp ;
> > Take ténderly inténi
> > What sóndes ar sént,
> > Els hármes shall ye hént
> > And lóthes you to láp.

In this form of stanza the different groups of lines or even single lines are frequently, as e. g. in the so-called *Processus Noe* (the *Play of the Flood*), very skilfully divided between several persons taking part in the dialogue. The interlaced rhyme in the long lines connects it with the stanza form of the lyric poem quoted above (p. 100), and the form of the 'cauda' relates it to that of the lyric poem quoted (p. 101), and in this respect is identical with that of *The Pistill of Susan*.

The rhythmic treatment of the verses is, both with regard to the relation between rhyme and the remnants of alliteration and to the use of the Middle English types of verse, on the whole the same as was described in §§ 62–4 treating of this form of verse in narrative poetry. The types A and A_1, B C and $B C_1$,

are chiefly met with ; now and then, however, type C₁ also occurs
in the second hemistich, as e. g. in the verses *that wold vówch
sáyf* 172, *of the tént máyne* 487, *wille com agáne sóne* 488, of the
Play of the Flood mentioned above.

But in the ' cauda' the difference explained in § 65 between
first and second short lines forming the close of a stanza is
often very regularly observed.

In other places of the *Towneley Mysteries* similar stanzas are
written in lines which have almost an alexandrine rhythm (cf.
Metrik, i. 229),while, on the other hand, in the *Coventry Mysteries*
we not unfrequently meet with stanzas of the same form written in
lines which, in consequence of their concise structure, approach
even-beat lines of four measures, or directly pass into this
metre. The intermixture of different kinds of line is even
carried here to such a length that to a *frons* of four-beat lines
is joined a *cauda* of even-beat lines of four or three measures
corresponding to King James VI's rule quoted above (p. 108) for
such stanzas ; and on the other hand to a *frons* of even-beat
lines of four measures is joined a *cauda* of two-beat short
lines.

§ 67. The distinctly four-beat line, however, still forms the
staple of the different kinds of verse occurring in these poems,
and was also used in them for simple forms of stanza. In the
further development of dramatic poetry it remained much in
use. Skelton's Moral Play *Magnificence*, and most of the
Moralities and Interludes contained in Dodsley's *Old Plays*
(ed. Hazlitt), vols. i–iv, are written chiefly in this popular metre.
As a rule it rhymes here in couplets, and under the influence of
the even-beat measures used in the same dramatic pieces it
gradually assumes a pretty regular iambic-anapaestic or trochaic-dactylic rhythm. This applies for the most part to the
humorous and popular parts; allegorical and historical per-
sonages are made to converse in even-beat verses.

Verses of an ascending (iambic-anapaestic) rhythm were
especially favoured, as might be expected from the fact that
the Middle English alliterative line in the preceding centuries
usually begins with one or two unaccented syllables before the
first accented one.

Of the different types used in the Middle English alliterative
line type C (C₁), which does not harmonize well with the even-
beat tendency of the rhythm, and which is only very seldom if
at all to be met with even in the *Coventry Plays*, becomes very
rare and tends to disappear altogether, type A (A₁) and (although

these are much less frequent) type $B C (B C_1)$ alone remaining in use.

§ 68. Of the more easily accessible pieces of Bishop John Bale (1495–1563) his *Comedye Concernynge Thre Lawes*, edited by A. Schröer (*Anglia*, v, pp. 137 ff., also separately, Halle, Niemeyer, 1882), is written in two-beat short lines and four-beat long lines, and his *King Johan* (c. 1548) (edited by Collier, Camden Society, 1838) entirely in this latter metre. The latter play has a peculiar interest of its own, containing as it does lines which, as in two Old English poems (cf. pp. 123, 124), consist either half or entirely of Latin words. Now, as the accentuation of the Latin lines or half-lines admits of no uncertainty, the four-beat scansion of the English verses of this play and of the long lines in *The Three Lawes* is put beyond doubt, though Schröer considers the latter as eight-beat long lines on the basis of the four-beat theory of the short line.

Some specimens may serve to illustrate the nature of these 'macaronic' verses, e. g. :

> *A péna et cúlpa* | *I desíre to be clére.* p. 33.
>
> *In nómine pátris,* | *of all that éver I hárd.* p. 28.
>
> *Iudicáte pupíllo,* | *deféndite víduam.* p. 6.

Other verses of the same kind occur, pp. 5, 6, 53, 62, 78, 92.

But apart from this irrefutable proof of the four-beat scansion of the long line, the rhythmic congruity of it with the rhyming alliterative lines discussed in § 67 can easily be demonstrated by the reoccurrence of the same types, although a difference between the first and the second hemistich no longer seems to exist.

Type A, of course, is the most frequent, and occurs in many sub-types, which are distinguished chiefly by monosyllabic, disyllabic, or polysyllabic anacruses, disyllabic or polysyllabic theses between the first and second arsis, and monosyllabic, disyllabic, or trisyllabic theses after the latter. The most usual form of this type corresponds to the scheme $(\times) \times \acute{} \times \times \acute{} \times$, while the form $\acute{} \times \times \acute{} \times$ is rarer. Type A_1 likewise admits of polysyllabic anacruses and theses, corresponding mostly to the formula $(\times) \times \acute{} \times \times \acute{}$, less frequently to $\acute{} \times \times \acute{}$. Type $B C$ $(\times) \times \times \acute{} \times \acute{} \times$ is rare, type $B C_1 (\times) \times \times \acute{} \times \acute{}$, on the other hand, very common; type $C (\times) \times \times \acute{} \acute{} \times$ still occurs now and then, but type $C_1 (\times) \times \times \acute{} \acute{}$ has become exceedingly scarce.

§ 69. Statistical investigations as to the frequency of occurrence, and especially on the grouping of these different types are still wanting, and would contribute greatly toward the more exact knowledge of the development of the iambic-anapaestic and the trochaic-dactylic metre out of the four-beat verse. Of course in such an investigation the use of anacrusis in the types A and A_1 should not be neglected. According to the presence or absence of anacrusis in the two hemistichs four different kinds of line may be distinguished:

1. Lines with anacrusis in both hemistichs. These are the most numerous of all, and are chiefly represented by the combinations of types $A (A_1) + A (A_1)$, $A (A_1) + B C_1 (B C)$:

A + A : *For by méasure, i wárne you, | we thýnke to be gýdyd.* Skelt. Magn. 186.

A + A_1 : *For mýschefe wyl máyster vs, | yf méasure vs forsáke.* ib. 156.

$A_1 + B C$: *Full gréat I do abhór | this your wícked sáying.*
Lusty Juventus, Dodsl. ii. 72.

$A_1 + B C_1$: *You may sáy you were síck, | and your héad did áche,*
That you lústed not this níght | any súpper máke.
Jack Juggler, ib. ii. 119.

$A_1 +$ A_1 : *And you nóthing regárd | what of mé may betíde?*
Jacob and Esau, ib. ii. 216.

$A_1 + B C_1$: *Our láwes are all óne, | though you do thré apére.*
Bale, Laws, line 63.

A + A_1 : *Whome dáyly the déuyll | to great sýnne doth allúre.* ib. 747.

$A_1 + B C_1$: *By hým haue I góte | thys fowle dyséase of bódye,*

$A_1 +$ A : *And, ás ye se hére, | am now thrówne in a léprye.*
ib. 749-50.

$A_1 + B C$: *Regárde not the pópe, | not yet hys whórysh kýngedom.* ib. 770.

$A_1 +$ A_1 : *Such lúbbers, as háth | dysgysed héads in their hóodes.* Bale, Johan, p. 2.

A + A : *Peccávi mea cúlpa : | I submýt me to yowr hólynes.*
ib. p. 62.

A + A : *With áll the ófsprynge, | of Ántichristes generácyon.*
ib. p. 102.

A + B C₁ :   *Maister Ráufe Royster Dóyster | is but déad and*
            gón.   Roister Doister, i. i. 43.

C +   A :   *And as thré téachers, | to hým we yow dyréct.*
            Bale, Laws, l. 67.

C + B C₁ :   *Of their fírst frédome, | to their most hýgh decáye.*
            ib. 82.

A₁ +   C₁ :   *Such an óther is nót | in the whóle sóuth.*
            ib. 1066.

2. Lines with anacrusis in the first section and without it in
the second. These are almost exclusively represented by the
combination A (A₁) + A (A₁); rarely by B C₁ (B C) + A (A₁) :

A   + A₁ :   *For wélthe without méasure | sódenly wyll slýde.*
            Skelton, Magn. 194.

A   + A₁ :   *Howe sódenly wórldly | wélth dothe dekáy,*

A   + A₁ :   *How wýsdom thórowe wántonnesse | ványisshyth*
            awáy.   ib. 2579–80.

A   + A₁ :   *Behóld, I práy you, | sée where they áre.*
            Four Elements, Dodsl. i. 10.

B C + A₁ :   *I am your éldest són, | Ésau by my náme.*
            Jacob and Esau, ib. ii. 249.

3. Lines without anacrusis in the first section and with
anacrusis in the second ; likewise chiefly represented by the
types A (A₁) + A (A₁), rarely by A (A₁) + B C (B C₁) :

A +   A₁ :   *Méasure contínwyth | prospérite and wélthe.*
            Skelton, Magn. 142.

A₁ +   A :   *Méasure and Í | will néuer be devýdyd.*   ib. 188.

A +   A₁ :   *Síghing and sóbbing | they wéep and they wáil.*
            Gammer Gurton's Needle, Prol.

A +   A :   *Ésau is gíven | to lóose and lewd líving.*
            Jacob and Esau, Dodsl. ii. 196.

A₁ +   A₁ :   *Líving in this wórld | from the wést to the éast.*
            Roister Doister, iii. iii. 28.

A +   A₁ :   *Chárge and enfórce hym | in the wáyes of vs to go.*
            Bale, Laws, line 102.

A +   A :   *Quáerite judícium, | subveníte opprésso.*
            Bale, Johan, p. 6.

A +B C : **F**ór *by conféssion | the holy* **f**áther knóweth.

ib. p. 11.

A +B C₁ : **D**ó *they so in* **d**éde *? | Well, they shall not* **d**ó *so lónge.* ib. p. 97.

4. Lines without anacrusis in either section, so that they are wholly dactylic in rhythm, only represented by A (A₁) + A₁ (A):

A + A : *Sáncte Francísse | óra pro nóbis !* Bale, Johan, p. 25.

A + A : *Péace, for with my spéctables | vádam et vidébo.*

ib. p. 30.

A + A : *Sýr, without ány | lónger délyaunce.*

Skelton, Magn. 239.

A + A₁ : *Wín her or lóse her, |* **t**rý *you the* **t**ráp.

Appius and Virginia, Dodsl. iv. 132.

A + A₁ : *Líkewise for a cómmonwealth | óccupied is hé.*

Four Elements, ib. i. 9.

A + A₁ : *Whát, you sáucy | málapert knáve.*

Jack Juggler, ib. ii. 145.

The numerical preponderance of types A + A₁ is at once perceptible, and usually these two types of hemistichs are combined in this order to form a long line.

The result is that in the course of time whole passages made up of lines of the same rhythmical structure (A + A₁) are common in the dramatic poetry of this period, as e. g. in the Prologue to *Gammer Gurton's Needle* :

> *As Gámmer Gúrton, with mánye a wýde stítch,*
> *Sat pésynge and pátching of Hódg her mans bríche,*
> *By chánce or misfórtune, as shée her gear tóst,*
> *In Hódge lether brýches her néedle shee lóst.*

Possibly this preference of the type A₁ in the second half line may go back to the influence of the difference between the rhythmical structure of the first and the second hemistich of the alliterative line in early Middle English poetry.

§ 70. This view derives additional probability from the manner in which lines rhythmically identical with the alliterative hemistich are combined into certain forms of stanza which are used in the above-mentioned dramatic poems, especially in Bale's *Three Lawes.*

For in this play those halves of tail-rhyme stanzas, which

I

form the 'wheels' of the alliterative-rhyming stanzas previously
described (§§ 61 and 66) as used in narrative poetry and in
the mysteries, are completed so as to form entire tail-rhyme
stanzas (of six or eight lines) similar to those mentioned in
§ 65. This will be evident from the following examples:

With holye óyle and wátter,
I can so clóyne and clátter,
That I cán at the látter
   Manye súttelties contrýve.
I can worke wýles in báttle,
If I do ónes but spáttle,
I can make córn and cáttle,
   That théy shall never thrýve.   ll. 439–446.

I have chármes for the plówgh,
And álso for the cówgh,
She shall geue mýlke ynówgh,
   So lóng as I am pléased.
Apace the mýlle shall gó,
So shall the crédle dó,
And the músterde querne alsó
   No mán therwith dyséased.   ll. 463–470.

The difference in rhythm which we have previously pointed
out between the lines of the body of the stanza (corresponding
to first halves of the alliterative line) and those of the tail
(corresponding to second halves) may again be observed in
most of the stanzas of this play, although not in all of them.

In other passages the sequence of rhymes is less regular;
e. g. in ll. 190–209, which rhyme according to the formulas
a a a b c c b, d d b e e b, e e e f g g f.

§ 71. Lastly, we must mention another kind of verse or stave
originating in the resolution of the four-beat alliterative line into
two sections, and their combination so as to form irregular tail-
rhyme stanzas, viz. the so-called Skeltonic verse. This kind of
verse, however, was not invented (as is erroneously stated in several
Histories of English Literature) by Skelton, but existed before
him, as is evident from the preceding remarks. The name
came to be given to the metre from the fact that Skelton, poet
laureate of King Henry VII, was fond of this metre, and used it
for several popular poems.

In Skelton's metre the strict form of the alliterative four-beat
line has arrived at the same stage of development which the
freer form had reached about three hundred years earlier in

Layamon's *Brut*, and afterwards in *King Horn*. That is to say, in Skelton's metre the long line is broken up by sectional rhyme into two short ones. The first specimens of this verse which occur in the *Towneley Mysteries*, in the *Chester Plays*, and in some of the Moralities, e. g. in *The World and the Child* (Dodsl. i), resemble Layamon's verse in so far as long lines (without sectional rhymes) and short rhyming half-lines occur in one and the same passage. On the other hand, they differ from it and approach nearer to the strophic form of the alliterative line (as occurring in the Miracle Plays) in that the short lines do not rhyme in couplets, but in a different and varied order of rhyme, mostly *a b a b* ; cf. the following passage (l. c., p. 247):

Ha, há, now Lúst and Líking is my náme.
Í am frésh as flówers in Máy,
Í am sémly-shápen ín sáme,
And próudly appáreled in gárments gáy :
My lóoks been full lóvely to a lády's éye,
And in lóve-lónging my héart is sore sét.
Might I fínd a fóode that were fáir and frée
To lie in héll till dómsday for lóve I would not lét,
My lóve for to wín,
All gáme and glée,
All mírth and mélody,
All rével and ríot,
And of bóast will I never blín, &c.

In Skelton's *Magnificence* the short lines rhyme in couplets like those of *King Horn*, in a passage taken from p. 257 (part of which may be quoted here):

Nowe lét me se abóut,
In áll this rówte,
Yf I cán fynde óut
So sémely a snówte
Amónge this prése :
Éven a hole mése—
Péase, man, péase !
I réde, we séase.
So farly fáyre as it lókys,
And her bécke so comely crókys,
Her naylys shárpe as tenter hókys !
I haue not képt her yet thre wókys
And howe stýll she dothe sýt ! &c., &c.

In other poems Skelton uses short lines of two beats, but rhyming in a varied order under the influence, it would seem, of the strophic system of the virelay, which rhymes in the order *a a a b   b b b c   c c c d*. But the succession of rhymes is more irregular in the Skeltonic metre, as e. g. in the passage :

> What cán it auáyle
> To drýue fórth a snáyle,
> Or to máke a sáyle
> Of an hérynges táyle ;
> To rýme or to ráyle,
> To wrýte or to endýte,
> Eyther for delýte,
> Or élles for despýte ;
> Or bókes to compýle
> Of dívers maner stýle, &c. Colin Cloute (i. 311).

In other cases short bob-lines of one beat only interchange with two-beat rhythms, as e. g. in Skelton's poem *Caudatos Anglos* (i. 193) :

> Gup, Scót,
> Ye blót :
> Laudáte
> Caudáte,
> Sét in bétter
> Thy péntaméter.
> This Dúndás,
> This Scóttishe ás,
> He rýmes and ráyles
> That Énglishman have táyles.
> Skeltónus laureátus,
> Ánglicus nátus,
> Próvocat Músas
> Cóntra Dúndas
> Spurcíssimum Scótum
> Úndique nótum, &c.

The mingling of Latin and English lines, as in this passage, is one of the characteristic features of the Skeltonic verse.

In some passages, as e. g. in the humorous poems *Phyllyp Sparowe* and *Elinour Rummyng*, the three-beat rhythm seems to prevail. In such cases it probably developed out of the two-beat rhythm in the same way as in *King Horn*.

> *Yet óne thynge ìs behýnde*
> *That nów còmmeth to mýnde ;*
> *An épytàphe I wold háue*
> *For Phýllỳppes gráue ;*
> *But fór I àm a máyde,*
> *Týmorous, hàlf afráyde,*
> *That néuer yèt asáyde*
> *Of Elycònys wéll,*
> *Whère the Múses dwéll ;* &c.

Phyllyp Sparowe (i. 69).

Skelton's verse was chiefly used by poets of the sixteenth and seventeenth centuries for satirical and burlesque poetry. One of its chief cultivators was John Taylor, the Water-poet. A list of Skeltonic poems is given in Dyce's edition of Skelton's poems, i. introduction, pp. cxxviii–cxxix.

C. Revival of the old four-beat alliterative verse in the Modern English period.

§ 72. If after what precedes any doubt were possible as to the scansion of the verses quoted on p. 113 from the Prologue to the Early Modern English comedy of *Gammer Gurton's Needle*, this doubt would be removed at once by the following couplet and by the accents put over the second line of it by the sixteenth-century metrician, George Gascoigne [1] :

> *No **w**ight in this **w**orld | that **w**ealth can attayne,*
> *Unlésse hè bèléve | thàt áll ìs bùt váyne.*

For the rhythm of these lines is perfectly identical with that of the lines of the above-mentioned prologue, and also with that of the alliterative line quoted ten years later (A. D. 1585), and called tumbling-verse by King James VI in his *Revlis and Cavtelis*, viz. :

> *Fetching fúde for to féid it | fast fúrth of the Fárie.*

This is the very same rhythm in which a good many songs and ballads of the fifteenth and sixteenth centuries are written, as e. g. the well-known ballad of *King John and the Abbot of Canterbury*, which begins with the following stanzas [2] :

---

[1] See G. Gascoigne, *Certayne Notes of Instruction concerning the making of verse or ryme in English*, 1575, in Arber's *Reprints*, together with *The Steele Glas*, &c., London, 1868, 8vo, p. 34.

[2] Bürger's version *Der Kaiser und der Abt* introduces a regular alterna-

An áncient stóry | I'le téll you anón
Of a nótable prínce, | that was cálled king Jóhn;
And he rúled Éngland | with máine and with míght,
For he díd great wróng, | and maintéin'd little ríght.

And I'le téll you a stóry, | a stóry so mérrye,
Concérning the Ábbot | of Cánterbúrye;
How for his hóuse-kéeping, | and hígh renówne,
They rode póst for hím | to faire Lóndon tówne.

This four-beat rhythm, which (as is proved by the definition King James VI givès of it) is the direct descendant of the old alliterative line, has continued in use in modern English poetry to the present day.

It occurs in the poem *The recured Lover*, by Sir Thomas Wyatt, one of the earliest Modern English poets, where it is intermixed sometimes with four-feet rhythms, as was the case also in several Early English poems. The general rhythm, however, is clearly of an iambic-anapaestic nature. Fifteen years after the death of Wyatt Thomas Tusser wrote part of his didactic poem *A hundred good points of Husbandry* in the same metre. In Tusser's hands the metre is very regular, the first foot generally being an iambus and the following feet anapaests :

Whom fáncy persuádeth | amóng. other cróps,
To háve for his spénding, | suffícient of hóps,
Must wíllingly fóllow, | of chóices to chóose.
Such léssons appróved, | as skílful do úse.

The four beats of the rhythm and the regular occurrence of the caesura are as marked characteristics of these verses as of the earlier specimens of the metre.

Spenser has written several eclogues of his *Shepheard's Calendar* in this metre (February, May, September), and Shakespeare uses it in some lyric pieces of his *King Henry IV*, Part II, but also for dialogues, as e.g. *Err.* III. i. 11–84. In more modern times Matthew Prior (1664–1715) wrote a ballad *Down Hall* to the tune, as he says, of *King John and the Abbot of Canterbury*, which clearly shows that he meant to imitate the ancient popular four-beat rhythm, which he did with perfect success. In other poems he used it for stanzas rhyming in the order *a b a b*.

tion of masculine and feminine couplets not observed in the original metre which he is copying.

Swift has used the same metre, and it became very popular in Scottish poetry through Allan Ramsay and Robert Burns, one of whose most famous poems is written in it, viz. :

> My héart's in the Híghlands, | my héart is not hére.;
> My héart's in the Híghlands, | a-chásing the déer ;
> Chásing the wíld deer | and fóllowing the róe,
> My héart's in the Híghlands | wheréver I gó.

Sir Walter Scott used it frequently for drinking-songs, and Thomas Moore wrote his *Letters of the Fudge Family* in it.

By Coleridge and Byron this metre was used in the same way as by Wyatt, viz. intermixed with regular four-foot verse according to the subject, the four-beat iambic-anapaestic rhythm for livelier passages, the pure iambic for passages of narration and reflection. Byron's *Prisoner of Chillon* and his *Siege of Corinth* are good specimens of this kind of metre.[1] On the other hand the regular four-foot rhythm, as will be shown below, if it is of a looser structure, develops into a kind of verse similar to the iambic-anapaestic rhythm—an additional reason for their existing side by side often in one poem.

A few variations of this metre remain to be mentioned, which occur as early as Tusser. The first variety arises from inter-laced rhyme, by which the two four-beat verses are broken up into four two-beat verses rhyming in the order *a b a b.*

> If húsbandry brággeth
> To gó with the bést,
> Good húsbandry bággeth
> Up góld in his chést.

On the model of these stanzas others were afterwards formed by Tusser consisting of three-beat verses of the same rhythm. The same verse was used for eight-line stanzas rhyming *a b a b c d c d* by Nicholas Rowe, Shenstone, Cowper, and in later times by Thackeray in one of his burlesque poems (*Malony's Lament* in *Ballads, the Rose and the Ring*, &c., p. 225). For examples of these variations see the sections treating of the iambic-anapaestic verses of three and two measures.

§ 73. In modern times a few attempts have been made to revive the old four-beat alliterative line without rhyme, but also without a regular use of alliteration. These attempts, however, have never become popular.

---

[1] Cf. the chapter on the four-foot iambic verse.

The following passage from William Morris's dramatic poem
Love is enough may give an idea of the structure of this kind of
verse:

> *Fáir Master Óliver, | thóu who at áll times*
> *Mayst ópen thy héart | to our lórd and máster,*
> *Téll us what tídings | thou hást to delíver;*
> *For our héarts are grown héavy, | and whére shall we*
>   *túrn to,*
> *If thús the king's glóry, | our gáin and salvátion,*
> *Must gó down the wínd | amid glóom and despáiring.*

The rhythm, together with the irregular use of alliteration,
places these four-beat alliterative lines on the same level with
those of the dramatic poems of the fifteenth and sixteenth
centuries.

The same kind of versification is found in Longfellow's translation of the late Old English poem on *The Grave*, and in
James M. Garnett's translations of *Beowulf* and Cynewulf's
Elene. On the other hand, George Stephens, in his translation
of the Old English poem on *The Phoenix*, published 1844,
not only adheres strictly to the laws of alliteration, but confines
himself to Germanic words, sometimes even using inflexional
forms peculiar to Middle English.

§ **74.** We shall conclude this survey of the development of
the four-beat alliterative line by giving a series of examples in
reversed chronological order, beginning with writers of the
present day and ending with the earliest remains of Old English
poetry, in order to illustrate the identity in rhythmic structure
of this metre in all periods of its history.

Nineteenth Century, End:

> *For níne days the kíng | hath slépt not an hóur*
> *And táketh no héed | of soft wórds or beseéching.*
>   W. Morris.

Nineteenth Century, Beginning:

> *So that wíldest of wáves, | in their ángriest móod,*
> *Scarce bréak on the boúnds | of the lánd for a róod.*
>   Byron, Siege of Corinth, 382–4.

Eighteenth Century, End:

> *My héart's in the Híghlands, | my héart is not hére;*
> *My héart's in the Híghlands, | a-chásing the déer.*   Burns.

Eighteenth Century, Middle :

> *A cóbbler there wás, | and he líved in a stáll.*[1]

Eighteenth Century, Beginning (1715):

> *I síng not old Jáson | who trável'd thro' Gréece*
> *To kíss the fair máids | and posséss the rich fléece.*
> Prior, Down-Hall, to the tune of King John and the Abbot.

Seventeenth Century, Beginning (or Sixteenth Century, End) :

> *An áncient stóry | I'le téll you anón*
> *Of a nótable prínce, | that was cálled king Jóhn.*
> King John and the Abbot of Canterbury.

Sixteenth Century, End (1585):

> *Fetching fúde for to féid it | fast fúrth of the Fárie.*[2]
> Montgomery.

Sixteenth Century (1575):

> *No wíght in this wórld | that wéalth can attáyne*
> *Unlésse hè beléve | thàt áll ìs bùt váyne.*[3] G. Gascoigne.

Sixteenth Century (before 1575) :

> *As Gámmer Gúrton, | with mánye a wyde stýche,*
> *Sat pésynge and pátching | of Hódg her mans brýche.*
> Gammer Gurton's Needle.

Sixteenth Century, Middle (about 1548) :

> *Such lúbbers as háth | dysgysed héads in their hóods.*
> Bale (*died* 1563), King Johan, p. 2.

> *Thýnke you a Róman | with the Rómans cannot lýe?*
> ibid. p. 84.

> *For as Chríste ded say to Péter, | Cáro et sánguis*
> *Non revelávit tíbi | sed Páter meus celéstis.* ibid. pp. 92–3.

---

[1] Recognized by Bishop Percy (1765) as rhythmically equivalent to

> *In a sómer séason, | when sóft was the sónne*
> *I shópe me into shróudes, | as I a shépe wére* (Piers Plowman).

and

> *Hám and héahsetl | héofena ríces* (Gen. 33).
> *Scéop þā and scýrede | scýppend úre* (ibid. 65).

[2] This alliterative-rhyming long line is scanned by the contemporary metrist King James VI in the manner indicated by the accents.

[3] The second of these lines is thus marked by Gascoigne as having four stresses.

A péna et cúlpa | I desýre to be clére,
And thén all the dévylles | of héll I wold not fére.
ibid. p. 33.

Judicáte pupíllo, | deféndite víduam:
Defénde the wýdowe, | whan she ís in dystrésse. ibid. p. 6.

Sáncte Domínice, | óra pro nóbis.
Sáncte pyld mónache, | I be-shrów vóbis.
Sáncte Francísse, | óra pro nóbis. ibid. p. 25.

Sixteenth Century, Beginning:

Apón the mídsummer évin, | mírriest of níchtis.
Dunbar, Twa Mariit Wemen, 1.

Fifteenth Century, Second Half:

In the chéiftyme of Chárlis, | that chósin chíftane.
Rauf Coilȝear, 1.

Fifteenth Century, ? First Half:

In the týme of Árthour, | as tréw men me táld.
Golagras and Gawane, 1.

Fourteenth Century, End:

Moste mýghty Máhowne | méng you with mýrthe,
Both of búrgh and of tówne, | by féllys and by fýrthe.
Towneley Mysteries, p. 140.

Oute, alás, I am góne! | oute apón the, mans wónder!
ibid. p. 30.

Fourteenth Century, Second Half:

In a sómer séson, | whan sóft was the sónne.
Piers Plowman, Prol. 1.

Þen com a vóis to Jóseph | and séide him þise wórdes.
Joseph of Arimathie, 21 (about 1350).

Fourteenth Century, Beginning:

Ich herde mén vpo móld | máke much món.
Wright's Pol. Songs.

Lýstneþ Lórdynges, | a newe sóng ichulle bigýnne.
ibid. p. 187.

Thirteenth Century, Middle:

Álle bèon he blíþe | þat tò my sóng líþe:
A sóng ihc schàl you sínge | of Múrry þe kínge.
King Horn, 1–4.

Thirteenth Century, Beginning :

And swá heo gùnnen wénden | fórð tò þan kínge.
Layamon, 13811–12.

Vmbe fíftene ʒér | þat fólc is isómned.   ibid. 13855–6.

Twelfth Century :

þat þe chíriche hàbbe grýþ | and þe chéorl bèo in frýþ
his sédes to sówen, | his médes to mówen.
Proverbs of Alfred, 91–4.

búte if he béo | in bóke iléred.   ibid. 65–6.

Eleventh Century, End :

þat he nám be wíhte | and mid mýcelan únrìhte.
Chron. an. 1087.

Eleventh Century, First Half :

súme hi man bénde, | súme hi man blénde.
Chron. an. 1037.

ne wearð drèorlìcre dǽd | gedón on þisan éarde.   ibid.

Eleventh Century, Beginning :

se of ǽðelre wǽs | vírginis pártū
clǽne acénned, | Chrístus in órbem.
Oratio Poetica, ed. Lumby.

hwǽt ! ic ǽna sǽt | ínnan béarwe,
mid hélme beþéaht, | hólte tō-míddes,
þǽr þā wǽterbúrnan | swégdon and úrnon,
on míddan gehǽge, | éal swā ic sécge.
Be Dōmes Dæge.

þæt Sámson se stránge | swā ofsléan míhte
ǽn þúsend mánna | mid þæs ássan cínbǽne.
Ælfric, Judges, 282–3.

Tenth Century, End :

ǽfre embe stúnde | he séalde sume wúnde,
þā hwíle þe hē wǽpna | wéaldan móste. Byrhtnoth, 271–2.

Ninth Century :

wýrmum bewúnden, | wítum gebúnden,
héarde gehǽfted | in hélle brýne.   Judith, 115–16.

Eighth Century:

> hắm and hếahsètle | héofena ríces. Genesis, 33.

> wúldre biwúnden | in þære wlítigan býrig.
> háfað ūs ālýfed | lúcis áuctor
> þæt wē mótun hếr | méruếrī [1]
> góddǽdum begíetan | gáudia in cǽlō. Phoenix, 666–9.

> onfêngon fúlwihte | and fréoðowǽre
> wúldres wédde | wítum āspédde. Andreas, 1632–3.

> þǽr wæs bórda gebréc | and béorna geþréc
> héard hándgeswìng | and hérga gríng,
> sýððan hēo éarhfære | ǽrest métton. Elene, 114–16.

> búgon þā tō bénce | blǽd-ágènde
> fýlle gefǽgon. | fǽgene geþǽgon
> médofull mánig | mágas þára. Beowulf, 1013–15.

Seventh Century:

> nu scýlun hérgan | héfænrícæs uárd,
> métudæs mǽcti | end his módgidanc. Cædmon's Hymn.

§ 75. The evidence contained in this chapter, with regard to the continuous survival, in its essential rhythmical features, of the Old English native verse down to modern times, may be briefly summed up as follows:—

1. In the oldest remains of English poetry (*Beowulf, Elene, Andreas, Judith, Phoenix,* &c.) we already find lines with combined alliteration and rhyme intermixed with, and rhythmically equivalent to, the purely alliterative lines, exactly as we do in late Old English and early Middle English poems such as *Byrhtnoth, Be Dōmes Dæge, Oratio Poetica, Chronicle* an. 1036, *Proverbs of Alfred,* and Layamon's *Brut.*

2. In some of these poems, viz. the *Phoenix* and the *Oratio Poetica,* Latin two-beat hemistichs are combined with English hemistichs of similar rhythm to form regular long lines, just as is done in Bale's play of *Kinge Johan* (sixteenth century).

3. The lines of this play agree in the general principle, and frequently in the details of their rhythmical structure, with alliterative-rhyming long lines which occur in lyric and epic poems of the same period, and which two contemporary metrists, Gascoigne and King James VI, recognized (independently of each other) as lines of four accents.

---

[1] We retain the MS. reading; see Sievers, *Altgerm. Metrik,* p. 17.

4. The rhythm of these sixteenth-century lines is indistinguish-able from that of a four-accent metre which is popular in English and German poetry down to the present day.

These facts appear to leave no room for doubt that the Germanic metre has had a continuous history in English poetry from the earliest times down to the present, and that the long line, in Old and Middle English as in Modern English, had four accents (two in each hemistich). The proof acquires additional force from the fact, established by recent investigations, that the most important of the metrical types of the Old English hemistich are found again in Middle and Modern English poetry.

PART II. FOREIGN METRES

DIVISION I. The Foreign Metres in General

CHAPTER V. INTRODUCTION

§ 76. It was not till about 150 years after the Norman Conquest that foreign metres were introduced in English literature under the influence of French and Low Latin versification. For these, too, the general law observed in all accentual poetry holds good, viz. that the word-accent and the syntactical accent must coincide with the rhythmical accent. This rule, however, was easier to observe in the old native four-beat alliterative metre, in which the proportion and order of accented and unaccented syllables admit of many variations, than in metres consisting of equal measures, which follow stricter rules in that respect. In the older native verse accordingly we seldom find deviations from this fundamental rule, whereas in the newer foreign metres they are more frequent and striking.

The ordinary native alliterative metre was founded, as we have seen, on the principle that four accented syllables had to occur in each long line, together with an undefined number of unaccented ones, the position and order of those different syllables admitting many variations. The new metres constructed on foreign models during the Middle English period differ from the earlier rhythmic forms by the regularity of the alternation of unaccented and accented syllables and by the uniformity of their feet or measures; they are accordingly styled even-measured or even-beat verses.

Four different kinds are to be distinguished, viz. ascending and descending disyllabic measures, and ascending and descending trisyllabic measures, commonly called *iambic*, *trochaic*, *anapaestic*, and *dactylic* measures. In Middle English poetry, however, only iambic rhythms were used. The three other kinds of rhythms did not come in till the beginning of the Modern English period.

With regard to the development of various even-measured rhythms from these four different kinds of feet, it will suffice to consider the iambic and trochaic metres only, as these are the most important, and the formation of the anapaestic and the dactylic metres is to be explained in the same way.

§ 77. According to the number of feet we may classify **the different kinds of line**—retaining the classical nomenclature —as dimeters, trimeters, tetrameters, &c.; (one meter always consisting of *two* iambic or trochaic, or anapaestic feet), so that, for instance, an iambic tetrameter contains eight iambic feet. Lines or rhythmical sections consisting of complete feet, i. e. of an equal number of accented and unaccented syllables, are called *acatalectic* or *complete* lines (dimeters, trimeters, &c.). If, however, the last foot of a line or of a rhythmical section be characterized by the omission of the last syllable, i. e. by a pause, the line is called *catalectic* or *incomplete*. The following examples will serve to illustrate the meaning of these terms:

Acatalectic iambic tetrameter:

Y spéke óf Ihésu, Márie sóne, | of álle Kínges hé is flóur,
Þat súffred déþ for ál man-kín, | he ís our álder créatóur.
Seynt Katerine, i. ll. 89–92.[1]

Come lísten tó my móurnful tále, | ye ténder héarts and lóvers
  déar ;
Nor wíll you scórn to héave a sígh, | nor wíll you blúsh to
  shéd a téar.   Shenstone, Jenny Dawson.

Catalectic iambic tetrameter:

Ne sólde nó man dón a fírst | ne sléuhþen wél to dónne ;
For mány man behóteð wél, | þet hít forȝét wel sóne.
Moral Ode, ll. 36–7.

They cáught their spéares, their hórses rán, | as thóugh there
  hád been thúnder,
And strúck them éach amídst their shíelds, | wherewíth they
  bróke in súnder.   Sir Lancelot du Lake, ll. 65–8.[2]*

Acatalectic trochaic tetrameter (not represented in Middle English):

Wérther hád a lóve for Chárlotte, | súch as wórds could néver
  útter ;
Wóuld you knów how fírst he mét her ? | shé was cútting
  bréad and bútter.

Thackeray, Sorrows of Werther, ll. 1, 2.

---

[1] Horstmann, *Altenglische Legenden, Neue Folge*, p. 244.
[2] Percy's *Reliques*, I. ii. 7.

Catalectic trochaic tetrameter:

Áh ! what pléasant vísions háunt me, | ás I gáze upón the séa :
Áll the óld romántic légends, | áll my dréams come báck to mé !
             Longfellow, Secret of the Sea, ll. 1, 2.

A line in which the whole last foot is supplied by a pause is called *brachycatalectic.*

Brachycatalectic iambic tetrameter:

The Brítons thús depárted hénce, | seven Kíngdoms hére begóne,
Where díverselý in dívers bróils | the Sáxons lóst and wón.
             Warner, Albion's England.[1]

Brachycatalectic trochaic tetrameter:

Hásten, Lórd, to réscue mé | and sét me sáue from tróuble;
Sháme thou thóse who séek my sóul, | rewárd their míschief
*   dóuble.*   Translation of Psalm lxix.

If both rhythmical sections of a tetrameter are brachycatalectic we get one of the four varieties of the Middle English Alexandrine—the only one that has continued in use in Modern English poetry.

Alexandrine:

Mid ývernésse and prúde | and ýssing wés that ón ;
He núste nouht þát he wés | bóþe gód and món.
             The Passion of our Lord, ll. 35, 36.

Of Álbion's glórious ísle | the wónders whílst I wríte,
The súndry várying sóils, | the pléasures ínfiníte.
             Drayton, Polyolbion, ll. 1, 2.

These are the principal forms of rhythmical sections made up of disyllabic feet that occur in Middle English and Modern English Poetry.

§ 78. **The breaking up of these long lines** (consisting of two rhythmical sections) into shorter lines is usually effected by rhyme. Thus, if both rhythmical sections of the acatalectic tetrameter are divided by what is called leonine rhyme we get the short four-foot couplet imitated from the French *vers octosyllabe,* as in the following verses taken from the Middle English *A lutel soth sermon* (ll. 17–20):

---

[1] Quoted in *Chambers's Cyclop. of Eng. Lit*, i. 242.

> *He máde him ínto hélle fálle,*
> *And éfter hím his chíldren álle;*
> *Þér he wás forló ure dríhte*
> *Híne bóhte míd his míhte.*

A Modern English example is—

> *Amóngst the mýrtles ás I wálk'd,*
> *Lóve and my síghs thus íntertálk'd:*
> *' Téll me,' said I in déep distréss,*
> *' Where I may fínd my shépherdéss.'*

Carew, Poets, iii, p. 703.

Another stanza of four lines is formed when the first rhythmical sections of two tetrameters rhyming together are also connected in the corresponding place (viz. before the caesura) by another species of rhyme, called *interlaced* or *crossed* rhyme (*rime entrelacée*) :

> *I spéke of Ihésu of hévene withín ;*
> *Off álle kýngys hé is flóur ;*
> *Þat súffryd déþ for álle mankýn,*
> *He ís our alle créatóur.*

Saynt Katerine, ii, ll. 89–92.

Cf. these verses with an earlier version of the same legend (quoted p. 127), where only the second sections are connected by rhyme.

A Modern English example is—

> *When yóuth had léd me hálf the ráce*
> *That Cúpid's scóurge had máde me rún ;*
> *I lóoked báck to méte the pláce*
> *From whénce my wéary cóurse begún.*

Surrey, Restless Lover, p. 4, ll. 1–4.

Corresponding short trochaic lines result from the acatalectic trochaic tetrameter broken by leonine or inserted rhyme. In Middle English poetry, however, they occur but very seldom in their pure form, i. e. with disyllabic rhymes; in most cases they have monosyllabic or alternate monosyllabic and disyllabic rhymes.

In like manner the catalectic iambic tetrameter is broken up by inserted rhyme into two short verses, viz. one of four feet with a monosyllabic ending, and one of three feet with a disyllabic ending, as in the following examples :

Bytwéne mérsh and áverýl,
  When spráy bigínneþ to springe,
þe lútel fóul haþ híre wýl
  On hýre lúd to sínge.
                    Wright's Spec. of Lyric Poetry, p. 27.

A chíeftain tó the híghlands bóund
  Cries: 'Bóatman, dó not tárry,
And I'll give thée a sílver póund
  To rów us ó'er the férry.'
                    Campbell, Lord Ullin's Daughter, ll. 1–4.

A tetrameter brachycatalectic in both sections may also be broken up either by leonine or by inserted rhyme. The following examples illustrate respectively these two methods:

Wiþ lónging ý am lád,
On mólde y wáxe mád,
Y gréde, y gróne, vnglád
For sélden ý am sád.
                    Wright's Spec. of Lyric Poetry, p. 29.

Lo, Ióseph, ít is Í,
  An ángelle sénd to thé;
We, léyf, I práy the, whý?
  What ís thy wýlle with mé?
                    Towneley Mysteries, p. 135.

In the same manner the verse of four feet mentioned above is broken up into two lines of two feet, and the two-feet line into two lines of one foot, as in the following examples:

Moost góod, most fáir,
Or thíngs as ráre,
To cáll you's lóst;
For áll the cóst . . . &c.
                    Drayton, An Amouret Anacreontic (Poets, iii. 582).

What shóuld I sáy
  Since fáith is déad,
And trúth awáy
  From mé is fléd? Wyatt, p. 130.

For might is riht,
Liht is niht,
And fiht is fliht.
Wright's Political Songs,
p. 254.

I ám the knight,
I cóme by night.
The Nutbrowne Mayd,
line 33.

§ 79. In the fourteenth century the **heroic verse** was added to these Middle English metres; a rhyming iambic line of five feet, formed after the model of the French line of ten syllables, e. g. :

A knight ther wás, | and thát a wórthy mán.
Chaucer, Prol. 43.

Finally, the verse used in the **tail-rhyme staves** (*rime couée*) must be mentioned. As this verse, however, usually appears only in that form in which it is broken up into three short ones which compose one half of the stave, its origin will be more properly discussed in the second Book, treating of the origin and form of the different stanzas. To begin with, however, it was simply a long line of three rhythmical sections. Indications of this are here and there found in the way in which it is arranged in MSS. and early printed books, e. g. in the first version of the *Legend of Alexius*,[1] where it is written in triple columns on the large folio pages of the Vernon MS. in the Bodleian Library :

Sitteþ stílle withóuten stríf, | And Í will télle yóu the líf |
Óf an hóly mán.
Álex wás his ríght náme, | To sérve gód thought hím no
sháme, | Therof néver hé ne blán.

§ 80. These are the simplest forms of verse used in Middle English poetry; they can be varied, however, in many ways. First, they are not restricted to monosyllabic or masculine endings or rhymes, but like their French models, admit also of disyllabic or feminine rhymes. Further, the caesura, where it occurs at all, may be masculine as well as feminine. The septenary line, however, in its strict form admits only of monosyllabic caesura and disyllabic ending.

Caesura and rhyme are in this respect closely analogous. For the difference between the two kinds of caesura and between the two kinds of rhyme is, that in the case of a masculine caesura or rhyme the pause occurs immediately after the last accented

[1] Ed. by J. Schipper, *Quellen und Forschungen*, xx.

K 2

syllable of the rhythmical section, whereas in the case of a feminine caesura or rhyme an unaccented syllable (sometimes even two or more unaccented syllables[1]) follows upon the last accented one before the pause takes place. Combinations of masculine caesura with masculine or with feminine line-endings or rhymes, or the reverse, are, of course, allowed and of frequent occurrence.

We quote in the first place some Middle English and Modern English examples of masculine caesura in the Septenary, in the Alexandrine, in lines of five and of four measures and—for the sake of comparison—in the four-beat verse:

> *They cáught their spéares, their hórses rán, | as thóugh there*
> *hád been thúnder.*   Percy's Rel. (cf. p. 127).
>
> *The lífe so shórt, so fráil, | that mórtal mén live hére.*
> Wyatt, p. 155.
>
> *A kníght there wás, | and thát a wórthy mán.*
> Chaucer, Prol. l. 43.
>
> *For wánt of wíll | in wóe I pláin.*   Wyatt, p. 44.
>
> *For wómen are shréws, | both shórt and táll.*
> Shakesp. 2 Hen. IV, v. iii. 36.

Of the feminine caesura there are two different kinds, viz. the so-called *Epic* and *Lyric* caesura.[2] In the Epic caesura in Iambic metre the pause occurs, as in the feminine rhyme, after a supernumerary syllable which follows upon the last accented one of the section the next iambic foot following upon it in the usual manner. In the Lyric caesura in Iambic metre, on the other hand, the pause occurs within a foot, i. e. after the regular unaccented syllable of an iambic foot.

These three different kinds of caesura may be more simply defined as follows: In the ordinary iambic line the caesura occurring after a regular unaccented syllable is a feminine Lyric one (thus: ... ◡ ∠́ ◡ | ∠́ ◡ ∠́ ...); the caesura occurring after an accented syllable is a masculine one (thus: ... ◡ ∠́ | ◡ ∠́ ◡ ∠́ ...); and that which occurs after a supernumerary unaccented syllable immediately following upon an accented one is a feminine Epic caesura (thus: ... ◡ ∠́ ◡ | ◡ ∠́ ◡ ∠́ ...).

---

[1] In the 'tumbling'—or, to use the German name, the 'gliding' (*gleitend*) caesura or rhyme.

[2] For the introduction and explanation of these technical terms cf. Fr. Diez, 'Über den epischen Vers,' in his *Altromanische Sprachdenkmale*, Bonn, 1846, 8vo, p. 53, and the author's *Englische Metrik*, i, pp. 438, 441; ii, pp. 24-6.

These different kinds of caesura strictly correspond to their French models. The Epic caesura, which to some extent disturbs the regular rhythmic flow of a verse, is by far the least frequent in metres of equal feet.

In the alliterative line, on the other hand, as this metre does not consist of equal feet, the feminine caesura, which is, from a rhythmical point of view, identical with the Epic, is commonly used both in the Old English and in the Middle English period, being produced by the natural quality of the types A, C, D, and by the resolution of the last accented syllable in the types B and D (of the Old English verse). For this reason it also occurs more frequently than the other kinds of caesura in the Modern English four-beat line.

This may be illustrated by the following examples:

Epic caesura:

To Cáunterbúry | with fúl devóut couráge.
Chaucer, Prol. line 22.

He knóweth how gréat Atrídës | that máde Troy frét.
Wyatt, p. 152.

And yét there ís anóther | betwéen those héavens twó.
Wyatt, p. 161.

Withóuten grúndwall | to bé lastánd: stand.
Cursor Mundi, line 125.

Lyric caesura:

Þer hé was fóurty dáwes | ál withúte méte.   Passion, line 29.

Se séttled hé his kíngdom | ánd confírmd his ríght.
Spenser, Faerie Queene, II. x. 60.

And wél we wéren ésed | átte béste.   Chaucer, Prol. 29.

Þat álre wúrste | þát hi wúste.   Owl and Night., line 10.

And Í should háve it | ás me líst.   Wyatt, p. 30.

All three kinds of caesura will have to be treated systematically later on in connexion with the iambic rhyming verse of five measures, the character of which they affect very much.

§ 81. The variety caused by the different kinds of caesura in the structure of the metres of equal measures, formed on the principle of a regular alternation of unaccented and accented syllables, is much increased by other causes arising from the different nature of Romanic and Germanic versification. These variations came into existence, partly because the poets, in the early days of the employment of equal-measured rhythms, found it difficult, owing to want of practice, to secure the exact co-incidence of the word-accent and the metrical accent, partly because for linguistic or (in the case of the later poets) for artistic reasons they considered it unnecessary to do so. They therefore either simply suffered the discord between the two kinds of accentuation to remain, or, in order to avoid it, permitted themselves licences that did violence either to the rhythmic laws of the verse itself, or to the customary pronunciation of the words as regards the value of syllables (i. e. their being elided or fully sounded) or word-accent.

The changes which the equal-measured rhythms have under-gone and still undergo from the causes mentioned thus have rela-tion partly to the rhythmic structure of the verse itself, partly to the value of syllables, and partly to the word-accent. From these three points of view we shall first consider the iambic equal-measured rhythm in general (this being the only species used in Middle English, and the one which in Modern English is of most frequent occurrence and influences all the rest), before we proceed to examine its individual varieties.

CHAPTER VI

VERSE-RHYTHM

§ **82.** As in Greek and Latin metre, so also in the equal-measured rhythms of Middle and Modern English, it is a general law that the beginning or end of a metrical foot should, so far as possible, not coincide with the beginning or end of a word, but should occur in the middle, so that the individual feet may be more closely connected with each other. When this law is not observed, there arises what is technically called *diaeresis*, that is to say, the breaking up of the line into separate portions, which as a rule renders the verse inharmonious. On this account lines composed entirely of monosyllables are to be avoided. This law is more frequently neglected in Modern English poetry than in that of earlier times, because the rarity of inflexional endings makes its constant observance difficult.

Even in Middle English poems, however, we often find lines, especially if they are short, which are composed of monosyllabic words only.

These observations may be illustrated by the following examples :

(*a*) Lines with diaeresis :

Ne ís no quéne so stárk ne stóur.
> Wright's Spec. of Lyr. Poetry, p. 87, l. 4.

And hé was cláud in cóote and hóod of gréne.
> Chaucer, Prol. line 103.

Had cást him óut from Héaven with áll his hóst.
> Milton, Parad. L. i. 37.

Had shóok his thróne.   What thóugh the field be lóst ?
> ib. 105.

(*b*) Lines without diaeresis :

Nou shrínkeþ róse and lýlie flour.
> Wright's Spec. of Lyr. Poetry, p. 87, line 1.

And smále fówles máken mélodíe.   Chaucer, Prol. line 9.
And réassémbling óur afflícted pówers.

Milton, Parad. L. i. 186.

§ 83. With regard to modulation, too, the lines with diaeresis
differ from those without it.   In lines with diaeresis all syllables
or words with a rhythmic accent upon them are pronounced
with nearly the same stress, while in lines without diaeresis the
difference between the accented syllables is more noticeable.
The two following examples taken from Milton's *Paradise Lost*
will serve to illustrate this, the difference of stress being indicated
by different numbers under the accented syllables :

Had cást him óut from Héaven with áll his hóst
   o   1   o 2   o   2   o   2   o   2

And réassémbling óur afflícted pówers.
   o   1o 2 o   1   o 3 o 2

As a general rule, the syllables which stand in an arsis are,
just because they bear the metrical stress, of course more strongly
accented than those which stand in a thesis.

Occasionally, however, a thesis-syllable may be more strongly
accented than an arsis-syllable in the same line which only
carries the rhythmical accent, but neither the word-accent nor
the logical accent of the sentence.

Thus in the following line from *Paradise Lost—*

Irreconcileable to our grand Foe,

the word *grand*, although it stands in a thesis, is certainly,
because of the rhetorical stress which it has, more strongly
accented than the preceding word *our* or the syllable *-ble*, both
of which have the rhythmical accent.   Milton's blank verse
abounds in such resolved discords, as they might be called.   In
not a few cases, however, they remain unresolved.   This occurs
chiefly in lines where the short unaccented syllables or unimportant monosyllabic words must be lengthened beyond their
natural quantity in order to fit in with the rhythm of the verse,
as in the following lines :

Of Thámuz yéarly wóunded : thé love-tále.   Par. L. i. 452.
Únivérsal repróach far wórse to béar.   Par. L. vi. 34.

On the other hand long syllables standing in a thesis may be
shortened without harshness, e. g. the words *brought* and *our* in
the following line :

Brought déath intó the wórld and áll our wóe.

§ **84.** With regard to the treatment of the rhythm the Middle
English even-beat metres in some respects are considerably
different from the Modern English metres, the reason being
that the earlier poets, as yet inexperienced in the art of
composing in even-beat measures, found it more difficult than
Modern English poets to make the rhythmic accent coincide with
the word-accent and the syntactic-accent (cf. pp. 126–7, 134).

Certain deviations from the ordinary iambic rhythm which
partly disturb the agreement of the number of accented and
unaccented syllables in a line are more frequent in Middle
English than in Modern English poetry. One of these licences
is the **suppression of the anacrusis** or the absence of the
first unaccented syllable of the line, or of the second rhythmical
section, e. g.

Pán sche séyd : ʒe trówe on hím | þát is lórd of swíche
pousté.
> Horstmann's Altengl. Legend. N. F., p. 250, ll. 333–4.

Gíf we léorniÐ gódes láre,
Þénne ofþúncheþ hít him sáre.   Pater Noster, 15–16.

Únnet líf ic hábbe iléd, | and ʒíet, me þíncÐ, ic léde.
> Moral Ode, l. 5.

Twénty bóokes, | clád in blák and réde.   Chaucer, Prol. 294.[1]

Sóme, that wátched | with the múrd'rer's knífe.   Surrey, p. 59.

Góod my Lórd, | give mé thy fávour stíll.
> Shakesp. Temp. iv. i. 204.

Nórfolk sprúng thee, | Lámbeth hólds thee déad.   Surrey, p. 62.

Vor mánies mánnes sóre iswínch | hábbeÐ ófte unhólde.
> Moral Ode, Ms. D. l. 34.

Enhástyng hím, | tíl he wás at lárge.
> Lydgate, Story of Thebes, 1075.

The tíme doth páss, | yét shall nót my lóve!   Wyatt, p. 130.

While this metrical licence may mostly be attributed to want
of technical skill in Middle English poets, it is frequently employed in the Modern English period, as the last example

---

[1] The occurrence of this licence in Chaucer's heroic verse has been
disputed by ten Brink (*Chaucer's Sprache und Verskunst*, p. 176) and
others, but see *Metrik*, i. 462–3, and Freudenberger, *Ueber das Fehlen des
Auftaktes in Chaucer's heroischem Verse*, Erlangen, 1889.

shows, with distinct artistic intention of giving a special emphasis to a particular word. Several Middle English poets, however, make but scant use of this licence, e. g. the author of *The Owl and the Nightingale* and Gower, while some of them, as Orm, never use it at all.

§ **85.** These latter poets, on the other hand, make very frequent use of another kind of rhythmical licence, viz. **level stress** or *hovering accent*, as Dr. Gummere calls it; i. e. they subordinate the word-accent or the syntactic accent to the rhythmic accent, and so far violate the principal law of all accentual metre, which demands *that those three accents should fall on one and the same syllable.*

This licence is found chiefly in metres of a certain length, e. g. in the Septenary or in the iambic five-foot line, but not so frequently in shorter metres, as the resulting interruption of the flow of the rhythm is not so perceptible in long as in short lines.

The least sensible irregularity of this kind occurs when the (syntactically) less emphatic of two consecutive monosyllabic words is placed in the arsis, as in the following lines:

For whý this ís more thén that cáuse is.

> Chaucer, H. of Fame, 20.

There ís a róck in thé salt flóod. Wyatt, p. 144.

Now seemeth féarful nó more thé dark cáve. ib. p. 210.

If the accented syllable of a word consisting of two or more syllables is placed in the thesis, and the unaccented one in the arsis, the licence is greater. This is a licence often met with in Middle English poetry, as e. g.:

I wílle not léyf you álle helpléss | as mén withóuten fréynd.

> Towneley Myst. p. 182.

Of clóth-makýng | she hádde súch an háunt.

> Chaucer, Prol. 447.

With blóod likewíse | ye múst seek yóur retúrn.

> Surrey, p. 117.

The effect is still more harsh, if inflexional endings are used in this way, though this does not often occur. The following are examples:

Þa béodes hé beodéþ therínne.   Pater Noster, 23.

Annd á33 aftérr þe Góddspell stánnt.   Orm. 33.

All þúss iss þátt hallghé goddspéll.   ib. 73.

In most cases dissonant rhythmical accentuations of this sort are caused by the rhyme, especially in Middle English poetry, e.g.:

> *Sównynge alwáy th' encrés of his wynnýnge.*
> *He wólde the sée were képt for ény thínge.*
>
> > Chaucer, Prol. 275.

Cf. also : *thing : writýng* ib. 325–6 ; *bremstóon : non* ib. 629–30 ; a*le-stáke : cake* ib. 667–8 ; *goddésse : gesse* Chaucer, Knightes Tale, 243–4 ; *herde : answérde* ib. 265–6 ; *assemblýnge : thynge* Barclay, Ship of Fools, p. 20 ; similar examples are even to be met with in early Modern English poetry, e. g.: *nothíng : bring* Sur. 15 ; *bem*oaní*ng : king* Wyatt, 206 ; *welfáre : snare* ib. 92 ; *goodnéss : accéss* ib. 209 ; *manére : chere* Surrey, 124, &c.

Sometimes it may be doubtful how a line should be scanned. In some cases of this kind the usage of the poet will decide the question; we know, for instance, that Orm never allows the omission of the first unaccented syllable. Where decisive evidence of this kind is wanting, the verse must be scanned in such a manner as to cause the least rhythmical difficulty. If a compound, or a word containing a syllable with secondary accent, does not fit in with the rhythmical accent, it is to be read, as a rule, with level stress when it occurs in the middle of a line (and, of course, always when it is the rhyme-word). On the other hand, if according to the rhythmical scheme of the line an unaccented syllable would be the bearer of the rhythmical stress, we must in most cases assume suppression of the anacrusis.

It would not be admissible therefore to scan:

> *Love, thát livéth | and réigneth ín my thóught,*
>
> > Surrey, p. 12.

but : *Lóve that líveth | and réigneth ín my thóught.*

The licence of displacement of accent is an offence against the fundamental law of accentual verse, and therefore becomes more and more rare as the technique of verse becomes more perfect.

§ **86.** Another metrical licence, which is not inadmissible, is **the absence of a thesis in the interior of a line.** This licence is not of the same origin in Middle English as in Modern English poetry.

In Middle English it generally appears to be a relic of the ancient alliterative verse (Types C and D) and to be analogous to the similar usage of the contemporary Middle English alliterative line, as e. g.:

Ne léve nó mán to múchel | to chílde ne to wíue.

Moral Ode, line 24.

Þet ís al sóth fúl iwís. Pater Noster, 2.

hálde wé gódes láʒe. ib. 21.

Óf the próphéte | that hátte Séynt Iohán. Passion, 26.

Not unfrequently, also, this licence is caused by the rhyme, as in the following examples:

Myd Hárald Árfáger, | kýng of Nórthwéy : eye.

Rob. of Glouc. 22.

As wás king Róbert of Scótlánd : hand. Barbour, Bruce, 27.

And gúd Schyr Iámes of Dóuglás : was. ib. 29.

Súmwhat óf his clóþíng : king.

Rob. Mannyng, Handlyng Sinne, l. 5703.

The same manner of treatment may be found applied to words which end in *-lyng*, *-esse*, *-nesse*, and similar syllables, and which have a secondary accent on the last syllable and the chief accent on the preceding root-syllable.

In Modern English verse the absence of a thesis between two accented syllables sometimes arises from phonetic conditions, i. e. from the pause which naturally takes place between two words which it is difficult to pronounce successively. This pause supplies the place of the missing thesis, as e. g. in the following lines:

And fírst cléns us fróm the fíend. Townl. Myst. p. 9.

An óld témple there stánds, | whereás some tíme. Surrey, p. 142.

And scórn the Stóry | thát the Kníght tóld. Wyatt, p. 192.

In other instances the emphasis laid upon a particular word compensates for the absence of the unaccented syllable, especially, if the accented syllable is long: e. g.

And thóu, Fáther, | recéive intó thy hánds. Surrey, p. 142.

Júst as you léft them | áll prísoners, sír. Shak. Temp. v. i. 8.

My ówn *lóve,* | *my ónly déar.* Moore.

Mórning, évening, | *nóon and níght*
Práise *Gód,* | *sang Théocríte.* R. Browning, ii. 158.

This licence is of frequent occurrence in even-beat measures.

§ 87. Another metrical peculiarity caused by the influence of the rhythm is the **lengthening** of a word by the introduction of an unaccented extra syllable, commonly an *e*, to supply a thesis lacking between two accented syllables.

This occurs in Middle English and in Modern English poetry also. (i) In disyllabic words, commonly those with a first syllable ending with a mute, the second beginning with a liquid, e. g. :

Of Éng(e)lónd | *to Cáunterbúry they wénde.*

Chauc. Prol. 16.

If yóu will tárry, | *hóly píl(e)grím.*

Shakesp. All's Well, III. v. 43.

(ii) In Modern English poetry only in certain monosyllabic words ending in *r* or *re*, preceded by a diphthong, as e. g. in *our, hour, fire,* &c., e. g. :

So dóth he féel | *his fíre mánifóld.* Wyatt, 205.

This peculiarity will be mentioned again in the next chapter.

§ 88. Another deviation from the regular iambic line is the **inversion of the rhythm**; i. e. the substitution of a trochee for an iambus at the beginning of a line or after the caesura. The rhythmical effect of this licence has some resemblance to that of the suppression of anacrusis. In both cases the rhythmic accent has to yield to the word-accent. But while in the latter case the whole verse becomes trochaic in consequence of the omission of the first syllable, in the former the trochaic cadence affects one foot only (generally the first), the rest of the verse being of a regular iambic rhythm. Hence the number of syllables in each line is the same as that in all the other regular lines (including those with level stress), whereas verses with suppressed anacrusis may easily be distinguished from the former by their smaller number of syllables. On the other hand, the number of syllables (being the same in both cases) affords no help in distinguishing between change of word-accent and inversion of rhythm. Which of these two kinds of licence is to be recognized in any particular case can be determined only by the position which the abnormal foot occupies in the line. Inversion of rhythm (i. e. the substitution of a trochee for an iambus) occurs, as a rule, only at the beginning of a line or hemistich, where the flow of the rhythm has not begun, so that the introduction of a trochee does not disturb it. If, therefore, the discord between normal word-stress and iambic rhythm occurs in any other position in the line, it must be regarded as a case of level stress.

The following examples will serve to illustrate the difference between these three species of metrical licence :

Omission of anacrusis :

Hérknet tó me góde men.   Hav. 1.   7 syll.

Nórfolk sprúng thee,   Lámbeth hólds thee déad.
                              Surrey, p. 62.   9   ,,

Level stress :

A stálworþí man ín a flok.   Hav. 24.   8   ,,

And Rýpheús that mét thee bý moonlíght.
                              Surrey, p. 126.   10   ,,

Inversion of rhythm :

Míchel was súch a kíng to préyse.   Hav. 60.   8   ,,

Míldly doth flów alóng the frúitful fíelds.
                              Surrey, p. 145.   10   ,,

Shróuding themsélves únder the désert shóre.
                              Surrey, p. 113.   10   ,,

Inversion of rhythm may be caused in the interior of a rhythmical series only when a particularly strong emphasis is laid upon a word, e. g. to express an antithesis or for similar reasons :

That íf góld ruste | whát shal ýren dó?
                              Chaucer, Prol. 500.

And wé'll nót fail | When Dúncan ís asléep.
                              Shakesp. Macb. i. vii. 61.

We may distinguish between two kinds of inversion of rhythm, viz. (1) *natural* inversion, and (2) *rhetorical* inversion. The former is caused by word-accent, the latter by the rhetorical accent, as illustrated by the last examples. The second kind differs very clearly from level stress, as the word in question or the first syllable of it (see the second line of the following quotation) is to be uttered with an unusually strong emphasis, e. g. :

Síck, or *in héalth,* | *in évil fáme or góod.*   Surrey, p. 17.

Lústy *of scháip,* lýght of *delíveránce.*

Dunbar, Thriss. and Rois 95.

In the second example inversion of rhythm occurs (as it often does) twice over, viz. at the beginning of the verse and after the caesura.

Not unfrequently also two inversions of rhythm follow immediately upon one another, e. g. :

Wórldly gládnes | *is mélled wíth affráy.*

Lydgate, Min. Poems, xxii, line 11.

Réigned óver | *so mány péoples and réalms.*   Surrey, p. 135.

Such verses, however, may also be looked upon as instances of the omission of anacrusis combined with epic caesura.

This would be the only admissible explanation in verses the first accented word of which is a word which usually does not bear an accent or is not accented rhetorically, e. g. :

Óf the wórdes | *that Týdeús had sáid.*

Lydgate, St. of Thebes, line 1082.

Tó have líved | *áfter the cíty táken.*   Surrey, p. 139.

But in a line with an emphasized first word inversion of rhythm is the more probable explanation : e. g.

Nát astónned, | *nor ín his hérte afférde.*

Lydgate, St. of Thebes, 1069.

Gód, that séndeth, | *withdráweth wínter shárp.*   Surrey, p. 58.

§ 89. Disyllabic or polysyllabic thesis.   Another important deviation from the regular iambic rhythm, which is clearly to be distinguished from the double thesis caused by inversion of rhythm, consists in the use of two or sometimes even more unaccented syllables instead of one to form a regular thesis of a verse.   This irregularity, which is almost as common in Modern English as it is in Early English poetry, may occur in any part of the verse.   If it occurs in the first foot, it may be called disyllabic or polysyllabic anacrusis, as in the following examples :

Gif we clépieþ híne féder þénne.   Pater Noster, 19.

Se þe múchel vólʒeð hís iwíl, | *him sélue hé biswíkeð.*

Moral Ode, 15.

To purvéie þám a skúlkyng, | *on þe Énglish éft to ríde.*
Rob. Mannyng, Chron. p. 3, l. 8.

With a thrédbare cópe, | *as ís a póure scolér.*
Chaucer, Prol. 260.

And why thís is a révelációun. Chaucer, H. of Fame, l. 8.

My comáundemént that kéeps trulý, | *and áfter ít will dó.*
Towneley Myst. p. 182.

There was néver nóthing | *móre me páin'd.* Wyatt, p. 57.

I beséech your Gráces | *bóth to párdon mé.*
Shakesp. Rich. III, i. i. 84.

By thy lóng grey béard and glíttering éye.
Coleridge, Anc. Mar. l. 3.

This metrical licence may occur also immediately after the caesura, e. g.:

Wel láte he léteþ úfel wéorc | *þe hit né may dón na máre.*
Moral Ode, 128.

And thríes hádde sche bén | *at Ierúsalém.* Chauc. Prol. 463.

My wíll confírm | *with the spírit of stéadfastnéss.*
Wyatt, p. 220.

But thén we'll trý | *what these dástard Frénchmen dáre.*
Shakesp. 1 Hen. VI, i. iv. 111.

It most frequently occurs, however, in the interior of the rhythmical sections, and there it is found in any of the feet, except the last, as will be seen by the following examples:

Intó þis ðhísternesse hér benéðen. Gen. and Exod. 66.

For þér we hit míhte fínden éft | *and hábben búten énde.*
Moral Ode, 52.

In Wéssex was thán a kíng, | *his náme wás Sir Íne.*
Rob. Mannyng, Chron. p. 2, l. 1.

Of Éngelónd | *to Cáunterbúry they wénde.* Chauc., Prol. 16.

So fervent hót, | *thy díssolute lífe.* Surrey, p. 68.

And Windsor, alás! | *doth cháse me fróm her síght.* ib. p. 14.

Succéeding his fáther Bólingbróke, | *did réign.*
Shakesp. 1 Hen. VI, ii. v. 83.

§ **90.** Unaccented extra syllables are found also before a caesura or at the end of the line. In the former case they constitute what is known as *epic caesura*, in the latter they form feminine or double endings (if there is only one extra syllable) or tumbling endings (if there are two extra syllables). In both cases this irregularity is softened or excused, so to say, by the pause, except where the accented or masculine ending of the hemistich is required by the very nature of the metre, viz. in the first acatalectic half of the Septenary line. It does, however, not unfrequently occur in some Early Middle English poems written in Septenary metre, e. g. in the *Moral Ode* and several others, but this may be only owing to want of skill or carelessness on the part of the authors of these poems. The following example taken from the *Moral Ode* may serve to illustrate this :

Nis nán wítnesse éal se múchel, | se mánnes ágen héorte. 114.

In the *Ormulum* irregularities of this kind never occur, a certain proof that Orm thought them metrically inadmissible, and felt that an extra syllable at the end of the first hemistich would disturb the flow of the rhythm.

Epic caesura certainly is more in place, or at any rate more common, in other kinds of verse, especially in the Middle English Alexandrine formed after the Old French model, e. g. :

Untó the Ínglis kínges, | þat hád it ín þer hónd.

Robert Mannyng, Chron. p. 2, l. 4.

In the four-foot and five-foot rhymed verse, and especially in blank verse, it is of frequent occurrence :

Why thís a fántom, | why thése orácles. Chauc. H. of F. 11.

To Cáunterbúry, | with fúl devóut coráge. id. Prol. 22.

What shólde he stúdie | and máke hym séluen wóod ? ib. 184.[1]

So crúel príson | how cóuld betíde, alás. Surrey, p. 19.

O míseráble sórrow ! | withóuten cúre. Wyatt, p. 124.

With hídden hélp or vántage, | or thát with bóth.

Shakesp. Macb. i. iv. 113.

---

[1] We therefore hold ten Brink to be wrong in asserting (*Chaucer's Sprache und Verskunst*, § 307, 3. Anm.) that no redundant or hypermetrical syllable is permissible in the caesural pause of Chaucer's iambic line of five accents, although he recognizes that in lines of four accents Chaucer admits the very same irregularity, which moreover has remained in use down to the present day. Cf. Skeat, *Chaucer Canon*, Oxford, 1900, pp. 31-3, and Schipper in Paul's *Grundriss*, ed. 2, II. ii, pp. 217-18. On

But hów of Cáwdor ? | The tháne of Cáwdor líves.

ib. i. iii. 72.

But thís delíver'd, | he sáw the ármies jóin.

Fletcher, Loyal Subj. ii. i. 333.

For íf my húsband táke you, | and táke you thús.

id. Rule a Wife, v. 495.

By vísion fóund thee ín the Témple, | and spáke.

Milton, Par. Reg. i. 256.

Creáted húgest | that swím the Ócean-stréam.

id. Par. L. i. 202.

And chíefly thóu, O Spírit ! | that dóst prefér. ib. i. 17.

Have fílled their víals | with sálutáry wráth.

Coleridge, Relig. Musings, 84.

§ **91.** Double or feminine endings are more frequent than epic caesuras, especially in Middle English poetry. They become rarer, however, in the course of time in Modern English in consequence of the gradual disappearance of the inflexional endings, e. g. :

Ꝟet wé don álle hís ibéden,
Ánd his wílle fór to réden. Pater Noster, 7–8.

Tó my wýtte | that cáuseth swévenes
Éyther on mórwes | ór on évenes. Chauc. H. of Fame, 3–4.

Áfter Éthelbért | com Élfríth his bróther,
Ꝧát was Égbrihtes sónne, | and ʒít ther wás an óper.

Robert Mannyng, Chron. p. 21, ll. 7–8.

Withóuten óther cómpainýe | in yóuthe,
But thérof néedeth nóught | to spéke as nóuthe.

Chauc. Prol. 461–2.

And ín her síght | the séas with dín confóunded ? Sur. p. 164.

Or whó can téll thy lóss, | if thóu mayst ónce recóver.

Wyatt, p. 154.

this point, as also on several others, Miss M. Bentinck Smith, the translator of ten Brink's work, is of our opinion (cf. her Remarks on Chapter III of ten Brink's *Chaucer's Sprache und Verskunst* in *The Modern Language Quarterly*, vol. v, No. 1, April, 1902, pp. 13–19). A contrary view with regard to ' extra syllables ' in the heroic and the blank-verse line (sixteenth and seventeenth centuries) is taken by A. P. van Dam and Cornelis Stoffel, *Chapters on English Printing, Prosody, and Pronunciation* (1550–1700), Heidelberg, 1902 (Anglistische Forschungen herausgegeben von Dr. Johannes Hoops, Heft 9), pp. 48–113.

Lie thére, my árt. | *Wípe thou thine éyes ; have cómfort.*

> Shakesp. Temp. i. ii. 25.

The dífference 'twíxt the cóvetous | *ánd the pródigall.*

> Ben Jonson, Staple of News, ii. 12.

Nothing at áll ! | *I'll téach you tó be treacherous.*

> Fletcher, Mad Lover, iii. 255.

Nó, Sir, | *I dáre not leave her* | *tó that sólitariness.*

> id. Rule a Wife, iv. 479.

What yóung thing's thís ?— | *Good mórrow, béauteous géntle-*
woman.

> id. Loy. Subj. v. ii. 402.

The two last quotations are noteworthy because the number of extra syllables after the last accented one is two, three, or even four, a peculiarity which is one of the characteristics of Fletcher's versification. Other poets, e. g. Shakespeare, preferred feminine endings in some periods of their literary career, so that it is possible to use the proportion of masculine and feminine endings occurring in a play, compared with others of the same poet, as a means of ascertaining the date of its origin.

It is also to be observed that in certain epochs or kinds of poetry feminine endings are more in favour than in others. In the eighteenth century they are very scarce, whereas they become more frequent again in the nineteenth century. Byron and Moore especially use them copiously in their satirical and humorous poems to produce burlesque effects.

§ **92.** Another metrical licence also connected with the end of the line is what is known as the **enjambement** or *run-on line*— that is to say, the carrying over of the end of a sentence into the following line.

The rule that the end of a line must coincide with the end of a sentence, is, from the nature of the case, more difficult to observe strictly—and, consequently, the run-on line is more readily admitted—in verse composed of short lines (which often do not afford room for a complete sentence) than where the lines are longer. In blank verse, also, the run-on line is more freely allowed than in rhymed verse, where the pause at the end of the line is more strongly marked.

Generally speaking, enjambement is not allowed to separate two short words that stand in close syntactical connexion and isolated from the rest of the sentence, though examples of this do occur (especially in the older poets) in which an adjective is separated from its substantive :

I wíll yive hím the álderbéste
Yífte, that éver he abóod his líve.   Chauc. Blaunche, 246.

My lúte awáke, perfórm the lást
Lábour, that thóu and Í shall wáste.   Wyatt, p. 29,

or a verb from its subject or object, formed by a monosyllabic
word :

To téllen shórtly, whán that hé
Was ín the sée, thús in this wíse.   Chauc. Blaunche, 68.

Me néed not lóng for tó beséech
Hér, that hath pówer me tó commánd.   Wyatt, p. 31.

But if, on the other hand, two closely connected parts of a
sentence are each of them long enough to fill up two measures,
they may be separated by enjambement :

Whan Zéphirús eek wíth his swéte bréethe
Enspíred háth in évery hólte and héethe
The téndre cróppes, ánd the yónge sónne
Háth in the Rám his hálfe cóurs irónne, &c.

Chauc. Prol. 5–8.

There áre a sórt of mén, whose vísagés
Do créam and mántle líke a stánding pónd.

Shakesp. Merch. i. i. 88–9.

The admissibility or inadmissibility, however, of run-on lines
depends on many different and complicated considerations, for
which the reader may be referred to ten Brink, *Chaucer's
Sprache und Verskunst,* §§ 317–20, and to our own larger work,
vol. ii, pp. 59–62.

In Shakespeare's versification, and probably also in that of
other poets, the more or less frequent use of run-on lines is
characteristic of certain periods of their literary career, and is
therefore looked upon as a valuable help in determining the
date of the different plays (cf. § 91). The largest percentage
of run-on lines probably occurs in Milton's epics.

§ 93. The judicious use of run-on lines is often resorted to
for the purpose of avoiding monotony. Another metrical licence
connected with the line-end, which is adopted for the same
purpose, is **rhyme-breaking**. This occurs chiefly in rhyming
couplets, and consists in ending the sentence with the first line
of the couplet, instead of continuing it (as is usually done) till
the end of the second line. Thus the close connexion of the
two lines of the couplet effected by the rhyme is broken up by
the logical or syntactic pause occurring at the end of the first

line. This is used rarely, and so to say unconsciously, by the earlier Middle English poets, but is frequently applied, and undoubtedly with artistic intention, by Chaucer and his successors. The following passage contains examples both of rhyme-breaking and of the more normal usage :

> *A Yéman hádde he, ánd servántz namó*
> *At thát tyme, fór him líste ríde sóo ;*
> *And hé was clád in cóte and hóod of gréne :*
> *A shéf of pécok árwes bríght and shéne*
> *Únder his bélt he bár ful thríftilý.*
> *Wél koude he drésse his tákel yémanlý ;* &c.

Chauc. Prol. ll. 101–6.

Rhyme-breaking may, of course, also take place in other metres, as e. g. in four-foot iambic verses :

> *Which hópe I kéep full súre in mé,*
> *As hé, that áll my cómfort ís.*
> *On yóu alone, which áre my blíss,* &c.

Surrey, pp. 79–80.

Chapman, in his translation of Homer, often uses it in Septenary verses as well as in five-foot iambic verses. In certain stanzas rhyme-breaking at particular places is a strict rule, as e. g. in the Rhyme-Royal stanza (*a b a b . b c c*), in the ballade-stanza of eight lines (*a b a b . b c b c*), and also between the two quatrains of the regular Italian sonnet.

On the other hand this licence is rare in the works of the poets of the eighteenth century who wrote under French influence, and in modern times (especially at the present day) it seems to be rather avoided than intentionally admitted.

§ 94. Another peculiarity of frequent but irregular occurrence in even-beat verse is **alliteration**, a feature which is derived from the old native metre, and is still (consciously or unconsciously) employed by many poets as an ornament of their verse.

The arbitrary use of alliteration in the freer form of the long line has been already discussed.

In the thirteenth and fourteenth centuries it is mostly used merely to give a stronger emphasis to those words of the verse which bear the logical and rhythmical accent,[1] but even as early as this we can observe a decided predilection for accumulated alliteration. Sometimes the same alliterative sound is retained through several successive lines. In other instances a fourth

---

[1] Cf. the lines from Wright's *Spec. of Lyr. Poetry*, p. 31, quoted on p. 98.

alliterating word is admitted in the line (as in the example referred to above). In the fifteenth and sixteenth centuries this striving after accumulation of alliteration was carried to such a length that it became a rule that as many words in the line as possible, whether accented or not, should begin with the same letter. This accounts for King James VI's metrical rule quoted above (p. 89), that in 'Tumbling verse' the line is to be 'literal'. Even Chaucer, in spite of his well-known hostile attitude to regular alliterative poetry,[1] allowed his diction to be influenced strongly by it, e. g.:

I wréche, which that wépe and wáylle thús,
Was whílom wýf to kýng Capáneús. Kn. Tale, ll. 73–4.

And hé him húrtleth with his hórs adóun. ib. line 1758.

This accumulation of alliterative sounds occurs in the works of many Modern English poets, some of whom, as Peele and Shakespeare, have themselves ridiculed it, but were unable, or were not careful, to avoid it altogether in their own practice.

And with sharp shrílling shríekes | doe bóotlesse crý.
Spens. F. Q. i. iii. 127.

Which with a rúshy wéapon | Í will wóund.
Peele, Old Wifes Tale, p. 467.

Théy love léast that lét men know their lóve. Shak. Rom. i. 3.

For particulars see *Neuengl. Metrik,* pp. 68–76, and the following treatises:

Die Alliteration im Layamon, by K. Regel; *Germanistische Studien,* ed. K. Bartsch, Vienna, 1874, i. 172 ff.
Die Alliteration bei Chaucer, by Dr. F. Lindner, *Jahrbuch f. rom. und engl. Literatur,* N. Ser. ii, p. 311 ff.
Die Alliteration in den Werken Chaucers mit Ausschluss der Canterbury Tales, by E. Petzold. Dissertation, Marburg, 1889.
Die alliterierenden Sprachformeln in Morris's Early English Alliterative Poems und im Sir Gawayne and the Green Knight, by Joh. Fuhrmann. Dissertation, Kiel, 1886.
Prof. Dr. K. Seitz, *Die Alliteration im Englischen vor und bei Shakspere,* and *Zur Alliteration im Neuenglischen.* Realschulprogramme i–iii, Marne, 1875, Itzehoe, 1883, 1884.
M. Zeuner, *Die Alliteration bei neuenglischen Dichtern.* Dissertation, Halle, 1880.
Die stabreimenden Wortverbindungen in den Dichtungen Walter Scott's, by Georg Apitz. Dissertation, Breslau, 1893.

[1] Cf. *Parson's Prologue,* 42–3.

CHAPTER VII

THE METRICAL TREATMENT OF SYLLABLES

§ 95. As the root-syllables of words (leaving out of account the words of Romanic origin) almost universally retain their full syllabic value, whether occurring in arsis or in thesis, they require no notice in this chapter. We therefore confine our remarks to the formative and inflexional syllables, which, though as a rule found only in thesis, admit of being treated metrically in three different ways. (1) A syllable of this kind may retain its full value, so as to form by itself the entire thesis of a foot. (2) It may be slurred, so that it combines with another unaccented syllable to form a thesis. (3) It may lose its syllabic value altogether, its vowel being elided and its consonantal part (if it has any) being attracted to the root-syllable. By the last-mentioned process, as is well known, the number of inflexional syllables has been greatly reduced in Modern as compared with Middle and Old English.

The inflexional endings which in Middle English (we are here considering chiefly the language of Chaucer) have ordinarily the value of independent syllables are the following :—

-es (*-is*, *-us*) in the gen. sing. and the plur. of the substantive, and in certain adverbs.

-en in the nom. plur. of some substantives of the weak declension, in certain prepositions, in the infinitive, in the strong past participle, in the plur. of the pres. of strong verbs, and in the pret. plur. of all verbs.

-er in the comparative.

-est in the superlative and the 2nd person pres.

-eth (*-ith*) in the 3rd person pres. sing., in the plur. pres. and plur. imperative.

-ed (*-id*, *-ud*) in the past participles of weak verbs, and often in the 1st and 3rd person sing. and the whole plur. pret. of the weak verbs with short root-syllable, instead of the fuller endings *-ede*, *-eden*, which also occur; in weak verbs with long root-syllable the endings are *-de*, *-den*.

-edest, or *-dest* in the 2nd pers. sing. pret. of the weak verb.

-e in a certain number of inflexional forms of the verb (as e. g. in the inf. and in the past part. of strong verbs, where *n* is dropped), and of the substantive and adjective, and as an ending of Romanic words, &c.

Of all these endings only the comparative and superlative suffixes *-er, -est* are preserved in an unreduced state in Modern English. The final *-e* has disappeared in pronunciation (with some exceptions occurring in Early Modern English). The important suffixes *-en, -es, -ed, -est* (2nd pers. sing.), *-eth* (for which *-s*, the northern ending, instead of *-es*, is commonly substituted) have been contracted through syncope so as to form one syllable with the root, except where the nature of the final consonant of the stem prevents syncope, e. g. in *-es* and *-est* after sibilants, in *-ed* after dentals, in *-en* after *v, s, t, d, k* (as in *houses, ended, risen, written, hidden, broken, driven*). As, however, these are always full syllables they may here be disregarded. The ending *-edest* has been shortened into *-edst*.

It is to be observed that the syncopation of the vowel (*e*) of the inflexional endings was not so nearly universal in Early Modern English as it is at present; and further, that it is still much less prevalent in poetry than in prose, because the poets for metrical reasons often preserve the fuller endings when in ordinary speech they are no longer used.[1] In examining the metrical treatment of the Early English inflexional endings, we shall therefore have occasion to consider the usage of the present day, notwithstanding the fact that some of these endings are obsolete in modern prose.

The chief difference between Early and Modern English with regard to the treatment of the inflexions is that in Early English poetry the full pronunciation is the rule—in accordance with the practice in ordinary speech—and the syncopation of the vowel (*e*, rarely *i* or *u*) is the exception; while in Modern English it is the shortened pronunciation that is normal, the full syllabic form being used only exceptionally as a poetic licence.

§ 96. The first point that requires notice is the treatment of the unaccented *e* of words of three and four syllables in Middle English. The following observations are founded on those of ten Brink, *Chaucer's Sprache und Verskunst*, § 256.

1. If each of the two last syllables of a trisyllabic word has

---

[1] In the reading of the Bible and Liturgy the older syllabic pronunciation of certain endings is still common, and it is occasionally heard in sermons, where a more elevated and poetical kind of diction is admissible than would be used in secular oratory.

an unaccented *e*, one of them is generally elided or slurred over under the influence of the rhythmical accent. Thus the past tense singular of the weak verbs *clepede, werede, makede, lovede* may be scanned either *clepte, werde, made, lovde,* or *cleped, wered, maked, loved.* Just in the same way the plural forms *clepeden, makeden,* &c., may be read either *clepten, maden,* &c., or *cleped, maked,* &c.; likewise the plural endings of nouns *faderes, hevenes* may be pronounced *fadres, hevnes* or *faders, hevens.* In Early Middle English, however, and also in the language of Chaucer, exceptions to this rule are found, trisyllabic scansion occurring chiefly in the plur. pret., e. g.:

> *Þatt úre Lóverrd Iésu Chríst, swa þóledé þe déofell.*
> Orm. 11822.

> *I dórste swére, they wéyedén ten póunde.*
> Chauc. Prol. 454.

Yélledén, id. N. Pr. Tale, 569; *wónedén,* id. Leg. 712, &c.

The *e* following upon an unaccented syllable which is capable of receiving the accent, whether in a word of Teutonic or Romanic origin, is commonly mute. E. g. *banere, manere, lovere, ladyes, housbondes, thousandes* are generally to be pronounced in verse (as, indeed, they were probably pronounced in prose) as, *baner, maner, lover, ladys, housbonds, thousands.* But this *e,* on the other hand, not unfrequently remains syllabic, especially in the *Ormulum,* where it is dropped only before a vowel or *h.* E. g. *cneolénn meoklík(e) annd lútenn* 11392, *meocnéss(e) is þrínne kíness* 10699, *Forr án godnéss(e) uss háveþþ dón* 185. Before a consonant or at the end of a line, however, it is always sounded: *Ennglísshe ménn to láre* 279, *God wórd and gód tiþénnde* 158, *forrþí birrþ áll Cristéne fóllc* 303. *Goddspélless hállȝhe láre* 14, 42, 54, *þa Góddspelléss neh álle* 30. Other examples are: *And þó þet wéren gítserés* Moral Ode, Ms. D. l. 269; *For thóusandés his hóndes máden dýe* Chauc. Troil. v, 1816; *enlúminéd* id. A B C 73.

In words of four syllables a final *e* which follows upon an unaccented syllable with a secondary accent may at pleasure either become mute or be fully pronounced. So words like *óut-rydère, sóudanèsse, émperòures, árgumèntes* may be read either as three or four syllables. Examples of *e* sounded: *Bifórr þe Rómanísshe kíng* Orm. 6902; *Annd síkerrlíke trówwenn* ib. 11412; *þurrh hállȝhe góddspellwríhhtess* ib. 160; *Till híse lérninngcníhhtess* ib. 235; *Annd þúrrh þin góddcunndnésse* ib. 11358; *An Gódd all únntodźeledd* ib. 11518; *I glúternésse fállenn* ib. 11636; *þurrh flźeshes únntrummnésse* ib. 11938; *in stránge ráketéȝe* Moral Ode, 281; *a thíng(e) unstédeféste* ib. 319; *bifóre héovenkínge* ib. 352, &c. Examples of *e* mute: *And þá, þe úntreownéss(e) dide þán* Moral Ode, 267; *þéosternéss(e) and éie* ib. 279. Orm has it only before vowels or *h*: *Forr són se glúternéss(e) iss dźed* 11663, &c.

§ 97. Special remarks on individual inflexional endings.

-es (gen. sing., nom. plur., and adverbial) is in disyllables (a) as a rule treated as a full syllable, e. g. *Ac þét we dóþ for gódes líue* Moral Ode 56; *from éuery shíres énde* Chauc. Prol. 15; *And élles cértain wére thei to blame* ib. 375; (b) seldom syncopated or slurred over, e. g. *Ure álre hláuerd fór his prélles* Moral Ode, 189; *He mákede físses in þére sé* ib. 83; *I sáugh his sléves purfíled* Chauc. Prol. 193; *The ármes of dáun Arcíte* id. Kn. Tale, 2033; *Or élles it wás* id. Sq. Tale, 209.

In trisyllables the reverse is the case; only Orm, who always, as is well known, carefully counts his syllables, treats the ending as a full syllable. Otherwise syncopation or slurring over of the last syllable is the rule in these words: *a sómeres dáy* Chauc. Sq. Tale, 64; *Gréyhoundes he hádde* id. Prol. 190; *hóusbondes át that tóun* id. Kn. Tale, 78; *the távernes wél* id. Prol. 240.

In Modern English in all these cases elision of the -*e* is the rule, those, of course, excepted in which the -*e* is still sounded at the present day (after sibilants, dentals, &c.) and which therefore we need not discuss here. The use of -*es* as a full syllable is otherwise quite exceptional, chiefly occurring in the Early Modern English poets, who use the sounded *e*, occasionally, to gain an unaccented syllable, e. g.:

The níghtës cár the stárs abóut doth bríng. Surrey, p. 15.

Sometíme to líve in lóvès blíss. Wyatt, p. 119.

That líke would nót for áll this wórldès wéalth.
Spens. F. Q. i. ix. 31.

The héat doth stráight forsáke the límbës cóld. Wyatt, p. 205.

Bé your éyës yét moon-próofe. Ben Jonson, i. 979.

The usual sound of these words is *night's, love's, world's, limbs, eyes,* and so in all similar cases.

The syncopation of the -*e* in the adverbial -*es* is indicated, as

is well known, by the spelling, in certain cases : e. g. in *else,
hence, thence, whence* (instead of the Middle English forms *elles,
hennes,* &c.) ; but even in words where it is preserved in writing,
as e. g. in *whiles, unawares,* it has become mute and has, as a
rule, no metrical value in Modern English poetry. The archaic
certes, however, is still always treated as a disyllable, e. g.

> *I wáil, I wáil, and cérẗes thát is trúe.*
>
> Mrs. Browning, i, p. 55.

§ **98.** The ending *-en* (plur. nom. of nouns; prepositions;
infinitive; strong past part.; plur. pres. and pret. of verbs) is
in Middle English (a) commonly treated as a full syllable during
the first period, and later on mostly, although not always, to
avoid hiatus, before vowels and *h*, e. g. *His éyen stépe* Chauc.
Prol. 201 ; *Bifórenn Críst allmáhhtig Gódd* Orm. 175 ; *Befóren
ánd behýnde* Alexius, ii. 393 ; *abóven álle nációuns* Chauc. Prol.
53 ; *þú schalt béren hím þis ríng* Floris and Blanch. 547 ; *Fór
to délen wíth no swích poráille* Chauc. Prol. 247 ; *bifrórenn* Orm.
13856 ; *forlórenn* ib. 1395 ; *Sche wás arísen ánd al rédy díght*
Chauc. Kn. T. 183 ; *Hir hósen wéren óf fyn scárlet réed* id. Prol.
456 ; *For thís ye knówen álso wél as I* ib. 730 ; *Swa þátt teȝȝ
shúlenn wúrrþen þǽr* Orm. 11867 ; *þatt háffdenn cwémmd himm
í þiss líf* ib. 210 ; *Al þet wé misdíden hére* Moral Ode, 99 ;
(b) syncopated or slurred, especially in later times, after the
n has been dropped already in prepositions and verbal inflexions, e. g. *His póre féren he delde* Alexius, ii. 210 ; *Hálles and
bóures, óxen and plóugh* ib. 12 ; *Bifórr þe Rómanísshe kíng*
(instead of *biforenn*) Orm. 6902 ; *Hastów had fléen al nýght*
Chauc. Manc. Prol. 17 ; *She bóthe hir yónge chíldren untó hir
cálleþ* id. Cl. T. 1081 ; *is bórn : þat wénten hím bifórn* id. Man
of Lawes T. 995–7 ; *withínne a lítel whýle* id. Sq. T. 590 ;
And únderfóngen his kínedóm Flor. and Blanch. 1264 ; *þei
máde sówen in þát cité* Alexius, i. 577 ; *Biddeþ his mén cómen
him nére* ib. 134 ; *Hórn : i-bórn* King Horn, 137–8 ; *forlóren :
Hórn* ib. 479–80 ; *Was rísen and rómede* Chauc. Kn. T. 207 ;
my líef is fáren on lónde id. N. Pr. T. 59 ; *And fórth we ríden
a lítel móre than þáas* id. Prol. 825 ; *þei drýven him ófte tó
skornínge* Alexius, i. 308 ; *þei rísen alle úp with blíþe chére*
ib. 367 ; *þei cásten upón his cróun* ib. 312 ; *And wíssheden þat
hé were déd* Alexius, ii. 335, &c.

In Modern English this ending is much more rare, and is
hardly ever used as a full syllable of the verse. The plural
ending *-en* of the substantive occurs now and then in Wyatt's

and Surrey's verse, as e. g. in *éyen* instead of *éyes*, both in rhyme,
e. g. *éyen : míne* Sur. 14, and in the interior of the line, ib. 126,
128 ; Wyatt 8, 17, &c.

Prepositions ending in *-en* are scarcely ever used now ; sometimes the archaic *withóuten* is to be met with in some Early
Modern English poets, and then, of course, as a trisyllable :
withóuten dréad Sur. 95 ; *withóuten énd* Spenser, F. Q. ii. ix. 58.
The obsolete infinitives in *-en* may also be found sometimes in
the writings of the same and other early Modern English poets :
in váyn : sdyen Sur. 31 ; *his flócke to víewën wíde* Spenser, F. Q.
i. i. 23 ; *to kíllën bád* Shak. Pericles, ii. Prol. 20. Likewise
certain antiquated plural forms of the verb in *-en* : *dischárgën
cléan* Sur. 30 ; *fen : lífedën* Spenser, F. Q. ii. x. 7 ; *and wáxën
in their mírth* Shak. M. N. Dr. ii. i. 56.

It is only the *-en* of the past participle that is at all often after
certain consonants treated as a full syllable, e. g. *the frózen héart*
Sur. 1 ; *gótten out* ib. 10 ; *the strícken déer* ib. 54 ; *hast táken páin*
Wyatt, 99. Here the full forms are preserved in the ordinary
language. It is only exceptionally that participles that have
undergone shortening, as *come*, reassume their *n* and regain an
extra syllable, e. g. *tíll he cómën háth* West (Poets, ix. 484).
Contracted forms like *grown, known, drawn*, always remain
monosyllabic, even in verse, and words like *fallen, swollen*,
which are normally disyllabic, are often contracted in poetry :
as *grown* Sur. 13 ; *known* ib. 45 ; *swoln* ib. 8 ; *befallen* ib. 26 ;
drawn Wyatt, 160. Complete contraction is effected either by
elision of the final consonant of the stem, e. g. *ta'en* (instead of
taken) Sur. 44, or by slurring of the ending, e. g. *hath gíven
a pláce* Sur. 108 ; *is béaten with wínd and stórm* ib. 157, &c.

§ 99. The comparative and superlative endings *-er*, *-est* are,
as a rule, syllabic. *Hórn is fáirer páne beo hé* King Horn, 330 ;
No lénger dwélle hý ne mýghte Alexius, ii. 85 ; *But ráther wólde
he yéven* Chauc. Prol. 487.

These endings are treated, moreover, as full syllables in the
unaccented rhymes *Hǽngest : fǽirest* Layamon, 13889–90 ;
Hǽngest : héndest ib. 13934–5. If an inflexional *-e* is added to
such words, so as to make them trisyllables, it is commonly
elided or apocopated, e. g. *Fór he ís the fáireste mán* Horn,
787 ; *hire grétteste óoth* Chauc. Prol. 120 ; *The férreste in his
párisshe* ib. 494. Slurring or syncopation takes place in the
following examples, *Sche móst wiþ hím no lénger abíde* Sir Orfeo,
line 328 ; *No lénger to héle óf he bráke* Alexius, ii. 127 ; more
rarely in the superlative, *Annd állre láttst he wúndedd wáss*

Orm. 11779, 11797; *Was thóu not fárist of ángels álle?* Towneley Myst. p. 4.

In Modern English these endings are treated similarly. The comparative-ending *-er* is mostly syllabic on account of the phonetic nature of the final *r*, and even if slurred, it does not entirely lose its syllabic character, e. g.:

The nígher my cómfort ís to mé. Surrey, p. 37.

Or dó him míghtier sérvice ás his thrálls.

Milton, Par. L. i. 149.

The ending of the superlative *-est*, too, is commonly syllabic, e. g.

In lóngest níght, or ín the shórtest dáy. Surrey, p. 16.

Now léss than smállest dwárfs, in nárrow róom.

Milton, P. L. i. 779.

Nevertheless many examples of syncopation are found, chiefly in the writings of the Early Modern English poets: e. g. *the méekest of mínd* Sur. 77; *the swéet'st compánions* Shak. Cymb. v. v. 349; *the stérn'st good níght* id. Macb. ii. ii. 4. Such forms are often used by Ben Jonson.

§ 100. The ending *-est* (2nd pers. pres. sing. ind. and pret. sing. of weak verbs) is in Middle English generally syllabic: *Annd séȝȝest swíllc annd swíllc was þú* Orm. 1512; *Annd ȝiff þu féȝesst þréo wiþ þréo, þa fíndesst tú þær séxe* id. 11523-4; *That bróughtest Tróye* Chauc. N. Pr. T. 408; *Thow wálkest nów* id. Kn. T; *þat gód þat þóu þénkest do mé* Alexius, ii. 304; *Hou mýȝtest þóu þus lónge wóne* Alexius, i. 445; *And wóldest névere ben aknówe* ib. 461.

Frequently, however, syncopation or slurring also occurs: *ȝiff þú seȝȝst tátt tu lúfesst Gódd* Orm. 5188; *þu wénest þat éch song béo grislích* Owl and Night. 315; *þu schríchest and ȝóllest to þíne fére* ib. 223; *Thou knówest him well* Chauc. Blaunche, 137; *Trówest thou? by our Lórd, I wíll thee sáy* ib. 551; *þou mýȝtest have bén a grét lordíng* Alexius, i. 511.

In Modern English syncopation is extremely common, e. g. *Now knówest thou áll* Sur. 27; *That mákest but gáme* Wyatt, 30, &c.; but the full syllabic pronunciation (in accordance with the modern prose usage) is also frequent, both in the poetry of the sixteenth century, e. g. *What frámëst thóu* Sur. 158; *And lóokèst tó commánd* Shak. H. VI. i. i. 38; and in that of recent times, e. g.:

Súch as thou stándëst, pále in thé drear líght.

Mrs. Browning, i. 4.

Wan Scúlptor, wéepëst thóu to táke the cást?

Tennyson, Early Sonn. 9.

§ 101. The ending *-eth*, in the North *-es*, *-is* (3rd pers. sing. pres., plur. pres., and 3rd pers. sing. imperative), is in most cases syllabic in Middle English, especially before the fifteenth century; e. g. *It túrrneþþ hémm till sínne* Orm. 150; *þat spékeþþ óff þe déofell* ib. 11944; *þat ǽfre annd ǽfre stándeþþ ínn* ib. 2617; *þánne hi cumeþ éft* Moral Ode, 236; *Hi wálkeþ éure* ib. 239; *So príkeþ hém natúre* Chauc. Prol. 11; *Cómeþ álle nów to mé* Alexius, ii. 337; *And a-fóngeþ ȝóure méde* ib. 375.

But already in the earlier portion of this epoch of the language slurring or syncopation is often to be met with, and it became gradually more and more frequent. *Boc séȝȝþ þe bírrþ wel ȝémenn þé* Orm. 11373, 11981; *Annd áȝȝ afflérr þe góddspell stánnt* ib. 33; *And thínkeþ, here cómeþ my mórtel énemý* Chauc. Kn. T. 785; *Comeþ nér, quoth hé* id. Prol. 839; *þat háveþ trav*á*ille* Alexius, i. 350; *Thai háldis this lánd agáyne resóune* Barbour's Bruce, i. 488.

In Modern English the endings *-eth* and *-es* (*'s*) were at first used promiscuously; later *-eth* is employed, if a full syllable is required, *-es* (*'s*) if syncopation is intended; but this rule is not strictly observed.

The dropping of *e* on the whole is the more usual: e. g. *begins* Sur. 1; *seems* ib. 2; *learns* Wyatt, 1; also if written *-eth*: *On hím that lóveth not mé* Wyatt, 57; *that séeth the héavens* Sur. 2. Treatment as a full syllable is less usual: *But áll too láte Love léarnëth mé* Sur. 5; *Lóve that lívëth and réignëth ín my thóught* Sur. 12. Shakespeare and his contemporaries still use it somewhat frequently (cf. Hertzberg in *Shakspeare-Jahrb.* xiii, pp. 255–7), and occasional instances are found even in later poets, as for instance in Keats, who rhymes: *death : ouershádowéth*, p. 336; Chr. Rossetti, *déath : fashionéth* p. 28, ii. ll. 5–6.

§ 102. The ending *-ed*, in the North *-id*, *-it* (past part. of weak verbs), is, as a rule, syllabic in Middle English: e. g. *Min Dríhhtin háfeþþ lénedd* Orm. 16; *Annd ícc itt háfe fórþedd té* ib. 25; *Annd tǽrfore háfe icc túrrnedd ítt* ib. 129; *ipróved ófte síthes* Chauc. Prol. 485; *hadde swówned wíth a dédly chére* ib. Kn. T. 55; *Nóu is Álex dwélled þóre* Alexius, i. 121; *Lóverd, ipánked bé þou áy* ib. 157; *A wéile gret quhíle thar duellyt hé* Barbour, Bruce, i. 359.

But slurring and syncopation likewise are of frequent occurrence : *þatt háffdenn cwémmd himm í þiss líf* ib. 211; *þet scúlle béo to déþe idémd* Moral Ode, 106 ; *His lónge héer was kémbd behýnde his bák* Chauc. Kn. T. 1285; *Fulfíld of íre* ib. 82; especially in words with the accent on the antepenultima, e. g. *Ybúried nór ibrént* ib. 88; *and hán hem cáried sófte* ib. 153; *And ben yhónowrid ás a kýng* Alexius, i. 5, 12 (Ms. N).

In this ending, too, syncopation (*-ed*, *'d*, *t*) is the rule already in the earliest Modern English poets : *offer'd* Sur. 6 ; *transgrést* ib. 11 ; *that prómised wás to thée* ib. 35. The use of it as a full syllable, however, is very frequently to be met with, chiefly in participles used as adjectives : *the párchëd gréen restórëd ís with sháde* Sur. 1 ; *by wéll assúrëd móan* Wyatt, 4 ; *but ármëd síghs* ib. 4 ; *false féignëd gráce* ib. 4. The dramatists of the Elizabethan time (cf. *Engl. Metrik*, ii. 336) similarly often use the full ending ; and even in modern poets it is not uncommon : *where wé've involvëd óthers* Burns, Remorse, l. 11 ; *The chármëd God begán* Keats, Lamia, p. 185, &c.

§103. The ending *-ed* (*-od*, *-ud*) of the 1st and 3rd pers. sing. pret. and the whole plur. pret. of weak verbs, which is shortened from *-ede*, *-ode*, *-ude*, *-eden*, *-oden*, *-uden* (cf. § 96), is in Middle English usually syllabic : e. g. *Mést al þét me líked(e) þó* Moral Ode, 7 ; *Oure lóverd þát al máked(e) iwís* Pop. Science, 2 ; *He énded(e) and cléped(e) yt Léicestre* Rob. of Glouc., p. 29 ; *The fáder hem lóued(e) álle ynóӡ* ib. ; *Híre overlíppe wýpud(e) sché so cléne* Chauc. Prol. 107 ; *An óutridére þat lóved(e) vénerýe* ib. 165; *Ne máked hím a spíced cónsciénce* ib. 526 ; *þei préced évere nére and nére* Alexius, i. 583 (Ms. V).

As several of these examples show, slurring occasionally takes place, so that the ending forms part of a disyllabic thesis, but real syncopation never occurs ; cf. further : *And asségit it rýgorouslý* Barbour, Bruce, i. 88 ; *and évere I hóped(e) of þé to hére* Alexius, ii. 482.

With regard to these endings from the beginning of the Modern English epoch onward syncopation ([*e*]*d*, *'d*, *t*) is the rule; *defied* Sur. 10 ; *sustain'd* ib. 15 ; *opprest* Wyatt, 107. But the full syllable not infrequently occurs : *I lóokëd báck* Sur. 4 ; *I néver próvëd nóne* Wyatt, 39. It is characteristic of Spenser's archaistic style, and is often met with in the Elizabethan dramatists ; Shakespeare, however, uses it much more frequently in his earlier than in his later plays. The more recent poets admit it in single cases : *said : vánishéd* Keats, Lamia, p. 202.

§ **104.** The final -*e* is treated in Modern English poetry in the same manner as in Modern High German : it may be either used as a thesis, or be slurred over, or become quite silent. In Middle English, however, the treatment of the final -*e* depends much more on the following word than on the etymological origin of the -*e*. It becomes mute, of course, mostly before *h* or a vowel, but is generally preserved (as a thesis) or slurred before a consonant. This rule has, however, many exceptions.

Orm and other poets of the beginning of the thirteenth century give the final *e* its full syllabic value in certain classes of words in which Chaucer[1] in the second half of the fourteenth century generally slurs it.

These words are the pronouns *hire, oure, ʒoure, here, myne, thyne* (also spelled without *e*), if they do not stand in rhyme ; the plural forms *thise, some, swiche, whiche*; the past part. of strong verbs with an originally short root, the inflexional *n* being apocopated, e. g. *come, write, stole*; the 2nd pers. sing. of the strong pret., e. g. *bare, tooke*, except such words as *songe, founde*, and others of the same group ; the preterites *were* and *made* ; the nouns *sone, wone*; the French words in -*ye*, -*aye*, -*eye*, and, finally, the words *before, tofore, there, heere*.

In most of these cases it is easy enough to give examples of the syllabic use of the -*e*, both from the earliest and from later poets : *Off úre sáwless néde* Orm. 11402 ; *þatt úre Láferrd Iésu Críst* ib. 11403, 11803, &c. ; *ʒérne hy þónkede óure dríghte* Alexius, ii. 35 ; *Annd ʒúre sáwless fóde íss éc* Orm. 11691, &c. ; *þatt ʒúre préostess hállʒhenn* ib. 11694 ; *Till híse déore þéowwess* ib. 11556 ; *Att álle þíne néde* ib. 11366, 11914, &c. ; Owl and Nightingale, 220, 221, &c. ; *Cástel gód an míne ríse* ib. 175, 282 ; *Forgíve hémm hére sínne* Orm. 86 ; *Annd wílle iss híre þrídde máhht* ib. 11509 ; *For híre héorte wás so grét* Owl and N. 43, 44, &c. ; *At súme síþe hérde ich télle* ib. 293 ; *þése wíkkede fóde* ib. 333 ; *And máde mé wíþ him ríde* Sir Orfeo, 153, &c.

All these words may, however, also be found with slurring or syncopation of the *e*, even in Early Middle English : *Annd þéowwtenn wél wiþþ áll þin máhht* Orm. 11393 ; *þa wǽre he þǽr bikǽchedd* ib. 11628 ; *Annd súme itt áll forrwérrþenn* ib. 11512 ; *Min héorte atflíhþ and fált mi túnge* Owl and N. 37 ; *þár þe úle sóng hir tíde* ib. 26, 441 ; *þát ich schúlle tó hire fléo* ib. 442 ; *he*

---

[1] See ten Brink, *Chaucer's Sprache und Verskunst*, § 260.

wére ischóte ib. 23, 53, &c. In later Middle English this is more common: *An ýmage óf hire sóne* Alexius i. 105; *þeróf to gód þei máde here móne* ib. 32; *Sómme þat óf þe ínne wére* Alexius ii. 325; *Fáste þey wére ysóught þoróugh* ib. 14; *And lóke síre at 3óure pilgríme* ib. 394; *And thére our óst bigán* Chauc. Prol. 827; *Entúned ín hire nóse* ib. 123; *Nought gréveth ús youre glórie ánd honóur* id. Kn. T. 59; *púrgh yóure géntilnésse* ib. 62; *ánd hire fálse whéel* ib. 67; *And pílgryms wére they álle* Chauc. Prol. 26, 59; *At níght was cóme intó that hóstelríe* ib. 23; *With hím ther wás his sóne, a yóung squyér* ib. 79; *In mótteléye and hígh* ib. 271; *cómpanýe in yóuthe* ib. 461; *no vílanýe is ít* ib. 740, &c.

§ 105. The following examples serve to show the arbitrary use of the final *-e* in other words, either (*a*) syllabic, or (*b*) slurred or syncopated.

1. **Infinitive**, (*a*) *And stónde úpe gódes knýght* Alexius ii. 269; *to télle yów áll the condícióun* Chauc. Prol. 38. (*b*) *to táke our wéy* ib. 34; *Mén mote 3eve sílver* ib. 232.

2. **Past part.** of strong verbs, (*a*) *ydráwe né ybóre* Sq. T. 336; *þó þe chíld ybóre wás* Alexius ii. 37; (*b*) *Ybóre he wás in Róme* ib. 6; *Though hé were cóme agáin* Chauc. Sq. T. 96; *ycóme from hís viáge* id. Prol. 77, &c.

3. Various **inflexional endings of the verb**, (*a*) *þát ich réde wé begínne* Cant. Creat. E. 225; *And yét I hópe, pár ma fáy* Chauc. Sir Thopas l. 2010; *and máde fórward* id. Prol. 33; *and wénte fór to dóon* ib. 78; *yet hádde hé but lítel góld in cóffre* ib. 298; *And séyde tó her þús* Alexius i. 69; *gládly wólde préche* Chauc. Prol. 480. (*b*) *devóutly wólde he téche* ib. 481; *I trówe ther nówher nón is* ib. 524; *I trówe some mén* id. Sq. T. 213; *So hádde I spóken* id. Prol. 31; *hádde he bé* ib. 60; *if thát sche sáwe a móus* ib. 144; *children betwéen them hédde þei nóne* Alexius i. 31; *Bote méte fóunde þe3 nón saundóute* Cant. Creat. O. 62.

4. **Inflexional endings of Germanic substantives**, (*a*) *His nékke whít* Chauc. Prol. 238; *Of wóodecráft* ib. 210; *whán the sónne wás to réste* ib. 30; *a spánne bróod* ib. 155; *At méte wél itáught* ib. 127; *Ne óf his spéche dáungeróus* ib. 517; *As wéll in spéche ás in cóntenánce* id. Sq. T. 93; *of sínne léche* Alexius i. 59; *He 3éde tó a chírche-héi* ib. 97; *ál for lóve míne* Alexius ii. 87; *of héwe bríght* ib. 100; *while gód in érþe máde mán* Cant. Creat. E. 26. (*b*) *Tróuthe and honóur* Chauc. Prol. 46; *Thát no drópe ne fílle* ib. 131; *In hópe to stónden* ib. 88; *And bý his sýde a swérd* ib. 112; *tó the pýne of hélle* Cant. Creat. O. 240; *þurch príde þat ín his wórd was lí3t* ib. E. 14.

5. **Romanic substantives**, (*a*) *átte síege hádde he bé* Chauc.

Prol. 56; *ín hire sáuce dépe* ib. 129; *Is sígne thát a mán* ib. 226.
(b) *And báthed éuery véyne in swích licóur* ib. 3; *of áge he wás*
ib. 81; *his bénefíce to hýre* ib. 507.

6. **Adjectives.** (a) Chiefly after the definite article, pronouns,
and in plural forms: *and ín the Gréte Sée* Chauc. Prol. 59;
The téndre cróppes ánd the yónge sónne ib. 7; *his hálfe cóurs
irónne* ib. 8; *wíth his swéete bréethe* ib. 5; *to séken stráunge
strondes* ib. 13; *the férste niʒt* Alexius i. 55; *þat ílke dáy* ib. 159;
þe déde córs ib. 420; *Póuere mén to clóþe and féde* ib. 10, 13, 93,
&c.; *cómen of hýe kínne* Alex. ii. 99; *with mílde stévene* ib. 72;
annd álle fúle lússtess Orm. 11656. (b) Chiefly after the indefinite article, but in other cases as well: *Annd álle þe fléeshess
kággerléʒʒc* Orm. 11655; *a fáyr forhéed* Chauc. Prol. 254; *as ís
a póure scolér* ib. 260; *as méke as ís a máyde* ib. 69; *a shéef of
pécock árwes bríght and kéne* ib. 104.

7. **Adverbs and prepositions.** (a) *Míldelíche hé him grétte*
Alexius ii. 296; *Ríght abóute nóne* ib. 387; *And sófte bróuʒte
hém obédde* ib. 23; *Ful ófte tíme* ib. 52; *Ful lúde sóngen* Chauc.
Sq. T. 55; *Abóute príme* id. Kn. T. 1331; *abóue érþe* Cant.
Creat. E. 573. (b) *Fáste þei wére ysóught þorúgh* Alexius ii. 14;
And éek as lóude as dóth Chauc. Prol. 171; *Ther ís namóre to
séyne* ib. 314; *stílle as ány stóon* id. Sq. T. 171; *Abóute this kýng*
id. Kn. T. 1321; *Chíldren betwéne hem hédde þei nóne* Alexius
i. 31; *wiþýnne a whýle* Cant. Creat. O. 29; *ʒif ʒít oure lórd
abóue þe ský* ib. O. 186.

8. **Numerals.** (a) *she hádde fýve* Chauc. Prol. 460; *Fúlle
séventéne ʒére* Alexius i. 179, 187, 321; *of fíue þóusende wínter
and ón* Cant. Creat. E. 462; *nóþer férste tíme ne lást* ib. O. 356.
(b) *and fíue and twénti wínter and mó* ib. E. 463; *táken þe ténde
part óf þy gúod* ib. O. 332; *álle þe béstis* ib. 173; *For séventene
ʒér hít is gán* Alexius i. 194.

§ 106. In poems written in more southern dialects the final *-e*
retains its syllabic value later than in those of the North, in
agreement with the actual usage of the dialects of these districts.
Sir Tristrem (c. 1300) has still many syllabic *e*'s in thesis; in
the *Cursor Mundi* (c. 1320) and the *Metrical Homilies* (c. 1330)
they are not so numerous, and they are still rarer in the poems
of Laurence Minot (c. 1352) and of Thomas of Erceldoune.
The editor of the last-mentioned poet, Prof. Alois Brandl, rejects
the syllabic final *-e* altogether in opposition to ten Brink and
Luick. In Barbour's *Bruce* (c. 1375) it is entirely silent.[1]

---

[1] Cf. Luick, *Anglia*, xi. 591-2.

But in the later poetry of the North, which was largely under the influence of southern English models, chiefly of Chaucer, many inflexional endings, especially various kinds of final -*e*, have a metrical value. King James I, one of the most eminent Scottish poets, e.g., is a strict follower of Chaucer in this respect, both in versification and language.[1] This will be shown by the following examples : *Myn éyen gán to smért* stanza 8; *To séken hélp* 99; *that néver chánge wóld* 83; *That féynen óutward* 136; *That ménen wéle* 137; *We wéren áll* 24; *Lýke to an hérte schápin vérilý* 48; *Thús sall on thé my chárge béne iláid* 120; *in lúfe fór a whíle* 134; *Now, swéte bírd, say ónes tó me pépe, I dée for wó; me thínk thou gýnnis slépe* 57; *And ón the smále gréne twístis sát* 33; *Withín a chámber, lárge, równ, and fáire* 77.

Other Scottish poets, like Dunbar, use the final *e* in the same way, but much more sparingly: *Amáng the gréne ríspis ánd the rédis* Terge 56; *And gréne lévis dóing of déw doun fléit* Thrissil and Rois 49; *scho sénd the swífte Ró* ib. 78; *when Mérche wés with váriand wíndis pást* ib. 1.

Only the inflexional endings of substantives and of verbs are used by Dunbar somewhat more frequently as full syllables, e. g.: *Had máid the bírdis to begín thair hóuris* Thrissil and Rois 5; *of flóuris fórgit néw* ib. 18; *the blástis óf his hórne* ib. 34; *In át the wíndow lúkit bý the dáy* ib. 10; *And hálsit mé* ib. 11; *Bálmit in déw* ib. 20; *The pérlit dróppis schúke* Terge 14. Even Lyndesay still uses certain full endings now and then in this way : *Eleméntis: inténl is* Monarchie 247–8; *thay cán nocht ús it : abúsit* Satire 2897–8; *Quhow Í ressávit cónfort* Monarchie 132; *Lyke áurient péirles ón the twístis háng* ib. 136. But the final -*e* is hardly ever found in his verses forming a thesis.

On the other hand some contemporary authors of the South, reckoned as included in the Modern English period, continue to admit in several cases the syllabic final -*e*, but this can only be regarded as an exception. E. g. *The sóte séason, that búd and blóom forth bríngs* Surrey, p. 3; *Thát the Gréeks bróught to Tróyë tówn* ib. 21; *Hersélf in shádow óf the clósë níght* ib. 138; *Agáinst the búlwark óf the fléshë fráil* Wyatt 207; *But tréated áfter á divérsë fáshion* ib. 7.

Spenser does not seem to admit syllabic final -*e*, in spite of his archaic style.

§ 107. Like the inflexional syllables, the suffixes of derivatives may be treated in a twofold manner. Those of Germanic origin

---

[1] Cf. King James I, *The Kingis Quair*, ed. by W. W. Skeat, 1883-4.

for the most part call for little remark, as many of them have coalesced with the root of the word, and others, as e. g. the syllables *-ing*, *-ness*, *-y*, *-ly*, can, on account of their phonetic character, only be metrically treated as full syllables. Only a few fluctuate in their metrical treatment, as e. g. *-en*, *-er*, *-le*, mostly after a consonant; these will be dealt with in the section on the slurring of syllables.

Of much greater importance are the formative endings of Romanic origin, especially those which begin with an *i*, *e*, or *u* + a vowel, as *-iage*, *-ian*, *-iaunt*, *-iance*, *-ience*, *-ient*, *-ier*, *-ioun*, *-ious*, *-eous*, *-uous*, *-ial*, *-ual*, *-iat*, *-iour*. Such endings may either have their full value, or be slurred in rhythm, i. e. they may be treated either as disyllabic or as monosyllabic.

The full forms do not occur frequently in the interior of the line, but mostly in the last foot, where the endings bear the last arsis and offer a convenient rhyme. Hence we conclude, that the slurred pronunciation (synizesis) had in the later Middle English period already become general in ordinary speech, although the full value is in rhyme-words certainly more common : e. g. *viáge : pílgrimáge* Chaucer, Prol. 77–8 ; *langáge : márriáge* ib. 211–12 ; *térciáne : báne* N. Pr. Tale 139–40 ; *córdiál : spéciál* Prol. 443–4 ; *ethériáll : impériáll* Lyndesay, Monarchie 139–40 ; *curát : licénciát* Chauc. Prol. 219–20 ; *láste : ecclésiáste* ib. 707–8 ; *réverénce : cónsciénce* ib. 225–6 ; *offénce : páciénce* Kn. T. 225–6 ; *dísposícioun : cónstellácioun* ib. 229–30 ; *prísoun : compássioun* ib. 251–2 ; *áscendént : páciént* Prol. 117–18 ; *obédiént : assént* ib. 851–2 ; *óriént : résplendént* Lyndesay, Monarchie 140–2 ; *gloríous : précióus* ib. 28–32, 44–5, 48–52, 75–9, 151–2, &c.; *ymágynácioun : impréssioun : illúsioun* James I, Kingis Quair, st. 12 ; *nácioun : mýlioun : méncioun* ib. st. 78. Slurred endings : *Ful wél bilóved and fámuliér was hé* Chauc. Prol. 215 ; *And spéciallý* ib. 15 ; *a cúrious pýn* ib. 196 ; *Perpétuellý, not ónly fór a yéer* Kn. T. 600 ; *Suspécious wás the* Clerk's T. 540 ; *This sérgeant cám* ib. 575, 582, &c.

Later on slurring becomes more frequent, mainly in the North, e. g. in Dunbar's poems : *with váriand wíndis pást* Thrissil and Rois 1 ; *wíth ane órient blást*, ib. 3 ; *So bústeous ár the blástis* ib. 35 ; *ane ínhibítioun tháir* ib. 64 (but *condítioun : renówn : fassóun* 79–82); *A rádius crówn* ib. 132 ; Lyndesay, Monarchie : *On sénsuall Lúste* 9 ; *Lyke áurient péirles* 136 ; *and búrial bémes* 142 ; *his régioun áuroráll* 148 ; *Quhilk síluate ár* 166 ; *melódious ármonýe* 195 ; *off thát mellífluous, fámous* 232 ; *And síc vaine súperstítioun tó refúse* 242 ; *The quhílk gaif sápience* 249.

In the Modern English period of the language slurring of such syllables is the rule, in conformity with the actual pronunciation in prose, contrary to the usage of Chaucer and other Early Middle English poets. Only exceptionally the unshortened use obtains chiefly in earlier Modern English, as the following examples show :

To wóe a máid in wáy of márriáge.
Shakesp. Merch. ii. ix. 13.

My búsiness cánnot bróok this dálliánce. id. Err. iv. i. 59.

Becáme the áccents óf the váliánt. id. 2 Henry IV, ii. iii. 25.

And yét 't is álmost 'gáinst my cónsciénce. id. Haml. v. ii. 307.

I dó volítient, nót obédiént. Mrs. Browning, i, p. 6.

The véry chúrches are fúll of sóldiérs.
Coleridge, Piccolomini. i. sc. 1.

And áfter hárd condítións of péace. Surrey, p. 173.

Áll the sad spáces óf oblívión. Keats, p. 257.

But Brútus sáys he wás ambítióus.
Shakesp. Caesar, iii. ii. 91.

And lóoking róund I sáw, as úsuál. D. G. Rossetti, i. p. 64.

For other examples cf. *Metrik*, ii. § 40.

§ 108. By the side of this artificial attribution of full syllabic value to Romanic endings which in ordinary pronunciation are contracted, there are many examples of the opposite process, namely the contraction, for metrical purposes, of words that are ordinarily pronounced in full. Both these devices serve the same purpose, that of adjusting the number of syllables to the requirements of the rhythm.

In the former case a syllable which commonly is pronounced quickly and indistinctly is uttered more distinctly and more slowly than in ordinary speech. In the latter, a couple of successive syllables or words are uttered more indistinctly and quickly than in ordinary speech, frequently so much so that a syllable may be entirely suppressed. Hence the slurring of syllables results, according to the degree of contraction, either in a disyllabic thesis, or in the complete coalescence of two syllables. The former takes place if the final unaccented vowel of a polysyllable is run into the following unaccented word consisting of, or beginning with, a vowel, e.g. :

For mány a mán | so hárd is óf his hérte.   Chauc. Prol. 229.

Nowhér so bísy a mán | as hé ther nás.   ib. 321.

Wél coude she cárie a mórsel | ánd wel képe.   ib. 130.

With múchel glórie | and grét solémpnitée.   id. Kn. T. 12.

Oh ! háppy are théy | that háve forgíveness gótt.   Wyatt 211.

My kíng, my cóuntry I séek, | for whóm I líve.   ib. 173.

Sórry am Í | to héar what Í have héard.
                        Shakesp. 2 Henry VI, ii. i. 193.

In cases like these it cannot be supposed that there is actual elision of a syllable, by which *many a, busy a, carie a, glorie and, happy are, country I, sorry am,* would be reduced to regular disyllabic feet.   In several of the instances such an assumption is forbidden not only by the indistinctness of pronunciation which it would involve, but also by the caesura.

Further, we find both in Middle and in Modern English poetry many examples of similar sequences in which there is neither elision nor slurring, the syllable ending with a vowel forming the thesis, and the following syllable beginning with a vowel forming the arsis.   Hiatus of this kind has always been perfectly admissible in English verse.

And yít he wás but ésy óf dispénse.   Chaucer, Prol. 441.

Mówbray's síns so héavy ín his bósom.
                        Shakesp. Rich. II, i. ii. 50.

§ 109. The second possibility, viz. complete amalgamation of two syllables, may occur if a word with an initial vowel or *h* is preceded by a monosyllabic word, standing in thesis, e. g. *th'estat, th'array* Chauc. Prol. 716 ; *th'ascendent* ib. 117 ; *t'allege (to allege)* Kn. T. 2142 ; *nys (ne ys)* ib. 43.   Even in Modern English poetry such contractions occur rather frequently : *Th'altar* Sur. 118; *t'assay* Wyatt 157 ; *N'other* ib. 21 ; often also the words are written in full, although the first vowel is metrically slurred or elided : *the ónly dárling* Shakesp. All 's Well, ii. i. 110.   Yet in all such cases the entire loss of the syllable must not be assumed unless the distinctness of the pronunciation—which must be the only guide in such matters, not the silent reading with the eyes—be sufficiently preserved.[1]

---

[1] Cf. *Metrik,* ii. 101-3 *note.*

Accordingly words like *the*, *to* are not so often contracted with the following word, as *ne*, the amalgamation of which, with the verb to which it belongs, is in accordance with normal Middle English usage : *nas = ne was, nil = ne wil, nolde = ne wolde, noot = ne woot, niste = ne wiste*, e. g. :

> *There nas no dore that he nolde heve of harre.*
> > Chauc. Prol. 550.

Neither in Middle English nor in Modern English poetry, however, is there any compulsion to use such contractions for the purpose of avoiding the *hiatus*, which never was prohibited. They merely serve the momentary need of the poet. Forms like *min* and *thin*, it is true, are regularly used by Middle English poets before vowels, and *my* and *thy* before consonants, and Chaucer applies—according to ten Brink—*from, oon, noon, an, -lych, -lyche* before vowels, and *fro, a, o, no, -ly* before consonants. But many examples of epic caesura show that ten Brink goes too far in maintaining that hiatus was strictly avoided, e. g. : *Whan théy were wónnë; | and ín the Gréete sée* Prol. 59. This is still more clearly shown by verses in which the final -*e* forms a necessary thesis before a vowel, e. g. :

> *Fro the senténcë | óf this trétis lýte.* Sir Thopas 2153.
>
> *Than hád yóur tálè | ál be tóld in váyn.* N. Pr. Prol. 3983.

§ 110. Slurring or contraction is still more frequently the result of indistinct pronunciation or entire elision of a vowel in the interior of a word. This is especially the case with *e* (or another vowel) in the sequence : conson.+*e*+*r*+vowel or *h*, where *e* is slurred over or syncopated : e. g. *And báthed év(e)ry véin* Chauc. Prol. 3 ; *Thy sóv(e)rein témple wól I móst honóuren* Kn. T. 1549 ; *and év(e)ry trée* Sur. 9 ; *the bóist(e)rous wínds* Sur. 21 ; *if ám(o)rous fáith* Wyatt 15 ; *a dáng(e)rous cáse* Sur. 4, &c. The full pronunciation is, of course, here also possible : *and dángeróus distréss* Sur. 150. Slurring of a vowel is also caused by this combination of sounds formed by two successive words : *a bétre envýned mán* Chauc. Prol. 342 ; *Forgétter of páin* Wyatt 33. Other words of the same kind are *adder, after, anger, beggar, chamber, silver, water*, &c.[1] The same rule applies to the group *e+l*+vowel or *h* (also *l+e+* vowel or *h*): *hire wýmpel ipynched was* Chauc. Prol. 151 ; *At*

---

[1] Cf. Ellis, *E. E. Pr.*, i. 367–8.

mány a nóble arríve ib. 60; *nóble and hígh* Wyatt 55; *the néedle his fínger prícks* Shak. Lucrece 319.

If a consonant takes the place of the vowel or *h* at the end of such a group of sounds, we have a disyllabic thesis instead of slurring: *With hórrible féar as óne that gréatly dréadeth* Wyatt 149; *The cómmon péople by númbers swárm to ús* Shak. 3 Hen. VI, IV. ii. 2. Similar slurrings are to be found—although more seldom and mainly in Modern English poetry—with other groups of sounds, e. g.: *én'mies swórd* Sur. 137; *threat'ner* ib. 162; *prís'ners* ib. 12. The vowel *i*, also, is sometimes slurred; *Incónt(i)nent* Wyatt, 110; *dést(i)ny* ib. 8, &c. In all these cases we must of course recognize only slurring, not syncopation of the vowel; and in general these words are used with their full syllabic value in the rhythm of a verse.

Another kind of slurring—occurring almost exclusively in Modern English poetry—is effected by contraction of a short vowel with a preceding long one, so that a disyllabic word becomes monosyllabic, e. g., *flower, lower, power, tower, coward, prayer, jewel, cruel, doing, going, being, seeing, dying, playing, praying, knowing*, &c.: *Whose pówer divíne* Sur. 118; *prayer: payr* Wyatt 26; *His crúel despíte* Sur. 7.

All these words are, of course, not less frequently used as disyllables sometimes even when their usual pronunciation is monosyllabic, e. g.:

> *How óft have Í, my déar and crúël fóe.*   Wyatt 14.

> *I'll práy a thóusand práyërs fór thy death.*
>
>   Shak. Meas. III. i. 146.

> *There ís no pówèr ín the tóngue of mán.*   id. Merch. IV. i. 241.

§ 111. Other groups of sounds which allow slurring are: vowel + *r* + vowel, where the second vowel may be slurred, e. g., *spirit, alarum, warrant, nourish, flourish*, &c.; *My fáther's spírit in árms!* Shak. Haml. I. ii. 255; *flóurishing péopled tówns* id. Gentl. v. iv. 3; *I wárrant, it wíll* id. Haml. I. ii. 243. In the group vowel + *v* + *e(i)* + cons. the *v* is slurred, if a consonant appears as the initial sound of the following word, and *e(i)* if the following word begins with a vowel. Such words are: *heaven, seven, eleven, devil, even, ever, never*, &c.; e. g., *and é'en the whóle* Wyatt 80; *had néver his fíll* id. 108; *disdáin they né'er so múch* Shak. I Hen. VI, v. iii. 98; *and drível on péarls* Wyatt 195. These words have, of course, not less frequently their full syllabic value: *Of Héaven gátes* Wyatt 222 ; *Then sét this drível óut of dóor* Sur. 79. Also *th* between vowels may be subjected to slurring, as in *whether, whither, hither, thither, either, neither, rather, further*, &c.; e. g., *go ásk him whíther he góes* Shak. 1 Hen. VI, 11. iii. 28 ; *Good Sír, say whéther you'll ánswer mé or nót*, id. Caes. v. iv. 30 ; *Whether óught to ús unknówn* id. Haml. 11. ii. 17.

When a syllabic inflexional ending forms one thesis with a following syllable, as in *The ímages of revólt* Shak. Lear, 11. iv. 91 ; *I hád not quóted him* id. Haml. 11. i. 112, &c., it is preferable to assume a disyllabic thesis rather than a slurring. Sometimes, however, the *-ed* of past participles (rarely of preterites) of verbs ending in *t* is actually cut off, as *torment* instead of *tormented* Wyatt 137 ; *deject* instead of *dejected* Shak. Haml. 111. i. 163.

Contractions of another kind—partly to be explained by negligent colloquial pronunciation—are: *ta'en* (=*taken*) Wyatt 182; *I'll* (=*I will*) Shak. Tempest, 11. ii. 419 ; *carry 'em* (=*carry them* id. 2 Hen. VI, 1. iv. 76, &c.; *Ma(d)am* id. Gent. 11. i. 6 ; *in's* (=*in his*), *doff* (=*do off*), *dout* (=*do out*), *o' the* (=*of the*), *w' us* (=*with us*), *let's* (=*let us*), *thou'rt* (=*thou art*), &c., &c.

Finally, we have to mention the apocopation, for metrical reasons, of unaccented prefixes, as *'bove* (*above*), *'cause* (*because*), *'longs* (*belongs*), &c., which on the whole cannot easily be misunderstood.[1]

§ 112. A contrast to these various forms of shortening is presented by the **lengthening** of words for metrical purposes, which we have already in part discussed in the preceding chapter (see for examples § 87). Disyllabic words are made trisyllabic by inserting an *e* (or rarely *i*) between mute and liquid, e. g., *wond(e)rous, pilg(e)rim, count(e)ry, breth(e)ren, ent(e)rance, child(e)ren, Eng(e)land, troub(e)lous, light(e)ning, short(e)ly, jugg(e)ler*, &c.[2]

Among the monosyllabic words or accented endings of words which admit of a disyllabic pronunciation for the sake of metre we have mainly to consider such as have a diphthong in their root, as *our, sour, devour, hour, desire, fire, ire, sire, hire, squire, inquire*, &c., or such as approach diphthongal pronunciation and therefore admit of being treated as disyllables, e. g., *dear, fear, hear, near, tear, clear, year*. The disyllabic use of words of the

---

[1] A long list of the words so treated is to be found in Abbott, *Shakespearian Grammar*, § 460.

[2] Cf. Abbott, § 477; Ellis, *E. E. Pr.*, iii. 951-2 ; *Metrik*, ii. 117-18.

latter class is very rare, though a striking example is afforded by the rhyme *see her : clear* Mrs. Browning, iii, p. 57. Some other words, phonetically analogous to these, but popularly apprehended as containing a simple long vowel, as *fair, fare, are, here, there, rare, sphere, were, more, door, your,* are added to the list by Abbott, but with doubtful correctness (cf. *Metrik,* ii. 115–17).

CHAPTER VIII

WORD-ACCENT

§ 113. In discussing the English Word-accent and its relationship to rhythmic accent it is necessary to consider the Middle English and the Modern English periods separately, for two reasons. First, because the inflexional endings which play an important part in Middle English are almost entirely lost in Modern English, and secondly, because the word-accent of the Romanic element of the language differs considerably in the Middle English period from what it became in Modern English. In the treatment of each period it will be convenient to separate Germanic from Romanic words.

I. Word-accent in Middle English.

A. Germanic words. The general laws of Germanic accentuation of words, as existing in Old English, have been mentioned above (cf. §§ 18, 19). The same laws are binding also for Middle English and Modern English.

The main law for all accentual versification is this, that verse-accent must always coincide with word-accent. This holds good for all even-beat kinds of verse, as well as for the alliterative line.

The language in all works of the same date and dialect, in whatever kinds of verse they may be written, must obey the same laws of accentuation. For this reason the results derived from the relation in which the word-accent and the metrical value of syllables stand to the verse-accent, with regard to the general laws of accentuation, and especially those of inflexional syllables, must be the same for the language of all even-beat kinds of verse as for that of the contemporary alliterative line, or the verse of Layamon's *Brut* and other works written in a similar form of verse and derived from the ancient native metre.

Now, when we wish to ascertain the state of accentuation of forms of words no longer spoken the evidence supplied by the even-beat rhythms is especially valuable. This is so, chiefly because it is much more difficult to make the word-accent agree with the verse-accent in this kind of rhythm, in which it is essential that accented and unaccented syllables should alternate continuously, than in the alliterative line, which allows greater freedom both in the relative position of accented and unaccented syllables and in the numerical proportion between the unaccented and the accented syllables.

In the alliterative line the position of the rhythmic accent depends on the accent of the words which make up the verse. In the even-beat metres on the other hand the regular succession of thesis and arsis is the ruling principle of the versification, on which the rhythmic accent depends, and it is the poet's task to choose his words according to that requirement. The difficulties to be surmounted in order to bring the word-accent into conformity with the verse-accent will frequently drive the poet using this kind of rhythm to do violence to the accented and, more frequently still, to the unaccented syllables of the word. He will be induced either to contract the unaccented syllables with the accented ones, or to elide the former altogether, or to leave it to the reader to make the word-accent agree with the verse-accent by making use of level stress, or by slurring over syllables, or by admitting disyllabic or even polysyllabic theses in a verse. On the other hand, the poet who writes in the native alliterative long line or in any of its descendants is allowed as a rule to use the words required for his verse in their usual accentuation or syllabic value, or at least in a way approximating very closely to their ordinary treatment in prose. Hence those unaccented syllables which, in even-beat rhythms, are found to be subjected to the same treatment (i. e. to be equally liable to slurring, elision, syncopation, or apocopation, according to the requirements of the verse) must be presumed to have been at least approximately equal in degree of accentual force.

Now when we examine the relation between word-accent and verse-accent in certain poetical works of the first half of the thirteenth century, viz. the *Ormulum* (which on account of its regularity of rhythm is our best guide), the *Pater Noster*, the *Moral Ode*, the *Passion*, and other poems, we arrive at the following results :—

§ 114. The difference in degree of stress among inflexional endings containing an *e* (sometimes *i* or another vowel) which is alleged by some scholars—viz. that such endings (in disyllabic words) have secondary stress when the root-syllable is long, and are wholly unaccented when it is short—has no existence : in both cases the endings are to be regarded as alike unaccented. For we find that in even-beat measures

(especially in the *Ormulum*) these endings, whether attached to
a long or to a short root-syllable, are treated precisely alike in
the following important respects :—

1. Those inflexional endings which normally occur in the
thesis, and which are naturally suited for that position, are
found in the arsis only in an extremely small number of instances, which must undoubtedly be imputed to lack of skill on
the part of the poet, as e. g. in *hallʒhe'* Orm. 70, *nemmnéd* ib. 75,
whereas this is very frequent in those disyllabic compounds, the
second part of which really has a secondary accent, as e. g.
larspéll ib. 51, *mannkínn* ib. 277.

2. It is no less remarkable, however, that such syllables as
those last mentioned, which undoubtedly bear a secondary
accent, are never used by Orm to form the catalectic end of the
septenary verse, evidently because they would in consequence
of their specially strong accent annul or at least injure the
regular unaccented feminine verse-ending.   On the other
hand, inflexional endings and unaccented terminations containing an *e* are generally used for that purpose, as on account
of their lightness of sound they do not endanger in any way
the feminine ending of the catalectic section of the verse.   In
any case, inflexional syllables following upon long root-syllables
cannot have the same degree of stress, and cannot be used for
the same rhythmic functions, as the end-syllables of disyllabic
compounds, which undoubtedly bear a secondary accent.

The *regular* rhythmic employment of the two last-mentioned
groups of syllables proves their characteristic difference of stress
—the former being wholly unaccented, the latter bearing a
secondary accent.   Further inquiry into the *irregular* rhythmic
employment of the two similar classes of inflexional endings,
those following upon long root-syllables, and those following
upon short ones, tends to prove no less precisely that they do
not differ in degree of stress, and so that they are both unaccented.   For it is easy to show that with regard to syncope, apocope, elision, and slurring they are treated quite in the same way.

Elision of the final *-e* before a vowel or an *h* takes place
quite in the same way in those inflexional syllables following
upon long root-syllables as it does in those less numerous
syllables which follow upon short ones, e. g. *Annd ʒéit ter
tákenn marę inóh* Orm. 37 ; *Wiþþ állę swillc rímę alls hér iss
séit* ib. 101 ; *For áll þat æfrę onn érþę is néd* ib. 121 ; *a wíntrę
and éc a lóre* Moral Ode 1 ; *Wel lóngę ic hábbe child ibíen* ib. 3 ;
Icc háfę itt dón forrþí þatt áll Orm. 115, &c.   It is the same

with apocopation : *Forr gluternésse wácneþþ áll Galnésses láþe strénnche, Annd állę þe flǽshess kággerlé33c Annd álle fúle lússtess* Orm. 11653–6 ; cf. also : *þatt hé wass hófenn úpp to kíng* ib. 8450, and *wass hófenn úpp to kínge* ib. 8370 ; *o fáderr hállf* ib. 2269, and *o fáderr hállfe* 2028, &c.; similarly with syncopation, cf. *3iff þú se33st tátt* ib. 5188, and *annd sé33est swíllc* ib. 1512 ; *þet scúlen bén to déaþe idémd* Moral Ode 106 ; *for bétere is án elmésse bifóren* ib. 26, &c.; and again with the slurring of syllables following upon long as well as upon short root-syllables, as the following examples occurring in the first acatalectic sections of septenary verse will show sufficiently : *Ál þet bétste þét we héfden* Moral Ode 51 ; *Gódes wísdom ís wel míchel* ib. 213, &c.

Now as a syllable bearing a secondary accent cannot become mute, as an unaccented syllable does, if required, it is evident that those inflexional syllables which follow upon long root-syllables and frequently do become silent cannot bear that secondary accent which has been ascribed to them by several scholars ; on the contrary, all syllables subject in the same way to elision, apocope, syncope, and slurring must have the same degree of stress (i. e. they must be alike unaccented) whether preceded by short or by long root-syllables.

Other terminations of disyllabic words which, though not inflexional, consist, like the inflexional endings, of *e* + consonant, are treated in the same way, e. g. words like *fader, moder, finger, heven, sadel, giver*, &c. Only those inflexional and derivational endings which are of a somewhat fuller sound, as e. g., -*ing*, -*ling*, -*ung*, -*and*, -*ish*, and now and then even the comparative and superlative endings -*er*, -*est*, and the suffixes -*lic*, -*lich*, -*ly*, -*y*, may be looked upon as bearing a secondary accent, as they may be used at will either in the arsis of the verse or lowered to the state of unaccented syllables as the thesis.

§ 115. In a trisyllabic simple word the root-syllable, of course, has the primary accent, and of the two following syllables, that which has the fuller sound, has the secondary accent, as in *áskedèst, wrítìnge, dággère, clénnèsse, hìèste.* If, however, the two last syllables are equally destitute of word-accent, as e. g. in *clepede, lufede,* they are both metrically unaccented ; and, as mentioned before (cf. § 96), may be shortened either to *lufde, clepte,* or to *lufed, cleped.* If they are used, however, as trisyllables in the iambic rhythm they naturally admit of the metrical accent on the last syllable.

It is the same with compounds of nouns or adjectives. The first syllable takes the chief accent, and of the two others that has the secondary accent which is the root-syllable of the second part of the compound, as in *fréendshìpe*, *shírrève*, but *wódecràft*, *bóldelỳ*.

In verbal compounds the primary accent, in conformity with the Old English usage, generally rests on the root-syllable of the verb, while the first and last syllable are mostly unaccented, as e. g. *alíhten*, *biséchen*, *forgíven*, *ibídden*, *ofpúnchen*. In denominatives, which in Old English have the primary accent on the first syllable, as e. g. *ándswarian*, both kinds of accentuation are allowed : *ánswere* and *answére*.

In disyllabic and trisyllabic compounds of nouns with certain prefixes, partly accented in Old English, as e. g. *al-*, *un-*, *for-*, *mis-*, *y-*, *a-*, *bi-*, the primary accent does not rest on these syllables, but on the second syllable, this being the root-syllable of the word, e. g. *almíhti*, *forgétful*, *unhéele*, *bihéeste* ; the first syllable in this case bears a secondary accent if it has a determinative signification, as e. g. *al-*, *mis-*, *un-*, but it is unaccented if it is indifferent to the meaning, as e. g. *a-*, *y-*, *bi-*.

§ 116. A peculiar rhythmical position is held by those words which we may call parathetic compounds.[1] To these belong certain compound nouns formed by two words of almost the same weight from a syntactical and metrical point of view, as e. g. *goodman*, *goodwyf*, *longswerd*, and also by similar composite particles, as e. g. *elleswhere*, *also*, *into*, *unto*. Although the regular colloquial pronunciation was probably in the Middle English period, as it is in Modern English, with the accent on the first syllable, they may be pronounced with the accent on the second syllable, or at least with level stress, as e. g. *goodmán*, *alsó*, *intó*, &c. To this class also belong certain compounds of adverbs with prepositions, as e. g. *herein*, *therefore*, *thereof*, the only difference being that the usual accent rests here on the last syllable, but may be placed also on the first, as in *heréin* and *hérein*, *theréof* and *théreof*, &c.

§ 117. These gradations of sound in the different words regulate their rhythmical treatment in the verse. In disyllabic words as a rule the syllable with the primary accent is placed in the arsis of the verse, the other syllable, whether it be an unaccented one, or have a secondary accent, is placed in the thesis. Such words as those described in the preceding section may much

---

[1] See ten Brink, *The Language and Metre of Chaucer* (English transl.), § 280, where the metrical treatment of these words is described. The German term used by ten Brink is *Anlehnungen*.

more easily be used with level stress than others. In that case
the rhythmical accent rests on the syllable which has the
secondary accent, while the syllable which in ordinary speech
has the chief accent is used as a thesis.

The ordinary as well as the abnormal use of one and the
same word will be illustrated by the following example:—

O mánnkinn swá þatt ítt mannkínn. Orm. 277.

With regard to the rhythmical treatment of trisyllables two
classes of such words are to be distinguished, namely, (1) those
in which the syllable bearing the primary accent is followed or
(rarely) preceded by a syllable bearing a secondary accent, as
e. g. *gódspèlles, énglìshe,* and (2) those in which the syllable
bearing the primary accent is preceded or followed by a syllable
wholly unaccented, as e. g. *bigínnen, òvercóme, crístendòm,
wéathercòck.* In the latter case level stress is hardly ever met
with, as the natural word-accent would be interfered with to an
intolerable extent by accentuations like *cristéndom, weathércock,
overcome, biginnén, forgottén, behavióur,* &c.

Words like these therefore can in regular iambic or trochaic
verse be used only with their natural accentuation, and hence
those syllables which either have the primary or the secondary
accent are always placed in the arsis, and the unaccented ones
in the thesis, e. g.: *To wínnenn únnder Crísstenndóm* Orm. Ded.
137; *off þátt ítt wáss bigúnnenn* ib. 88; *Though the séas thréaten,
théy are mércifúl* Shakesp. Temp. v. 178; *Ónly compóund me wíth
forgótten dúst* id. 2 Hen. IV, IV. v. 116, &c. On the other hand,
when primary and secondary accent occur in two adjacent
syllables level stress is very common, in Middle English,
especially between the first and the second syllable, as *godspélles
hállʒhe láre* Orm. 14, more rarely between the second and the
third syllable, as *þa Góddspelléss neh álle* ib. 30; it also occurs
in Chaucer's poems, as *For thóusandés his hóndes máden dýe*
Troil. v. 1816; in the same way Modern English words are
treated to fit the rhythm, as e. g. *mídsùmmer, fáinthèárted,* in
Farewéll, fáint-héarted ánd degénerate kíng Shak. 3 Hen. VI.
I. i. 138; *And górgeous ás the sún at mídsummér* 1 Hen. IV,
IV. i. 102. With the more recent poets this latter kind of
rhythmical accentuation becomes the more usual of the two,
although the nature and the meaning of the compound word
always play an important part in such cases.

With regard to their accentuation and metrical employment
words of four syllables also fall into three classes: 1. Inflected

forms of words belonging to the first group of trisyllables, like *crístendómes*, which can be used in the rhythm of the verse only with their natural accentuation; 2. words like *fordémde* (first and last syllable unaccented, the second syllable having the chief accent) with a determinative prefix, as e. g. *únfordémde*; these likewise are used in the rhythm of the verse according to their natural accentuation; 3. words of the third group with a prefix which either has the secondary accent, or is unaccented, as *únwíslìce* or *iwítnèsse*; the metrical usage of these is regulated according to the rules for the trisyllabic words. The same is to be observed with regard to words of five and six syllables like * únderstándìnge*, *únimételiche*, which, however, are only of rare occurrence.

§ **118. B. Romanic words.** It was not till the thirteenth and fourteenth centuries that Romanic words passed in considerable numbers into the English language; and they were then accommodated to the general laws of accentuation of English. The transition, however, from Romanic to Germanic accentuation certainly did not take place at once, but gradually, and earlier in some districts and in some classes of society than in others; in educated circles undoubtedly later than amongst the common people. The accentuation of the newly introduced Romanic words thus being in a vacillating state, we easily see how the poets writing at that period in foreign even-beat rhythms, of whom Chaucer may serve as a representative, could use those words with whichever accentuation best suited their need at the moment, admitting the Romanic accentuation chiefly in rhymes, where it afforded them great facilities, and the usual Germanic accentuation mostly in the interior of the line. A few examples will suffice to illustrate this well-known fact. We arrange them in five classes according to the number of syllables in the words; the principles of metrical accentuation not being precisely identical in the several classes.

Disyllabic words. I. Words whose final syllable is accented in French. They are used in even-beat rhythms (1) with the original accentuation, e. g. *prisóun : raunsóun* Kn. T. 317–18; *pítouslý : mercý* ib. 91–2; *pitóus : móus* Prol. 143–4; (2) with the accent on the first syllable according to the accentuation which had already become prevalent in ordinary English speech, e. g. *This prísoun cáusede me* Kn. T. 237; *With hérte pítous* ib. 95; *But wé beséken mércy ánd socóur* ib. 60.

II. Words having in French the accent on the first syllable, the last syllable being unaccented. These words, partly substantives or adjectives, as *people, nombre, propre*, partly verbs, as *praye, suffre, crie* (in which case the accentuation of the sing. of the present tense prevails), are always used in verse with the original accentuation, the second unaccented syllable either (1) forming a full thesis of the verse, as in *the péple préseth thíderward* Kn. T. 1672; *bý his própre gód* Prol. 581, or (2) being elided or slurred and forming only part of the thesis, as in *the nómbre and éek the cáuse* ib. 716; *and crýe as hé were wóod* ib. 636.

As a rule also the original and usual accent is retained by disyllabic words containing an unaccented prefix, as in *accord, abet, desyr, defence,* &c. Only words composed with the prefix *dis-* occur with either accentuation, as *díscreet* and *discréet*.

§ 119. **Trisyllabic words.** I. Words, the last syllable of which in French has the chief accent, the first having a second-ary accent. In these words the two accents are transposed in English, so that the first syllable bears the chief accent, the last the secondary accent, and both of them as a rule receive the rhythmical accent: *émperóur, árgumént*. But if two syllables of such a word form a disyllabic thesis, generally the last syllable which has the secondary accent is lowered to the unaccented grade: *árgument, émperour*.

II. Words which in French have the chief accent on the middle syllable, the last being unaccented. These are some-times used with the original accentuation, mostly as feminine rhymes, e. g.: *viságe : uságe* Prol. 109–10; *chére : manére* ib. 139–40; *penánce : pitánce* ib. 233–4; *poráille : vitáille* ib. 247–8; *prudénce : senténce* ib. 305–6; *office : áccomplíce* Kn. T. 2005–6, &c.; more rarely in the interior of the verse, where the last syllable may either form a thesis as in *Ál your plesánce férme and stáble I hólde* Cl. T. 663, or part of it, being elided or slurred, as in *The sáme lúst was híre plesánce alsó* ib. 717. In other instances, mostly in the interior of the verse, they have the accent on the first syllable, the last being always elided or slurred: *And sáugh his vísage was in anóther kýnde* Kn. T. 543; *He fél in óffice wíth a chámberléyn* ib. 561.

Verbs ending in *-ice (-isse), -ishe, -ie*, as e. g. *chérisse, púnishe, stúdie, cárrie, tárrie*, nearly always have the accent on the first syllable, the last syllable being elided or apocopated, except where it is strengthened by a final consonant, as e. g. *chérishĕd, tárriĕd*. If the first syllable of a trisyllabic word be formed by an unaccented particle, the root-syllable of the word, in this

case the middle one, likewise retains the accent, as e. g. in
despíse, remaíne.

§ 120. **Four-syllable words** of French origin when they
are substantives or adjectives frequently have disyllabic or trisyllabic suffixes such as : *-age, -iage, -ian, -iant, -aunce, -iance,
-iaunce, -ence, -ience, -ient, -ier, -ioun, -ious, -eous, -uous, -ial, -ual,
-iat, -iour, -ure, -ie (-ye)*. As most of these words already have
a trochaic or iambic rhythm, they are used without difficulty in
even-beat disyllabic verses, chiefly in rhymes, and then always
with their full syllabic value, as e. g.: *pílgrimáge : coráge* Prol.
11–12 ; *hóstelrýe : cómpanýe* ib. 23–4; *resóun : condícióun* ib. 37–8;
chývalrýe : cúrtesýe ib. 45–6 ; *chívachíe : Pícardíe* ib. 185–6 ;
cónsciénce : réverénce ib. 141–2 ; *tóun : conféssióun* ib. 217–18 ;
curát : licénciát 219–20 ; *góvernáunce : chévysáunce* ib. 291–2, &c.
In the interior of a verse also the words not ending in an unaccented *e* are always metrically treated according to their full
syllabic value, e. g.: *That héeld opínyóun that pléyn delýt* Prol.
337 ; *Of hís compléxióun he wás sangwýn* ib. 333. In those
words, on the other hand, which end in an unaccented *e*, this
vowel is in the interior of the verse generally elided or apocopated : *no vílanýe is ít* ib. 740 ; *in that óstelríe alíght* ib. 720 ;
So móche of dáliáunce and fáir langáge ib. 211 ; *And ál was
cónsciénce and téndre hérte* ib. 150.

Further shortenings, however, which transform an originally
four-syllable word into a disyllabic one, as in the present pronunciation of the word *conscience,* do not take place in Middle
English before the transition to the Modern English period.
In Lyndesay's *Monarchie* we meet with accentuations of this
kind, as e. g. :

> *The quhílk gaif sápience tó king Sálomóne.*   249.
> *Be tháy contént, mak réverence tó the rést.*   36.

In a similar way adjectives ending in *-able* and verbs ending in
-ice, -ye adapt themselves to the disyllabic rhythm, and likewise
verbs ending in *-ine* (Old French *-iner*); only it must be noticed
that in the preterite and in the past participle verbs of the
latter class tend to throw the accents on the antepenultimate and
last syllables, e. g. *enlúminéd, emprísonéd.*

Words of five syllables almost without exception have
an iambic rhythm of themselves and are used accordingly in
even-beat verses, as e. g. *expériénce*; the same is the case with
words which have Germanic endings, like *-ing, -inge, -nesse,*
e. g. *discónfytýnge.*

The rhythmic accentuation of foreign proper names both in disyllables and in polysyllables varies. Thus we may notice the accentuations *Junó*, *Plató*, *Venús*, and, on the other hand, *Júno*, *Pláto*, *Vénus*; *Arcíte*, *Athénes*, and *Árcíte*, *Áthenes*; *Antónie* and *Antoníe*. Wherever in such cases level stress may help to smooth the rhythm it certainly is to be assumed in reading.

II. Word-accent in Modern English.

§ 121. Modern English accentuation deviates little from that of the Old English and Middle English; the inflexional endings, however, play a much less important part; further, in many cases the Romanic accentuation of Middle English is still in existence, or at least has influence, in words of French or Latin origin. This is evident from many deviations in the rhythmic accentuation of such words from the modern accentuation which we here regard as normal, though it is to be noted that in the beginning of the Modern English epoch, i. e. in the sixteenth century, the actual accentuation in many cases was still in conformity with the earlier conditions.

Only these real and apparent anomalies are noticed here. We have first to consider the **Romanic endings** -*ace*, -*age*, -*ail*, -*el*, -*ain*, -*al*, -*ance*, -*ence*, -*ant*, -*ent*, -*er*, -*ess* (Old French -*esse*), -*ice*, -*ile*, -*in*, -*on*, -*or*, -*our*, -*une*, -*ure*, -*y*(*e*) (in disyllabic words). As the final *e* has become mute, all these endings are monosyllabic.

In the works of the earlier Modern English poets some words ending in these syllables are only exceptionally used with the accent on the last syllable according to the Old French or Middle English accentuation, the Modern English accentuation being the usual one; others are employed more frequently or even exclusively with the earlier accentuation, e. g. *paláce* Sur. 174, *bondáge* Wyatt 224, *travául* Sur. 82, Wyatt 19, *certáin* ib. 179, *mountáin* Sur. 37, *chieftáin* ib. 112, *cristál* Wyatt 156, *presénce* ib. 81, *grievánce* ib. 55, *penánce* ib. 209, *balánce* ib. 173, *pleasánt* ib. 130, *tormént* (subst.) ib. 72, *fevér*, *fervóur* ib. 210, *mistréss* ib. 109, *richés* ib. 209, *justíce* ib. 229, *servíce* ib. 177, *engíne* Sur. 130, *seasón* ib. 149, *honóur* ib. 166, *armóur* 148, *colóur : therefóre* Wyatt 6, *terrór : succóur* ib. 210, &c., *fortúne : tune* ib. 152, Sur. 115, *measúre* Wyatt 125, *natúre : unsúre* ib. 144, *glorý : mercý* ib. 208.

In almost all these cases and in many other words with the same endings this accentuation seems to be due to the requirements of the rhythm, in which case level stress must be assumed.

§ 122. It is the same with many other disyllabic words, especially those both syllables of which are almost of equal sound-value and degree of stress, as in cases in which two different meanings of one and the same word are indicated by different accentuation, a distinction not unfrequently neglected in the metrical treatment of these words.

So the following adjectives and participles are used by Shakespeare and other poets with variable accentuation: *complete, adverse, benign, contrived, corrupt, despised, dispersed, distinct, distract, diverse, eterne, exact, exhaled, exiled, expired, express, extreme, famous, insane, invised, misplaced, misprised, obscure, perfect, profane, profound, remiss, secure, severe, sincere, supreme, terrene*; and so are also the many adjectives and participles compounded with the prefix *un-*, as e. g. *unborn, unchaste, unkind*, &c. (cf. Alexander Schmidt, *Shakespeare-Lexicon*).

Substantives and verbs are treated in a similar way, e. g. *comfórt* (subst.) Wyatt 14, *recórd* ib. 156, *discórd* Sur. 6, *conflíct* ib. 85, *purcháse* ib. 58, *mischíef* Wyatt 78, *safeguárd* ib. 212, *Madáme* ib. 149, *proméss* ib. 25. So also in Shakespeare (cf. Alexander Schmidt, l. c.): *áccess, aspéct, commérce, consórt, contráct, compáct, edíct, instínct, outráge, precépts, cément, cónduct* (vb.), *cónfine, púrsue, rélapse* (cf. *Metrik*, ii. § 62).

§ 123. Trisyllabic and polysyllabic words, too, of French or Latin origin are still used frequently in the beginning of the Modern English period with an accentuation contrary to present usage. Words e. g. which now have the chief accent on the second syllable, the first and third syllable being unaccented, are often used with the rhythmical accents on these two syllables, e. g.: *cónfessór* Meas. IV. iii. 133, *cóntínue* Wyatt 189; *départúre* ib. 129; *répentánce* ib. 205, *éndeavóur* ib. 232; *détestáble* John III. iv. 29, *rhéumatíc* Ven. 135, &c. Likewise in words the first and third syllables of which are now accented and the second unaccented, the rhythmical accent is placed on this very syllable, e. g. *charácter* Lucr. 807, *confíscate* Cymb. v. v. 323, *contráry* Wyatt 8, *impórtune* Ant. IV. xv. 19, *oppórtune* Temp. IV. i. 26, *perséver* All's Well IV. ii. 37, *prescíence* Troil. I. iii. 199, *siníster* Troil. IV. v. 128. Certain verbs also in *-ise, -ize* are used with fluctuating accentuation; Shakespeare e. g. always has *advértise* Meas. i. 142, *authórise* Sonn. 35, *canónize* Troil. II. ii. 202; sometimes also *solémnize* Temp. v. 309 (cf. *Metrik*, ii. §§ 64, 65).

Foreign proper names especially in many cases are subject, as in earlier times, to variable accentuation, as e. g.: *Ajáx* Sur.

129, *Cæsár* Wyatt 191, *Cató* ib. 191, the more usual accentuation also occurring in the writings of the same poets; similarly *Átrídés* Sur. 129 and *Atríde* ib. 116, *Cárthages* ib. 149 and *Carthágé* 175. Shakespeare has always the unclassical *Andrónicus, Hypérion, Cleopátra*, but for rhythmical reasons *Nórthamptón* Rich. III, II. iv. 1 instead of *Northámpton*, and so in several other cases (cf. *Metrik*, ii. § 67).

§ **124.** Amongst the **Germanic vocables** the parathetic compounds chiefly call for notice, as their accentuation in common speech also approaches level stress, and for this reason they may be used with either accentuation. This group includes compounds like *moonlight, welfare, farewell*, and some conjunctions, prepositions, and pronouns, as *therefore, wherefore, something, nothing, sometimes, into, unto, towards, without*, as e. g. : *thérefore* Wyatt 24, &c., *theréfóre* ib. 42, *nóthing* Rich. II, II. ii. 12, *nothíng* Rich. III, I. i. 236, *únto* Sur. 125, *untó* Sur. 117 (cf. *Metrik*, ii. § 58).

Greater arbitrariness in the treatment of word-accent, explained best by the influence of Middle English usage, is shown in the rhythmical accentuation of the final syllable *-ing* in words like *endíng : thing* Wyatt 27 ; and of the suffixes *-ness, -ly, -y, -ow*, e. g. *goodnéss : excéss* Wyatt 206, *free : trulý* 147 ; *borrów : sorrów : overthrów* ib. 227. Less admissible still are such accentuations with the endings *-er, -est*, used on the whole only by the earlier Modern English poets, e. g. *earnést* Wyatt 11, *aftér* ib. 207, and least of all with inflexional endings, e. g. *scornéd* Sur. 170, *causéth* Wyatt 33 (cf. *Metrik*, ii. §§ 59–61).

As a rule, however, such unnatural accentuations can be avoided by assuming the omission of a thesis at the beginning or in the interior of a line. With regard to trisyllabic and polysyllabic words the remarks on pp. 176–7 are to be compared.

DIVISION II

Verse-forms common to the Middle and Modern English Periods

CHAPTER IX

LINES OF EIGHT FEET, FOUR FEET, TWO FEET, AND ONE FOOT

§ 125. Among the metres introduced into Middle English poetry in imitation of foreign models, perhaps the oldest is the four-foot verse, rhyming in couplets. This metre may be regarded as having originally arisen by halving the eight-foot line, although only an isolated example of this, dating from about the middle of the thirteenth century, quoted above (p. 127), is known in Middle English poetry. This, however, serves with special clearness to illustrate the resolution, by means of inserted rhyme, of the eight-foot long-line couplet into four-foot lines rhyming alternately (cf. § 78).

In the manuscript the verses, though rhyming in long lines, are written as short lines, with intermittent rhyme *a b c b d b e b*, just as the example of Modern English eight-foot iambic verse, quoted before (p. 127), is found printed with this arrangement, as is indeed generally the case with most long-line forms of that type. This metre calls for no other remarks on its rhythmical structure than will have to be made with regard to the four-foot verse.

§ 126. The four-foot line, rhyming in couplets, first appears in a paraphrase of the *Pater Noster* of the end of the twelfth century,[1] doubtless in imitation of the Old French *vers octosyllabe* made known in England by Anglo-Norman poets, such as Gaimar, Wace, Benoit, &c.

This French metre consists of eight syllables when the ending is monosyllabic, and nine when it is disyllabic.

---

[1] *Old English Homilies*, ed. R. Morris, First Series, Part I, E. E. T. S., No. 29, pp. 55-71.

The lines are always connected in couplets by rhyme, but masculine and feminine rhymes need not alternate with one another.

It is exactly the same with the Middle English four-foot line, except that the rising iambic rhythm comes out more clearly in it, and that, instead of the Romanic principle of counting the syllables, that of the equality of beats is perceptible, so that the equality of the number of syllables in the verses is not so strictly observed. Hence, all the deviations before mentioned from the strict formal structure of even-beat verses occur even in this early poem, and quite regularly constructed couplets are indeed but rare in it. Examples of this type are the following:

> *Ah, láverd gód, her úre béne,*
> *Of úre súnne máke us cléne,*
> *Þet hé us ȝéue alswá he méi,*
> *Þet ús bihóueð úlche déi.* ll. 167–170.

The first ten lines of the poem give a sufficient idea of the structure of the verse, and its characteristics:

> *Ure féder þét in héouene ís,*
> *Þet ís all sóþ fúl iwís !*
> *Weo móten tó þeos wéordes iséon,*
> *Þet to líue and to sáule góde béon,*
> *Þet wéo beon swá his súnes ibórene,*
> *Þet hé beo féder and wé him icórene,*
> *Þet wé don álle hís ibéden*
> *Ánd his wílle fór to réden.*
> *Lóke weo ús wíð hím misdón*
> *Þurh béelzebúbes swíkedóm.*

Here we find almost all the rhythmical licences to be found in even-beat metres. Thus we have suppression of the anacrusis in line 8 and again in two consecutive lines, such as 15, 16:

> *Gíf we léornið gódes láre,*
> *Þénne of-þúnceð hít him sáre ;*

and very often in the course of the poem, e. g. ll. 22, 29, 30, 37, &c., so that it acquires a loose, iambic-trochaic cadence; further, the absence of an unaccented syllable in the middle of the line (line 2); inversion of accent in line 9, and again in line 81, *Láverd he ís of álle scáfte*; two unaccented syllables at the beginning and in the interior of the verse in 4; light slurrings ll. 1, 3, 5; only ll. 7 and 10 are regularly constructed throughout. The same proportion of regular to irregular verses runs through the whole poem, in which, besides the licences mentioned, that of level stress is also often to be met with, especially in rhymes like *wurþing : héovenkíng* 99–100 ; *hating : king* 193–4, 219–20 ; *fóndúnge : swinkúnge* 242–3.

§ 127. The treatment of the caesura in this metre also deserves special mention, for this, as has already been stated, is one of the chief points in which the four-foot even-beat metre differs from the four-stress metre, as represented either by the old alliterative long line or by the later non-alliterating line. For there must be a caesura in every four-beat verse, and it must always be found in one definite place, viz. after the second beat next to any unaccented syllable or syllables that follow the beat, the line being thus divided into two rhythmically fairly equal halves. On the other hand, for the four-foot verse, not only in this, its earliest appearance, but in the rest of Middle and Modern English literature, the caesura is not obligatory, and when it does occur it may, theoretically speaking, stand in any place in the line, although it most frequently appears after the second foot, particularly in the oldest period.

The caesura may (§ 80) be of three kinds :

(1) Monosyllabic or masculine caesura :

> *Ne képeð he nóht | þet wé beon súne.* 18.

(2) Disyllabic or feminine caesura, two kinds of which are to be distinguished, viz.

(*a*) Lyric caesura, within a foot :

> *And 3éfe us mihte | þúrh his héld.* 240.

(*b*) Epic caesura caused by a supernumerary unaccented syllable before the pause :

> *Ure gúltes, láverd, | bon ús for3éven.* 173.

These three kinds of caesura, the last of which, it is true, we meet here only sporadically, may thus in four-foot verse also occur *after*, as well as *in* the other feet. Thus we find in the very first line, a lyrical caesura after the first foot :

> *Ure féder | þét in héouene ís.*

This, however, seldom happens in the oldest examples, in which caesuras sharply dividing the line are rare, enjambement being only seldom admitted. Examples of verses without caesuras are to be found, among others, in the following : *púrh béelzebúbes swíkedóm* 10, *Intó þe pósternésse héllen* 104. As a rule, in the four-foot verse as well as in French octosyllabics, a pause does not occur until the end, on account of the shortness of this metre, which generally only suffices for one rhythmic section, while in four-beat verse a regular division into two rhythmic sections, and consequently the constant occurrence of a caesura, is rendered possible by the greater number of unaccented syllables.

The end of the line may, in any order, have either a masculine rhyme, as in ll. 1–4, 9, 10, or a feminine rhyme, as in ll. 7 and 8. There occur besides, but seldom, trisyllabic rhymes, such as those in ll. 5–6, or *súnegen : múnegen* 141–2.

§ **128.** This metre continued to be very popular in Middle and Modern English poetry, and is still extensively used. As a rule its structure constantly remained the same ; nevertheless we may, in both periods, distinguish between two well-marked ways of treating it. It was, for instance, at the end of the thirteenth and in the first half of the fourteenth century, very freely handled in the North of England in the *Surtees Psalter*, further by Robert Mannyng in his *Handlyng Sinne*, and by Richard Rolle de Hampole in his *Pricke of Conscience*. Their treatment of this verse is characterized, for instance, by the remarkably frequent occurrence of two and even three unaccented syllables at the beginning and in the middle of the line, e. g. :

> *In þi rightwísenésses biþénke I sál*
> *Þine sághes nóght forgéte withál.* Psalm cxviii, v. 16.

> *And rékened þe cústome hóuses echóne,*
> *At whých þey had góde and at whýche nóne.*
> Mannyng, Handlyng Sinne, ll. 5585–6.

Other rhythmical licences, such as the omission of unaccented syllables in the middle of a verse, and inversion of accent, are frequent in these compositions. Level stress, on the other hand, for the most part is found only in rhyme, as *shenshéþe : keþe* Hampole 380–1 ; *come : boghsóme* ib. 394–5.

The other extreme of strict regularity in the number of syllables is exhibited in another group of North English and Scottish compositions of the fourteenth century, such as the *Metrical Homilies*, the *Cursor Mundi*, Barbour's *Bruce*, Wyntoun's *Chronykyl*. The metrical licences most frequent here are level

stress, suppression of the anacrusis, and the omission of unaccented syllables in the middle of the line, in the *Metrical
Homilies*. The rhythm is, however, as a rule, strictly iambic,
and the number of syllables eight or nine, according as the
rhymes are masculine or feminine.

§ **129.** The contemporaneous literary productions of the Midlands and South written in this metre generally observe a mean
between the free and the strict versification of the two northern
groups.

These are inter alia *The Story of Genesis and Exodus, The
Owl and Nightingale, The Lay of Havelok, Sir Orfeo, King
Alisander*, several compositions of Chaucer's,[1] as, for instance,
The Book of the Duchesse, The House of Fame, Gower's *Confessio
Amantis*, and others. The last work, as well as *The Owl and
Nightingale*, is written in almost perfectly regular iambic verses,
in which the syllables are strictly counted. The other compositions more frequently admit the familiar rhythmical licences and
have a freer movement, but none to the same extent as the
Pater Noster. In artistic perfection this metre presents itself to
us in Chaucer, who was particularly skilful in employing and
varying the enjambement. A short specimen from his *House
of Fame* (ll. 151–74) will illustrate this :

> Fírst sawgh I thé destrúcción
> Of Tróy, thórgh the Gréke Synóun,
> Wíth his fálse fórswerýnge,
> And his chére and hís lesýnge
> Máde the hórs broght ínto Tróye,
> Thorgh which Tróyens lost ál her joýe.
> And áfter thís was gráve, allás,
> How Ílyóun assáyled wás
> And wónne, and kýnge Príam ysláyne
> And Políte his sóne, certáyne,
> Dispítouslý of dáun Pírrús,
> And néxt that sáwgh I hów Venús,
> Whan thát she sáwgh the cástel brénde,
> Dóune fro the hévene gán descénde,
> And bád hir sóne Enéas flée ;
> And hów he fléd, and hów that hé
> Escáped wás from ál the prés,
> And tóoke his fáder, Ánchisés,

[1] Cf. Charles L. Crow, *On the History of the Short Couplet in Middle
English*. Dissert., Göttingen, 1892.

> *And báre hym ón hys bákke awáy,*
> *Crýinge 'Allás and wélawáy !'*
> *The whíche Anchíses ín hys hónde*
> *Báre the góddes óf the lónde,*
> *Thílke thát unbrénde wére.*
> *And Í saugh néxt in ál hys fére,* &c.

§ **130.** Four-foot verses often occur also in Middle English in connexion with other metrical forms, especially with three-foot verses, e. g. in the Septenary, which is resolved by the rhyme into two short lines, and in the tail-rhyme stanza, or *rime couée* (cf. §§ 78, 79).

In these combinations the structure of the metre remains essentially the same, only there are in many poems more frequent instances of suppression of the anacrusis, so that the metre assumes a variable cadence, partly trochaic, partly iambic. At the end of the Middle English period the four-foot verse was, along with other metrical forms, employed by preference in the earlier dramatic productions, and was skilfully used by Heywood, among others, in his interlude, *The Four P.'s.*[1]

§ **131.** In the Modern English period this metre has also found great favour, and we may, as in the case of other metres, distinguish between a strict and a freer variety of it.   The strict form was, and is, mostly represented in lyric poetry, in verses rhyming in couplets or in cross rhyme.   The rhythm is generally in this case (since the separation between iambic and trochaic verse-forms became definitely established) strictly iambic, generally with monosyllabic rhymes.

A greater interest attaches to the freer variety of the metre, which is to be regarded as a direct continuation of the Middle English four-foot verse, inasmuch as it was practised by the poets of the first Modern English period in imitation of earlier models, and has been further cultivated by their successors down to the most recent times.   The characteristic feature in this treatment of the four-foot verse is the frequent suppression of the anacrusis, by which it comes to resemble the four-beat verse, along with which it is often used.   But whilst the latter generally has an iambic-anapaestic or trochaic-dactylic structure, and is constantly divided by the caesura into two halves, the Modern English four-foot verse of the freer type has, as a rule, an alternately iambic and trochaic rhythm, with a rare occurrence of caesuras.   Shakespeare. and other dramatists often employ this metre for lyrical passages in

---

[1] Cf. *John Heywood als Dramatiker*, von Wilh. Swoboda, 1888, p. 83 ff.

their dramas. Of longer poems in the earlier period Milton's
L'Allegro and *Il Penseroso* are conspicuous examples.

The following passage from *L'Allegro* (ll. 11–16) may serve
as a specimen:

> *But cóme thou Góddess fáir and frée,*
> *In héaven yclépt Euphrósyné,*
> *And by mén héart-easing Mírth,*
> *Whom lóvely Vénus, át a bírth,*
> *With two síster Gráces móre,*
> *To ívy-crównèd Bácchus bóre, &c.*

The structure of the verse is essentially iambic, though the
iambic metre frequently, by suppression of the initial theses, as
in the thirteenth and fifteenth lines of this passage, falls into
a trochaic cadence.   Pure trochaic verses, i. e. those that begin
with an accented syllable and end with an unaccented one,
occur in these two poems, in couplets, only once, *L'Allegro*
(ll. 69–70):

> *Stráight mine éye hath cáught new pléasures,*
> *Whíles the lándscape róund it méasures.*

With masculine endings such couplets are frequent, e. g.
Il Penseroso, 67–8:

> *Tó behóld the wándering móon,*
> *Ríding néar the híghest nóon;*

further, ll. 75–6, 81–2, 141–2, &c.

As a rule, pure iambic lines rhyme together, or an iambic
with a line that has a trochaic cadence, as, for instance, in the
above specimen, *L'Allegro*, 13–14 and 15–16.

Besides initial truncation there also occur here the other
metrical licences observed in iambic rhythm.

§ 132. Many sections of the narrative poems of Coleridge,
Scott, and Byron, e. g. the latter's *Siege of Corinth*, are written
in this form, with which, in especially animated passages, four-
beat verses often alternate. Cf., for instance, the following
passage, xvi, from the last-named poem:

> *Stíll by the shóre Alp mútely músed,*
> *And wóo'd the fréshness níght diffúsed.*
> *There shrínks no ébb in that tídeless séa,*
> *Which chángeless rólls etérnallý;*
> *So that wíldest of wáves, in their ángriest móod,*
> *Scarce bréak on the bóunds of the lánd for a róod;*

And the pówerless móon behólds them flów
Héedless if she cóme or gó :
Cálm or hígh, in máin or báy,
Ón their cóurse she háth no swáy.

Lines 5–7 can be at once recognized as four-stress verses by
the iambic-anapaestic rhythm, as well as by the strongly-marked
caesura, which, in the four-foot verses 4, and especially 8 and 10,
is entirely or almost entirely absent (cf. pp. 98–9); and both
metrical forms, the calmer four-foot verse and the more animated
four-stress metre, are in harmonious agreement with the tone of
this passage.

Four-foot lines, forming component parts of metrically heterogeneous types of stanzas, such, for instance, as the tail-rhyme
stave, are generally more regularly constructed than in the
Middle English period.

§ 133. Among the metrical forms which took their rise from
the four-foot line, the most noteworthy are the two-foot and the
one-foot verse, the former the result of halving the four-foot
verse, the latter of dividing the two-foot verse, as a rule, by
means of the rhyme. These verse-forms only seldom occur in
the Middle English period, as a rule in anisometrical stanzas in
connexion with verses of greater length. Thus, in the poem
in Wright's *Specimens of Lyric Poetry*, p. 38, composed in the
entwined tail-rhyme stanza, the short lines have two accents :
wipóute stríf : y wýte, a wýf 10–12 ; *in tóune tréwe : while ý
may gléwe* 4–6. The eighteen-lined enlarged tail-rhyme stave
of the ballad, *The Nut-brown Maid* (Percy's *Reliques*, iii. 6),
also consists of two- and three-foot lines ; in this case the
two-foot lines may be conceived as the result of halving the
first hemistich of the septenary line.

In Modern English two-foot lines are also rare and are chiefly
found in anisometrical stanzas. They do occur, however, here
and there in isometrical poems, either written in couplets or in
stanzas of lines rhyming alternately ; as, for instance, in Drayton,
An Amouret Anacreontic :

Most góod, most fáir,
Or thíngs as ráre
To cáll you's lóst ;
For áll the cóst
Wórds can bestów,
Só póorly shów

> *Upón your práise*
> *That áll the wáys*
> *Sénse hath, come shórt,* &c.

The commonest rhythmical licences are inversion of accent and initial truncation. In stanzas verses of this sort occur, for the most part it seems, with the rhyme-order *a b c b*, for instance in Burns, *The Cats like Kitchen,* and Moore, *When Love is Kind,* so that these verses might be regarded as four-foot lines rhyming in couplets.

§ 134. One-foot lines, both with single and with double ending, likewise occur in Middle English only as component parts of anisometrical stanzas, as a rule as *bob*-verses in what are called *bob-wheel* staves; as, for instance, in a poem in Wright's *Songs and Carols* (Percy Society, 1847), the line *With áye* rhyming with the three-foot line *Aye, áye, I dár well sáy*; in the *Towneley Mysteries,* the verse *Alás* rhyming with *A góod máster he wás*; in an *Easter Carol* (Morris, *An Old Engl. Miscellany,* pp. 197–9), the line *So strónge* rhyming with *Jóye hím wit sónge,* or *In lónde* and *of hónde* rhyming with *Al with jóye þát is fúnde.*

Metrical licences can naturally only seldom occur in such short lines.

One-foot iambic lines occur also in the Modern English period almost exclusively in anisometrical stanzas. A little poem entitled *Upon his Departure hence,* in Herrick's *Hesperides,* may be quoted as a curiosity, as it is written in continuous one-foot lines of this kind, rhyming in triplets:

Thus Í,	*As óne*	*I'm máde*	*I' the gráve,*	*Where téll*
Passe bý,	*Unknówn,*	*A sháde*	*There háve,*	*I dwéll.*
And díe,	*And góne,*	*And láid*	*My cáve:*	*Farewéll.*

One-foot lines with feminine ending are employed by Moore as the middle member of the stanza in the poem *Joys of Youth, how fleeting*.

CHAPTER X

THE SEPTENARY, THE ALEXANDRINE, AND THE THREE-FOOT LINE

§ 135. The Septenary is a favourite Middle English metre, going back to a Mediaeval Latin model. It cannot, however, be definitely determined whether this is to be found in the (accentual) catalectic iambic tetrameter, an example of which is preserved, among other instances, in the *Planctus Bonaventurae* (1221–74) printed by Mone in his *Latin Hymns of the Middle Ages*, which begins as follows:

> *O crux, frutex salvificus, | vivo fonte rigatus,*
> *Quem flos exornat fulgidus, | fructus fecundat gratus,*

or possibly in another Latin metre which was a far greater favourite with the Anglo-Norman Latin poets. This is the (accentual) brachycatalectic trochaic tetrameter, which frequently occurs, among other instances, in the poems ascribed to Walter Map, e. g. in the still popular verses:

> *Mihi est propositum | in taberna mori,*
> *Vinum sit appositum | morientis ori.*

The result of an attempt to adopt this metre in Middle English might, on account of the preference of the language for iambic rhythm, very naturally be to transform it into the iambic catalectic tetrameter by the frequent addition of an unaccented opening syllable at the beginning of each half-line. Probably the latter verse-form was the model, as may be seen from Leigh Hunt's Modern English translation of the Latin drinking-song just quoted.[1]

Moreover, many mediaeval Latin verses also have a wavering rhythm resulting in a form at times characterized by level stress, e. g.

> *Fortunae rota volvitur ; | descendo minoratus,*
> *Alter in altum tollitur | nimis exaltatus.*
> *Rex sedet in vertice, | caveat ruinam,*
> *Nam sub axe legimus | ' Hecubam' reginam.*

Carmina Burana, lxxvii.

---

[1] Cf. our metrical notes ('Metrische Randglossen') in *Engl. Studien*, x, p. 192 seq.

136. These verses correspond pretty exactly, in their metrical structure, to the opening lines of the *Moral Ode*, which, as far as is known, is the earliest Middle English poem in septenary lines, and dates from the twelfth century :

Íc am élder þánne ic wés, | a wíntre and éc a lóre;
ic éaldi móre þánne ic déde: | mi wít oʒhte tó bi móre.
Wel lónge ic hábbe chíld ibíen | on wórde ánd on déde;
þéʒh ic bí on wíntren éald, | to ʒíung ic ám on réde.

The other common licences of even-beat metre which affect the rhythm of the line, the metrical value of syllables, and the word-accent, also occur in the *Moral Ode*. Suppression of the anacrusis is very often met with; it occurs, for instance, in the first hemistich, in lines 1 and 4 above; in the second hemistich, *ér ic hít iwíste* l. 17, in both, *þó þet hábbeð wél idón | éfter híre míhte*, l. 175; so that a pure iambic couplet seldom occurs, although the iambic rhythm is, on the whole, predominant. The omission of unaccented syllables in the middle of the line is also often found (although many verses of this kind probably require emendation), as *Ne léve nó mán to múchel* 24; also in the second hemistich, as *and wól éche dede* 88. Transpositions of the accent are quite usual at the beginning of the first as well as of the second hemistich : *Elde me ís bestólen ón* 17; *síðen ic spéke cúðe* 9. Level stress is also not absent : *For bétere is án elmésse bifóre* 28. We often meet with elision, apocope, syncope, slurring of syllables, and the use of a disyllabic thesis both at the beginning of the line and in other positions : *þo þet wél ne dóeþ þe wíle he múʒe* 19; *nís hit búte gámen and glíe* 188. A noteworthy indication of want of skill in the handling of the Septenary in this first attempt is the frequent occurrence of a superfluous syllable at the close of the first hemistich, which should only admit of an acatalectic ending, e. g.: *Hé scal cúme on úuele stéde | búte him Gód beo mílde* 26; *Eíðer to lútel ánd to múchel | scal þúnchen éft hem báthe* 62, &c. The end of the second hemistich, on the other hand, in accordance with the structure of the metre, is in this poem always catalectic.

§ **137.** The irregularity of the structure of the Septenary rhyming line of the *Moral Ode* stands in marked contrast with the regularity of the rhymeless Septenary verse of the *Ormulum*. The first hemistich here is always acatalectic, the second catalectic, and the whole line has never more nor less than fifteen syllables.

Hence the only metrical licences that occur here are elision, syncope, and apocope of the unaccented *e* of some inflexional endings, and the very frequent admission of level stress in disyllabic and polysyllabic words, which are to be found in all places in the line :

> *Icc þátt tiss Énnglissh háfe sétt* | *Ennglísshe ménn to láre,*
> *Icc wáss þær þær I crísstnedd wáss* | *Orrmín bi náme némmnedd,*
> *Annd ícc Orrmín full ínnwarrdlíʒ* | *wiþþ mú∂ annd éc wiþþ*
> *hérrte.* Dedic. 322–7.

In all such cases, in the versification of Orm, whose practice is to count the syllables, there can only be a question of level stress, not of inversion of accent. *Ennglísshe* at the beginning of the second hemistich of the above line, 322, is no more an example of inversion of rhythm than in the hemistich *Icc háfe wénnd inntill Ennglíssh* l. 13.

§ 138. After the *Moral Ode* and the *Ormulum* the Septenary often occurs in combination with other metres, especially the Alexandrine, of which we shall speak later on.

In some works of the thirteenth and fourteenth centuries the Septenary was, however, employed in a fairly unmixed form, as, for instance, in the *Lives of Saints*, ed. Furnivall, 1862, the *Fragment of Popular Science*, ed. Wright in *Popular Treatises on Science*, London, 1841, and several others.

The most important deviation from the Septenary of Orm and of the *Moral Ode* is the frequent occurrence of long lines with a masculine instead of the usual feminine ending. Both forms are to be found in the opening lines of the *Fragment of Popular Science* :

> *The ríʒte pút of hélle ís* | *amídde the úrþe wiþínne,*
> *Oure Lóverd þát al mákede iwís,* | *quéinte ís of gýnne,*
> *Héuene and úrþe ymákede iwís,* | *and síþþe alle þíng þat ís.*
> *Úrþe is a lútel húrfte* | *aʒén héuene iwís.*

It may fairly be assumed that the structure of the Alexandrine (which, according to French models, might have either a masculine or a feminine ending) may have greatly furthered the intrusion of monosyllabic feet into the Septenary verse, although the gradual decay of the final inflexions may likewise have contributed to this end. For the rest, all the rhythmic licences of the Septenary occurring in the *Moral Ode* are also to be met with here ; as, for instance, the suppression of the anacrusis in the first hemistich of l. 4 of the passage quoted, and in the second of l. 2, and the omission of the unaccented syllable in the second hemistich of the fourth line, the inversion of accent and disyllabic thesis in the first hemistich of the third line, and other licences, such as the anapaestic beginning of the line, &c., in other places in these poems (cf. *Metrik*, i, p. 246).

§ **139.** In lyrical poems of this time and in later popular ballad poetry the Septenary is employed in another manner, namely, in four-lined stanzas of four- and three-foot verse, rhyming crosswise, each of which must be looked on as consisting of pairs of Septenaries with middle rhyme inserted (interlaced rhyme), as is clearly shown by the Latin models of these metrical forms quoted above (p. 192). Latin and English lines are thus found connected, so as to form a stanza, in a poem of the fifteenth century :

> *Fréeres, fréeres, wó ʒe bé!*
> *Ministrí malórum,*
> *For mány a mánnes sóule bringe ʒé*
> *Ad póenas infernórum.*   Political Poems, ii. 249.

In many lyrical poems of the older period some stanzas rhyme in long lines, others rhyme in short lines, which shows the gradual genesis of the short-lined metre, rhyming throughout. Thus, in the poem in Wright's *Spec. of Lyr. P.*, p. 90, the opening verses of the first stanza rhyme in long lines :

> *My déþ y lóue, my lýf ich háte, | fór a léuedy shéne,*
> *Héo is bríht so daíes líht, | þat ís on mé wel séne,*

whereas those of the second rhyme in short lines :

> *Sórewe and sýke and dréri mód | býndeþ mé so fáste,*
> *Þát y wéne to wálke wód, | ʒef hít me léngore láste.*

Instances of this kind are frequent ; but the four lines of the single stanzas are never completely rhymed throughout as short-lines, as, for instance, is the case in the opening parts or 'frontes' of the stanzas of the poems in Wright's *Spec. of Lyr. P.*, pp. 27 and 83, the lines of which are far more regularly constructed. The rhymes are in these compositions still generally disyllabic.

The metrical structure of the old ballads *The Battle of Otterborn* and *Chevy Chase* is similar to that of the poem just quoted. In those ballads some original long lines are provided with middle rhyme, others not, so that the stanzas partly rhyme according to the formula *a b c b*, partly according to the formula *a b a b*. The versification is, moreover, very uneven, and the endings are, as a rule, if not without exception, masculine:

> *Sir Hárry Pérssy cam to the wálles,*
> *The Skóttish óste for to sé;*
> *And sáyd, and thou hast brént Northómberlónd,*
> *Full sóre it réwyth mé.*

The ballads of the end of the Middle English period are generally composed in far more regular lines or stanzas. The feminine endings of the Septenary are, however, as a rule replaced by masculine endings, whether the lines rhyme cross-wise or only in the three-foot verses. Cf. the ballad, *The Lady's Fall* (Ritson, ii. 110), which, however, was probably composed as late as the Modern English period:

> *Mark wéll my héavy dóleful tále,*
> *You lóyal lóvers áll,*
> *And héedfullý béar in your bréast*
> *A gállant lády's fáll.*

§ **140.** In Modern English the Septenary has been extensively used, both in long and in short rhyming lines. One special variety of it, consisting of stanzas of four lines, alternately of eight and six syllables (always with masculine ending), is designated in hymn-books by the name of Common Metre.

In the long-lined form this metre occurs at the beginning of this period in poems of some length, as, for instance, in William Warner's *Albion's England*, and in Chapman's translation of the *Iliad*. Here, too, the ending of the line is almost without exception masculine, and the rhythm, on the whole, pretty regular, although this regularity, especially in Chapman, is, in accordance with the contemporary practice, only attained by alternate full pronunciation and slurring of the same syllables (Romanic -*ion*, -*ious*, &c., and Germanic -*ed*, &c.) and by inversion of accent. The caesura is always masculine at the end of the first hemistich, but masculine or feminine minor caesuras are often met with after the second or in the third foot, sometimes also after the first or in the second:

> *Occásioned thús:* | *Chrýses the priest* ‖ *cáme to the fléet to búy.* i. 11.

> *To plágue the ármy,* | *ánd to déath* ‖ *by tróops the sóldiers wént.* ib. 10.

Secondary caesuras also occur, though less frequently, in other places in the line, particularly in the second hemistich :

> *But íf thou wílt be sáfe begóne.* || *This sáid,* | *the séa-beat shóre.*   ib. 32.

> *All mén in óne aróse and sáid:* || *Atrídes,* | *nów I sée.*
> ib. 54.

These last examples suffice to show the rich variety of the caesura, which may be referred perhaps to the influence of blank verse, in the management of which Chapman displays great skill, and to the frequent use which he makes of the enjambement. Rhyme-breaking also sometimes occurs in his verse. Occasionally three consecutive lines rhyme together, as in W. Warner, whose versification is otherwise extremely regular, similar to that of lyrical poetry. In this branch of poetry the Septenary, with the simple rhyme-order *a b c b* and especially with the more artistic form *a b a b*, has continued to be very popular from the time of Wyatt down to the present day. The three-foot line has naturally in most instances a masculine ending, but lines also occasionally occur with feminine rhyme. In many poems the feminine rhyme is, moreover, regularly employed in this metre; as, for instance, in Burns's *To John Taylor* (p. 158) :

> *With Pégasús upón a dáy,*
> *Apóllo wéary flýing,*
> *Through frósty hílls the jóurney láy,*
> *On fóot the wáy was plýing.*

In ballad poetry, on the other hand, the Septenary metre tends to assume a somewhat freer construction, similar to, though not so capricious as that in the old ballads edited by Percy. A well-known example is offered by Coleridge's *Rime of the Ancient Mariner* :

> *It ís an áncient Márinér,* | *And he stoppeth óne of thrée:*
> *'By thy lóng grey béard and glíttering éye,* | *Now whérefore stópp'st thou mé?'*

Two unaccented opening syllables and two unaccented syllables in the middle of the line are, in particular, often met with.

§ 141. **The Septenary in combination with other metres.** After its occurrence in the *Moral Ode* and the *Ormulum* the Septenary, as we have seen, appears at first very seldom by itself, but generally in connexion with other metres, especially the old long line in its freer development, the four-foot metre (though more rarely), and, particularly, the Alexandrine.

The Middle English Alexandrine was constructed on the model of the Old French Alexandrine—except for the use of Teutonic licences in even-beat rhythm—and it thus possessed four different types, which the following examples from *On god Ureison of ure Lefdi*[1] may serve to illustrate. We give the corresponding Old French metrical types from the *Roman d'Alixandre* (Bartsch, *Chrestomathie de l'ancien français*, p. 175).

a. Masculine caesura with masculine line-ending:

En icele forest, | dont voz m'oëz conter. 24.

Nim nu ʒéme to mé, | so me bést a béo ðe béo. 129.

b. Feminine (epic) caesura with masculine line-ending:

nesune male choze | ne puet laianz entrer. 25.

vor þín is þé wurchípe, | ʒif ich wrécche wel iþéo. 130.

c. Masculine caesura with feminine line-ending:

Moult fut biaus li vregiers | et gente la praèle. 1.

Píne blísse ne méi | nówiht únderstónden. 31.

d. Feminine (epic) caesura with feminine line-ending:

Moult souëf i flairoient | radise et canele. 2.

Vor ál is gódes ríche | an únder þíne hónden. 32.

Alexandrines of this sort, particularly of the last type, are found in a group of poems of the close of the twelfth, or beginning of the thirteenth century, intermingled with Septenaries, and also, though more seldom, combined with four-beat alliterative rhyming long lines and with four-foot verses. Such poems are *On god Ureison of ure Lefdi* (quoted above), *A lutel soth sermon* (*Old English Miscellany*, ed. R. Morris, pp. 186 ff.), and *A Bestiary* (ib. pp. 1–25).

The following lines from *A lutel soth sermon* may serve to illustrate this mixture:

Hérknied àlle góde mèn, | and stílle sùtteþ adún,
And ích ou wùle téllen | a lútel sòþ sermún.
Wél we wìten álle, | þag ìch eou nóʒt ne télle,
Hu ádam ùre vórme fàder | adún vel ìnto hélle.

[1] In *Old English Homilies*, ed. R. Morris, pp. 190 ff.

Schómeliche hè vorlés | þe blísse þàt he hédde ;
To zívernèsse and prúde | nóne nèode he nédde.
He nòm þen áppel òf the trè | þat hìm forbóde wás :
So reúpful dède idón | néuer nòn nás.
He máde him ìnto hélle fàlle, | and éfter hìm his chíldren
    àlle ;
Þér he wàs fort ùre dríhte | hìne bóhte mìd his míhte.
He hìne alésede mìd his blóde, | þàt he schédde upòn the
    róde,
To dèþe he zèf him fòr us álle, | þó we wèren so strònge
    at-fálle.
Álle bácbìteres | wéndet to hélle,
Róbberes and réueres, | and þe mónquélle,
Léchurs and hórlinges | þíder sculen wénde,
And þér heo sculen wúnien | évere buten énde.

Here we have Septenaries (ll. 1, 4, 7) and Alexandrines
(ll. 2, 3, 5, 6, 8) intermixed in ll. 1–8, eight-foot long lines
resolved by means of *sectional rhyme* into four-foot lines in
ll. 9–12, and four-beat rhyming alliterative long lines of the freer
type in ll. 13–16. The easy intermixture of metres may be
explained by the fact that in all these different long-lined
metrical forms four *principal stresses* are prominent amid the
rest, as we have indicated by accents (').

§ 142. In the *Bestiary* this mixture of metrical forms has
assumed still greater proportions, inasmuch as alongside of the
long-lined rhyming Septenaries and alliterative long lines there
are found also Layamon's short-lined rhyming verses and
Septenary lines resolved into short verses by middle rhyme.

The following passages may more closely illustrate the
metrical construction of this poem; in the first place, ll. 384–
97 :

A wìlde dér is, þàt is fúl | of féle wíles,
Fóx *is hère tó-nàme, | for hìre quéðscípe ;*
Húsebondes hìre **h**áten, | *for hère* **h**árm-dédes :
þe **c**óc *and tè* **c**apún | *ge fècheð ófte ìn ðe tún,*
And te **g**ándre ànd te **g**ós, | bì ðe **n**écke and bì ðe **n**óz,
Háleð *is tò hire* **h**óle ; | *forðí man hìre* **h**átieð,
Hátien *and* **h**úlen | *bòðe* **m**én *and* **f**úles.

Here we have unmistakable long lines of the freer type.
In other passages the alliterative long lines pass into Septenaries, as, for instance, ll. 273–98 :

ðe míre múneð us | méte to tílen,
lóng lívenoðe, | ðis lítle wíle
ðe we on ðis wérld wúnen : | for ðanne we óf wénden,
ðánne is ure wínter : | we sulen húnger háuen
and hárde súres, | buten we ben wár hére.
Do wé forðí so dóð ðis dér, | ðánne wé be dérue
Ón ðat dái ðat dóm sal bén, | ðát ít ne us hárde réwe:

. . . .

þe córn ðat gé to cáue béreð, | áll ge it bít otwínne,
ðe láge us léreð to dón gód, | ánd forbédeð us sínne, &c.

In a third instance (ll. 628–35) Septenary and four-foot
lines run into one another :

> *Hú he résteð hím ðis dér,*
> *ðánne he wálkeð wíde,*
> *hérkne wú it télleð hér,*
> *for hé is ál unríde.*
> *A tré he sékeð to fúligewís*
> *ðát is stróng and stédefast ís,*
> *and léneð hím trostlíke ðerbí,*
> *ðánne he ís of wálke werí.*

In many passages in the poem one or other of these different
types of verse occurs unmixed with others. Thus we have
short couplets in the section 444–5; in ll. 1–39 alliterative
rhymeless verse, occasionally of marked archaic construction,
concluding with a hemistich (39) which rhymes with the preceding hemistich so as to form a transition to the following
section (ll. 40–52), which again consists of four-foot and
Septenary verses. These are followed by a section (ll. 53–87)
in which four-foot and three-foot lines (that is to say, Alexandrines) rhyming in couplets are blended; and this is succeeded
by a further section (ll. 88–119) mostly consisting of Septenaries resolved by the rhyme into short lines. (Cf. *Metrik*, i,
§§ 79–84.)

Hence we may say that the poet, in accordance with his
Latin model (likewise composed in various metres), has purposely made use of these different metrical forms, and that the
assertion made by Trautmann and others,[1] that the Septenary
of the *Ormulum* and the *Moral Ode*, which is contemporary
with Layamon, represents the final result of the development of

---

[1] Trautmann, *Anglia*, v, Anz., p. 124; Einenkel, ibid., 74; Menthel,
Anglia, viii, Anz., p. 70.

Layamon's verse (the freer alliterative long line), must be
erroneous.

§143. In *On god Ureison of ure Lefdi*, on the other hand,
the alliterative long lines play only an insignificant part, a part
which is confined to an occasional use of a two-beat rhythm in
the hemistichs and the frequent introduction of alliteration.
Septenaries and Alexandrines here interchange *ad libitum*.

The following short passage (ll. 23–34) will suffice to illustrate these combinations of metres:

> Nís no wúmmen ibóren | þét þe béo ilíche,
> Ne nón þer nís þin éfning | wiðínne héoueríche.
> Héih is þi kínestól | onúppe chérubíne,
> Biuóren ðíne léoue súne | wiðínnen séraphíne.
> Múrie dréameð éngles | biuóren þín onséne,
> Pleieð and swéieð | and síngeð bitwéonen.
> Swúðe wél ham líkeð | biuóren þe to béonne,
> Vor heo néuer né beoð séad | þi uéir to iséonne.
> Þíne blísse ne méi | nówiht únderstónden,
> Vor ál is gódes ríche | anúnder þíne hónden.
> Álle þíne uréondes | þu mákest ríche kínges ;
> Þú ham ȝíuest kínescrúd, | béies and góldrínges.

Lines 26 and 34, perhaps also 25 and 30, are Septenaries,
l. 28 is the only line of the poem which contains two beats
in both hemistichs (hemistichs of this sort are further found in
the first hemistich of ll. 3, 12, 44, 72, 77, and in the second of
ll. 30, 45, 46, 52, and 70); the remaining lines of this passage
are most naturally scanned as Alexandrines. ·

§144. Now, this unsystematic combination of Alexandrines
and Septenaries is a metre which was especially in vogue in the
Middle English period. In this metrical form two religious
poems, *The Passion of our Lord* and *The Woman of Samaria*
(Morris, *Old English Miscellany*), were composed so early as
the beginning of the thirteenth century. From the first we
quote ll. 21–4 :

> Léuedi þu bére þat béste chíld, | þat éuer wés ibóre ;
> Of þé he mákede his móder, | vor hé þe hédde ycóre.
> Ádam ánd his ófsprung | ál hit wére furlóre,
> Ýf þi súne nére, | ibléssed þu béo þervóre.

Many lines of these poems may be scanned in both ways ;
in the third line of the preceding extract, for instance, we may

either take the second syllable of the word *ofsprung*, in the manner of the usual even-beat rhythm, to form a thesis (in this case hypermetrical, yielding an epic caesura), or we may regard it as forming, according to ancient Germanic usage, a fourth arsis of the hemistich, which would then belong to a Septenary. At any rate, this scansion would, in this case, be quite admissible, as indeed the other licences of even-beat rhythm all occur here.

It is in this metre that the South English Legends of Saints (*Ms. Harleian* 2277) and other poems in the same MS., as the *Fragment on Popular Science* (fourteenth century), are written. The same holds good for Robert of Gloucester's Rhyming Chronicle (cf. *Metrik*, i, §§ 113, 114). Mätzner (in his *Altengl. Sprachproben*, p. 155), and Ten Brink (*Literaturge-schichte*, i, pp. 334, 345) concur in this opinion, while Trautmann (in *Anglia*, v, Anz., pp. 123–5), on a theory of metrical accentuation which we hold to be untenable, pronounces the verses to be Septenaries.

The following passage (Mätzner, *Altengl. Sprachproben*, i, p. 155) may serve to illustrate the versification of Robert of Gloucester:

Áftur kýng Báthulf | Léir ys sóne was kýng,
And régned síxti zér | wél þoru álle þýng.
Up þe wáter of Sóure | a cíty óf gret fáme
He éndede, and clépede yt Léicestre, | áftur is ówne náme.
Þre dóztren þis kýng hádde, | þe éldeste Górnorílle,
Þe mýdmost hátte Régan, | þe zóngost Córdeílle.
Þe fáder hem lóuede álle ynóz, | ác þe zóngost mést:
For héo was bést an fáirest, | and to háutenésse drow lést.
Þó þe kýng to élde cóm, | álle þré he brózte
Hys dóztren tofóre hým, | to wýte of hére póuzte.

§ 145. At the end of the thirteenth century the Septenary and Alexandrine were, however, relegated to a subordinate position by the new fashionable five-foot iambic verse. But we soon meet them again in popular works of another kind, viz. in the Miracle Plays, especially in some plays of the *Towneley Collection*, like the *Conspiratio et Capcio* (p. 182), and actually employed quite in the arbitrary sequence hitherto observed, Alexandrine sometimes rhyming with Alexandrine, Septenary with Septenary, but, more frequently, Alexandrine with Septenary. A passage from the Towneley Mysteries may make this clear:

Now háve ye hárt what Í have sáyde, | I gó and cóm agáyn,
Therfór looke yé be páyde | and álso glád and fáyn,

For tó my fáder I wéynd, | for móre then Í is hé,
I lét you wýtt, as fáythfulle fréynd, | or thát it dóne bé.
That yé may trów when ít is dóne, | for cértes, I máy noght nów
Many thýnges so sóyn | at thís tyme spéak with yóu.

This metre is also employed in many Moral Plays with a similar liberty in the succession of the two metrical forms.

But we may often observe in these works, as, for instance, in Redford's *Marriage of Wit and Science* (Dodsley, ii, p. 325 sq.), that Alexandrines and Septenaries are used interchangeably, though not according to any fixed plan, so that sometimes the Septenary and sometimes the Alexandrine precedes in the couplet, as, for instance, in the last four lines of the following passage (Dodsley, ii, p. 386) :

O lét me bréathe a whíle, | and hóld thy héavy hánd,
My gríevous fáults with sháme | enóugh I únderstánd.
Take rúth and píty ón my pláint, | or élse I ám forlórn ;
Let nót the wórld contínue thús | in láughing mé to scórn.
Mádam, if Í be hé, | to whóm you ónce were bént,
With whóm to spénd your tíme | sometíme you wére contént :
If ány hópe be léft, | if ány récompénse
Be áble tó recóver thís | forpássed néglig énce,
O, hélp me nów poor wrétch | in thís most héavy plíght,
And fúrnish mé yet ónce agáin | with Tédiousnéss to fíght.

§ **146.** In other passages in this drama, e. g. in the speech of *Wit*, p. 359, this combination (Alexandrine with Septenary following) occurs in a sequence of some length. It existed, however, before Redford's time, as a favourite form of stave, in lyrical as well as in narrative poetry, and was well known to the first Tudor English prosodists under the name of *The Poulter's Measure*.[1]

The opening lines of Surrey's *Complaint of a dying Lover* (p. 24) present an example of its cadence :

In wínter's just retúrn, | when Bóreas gán his réign,
And évery trée unclóthed fást, | as Náture táught them pláin:
In místy mórning dárk, | as shéep are thén in hóld,
I híed me fást, it sát me ón, | my shéep for tó unfóld.

Brooke's narrative poem *Romeus and Juliet*, utilized by Shakespeare for his drama of the same name, is in this metre. Probably the strict iambic cadence and the fixed position of the caesura

---

[1] According to Guest (ii. 233) ' because the poulterer, as Gascoigne tells us, giveth twelve for one dozen and fourteen for another '.

caused this metre to appear especially adapted for cultured poetry, at a time when rising and falling rhythms were first sharply distinguished. It was, however, not long popular, though isolated examples are found in modern poets, as, for instance, Cowper and Watts. Thackeray uses it for comic poems, for which it appears especially suitable, sometimes using the two kinds of verse promiscuously, as Dean Swift had done before him, and sometimes employing the Alexandrine and Septenary in regular alternation.

§ 147. **The Alexandrine** runs more smoothly than the Septenary. The Middle English Alexandrine is a six-foot iambic line with a caesura after the third foot. This caesura, like the end of the line, may be either masculine or feminine.

This metre was probably employed for the first time in Robert Mannyng's translation of Peter Langtoft's rhythmical Chronicle, partly composed in French Alexandrines. The four metrical types of the model mentioned above (p. 198) naturally also make their appearance here.

a. *Méssengérs he sent | þórghout Inglónd*
b. *Untó the Inglis kýnges | þat hád it ín þer hónd.*

p. 2, ll. 3–4.

c. *After Éthelbért | com Élfríth his bróther,*
d. *Þát was Égbrihtes sónne, | and ʒít þer wás an óþer ;*

p. 21, ll. 7–8.

The Germanic licences incidental to even-beat rhythm are strikingly perceptible throughout.

In the first line we have to note in both hemistichs suppression of the anacrusis, in the second either the omission of an unaccented syllable or lengthening of a word (*Ing(e)lond*). The second line has a regular structure : in the third the suppression of the anacrusis is to be noted and the absence of an unaccented syllable in the second hemistich. The last line has the regular number of syllables, but double inversion of accent in the first hemistich. A disyllabic thesis at the beginning or in the middle of the line also frequently occurs.

To purvéie þám a skúlking, | on the Énglish éft to ríde ;

p. 3, l. 8.

Bot soiórned þám a whíle | in rést a Bángóre ;

p. 3, l. 16.

In Wéstsex was þán a kýng, | his náme wás Sir Íne ;

p. 2, l. 1.

There is less freedom of structure in the Alexandrine as used in the lyrical poems of this period, in which, however, the verse is generally resolved by middle rhyme into short lines, as may be seen from the examples in § 150.

§ 148. The structure of the Alexandrine is, on the other hand, extremely irregular in the late Middle English Mysteries and the Early English Moral Plays, where, so far as we have observed, it is not employed in any piece as the exclusive metre, but mostly occurs either as the first member of the above-mentioned *Poulter's Measure*, and occasionally in uninterrupted sequence in speeches of considerable length. We cannot therefore always say with certainty whether we have in many passages of *Jacob and Esau* (Dodsley's *Old Plays*, ed. Hazlitt, vol. ii, pp. 185 ff.) to deal with four-beat lines or with unpolished Alexandrines (cf. Act II, Sc. i). In other pieces, on the other hand, the Alexandrine, where it appears in passages of some length, is pretty regularly constructed, as, for instance, in Redford's *Marriage of Wit and Science* (Dodsley, ii, pp. 325 ff.), e. g. in Act II. Sc. ii (pp. 340–1):

> *How mány séek, that cóme | too shórt of théir desíre :*
> *How mány dó attémpt, | that daíly dó retíre.*
> *How mány róve abóut | the márk on évery síde :*
> *How mány thínk to hít, | when théy are múch too wíde :*
> *How mány rún too fár, | how mány líght too lów :*
> *How féw to goód efféct | their trávail dó bestów !* &c.

The caesura and close of the line are in this passage, which comprises eighteen lines, monosyllabic throughout.

§ 149. In Modern English the Alexandrine is also found in a long-lined rhyming form, as, for instance, in the sixteenth century in certain poems by Sidney, but notably in Drayton's *Polyolbion*.

The Modern English Alexandrine is particularly distinguished from the Middle English variety by the fact that the four types of the Middle English Alexandrine are reduced to one, the caesura being regularly masculine and the close of the line nearly always so; further by the very scanty employment of the Teutonic rhythmical licences; cf. the opening lines of the *Polyolbion* (*Poets*, iii, pp. 239 ff.) :

> *Of Álbion's glórious ísle | the wónders whílst I wríte,*
> *The súndry várying sóils, | the pléasures ínfiníte,*
> *Where héat kills nót the cóld, | nor cóld expéls the héat,*
> *The cálms too míldly smáll, | nor wínds too róughly gréat, &c.*

Minor caesuras seldom occur, and generally in the second hemistich, as, e. g., minor lyric caesuras after the first foot:

> *Wise génius, | bý thy hélp ‖ that só I máy descrý.* 240 a;

or masculine caesura after the second foot:

> *Ye sácred bárds | that to ‖ your hárps' melódious stríngs.* ib.

Enjambement is only sporadically met with; breaking of the rhyme still more seldom.

Less significance is to be attached to the fact that Brysket, in a poem on Sidney's death, entitled *The Mourning Muse of Thestylis* (printed with Spenser's works, Globe edition, p. 563), makes Alexandrines rhyme together, not in couplets, but in an arbitrary order; further, that Surrey and Blennerhasset occasionally composed in similarly constructed rhymeless Alexandrines (cf. *Metrik*, ii, p. 83).

Of greater importance is the structure of the Alexandrine when used as the concluding line of the Spenserian stanza and of its imitations.

It is here noteworthy that the lyric caesura, unusual in Middle English, often occurs in Spenser after the first hemistich:

> *That súch a cúrsed créature ‖ lives so lóng a spáce.*
>   F. Q. i. i. 31;

as well as in connexion with minor caesuras:

> *Upón his fóe, | a Drágon, ‖ hórriblé and stéarne.* ib. i. i. 3.

The closing line of the Spenserian stanza is similarly handled by other poets, such as Thomson, Scott, Wordsworth, while poets like Pope, Byron, Shelley, and others admit only masculine caesuras after the third foot. By itself the Alexandrine has not often been employed in Modern English.

Connected in couplets it occurs in the nineteenth century in Wordsworth's verse, e. g. in *The Pet Lamb* (ii. 149), and is in this use as well as in the Spenserian stanza treated by this poet with greater freedom than by others, two opening and medial disyllabic theses as well as suppression of anacrusis, being frequently admitted, while on the other hand the caesura and close of the verse are always monosyllabic.

§ **150. The three-foot line** has its origin theoretically, and as a rule also actually, in a halving of the Alexandrine, and this is effected less frequently by the use of leonine than by cross rhyme.

Two Alexandrine long lines are, for instance, frequently

resolved in this metrical type into four three-foot short lines
with crossed rhymes, as, e. g., in Robert Mannyng's *Chronicle*,
from p. 69 of Hearne's edition onwards.

From our previous description of the four types of the Middle
English Alexandrine, determined by the caesura and the close
of the verse, it is clear that the short verses resulting from
them may rhyme either with masculine or feminine endings,
as, e. g., on p. 78, ll. 1, 2 :

Wílliam the Cónqueróur   *Óut of his fírst erróur*
Chángis his wícked wíll ;   *repéntis óf his ílle.*

In accordance with the general character of the metre the
verses in this Chronicle are, even when rhyming as short lines,
printed as long lines, especially as this order of rhymes is not
consistently observed in all places in which they occur.

In lyrical poetry this metre is naturally chiefly found arranged
in short lines, as in the following examples :

Wright's Spec. of L. P., 97 :   Minot, ed. Hall, 17 :

Máyden móder mílde,   *Tówrenay, ȝów has tíght*
oiéz cel óreysóun ;   *To tímber tréy and téne*
from sháme þóu me shílde,   *A bóre, with brénis bríght*
e dé ly málfelóun.   *Es bróght opón ȝowre gréne.*

With another order of rhymes these verses are also met
with in tail-rhyme stanzas of different kinds, as, for instance,
in Wright's *Spec. of L. P.*, p. 41 :

Of a món mátheu póhte,   *In márewe mén he sóhte,*
þo hé þe wýnȝord wróhte ;   *at únder mó he bróhte,*
and wrót hit ón ys bóc.   *and nóm, ant nón forsóc.*

As a rule, the verses in such lyrical compositions intended
to be sung are more regularly constructed than in those of
narrative poetry, where the usual Germanic metrical licences
occur more frequently.

In Modern English the three-foot verse has remained a
favourite, chiefly in lyrical poetry, and occurs there as well with
monosyllabic as with disyllabic rhymes, which may either follow
one another or be crossed, e. g. :

Surrey, p. 128 :   Surrey, p. 39 :

Me líst no móre to síng   *Though Í regárded nót*
Of lóve, nor óf such thing,   *The prómise máde by mé ;*
How sóre that ít me wríng ;   *Or pássed nót to spót*
For whát I súng or spáke,   *My fáith and hónestý :*
Mén did my sóngs mistáke.   *Yét were my fáncy stránge,* &c.

We seldom find three-foot verses with disyllabic rhymes throughout. There is, on the other hand, in lyrical poetry a predilection for stanzas in which disyllabic rhymes alternate with monosyllabic, as, for instance, in Sheffield, *On the Loss of an only Son* :

> *Our mórning's gáy and shíning,*
> *The dáys our jóys declàre ;*
> *At évening nó repíning,*
> *And níght's all vóid of cáre.*
> *A fónd transpórted móther*
> *Was óften héard to crý,*
> *Oh, whére is súch anóther*
> *So bléss'd by Héaven as Í ?* &c.

Rhythmical licences, such as suppression of the anacrusis, seldom occur in such short lines. The species of licence that is most frequent appears to be inversion of accent.

CHAPTER XI

THE RHYMED FIVE-FOOT VERSE

§ **151.** Among all English metres the five-foot verse may be said to be the metre which has been employed in the greatest number of poems, and in those of highest merit.

Two forms can be distinguished, namely, the rhymed and the rhymeless five-foot verse (the latter being known as *blank verse*), which are of equal importance, though not of equal antiquity.

The rhymed five-foot verse was known in English poetry as far back as the second half of the thirteenth century, and has been a favourite metre from Chaucer's first poetic attempts onward to the present, whilst the blank verse was first introduced into English literature about the year 1540 by the Earl of Surrey (1518–47), and has been frequently employed ever since that time. The rhymed five-foot verse was, and has continued to be, mainly preferred for lyrical and epic, the blank verse for dramatic poetry. The latter, however, has been employed e. g. by Milton, and after him by Thomson and many others for the epic and allied species of poetry ; while rhymed five-foot verse was used during a certain period for dramatic poetry, e. g. by Davenant and Dryden, but by the latter only for a short time.

Rhymed five-accent verse occurs in Middle English both in poems composed in stanza form and (since Chaucer's *Legend of Good Women*, c. 1386) in couplets.

This metre, apart from differences in the length of the line and in number of accents, is by no means to be looked upon as different from the remaining even-stressed metres of that time. For, like the Middle English four-foot verse and the Alexandrine, it derives its origin from a French source, its prototype being the French decasyllabic verse. This is a metre with rising rhythm, in which the caesura generally comes after the fourth syllable, as e. g. in the line :

Ja mais n'iert tels | com fut as anceisors. Saint Alexis, l. 5.

P

To this verse the following line of Chaucer's corresponds exactly in point of structure:

A kníght ther wás, | and thát a wórthy mán.

Cant. Tales, Prol. 43.

§ 152. The English verse, like the French decasyllabic, admits feminine caesuras and feminine line-endings, and the first thesis (anacrusis) may be absent; there are, therefore, sixteen varieties theoretically possible.

I. Principal Types.		II. With Initial Truncation (omission of the first thesis).	
1. ∪–∪– ∪–∪–∪– 10 syll.		5. –∪– ∪–∪–∪– 9 syll.	
2. ∪–∪–∪ ∪–∪–∪– 11 „		6. –∪–∪ ∪–∪–∪– 10 „	
3. ∪–∪– ∪–∪–∪–∪ 11 „		7. –∪– ∪–∪–∪–∪ 10 „	
4. ∪–∪–∪ ∪–∪–∪–∪ 12 „		8. –∪–∪ ∪–∪–∪–∪ 11 „	

III. With Internal Truncation (omission of the thesis after the caesura).		IV. With both Initial and Internal Truncation.	
9. ∪–∪– –∪–∪– 9 syll.		13. –∪– –∪–∪– 8 syll.	
10. ∪–∪–∪ –∪–∪– 10 „		14. –∪–∪ –∪–∪– 9 „	
11. ∪–∪– –∪–∪–∪ 10 „		15. –∪– –∪–∪–∪ 9 „	
12. ∪–∪–∪ –∪–∪–∪ 11 „		16. –∪–∪ –∪–∪–∪ 10 „	

This table at the same time also contains the formal exposition, and indeed possibly the actual explanation (by suppression of the thesis following the epic caesura), of such lines as may be regarded as lines with lyric caesura, and are identical with these in regard to rhythm and number of syllables. To this class belong the forms given under 10, 12, 14, and 16.

The following examples will serve to illustrate these sixteen types:

I. Principal Types.

1. *A kníght ther wás, | and thát a wórthy mán.* Prol. 43.
2. *What schúlde he stúdie, | and máke himsélven wóod ?*
ib. 184.
3. *But thílke téxt | held hé not wórth an óystre.* ib. 182.
4. *To Cáunterbúry | with fúl devóut coráge.* ib. 22.

II. With Initial Truncation.

5. *Úpon whích | he wíl auénged bé.*
> Lydgate, Story of Thebes, 1086.

6. *Óf the wórdes | that Týdeús had sáid.*   ib. 1082.

7. *Fró the kíng | he gán his fáce tóurne.*   ib. 1068.

8. *Nát astónned, | nor ín his hért afêrde.*   ib. 1069.

III. With Internal Truncation after the caesura.

9. *A stérne pás | thórgh the hálle he góth.*   ib. 1072.

10. *And whích they wéren, | ánd of whát degré.*
> Chaucer, Prol. 40.

11. *And yét therbý | sháll they néuer thrýve ?*
> Barclay, Ship of Fooles, p. 20.

12. *And máde fórward | érly fór to rýse.*
> Chaucer, Prol. 33.

IV. With Initial Truncation and Truncation after the caesura.

13. *Ín al hást | Týdeús to swé.*
> Lydgate, Story of Thebes, 1093.

14. *Twénty bókes, | clád in blák and réed.*
> Chaucer, Prol. 294.

15. *Spáred nát | wómen gréet with chýlde.*
> Lydgate, Guy of Warwick, 16.

16. *Fór to délen | with no súch poráille.*
> Chaucer, Prol. 247.

In this five-foot metre all the Germanic licences of the even-beat rhythm may occur in the same way as in the other even-beat metres. The caesura, for instance, may occur in both (or all three) varieties in the five-foot verse of Chaucer and of many other poets, either after or within any of the remaining feet. Hence the structure of this metrical form gains to an extraordinary degree in complexity.

By the mere fact that the variations adduced above may also occur after the first, third, and fourth foot, the number of verse-forms produced by the above-mentioned types of caesura in

combination with initial truncation and the different kinds of
verse-ending rises to sixty-four, to say nothing of the other
metrical licences due to inversion of accent, level stress, and the
presence of hypermetrical unaccented syllables at the beginning,
or in the middle and the end of the line. At any rate, the
varieties of even-beat metres, especially of the five-foot verse,
resulting from these metrical licences, are much more numerous
than those connected with the five main types of the alliterative
hemistich. The great diversity of rhythm allowed by this
metrical theory has, indeed, been objected to, but evidently
without sufficient reason, and, as it seems, only because of
the unfamiliarity of the idea.

§ 153. This variable position of the caesura is, however, not
found in the earliest specimens of this metre presented to us in the
two poems in the Harl. MS. 2253 dating from the second half
of the thirteenth century, which are edited in Wright's *Specimens
of Lyric Poetry*, Nos. xl and xli (wrongly numbered xlii).[1] These
are written in tripartite eight-lined, anisometrical stanzas of the
form $a_4 b_3 a_4 b_3 c_5 c_5 d_7 d_5$, in which the fifth, sixth, and eighth
lines are evidently of five feet. Ten Brink,[2] it is true, says that
he has not been able ' to convince himself that this was a genuine
instance of a metre which—whether in origin or character—
might be identified with Chaucer's heroic verse, although in
isolated instances it seems to coincide with it '. According to
my conviction, there is not the slightest doubt as to the structure
of these verses as lines of five feet, and Ten Brink has not
expressed any opinion as to the nature of the verse to which
they must otherwise be referred.[3]

In both these poems there occur only verses of the type
indicated by the formulas 3, 4, 7, 12 :

3. *His hérte blód | he ȝéf for ál monkúnne.*　xl. 35.

4. *Upón þe róde | why núlle we táken héde?*　ib. 27.

7. *Ȝéf þou dóst, | hit wól me réowe sóre.*　xli. 20.

12. *Bote héo me lóuye, | sóre hit wól me réwe.*　ib. 27.

[1] These poems are also printed in Böddeker, *Altengl. Dichtungen*,
Geistl. Lieder, xviii, Weltl. Lieder, xiv.

[2] *Chaucer's Sprache und Verskunst*, § 305, note.

[3] The verses he calls five-foot lines have, on the other hand, decidedly
not this structure, but are four-foot lines with unaccented rhymes; for
a final word in the line, such us *wrécful*, as is assumed by Ten Brink, with
the omission of an unaccented syllable between the last two accents, would
be utterly inconsistent with the whole character of this metre.

Among the Germanic licences the presence of a disyllabic initial or internal thesis is most noticeable in these which are, so far as is known, the earliest five-foot verses in English poetry; as, e. g. in xli. 33, 34 :

> *Ase stérres beþ in wélkne,* | *and gráses sóur ant suéte ;*
> *Whose lóueþ vntréwe,* | *his hérte is sélde séete.*

§ 154. The main difference between Chaucer's five-foot verse and these early specimens of this metre is that the caesura does not always occupy a fixed place in it, but is liable to shift its position.[1] It is either masculine, epic, or lyric, and occurs chiefly after the second or in and after the third foot, or in the fourth, so that there are thus (in Chaucer's verse and that of most of the following poets) **six main types of caesura** :

1. Masculine (monosyllabic) caesura after the second foot; the principal kind (types 1 and 3) :

> *Whan Zéphirús* | *eek wíth his swéte bréethe.*   Prol. 5.

2. Feminine (disyllabic) epic caesura after the second foot; far rarer (types 2 and 4) :

> *To Cáunterbúry* [2] | *with fúl devóut coráge.*   ib. 22.

3. Feminine (disyllabic) lyric caesura in the third foot; more frequent than the preceding (types 10 and 12) :

> *And máde fórward* | *érly fór to rýse.*   ib. 83.

4. Masculine (monosyllabic) caesura after the third foot (first subordinate type to 1 and 3 = 1 a and 3 a) :

> *That slépen ál the níght* | *with ópen éye.*   ib. 10.

[1] According to Ten Brink, *Chaucer's Sprache und Verskunst*, § 305, the shifting character of Chaucer's caesura was chiefly caused by his acquaintance with the Italian *endecasillabo*. This influence may have come in later, but even in Chaucer's early *Compleynt to Pitee* (according to Ten Brink, *Geschichte der englischen Literatur*, ii. p. 49, his first poem written under the influence of the French decasyllabic verse) the caesura is here moveable, though not to the same extent as in the later poems. The liability of the caesura to shift its position was certainly considerably increased by the accentual character of English rhythm. On the untenableness of his assertion, that in Chaucer's five-accent verse the epic caesura is unknown, cf. p. 145 (footnote), *Metrik*, ii. 101-3 note, and Schipper in Paul's *Grundriss*, ed. 2, II. ii, pp. 217-21.

[2] For the accentuation of the word cf. *inter alia* rhymes such as *mérie : Cáunterbúry*, Prol. 801-2, and Schipper, l. c., pp. 217-18.

5. Feminine (disyllabic) epic caesura after the third foot, rare (first subordinate type to 2 and 4 = 2 a and 4 a):

Ther ás he wás ful mérye | and wél át ése.

Nonne Pr. T. 438.

6. Feminine lyric caesura in the fourth foot (first subordinate type to 10 and 12 = 10 a and 12 a):

An ánlas ánd a gípser | ál of sílk. Prol. 357.

Besides these six principal caesuras we also find all the three types occurring in rarer instances in the corresponding remaining positions of the verse, namely, after the first or in the second foot, and after the fourth or in the fifth foot. Enjambement often gives rise to logical caesuras in unusual positions, alongside of which another metrical caesura is generally noticeable in one of the usual positions:

Byfél, ‖ that ín that sésoun | ón a dáy. Prol. 18.

In Sóuthwerk | át the Tábard ‖ ás I láy. ib. 20.

Farwél, ‖ for Í ne máy | no lénger dwélle. Kn. T. 1496.

O régne, ‖ that wólt no félawe | hán with thé. ib. 766.

Now cértes, ‖ Í wol dó | my díligénce. Prioresse T. 1729.

Is ín this lárge | wórlde ysprád ‖ —quod shé. ib. 1644.

To Médes ánd | to Pérses yíuen ‖ quod hé.

Monkes T. 3425.

And sófte untó himsélf | he séyde | : Fý. Kn. T. 915.

By the various combinations of such principal and subordinate caesuras the number of the varieties of this metre is increased to an almost unlimited extent. Many lines also are devoid of the caesura completely, or, at most, admit, under the influence of the general rhythm, a light metrical caesura without any strict logical need, as, for instance, when it occurs after a conjunction or a preposition, as in the verses:

By fórward ánd | by cómposícióun. Prol. 848.

That Í was óf | here félaweschípe anón. ib. 32.

§ 155. The end also of the line may be either masculine or feminine. Both kinds occur side by side on a perfectly equal footing, the feminine endings probably somewhat oftener in Chaucer's verse owing to the numerous terminations consisting of *e* or *e* + consonant which were still pronounced at his time. Besides the variety in the caesura and the end of the verse, the well-known licences of even-beat rhythm play a considerable part; as, for instance, inversion of accent, ordinary and rhetorical, at the beginning of the verse and after the caesura: rédy *to wénden* Prol. 21; Sýngynge *he wás* ib. 91; Schórt *was his góune* ib. 93; Tróuthe *and honóur*, frédom *and córteisíe* ib. 46.

Although omission of the anacrusis is on the whole unfrequent, it yet undoubtedly occurs (cf. p. 137, footnote):

> Ál besmótered | *wíth his hábergeóun.*   Prol. 76.

> Gýnglen *ín a* | *whístlyng wýnd as clére.*   ib. 170.

Disyllabic theses are often found initially and internally.

> *With a thrédbare cópe* | *as ís a póure schóler.*   Prol. 262.

> *Of Éngelónd,* | *to Cáunterbúry they wénde.*   ib. 16.

Similar rhythmical phenomena are caused by the slurring of syllables, such, e. g., as *Many a, tharray* from *the array*, &c., &c., in regard to which reference should be made to the chapter on the metrical value of syllables.

Level stress occurs most frequently in Chaucer in rhyme: *fiftíne : Trámasséne* 61–2; *daggére: spere* 113–14; *thing : writýng* 325–6. Enjambement and rhyme-breaking are used by him with great skill (cf. §§ 92, 93).

§ 156. In later Middle English this metre on the whole retained the same character, and individual poets vary from one another only in a few points.

Of Gower's five-foot verse only short specimens are preserved. Like his four-foot verse, they are very generally regular. Inversion of accent is the licence he most often employs. Gower uses almost exclusively the masculine caesura after the second foot and the lyric caesura in the third foot. But epic caesura also occasionally occurs in his verse:

> Fór of batáille | *the fínal énde is pés.* Praise of Peace, 66.

A decline in the technique of the five-foot verse begins with Lydgate and Hoccleve.

These writers deprived the caesura of its mobility and admitted it almost exclusively after the second beat. Hoccleve uses hardly any caesuras but the masculine and lyric, whilst in Lydgate's verse epic caesura is often met with (cf. p. 211). Both indulge in the licences of initial truncation and omission of the unaccented syllable after the caesura (cf. l. c.) as well as level stress and the admission of several unaccented syllables at the beginning of the verse and internally; there are even cases of the omission of unaccented syllables in the middle of the verse :

Of hárd márble | they díde anóther mǎke. Min. P., p. 85, 24.

The slight licence of inversion of accent is also taken advantage of.

Stephen Hawes and Barclay again imparted to this line greater freedom with regard to the caesura. And yet the metre exhibits under their hands, in consequence of the frequent occurrence of disyllabic initial and internal theses, a somewhat uneven rhythm.

The ablest of the successors of Chaucer, in technique as in other respects, are the Scots : Blind Harry, Henrysoun, King James I, Douglas, and Dunbar. The verse of Dunbar, in particular, stands on an equality with Chaucer's in rhythmical euphony, while David Lyndesay often struggles with difficulties of form, and, by frequent use of level stress, offends against the first principle of even-beat rhythm, viz. the coincidence of the metrical accent with the natural accentuation of the word and sentence.

§ 157. In Modern English the rhymed five-foot verse remains essentially the same as in the Middle English period. Feminine rhymes are indeed rarer than in Middle English poetry in consequence of the disuse of flexional endings.

For the same reason, and owing to the advance in technical execution, the epic caesura is also rarer. Still, examples of this as well as of the other kind of caesuras employed by Chaucer are found in Modern English :

I. *The níghtingále | with féathers néw she síngs.* Sur. p. 3.

II. *The sóte séason | that búd and blóom forthbríngs.* ib. p. 3.

III. *Itsélf from trávail | óf the dáys unrést.* ib. p. 2.

IV. *The sún hath twíce brought fórth | his ténder gréen.*

V. *He knóweth how gréat Atrídes, | that máde Troy frét.*
Wyatt, 152.

VI. *At lást she ásked sóftly, | whó was thére.* ib. 187.

In positions nearer to the beginning or the end of the line the different kinds of caesura are also rare in Modern English, and occur mostly in consequence of enjambements.

In Wyatt's poems epic caesuras are found in comparatively

large number; in Spenser, on the other hand, they are probably entirely lacking, owing to a finer feeling for the technique of the verse.

Inversions of accent occur in the usual positions and at all times with all the poets. Level stress, on the other hand, is more frequently detected in such poets as do not excel in technical skill, as, for instance, in Wyatt and Donne, who also admit initial truncation, and more rarely the omission of a thesis in the middle of the line. In their poems disyllabic theses also often occur initially and internally, while more careful poets more rarely permit themselves these licences. To Wyatt's charge must be laid further the unusual and uncouth licence of unaccented rhyme, such rhymes, for example, as *begínnìng : eclípsìng*, p. 56, 1–3; *dréadèth : séekèth, inclósèd : oppréssèd* 54, &c. In other poets this peculiarity is hardly ever found.

§ 158. In narrative poetry the five-foot verse rhyming in couplets, *heroic verse*, was a favourite metre. As a close in the sense coincides with that of each couplet, this metre tends to assume an epigrammatic tone, especially since enjambement seldom occurs after the Restoration. To avoid the monotony thus occasioned, many Restoration poets linked three verses together by one and the same rhyme, whereby the regular sequence of couplets was then interrupted wherever they pleased. Sometimes such threefold rhymes (*triplets*) serve the purpose of laying a special stress on particular passages, a practice which is, moreover, to be observed as early as in some contemporaries of Shakespeare, e.g. in Donne. A somewhat freer structure than that of the heroic verse is, as a rule, exhibited by the five-foot line when employed in poems in stanza form. In this verse a considerable part is played by enjambement. This also holds good for the rhymed five-foot verse employed in dramatic poetry, which usually rhymes in couplets, though alternate rhymes are occasionally used.

After Lyly's *The Maid's Metamorphosis*, entirely written in heroic verse, this metre was chiefly employed by Shakespeare and his contemporaries for prologues and epilogues. Rhymed five-foot verses frequently occur in Shakespeare's earlier dramas, e.g. in *Romeo and Juliet*, where their technical structure is found to be fairly strict. In his later dramas, on the other hand, e.g. in the Prologue and Epilogue to *Henry VIII*, the heroic verse is, on the analogy of the freer treatment of his later blank verse, also more loosely constructed. Enjambement, and the caesuras connected with it after the first and fourth accents, are often met with.

§ **159.** Dryden's dramatic heroic verse does not differ essentially from that of his satirical poems and translations. After Dryden returned to blank verse for dramatic writing, heroic verse ceased to be employed for this purpose. Rhymed verse, rhyming in couplets and stanzas, however, still continued to be in vogue in lyrical, satirical, didactic, and narrative poetry.

Pope's heroic verse is still more uniformly constructed than that of Dryden. Both poets hardly ever employ any caesura but the masculine and the lyric after the second and third beat, and the end of the line is almost exclusively masculine. Initial truncation or the absence of an unaccented syllable internally is hardly to be met with in their poems. The earlier diversity in the structure of this line was (under the influence of the French models whom they closely imitated) considerably restricted. Even transposition of accent occurs comparatively seldom, so that the word-accent generally exactly coincides with the rhythmical accent. Enjambement is, however, employed more frequently by Dryden than by Pope ; and the former, moreover, occasionally admits at the close of a triplet a verse of six feet, while Pope, in his original poems, completely avoids triplets as well as six-accent lines. The breaking of rhyme both poets purposely exclude.

A similar uniform character is exhibited by the heroic verse of most of the poets of the eighteenth century. It is not before the nineteenth century that this metre, in spite of the persistence of individual poets, e. g. Byron, in adhering to the fashion set by Pope, again acquires greater freedom. Shelley and Browning, for instance, are fond of combining lines of heroic verse by enjambement so as to form periods of some length. Wordsworth, Coleridge, Southey and others again admit couplets and triplets with occasional six-foot lines at the close. But the caesura remains nearly always restricted to the places which it occupies in Pope's verse, and the close of the line is masculine. Keats only often indulges in feminine rhymes.

It is, however, remarkable that such rhymes more often occur in five-foot verses combined in stanzas when employed for satirical and comic compositions, as e. g. in Byron's *Beppo* and *Don Juan*. In these poems the disyllabic thesis, the slurring of syllables, and other rhythmical licences, also more frequently occur.

DIVISION III

VERSE-FORMS OCCURRING IN MODERN ENGLISH POETRY ONLY

CHAPTER XII

BLANK VERSE

§ 160. The Beginnings of Modern English Poetry. Puttenham, in his *Arte of English Poesie*, i. 31, speaks of Surrey and Wyatt as having originated the modern period of English poetry. This is true in so far as their poems are the first to show clearly—especially in metrical form—the influence of the spirit of the Renaissance, which had been making itself felt in English Literature for some time past. The new tendencies manifested themselves not only in the actual introduction of new rhythms and verse-forms borrowed from Classical and Italian poetry, but also in the endeavour to regulate and reform the native poetry according to the metrical laws and peculiarities of foreign models, especially of the ancient classics.

There were, indeed, several features of classical poetry which invited imitation, and the introduction of which produced the chief differences between Modern English and Middle English versification. These features are :

First, the quantitative character of the ancient rhythms as opposed to the accentual character of English verse. Secondly, the strict separation of rising and falling rhythms. In Middle English we have only the rising rhythm, which, however, sometimes becomes a falling one if the first thesis is wanting. Finally, the absence of rhyme in the poetry of the ancients, whereas in late Middle English poetry—apart from some North-English and Scottish productions written in the conservative, rhymeless form of the alliterative line—rhyme is all but universal.

§ 161. The heroic couplet, the most popular and most important metre in later Middle English poetry, was, naturally, first of all influenced by the new classical movement.

It was the Earl of Surrey who, by dispensing with the rhyme, first transformed this metre into what is now known as Blank Verse. He adopted the unrhymed decasyllabic line as the most suitable vehicle for his translation of the second and fourth books of the *Aeneid*, written about 1540. In so doing, he enriched modern literature with a new form of verse which was destined to take a far more important place in English poetry than he can have foreseen for it. In its original function, as appropriate to the translation of ancient epic poetry, it has been employed by many late writers, e. g. by Cowper in his version of Homer; but this is only one, and the least considerable, of its many applications. Shortly after Surrey's time blank verse was used for court drama by Sackville and Norton in their tragedy of *Gorboduc* (1561), and for popular drama by Marlowe in *Tamburlaine the Great* (1587).

From the latter part of the sixteenth century onwards it has continued to be the prevailing metre for dramatic poetry, except for a short time, when its supremacy was disputed by the heroic couplet used by Lord Orrery, Davenant, Dryden, and others. Meanwhile blank verse had also become the metre of original epic poetry through Milton's use of it in his *Paradise Lost*; and in the eighteenth century it was applied to descriptive and reflective poetry by Thomson and Young.

It is uncertain whether Surrey invented it himself on the basis of his studies in classical rhymeless poetry, or whether he was influenced by the example of the Italian poet Trissino (1478–1550), who, in his epic *Italia liberata dai Goti* and in his drama *Sofonisba*, introduced into Italian poetry the rhymeless, eleven-syllabled verses known as *versi sciolti* (sc. *della rima*, i. e. freed from rhyme). There are at least no conclusive grounds for accepting the latter view, as there are some peculiarities in Surrey's blank verse which are not met with in Trissino, e. g. the occurrence of incomplete lines, which may have been introduced after the model of the unfinished lines found occasionally amongst Vergil's Latin hexameters.

Blank verse being in its origin only heroic verse without rhyme,[1] we may refer for its general rhythmical structure to what we have said on this metre. The rhythmical licences of this and the other iambic metres discussed in §§ 82–8 are common also to blank verse. But in addition to these, blank

---

[1] This definition is also given by Milton in his introductory note on 'The Verse' prefixed in 1668 to *Paradise Lost*.

verse has several other deviations from the normal rhymed five-foot iambic verse, the emancipation from rhyme having had the effect of producing greater variability of metrical structure. It is for this reason it has been thought advisable to treat heroic verse and blank verse in separate chapters.

At first, it is true, the two metres are very similar in character, especially in Surrey; with the further and independent development of blank verse, however, they diverge more and more.

§ 162. In conformity with Surrey's practice in his heroic verse, which, as we have seen, usually had masculine rhymes, his blank verse has also as a rule masculine endings, and is thus distinguished not only from Chaucer's heroic verse, which frequently had feminine endings, but from the blank verse of later poets like Shakespeare and some of his contemporaries.

As to the principal kinds of the caesura after the second and third foot there is no material difference between Surrey's blank verse and the heroic verse of the same period (cf. §§ 154, 157).

The Epic caesura occurs occasionally after the second foot, e. g.:

Líke to the ádder | with vénomous hérbes féd. p. 131;

but apparently not after the third, although it does not seem to have been avoided on principle, as we often find lyric caesuras in this place, and even after the fourth foot:

His tále with ús | did púrchase crédit; || sóme
Trápt by decéit; | some fórced bý his téars. p. 120.

The run-on line (or enjambement) is already pretty frequently used by Surrey (35 times in the first 250 lines), and this is one of the chief distinctions between blank verse and heroic verse. In most instances the use of run-on lines is deliberately adopted with a view to artistic effect. The same may be said of the frequent inversion of rhythm. On the other hand, it seldom happens that the flow of the metre is interrupted by level stress, missing thesis, or the use of a disyllabic thesis at the beginning or in the interior of the verse.[1]

As to the peculiarities of the word-stress and the metrical treatment of syllables in Surrey, the respective sections of the introductory remarks should be consulted. Apart then from the metrical licences, of which it admits in common with heroic verse, the most important peculiarities of Surrey's blank verse are the masculine endings, which are almost exclusively used, and the frequent use of run-on lines.

[1] Cf. *Metrik*, ii. §§ 132-5.

Cf. the opening lines of the fourth book of his *Aeneid* :

> *But nów the wóunded Quéen, | with héavy cáre,*
> *Throughóut the véins | she nóurishéth the pláie,*
> *Surprisëd with blind fláme ; | and tó her mínd*
> *'Gan éke resórt | the prówess óf the mán,*
> *And hónour óf his ráce : | while in her bréast*
> *Imprínted stáck his wórds, | and píctures fórm.*
> *Né to her límbs | care gránteth quíet rést.*
> *The néxt mórrow, | with Phóebus' lámp the éarth*
> *Alíghted cléar ; | and éke the dáwning dáy*
> *The shádows dárk | 'gan fróm the póle remóve :*
> *When áll unsóund, | her síster óf like mínd*
> *Thús spake she tó : | ' O ! Síster Ánne, what dréams*
> *Be thése, | that mé torménted | thús affráy ?*
> *What new guést is thís, | that tó our réalm is cóme ?*
> *Whát one of chéer ? | how stóut of héart in árms ?*
> *Trúly I thínk | (ne váin is mý belíef)*
> *Of Góddish ráce | some óffspring shóuld he bé.'*

§ **163.** With regard to the further development of this metre in the drama of the second half of the sixteenth and the first half of the seventeenth centuries we must restrict ourselves to a brief summary of its most important peculiarities, for details referring the reader to *Metrik*, ii, pp. 256–375 ; for bibliography see ib., pp. 259–60.

The employment of blank verse in the court drama hardly brought about any change in its structure. In *Gorboduc*, apart from a few instances in which a line is divided in the dialogue between two speakers (generally two and three feet) and the occasional (for the most part no doubt accidental) use of rhyme, the blank verse is exceedingly similar to that of Surrey, having masculine endings with hardly any exceptions.

This character was maintained by blank verse in all the other court plays of this time, only occasionally rhyming couplets are used at the end of a scene in Gascoigne's *Iocasta*, and prose passages now and then occur in Lyly's *The Woman in the Moon*.

The next and greatest step in the further development of the metre was its introduction into the popular drama by no less a poet than Marlowe in his drama *Tamburlaine the Great* (1587). Marlowe's mastery over this metrical form was supreme. His skill is shown in his use of the inversion of accent, particularly the rhetorical inversion, to give variety to his rhythm, e. g. :

Áh, sacred Máhomet, | thóu that hast seen
Míllions of Túrks | pérish by Támburláine. Tam. ii, p. 213.

But stíll the pórts were shút : | víllain, I sáy. ib., p. 206.

And hágs hówl for my déath | at Cháron's shóre.

Vol. ii. 255.

In his practice with regard to the caesura, the suppression of the anacrusis, and the use of disyllabic theses in the interior of the verse, he differs little from his predecessors. One distinctive feature of his verse is that he usually gives their full syllabic value to the Teutonic inflexional endings (*-ed, -est*), as well as to the Romanic noun- and adjective-suffixes ; as *-iage, -iance, -ion, -eous, -ial*, &c. (cf. §§ 102–7).

By a frequent use of these endings as full syllables which is not always in conformity with the spoken language of his time, his verse obtains a certain dignity and pathos ; cf. the following lines :

Yét in my thóughts | shall Chríst be hónouréd.

Tamb. ii, p. 148.

They sáy, | we áre a scáttered | nátión. Jew of M. 1, Sc. i.

These métaphýsics | óf magíciáns. Faust. 1, Sc. ii.

Allied with this is the fact that Marlowe still has a great predilection for masculine endings, although feminine endings are also met with now and then, especially in his later plays. Run-on lines do not often occur, but many two- and three-foot lines as well as heroic couplets are found at the end of longer speeches, scenes, and acts.

The blank verse of Greene, Peele, Kyd, and Lodge has a similar structure to that of Marlowe, especially as regards the prevalence of masculine endings. The verse of Greene and Peele, however, is rather monotonous, because generally the caesura occurs after the second foot. On the other hand, the metre of Kyd and Lodge stands in this respect much nearer to that of Marlowe and in general shows greater variety.[1]

§ 164. The blank verse of Shakespeare,[2] which is of great interest in itself, and moreover has been carefully examined

---

[1] Cf. *Metrik*, ii. §§ 136–46.

[2] Cf. on this subject the essays and treatises by T. Mommsen, Abbott, Furnivall, Ingram, Hertzberg, Fleay, A. J. Ellis (*On Early English Pronunciation*, iii), &c. (quoted *Metrik*, ii, p. 259) ; besides G. König, *Der Vers in Shakspere's Dramen*, Strassburg, Trübner, 1888, 8° (*Quellen und Forschungen*, 61) ; *Der Couplet-Reim in Shakspere's Dramen* (Dissertation),

during the last decades from different points of view, requires to be discussed somewhat more fully.

It is of the first importance to notice that Shakespeare's rhythms have different characteristic marks in each of the four periods of his career which are generally accepted.[1] For the determination of the dates of his plays the metrical peculiarities are often of great value in the absence of other evidence, or as confirming conclusions based on chronological indications of a different kind; but theories on the dates of the plays should not be built solely upon these metrical tests, as has been done, for instance, by Fleay. Such criticisms, generally speaking, have only a subordinate value, as, amongst others, F. J. Furnivall has shown in his treatise *The Succession of Shakespeare's works and the use of metrical tests in settling it* (London, Smith, Elder & Co., 1877. 8º).

The differences in the treatment of the verse which are of greatest importance as distinctive of the several periods of Shakespeare's work are the following:

§ **165.** In the first place the numerical proportion of the rhymed and rhymeless lines in a play deserves attention. Blank verse, it is true, prevails in all Shakespeare's plays; but in his undoubtedly earlier plays we find a very large proportion of rhymed verse, while in the later plays the proportion becomes very small.

Some statistical examples, based on careful researches by English and German scholars, may be quoted to prove this; for the rest we refer to the special investigations themselves.

In *Love's Labour's Lost*, one of Shakespeare's earliest plays, we have 1028 rhymed lines and 579 unrhymed. In *The Tempest*, one of his last plays, we find 1458 unrhymed and only two rhymed five-foot lines. In the plays that lie between the dates of these two dramas the proportion of rhymed and unrhymed verse lies between these two numbers. In *Romeo and Juliet*, e.g. (which belongs to the end of Shakespeare's first

von J. Heuser, Marburg, 1893, 8; H. Krumm, *Die Verwendung des Reims in dem Blankverse des englischen Dramas zur Zeit Shaksperes*, Kiel, 1889; H. Conrad, *Metrische Untersuchungen zur Feststellung der Abfassungszeit von Shakspere's Dramen* (*Shakespeare-Jahrbuch*, xxx. 318-353); *William Shakespeare, Prosody and Text*, by B. A. P. van Dam and C. Stoffel, Leyden, 1900, 8º; *Chapters on English Printing Prosody, and Pronunciation* (1550-1700),' by B. A. P. van Dam and C. Stoffel, Heidelberg, 1902 (*Anglistische Forschungen*, ix).

[1] I. 1587-1592; II. 1593-1600; III. 1600-1606; IV. 1606-1613; according to Dowden.

period, though Fleay thought it a very early play) we have
2111 unrhymed and 486 rhymed five-foot lines; in *Hamlet*
(belonging to the third period) there are 2490 unrhymed and
81 rhymed lines.

In many cases, however, the use of rhyme in a play is connected with its whole tone and character, or with that of certain
scenes in it. The frequency of rhymes in *Romeo and Juliet*
finds its explanation in the lyrical character of this play. For
the same reason *A Midsummer Night's Dream*, although it is
certainly later than *Love's Labour's Lost* and *Romeo and Juliet*,
shows a larger proportion of rhymed lines (878 blank: 731
rhymes). This seems sufficient to show that we cannot rely
exclusively on the statistical proportion of rhymed and unrhymed verses in the different plays in order to determine their
chronological order.

§ 166. The numerical proportion of feminine and masculine
endings is of similar value. In the early plays we find both
masculine and feminine endings; the masculine, however, prevail. The number of feminine endings increases in the later
plays. On this point Hertzberg has made accurate statistical
researches. According to him the proportion of feminine to
masculine endings is as follows :

Love's Labour's Lost 4 per cent., *Romeo and Juliet* 7 per
cent., *Richard III* 18 per cent., *Hamlet* 25 per cent., *Henry
VIII* 45·6 per cent.[1] This proportion, however, as has
been shown by later inquiries,[2] does not depend solely on the
date of the composition, but also on the contents and the tone
of the diction, lines with masculine endings prevailing in pathetic
passages, and feminine endings in unemotional dialogue, but also
in passionate scenes, in disputations, questions, &c.

§ 167. The numerical proportion of what are called 'weak'
and 'light' endings to the total number of verses in the different plays is similarly of importance. These are a separate
subdivision of the masculine endings and are not to be confused
with the feminine. They are formed by monosyllabic words,
which are of subordinate importance in the syntactical structure
of a sentence and therefore stand generally in thesis (sometimes even forming part of the feminine ending of a line),
but which under the influence of the rhythm are used to carry
the arsis. To the 'weak' endings belong the monosyllabic con-

---

[1] Cf. Furnivall, p. xxviii.
[2] Cf. Mayor, *Chapters on English Metre*, pp. 174–7.

junctions and prepositions if used in this way: *and, as, at, but* (*except*), *by, for, in, if, on, nor, than, that, to, with*; as e. g. in the three middle lines of the following passage taken from *Henry VIII* (III. ii. 97–101):

> *What thóugh I knów her vértuous*
> *And wéll desérving ? | Yét I knów her fór*
> *A spléeny Lútheran, | ánd not whólsome tó*
> *Our cáuse, | that shé should lýe | i' th' bósom óf*
> *Our hárd-rul'd kíng.*

The 'light' endings include a number of other monosyllabic words, viz. articles, pronouns, auxiliary verbs, that are used by Shakespeare in a similar way.

These are, according to Ingram, *am, are, art, be, been, but* (=*only*), *can, could, did*(2), *do*(2), *does*(2), *dost*(2), *ere, had*(2), *has* (2), *hast* (2), *have* (2), *he, how*(3), *I, into, is, like, may, might, shall, shalt, she, should, since, so* (4), *such* (4), *they, thou, though, through, till, upon, was, we, were, what* (3), *when* (3), *where* (3), *which, while, whilst, who* (3), *whom*(3), *why*(3), *will, would, yet* (=*tamen*), *you*.

According to Ingram, the words marked (2) are to be regarded as light endings 'only when used as auxiliaries'; those marked (3), 'when not directly interrogative'; those marked (4), 'when followed immediately by *as*.' *Such* belongs to this class, 'when followed by a substantive with an indefinite article, as *Such a man*.'

There are hardly any weak or light endings in the first and second periods of Shakespeare's work. In the third they occur now and then and become more frequent in the last period. So we have e.g. in *Antony and Cleopatra* (1600) 3·53 per cent.; in *The Tempest* (1610) 4·59 per cent.; in *Winter's Tale* (1611) 5·48 per cent.

In the application of this test we must chiefly keep in mind that these two groups of words are only to be considered as 'weak' and 'light' endings when they form the last arsis of the line, as is the case in the lines quoted from *Henry VIII*; but they are to be looked upon as part of a disyllabic or feminine ending if they form a supernumerary thesis following upon the last arsis:

> *Upón this gróund; | and móre it woúld contént me.*
> Wint. II. i. 159.

§ **168.** Intimately connected with the quality of the line-endings is the proportion of unstopt or 'run-on' and 'end-stopt' lines, or the frequent or rare use the poet makes of enjambement. Like the feminine, weak, and light endings, this metrical peculiarity also occurs much more rarely in Shake-speare's earlier than in his later plays. According to Furnivall's statistics, e. g. in *Love's Labour's Lost* one run-on line occurs in 18·14 lines; in *The Tempest*, on the other hand, we have one run-on line in 3·02 lines; in *Winter's Tale* the proportion rises to one in 2·12.

As in the later plays run-on lines are often the result of the use of weak and light endings, we may perhaps assume with Hertzberg that at times the poet deliberately intended to give a greater regularity to the verse, if only by introducing the more customary masculine endings. From this point of view, then, both the weak and light endings and the run-on lines would have much less importance as metrical and chronological tests than they otherwise might have had.

§ 169. But there is another peculiarity of Shakespeare's rhythms noticed by Hertzberg which is of greater value as a metrical test; viz. the use of the full syllabic forms of the suffixes *-est*, and especially of *-es* or *-eth* in the second and third pers. sing., as well as that of *-ed* of the preterite and of the past participle. These tests are all the more trustworthy because they do not so much arise from a conscious choice on the part of the poet as from the historical development of the language. This is indicated by the fact that the slurring of these endings prevails more and more in the later plays.

According to Hertzberg's statistics the proportion of fully sounded and slurred *e* is as follows:

	1 *H. VI.*	*T. Andr.*	1 *H. IV.*	*H. VIII.*
3 Pers. Sing.	15·58 %	6·4 %	2·25 %	0 %
Pret. and P. P.	20·9 %	21·72 %	15·41 %	4·2 %

It thus appears that in this respect also there is a decided progress from a more archaic and rigorous to a more modern usage.

These are the five chief distinctive marks of Shakespeare's verse in the different periods of his dramatic work. Besides these, Fleay has pointed out some other characteristics distinctive of the first period, namely, the more sparing use of Alexandrines, of shortened verses, and of prose, and the more frequent use of doggerel verses, stanzas, sonnets, and crossed rhymes.

§ 170. There are, however, some other rhythmical characteristics that have not yet been sufficiently noticed by English or
German scholars, probably because they cannot be so easily
represented by means of statistics.

The caesura is of special importance. Although from the first
Shakespeare always allowed himself a great degree of variety
in the caesura, he prefers during his first and second period the
masculine and lyrical caesura after the second foot; in his third
period, in *Macbeth* especially, both the masculine and lyrical
caesura occur as frequently after the third foot, and side by
side with these the epic caesura after the second and third foot
pretty often (§ 90); during the fourth period a great many double
caesuras occur corresponding to the numerous run-on lines.[1]

The old-fashioned disyllabic pronunciation of certain Romanic
terminations (as *-ion*, *-ier*, *-iage*, *-ial*, &c.), so often met with in
Marlowe, is not uncommon in Shakespeare, chiefly in his early
plays, but also in those of later date (cf. § 107).

As to inversion of rhythm (cf. § 88), it is a noteworthy feature
that during the first period it occurs chiefly in the first foot
and afterwards often in the third also.

Disyllabic theses may be found in each of the five feet,
sometimes even two at the same time:

Having Gód, her cónscience, | ánd these bárs agaínst me.
R. III, i. ii. 235.

Succéeding his fáther Bólingbróke, | did réign.
1 H. VI, ii. v. 83.

But thén we'll trý | what these dástard Frénchmen dáre.
1 H. VI, i. iii. 111.

Thén is he móre behólding | to yóu than Í. R. III, iii. i. 107.
Pút in their hánds | thy brúising írons of wráth.
R. III, v. iii. 110.

My survéyor is fálse ; | the ó'ergreat cárdinál.
H. VIII, i. i. 222.

Disyllabic or polysyllabic line-endings are likewise of frequent occurrence:

I dáre avóuch it, sír, what, fífty fóllowers ? Lear, ii. iv. 240.
To yóur own cónscience, sír, befóre Políxenes. Wint. iii. ii. 47.

[1] Cf. Metrik, ii, § 154.

Slurring and other modifications of words to make them fit into the rhythm are very numerous and of great variety in Shakespeare; we have referred to them before, §§ 108–11; here only some examples may be repeated, as (a)*bove*, (*be*)*cause*, (*ar*)*rested*, *th' other*, *th' earth*, *whe*(*th*)*er*, *ha*(*v*)*ing*, *e*(*v*)*il*, *eas*(*i*)*ly*, *barb*(*a*)*rous*, *inn*(*o*)*cent*, *acquit* for *acquitted*, *deject* for *dejected*, &c.

On the other hand, many lengthenings also occur, as *wrest*(*e*)*ler* A. Y. L. ii. ii, 13; *pilg*(*e*)*rim* All's Well, iii. v. 43, &c. (Cf. §§ 87, 112.)

In some monosyllabic words, as *fear, dear, hear, wear, tear, year*, it is not always necessary to assume with Abbott (§§ 480–6) a disyllabic pronunciation, e. g. *dèàr, yèàr*. On the contrary, in many cases it is more probable that the emphasis laid on the monosyllable takes the place of the missing thesis, e. g.:

The kíng would spéak with Córnwall: | the déar fáther.
Lear, ii. iv. 102.

Déar my lórd, | if you in yóur own próof. Ado, iv. i. 46.

Hor. *Whére my lórd?* | Haml. *In my mínd's éye, Horátio.*
Ham. i. ii. 185.

The two last examples also show the absence of the first thesis, which often occurs in Shakespeare; frequently, as in these cases, it is compensated by an extra stress laid on the first accented syllable (cf. § 84); e. g.:

Stáy! | the kíng has thrówn | his wárder dówn.
Rich. II, i. iii. 118.

Upón your Gráce's part; | bláck and féarful.
All's Well, iii. i. 4.

For the same reason a thesis is sometimes wanting in the interior of a line:

Of góodly thóusands. | Bút, for áll thís.   Macb. iv. iii. 44;

or for phonetic reasons (cf. § 86):

A thírd thínks, | withóut expénse at áll. 1 Hen. VI, i. i. 76.

With respect to the word-stress and the metrical value of syllables there are in Shakespeare many archaic peculiarities. Some of those we have already dealt with; for the rest the reader must consult the works in which they are specially discussed.

§ 171. Of great interest are the other metres that occur in combination with blank verse in Shakespeare's plays.

Alexandrines are frequently met with, especially where one line is divided between two speakers :

Macb. *I'll cóme to yóu anón.* | Murd. *We áre resólved, my lórd.* Macb. III. i. 139.

Macb. *Hów does your pátient, dóctor ?* | Doct. *Nót so síck, my lórd.* ib. v. iii. 37 ;

but also in many other cases :

Hów dares thy hársh rude tóngue | *sound thís unpléasing néws ?* R. II, III. iv. 74.

And thése does shé applý | *for wárnings, ánd porténts.* Caes. II. ii. 80.

Frequently, however, such apparent Alexandrines can easily be read as regular five-foot lines, for which they were certainly intended by the poet, by means of the ordinary metrical licences, as slurring, double theses, epic caesuras, or feminine endings [1]; e. g. :

I had thóught, my lórd, | *to have léarn'd his héalth of yóu.* R. II, II. iii. 24.

I prómise you, | *Í am afráid* | *to héar you téll it.* R. III, I. iv. 65.

O'erbéars your ófficers; | *the rábble cáll him lórd.* Haml. IV. v. 102.

Among the blank verse lines in Shakespeare's plays there are sometimes interspersed examples of the native four-beat long line. This occurs, apart from lyrical passages, most frequently in the early plays, e. g. in *Love's Labour's Lost* and in *The Comedy of Errors*, III. i. 11–84, from which the following specimen is taken :

Ant. E. *I thínk thou art an áss.* |
Dro. E.   *Marry, só it doth appéar*
By the wróngs I súffer | *and the blóws I béar.*
I should kíck, being kíck'd ; | *and, béing at that páss,*
You would kéep from my héels | *and bewáre of an áss.*
Ant. E. *You're sád, Signior Bálthasar :* | *pray Gód our chéer*
May ánswer my good wíll | *and your good wélcome hére.*

---

[1] Cf. *Metrik*, ii, § 161.

Occasionally these verses exhibit a somewhat more extended structure, so that they might pass for Alexandrines; mostly, however, a line of this type is connected by rhyme with an unmistakable four-beat line; cf.

> *If thóu hadst been, Drómio, | to dáy in my pláce,*
> *Thou wouldst have changed thy fáce for a náme, | or thy*
>   *náme for an áss.*   Com. of Err. III. i. 47.

For this reason the second line also is to be scanned somehow or other in conformity with the general four-beat rhythm of the passage; possibly we should assume an initial thesis of five syllables. In lyrical passages four-beat lines are often combined also with four-foot iambic verse of the freer type (cf. § 132); e. g. in the following passage from *Midsummer Night's Dream*, II. i. 2–7:

> *Over híll, over dále, | thorough búsh, thorough bríer,*
> *Over párk, over pále, | thorough flóod, thorough fíre,*
> *I do wánder évery whére,*
> *Swífter thán the móon's sphére;*
> *And I sérve the fáiry quéen,*
> *To déw her órbs upón the gréen,* &c.

The two first lines belong to the first, the following to the latter species. Sometimes the rhythm of such rhymed four-foot verses is purely trochaic, e. g. in the witches' song in Macbeth, IV, sc. i.

There are also unrhymed iambic lines of four feet, which usually have a caesura in the middle; e. g. :

> *The mátch is máde, | and áll is dóne.*   Shrew, IV. iv. 46.

> *Befóre the kíngs | and quéens of France.*   Hen. VI, I. vi. 27.

Not unfrequently, however, such verses only apparently have four feet, one missing foot or part of it being supplied by a pause (cf. *Metrik*, ii, § 164):

> *He's tá'en ∪ ⏜ (Shout). ‖ And hark! | they shóut for jóy.*
>   Caes. v. iii. 32.

> Mal. *As thóu didst léave it. ⏜ ‖* Serg. *Dóubtful it stóod.*
>   Macb. I. ii. 7.

> *Thínk on lord Hástings. ⏜ ‖ Despáir and díe!*
>   Rich. III, v. iii. 134.

Isolated two- and three-foot lines occur mostly at the beginning or at the end of a speech, or in pathetic passages of
monologues ; this usually causes a somewhat longer pause,
such as is suitable to the state of feeling of the speaker.

Short exclamations as *Why, Fie, Alack, Farewell* are often
to be regarded as extra-metrical.

Prose also is often used for common speeches not requiring
poetic diction.[1]

§172. One passage from an early play of Shakespeare, and
another, chosen from one of his last plays, will sufficiently
exhibit the metrical differences between these periods of his
work. (For other specimens cf. *Metrik*, ii, § 166.)

Capulet. *But Móntagúe | is bóund as wéll as Í,*
        In pénaltý alíke ; | and 'tis not hárd, I thínk,
        For mén so óld as wé | to kéep the péace.
Paris. *Of hónouráble réckoning | áre you bóth ;*
        And píty 'tís | you líved at ódds so lóng.
        But nów, my lórd, | what sáy you tó my súit ?
Capulet. *But sáying ó'er | what Í have sáid befóre :*
        My chíld is yét | a stránger ín the wórld ;
        She hás not séen | the chánge of fóurteen yéars :
        Let twó more súmmers | wíther ín their príde,
        Ére we may thínk her rípe | to bé a bríde.
Paris. *Yóunger than shé | are háppy móthers máde.*
Capulet. *And tóo soon márr'd | are thóse so éarly máde.*
        The éarth hath swállow'd | áll my hópes but shé,
        Shé is the hópeful lády | óf mý éarth :
        But wóo her, géntle Páris, | gét her héart,
        My wíll to hér consént | is bút a párt ; &c.

                              Romeo and Juliet, I. ii. 1–19.

Miranda. *Íf by your árt, | my déarest fáther, you háve*
        Pút the wild wáters | ín this róar, | alláy them.
        The ský, it séems, | would póur down stínking pítch,
        Bút that the séa, | móunting to the wélkin's chéek,
        Dáshes the fíre out. | Ó, I have súffered
        With thóse thát I saw súffer : | a bráve véssel,
        Who hád, no dóubt, | some nóble créature ín her,
        Dash'd áll to píeces. | Ó, the crý did knóck
        Against my véry héart. | Poor sóuls, they pérish'd.

---

[1] Cf. N. Delius, *Die Prosa in Shakespeares Dramen* (Jahrbuch d.
deutschen Shakespeare-Gesellschaft, v. 227–73).

Had Í been ány gód of pówer, | *I wóuld*
Have súnk the séa | *withín the éarth,* | *or ére*
It shóuld the góod ship | *só have swállow'd* | *ánd*
The fráughting sóuls withín her. |

Prospero.   *Bé collécted :*
No móre amázement : | *téll your píteous héart*
There's nó harm dóne. |

Miranda.   *O wóe the dáy!*
Prospero.   *No hárm!*
Í have done nóthing | *bút in cáre of thée,*
Of thée, my déar one, | *thée, my dáughter,* | *whó*
Art ígnoránt of whát thou árt, | *nought knówing*
Of whénce I ám, | *nór that I ám more bétter*
Than Próspero, | *máster óf a fúll poor céll,*
And thý no gréater fáther. |

Miranda.   *Móre to knów*
Did néver méddle with my thóughts. | &c.
                           Tempest, i. ii. 1—22.

§ 173. The further development of blank verse can be dealt
with here only very briefly.

For the dramatic blank verse of Shakespeare's contemporaries
and immediate successors see *Metrik,* vol. ii, §§ 167—78, and the
works there enumerated. The reader may also be referred to
various special treatises[1] of later date, which supply detailed
evidence in the main confirming the correctness of the author's
former observations.

In this place we mention only the characteristic peculiarities
of the most important poets of that group.

Ben Jonson's blank verse is not so melodious as that of
Shakespeare.

There is often a conflict between the logical and the rhythmical stress, as e. g. :

Be éver cáll'd | *the fóuntayne óf selfe-lóve.*   Cynthia's Rev. i. ii.

Theses of two and even more syllables likewise occur in many
verses, e. g. :

---

[1] Cf. the Halle dissertations by *Hannemann* (on Ford, Oxford, 1889);
Penner (on Peele, Braunschweig, 1890); *Knaut* (on Greene, 1890); *Schulz*
(on Middleton, 1892); *Elste* (on Chapman, 1892); *Kupka* (on Th. Dekker,
1893); *Meiners* (on Webster, 1893); *Clages* (on Thomson and Young,
1892); and the criticism of some of them by Boyle, *Engl. Studien,* xix.
274-9.

Sir Péter Túb was his fáther, | a saltpétre mán.

Tale of a Tub, i. 22 ;

frequently also feminine or even disyllabic unaccented endings
are used:

The dífference 'twíxt | the cóvetous ánd the pródigal.

Staple of News, i. iii. 39.

These licences often give to his verse an uneven and rugged
rhythm.

There are only slight differences from Shakespeare's usage
with regard to the caesura, inversion of accent, &c. Run-on
lines, as well as rhyme and the use of prose, are common in his
plays ; some of his comedies are almost entirely written in prose.

§ 174. In **Fletcher**, on the contrary, run-on lines, rhymed
verses, and prose are exceedingly rare.

Feminine and gliding endings, however (sometimes of three,
and even of four supernumerary syllables), are often used ; in
some plays even more often than masculine ones. (For specimens cf. § 91.)

Feminine endings, combined with disyllabic or polysyllabic
first thesis, are common; now and then we find epic caesuras
or other theses in the interior of the line:

They are too hígh a méat that wáy, | they rún to jelly.

Loyal Subj. i. i. 371.

A cóach and four hórses | cánnot dráw me fróm it.

ib. iii. ii. 361.

Thís was hard fórtune ; | but íf alíve and táken.

Hum. Lieut. i. i. 7.

You máy surpríse them éasily ; | they wéar no pístols.

Loyal Subj. i. ii. 314.

It deserves particular notice that in such feminine endings
or epic caesuras, where the superfluous thesis consists of one
monosyllabic word, this very often has something of a subordinate accent :

And lét sóme létters | tó that énd be féign'd tòo.

Mad Lov. iii. 268.

That spírits háve no séxes, | I belíeve nòt. ib. 272.

You múst look wondrous sád tòo.— | I néed not lóok sò.

ib. v. iii. 105.

The following passage from *The Maid's Tragedy* [1] shows the character of Fletcher's rhythms :

Mel.   *Fórce my swoll'n héart no fúrther; | Í would sáve thee.*
        Your gréat maintáiners áre not hére, | they dáre not:
        'Wóuld they were áll, and árm'd ! | I wóuld speak lóud ;
        Here's óne should thúnder tó them ! | will you téll me ?
        Thou hást no hópe to 'scápe ; | Hé that dares móst,
        And dámns awáy his sóul | to dó thee sérvice,
        Wíll sóoner fetch méat | fróm a húngry líon,
        Than cóme to réscue thée ; | thou'st déath abóut thee.
        Who hás undóne thine hónour, | póison'd thy vírtue,
        Ánd, of a lóvely róse, | léft thee a cánker ?

Evadne. *Lét me consíder. |*
Mel.   *Dó, whose chíld thou wért,*
        Whose hónour thóu hast múrder'd, | whose gráve open'd
        And só pull'd ón the góds, | thát in their jústice
        They múst restóre him | flésh agáin, | and lífe,
        And ráise his drý bònes | tó revénge his scándal.

§ 175. There are no plays extant written by **Beaumont** alone; plays, however, from Fletcher's pen alone do exist, and we can thus gain a clear insight into the distinctive features of his rhythm and style, and are so enabled to determine with some prospect of certainty the share which Beaumont had in the plays due to their joint-authorship. This has been attempted with some success by Fleay, and especially by Boyle.[2]

The characteristics of Beaumont's style and versification may be summed up as follows :

He often uses prose and verse, rhymed and unrhymed verses in the same speech; feminine endings occur rarely, but there are many run-on lines; occasionally we find 'light' and 'weak' endings; double theses at the beginning and in the interior of the line are met with only very seldom. His verse, therefore, is widely different from Fletcher's; cf. the following passage from *The Maid's Tragedy* (II. i, pp. 24–5) :

Evadne. *I thánk thee, Dúla ; | 'wóuld, thou cóuld'st instíl*
        Sóme of thy mírth | intó Aspátiá !
        Nóthing but sád thòughts | in her bréast do dwéll:
        Methínks, a méan betwíxt you | wóuld do wéll.

---

[1] IV. i, p. 66, cf. *Engl. Studien*, v, p. 76.
[2] *Engl. Studien*, iv–vii.

Dula. *Shé is in lóve: | Háng me, if Í were só,*
　　　But Í could rún my cóuntry. | Í love, tóo,
　　　To dó those thíngs | that péople ín love dó.

Asp. *It wére a tímeless smíle | should próve my chéek:*
　　　It wére a fítter hóur | for mé to láugh,
　　　When át the áltar | thé relígious príest
　　　Were pácifýing | thé offénded pówers
　　　With sácrifíce, than nów. | Thís should have béen
　　　My níght; and áll your hánds | have béen emplóy'd
　　　In gíving mé | a spótless óffering
　　　To yóung Amíntor's béd, | as wé are nów
　　　For yóu. | Párdon, Evádne; 'wóuld, my wórth
　　　Were gréat as yóurs, | ór that the kíng, or hé,
　　　Or bóth thought só! | Perháps, he fóund me wórthless:
　　　But, tíll he díd so, | ín these éars of míne,
　　　These crédulous éars, | he póur'd the swéetest wórds
　　　That árt or lóve could fráme. | Íf he were fálse,
　　　Párdon it Héaven! | ánd if Í did wánt
　　　Vírtue, | you sáfely máy | forgíve that tóo;
　　　For Í have lóst | nóne that Í hád from yóu.

§ 176. Fewer peculiarities appear in the verse of **Massinger**, who (according to Fleay and Boyle) wrote many plays in partnership with Beaumont and Fletcher; for this reason his verse has been examined by those scholars in connexion with that of Beaumont and Fletcher. Like Fletcher, Massinger uses a great many feminine endings; but he has many run-on lines as well as 'light' and 'weak' endings. In contradistinction to Beaumont's practice, he seldom uses prose and rhyme, but he has a great many double endings. His verse is very melodious, similar on the whole to that of Shakespeare's middle period.

The following passage may serve as an example:

Tib. *It ís the dúchess' bírthday, | ónce a yéar*
　　　Solémnized with all pómp | and céremóny;
　　　In whích the dúke is nót his ówn, | but hérs:
　　　Nay, évery dáy, indéed, | he ís her créature,
　　　For néver mán so dóated;— | bút to téll
　　　The ténth part óf his fóndness | to a stránger,
　　　Would árgue mé of fíction. | Steph. Shé's, indéed,
　　　A lády óf most éxquisite fórm. | Tib. She knóws it,
　　　And hów to príze it. | Steph. I néver héard her tainted
　　　In ány póint of hónour. | Tib. Ón my lífe,

She's cónstant tó his béd, | and wéll desérves
His lárgest fávours. | Bút, when béauty is
Stámp'd on great wómen, | gréat in bírth and fórtune,
And blówn by flátterers | gréater thán it ís,
'Tis séldom únaccómpanied | with príde ;
Nor ís she thát way frée : | presúming ón
The dúke's afféction, | ánd her ówn desért,
She béars hersélf | with súch a májestý,
Lóoking with scórn on áll | as thíngs benéath her,
That Sfórza's móther, | thát would lóse no párt
Of whát was ónce her ówn, | nor hís fair síster,
A lády tóo | acquáinted wíth her wórth,
Will bróok it wéll; | and hówsoé'er their háte
Is smóther'd fór a tíme, | 'tis móre than féar'd
It will at léngth break óut. | Steph. *Hé in whose pówer it ís,*
Turn áll to the bést. | Tib. *Come, lét us tó the cóurt ;*
We thére shall sée all bráverý and cóst,
That árt can bóast of. | Steph. *I'll béar you cómpaný.*

Massinger, Duke of Milan, 1. i. end.

The versification of the other dramatists of this time cannot
be discussed in this place. It must suffice to say that the more
defined and artistic blank verse, introduced by Marlowe and
Shakespeare, was cultivated by Beaumont, Massinger, Chapman, Dekker, Ford, &c.; a less artistic verse, on the other
hand, so irregular as sometimes to approximate to prose, is
found in Ben Jonson and Fletcher, and to a less degree in
Middleton, Marston, and Shirley. (Cf. *Metrik*, ii. §§ 171–8.)

§ 177. **The blank verse of Milton**, who was the first since
Surrey to use it for epic poetry, is of greater importance than
that of the minor dramatists, and is itself of particular interest. Milton's verse, it is true, cannot be said to be always
very melodious. On the contrary, it sometimes can be brought
into conformity with the regular scheme of the five-foot verse
only by level stress and by assigning full value to syllables
that in ordinary pronunciation are slurred or elided (see § 83).

Generally, however, Milton's blank verse has a stately rhythmical structure all its own, due to his masterly employment
of the whole range of metrical artifices. In the first place, he
frequently employs inversion of accent, both at the beginning of
a line and after a caesura; sometimes together with double
thesis in the interior of the line, as e.g. :

Báck to the gátes of Héaven ; | the súlphurous háil.

Par. Lost, I. 171.

Quite peculiar, however, to Milton's blank verse is the extensive use he makes of run-on lines, and in connexion with the great variety in his treatment of the caesura.

Milton has more than 50 per cent. run-on lines; sometimes we have from three to six lines in succession that are not stopt.

As to the caesura, we mostly have masculine and lyric caesura (more seldom epic caesuras) after the second or third foot; besides, we have frequent double caesuras (generally caused by run-on lines), about 12 per cent.[1]

Finally, as the third peculiarity of Milton's epic blank verse, the almost exclusive use of masculine endings deserves mention. The number of feminine endings in the various books of *Paradise Lost* and of *Paradise Regained* is only from 1 to 5 per cent.; in *Samson Agonistes*, on the other hand, we have about 16 per cent., nearly as many as in the plays of Shakespeare's second period.[2]

The following example (*Paradise Lost*, v. 1-25) may illustrate Milton's blank verse:

Now Mórn, | her rósy stéps | in the éastern clíme
Advráncing, | sówed the éarth with órient péarl,
When Ádam wáked, so cústomed; | fór his sléep
Was áery líght, | from púre digéstion bréd,
And témperate vápours blánd, | which the ónly sóund
Of léaves and fúming rílls, | Auróra's fán,
Líghtly dispérsed, | ánd the shrill mátin sóng
Of bírds on évery bóugh. | So múch the móre
His wónder wás | to fínd unwákened Éve,
With trésses díscompósed, | and glówing chéek,
As thróugh unquíet rést. | Hé, on his síde
Léaning half ráised, | with lóoks of córdial lóve
Hung óver hér enámoured, | ánd behéld
Béauty | whích, whéther wáking | ór asléep,
Shot fórth pecúliar gráces; | thén, with vóice
Míld as when Zéphyrús | on Flóra bréathes,
Her hánd soft tóuching, | whíspered thús:— | ' Awáke,
My fáirest, mý espóused, | my látest fóund,
Heaven's lást best gíft, | my éver-néw delíght!
Awáke! | the mórning shínes, | ánd the fresh fíeld
Cálls us; | we lóse the príme | to márk how spríng

---

[1] On the many combinations of the three kinds of caesura in the different places of the verse, cf. *Metrik*, ii, pp. 28-31.
[2] Cf. *Metrik*, ii, §§ 179-185.

Our ténded plánts, | how blóws the cítron gróve,
What dróps the mýrrh, | and whát the bálmy réed,
How Náture páints her cólours, | hów the bée
Síts on the blóom | extrácting líquid swéet.'

§178. **The dramatic blank verse of the Restoration** is strongly influenced by the heroic verse of the same period, and is on this account very different from the blank verse of Shakespeare and his contemporaries.

For this period the blank verse of Dryden is most interesting ; he uses it with great skill, but also with great restriction of its former licences.

Even the number of the inversions of accent decreases considerably and is only about 12 per cent. We find scarcely any examples of double thesis, slurring of syllables, missing theses in the beginning or in the interior of the line, &c.

The caesura, which is the chief means by which variety is imparted to the metre, is generally masculine or lyric, and as a rule occurs after the second or third foot; occasionally we have double caesuras. Epic caesuras are rare, if they occur at all. Feminine endings are frequent, their proportion being about 25 to 28 per cent. Light and weak endings are rarely to be found amongst the masculine endings, nor are run-on lines (about 20 per cent.) frequently used by Dryden.

Most of the characteristic features of his blank verse will be found exemplified in the following extract :

Emperor. *Márry'd ! | I'll nót belíeve it ; || 'tis impósture ;*
　　　　　Impróbable | they shóu'd presúme t'attémpt,
　　　　　Impóssible | they shóu'd efféct their wísh.
Benducar. *Have pátience tíll I cléar it. |*
Emperor.　　　　　　　　　　　　　*Í have nóne :*
　　　　　Go bíd our móving Pláins of Sánd | lie stíll,
　　　　　And stír not, | whén the stórmy Sóuth blows hígh :
　　　　　From tóp to bóttom | thóu hast tóss'd my Sóul,
　　　　　And nów 'tis ín the mádness | of the Whírl.
　　　　　Requír'st a súdden stóp ? | unsáy thy lýfe,
　　　　　That máy in týme do sómewhat. |
Benducar.　　　　　　　　　　　　　*Í have dóne.*
　　　　　For, sínce it pléases yóu | it shóu'd be fórg'd
　　　　　'Tis fít it shóu'd : | Fár be it fróm your Sláve,
　　　　　To ráise distúrbance | in your Sácred Bréast.
Emperor. *Sebástian ís my Sláve | as wéll as thóu ;*
　　　　　Nor dúrst offénd my Lóve, | but thát Presúmption . . .

Benducar. *Most súre he óught not.* |
Emperor.   *Thén all méans were wánting ;*
    No Príest, no Céremónies | óf their Séct:
    Or, gránt we thése deféchts | cou'd bé supplý'd,
    Hów cou'd our Próphet dó | an áct so báse,
    Só to resúme his Gífts, | and cúrse my Cónquests,
    By máking mé unháppy ! | Nó, the Sláve
    That tóld thee só absúrd a stóry, | lý'd.

                                  Dryden, Sebastian, iii.

The blank verse of Lee, Otway, N. Rowe, and Addison[1] is
of similar structure.

§ 179. Blank verse was treated even more strictly by **Thomson** in *The Seasons.* Thomson followed Dryden with regard to
his treatment of the caesura and the inversion of accent, but
made no use at all of feminine endings. Cf. the following
passage from *Summer* :

    From bríghtening fíelds of éther | fáir disclós'd,
    Chíld of the sún, | refúlgent Súmmer cómes,
    In pride of yóuth, | and félt through náture's dépth:
    He cómes atténded | bý the súltry hóurs,
    And éver-fánning bréezes, | ón his wáy ;
    Whíle, from his árdent lóok, | the túrning Spríng
    Avérts her blúshful fáce ; | and éarth, and skíes
    All smíling, | to his hót domínion léaves.

      Hénce let me háste | intó the míd-wood sháde,
    Where scárce a sún-beam | wánders thróugh the glóom ;
    And ón the dárk-green gráss, | besíde the brínk
    Of háunted stréam, | that bý the róots of óak
    Rólls o'er the rócky chánnel, | líe at lárge,
    And síng the glóries | óf the círcling yéar.

The blank verse of Young (*Night Thoughts*), Cowper (*The
Task*), and other less important poets of the eighteenth century
is of a similar uniform structure; cf. *Metrik,* ii, § 193.

§ 180. In the blank verse of the nineteenth century
we find both tendencies, the strict and the free treatment of this
verse-form ; according to their predominant employment in epic
and dramatic poetry respectively, we may call them the epic
and the dramatic form of the verse. They may be chiefly
distinguished by the peculiarities to be observed in the blank

---

[1] See *Englische Metrik,* ii, §§ 188–90.

verse of Milton and Thomson on the one hand, and of Dryden on the other; i. e. by the admission or exclusion of feminine endings.

The strict form of the epic blank verse, with masculine endings, is preferred in the narrative or reflective poems of Coleridge, Wordsworth, Southey, Shelley, Keats, W. S. Landor, Longfellow, D. G. Rossetti, Mrs. Browning, Robert Browning, Matthew Arnold, Tennyson, Swinburne, and Edwin Arnold.[1]

The free form is represented, mainly, in the dramatic verse of the same and other poets, being used by Coleridge (in his translation of *The Piccolomini*), Wordsworth, Southey, Lamb, Byron, Shelley, W. S. Landor, Tennyson, Matthew Arnold, and others.[2]

[1] Cf. *Metrik*, ii, §§ 195–201.
[2] Cf. *Metrik*, ii, §§ 202–6.

CHAPTER XIII

TROCHAIC METRES

§ **181**. TROCHAIC metres, which, generally speaking, are less common in English poetry than iambics, were not used at all till the Modern English Period. The old metrical writers (Gascoigne, James VI, W. Webbe) only know rising metres.

Puttenham (1589) is the first metrician who quotes four-foot trochaic lines; similar verses also occur during the same period in Shakespeare's *Love's Labour's Lost*, *A Midsummer Night's Dream*, and other plays.

Whether they were introduced directly on foreign models, or originated indirectly from the influence of the study of the ancients by means of a regular omission of the first thesis of the iambic metres, we do not know. It is likewise uncertain who was the first to use strict trochaic verses deliberately in English, or in what chronological order the various trochaic metres formed in analogy with the iambic ones entered into English poetry.

The longest trochaic lines, to which we first turn our attention, seem to be of comparatively late date.

The **eight-foot trochaic line**, more exactly definable as the acatalectic trochaic tetrameter (cf. § 77), is the longest trochaic metre we find in English poetry. As a specimen of this metre the first stanza of a short poem by Thackeray written in this form has been quoted already on page 127. As a rule, however, this acatalectic feminine line is mingled with catalectic verses with masculine endings, as e. g. in the following burlesque by Thackeray, *Damages Two Hundred Pounds*:

Só, God bléss the Spécial Júry! | príde and jóy of Énglish
  gróund,
And the háppy lánd of Éngland, | whére true jústice dóes
  abóund!
Brítish júrymén and húsbands, | lét us háil this vérdict
  próper:
If a Brítish wife offénds you, | Brítons, yóu've a right to
  whóp her.

While the catalectic iambic tetrameter is a line of seven feet (the last arsis being omitted), the catalectic trochaic tetrameter loses only the last thesis, but keeps the preceding arsis; and on this account it remains a metre of eight feet.

Rhyming couplets of this kind of verse, when broken up into short lines, give rise to stanzas with the formulas $a \sim b\, c \sim b_4$, $d \sim e \sim f \sim e \sim_4$; or, if inserted rhymes are used, we have the form $a \sim b\, a \sim b_4$ (alternating masculine and feminine endings), or $a \sim b \sim a \sim b \sim_4$ (if there are feminine endings only). In both these cases the eight-foot rhythm is distinctly preserved to the ear. But this is no longer the case in another trochaic metre of eight feet, where the theses of both the fourth and the eighth foot are wanting, as may be noticed in Swinburne, *A Midsummer Holiday*, p. 132 :

Scárce two húndred yéars are góne, | ánd the wórld is pást awáy
As a nóise of bráwling wínd, | ás a flásh of bréaking fóam,
Thát behéld the sínger bórn | whó raised úp the déad of Róme ;
Ánd a míghtier nów than hé | bíds him tóo rise úp to-dáy ;

still less when such lines are broken up by inserted rhyme in stanzas of the form $a\, b\, a\, b_4$. In cases, too, where the eight-foot trochaic verse is broken up by leonine rhyme, the rhythm has a decided four-foot cadence on account of the rapid recurrence of the rhyme.

§ 182. The **seven-foot trochaic line** is theoretically either a brachycatalectic tetrameter with a feminine or a hypercatalectic trimeter with a masculine ending. An example of the first kind we had on p. 128. A more correct specimen is the following line from the same poem :

Hásten, Lórd, who árt my Hélper; | lét thine áid be spéedy.

The verses quoted on p. 128 are incorrect in so far as the caesura occurs at an unusual place, viz. in the middle of the fourth foot, instead of after it, as in the example just quoted.

They show, however, the origin of a pretty frequently occurring anisorhythmical stanza, which is derived from this metre by means of the use of inserted rhyme; lines 1 and 3 having a trochaic, lines 2 and 4, on the other hand, an iambic rhythm; cf. e. g. the following stanza from a poem by Suckling (*Poets*, iii. 741):

> Sáy, but díd you lóve so lóng?
>   In trúth I néeds must bláme you:
> Pássion díd your júdgement wróng,
>   Or wánt of réason sháme you.

When there are masculine rhymes throughout, the stanza is felt distinctly as consisting of alternate lines of four and three feet $(a_4\, b_3\, a_4\, b_3)$.

The seven-foot rhythm, however, remains, if the three-foot half-lines only have masculine endings, and the four-foot half-lines remain feminine; as is the case in Swinburne's poem *Clear the Way* (*Mids. Hol.*, p. 143):

> Cléar the wáy, my lórds and láckeys, | yóu have hád your dáy.
> Hére you háve your ánswer, Éngland's | yéa agáinst your náy;
> Lóng enóugh your hóuse has héld you: | úp, and cléar the wáy!

This, of course, is likewise the case, if the verses are broken up into stanzas by inserted rhyme $(a_4\, b_3\, a_4\, b_3)$.

More frequently than this correct seven-foot verse, with either a feminine or masculine ending, we find the incorrect type, consisting of a catalectic and a brachycatalectic dimeter, according to the model of the well-known Low Latin verse:

> Mihi est propositum | in taberna mori,

which is often confounded with the former (cf. § 135). The following first stanza of a poem by Suckling (*Poets*, iii. 471) is written in exact imitation of this metre:

> Óut upón it, Í have lóved | thrée whole dáys tógether;
> And am líke to lóve three móre, | if it próve fair wéather.

Although only the long lines rhyme, the stanza is commonly printed in short lines $(a_4\, b_3 \sim c_4\, b_3 \sim)$. Still more frequently we find short-lined stanzas of the kind $(a_4\, b_3 \sim a_4\, b_3 \sim)$ as well as the other sub-species with masculine rhymes only: $a_4\, b_3\, a_4\, b_3$.

§ 183. The **six-foot trochaic line** occurs chiefly in Modern English, and appears both in acatalectic (feminine) and catalectic (masculine) form; e.g. in Swinburne *The Last Oracle* (*Poems and Ballads*, ii. 1):

> *Dáy by dáy thy shádow | shínes in héaven behólden,*
> *Éven the sún, the shíning | shádow óf thy fáce:*
> *Kíng, the wáys of héaven | befóre thy féet grow gólden;*
> *Gód, the sóul of éarth | is kíndled wíth thy gráce.*

Strictly the caesura ought to occur after the third foot, as it does in the first line; generally, however, it is within the third foot, and so this metre as well as the stanza formed by insertion of rhyme acquires an anisorhythmical character, as e.g. in the following quatrain by Moore:

> *Áll that's bríght must fáde,—*
> *The bríghtest stíll the fléetest;*
> *Áll that's swéet was máde*
> *Bút to be lóst when swéetest.*

When masculine rhymes are used throughout, the six-foot rhythm is preserved in anisorhythmical stanzas of this kind just as well as when lines like the first of those in the example quoted above, *Day by day*, &c., are broken up by inserted rhymes $(a \sim b \sim a \sim b_3 \sim)$; or again when they have masculine endings in the second half-lines $(a \sim b \, a \sim b_3)$. If the first half is masculine however, and the second feminine (or if both have masculine endings on account of a pause caused by the missing thesis), the verses have a three-foot character, e. g. in Moore:

> *Whíle I tóuch the stríng,*
> *Wréathe my bróws with láurel,*
> *Fór the tále I síng*
> *Hás for ónce a móral.*

§ 184. The **five-foot trochaic line** also occurs both in acatalectic (feminine) and catalectic (masculine) form, and each of them is found in stanzas rhyming alternately, as e.g. in Mrs. Hemans's *O ye voices* (vii. 57):

> *Ó ye vóices róund | my ówn hearth sínging!*
> *Ás the winds of Máy | to mémory swéet,*
> *Míght I yét retúrn, | a wórn heart brínging,*
> *Wóuld those vérnal tónes | the wánderer gréet?*

Such verses, of course, can be used also in stanzas with either masculine or feminine endings only.

As in the five-foot iambic verse, the caesura generally occurs
either after the second or third foot (in which case it is
feminine), or usually within the second or third foot (masculine
caesura).

In a few cases this metre is also used without rhyme; e. g.
in Robert Browning's *One Word More* (v. 313–21); feminine
endings are used here throughout; run-on lines occasionally
occur, and the caesura shows still greater variety in consequence.   A specimen is given in *Metrik*, ii, § 217.

§ 185. The **four-foot trochaic line** (discussed above in its
relationship to the eight- and seven-foot verse) is the most
frequent of all trochaic metres.   It likewise occurs either with
alternate feminine and masculine rhymes or with rhymes of one
kind only.   We find it both in stanzas and in continuous verse.
The latter form, with feminine rhymes only, we have in Shakespeare's *Tempest*, IV. i. 106–9 :

> *Hónour, ríches, márriage-bléssing,*
> *Lóng contínuance, ánd incréasing,*
> *Hóurly jóys be stíll upón you!*
> *Júno síngs her bléssings ón you,* &c.

With masculine endings only it is found in *Love's Labour's Lost*,
IV. iii. 101 :

> *Ón a dáy—aláck the dáy!—*
> *Lóve, whose mónth is éver Máy,*
> *Spíed a blóssom pássing fáir*
> *Pláying ín the wánton áir.*

As in the five-foot verse, here also the caesura if used at all
may fall at different places; mostly its place is after or within
the second foot.

Generally speaking this metre is used in continuous verse in
such a way that masculine and feminine couplets are intermixed
without regular order;[1] when it is used in stanzas the forms
previously mentioned in § 181 are usually adopted.

This metre is used also, in an unrhymed form and with
feminine endings throughout, in Longfellow's *Song of Hiawatha*,
in which there are noticeably more run-on lines than in rhymed
four-foot trochaics.

§ 186. The **three-foot trochaic line**, both with feminine

---

[1] For examples see *Metrik*, ii, § 218.

and with masculine endings, has been discussed in previous
sections (§§ 182–3) so far as it is derived from seven- and six-
foot verse.   It may also be derived from the six-foot metre
through the breaking up of the line by means of leonine
rhyme, as in the following rhyming couplets :

> Áge, I dó abhór thee,
> Yóuth, I dó adóre thee ;
> Yóuth ís fúll of spórt,
> Áge's bréath ís shórt.
>
> Passionate Pilgrim, No. 12.

§ 187.   **Two-foot trochaic lines** generally occur among
longer lines of anisometrical stanzas ; but we also find them now
and then without longer lines in stanzas and poems.   Feminine
verses of this kind, which may be regarded as four-foot lines
broken up by leonine rhyme, we have in Dodsley (*Poets*,
xi. 112):

> Lóve comméncing,
> Jóys dispénsing ;
> Béauty smíling,
> Wít beguíling ;

and masculine ones in a short poem, possibly by Pope, *To Quinbus
Flestrin, the Man-Mountain* (p. 481):

> Ín a máze,
> Lóst, I gáze,
> Cán our éyes
> Réach thy síze ?
> Máy my láys
> Swéll with práise, &c.

§ 188.   **One-foot trochaic lines** seem only to occur among
longer verses in regular stanzas, as e. g. in a stanza of Addison's opera *Rosamund* (i. ii. 38):

> Túrning,
> Búrning,
> Chánging,
> Ránging.

We even find sometimes a line consisting of a single (of
course accented) syllable in Swinburne, as e. g. in his poem

in trochaic verse, *A Dead Friend* (*A Century of Roundels*, pp. 12–19):

> Góne, O géntle héart and trúe,
> Fríend of hópes forgóne,
> Hópes and hópeful dáys with yóu,
> Góne ?

It is common to all these trochaic metres that their structure, especially that of the longer ones, is (except for the varying caesura) very regular, and that they have only very few rhythmical licences, chiefly slight slurring.

CHAPTER XIV

IAMBIC-ANAPAESTIC AND TROCHAIC-DACTYLIC METRES

§ 189. THE **iambic-anapaestic rhythm** has been touched on before in connexion with the four-stressed verse (cf. § 72) which was developed from the alliterative long line, and which at the end of the Middle English and in the beginning of the Modern English period, under the growing influence of the even-beat metres, had assumed more or less regular iambic-anapaestic character.

When during the same period a definitive separation of the rising and falling rhythms took place, the even-measured rhythm of this four-stressed modern metre became more conspicuous and was made up frequently, although not always, of a regular series of iambic-anapaestic measures. It was thus differentiated still more distinctly from the uneven-beat Old and Middle English long line, the character of which mainly rested on the four well-marked beats only. It deserves notice further that it was not until the Modern English period that the rest of the iambic-anapaestic and trochaic-dactylic metres (the eight-, seven-, six-, five-, four-, three-, and two-foot verses) were imitated from the then common corresponding iambic rhythms.

In the sixteenth century Puttenham quotes four-foot dactylics, and in his time the dactylic hexameter had already been imitated in English. But most of the other trisyllabic rising and falling metres, except the Septenary, occur first in English poetry at the end of the eighteenth and during the course of the nineteenth century.

It must also be noted that in many cases, especially in the eight-, four-, and two-foot verses of this kind (i. e. in those metres that are connected with the old four-stressed verse), the rising and falling rhythms are not strictly separated, but frequently intermingle and even supplement one another.

I. Iambic-anapaestic Metres.

§ **190.** **Eight-foot iambic-anapaestic verses** rhyming in long lines are very rare, but appear in the following four-lined stanza of four-foot verses by Burns, *The Chevalier's Lament* (p. 343):

> *The smáll birds rejóice in the gréen leaves retúrning,*
> *The múrmuring stréamlet winds cléar thro' the vále;*
> *The háwthorn trees blów in the déws of the mórning,*
> *And wíld scatter'd cówslips bedéck the green dále.*

In this metre each of the two periods begins with an iambic measure and then passes into anapaests, the feminine ending of the first (or third) line and the iambic beginning of the second (or fourth) forming together an anapaest.

In a poem by Swinburne (*Poems*, ii. 144) four-foot anapaestic and dactylic lines alternate so as to form anapaestic periods:

> *For a dáy and a níght Love sáng to us, pláyed with us,*
> *Fólded us róund from the dárk and the líght*, &c.

For other less correct specimens of such combinations of verse cf. *Metrik*, ii, § 225.

§ **191.** The **seven-foot iambic-anapaestic verse** would seem to be of rare occurrence except in the most recent period; in long lines and masculine rhymes it has been used by Swinburne, as e.g. in *The Death of Richard Wagner*;[2] we quote the middle stanza:

> *As a vísion of héaven from the hóllows of ócean,* | *that nóne but a gód might sée,*
> *Rose óut of the sílence of things unknówn* | *of a présence, a fórm, a míght,*
> *And we héard as a próphet that héars God's méssage* | *agáinst him, and máy not flée.*

The occurrence of an iambus or a spondee at the end and sometimes in the middle of the verse is remarkable, as well as the arbitrary treatment of the caesura, which does not, as in the iambic Septenary verse, always come after the fourth foot (as in the second line), but sometimes in other places; in the first and third lines, for instance, there is a feminine caesura in the fifth foot.

---

[1] *A Century of Roundels*, p. 30.

More often this Septenary metre occurs in short lines (and therefore with fixed masculine caesura). In this form it appears as early as the seventeenth century in a poem by the Earl of Dorset, *To Chloris* :

> *Ah ! Chlóris, 'tis tíme to disárm your bright éyes,*
>   *And lay bý those térrible glánces ;*
> *We líve in an áge that's more cívil and wíse,*
>   *Than to fóllow the rúles of románces.*

Poets, vii. 513.

Another specimen of the same rhythm, very artistically handled (cf. *Metrik*, i, § 226) is Charles Wolfe's well-known poem *The Burial of Sir John Moore*. The same metre also occurs with masculine rhymes.

§ 192. The **six-foot iambic-anapaestic verse** sometimes occurs in Modern English poets, as Tennyson, *The Grandmother*, *Maud*, &c., Robert Browning, *Abt Vogler*, Mrs. Browning, *Confessions*, Swinburne, *Hymn to Proserpine*, &c.

We quote the following verses from Tennyson's *Maud* to illustrate this metre, which, however, in consequence of the fluctuating proportion of iambic and anapaestic measures occurring in it is handled very differently by different poets (cf. *Metrik*, ii, § 227):

> *Did he flíng himself dówn ? who knóws ? | for a vást specu-*
>   *látion had fáil'd,*
> *And éver he mútter'd and mádden'd, | and éver wánn'd with*
>   *despáir,*
> *And óut he wálk'd when the wínd | like a bróken wórldling*
>   *wáil'd,*
> *And the flýing góld of the rúin'd wóodlands | dróve thro' the*
>   *áir.*

The caesura is sometimes masculine after the third foot (as in lines 1 and 3), sometimes feminine in the fourth (line 2) or the fifth (line 4) ; so that its position is quite indeterminate. The rhymes are mostly masculine, but feminine rhymes are also met with, as e. g. in Mrs. Browning's *Confessions*. Swinburne's verses are printed in long lines, it is true, but they are broken into short lines by inserted masculine and feminine rhymes.

§ 193. The **five-foot iambic-anapaestic verse** likewise does not occur till recent times, and is chiefly used by the poets just mentioned. Rhymed in couplets it occurs in Mrs. Browning's *The Daughters of Pandarus*, Version II (vol. iv, p. 200):

*So the stórms bore the dáughters of Pándarus | óut into
    thráll—
The góds slew their párents; | the órphans were léft in the
    háll.
And there cáme, to féed their young líves, Aphrodíte divíne,
With the íncense, the swéet-tasting hóney, the swéet-smelling
    wíne.*

The rhythm is here almost entirely anapaestic; the caesura
occurs in the most diverse places and may be either masculine
or feminine. The ending of the line is masculine throughout,
as well as in Robert Browning's *Saul* (iii. 146–96), but with many
run-on lines.

In Swinburne's *A Word from the Psalmist* (*A Mids. Holiday*,
p. 176) we have another treatment of this metre. As a rule
the line begins with an anapaest, and continues in pure iambic
rhythm :

*But a lóuder | thán the Chúrch's écho | thúnders
    In the éars of mén | who máy not chóose but héar ;
And the héart in hím | that héars it léaps and wónders,
    With triúmphant hópe | astónished, ór with féar.*

In other examples it has an iambic or spondaic rhythm at the
beginning and end, with an anapaestic part in the middle, as in
The Seaboard (ib., p. 3) by the same poet:

*The séa is at ébb, | and the sóund of her útmost wórd,
    Is sóft as the léast wave's lápse | in a stíll small réach.
From báy into báy, | on quést of a góal deférred,
    From héadland éver to héadland | and bréach to bréach,
Where éarth gives éar | to the méssage that áll days préach.*

In *A Century of Roundels*, p. 1, &c., Swinburne uses this
metre, which also occurs in Tennyson's *Maud*, with feminine
and masculine endings alternately.

§ 194. The **four-foot iambic-anapaestic verse** is essentially identical with the four-stressed verse treated of above
(§ 72), except that it has assumed a still more regular, even-beat
rhythm in modern times; generally it begins with an iambus
and anapaests follow, as in the stanza quoted from Burns
(§ 190). Occasionally this metre has an almost entirely anapaestic structure; as e. g. in Moore, *In the Morning of Life*:

In the mórning of lífe, | when its cáres are unknówn,
  And its pléasures in áll | their new lústre begín,
When we líve in a bríght-beaming | wórld of our ówn,
  And the líght that surróunds us | is áll from withín.

In other examples the rhythm is chiefly iambic, intermingled with occasional anapaests; as e.g. in Moore's *You Remember Ellen*:

  You remémber Éllen, | our hámlet's príde
    How méekly she bléssed | her húmble lót,
  When the stránger Wílliam, | had máde her his bríde,
    And lóve was the líght | of her lówly cót.

Verses like these, which in their structure recall the earlier four-stressed verses, frequently occur (see §§ 72, 132) mixed with four-foot verses of a somewhat freer build in the narrative poems of Coleridge, Scott, and Byron.

§ 195. The **three-foot iambic-anapaestic verse** took its origin by analogy to the corresponding four-foot line, or perhaps to the two-foot line derived from it by inserted rhymes; it occurs as early as Tusser, *Five Hundred Points of Good Husbandry* (cf. Guest, ii, p. 251):

      What lóokest thou hérein to háve ?
      Fíne vérses thy fáncy to pléase ?
      Of mány my bétters that cráve ;
      Look nóthing but rúdeness in thése.

We have the same metre (two anapaests following the first iambic measure) in Rowe, Shenstone, Moore, and others, sometimes with alternate masculine and feminine rhymes.

§ 196. The **two-foot iambic-anapaestic verse** sprang from the breaking-up of the corresponding four-foot (or four-stressed) line by inserted or leonine rhyme, as we find it even in the Middle English bob-wheel stanzas; in Modern English we have it in Tusser for the first time:

      Ill húsbandry brággeth
      To gó with the bést,
      Good húsbandry bággeth
      Up góld in his chést.
      Ill húsbandry lóseth
      For lácke of good fénce,
      Good húsbandry clóseth
      And gaíneth the pénce.

This metre is used by Gay, Goldsmith, Scott, Moore, Long-fellow, Robert Browning, and others; it is also found with an anapaest following the first iambic measure, and either with masculine and feminine rhymes alternately, as in the example quoted above, or (as is most usual) with these rhymes in indiscriminate succession.

§ 197. The **one-foot iambic-anapaestic verse** occasionally occurs in the Middle English bob-wheel stanzas. In Modern English we find it only as an element in anisometrical stanzas, as e.g. in the following half-stanza of Shelley's *Autumn* (iii. 65):

> *The chill rain is fálling, the nípt worm is cráwling,*
> *The rívers are swélling, the thúnder is knélling*
> > *For the yéar;*
> *The blithe swállows are flówn, and the lízards each góne*
> > *To his dwélling.*

In Shakespeare's *Midsummer Night's Dream*, III. ii. 448–63 (apart from the four-foot trochaic end-lines of the half-stanzas), we also have such verses apparently; the iambic-anapaestic character being clearly shown by a couplet like the following:

> *When thou wákest,*
> *Thou tákest.*[1]

II. Trochaic-dactylic Metres.

§ 198. These are much rarer than the iambic-anapaestic metres. Specimens of all of them are quoted, but some are only theoretical examples invented by, and repeated from, English or American metrists.

Theoretically the acatalectic dactylic verse in its rhymed form ought always to have trisyllabic or at least feminine caesura and ending. As a fact, however, these metres have just as frequently or perhaps more frequently masculine caesuras and rhymes.

The **eight-foot trochaic-dactylic verse**, alternating occasionally with iambic-anapaestic lines, occurs in Longfellow's *The Golden Legend*, iv:[2]

[1] Cf. *Metrik*, ii, § 232.
[2] *Prince Henry and Elsie*, pp. 249–51.

Elsie.

> *Ónward and ónward the híghway rúns* ‖ *to the dístant cíty,* |
>   *impátiently béaring*
> *Tídings of húman jóy and disáster,* ‖ *of lóve and of háte,* |
>   *of dóing and dáring !*

Prince Henry.

> *This lífe of óurs* | *is a wíld aeólian hárp* | *of mány a jóyous*
>   *stráin,*
> *But únder them áll there rúns* | *a lóud perpétual wáil,* | *as*
>   *of sóuls in páin.*

Elsie.

> *Fáith alóne can intérpret lífe,* ‖ *and the héart that áches and*
>   *bléeds with the stígma*
> *Of páin,* | *alóne bears the likeness of Chríst,* ‖ *and cán com-*
>   *prehénd its dárk enígma.*

There are, as appears from this specimen, a great many
licences in these verses; the caesura, mostly in the fourth foot,
is masculine in lines 1, 5, 6, feminine in 2 ; so that the second
half of the line has an iambic-anapaestic rhythm. Besides this
most of the lines have secondary caesuras in different places of
the verse ; iambic-anapaestic verses (like 3, 4, 6) are decidedly
in the minority. The rhymes are both feminine and masculine,
but there is no regular alternation between them, as might be
supposed from the above short specimen.

§ **199.** The form of the **seven-foot trochaic-dactylic verse**
may be illustrated by the following theoretical specimen, quoted
from *The Grammar of English Grammars* (p. 880), by Goold
Brown :

> *Óut of the kíngdom of Chríst shall be gáthered,* | *by ángels*
>   *o'er Sátan victórious,*
> *Áll that offéndeth, that líeth, that fáileth* | *to hónour his náme*
>   *ever glórious.*

Verses of this form with masculine endings printed in short
lines occur in a song by Burns (p. 217):

> *Whére are the jóys I have mét in the mórning,* | *that dánc'd*
>   *to the lárk's early sáng ?*
> *Whére is the péace that awáited my wánd'ring* | *at évening*
>   *the wíld woods amáng ?*

§ **200.** The **six-foot trochaic-dactylic verse** may be illustrated by a theoretical specimen from Goold Brown (p. 880), which is strictly dactylic, with inserted rhymes :

> Tíme, thou art éver in mótion, | on whéels of the dáys, years
>   and áges ;
> Réstless as wáves of the ócean, | when Eúrus or Bóreas
>   ráges.

Generally this metre is combined with iambic-anapaestic verses, as e. g. in Mrs. Browning's *Confessions* (iii. 60) mentioned above, § 192, which is, for the greatest part, written in this form :

> Fáce to fáce in my chámber, | my sílent chámber, I sáw her :
> Gód and shé and I ónly, | there Í sate dówn to dráw her
> Sóul through the cléfts of conféssion,— | spéak, I am hólding
>   thee fást
> As the ángel of résurréction | shall dó it át the lást!

§ 201. The **five-foot trochaic-dactylic verse** occurs now and then in Swinburne's *A Century of Roundels*, as e. g. on p. 5 :

> Súrely the thóught | in a mán's heart hópes or féars
> Nów that forgétfulness | néeds must hére have strícken
> Ánguish, | and swéetened the séaled-up spríngs | of téars, &c.

The verses are trochaic with two dactyls at the beginning. The caesura is variable ; masculine in line 1 ; trisyllabic after the second arsis in line 2 ; a double caesura occurs in line 3, viz. a feminine one in the first foot, a masculine one in the fourth. The rhymes are both masculine and feminine.

§ 202. The **four-foot trochaic-dactylic verse** is mentioned first by Puttenham (p. 140), and occurs pretty often ; seldom unrhymed as in Southey, *The Soldier's Wife* ;[1] mostly rhymed, as e. g. in Thackeray, *The Willow Tree* (p. 261):

> Lóng by the wíllow-trees | váinly they sóught her,
> Wíld rang the móther's screams | ó'er the grey wáter :
> Whére is my lóvely one ? | whére is my dáughter ?

For other specimens with occasional masculine rhymes see *Metrik*, ii, § 238; amongst them is one from Swinburne's *A Century of Roundels*, of principally trochaic rhythm.

[1] Cf. *Metrik*, ii, § 238.

§ **203.** The **three-foot trochaic-dactylic verse** with feminine rhymes occurs in R. Browning, *The Glove* (iv. 171):

> Héigho, yawned óne day King Fráncis,
> Dístance all válue enhánces !
> Whén a man's búsy, why, léisure
> Stríkes him as wónderful pléasure.

Masculine rhymes occur in a song by Moore :

> Whére shall we búry our Sháme ?
> Whére, in what désolate pláce,
> Híde the last wréck of a náme,
> Bróken and stáin'd by disgráce ?

We have a strict dactylic rhythm, extending to the end of the line, in a short poem, *To the Katydid*, quoted by Goold Brown.[1]

§ **204.** **Two-foot dactylic** or **trochaic-dactylic verses** (derived from the corresponding four-foot verses by means of inserted or leonine rhyme) are fairly common ; generally, it is true, they have intermittent rhyme (*a b c b*), so that they are in reality four-foot rhyming couplets, merely printed in a two-foot arrangement, as in Tennyson, *The Charge of the Light Brigade* (p. 260). There are, however, also some poems consisting of real short lines of this metre, i. e. of two-foot lines with alternately tumbling and feminine or tumbling and masculine rhymes; as, e. g., in Burns's *Jamie, come try me* (p. 258), and in Hood, *The Bridge of Sighs* (p. 1):

Burns.	Hood.
Íf thou should ásk my love,	Óne more unfórtunate,
Cóuld I dený thee ?	Wéary of bréath,
Íf thou would wín my love,	Ráshly impórtunate,
Jámie, come trý me.	Góne to her déath !

Masculine rhymes throughout occur in Thackeray, *The Mahogany Tree* (p. 51), and in an imitation of the old four-stressed alliterative long line in Longfellow, *The Saga of King Olaf I* (p. 546):

[1] Cf. *Metrik*, ii, § 239.

Thackeray.	Longfellow.
Chrístmas is hére:	*Í am the Gód Thor,*
Wínds whístle shríll,	*Í am the Wár God,*
Ícy and chíll,	*Í am the Thúnderer !*
Líttle care wé:	*Hére in my Nórthland,*
Líttle we féar	*My fástness and fórtress,*
Wéather withóut,	*Réign I for éver !*
Shéltered abóut	*Hére amid ícebergs*
The Mahógany Trée.	*Rúle I the nátions.*

§ 205. **One-foot dactylic verses** are not likely to occur except in anisometrical stanzas. We are unable to quote any proper example of them, but the following two four-lined half-stanzas from Scott's *Pibroch of Donald Dhu* (p. 488), in which some of the two-foot lines admit of being resolved into verses of one foot, may serve to illustrate this metre:

Cóme away,	*Fáster come,*
Cóme away,	*Fáster come,*
Hárk to the súmmons !	*Fáster and fáster,*
Cóme in your	*Chíef, vassal,*
Wár-array,	*Páge and groom,*
Géntles and cómmons.	*Ténant and Máster.*

CHAPTER XV

NON-STROPHIC, ANISOMETRICAL COMBINATIONS OF RHYMED VERSE

§ **206**. NON-STROPHIC anisometrical combinations of rhymed verse consist of lines of different metres, rhyming in pairs, and recurring in a definite order of succession. One of these combinations, known as the **Poulter's Measure** (Alexandrine + Septenary), already occurs in the Middle English Period (cf. § 146) and has remained in use down to the present day. It was at one time extremely popular, and has in the Modern English Period been imitated in other metres.

The most common variety of this metre is that in which the verses have an iambic-anapaestic rhythm; they are usually printed in short lines, as e. g. in a poem by Charles Kingsley:

> When Í was a gréenhorn and yóung,
>   And wánted to bé and to dó,
> I púzzled my bráins about chóosing my líne,
>   Till I fóund out the wáy that things gó.

Before his time Burns had composed a poem in the same metre, *Here's a Health to them that's awa* (p. 245); and at the end of the seventeenth century Philips (*Poets*, vi. 560) wrote a *Bacchanalian Song* in similar verses.

In the same metre are the *Nonsense Rhymes* by Edward Lear,[1] as well as many other quatrains of a similar kind, the humour of which is often somewhat coarse.

An unusual sub-species of this metre, consisting of trochaic verses, occurs only very rarely in Leigh Hunt, e. g. in *Wealth and Womanhood* (p. 277):

> Háve you séen an héiress ín her jéwels móunted,
> Till her wéalth and shé seem'd óne, ánd she míght be cóunted?
> Háve you séen a bósom wíth one róse betwíxt it?
> And díd you márk the gráteful blúsh, whén the brídegroom
>   fix'd it?

[1] *Book of Nonsense*, London, Routledge, 1843.

§ **207.** Other anisometrical combinations consist of a five-foot line followed by one consisting of four, three, or two feet. This form we find pretty often ; Ben Jonson, e. g., uses it (five + four feet) in his translation of Horace, *Odes* v. 11 (*Poets*, iv. 596):

> *Háppy is hé, that fróm all búsiness cléar,*
> *As the old ráce of mánkind wére,*
> *With his own óxen tílls his síre's left lánds,*
> *And ís not ín the úsurer's bánds;*
> *Nor sóldier-líke, stárted with róugh alárms,*
> *Nor dréads the séa's enráged hárms,* &c.

He used the reverse order in *Odes* iv. 1. In Wordsworth's poem *The Gipsies* (iv. 68) we have the couplets : $a\ a_5\ b\ b_4\ c\ c_5\ d\ d_4$, &c., but not divided into stanzas.

Five- and three-foot lines $a_5\ a_3\ b_5\ b_3\ c_5\ c_3\ d_5\ d_3$, &c., occur in Ben Jonson, *The Forest, XI. Epode* (*Poets*, vi, pp. 555–6); and with reverse order $(a_3\ a_5\ b_3\ b_5\ c_3\ c_5,$ &c.) in his *Epigrams* (*Poets*, iv. 546).

The combination of five- and two-foot lines seems to occur in modern poets only ; e. g. in W. S. Landor, *Miscellanies*, clxxv (ii. 649):

> *Néver may stórm thy péaceful bósom véx,*
> *Thou lóvely Éxe !*
> *O'er whóse pure stréam that músic yésternight*
> *Pour'd frésh delíght,*
> *And léft a vísion for the éye of Mórn*
> *To láugh to scórn,* &c.

With crossed rhymes (feminine and masculine rhymes, alternately) this combination occurs in Mrs. Browning, *A Drama of Exile* (i. 12), where the scheme is $a \sim_5 b_2\ a \sim_5 b_2\ c \sim_5 d_2\ c \sim_5 d_2$, and in R. Browning, *A Grammarian's Funeral* (iv. 270), the formula being $a_5\ b \sim_2 a_5\ b \sim_2 c_5\ d \sim_2 c_5\ d \sim_2$, &c.

§ **208.** Combinations of four- and two-foot lines (masculine and feminine endings) occur in Ben Jonson, *Epigrams*, cxx (*Poets*, iv. 545); iambic and anapaestic verses similarly combined in R. Browning, *Prospice*, vi. 152.

In the same poet we have three- and two-foot iambic-anapaestic lines with the formula $a \sim_3 b_2\ c \sim_3 b_2\ d \sim_3 e_2 f \sim_3 e_2$; in *The Englishman in Italy* (iv. 186):

> *Fortú, Fortú, my belóved one,*
> *Sit hére by my síde,*
> *On my knées put up bóth little féet !*
> *I was súre, if I tried,* &c.

In Mrs. Browning we find this metre, which might be taken also as five-foot iambic-anapaestic couplets, broken up by internal rhyme (according to the formula $a \sim_3 b_2 a \sim_3 b_2 c \sim_3 d_2 c \sim_3 d_2$, &c.) in *A Drama of Exile* (i. 3). For other specimens see *Metrik*, ii, §§ 244–8.

A number of other anisometrical combinations of verses will be mentioned in Book II, in the chapter on the non-strophic odes.

CHAPTER XVI

IMITATIONS OF CLASSICAL FORMS OF VERSE AND STANZA

§ 209. The English hexameter. Of all imitations of classical metres in English the best known and most popular is the hexameter. In the history of its development we have to distinguish two epochs—that of the first and somewhat grotesque attempts to introduce it into English poetry in the second half of the sixteenth century, and that of its revival in the eighteenth and nineteenth centuries.

The hexameter was introduced into English poetry by Gabriel Harvey (1545–1630), who, in his *Encomium Lauri*, attempted to imitate the quantitative classic verse in the accentual English language, paying attention as much as possible to the quantity of the English words.

Sir Philip Sidney followed with some poetical portions of his *Arcadia* written in this metre; Stanyhurst (1545–1618) translated the first four books of Virgil in quantitative hexameters; in 1591 Abraham Fraunce translated Virgil's *Alexis*, and William Webbe, the metrist, turned into English the *Georgics* and two eclogues of the same poet, also in quantitative hexameters; but all these efforts had little success on account of the unfitness of English for quantitative treatment. Robert Greene also employed this metre in some of his minor poems, but followed the accentual system; on this account he was more successful, but he found no imitators, and during the latter part of the seventeenth century the metre fell altogether into disuse.

In one isolated case about the middle of the eighteenth century it was revived by an anonymous translator of Virgil's first and fourth eclogues. But English hexameters did not begin to come into favour again before the close of the eighteenth century, when the influence of the study of German poetry began to make itself felt. Parts of Klopstock's *Messiah* were translated by William Taylor (1765–1836) in the metre of the original. He also turned several passages of Ossian into hexameters (published in June, 1796, in the *Monthly*

Magazine), and maintained that the hexameter, modified after the German fashion by the substitution of the accentual for the quantitative principle and the use of trochees instead of spondees, could be used with as good effect in English as in German. About the same time, Coleridge used the hexameter in some of his minor poems, *Hymn to the Earth, Mahomet,* &c., and Southey chose this form for his longer poem, *A Vision of Judgement.*

But it was not till the middle of the nineteenth century that the English hexameter came into somewhat more extensive use. It was at first chiefly employed in translations from the German. Goethe's *Hermann und Dorothea* has been translated five times at least (for the first time by Cochrane, Oxford, 1850). The metre has also been employed in translations of classical poetry, especially Homer and Virgil, and in original poems, none of which, however, have attained general popularity except those by Longfellow, especially his *Evangeline* and *The Courtship of Miles Standish.*

§ 210. The hexameter is a six-foot catalectic verse theoretically consisting of five successive dactyls and a trochee. But the greatest rhythmical variety is given to this verse by the rule which allows a spondee to be used instead of any of the dactyls; in the fifth foot, however, this rarely occurs. In the sixth foot, moreover, the spondee is admissible instead of the trochee. The structure of the verse may thus be expressed by the following formula :

$$\acute{\smile}\,\bar{\smile}\bar{\smile}\,\acute{\smile}\,\bar{\smile}\bar{\smile}\,\acute{\smile}\,\bar{\smile}\bar{\smile}\,\acute{\smile}\,\bar{\smile}\bar{\smile}\,\acute{\smile}\,\smile\smile\,\acute{\smile}\,\bar{\smile}.$$

The main difficulty in imitating this metre in English is caused by the large number of monosyllabic words in the English language, and especially by its lack of words with a spondaic measurement.

Some recent attempts to imitate the hexameter in English according to the principles of quantity have been altogether unsuccessful, as e. g. Cayley's (*Transactions of the Philological Society,* 1862–3, Part i, pp. 67–85). Matthew Arnold's method too proved impracticable (*On Translating Homer,* London, 1862); he attempted and recommended the regulation of the rhythm of the verse by the accent and at the same time sought not to neglect the quantity altogether. But the only successful method of adapting the hexameter to English use is that adopted by William Taylor, who followed the example of the

Germans in observing only the accentual system and substituting the accentual trochee for the spondee. Sir John Herschel in his translation of Homer and Longfellow in his original poems have done the same.

Even with these modifications a certain harshness now and then is inevitable in hexameters both in German and particularly in English, where many lines occur consisting nearly throughout of monosyllables only, as e. g. the following lines from Longfellow's *Evangeline*:

> *White as the snów were his lócks, and his chéeks as brówn*
> *   as the óak-leaves.*
> *Ánd the great séal of the láw was sét like a sún on a*
> *   márgin.*

Other passages, however, prove the English hexameter to be as capable of harmony as the German if treated in this way; cf. e. g. the introductory verses of the same poem : [1]

> *Thís is the fórest priméval.   The múrmuring pínes and the*
> *   hémlocks,*
> *Béarded with móss, and in gárments gréen, indistínct in the*
> *   twílight,*
> *Stánd like Drúids of éld, with vóices sád and prophétic,*
> *Stánd like hárpers hóar, with béards that rést on their*
> *   bósoms.*
> *Lóud from its rócky cáverns, the déep-voiced néighbouring*
> *   ócean*
> *Spéaks, and in áccents discónsolate ánswers the wáil of the*
> *   fórest.*

§ **211.** Besides these repeated attempts to naturalize the hexameter in English, many other kinds of classical verses and stanzas have been imitated in English literature from the middle of the sixteenth and afterwards during the eighteenth and nineteenth centuries. Among these the **Elegiac** verse of the ancients (hexameter alternating with pentameter) was attempted by Sidney in his *Arcadia*. Of more modern experiments in accordance with the accentual principle, Coleridge's translation of Schiller's well-known distich may be quoted:

---

[1] Specimens of earlier hexameter verse with detailed bibliographical information may be found in our *Metrik*, ii, §§ 249–50 ; and especially in C. Elze's thorough treatise on the subject, *Der englische Hexameter*. Programm des Gymnasiums zu Danzig, 1867. (Cf. F. E. Schelling, *Mod. Lang. Notes*, 1890, vii. 423–7.)

In the hexámeter ríses the fóuntain's sílvery cólumn,
In the pentámeter áye fálling in mélody báck.

Swinburne, among others, has written his *Hesperia* (*Poems
and Ballads*, i, 1868, p. 200) in rhymed verses of this kind :

Óut of the gólden remóte wild wést, where the séa without
    shóre ís,
Fúll of the súnset, and sád, if at áll, with the fúllness
    of jóy,
As a wínd sets ín with the áutumn that blóws from the
    région of stóries,
Blóws from a pérfume of sóngs and of mémories belóved
    fróm a bóy.

The third line is remarkable for its anacrusis, which occasionally occurs also in other English hexameters.

Sidney in his *Arcadia*, p. 229 (333, xxxvii), also tried the
minor Asclepiad, which has the following scheme :

$$\_\smile\_\smile\smile\_\mid\_\smile\smile\_\smile\_.$$

Ó sweet wóods, the delíght | óf solitáriness !
Ó how múch I do líke | yóur solitárinesse !
Whére man's mínde hath a fréed | cónsiderátion,
Óf goodnésse to recéive | lóvely diréction, &c.

As an example of Spenser's **six-foot iambic line** Guest
(ii. 270) quotes the verses :

Nów doe I níghtly wáste, | wánting my kíndely réste,
Nów doe I dáily stárve, | wánting my lívely fóode,
Nów doe I álwayes dýe, | wánting my tímely mírth.

In his *Arcadia*, p. 228 (232, xxxvi), Sidney used the **Phaleuciac**
verse of eleven syllables in stanzas of six lines marked by the
recurrence of a refrain. The rhythm is the same as in the
Hendecasyllabics of modern poets, in the following lines of
Swinburne (*Poems*, i. 233):

In the mónth of the lóng declíne of róses
Í behólding the súmmer déad befóre me,
Sét my fáce to the séa and jóurneyed sílent, &c.

The same metre was inaccurately imitated by Coleridge
(p. 252) who put a dactyl in the first foot :

Héar, my belóvëd, an old Milésian stóry !
Hígh and embósom'd in cóngregáted laúrels,
Glímmer'd a témple upón a bréezy héadland, &c.

Finally, the **rhymed Choriambics** may be mentioned, used also by Swinburne (*Poems*, ii. 141–3):

> *Lóve, what áiled thee to léave lífe that was máde lóvely, we*
>   *thóught, with lòve?*
> *Whát sweet vísions of sléep lúred thee awáy, dówn from the*
>   *líght abòve?*
> *Whát strànge fáces of drèams, vóices that cálled, hánds that*
>   *were ráised to wàve,*
> *Lúred or léd thee, alás, óut of the sún, dówn to the súnless*
>   *gràve?* &c.

§ **212.** Among the **classical stanzas**, which may appropriately be discussed in this connexion, the **Sapphic metre** deserves the first place, as it has been imitated pretty often; its scheme is as follows:

It is certainly not an easy task to write in this form of stanza, as it is rather difficult in English to imitate feet of three or even two long syllables (Molossus and Spondee). Yet it has been used by several poets, as by Sidney and his contemporary, the metrist William Webbe; in the eighteenth century by Dr. Watts, Cowper, and Southey (cf. *Metrik*, ii, § 253); and in later times by Swinburne, from whose *Poems and Ballads* a specimen may be quoted:

> *Áll the níght sleēp cǎme not upǒn my éyelǐds,*
> *Shěd not děw, nōr shǒok nor unclósed a fěather,*
> *Yét with lǐps shǔt clóse and with éyes of íron*
>   *Stóod and behěld me.*

Of other kinds of classical verses and stanzas the **Alcaic metre** has occasionally been imitated, e. g. by Tennyson. The scheme of the Latin original is as follows:

Tennyson's poem is an *Ode to Milton* (p. 281):

> *O mĭ́ghty mŏ́uth'd ĭnvĕ́ntŏr ŏ̆f hărmŏ̆nĭes,*
> *O skĭ́lled tŏ sĭ́ng ŏf Tĭ́me ŏr Ĕtĕ́rnĭty,*
> *Gŏ̄dgĭ́ftĕd ŏrgān-vŏ́ice ŏ̆f Ĕ́nglānd,*
> *Mĭ́ltŏn, ă̆ nắme tŏ rĕsŏ́und fŏr ă̆gĕ̆s.*

There are besides in Sidney's *Arcadia*, pp. 227 (232, xxxv) and 533, **Anacreontic stanzas** of varying length, consisting of 3–11 verses and constructed in this way:

> *My Mŭ́se, what áiles this árdour ?*
> *To bláse my ónely sécrets ?*
> *Alás, it ís no glóry*
> *To síng mine ówne decáid state.*

§ **213.** In connexion with these imitations of classical verses and stanzas without rhyme some other forms should be mentioned which took their rise from an attempt to get rid of end-rhyme. Orm was the first to make the experiment in his rhymeless Septenary, but he found no followers in the Middle English period; Surrey, several centuries later, on the other hand, did achieve success with his blank verse. In the beginning of the seventeenth century Thomas Campion, in his *Observations on the Arte of English Poesy* (London, 1602), tried to introduce certain kinds of rhymeless verses and stanzas, mostly trochaic; e. g. trochaic verses of three measures (with masculine endings) and of five measures (with feminine endings); distichs consisting of one five-foot iambic and one six-foot trochaic verse (both masculine); then a free imitation of the Sapphic metre and other kinds of rhymeless stanzas, quoted and discussed in *Metrik*, ii, § 254. But these early and isolated attempts need not engage our attention in this place, as they had probably no influence on similar experiments of later poets.

In Milton, e. g., we find a stanza corresponding to the formula $a\, b_5\, c\, d_3$ in his imitation of the fifth Ode of Horace, Book I, used also by Collins, *Ode to Evening* (*Poets,* ix. 526):

> *If áught of oáten ʂtóp or pástoral sóng*
> *May hópe, chast Éve, to soóthe thy módest éar*
> *Like thý own sólemn spríngs*
> *Thy spríngs and dýing gáles.*

Southey uses the same stanza (ii. 145); to him we owe several other rhymeless stanzas of the form $a\, b_4\, c\, d_3$ (ii. 212), $a_3\, b\, c_4\, d_3$ (ii. 210) (both of anapaestic verses), $a\, b\, c_4\, d_3$ (ii. 148),

$a_3\,b\,c_5\,d_3$ (ii. 159), $a_4\,b\,c_3\,d_5$ (ii. 182), $a\,b_4\,c_5\,d_3$ (ii. 187), $a_4\,b_3\,c_5\,d_3$ (ii. 189); all consisting of iambic verses.

The same poet also uses a stanza of five iambic lines of the form $a_5\,b_3\,c_4\,d\,e_3$ (iii. 255), and another of the form $a_5\,b_3\,c_5\,d_4\,e_3$ in his ode *The Battle of Algiers* (iii. 253):

> One dáy of dréadful occupátion móre,
> > Ere Éngland's gállant shíps
> Shall, of their béauty, pómp, and pówer disróbed,
> > Like séa-birds ón the súnny máin,
> > Rock ídly ín the pórt.

A stanza of similar construction (formula $a\,b\,c_5\,d\,e_3$) is used by Mrs. Browning in *The Measure* (iii. 114).

Various isometrical and anisometrical stanzas of this kind occur in Lord Lytton's *Lost Tales of Miletus*; one of these consists of three of Coleridge's Hendecasyllabics, followed by one masculine verse of similar form, and has the formula $a \sim b \sim c \sim d_5$; it is used, e. g., in *Cydippe*:

> Fáirest and hárdiest óf the yóuths in Céos
> Flóurish'd Acóntius frée from lóve's sweet tróuble,
> Púre as when fírst a chíld, in hér child-chórus,
> > Chánting the góddess óf the silver bów.

In another stanza used in *The Wife of Miletus* an ordinary masculine blank verse alternates with a Hendecasyllabic; a third of the form $a\,b\,c\,d_4$ consists of trochaic verses.

Other stanzas of ordinary five- and three-foot verses used by him in the *Lost Tales* have the formulas $a\,b_5\,c_3\,d_5$, $a\,b\,c_5\,d_3$, $a \sim b \sim_5 c_3\,d_5$.

In another stanza (*Corinna*), constructed after the formula $a\,b_4\,c\,d_3$, a dactylic rhythm prevails:

> Gláucon of Lésbos, the són of Euphórion,
> Búrned for Corinna, the blúe-eyed Milésian.
> > Nor móther nor fáther hád she;
> > Béauty and wéalth had the órphan.

Stanzas of a similar kind consisting of trochaic verses are used by Longfellow; one of the form $a_3\,b\,c_4\,d \sim_2$ in *To an old Danish Song Book*, and another which corresponds to the formula $a\,b_5\,c_2\,d_5$ in *The Golden Mile-Stone*.

Iambic-anapaestic verses of two stresses and feminine ending are found in Longfellow's poem *The Men of Nidaros* (p. 579); the arrangement into stanzas of six lines being marked only by the syntactical order, in the same way as in Southey's poem *The Soldier's Wife* (ii. 140), in which, too, four-foot dactylic verses are combined in stanzas of three lines. Two-foot dactylic and dactylic-trochaic verses of a similar structure to those mentioned in Book I, § 73, are joined to rhymeless stanzas of five lines (the first four have feminine endings, the last a masculine one) by Matthew Arnold in his poem *Consolation* (p. 50). Stanzas of five iambic verses of three and five measures, corresponding to the formula $a_3 b_5 c_3 d_5 e_3$, occur in his poem *Growing Old* (p. 527). In Charles Lamb's well-known poem, *The Old Familiar Faces*, written in stanzas of three lines, consisting of five-foot verses with feminine endings, the division into stanzas is marked by a refrain at the end of each stanza. For examples of these different kinds of verses the reader is referred to the author's *Metrik*, ii, §§ 255–8.

In conclusion it may be mentioned that many of the irregular, so-called Pindaric Odes (cf. Book II, chap. viii) are likewise written in rhymeless anisometrical stanzas.

BOOK II. THE STRUCTURE OF STANZAS

PART I

CHAPTER I. DEFINITIONS

STANZA, RHYME, VARIETIES OF RHYME

§ **214.** THE strophe in ancient poetry, and the stanza in mediaeval and modern analogues and derivatives of that poetic form, are combinations of single lines into a unity of which the lines are the parts. The word *strophe*[1] in its literal sense means a turning, and originally denoted the return of the song to the melody with which it began. The melody, which is a series of musical sounds arranged in accordance with the laws of rhythm and modulation, has in poetry its counterpart in a parallel series of significant sounds or words arranged according to the laws of rhythm; and the melodic termination of the musical series has its analogue in the logical completion of the thought. But within the stanza itself again there are well-marked resting places, divisions closely connected with the periods or sentences of which the stanza is made up. The periods are built up of rhythmical sequences which are combinations of single feet, dominated by a rhythmical main accent. In shorter lines the end of the rhythmical sequence as a rule coincides with the end of the verse; but if the line is of some length it generally contains two or even more rhythmical sequences.[2] The essential constituents of the stanza are the lines; and the structure of the stanzas connected together to make up a poem is in classical as well as in mediaeval and modern poetry subject to the rule that

---

[1] The word stanza is explained by Skeat, *Conc. Etym. Dict.*, as follows: 'STANZA. Ital. stanza, O.Ital. *stantia*, "a lodging, chamber, dwelling, also *stance* or staffe of verses;" Florio. So called from the stop or *pause* at the end of it. ─ Low Lat. *stantia*, an abode. ─ Lat. *stant-*, stem of pres. pt. of *stare*.'

[2] Cf. §§ 8, 223-7.

the lines of each stanza of the poem must resemble those of the other stanzas in number, length (i. e. the number of feet or measures), rhythmical structure, and arrangement. (This rule, however, is not without exceptions in modern poetry.) In the versification of the ancients it was sufficient for the construction of a strophic poem that its verses should be combined in a certain number of groups which resembled each other in these respects. In modern poetry, also, such an arrangement of the verses may be sufficient for the construction of stanzas; but this is only exceptionally the case, and, as a rule, only in imitation of the classic metrical forms (cf. §§ 212–13). The stanza, as it is found in the mediaeval and modern poetry of the nations of western Europe, exhibits an additional structural element of the greatest importance, viz. the connexion of the single lines of the stanza by end-rhyme; and with regard to this a rule analogous to the previously mentioned law regarding the equality in number and nature of verses forming a stanza holds good, viz. that the arrangement of the rhymes which link the verses together to form stanzas, must be the same in all the stanzas of a poem.

§ 215. Of the three chief kinds of rhyme, in its widest sense (mentioned § 10), i. e. alliteration, assonance, and end-rhyme, only the last need be taken into consideration here. There are, indeed, some poems in Old English in which end-rhyme is used consciously and intentionally (see §§ 40–1), but it was never used in that period for the construction of stanzas. This took place first in Middle English under the influence and after the model of the Low Latin and the Romanic lyrics.

The influence of the Low Latin lyrical and hymnodic poetry on the Old English stanzas is easily explicable from the position of the Latin language as the international tongue of the church and of learning during the Middle Ages. The influence of the lyrical forms of Provence and of Northern France on Middle English poetry was rendered possible by various circumstances. In the first place, during the crusades the nations of Western Europe frequently came into close contact with each other. A more important factor, however, was the Norman Conquest, in consequence of which the Norman-French language during a considerable time predominated in the British Isles and acted as a channel of communication of literature with the continent. One historical event deserves in this connexion special mention— the marriage in the year 1152 of Henry, Duke of Normandy (who came to the throne of England in 1154), and Eleonore of

Poitou, widow of Louis VII of France; in her train Bernard
de Ventadorn, the troubadour, came to England, whither many
other poets and minstrels soon followed him, both in the reign
of Henry and of his successor Richard Cœur de Lion, who
himself composed songs in the Provençal and in the French
language. The effect of the spread of songs like these in
Provençal and French in England was to give a stimulus and
add new forms to the native lyrical poetry which was gradually
reviving. At first indeed the somewhat complicated strophic
forms of the Provençal and Northern French lyrics did not
greatly appeal to English tastes, and were little adapted to the
less flexible character of the English tongue. Hence many of
the more elaborate rhyme-systems of Provençal and Northern
French lyrical versification were not imitated at all in English ;
others were reproduced only in a modified and often very
original form; and only the simpler forms, which occurred
mostly in Low Latin poetry as well, were imitated somewhat
early and with little or no modification.

§ 216. The end-rhyme, which is so important a factor in the
formation of stanzas, has many varieties, which may be classified
in three ways :

A. According to the **number** of the rhyming syllables.

B. According to the **quality** of these syllables.

C. According to the **position of the rhyme** in relation to
the line and the stanza.

Intimately connected with this last point is the use of rhyme
as an element in the structure of the stanza.

A. With regard to the number of the syllables, rhymes are
divided into three classes, viz. :

1. The **monosyllabic** or **single rhyme** (also called **masculine**), e. g. *hand : land, face : grace.*

2. The **disyllabic** or **double rhyme** (also called **feminine**),
as *ever : never, brother : mother, treasure : measure, suppression :
transgression*; or *owe me : know me* Shakesp. Ven. and Ad.
523–5, *bereft me : left me* ib. 439–41. The terms *masculine* and
feminine originated with the Provençal poets and metrists, who
were the first among the people of Western Europe to theorize
on the structure of the verses which they employed, and introduced these terms in reference to the forms of the Provençal
adjective, which were monosyllabic or accented on the last
syllable in the masculine, and disyllabic or accented on the last
syllable but one in the feminine : *bos–bona, amatz–amada.*

3. The **trisyllabic, triple,** or **tumbling rhyme**, called

gleitender (i. e. gliding) *Reim* in German. Of this variety of rhyme, which is less common than the two others, examples are *gymnastical : ecclesiastical* Byron, Beppo, 3; *quality : liberality* ib. 30; *láugh of them : hálf of them* ib. 98. Rhymes like this last, which are made up of more words than two, might, like those given above under the disyllables, such as *owe me : know me,* also form a separate sub-species as **compound rhymes,** as they resemble the broken rhymes (cf. § 217, B. 3) and have, like these, mostly a burlesque effect.

§ **217.** B. According to the second principle of classification, by the quality of the rhyming syllables, the species of rhyme are as follows :

1. The **rich rhyme** (in French *rime riche*), i.e. two words completely alike in sound but unlike in meaning rhyming with each other. Of this three special cases are possible :

a. Two simple words rhyming with each other, as *londe* (inf.) *: londe* (noun) K. Horn, 753–4; *armes* (arms) *: armes* (weapons) Chaucer, Compleynt of Mars, ll. 76–7; *steepe* (adj.) *: steepe* (inf.) Spenser, F. Q. i. i. 39; *sent* (perf.) *: sent* (=*scent,* noun) ib. 43; *can* (noun) *: can* (verb) ib. i. iv. 22, &c. In the earlier Modern English poetry we find many rhymes of this class between words that are alike or similar in sound, but of different spelling, as *night : knight, foul : fowl, gilt : guilt, hart : heart,* &c. (cf. Ellis, 'Shakespere's Puns' in *Early Engl. Pron.* iii. 920, iv. 1018).

b. A simple and a compound word rhyming together, as *leue : bileue* K. Horn, 741–2; *like : sellike* Sir Tristr. 1222–4; *ymake : make* Wright's Spec. of Lyr. Poetry, p. 27, ll. 16–18; *apart : part* Spenser, F. Q. i. ii. 21, *hold : behold* ib. i. iii. 40; here also identity of sound and difference of spelling is possible, as *renew : knew* ib. i. iii. 25.

c. Two compound words rhyming together, as *recorde : accorde* Chaucer, C. T. Prol. 828–9; *affirmed : confirmed* Wyatt, p. 98; *expeld : compeld* Spenser, F. Q. i. i. 5.

2. The **identical rhyme.** This is, properly speaking, no rhyme at all, but only a repetition of the same word intended as a substitute for rhyme; and therefore was and is avoided by careful and skilful poets; *sette : sette* K. Horn, 757–8; *other : other* Wyatt, p. 45; *down : down* ib. p. 194; *sight : sight* Spenser, F. Q. i. i. 45, &c.

3. The **broken rhyme** has two sub-species :

a. In the first of these one part of the rhyme is composed of two or three words (unlike the rhymes spoken of under A. 3, consisting of two words each), e. g. *time : bi me* K. Horn, 533–4; *scolis : fole is*, Chaucer, Troil. i. 634–5; *tyrant : high rent* Moore, Fudge Fam., Letter iv; *wide as : Midas* ib.; *well a day : melody* ib. x; *Verona : known a* Byron, Beppo, 17; *sad knee : Ariadne* ib. 28; *endure a : seccatura* ib. 31; *estrangement : change meant* ib. 53; *quote is : notice* ib. 48; *exhibit 'em : libitum* ib. 70; *Julia : truly a : newly a* Byron, Don Juan, ii. 208.

b. In the second sub-species the rhyme to a common word is formed by the first part only of a longer word, the remainder standing at the beginning of the following line. This sort of rhyme seems to be unknown in Middle English literature; modern poets, however, use it not unfrequently in burlesque, as well as the previously mentioned sub-species, e. g. *kind : blind-(ness)* Pope, Satire iii. 67; *forget-(ful) : debt* ib. iv. 13; *beg : egge-(shells)* ib. iv. 104; *nice hence-(forward) : licence* Byron, Don Juan, i. 120; Thackeray, Ballads, p. 133:

> *Winter and summer, night and morn,*
> *I languish at this table dark;*
> *My office window has a corn-*
> *er looks into St. James's Park.*

4. The **double rhyme**. This is always trisyllabic like that mentioned under A. 3; but there is a difference between them, in that the two closing syllables of the gliding rhyme stand outside the regular rhythm of the verse; while the first and the third syllable of the double rhyme bear the second last and last arsis of the verse.

> *For dóuteth nóthinge, mýn inténción*
> *Nis nót to yów of reprehénción.*
>
> Chaucer, Troil. i. 683–4.

This sort of rhyme does on the whole not very often occur in Modern English poetry, and even in Middle English literature we ought to regard it as accidental. The same is the case with another (more frequent) species, namely,

5. The **extended rhyme**, in which an unaccented syllable preceding the rhyme proper, or an unaccented word in thesis, forms part of the rhyme, e. g. *biforne : iborne* Chaucer, Troil. ii. 296–8; *in joye : in Troye* ib. i. 118–19; *to quyken : to stiken* ib. 295–7; *the past : me last* Byron, Ch. Harold, ii. 96; *the limb : the brim* ib. iii. 8, &c.

6. The **unaccented rhyme**, an imperfect kind of rhyme, because only the unaccented syllables of disyllabic or poly-

syllabic words, mostly of Germanic origin and accentuation, rhyme together, and not their accented syllables as the ordinary rule would demand, e. g. *láweles, lóreless, námeless; wrécful, wróngful, sínful* Song of the Magna Charta, ll. 30–2, 66–8; many rhymes of this kind occur in the alliterative-rhyming long line combined into stanzas.[1] In Modern English we find this kind of rhyme pretty often in Wyatt[2]; e. g.:

> *Consider well thy ground and thy beginning;*
> *And gives the moon her horns, and her eclipsing.* p. 56.

> *With horrible fear, as one that greatly dreadeth*
> *A wrongful death, and justice alway seeketh.* p. 149.

Such rhymes in dactylic feet, as in the following verses by Moore (*Beauty and Song*, ll. 1–4),

> *Dówn in yon súmmer vale,*
> *Whére the rill flóws,*
> *Thús said the Níghtingale*
> *Tó his loved Róse,*

are not harsh, because in this case the unaccented syllable which bears the rhyme is separated from the accented syllable by a thesis. A variety of the unaccented rhyme is called the **accented-unaccented**; examples have been quoted before in the chapter treating of the alliterative-rhyming long line (§§ 61, 62). In the same place some other verses of the above-quoted song of Moore are given, showing the admissibility of rhymes between gliding or trisyllabic and masculine rhyming-syllables or -words (*mélodỳ : thée, Róse bè : thée*). In these cases the subordinate accent of the third syllable in *mélody* or the word *bè* in the equally long *Róse bè* is strong enough to make a rhyme with *thee* possible, although this last word has a strong syntactical and rhythmical accent. As a rule such accented-unaccented rhymes, in which masculine endings rhyme with feminine endings, are very harsh, as is often the case in Wyatt's poems (cf. Alscher, pp. 123–6), e. g.

> *So chánced mé that évery pássión*
> *Wherebỳ if thát I láugh at ány séason.* p. 7.

---

[1] Cf. §§ 60–2 and the author's 'Metrische Randglossen, II.', *Engl. Stud.*, x, pp. 196–200.

[2] Cf. *Sir Thomas Wyatt*, von R. Alscher, Wien, 1886 pp. 119–23.

§ **218**. C. According to the third principle of classification, by the position of the rhyming syllable, the varieties of rhyme are as follows:

1. The **sectional rhyme**, so called because it consists of two rhyming words within one section or hemistich.[1] This kind of rhyme occurs now and then even in Old English poetry, but it is usually unintentional (cf. §§ 40–2), e. g. *sǣla and mǣla*; *þæt is sōð metod* Beow. 1611; in Middle English literature it is frequent, as in Barbour's Bruce: *and till Ingland agayne is gayne* i. 144, iii. 185; *That eftyr him dar na man ga* iii. 166. In Modern English poetry this kind of rhyme is more frequent, and often intentionally used for artistic effect:

> *Then up with your cup, | till you stagger in speech,*
> *And match me this catch, | though you swagger and screech,*
> *Ah, drink till you wink, | my merry men, each.*
>
> Walter Scott, Song from Kenilworth.

2. Very closely related to this is the **inverse rhyme** (as Guest called it), which occurs when the last accented syllable of the first hemistich of a verse rhymes with the first accented syllable of the second hemistich:

> *These steps both reach | and teach thee shall*
> *To come by thrift | to shift withall.* Tusser.

This kind of rhyme is generally met with in the popular national long line of four stresses. Guest gives a much wider range to it. But when it occurs in other kinds of verse, as in the iambic verse of four or five feet, it is not to be looked upon as an intentional rhyme, but only as a consonance caused by rhetorical repetition (the examples are quoted by Guest):

> *And art thou gone and gone for ever?* Burns.
> *I followed fast, but faster did he fly.* Shak. Mids. III. ii. 416.

3. The **Leonine**[2] **rhyme** or **middle rhyme,** which recurs throughout the Old English *Rhyming Poem*, and is occasionally used in other Old English poems. This rhyme connects the two hemistichs of an alliterative line with each other by end-rhyme and, at the same time, causes the gradual breaking up of

---

[1] By the German metrists it is called *Binnenreim*, or *Innenreim*.

[2] So called from a poet Leo of the Middle Ages (c. 1150) who wrote in hexameters rhyming in the middle and at the end. Similar verses, however, had been used occasionally in classic Latin poetry, as e. g. *Quot caelum stellas, tot habet tua Roma puellas*, Ovid, Ars Amat. i. 59.

it into two short lines; we find it in certain parts of the *Anglo-Saxon Chronicle*, in Layamon, in the *Proverbs of Alfred*, and other poems, e. g.: *his sedes to* sowen, *his medes to* mowen Prov. 93–4; *þus we uerden* þere, *and for þi beoþ nu* here Lay. 1879–80. See §§ 49, 57–58, 78 for examples from Middle and Modern English literature of this kind of rhyme (called by the French *rimes plates*) as well as of the following kind, when used in even-beat metres.

4. The **interlaced rhyme** (*rime entrelacée*), by means of which two long-lined rhyming couplets are connected a second time in corresponding places (before the caesura) by another rhyme, so that they seem to be broken up into four short verses of alternate or cross-rhyme (*a b a b*), e. g. in the latter part of Robert Mannyng's *Rhyming Chronicle* (from p. 69 of Hearne's edition), or in the second version of *Saynt Katerine* (cf. the quotations, §§ 77, 78, 150). When, however, long verses without interlaced rhyme are broken up only by the arrangement of the writer or printer into short lines, we have

5. The **intermittent rhyme**, whose formula is *a b c b* (cf. p. 196). Both sorts of rhyme may also be used, of course, in other kinds of verse, shorter or longer; as a rule, however, the intermittent rhyme is employed for shorter, the alternate or cross-rhyme for longer verses, as, for example, those of five feet.

6. The **enclosing rhyme**, corresponding to the formula *a b b a*, e. g. in *spray, still, fill, May*, as in the quartets of the sonnet formed after the Italian model (cf. below, Book II, chap. ix). This sort of rhyme does not often occur in Middle English poetry; but we find it later, e. g. in the tail or veer of a variety of stanza used by Dunbar and Kennedy in their *Flyting Poem*.

7. The **tail-rhyme** (in French called *rime couée*, in German *Schweifreim*), the formula of which is *a a b c c b*. (For a specimen see § 79.)

This arrangement of rhymes originated from two long lines of the same structure, formed into a couplet by end-rhyme, each of the lines being divided into three sections (whence the name *versus tripertiti caudati*). This couplet, the formula of which was $-a-a-b \parallel -c-c-b$, is, in the form in which it actually appears, broken up into a stanza of six short lines, viz. two longer couplets *a a, c c*, and a pair of shorter lines rhyming together as *b b*, the order of rhymes being *a a b c c b*. (For remarks on the origin of this stanza see § 240.)

§ **219.** As to the quality of the rhyme, purity or exactness, of course, is and always has been a chief requirement. It is, however, well known that the need for this exactness is frequently disregarded not only in Old and Middle English poetry (cf. e. g. the Old English assonances meant for rhymes, § 40, or the often very defective rhymes of Layamon, § 45) but even in Modern English poetry. Many instructive examples of defective rhymes from Spenser, Sidney, Shakespeare, and Dryden are given by A. J. Ellis, *On Early Engl. Pronunciation*, iii. 858–74, 953–66, iv. 1033–9.

From these collections of instances we see how a class of imperfect rhymes came into existence in consequence of the change in the pronunciation of certain vowels, from which it resulted that many pairs of words that originally rhymed together, more or less perfectly, ceased to be rhymes at all to the ear, although, as the spelling remained unaltered, they retained in their written form a delusive appearance of correspondence. These 'eye-rhymes', as they are called, play an important part in English poetry, being frequently admitted by later poets, who continue to rhyme together words such as *eye : majesty* Pope, Temple of Fame, 202–3; *crowns : owns* ib. 242–3; *own'd : found* id. Wife of Bath, 32–3, notwithstanding the fact that the vowel of the two words, which at first formed perfect rhymes, had long before been diphthongized or otherwise changed while the other word still kept its original vowel-sound.

CHAPTER II

THE RHYME AS A STRUCTURAL ELEMENT OF THE STANZA

§ **220.** On the model of the Provençal and Northern French lyrics, where the rhyme was indispensable in the construction of stanzas, rhyme found a similar employment in Middle English poetry. Certain simple kinds of stanzas, however, were in their formation just as much influenced by the Low Latin hymn forms, in which at that time rhyme had long been in vogue.

But the rules prescribed for the formation of stanzas by the Provençal poets in theory and practice were observed neither by the Northern French, nor by the Middle English poets with equal rigour, although later on, it is true, in the court-poetry greater strictness prevailed than in popular lyrical poetry.

One of the chief general laws relating to the use of rhyme in the formation of stanzas has already been mentioned in § 214 (at the end). A few other points of special importance require to be noticed here.

Both in Middle English and in Romanic poetry we find stanzas with a single rhyme only and stanzas with varied rhymes. But the use of the same rhymes throughout all the stanzas of one poem (in German called *Durchreimung*), so frequent in Romanic literature, occurs in Middle English poetry only in some later poems imitated directly from Romanic models. As a rule, both where the rhyme in the same stanza is single and where it is varied, all the stanzas have different rhymes, and only the rhyme-system, the arrangement of rhymes, is the same throughout the poem. It is, however, very rarely and only in Modern English literary poetry that the several stanzas are strictly uniform with regard to the use of masculine and feminine rhyme; as a rule the two kinds are employed. Sometimes, it is true, in the anisometrical 'lays', as they are called, as well as in the later popular ballads (e. g. in *Chevy Chace* and *The Battle of Otterbourne*), we find single stanzas deviating from the rest in rhyme-arrangement as well as in number of lines, the stanzas consisting of Septenary lines with cross-rhymes and intermittent rhymes (*a b a b*, and *a b c b*) being combined now and then with tail-rhyme. This is found to a still greater extent in lyrical poetry of the seventeenth century (e. g. Cowley, G. Herbert, &c.) as well as in odic stanzas of the same or a somewhat later period.

§ 221. It does not often happen in Middle English poetry that a line is not connected by rhyme with a corresponding line in the same stanza to which it belongs, but only with one in the next stanza. In Modern English poetry this peculiarity, corresponding to what are called *Körner* in German metres, may not unfrequently be observed in certain poetic forms of Italian origin, as the terza rima or the sestain. Of equally rare occurrence in English strophic poetry are lines without any rhyme (analogous to the *Waisen*—literally 'orphans'—of Middle High German poetry), which were strictly prohibited in Provençal poetry. In Middle English literature they hardly ever occur, but are somewhat more frequent in Modern English poetry, where they generally come at the end of the stanza. On the other hand the mode of connecting successive stanzas, technically called *Concatenatio* (rhyme-linking), so frequently used by the Provençal and Northern French poets, is very common in Middle English verse. Three different varieties of this device are to be distinguished, viz.:

1. The repetition of the rhyme-word (or of a word standing close by it) of the last line of a stanza, at the beginning of the first line of the following stanza.

2. The repetition of the whole last line of a stanza, including the rhyme-word, as the initial line of the following stanza (not very common); and

3. The repetition of the last rhyme of a stanza as the first rhyme of the following one; so that the last rhyme-word of one stanza and the first rhyme-word of the next not only rhyme with the corresponding rhyme-words of their own stanzas, but also with one another. Such 'concatenations' frequently connect the first and the last part (i. e. the *frons* and the *cauda*) of a stanza with each other. They even connect the single lines of the same stanza and sometimes of a whole poem, with each other, as e. g. in the 'Rhyme-beginning Fragment' in Furnivall's *Early English Poems and Lives of Saints*, p. 21 (cf. *Metrik*, i, p. 317).

§ 222. Another and more usual means of connecting the single stanzas of a poem with each other is the **refrain** (called by the Provençal poets *refrim*, i. e. 'echo'; by German metrists sometimes called *Kehrreim*, i. e. recurrent rhyme). The refrain is of popular origin, arising from the part taken by the people in popular songs or ecclesiastical hymns by repeating certain exclamations, words, or sentences at the end of single lines or stanzas. The refrain generally occurs at the end of a stanza, rarely in the interior of a stanza or in both places, as in a late ballad quoted by Ritson, *Ancient Songs and Ballads*, ii. 75.

In Old English poetry the refrain is used in one poem only, viz. in *Deor's Complaint*, as the repetition of a whole line. In Middle and Modern English poetry the refrain is much more extensively employed. Its simplest form, consisting of the repetition of certain exclamations or single words after each stanza, occurs pretty often in Middle English. Frequent use is also made of the other form, in which one line is partially or entirely repeated. Sometimes, indeed, two or even more lines are repeated, or a whole stanza is added as refrain to each of the main stanzas, and is then placed at the beginning of the poem (cf. Wright's *Spec. of Lyr. Poetry*, p. 51).

In English the refrain is also called *burthen*, and consists (according to Guest) of the entire or at least partial repetition of the same words. Distinct from the burthen or refrain is the *wheel*, which is only the repetition of the same rhythm as an addition to a stanza. In Middle English poetry especially a favourite form was that in which a stanza consisting mostly of alliterative-rhyming verses or half-verses (cf. §§ 60, 61, 66) is followed by an addition (the *cauda*), differing very much from the rhythmical structure of the main part (the *frons*) of the stanza, and connected with it by means of a very short verse consisting of only one arsis and the syllable or syllables forming the thesis. This short verse is called by Guest *bob-verse*, and the *cauda*, connected with the chief stanza by means of such a verse, he calls *bob-wheel*, so that the whole stanza, which is of a very remarkable form, might be called the *bob-wheel stanza*. The similar form of stanza, also very common, where the chief part of the stanza is connected with the ' cauda', not by a ' bob-verse' but by an ordinary long line, might be called the *wheel-stanza*. These remarks now bring us to other considerations of importance with regard to the formation of the stanza, which will be treated of in the next section.

§ 223. The structure and arrangement of the different parts of the stanza in Middle English poetry were also modelled on Low Latin and especially on Romanic forms.

The theory of the structure of stanzas in Provençal and Italian is given along with much interesting matter in Dante's treatise *De vulgari eloquentia*,[1] where the original Romanic technical terms are found. Several terms used in this book have also been taken from German metrics.

In the history of Middle English poetry two groups of stanzas must be distinguished : *divisible* and *indivisible* stanzas (the *one-rhymed* stanzas being included in the latter class). The divisible stanzas consist either of two equal parts (*bipartite equal-membered stanzas*) or of two unequal parts (*bipartite unequal-membered stanzas*) or thirdly of two equal parts and an unequal one (*tripartite stanzas*). Now and then (especially in Modern English poetry) they consist of three equal parts. These three types are common to Middle and Modern English poetry. A fourth class is met with in Modern English poetry only, viz. stanzas generally consisting of *three*, sometimes of *four* or more *unequal parts*.

All the kinds of verse that have been previously described in this work can be used in these different classes of stanzas, both separately and conjointly. In each group, accordingly, *isometrical* and *anisometrical* stanzas must be distinguished. Very rarely, and only in Modern English, we find that even the rhythm of the separate verses of a stanza is not uniform ; iambic and trochaic, anapaestic and dactylic, or iambic and anapaestic verses interchanging with each other, so that a further distinction between *isorhythmical* and *anisorhythmical* stanzas is possible.

§ 224. The **bipartite equal-membered** stanzas, in their simplest form, consist of two equal periods, each composed of a prior and a succeeding member. They are to be regarded as the primary forms of all strophic poetry.

The two periods may be composed either of two rhyming couplets or of four verses rhyming alternately with each other. Specimens of both classes have been quoted above (§ 78). Such equal-membered stanzas can be extended, of course, in each part uniformly without changing the isometrical character of the stanza.

§ 225. The **bipartite unequal-membered** stanzas belong to a more advanced stage in the formation of the stanza. They are, however, found already in Provençal poetry, and consist of the 'forehead' (*frons*) and the 'tail' or veer (*cauda*). The *frons* and the *cauda* differ sometimes only in the number of

---

[1] See *The Oxford Dante*, pp. 379–400, or *Opere minori di Dante Alighieri*, ed. Pietro Fraticelli, vol. ii, p. 146, Florence, 1858, and Böhmer's essay, *Über Dante's Schrift de vulgari eloquentia*, Halle, 1868.

verses, and consequently, in the order of the rhymes, and
sometimes also in the nature of the verse. The two parts may
either have quite different rhymes or be connected together by
one or several common rhymes. As a simple specimen of this
sort of stanza the first stanza of Dunbar's *None may assure in
this warld* may be quoted here :

frons : $\begin{cases} \textit{Quhome to sall I complene my wo,} \\ \textit{And kyth my kairis on or mo?} \end{cases}$

cauda : $\begin{cases} \textit{I knaw nocht, amang riche nor pure,} \\ \textit{Quha is my freynd, quha is my fo;} \\ \textit{For in this warld may non assure.} \end{cases}$

In literary poetry, however, the tripartite stanzas are commoner than the bipartite unequal-membered stanzas just
noticed; they are as much in favour as the bipartite, equal-
membered stanzas are in popular poetry. In Provençal and
Northern French poetry the principle of a triple partition in
the structure of stanzas was developed very early. Stanzas
on these models were very soon imported into Middle English
poetry.

§ 226. The **tripartite** stanzas generally (apart from Modern
English forms) consist of two equal parts and one unequal part,
which admit of being arranged in different ways. They have
accordingly different names. If the two equal parts precede they
are called *pedes*, both together the *opening* (in German *Aufgesang*
='upsong'); the unequal part that concludes the stanza is called
the *conclusion* or the *veer, tail,* or *cauda* (in German *Abgesang*
='downsong'). If the unequal part precedes it is called *frons*
(='forehead'); the two equal parts that form the end of the
stanza are called *versus* ('turns,' in German *Wenden*). The
former arrangement, however, is by far the more frequent.

There are various ways of separating the first from the last
part of the stanza : (a) by a pause, which, as a rule, in Romanic
as well as in Middle English poetry occurs between the two
chief parts ; (b) by a difference in their structure (whether in
rhyme-arrangement only, or both in regard to the kinds and the
number of verses). But even then the two chief parts are
generally separated by a pause. We thus obtain three kinds of
tripartite stanzas :

1. Stanzas in which the first and the last part differ in
versification; the lines of the last part may either be longer or
shorter than those of the 'pedes'. Difference in rhythmical
structure as well as in length of line is in Middle English

poetry confined to the *bob-wheel* stanzas, and is not otherwise
common except in Modern English poetry.

2. Stanzas in which the parts differ in *number of verses*. The
number may be either greater or smaller in the last part than in
the two ' pedes ', which, of course, involves at the same time
a difference in the order of the rhymes. Change of length,
however, and change of versification in the last part in comparison with the half of the first part are generally combined.

3. Stanzas in which the parts agree in versification but *differ
in the arrangement of the rhymes*; the number of verses in the
cauda being either the same as that of one of the *pedes*, or (as
commonly the case) different from it.

In all these cases the first and the last part of the stanza may
have quite different rhymes, or they may, in stanzas of more
artistic construction, have one or several rhymes in common.

If the *frons* precedes the *versus*, the same distinctions, of
course, are possible between the two chief parts.

§ **227.** The following specimens illustrate first of all the
two chief kinds of arrangement ; i. e. the *pedes* preceding the
cauda, and the *frons* preceding the *versus* :

I. pes :
> *With longyng y am lad,*
> *On molde y waxe mad,*
>   *A maide marreþ me ;*

II. pes :
> *Y grede, y grone, vnglad,*
> *For selden y am sad*
>   *Þat semly for te se.*

cauda :
>   *Leuedy, þou rewe me !*
> *To rouþe þou hauest me rad,*
> *Be bote of þat y bad,*
>   *My lyf is long on þe.*
>   Wright's Spec. of Lyr. Poetry, p. 29.

frons :
> *Jesu, for þi muchele miht,*
>   *Þou ȝef vs of þi grace,*
> *Þat we mowe dai and nyht*
>   *Þenken o þi face.*

I. versus :
> *In myn herte hit doþ me god,*
> *When y þenke on iesu blod,*
>   *Þat ran doun bi ys syde,*

II. versus :
> *From is herte doun to is fot ;*
> *For ous he spradde is herte blod,*
>   *His woundes were so wyde.*   ib. p. 83.

Theoretically, the second stanza might also be regarded as a stanza consisting of two *pedes* and two *versus*, or, in other words, as a four-part stanza of two equal parts in each half. Stanzas of this kind occur pretty often in Middle and Modern English poetry. They mostly, however, convey the effect of a tripartite stanza on account of the greater extent of the one pair of equal parts of the stanza.

The tripartition effected only by a difference in the arrangement of rhymes either in the *pedes* and the *cauda*, or in the *frons* and the *versus*, will be illustrated by the following specimens:

I. pes:
{ *Take, oh take those lips away,*
That so sweetly were forsworne ;

II. pes:
{ *And those eyes, the breake of day,*
Lights that doe mislead the morne.

cauda:
{ *But my kisses bring againe,*
Seales of love, but seal'd in vaine.

Shak., Meas. IV. i. 4.

frons:
{ *As by the shore, at break of day,*
A vanquish'd Chief expiring lay,

I. versus:
{ *Upon the sands, with broken sword,*
He traced his farewell to the Free ;

II. versus:
{ *And, there, the last unfinish'd word*
He dying wrote was 'Liberty'.

Moore, Song.

A very rare variety of tripartition that, as far as we know, does not occur till Modern English times, is that by which the *cauda* is placed between the two *pedes*. This arrangement, of course, may occur in each of the three kinds of tripartition. A specimen of the last kind (viz. that in which the *cauda* is distinguished from the *pedes* by a different arrangement of rhymes) may suffice to explain it:

I. pes:
{ *Nine years old !   The first of any*
Seem the happiest years that come :

cauda:
{ *Yet when I was nine, I said*
No such word !   I thought instead

II. pes:
{ *That the Greeks had used as many*
In besieging Ilium.

Mrs. Browning, ii. 215.

Lastly, it is to be remarked that the inequality of Modern English stanzas, which may be composed of two or three or several parts, admits, of course, of many varieties. Generally, however, their structure is somewhat analogous to that of the regular tripartite stanzas (cf. below, Book II, chap. vi).

In Romanic poetry the tripartite structure sometimes was carried on also through the whole song, it being composed either of three or six stanzas (that is to say, of three equal groups of stanzas), or, what is more usual, of seven or five stanzas (i. e. of two equal parts and an unequal part). In Middle English literary poetry, too, this practice is fairly common;[1] in Modern English poetry, on the other hand, it occurs only in the most recent times, being chiefly adopted in imitations of Romanic forms of stanza, especially the *ballade*.

§ **228. The envoi.** Closely connected with the last-mentioned point, viz. the partition of the whole poem, is the structural element in German called *Geleit*, in Provençal poetry *tornada* (i. e. 'turning', 'apostrophe', or 'address'), in Northern French poetry *envoi*, a term which was retained sometimes by Middle English poets as the title for this kind of stanza (occasionally even for a whole poem). The tornada used chiefly in the ballade is a sort of epilogue to the poem proper. It was a rule in Provençal poetry (observed often in Old French also) that it must agree in form with the concluding part of the preceding stanza. It was also necessary that with regard to its tenor it should have some sort of connexion with the poem; although, as a rule, its purpose was to give expression to personal feelings. The tornada is either a sort of farewell which the poet addresses to the poem itself, or it contains the order to a messenger to deliver the poem to the poet's mistress or to one of his patrons; sometimes these persons are directly praised or complimented. In Middle English poetry the envoi mostly serves the same purposes. But there are some variations from the Provençal custom both as to contents and especially as to form.

§ **229.** We may distinguish *three kinds* of so-called envois in Middle English poetry: (1) Real envois. (2) Concluding stanzas resembling envois as to their form. (3) Concluding stanzas resembling envois as to their contents.

The most important are the *real envois*. Of these, two subordinate species can be distinguished: (*a*) when the form of

---

[1] See B. ten Brink, *The Language and Metre of Chaucer*, translated by M. Bentinck Smith. London, Macmillan & Co., 1901, 8°, § 350.

the envoi differs from the form of the stanza, as in Wright's *Spec. of Lyr. Poetry*, p. 92, and even more markedly in Chaucer's *Compleynt to his Purse*, a poem of stanzas of seven lines, the envoi of which addressed to the king consists of five verses only; (*b*) when the form of the envoi is the same as that of the other stanzas of the poem, as e. g. in Wright's *Spec. of Lyr. Poetry*, p. 111 (a greeting to a mistress), in Dunbar's *Goldin Targe* (address to the poem itself).

When the poem is of some length the envoi may consist of several stanzas ; thus in Chaucer's *Clerkes Tale* (stanzas of seven lines) the envoi has six stanzas of six lines each.

Concluding stanzas resembling envois in their form are generally shorter than the chief stanzas, but of similar structure. Generally speaking they are not very common. Specimens may be found in Wright's *Spec. of Lyr. Poetry*, pp. 38, 47, &c.

Concluding stanzas resembling envois in their contents. An example occurs in Wright's *Spec. of Lyr. Poetry*, p. 31, where the concluding stanza contains an address to another poet. Religious poems end with addresses to God, Christ, the Virgin, invitations to prayer, &c.; for examples see Wright's *Spec. of Lyr. Poetry*, p. 111, and *Hymns to the Virgin* (ed. Furnivall, E. E. T. S. 24), p. 39, &c. All these may possibly fall under this category.

Even in Modern English poetry the envoi has not quite gone out of use. Short envois occur in Spenser, *Epithalamium*; S. Daniel, *To the Angel Spirit of Sir Philip Sidney* (Poets, iv. 228); W. Scott, *Marmion* (Envoy, consisting of four-foot verses rhyming in couplets), *Harold, Lord of the Isles, Lady of the Lake* (Spenserian stanzas); Southey, *Lay of the Laureate* (x. 139–74), &c.; Swinburne, *Poems and Ballads*, i, pp. 1, 5, 141, &c.

Concluding stanzas resembling envois occur pretty often in poets of the seventeenth and eighteenth centuries, as Carew, Donne, Cowley, Waller, Dodsley, &c. (cf. *Metrik*, ii, p. 794 note).

PART II

STANZAS COMMON TO MIDDLE AND MODERN ENGLISH, AND OTHERS FORMED ON THE ANALOGY OF THESE

CHAPTER III

BIPARTITE EQUAL-MEMBERED STANZAS

I. *Isometrical stanzas.*

§ 230. **Two-line stanzas.** The simplest bipartite equal-membered stanza is that of two isometrical verses only. In the Northern English translation of the Psalms (*Surtees Society*, vols. xvi and xix) we find, for the most part, two-line stanzas of four-foot verses rhyming in couplets, occasionally alternating with stanzas of four, six, eight, or more lines.

In Middle English poetry, however, this form was generally used for longer poems that were not arranged in stanzas. Although it would be possible to divide some of these (e. g. the *Moral Ode*), either throughout or in certain parts, into bipartite stanzas, there is no reason to suppose that any strophic arrangement was intended.

In Modern English, on the other hand, such an arrangement is often intentional, as in R. Browning, *The Boy and the Angel* (iv. 158), a poem of four-foot trochaic verses :

> *Morning, evening, noon and night*
> *' Praise God !' sang Theocrite.*
>
> *Then to his poor trade he turned,*
> *Whereby the daily meal was earned.*

Similar stanzas in other metres occur in Longfellow, Tennyson, Thackeray, Rossetti, &c.; among them we find e. g. eight-foot trochaic and iambic-anapaestic verses (cf. *Metrik*, ii, § 3).

§ **231.** More frequently we find **four-line stanzas,** consisting of couplets. In Middle English lyric poetry such stanzas of two short couplets are occasionally met with as early as in the

Surtees Psalms, but they occur more frequently in Modern English, e. g. in M. Arnold, *Urania* (p. 217), and in Carew, e. g. *The Inquiry* (Poets, iii):

> *Amongst the myrtles as I walk'd,*
> *Love and my sighs thus intertalk'd:*
> *'Tell me,' said I, in deep distress,*
> *'Where I may find my shepherdess.'*

Regular alternation of masculine and feminine rhymes is very rarely found in this simple stanza (or indeed in any Middle English stanzas); it is, properly speaking, only a series of rhyming couplets with a stop after every fourth line.

This stanza is very popular, as are also various analogous four-line stanzas in other metres. One of these is the quatrain of four-foot trochaic verses, as used by M. Arnold in *The Last Word*, and by Milton, e. g. in *Psalm CXXXVI*, where the two last lines form the refrain, so that the strophic arrangement is more distinctly marked. Stanzas of four-foot iambic-anapaestic lines we find e. g. in Moore, *'Tis the last Rose of Summer*, and similar stanzas of five-foot iambic verses in Cowper, pp. 359, 410; M. Arnold, *Self-Dependence* (last stanza).

Less common are the quatrains of four-foot dactylic lines, of three-foot iambic-anapaestic lines, of six-foot iambic and trochaic lines, of seven-foot iambic lines, and of eight-foot trochaic lines. But specimens of each of these varieties are occasionally met with (cf. *Metrik*, ii, § 261).

§ 232. The double stanza, i. e. that of eight lines of the same structure ($a\,a\,b\,b\,c\,c\,d\,d$), occurs in different kinds of verse. With lines of four measures it is found, e. g. in Suckling's poem, *The Expostulation* (Poets, iii. 749):

> *Tell me, ye juster deities,*
> *That pity lover's miseries,*
> *Why should my own unworthiness*
> *Light me to seek my happiness?*
> *It is as natural, as just,*
> *Him for to love whom needs I must:*
> *All men confess that love's a fire,*
> *Then who denies it to aspire?*

This stanza comes to a better conclusion when it winds up with a refrain, as in Percy's *Reliques*, II. ii. 13. One very popular form of it consists of four-foot trochaic lines, e. g. in

Burns, p. 197, M. Arnold, *A Memory Picture*, p. 23 (the two last lines of each stanza forming a refrain), or of four-foot iambic-anapaestic lines (Burns, *My heart's in the Highlands*). Somewhat rarely it is made up of five-foot iambic or septenaric lines (cf. *Metrik*, ii, § 262).[1]

§ 233. We have next to consider the stanzas of four isometrical lines with intermittent rhyme (*a b c b*). As a rule they consist of three- or four-foot verses, which are really Alexandrines or acatalectic tetrameters rhyming in long couplets, and only in their written or printed arrangement broken up into short lines; as, e. g., in the following half-stanza from the older version of the *Legend of St. Katherine*, really written in eight-lined stanzas (ed. Horstmann, *Altenglische Legenden, Neue Folge*, Heilbronn, 1881, p. 242):

> He that made heven and erthe
> and sonne and mone for to schine,
> Bring ous into his riche
> and scheld ous fram helle pine !

Examples of such stanzas of four-foot trochaic and three-foot iambic verses that occur chiefly in Percy's *Reliques* (cf. *Metrik*, ii, § 264), but also in M. Arnold, *Calais Sands* (p. 219), *The Church of Brou, I., The Castle* (p. 13, feminine and masculine verse-endings alternating), *New Rome*, p. 229, *Parting*, p. 191 (iambic-anapaestic three-beat and two-beat verses), *Iseult of Ireland*, p. 150 (iambic verses of five measures); cf. *Metrik*, ii, § 264.

§ 234. Stanzas of eight lines result from this stanza by doubling, i. e. by adding a second couplet of the same structure and rhyme to the original long-line couplet. Such a form with the scheme *a b c b d b e b* we meet in the complete stanza of the older *Legend of St. Katherine* just referred to:

> He that made heven and erthe
> and sonne and mone for to schine,
> Bring ous into his riche
> and scheld ous fram helle pine !
> Herken, and y you wile telle
> the liif of an holy virgine,
> That treuli trowed in Jhesu Crist:
> hir name was hoten Katerine,

---

[1] Stanzas of six and twelve lines formed on the same principle (*a a a b b b* and *a a b b c c d d e e f f*) are very rare. For specimens see *Metrik*, ii, § 363.

This sort of doubling, however, occurs in Modern English poetry more rarely than that which is produced by adding a second long-lined couplet, but with a new rhyme, so that when the stanza is arranged in short lines we have the scheme *a b c b d e f e*.

A stanza like this of trochaic lines we find in *Hymns Ancient and Modern*, No. 419:

> *King of Saints, to whom the number*
> *Of Thy starry host is known,*
> *Many a name, by man forgotten,*
> *Lives for ever round Thy Throne ;*
> *Lights, which earth-born mists have darkened,*
> *There are shining full and clear,*
> *Princes in the court of heaven,*
> *Nameless, unremembered here.*

Still more frequent are stanzas of this kind consisting of four-foot and three-foot iambic lines, or of two-foot iambic-anapaestic and trochaic-dactylic lines (cf. *Metrik*, ii, § 265).

§ 235. More popular than the stanza just noticed is that developed from the long-lined couplets by inserted rhyme. A very instructive example of this development is given in the later version of the *Legend of St. Katherine* (ed. by Horstmann) which is a paraphrase of the older.

The first half-stanza is as follows:

> *He that made bothe sunne and mone*
> *In heuene and erthe for to schyne,*
> *Bringe vs to heuene, with him to wone,*
> *And schylde vs from helle pyne !*

Stanzas like this, which are frequent in Low Latin, Provençal, and Old French poetry, are very common in Middle and Modern English poetry. Examples may be found in Ritson's *Ancient Songs*, i, p. 40, Surrey, pp. 37, 56, &c., Burns, p. 97, &c., M. Arnold, *Saint Brandan*, p. 165, &c. Masculine and feminine rhymes do not alternate very often (cf. Percy's *Reliques*, I. iii. 13). More frequently we find stanzas with refrain verses, e. g. Wyatt, p. 70.

Stanzas of this kind consisting of four- or three-foot iambic, trochaic, iambic-anapaestic, trochaic-dactylic lines, of three-foot iambic lines, or of two-foot dactylic or other lines are also very common, e. g. in M. Arnold's *A Modern Sappho* (with alternating masculine and feminine verse-endings), *Pis Aller* (p. 230), *Requiescat* (p. 21).

Another stanza of great importance is what is called the elegiac stanza, which consists of four five-foot verses with crossed rhymes. In Middle English literature it was only used as a part of the *Rhyme-Royal* and of the eight-lined stanza. In Modern English, however, it has been used from the beginning more frequently; it occurs already in Wyatt (p. 58):

> *Heaven and earth and all that hear me plain*
> > *Do well perceive what care doth make me cry*
> *Save you alone, to whom I cry in vain;*
> > *Mercy, Madam, alas! I die, I die!*

Other examples are found in M. Arnold's poems *Palladium* (p. 251), *Revolutions* (p. 254), *Self Deception* (p. 225, with alternate masculine and feminine rhymes). This stanza is very popular throughout the Modern English period (cf. *Metrik*, ii, § 267).

Stanzas of this kind, however, consisting of trochaic verses, of six-foot (as in Tennyson's *Maud*), seven- and eight-foot metres are not very frequently met with (cf. *Metrik*, ii, § 269).

§ **236**. The four-lined, cross-rhyming stanza gives rise by doubling to the eight-lined (*a b a b a b a b*), which occurs very often in Middle English, as in Wright's *Spec. of Lyr. Poetry*, p. 99, or in the *Luve-Rone* by Thomas de Hales, ed. Morris (*Old Eng. Misc.*, p. 93), where both masculine and feminine rhymes are used:

> *A Mayde cristes me bit yorne,*
> > *þat ich hire wurche a luue ron:*
> *For hwan heo myhte best ileorne*
> > *to taken on oþer soþ lefmon,*
> *Þat treowest were of alle berne*
> > *and beste wyte cuþe a freo wymmon;*
> *Ich hire nule nowiht werne,*
> > *ich hire wule teche as ic con.*

Stanzas of this kind are met with also in Modern English, as in Burns (p. 262); stanzas of four-stressed lines are found in Wright's *Spec. of Lyr. Poetry*, p. 110, and others of three-foot verses in *Polit. Poems*, i. 270.

There is still another mode of doubling, by which the four originally long-lined verses are broken up by the use of two

different inserted rhymes; the scheme is then: $a b a b c b c b$.
This is the stanza to which the second version of the *Legend of
St. Katherine* has been adapted in paraphrasing it from the first
(cf. §§ 77, 78, 235):

> *He that made bothe sunne and mone*
> *In heuene and erthe for to schyne,*
> *Bringe vs to heuene, with him to wone,*
> *And schylde vs from helle pyne!*
> *Lystnys, and I schal you telle*
> *The lyff off an holy virgyne,*
> *That trewely Jhesu louede wel :*
> *Here name was callyd Kateryne.*

This stanza occurs, e.g., in Burns (p. 201). Less common is
the form of stanza $a b a b a c a c$ (e. g. in Wyatt, p. 48) resulting
from the breaking up two rhyming couplets of long lines by
inserted rhyme (not from four long lines with one rhyme).

The common mode of doubling is by adding to a four-lined
stanza a second of exactly the same structure, but with new
rhymes. Some few examples occur in Middle English in the
Surtees Psalter, Ps. xliv, ll. 11, 12. Very frequently, however,
we find it in Modern English constructed of the most varying
metres, as, e. g., of five-foot iambic verses in Milton, *Psalm VIII*
(vol. iii, p. 29):

> *O Jehovah our Lord, how wondrous great*
> *And glorious is thy name through all the earth,*
> *So as above the heavens thy praise to set !*
> *Out of the tender mouths of latest birth,*
> *Out of the mouths of babes and sucklings thou*
> *Hast founded strength, because of all thy foes,*
> *To stint the enemy, and slack the avenger's brow,*
> *That bends his rage thy providence to oppose.*

More popular are stanzas of this kind consisting of three- or
four-foot iambic, trochaic, and iambic-anapaestic verses, sometimes with alternate masculine and feminine rhymes. (For
specimens see *Metrik*, ii, § 271.)

§ **237**. Only very few examples occur of the sixteen-
lined doubling of this stanza, according to the scheme
$a b a b c d c d e f e f g h g h_2$; it occurs, e. g., in Moore, *When
Night brings the Hour*. Another form of eight lines
($a b c d . a b c d_3$) is met with in Rossetti, *The Shadows* (ii. 249);

it seems to be constructed on the analogy of a six-lined stanza
($a\,b\,c\,.\,a\,b\,c$), which is used pretty often.   This stanza, which is
closely allied to the tail-rhyme stanza described in § 238, consists
most commonly of four-foot iambic verses; it occurs, e. g., in
Campbell, *Ode to the Memory of Burns* (p. 19):

> *Soul of the Poet! whereso'er*
> *Reclaim'd from earth, thy genius plume*
>   *Her wings of immortality:*
> *Suspend thy harp in happier sphere,*
> *And with thine influence illume*
>   *The gladness of our jubilee.*

Specimens of forms of stanzas like this, consisting of other
kinds of verse, e.g. of three-foot trochaic-dactylic verse, as in
M. Arnold's *The Lord's Messenger* (p. 231), are given in *Metrik*,
ii, § 272.

§ 238. From the four- and eight-lined bipartite equal-
membered isometrical stanzas, dealt with in the preceding
paragraphs, it will be convenient to proceed to the six-lined
stanzas of similar structure.   To these belongs a certain form of
the tail-rhyme stanza, the nature and origin of which will be
discussed when we treat of the chief form, which consists of
unequal verses.   The isometrical six-lined stanzas to be discussed here show the same structure as the common tail-rhyme
stanza, viz. $a\,a\,b\,c\,c\,b$.   An example is afforded in a song,
Ritson, i. 10:

> *Sith Gabriel gan grete*
> *Ure ledi Mari swete,*
>   *That godde wold in hir lighte,*
> *A thousand yer hit isse,*
> *Thre hundred ful iwisse,*
>   *Ant over yeris eighte.*

In Modern English this stanza occurs very often, e.g. in
Drayton, *To the New Year* (Poets, iii. 579); as a rule, however,
it consists of four-foot iambic verses; e.g. in Suckling in a song
(*Poets*, iii. 748):

> *When, dearest, I but think of thee,*
> *Methinks all things that lovely be*
>   *Are present, and my soul delighted:*
> *For beauties that from worth arise,*
> *Are like the grace of deities,*
>   *Still present with us though unsighted.*

In this poem all the tail-verses are feminine throughout; in other cases there are masculine and feminine verses, more often we find masculine or feminine exclusively; but usually they interchange without any rule. Examples of these varieties, and also of similar stanzas consisting of three-foot trochaic verses, of two- and three-foot iambic-anapaestic, and of five-foot iambic lines are given in *Metrik*, ii, § 273.

Stanzas of this form consisting of two-stressed verses occurring in Middle English poems have been quoted in § 65.

§ **239**. A variety that belongs to Modern English only is that in which the tail-verses are placed at the head of the half-stanzas, according to the formula *a b b a c c*. It occurs in Ben Jonson's *Hymn to God* (Poets, iv. 561), consisting of two-foot iambic verses; another example, with four-foot trochaic verses, occurs in Mrs. Browning, *A Portrait* (iii. 57); cf. *Metrik*, ii, § 274.

A twelve-lined stanza, resulting from the doubling of the six-line stanza, is found only in Middle English poetry, its arrangement of rhymes being *a a b c c b d d b e e b*; or with a more elaborate rhyme-order, *a a b a a b c c b c c b*, as in Wright's *Spec. of Lyr. Poetry*, p. 41.

Still another modification of the simple six-lined stanza consists in the addition of a third rhyme-verse to the two rhyming couplets of each half-stanza; so that an eight-lined stanza results with the scheme *a a a b c c c b*. Two specimens of this kind of stanza, consisting of two-stressed lines and occurring in Early English dramatic poetry, have been quoted above, § 70.

The same stanza of two-foot verses occurs in the *Coventry Mysteries*, p. 342. In Modern English, too, we find it sometimes, consisting of three-foot iambic verses, as in Longfellow, *King Olaf's Death Drink* (p. 577). Stanzas of five-, four-, and two-foot iambic verses and other metres are likewise in use. (For examples see *Metrik*, ii, § 275.)

Some rarely occurring extended forms of this stanza are exemplified in *Metrik*, ii, § 277, their schemes being $a \sim a \sim b \sim c d \sim d \sim b \sim c_4$, $a \sim b \sim c \sim d e \sim f \sim g \sim d_3$, $a b b c a d d c_4$, $a a a a b c c c c b_4$.

Sixteen-lined stanzas of this kind of two-stressed verses (rhyming *a a a b c c c b d d d b e e e b*) that were frequently used in Middle English Romances have been quoted and discussed above, § 65.

II. *Anisometrical Stanzas.*

§ **240.** In connexion with the last section, the chief species of
the **tail-rhyme stanza** may be discussed here first of all. This
stanza, as a rule, consists of four four-foot and two three-foot
verses, rhyming according to the scheme $a\,a_4\,b_3\,c\,c_4\,b_3$; cf. the
following specimen (Wright's *Spec. of Lyr. Poetry*, p. 101):

> *Lustneþ alle a lutel prowe,*
> *Ʒe þat wolleþ ou selue yknowe,*
> *Unwys þah y be :*
> *Ichulle telle ou ase y con,*
> *Hou holy wryt spekeþ of mon ;*
> *Herkneþ nou to me.*

The last line of each half-stanza, the tail-verse proper, was
originally simply a refrain. The tripartite character of the half-
stanza and the popular origin of the stanza was shown long ago
by Wolf, *Über die Lais, Sequenzen und Leiche*, p. 27 (cf. *Engl.
Metrik*, i, pp. 353–7). According to him this stanza was
developed first of all from choruses sung in turn by the people
and from the ecclesiastical responses which also had a popular
origin, and lastly from the sequences and 'proses' of the
middle ages.

A sequence-verse such as :

> *Egidio psallat coetus | iste laetus | Alleluia,*

in its tripartition corresponds to the first half of the above-
quoted Middle English tail-rhyme stanza :

> *Lustneþ alle a lutel prowe | Ʒe þat wolleþ ou selue yknowe |*
> *Unwys þah y be.*

When two long lines like this, connected with each other by
the rhyme of the last section, the two first sections of each line
being also combined by leonine rhyme, are broken up into six
short verses, we have the tail-rhyme stanza in the form above
described. This form was frequently used in Low Latin poetry,
and thence passed into Romanic and Teutonic literature.

A form even more extensively used in Middle and Modern
English poetry is that in which the tail-verse has feminine
instead of masculine endings. A Modern English specimen
from Drayton's poem *To Sir Henry Goodere* (*Poets*, iii. 576)
may be quoted ; it begins :

> *These lyric pieces, short and few,*
> *Most worthy Sir, I send to you,*
> > *To read them be not weary:*
> *They may become John Hewes his lyre,*
> *Which oft at Powlsworth by the fire*
> > *Hath made us gravely merry.*

This, the chief form of the tail-rhyme stanza, has been in use throughout the whole Modern English period. There has, however, never been any fixed rule as to the employment of feminine or masculine rhymes. Sometimes feminine tail-rhymes with masculine couplets are used (as in the example above), sometimes masculine rhymes only, while in other instances masculine and feminine rhymes are employed indiscriminately.

Iambic-anapaestic verses of four or three measures were also sometimes used in this form of stanza, as in Moore, *Hero and Leander.*

There are a great many varieties of this main form; the stanza may consist, for instance, of four- and two-foot iambic or trochaic lines, or of iambic lines of three and two, five and three, five and two measures, according to the schemes $a\,a_4\,b_2\,c\,c_4\,b_2$, $a\,a_3\,b_2\,c\,c_3\,b_2$, $a\,a_5\,b_3\,c\,c_5\,b_3$, $a\,a_5\,b_2\,c\,c_5\,b_2$, and $a_3\,b\,b_5\,a_3\,c\,c_5$ (the tail-verses in front). For examples see *Metrik*, ii, § 279.

§ 241. The next step in the development of this stanza was its enlargement to twelve lines ($a\,a_4\,b_3\,c\,c_4\,b_3\,d\,d_4\,b_3\,e\,e_4\,b_3$) by doubling. This form occurs in Wright's *Spec. of Lyr. Poetry*, p. 43:

> *Lenten is come wiþ loue to toune,*
> *Wiþ blosmen and wiþ briddes roune,*
> > *Þat all þis blisse bryngeþ:*
> *Dayes eȝes in þis dales,*
> *Notes suete of nyhtegales,*
> > *Vch foule song singeþ.*
> *Þe þrestlecoc him þreteþ oo;*
> *Away is huere wynter woo,*
> > *When woderoue springeþ.*
> *Þis foules singeþ ferli fele,*
> *Ant wlyteþ on huere wynter wele,*
> > *Þat al þe wode ryngeþ.*

We are not in a position to quote a Modern English specimen of this stanza, but it was very popular in Middle English poetry, both in lyrics and in legends or romances, and in later dramatic poetry.[1]

§ **242**. As to the **further development of the tail-rhyme stanza**, the enlarged forms must first be mentioned. They are produced by adding a third line to the principal lines of each half-stanza; the result being an eight-lined stanza of the formula $a\,a\,a_4\,b_3\,c\,c\,c_4\,b_3$. Stanzas of this form occur in Early Middle English lyrics, e. g. in Wright's *Spec. of Lyr. Poetry*, p. 51 (with a refrain-stanza) and *Polit. Songs*, p. 187 (four-stressed main verses and two-stressed tail-verses, the latter having occasionally the appearance of being in three-beat rhythm).

A later example is found in Dunbar's poem *Off the Fenʒeit Freir of Tungland*; in the Miracle Plays the form was also in favour. Isometrical stanzas of this kind have been mentioned above (§§ 238, 239).

In Modern English poetry this stanza is extensively used. We find it in Drayton, *Nymphidia* (Poets, iii. 177), with feminine tail-verses:

> *Old Chaucer doth of Topas tell,*
> *Mad Rablais of Pantagruel,*
> *A later third of Dowsabel,*
>   *With such poor trifles playing:*
> *Others the like have labour'd at,*
> *Some of this thing and some of that,*
> *And many of they know not what,*
>   *But that they must be saying.*

Other examples of this stanza, as of similar ones, consisting of four- and three-foot trochaic and iambic-anapaestic verses, are given in *Metrik*, ii, § 280.

There are some subdivisions of this stanza consisting of verses of three and two measures, of four and two measures, four and one measure, five and two, and five and one measure, according to the formulae $a\,a\,a_3\,b_2\,c\,c\,c_3\,b_2$, $a\,a\,a_4\,b_2\,c\,c\,c_4\,b_2$, $a\,a\,a_4\,b_1\,c\,c\,c_4\,b_1$, $a\,a\,a_5\,b_2\,c\,c\,c_5\,b_2$, $a\,a\,a_5\,b_1\,c\,c\,c_5\,b_1$. For specimens see *Metrik*, ii, § 281.

The ten-lined tail-rhyme stanza occurs very rarely; we have an example in Longfellow's *The Goblet of Life* (p. 114), its formula being $a\,a\,a\,a_4\,b_3\,c\,c\,c\,c_4\,b_3$.

§ **243**. We find, however, pretty often—though only in Modern English—certain variant forms of the enlarged eight- and ten-

---

[1] Cf. O. Wilda, *Über die örtliche Verbreitung der zwölfzeiligen Schweifreimstrophe in England*, Breslau Dissertation, Breslau, 1887.

lined tail-rhyme stanzas, the chief verses of which are of unequal length in each half-stanza ; as in Congreve's poem, *On Miss Temple* (Poets, vii. 568). In this poem the first verse of each half-stanza is shortened by one foot, in accordance with the formula $a_3\, a\, a_4\, b_3\, c_3\, c\, c_4\, b_3$:

> *Leave, leave the drawing-room,*
> *Where flowers of beauty us'd to bloom ;*
> *The nymph that's fated to o'ercome,*
>   *Now triumphs at the wells.*
> *Her shape, and air, and eyes,*
> *Her face, the gay, the grave, the wise,*
> *The beau, in spite of box and dice,*
>   *Acknowledge, all excels.*

Stanzas of cognate form are quoted in *Metrik*, ii, §§ 283–5, constructed according to the schemes : $a\, a_2\, a_4\, b_3\, c\, c_2\, c_4\, b_3$, $a_3\, b\, b_4\, c \sim_2 a_3\, d\, d_4\, c \sim_2$ (with a varying first rhyme in the chief verses), $a\, a\, b\, b_4\, c_2\, d\, d\, e\, e_4\, c_2$ (ten lines, with a new rhyming couplet in the half-stanza), $a\, a\, b\, b\, c_3\, C_2\, a\, a\, b\, b\, c_3\, C_2$ (an analogous twelve-lined stanza, extended by refrain in each half-stanza), $a\, b\, a\, b_5\, c_3\, d\, e\, d\, e_5\, c_3$ (crossed rhymes in the principal verses).

Two uncommon variations that do not, strictly speaking, belong to the isocolic stanzas, correspond to the formulas $a\, b\, b_5\, c_2\, c\, d\, d_5\, a_2$, $a\, b\, a_4\, c \sim_2 b\, a\, b_4\, c \sim_2$.

§ 244. Another step in the development of the tail-rhyme stanza consisted in making the principal verses of the half-stanza shorter than the tail-verse. Models for this form existed in Low Latin, Provençal, and Old French poetry (cf. *Metrik*, i, § 366). In Middle English, however, there are not many stanzas of this form. We have an example in Dunbar's poem *Of the Ladyis Solistaris at Court* ($a\, a_2\, b_3\, c\, c_2\, b_3\, d\, d_2\, e_3\, f\, f_2\, e_3$) :

> *Thir Ladyis fair,*
> *That makis repair,*
> *And in the Court ar kend,*
> *Thre dayis thair*
> *Thay will do mair,*
> *Ane mater for till end,*
> *Than thair gud men*
> *Will do in ten,*
> *For ony craft thay can ;*
> *So weill thay ken*
> *Quhat tyme and quhen*
> *Thair menes thay sowld mak than.*

The same rhythmical structure is found in the old ballad, *The Notbrowne Maid*, in Percy's *Reliques*, vol. ii. In this collection the poem is printed in twelve-lined stanzas of four- and three-foot verses. Skeat, however, in his *Specimens of English Literature*, printed it in stanzas of six long lines.

In either arrangement the relationship of the metre to the Septenary verse comes clearly out.

In Modern English this stanza is also very popular. It occurs in Scott (p. 460, $a\,a_2\,b_3\,c\,c_2\,b_3$), Burns (doubled, p. 61, $a\,a_2\,b_3\,c\,c_2\,b_3\,d\,d_2\,e_3\,f\,f_2\,e_3$, p. 211, $a\,a_2\,b_3\,c\,c_2\,b_3\,d\,d_2\,b_3\,e\,e_2\,b_3$).

Often there are also two- and three-foot iambic-anapaestic verses combined in stanzas of this kind, as in Cowper (p. 427), Burns (p. 244), &c.

Subordinate varieties of this stanza consisting of other verses are quoted, with specimens, in *Metrik*, ii, §§ 286–8, after the formulas: $a\,a_4\,b_5\,c\,c_4\,b_5$, $a\,a_4\,b_6\,c\,c_4\,b_6$, $a\,a_3\,b_5\,c\,c_3\,b_5$, $a\,a_3\,b_4\,c\,c_3\,b_4$, $a\,a_2\,b_4\,c\,c_2\,b_4$, $a \sim a \sim b \sim b \sim_2 c_3\,d \sim d \sim e \sim e \sim_2 c_3$.

§ **245.** A small group of tail-rhyme stanzas consists of those in which the second chief verses are shorter than the first.

Such a variety occurs in a tail-rhyme stanza of four-foot trochaic verses, the second verse of each half-stanza being shortened by two measures. It was used by Donne in his translation of Psalm 137 (*Poets*, iv. 43):

> By Euphrates' flow'ry side
> We did 'bide,
> > From dear Juda far absented,
> Tearing the air with our cries,
> And our eyes
> > With their streams his stream augmented.

The same stanza we find in Longfellow, *Tales of a Wayside Inn*, v (p. 552). Similar stanzas are quoted in *Metrik*, ii, § 289, their schemes being $a_3\,a_2\,b_3\,c_3\,c_2\,b_3$, $a_3\,a_2\,b_5\,c_3\,c_2\,b_5$, $a_4\,b_3\,b_2\,a_4\,c_3\,c_2$ (the tail-rhyme verse put in front).

§ **246.** There are also some stanzas ($a\,b_4\,c_3\,a\,b_4\,c_3$) which may be looked upon as modelled on the tail-rhyme stanza; such a stanza we find in Mrs. Browning's poem, *A Sabbath morning at Sea* (iii. 74); its formula being $a\,b_4\,c_3\,a\,b_4\,c_3$:

> The ship went on with solemn face:
> To meet the darkness on the deep,
> > The solemn ship went onward:
> I bowed down weary in the place,
> For parting tears and present sleep
> > Had weighed mine eyelids downward.

Other stanzas of this kind show the scheme: $a_4 b_5 c_3 a_4 b_5 c_3$, $a b_2 c_4 a b_2 c_4$, $a_2 b_3 c_1 a_2 b_3 c_1$, $a \sim b a \sim b_4 c \sim_6 d \sim e d \sim e_4 c \sim_6$; cf. *Metrik*, ii, § 290.

A stanza belonging to this group, and consisting of ten lines rhyming according to the formula $a b a b_3 c_6 d e d e_3 c_6$, occurs in M. Arnold's *Empedocles on Etna*, p. 446 (printed in stanzas of five lines).

§ **247.** Another metre, which was equally popular with the tail-rhyme stanza with its many varieties, is the stanza formed of two Septenary verses (catalectic tetrameters). In the Middle English period we find it used with feminine rhymes only; afterwards, however, there are both feminine and masculine rhymes, and in modern times the feminine ending is quite exceptional. This metre, broken up into four lines, is one of the oldest and most popular of equal-membered stanzas. One of its forms[1] has in hymn-books the designation of *Common Metre*.

Middle and Modern English specimens of this simple form have been given above (§§ 77, 78, 136, 138–40); in some of them the verses rhyme and are printed as long lines; in others the verses rhyme in long lines but are printed as short ones ($a b c b$), and in others, again, the verses both rhyme and are printed as short lines ($a b a b$).

On the analogy of this stanza, especially of the short-lined rhyming form, and of the doubled form with intermittent rhyme (which is, properly speaking, a stanza rhyming in long lines), there have been developed many new strophic forms. One of the most popular of these is the stanza consisting alternately of four- and three-foot iambic-anapaestic verses. In this form is written, e. g. the celebrated poem of Charles Wolfe, *The Burial of Sir John Moore* (cf. § 191):

> *Not a drum was heard, not a funeral note,*
> *As his corpse to the rampart we hurried;*
> *Not a soldier discharged his farewell shot*
> *O'er the grave where our hero we buried.*

In other poems there are masculine rhymes only, as in Cowper (p. 429).

Stanzas of this structure, composed of trochaic verses or of trochaic mixed with iambic or of dactylic mixed with iambic-

---

[1] This is a stanza of four iambic lines alternately of four and three feet with masculine endings, usually rhyming $a b a b$.

anapaestic verses, are not frequent. (For examples see *Metrik*, ii, § 292.)

§ **248.** Some other analogical developments from this type, however, occur pretty often; a stanza of alternate four- and two-foot verses $(a_4 \, b \sim_2 a_4 \, b \sim_2)$ is used, for example, by Ben Jonson (*Poets*, iv. 545):

> Weep with me all you that read
>   This little story ;
> And know, for whom a tear you shed,
>   Death's self is sorry.

Another of five- and four-foot verses $(a_5 \, b_4 \, a_5' b_4)$ occurs in Cowley, *The long Life* (Poets, v. 264):

> Love from Time's wings hath stol'n the feathers sure,
>   He has, and put them to his own,
> For hours, of late, as long as days endure,
>   And very minutes hours are grown.

Other less common analogous forms are given in *Metrik*, ii, § 298, the formulas being $a_5 \, b_3 \, a_5' \, b_3$, $a_3 \, b_5 \, a_3 \, b_5$, $a_5 \, b_2 \, a_5 \, b_2$, $a_2 \, b_5 \, a_2 \, b_5$.
There are also stanzas of anisometrical verses rhyming in couplets, but they occur very rarely. An example is Donne's *The Paradox* (Poets, iv. 397), after the scheme $a_5 \, a_3 \, b_5 \, b_3$:

> No lover saith I love, nor any other
>   Can judge a perfect lover :
> He thinks that else none can or will agree
>   That any loves but he.

§ **249.** Pretty often we find—not indeed in middle English, but in Modern English poetry—eight-lined (doubled) forms of the different four-lined stanzas. Only doubled forms, however, of the formula $a_4 \, b_3 \, a_4 \, b_3 \, c_4 \, d_3 \, c_4 \, d_3$ are employed with any frequency; they have either only masculine rhymes or rhymes which vary between masculine and feminine. An example of the latter kind we have in Drayton's *To his coy Love* (Poets, iii. 585) :

> I pray thee, love, love me no more,
>   Call home the heart you gave me,
> I but in vain that saint adore,
>   That can, but will not save me :
> These poor half kisses kill me quite ;
>   Was ever man thus served ?
> Amidst an ocean of delight,
>   For pleasure to be starved.

Eight-lined stanzas with the following schemes are not common :—$a_4 b_3 c_4 b_3 a_4 b_3 c_4 b_3$, $a_4 b_3 a_4 b_3 c_4 b_3 c_4 b_3$, $a_4 b_3 a_4 b_3 a_4 b_3 a_4 b_3$, $a \sim_3 b_4 a \sim_3 b_4 c \sim_3 d_4 c \sim_3 d_4$, $a_4 b_3 c_4 b_3 d_4 e_3 f_4 e_3$. Only in the last stanza and in the usual form $a\, b\, a\, b\, c\, d\, c\, d$ we find trochaic and iambic-anapaestic verses. An example of the latter sort which is pretty often met with we have in Cunningham's *The Sycamore Shade* (Poets, x. 717):

> T''other day as I sat in the sycamore shade,
>   Young Damon came whistling along,
> I trembled—I blush'd—a poor innocent maid!
>   And my heart caper'd up to my tongue:
> Silly heart, I cry'd, fie! What a flutter is here!
>   Young Damon designs you no ill,
> The shepherd's so civil, you've nothing to fear,
>   Then prythee, fond urchin, lie still.

For specimens of the other subordinate varieties and of the rare twelve-lined stanza ($a_4 b_3 c_4 b_3 d_4 b_3 e_4 f_3 d_4 f_3 g_4 f_3$ and $a_4 b \sim_3 a_4 b \sim_3 a_4 b \sim_3 c_4 d \sim_3 c_4 d \sim_3 c_4 d \sim_3$) see *Metrik*, ii, §§ 295, 296.

§ 250. There are also doubled forms of the before-mentioned analogical development of the Septenary, the schemes of which are as follows:

$a_4 b \sim_2 a_4 b \sim_2 a_4 b \sim_2 a_4 b \sim_2$, $a_3 b \sim_2 a_3 b \sim_2 c_3 d \sim_2 c_3 d \sim_2$,
$a \sim_2 b_3 a \sim_2 b_3 c \sim_2 d_3 c \sim_2 d_3$, $a \sim_4 b_5 a \sim_4 b_5 c \sim_4 d_5 c \sim_4 d_5$,   and
$a_5 a_4 b_5 b_4 c_5 c_4 d_5 d_4$.

We must here refer to some eight-lined stanzas which have this common feature that the two half-stanzas are exactly alike, but the half-stanzas themselves consist of unequal members. These, however, will be treated in the next chapter.

In this connexion may be also mentioned the doubled *Poulter's Measure*, which occurs somewhat frequently, as in *Hymns Ancient and Modern*, No. 149 :

> Thou art gone up on high,
>   To mansions in the skies;
> And round Thy Throne unceasingly
>   The songs of praise arise.
> But we are lingering here,
>   With sin and care oppressed;
> Lord, send Thy promised Comforter,
>   And lead us to Thy rest.

The same form of stanza was used in Hood's well-known *Song of the Shirt* (p. 183).

Other stanzas of similar structure are given with specimens in *Metrik*, ii, §§ 300, 301; their formulas are $a_4 a_4 b_2 b_5 c_4 c_4 d_2 d_5$, $a b a_4 b_3 c d c_4 d_3$ (Moore, *Dreaming for ever*), $a_3 b b_4 a_3 c_3 d d_4 c_3$, $a b a_3 b_2 c d c_3 d_2$, $a_3 b_2 c_4 a_2 d_3 b_2 c_4 d_2$; in the same place we have mentioned some ten-lined stanzas of the forms $a a_4 b b_2 a_4 c c_4 d d_2 c_4$ (Moore, *The Young May Moon*) and $a_3 a_2 b_5 b_2 c_4 d_3 d_2 e_5 e_2 c_4$, &c.

CHAPTER IV

ONE-RHYMED INDIVISIBLE AND BIPARTITE UNEQUAL-MEMBERED STANZAS

§ **251.** THESE different kinds of stanzas may be conveniently treated together, since they are closely allied with each other, in that both of them—the indivisible stanzas usually, and the bipartite unequal-membered stanzas frequently—exhibit a one-rhymed principal part.

I. *One-rhymed and indivisible stanzas.*

The **one-rhymed stanzas**, taken as a whole, cannot without qualification be ranged under any of the other kinds of stanza. The four-lined and eight-lined stanzas of this form, it is true, do for the most part seem to belong so far as their syntactical structure is concerned to the bipartite, equal-membered class (*a a, a a*; *a a a a, a a a a*). But those of six lines may belong either to the bipartite (*a a a, a a a*) or to the tripartite class (*a a, a a, a a*). It is even more difficult to draw a sharp line of distinction when the strophes have an odd number of lines.

In no case is there such a definite demarcation between the chief parts in these one-rhymed stanzas as exists in stanzas with varied rhymes, whether based upon crossed rhymes or on rhyming couplets.

Three-lined stanzas of the same structure as the four-lined stanzas to be described in the next section were not used before the Modern period. They occur pretty often, and are constructed of widely different kinds of verse; in Drayton's *The Heart* (Poets, iii. 580) three-foot lines are used:

> *If thus we needs must go,*
> *What shall our one heart do,*
> *This one made of our two?*

Stanzas of this kind, consisting of three-foot trochaic and dactylic verses, as well as stanzas of four-foot iambic, iambic-anapaestic, trochaic, and dactylic verses, are also met with in the Modern period. Even more popular, however, are those of five-foot iambic verses, as e. g. in Dryden, pp. 393, 400, &c. Stanzas of longer verses, on the other hand, e. g. six-foot dactylic, seven-foot trochaic, iambic, or iambic-anapaestic and eight-foot trochaic verses, occur only occasionally in the more recent poets, e. g. Tennyson, Swinburne, R. Browning, D. G. Rossetti, &c. (cf. *Metrik*, ii, §§ 303-4).

Some other Modern English anisometrical stanzas may also be mentioned, as one in Cowley with the formula $a_5 a_4 a_5$ in *Love's Visibility* (Poets, v. 273):

> With much of pain, and all the art I knew
> Have I endeavour'd hitherto
> To hide my love, and yet all will not do.

For other forms see *Metrik*, ii, § 305.

§ 252. **Four-lined, one-rhymed stanzas** of four-foot verses (used in Low Latin, Provençal and Old French poetry, cf. *Metrik*, i, p. 369) are early met with in Middle English poems, as in Wright's *Spec. of Lyr. Poetry*, pp. 57 and 68.

The first begins with these verses, which happen to show a prevailing trochaic rhythm.

> Suete iesu, king of blysse,
> Myn huerte loue, min huerte lisse,
> Þou art suete myd ywisse,
> Wo is him þat þe shall misse.

> Suete iesu, myn huerte lyht,
> Þou art day withoute nyht;
> Þou ȝeue me streinþe ant eke myht,
> Forte louien þe aryht.

This simple form of stanza is also found in Modern English poetry; apparently, however, only in one of the earliest poets, viz. Wyatt (p. 36).

It occurs also in Middle English, consisting of four-stressed, rhyming-alliterative long-lines, as e. g. in Wright's *Spec. of Lyr. Poetry*, p. 237; and of simple four-stressed long lines in Wyatt (p. 147), and Burns (pp. 253, 265, &c.).

In Middle English poetry Septenary verses are often used in this way on the Low Latin model (cf. *Metrik*, i, pp. 90, 91, 370), as well as Septenary-Alexandrine verses, e. g. Wright's *Spec. of Lyr. Poetry*, p. 93:

Blessed be þou, leuedy, ful of heouene blisse,
Suete flur of parays, moder of mildenesse,
Preyƺe iesu, þy sone, þat he me rede and wysse
So my wey forte gon, þat he me neuer misse.

In Modern English stanzas of this kind, consisting of Sep-tenary verses, are of rare occurrence. We have an example in Leigh Hunt's *The jovial Priest's Confession* (p. 338), a translation of the well-known poem ascribed to Walter Map, *Mihi est propositum in taberna mori* (cf. §§ 135, 182).

Shorter verses, e. g. iambic lines of three measures, are also very rarely used for such stanzas; e. g. in Donne and Denham (*Poets*, iv. 48 and v. 611).

§ **253.** A small group of other stanzas connected with the above may be called **indivisible stanzas**. They consist of a one-rhymed main part mostly of three, more rarely of two or four lines, followed by a shorter refrain-verse, a *cauda*, as it were, but in itself too unimportant to lend a bipartite character to the stanza. Otherwise, stanzas like these might be looked upon as bipartite unequal-membered stanzas, with which, indeed, they stand in close relationship. Three-lined stanzas of this kind occur in Modern English only; as e. g. a stanza consisting of an heroic couplet and a two-foot refrain verse of different rhythm: $a\,a_5\,B_2$ in Moore's Song:

Oh! where are they, who heard in former hours,
The voice of song in these neglected bowers?
They are gone—all gone!

Other stanzas show the formulas $a\,a_5\,b_3$ and $a\,a_4\,b_3$. Their structure evidently is analogous to that of a four-lined Middle English stanza $a\,a\,a_4\,B_3$, the model of which we find in Low Latin and Provençal poetry (cf. *Metrik*, i. 373) and in Furnivall's *Political, Religious, and Love Poems*, p. 4:

Sithe god hathe chose þe to be his knyƺt,
And posseside þe in þi right,
Thou hime honour with al thi myght,
Edwardus Dei gracia.

Similar stanzas occur also in Modern English poets: $a\,a\,a_4\,B_2$ in Wyatt, p. 99, $a\,a\,a_5\,B_3$ in G. Herbert, p. 18, &c. We find others with the formula $a\,a\,a_4\,b_2$ $a\,a\,a_4\,b_2$ in Dunbar's *Inconstancy of Love*, and with the formula $a\,a\,a_4\,b_3$ $c\,c\,c_4\,b_3$ $d\,d\,d_4\,b_3$, in Dorset (*Poets*,

vi. 512); there are also stanzas of five lines, e. g. $a\,a\,a\,a_4\,B_2$ (Wyatt, p. 80).

An older poem in Ritson's *Anc. Songs*, i. 140 (*Welcom Yol*), has the same metre and form of stanza, but with a refrain verse of two measures and a two-lined refrain prefixed to the first stanza : $A\,B_4$ $a\,a\,a_4\,B_2$ $c\,c\,c_4\,B_2$. A similar extended stanza is found in Wyatt (p. 108) A_3 $b\,b\,b_3$ $A_3\,B_2$; A_3 $c\,c\,c_3$ $A_3\,B_2$. There are also in modern poetry similar isometrical stanzas, as in Swinburne (*Poems*, ii. 108) on the scheme $a\,a\,a\,b_5$, $c\,c\,c\,b_5$, $d\,d\,d\,b_5$, $e\,e\,e\,f_5$, $g\,g\,g\,f_5$, $h\,h\,h\,f_5$; in Campbell (p. 73) $a\,a\,a\,b_4$, $c\,c\,c\,b_4$, $d\,d\,d\,b_4$; and in M. Arnold, *The Second Best* (p. 49), with feminine endings in the main part of the stanza, $a \sim a \sim a \sim b_4$, $c \sim c \sim c \sim b_4$, $d \sim d \sim d \sim b_4$, &c.

II. *Bipartite unequal-membered isometrical stanzas.*

§ 254. These are of greater number and variety. The shortest of them, however, viz. **stanzas of four lines**, are found only in Modern English ; first of all, stanzas arranged according to the formula $a\,a\,b\,a$; in this case b can be used as refrain also, as in Sidney, *Astrophel and Stella*, Song I (Grosart, i. 75):

> *Doubt you to whom my Muse these notes entendeth,*
> *Which now my breast, surcharg'd to musick lendeth!*
> *To you, to you, all song of praise is due,*
> *Only in you my song begins and endeth.*

Similar stanzas of four-foot iambic and of two-foot iambic-anapaestic lines occur in Tennyson, *The Daisy* (p. 270), and in Longfellow, *King Olaf and Earl Sigwald* (p. 573).

Stanzas with the scheme $a\,b\,b\,a$ also belong to this group, the two halves not being exactly equal, but only similar to each other on account of the unequal arrangement of rhymes.

Such a stanza of four-foot iambic verses occurs in an elegy of Ben Jonson's (*Poets*, iv. 571):

> *Though beauty be the mark of praise,*
> *And yours of whom I sing be such,*
> *As not the world can praise too much,*
> *· Yet is't your virtue now I raise.*

and notably in Tennyson's *In Memoriam*. Both this stanza and the similar stanza of trochaic verses are found pretty often (cf. *Metrik*, ii, § 311).

§ 255. More frequently **five-lined stanzas** occur. One on the scheme $a\,b\,b\,a\,a_4$, similar to that just mentioned, is used in Sidney, *Psalm XXVIII*; others, composed in various metres, have a one-rhymed *frons* or *cauda*, e. g. $a\,a\,a\,b\,b_3$ in Wyatt, p. 128, $a\,a\,b\,b\,b_4$ in Moore (*Still when Daylight*) and other poets. Of greater importance are some stanzas on the formula $a\,a\,b\,a\,b$; they may be looked upon as isometrical tail-rhyme-stanzas, shortened by one chief verse; as $a\,a\,b\,a\,B_4$, often occurring in Dunbar, e. g. in *The Devil's Inquest*, and in Wyatt, p. 29 :

> *My lute awake, perform the last*
> *Labour, that thou and I shall waste,*
>   *And end that I have now begun ;*
> *And when this song is sung and past,*
>   *My lute ! be still, for I have done.*

Another form of this stanza, consisting of five-foot lines with refrain, occurs in Swinburne, *In an Orchard* (*Poems*, i. 116), and a variety consisting of three-foot verses is found in Drayton's *Ode to Himself* (Poets, iii, p. 587). More frequently this stanza is found with the two parts in inverted order ($a\,b\,a\,a\,b_4$), as in Moore :

> *Take back the sigh, thy lips of art*
>   *In passion's moment breath'd to me :*
> *Yet, no—it must not, will not part,*
> *'Tis now the life-breath of my heart,*
>   *And has become too pure for thee.*

There are also five-foot iambic and three-foot iambic-anapaestic and other lines connected in this way, as in G. Herbert (p. 82); in Longfellow, *Enceladus* (p. 595); on the scheme $a\,b\,c\,c\,b_3$ in Wordsworth, i. 248 ; and in R. Browning according to the formula $a\,b\,c\,c\,b_4$ (vi. 77). The allied form of stanza, $a\,a\,b\,b\,a$, probably originating by inversion of the two last verses of the former stanza ($a\,a\,b\,a\,b$), occurs in Middle English in the poem *Of the Cuckoo and the Nightingale*.[1]

> *The god of love,—a ! benedicite,*
> *How mighty and how greet a lord is he !*
> *For he can make of lowe hertes hye,*
>   *And of hye lowe, and lyke for to dye,*
> *And harde hertes he can maken free.*

---

[1] *Chaucerian and other Pieces, &c.*, ed. Skeat, Oxford, 1897, p. 347.

The same stanza, both of four- and five-foot lines, is frequently employed by Dunbar; e. g. *On his Heid-Ake*, *The Visitation of St. Francis*, &c. We find it also in modern poets, composed of the same, or of other verses; Moore, e. g., has used it with five-foot iambic-anapaestic lines, in *At the mid hour of Night*.

A stanza on the model *a b a b b* is a favourite in Modern English; it is formed from the four-lined stanza (*a b a b*) by repeating the last rhyme. It consists of the most different kinds of verse; an example is Carew's *To my inconstant Mistress* (Poets, iii. 678):

> *When thou, poor excommunicate*
> *From all the joys of love, shalt see*
> *The full reward, and glorious fate,*
> *Which my strong faith shall purchase me,*
> *Then curse thine own inconstancy.*

For other specimens in lines of five, three, and four feet see *Metrik*, ii. 307.

Much less common is the form *a b b a b*, which occurs e. g. in Coleridge's *Recollections of Love* (*a b b a b₄*).

Five-lined stanzas of crossed rhymes are not very rare; an example of the form *a b a b a₄* is found in R. Browning's *The Patriot* (iv. 149):

> *It was roses, roses, all the way,*
> *With myrtle mixed in my path like mad:*
> *The house-roofs seemed to heave and sway,*
> *The church-spires flamed, such flags they had,*
> *A year ago on this very day.*

For specimens of other forms see *Metrik*, ii, § 318.

§ 256. The simplest kind of isometrical stanzas of this group is that in which the four-lined one-rhymed stanza is extended by the addition of a couplet with a new rhyme, so that it forms a **six-lined stanza**. A Latin stanza of this kind consisting of Septenary verses is given in Wright's *Pol. Poems*, i. 253, and a Middle English imitation of it, ib. p. 268, in the poem *On the Minorite Friars*. The same stanza composed of four-stressed verses is used by Minot in his poem *Of the batayl of Banocburn* (ib. i. 61):

> *Skottes out of Berwik and of Abirdene,*
> *At the Bannok burn war ʒe to kene;*
> *Thare slogh ʒe many sakles, als it was sene;*
> *And now has king Edward wroken it, I wene.*
> > *It es wrokin, I wene, wele wurth the while;*
> > *War ʒit with the Skottes, for thai er ful of gile.*

Here the *frons* is connected with the *cauda*, which recurs in each stanza as a kind of refrain, by means of *concatenatio*. Two other poems of Minot's (v, ix) are written in similar stanzas of six and eight lines. In the ten-lined stanza of the poem in Wright's *Spec. of Lyr. Poetry*, p. 25, which is of similar structure, we find the doubling of the *frons*.

A six-lined stanza of this kind, which has the formula *a a a b B B* (*BB* being refrain-verses), is used by Dunbar in his *Gray-Horse* poem and in *Luve Erdly and Divine*. The latter begins:

> *Now culit is Dame Venus brand;*
> *Trew Luvis fyre is ay kindilland,*
> *And I begyn to undirstand,*
> *In feynit luve quhat foly bene;*
> > *Now cumis Aige quhair Yowth hes bene,*
> > *And true Luve rysis fro the splene.*

The same kind of stanza occurs in Wyatt, p. 137. Other forms are: $a a b a b b_5$, in Wyatt, p. 71; $a b c c b a_4$ in John Scott, *Conclusion* (Poets, ix. 773); $a b c b c a_4$ in Tennyson, *A Character* (p. 12):

> *With a half-glance upon the sky*
> *At night he said, 'The wanderings*
> *Of this most intricate Universe*
> *Teach me the nothingness of things.'*
> *Yet could not all creation pierce*
> *Beyond the bottom of his eye.*

Longer isometrical stanzas are unfrequent, and need hardly be mentioned here (cf. *Metrik*, ii, p. 556).

III. *Bipartite unequal-membered anisometrical stanzas.*

§ 257. **Two-lined** and **four-lined stanzas.** The shortest stanzas of this kind consist of two anisometrical lines, rhyming in couplets, e. g. four- and five-foot, five- and three-foot lines, &c.

These have been mentioned before (§ 207); but as a rule they are used, like the heroic couplet, in continuous systems only, without strophic arrangement.

The *Poulter's Measure* (§§ 146, 206) must be mentioned in this place. This metre, also, is in narrative poetry employed without strophic arrangement; but in lyrical poetry it is sometimes written in stanzas. In this case it is mostly printed as a stanza of four lines, even when rhyming in long lines, i. e. with intermittent rhyme ($a\,b_3\,c_4\,b_3$); e.g. in Tennyson, *Marriage Morning* (p. 285):

> *Light, so low upon earth,*
>   *You send a flash to the sun,*
> *Here is the golden close of love,*
>   *All my wooing is done.*

The division into stanzas is still more distinctly recognizable when there are crossed rhymes ($a\,b_3\,a_4\,b_3$), as e. g. in a song in Percy's *Reliques*, I. ii. 2, *The Aged Lover renounceth Love* (quoted by the grave-digger in Shakespeare's *Hamlet*):

> *I lothe that I did love,*
>   *In youth that I thought swete,*
> *As time requires: for my behove*
>   *Me thinkes they are not mete.*

This stanza occurs very frequently (cf. *Metrik*, ii, § 321), but is rarely formed of trochaic verses.

Another rare variety on the scheme $a \sim b_3\,c_4\,b_3$ is found in Mrs. Hemans, *The Stream is free* (vii. 42), and in M. Arnold's *The Neckan* (p. 167).

Similar to the common *Poulter's Measure* stanza is another stanza of iambic-anapaestic verses on the formula $a\,a_3\,b_4\,a_3$ (in b middle-rhyme is used, so that the scheme may also be given as $a\,a_3\,b\,b_2\,a_3$). We find it in Burns, the a-rhymes being masculine (p. 245) and feminine (p. 218).

Four-lined stanzas of two rhyming couplets of unequal length are fairly common; as e. g. on the model $a\,a_5\,b\,b_4$ in Dryden, *Hymn for St. John's Eve*:

> *O sylvan prophet! whose eternal fame*
> *Echoes from Judah's hills and Jordan's stream,*
>   *The music of our numbers raise,*
>   *And tune our voices to thy praise.*

Other schemes that occur are $a\,a_4\,b\,b_5$, $a\,a\,b_4\,b_5$, $a\,a\,b_4\,b_2$, $a\,a_4\,b_3\,b_2$, $a_4\,a_2\,b\,b_4$, $a_5\,a_3\,b\,b_5$; there are even forms with lines of unequal length in each part, as e.g.: $a_4\,a_5\,b_7\,b_5$, $a_7\,a_4\,b_2\,b_6$, $a_5\,a_3\,b_5\,b_4$, $a_5\,a_4\,b_4\,b_5$. For examples see *Metrik*, ii (§§ 322–4).

Enclosing rhymes are also found; and in this case the lines of the same length usually rhyme together, as in the formula $a_3\,b\,b_5\,a_3$ in Mrs. Hemans, *The Song of Night* (vi. 94):

> *I come to thee, O Earth!*
> *With all my gifts!—for every flower sweet dew*
> *In bell, and urn, and chalice, to renew*
> *The glory of its birth.*

Sometimes verses are used partly of unequal length: $a_3\,b_5\,b_3\,a_4$ in M. Arnold, *A Nameless Epitaph* (p. 232), or $a_5\,b_2\,b_4\,a_5$, $a\,b\,b_4\,a_3$, &c. (cf. *Metrik*, ii, § 325).

§ **258.** Stanzas of this kind frequently occur with crossed rhymes. Most commonly two longer verses are placed between two shorter ones, or vice versa; thus we have the formula $a_3\,b\,a_5\,b_3$ in Southey's *The Ebb-Tide* (ii. 193):

> *Slowly thy flowing tide*
> *Came in, old Avon! scarcely did mine eyes,*
> *As watchfully I roam'd thy green-wood side,*
> *Perceive its gentle rise.*

Other forms are $a_2\,b\,a_3\,b_2$, $a_4\,b\,a_5\,b_4$, $a_5\,b\,a_4\,b_5$ (cf. *Metrik*, ii, § 326).

Three isometrical verses and one shorter or longer end-verse can also be so connected, as e.g. on the scheme $a\,b\,a_4\,b_2$ in Pope, *Ode on Solitude* (p. 45):

> *Happy the man whose wish and care*
> *A few paternal acres bound,*
> *Content to breathe his native air,*
> *In his own ground;*

or in Cowper on the model $a\,b\,a_4\,b_5$ in *Divine Love endures no Rival* (p. 418):

> *Love is the Lord whom I obey,*
> *Whose will transported I perform;*
> *The centre of my rest, my stay,*
> *Love's all in all to me, myself a worm.*

Similar stanzas both with this and other arrangements of rhymes (as e.g. $a\,b\,a_5\,b_3$, $a\,b\,a_4\,b_2$, $a\,b\,a_3\,b_5$) are very popular.

A specimen of the first of these formulas is found in M. Arnold's *Progress* (p. 252), and one of the second in his *A Southern Night* (p. 294). For other examples see *Metrik*, ii, §§ 326-7.

More rarely a short verse begins the stanza (e. g. $a_3 b a b_5$ in Mrs. Hemans, *The Wish*, vi. 249), or is placed in the middle on the scheme $a_5 b_2 a b_5$ (as in G. Herbert, *Church Lock and Key*, p. 61). For specimens see *Metrik*, ii, §§ 328, 329.

Stanzas of one isometrical and another anisometrical half are not frequently met with; a specimen of the form $a b_4 a_5 b_2$ is found in G. Herbert's *Employment* (p. 51).

More common are stanzas of two anisometrical halves; in this case either the two middle or the isolated verses are generally isometrical; e. g. on the scheme $a_5 b a_4 b_3$ in G. Herbert, *The Temper* (p. 49):

> *How should I praise thee, Lord! how should my rymes*
>   *Gladly engrave thy love in steel,*
>   *If what my soul doth feel sometimes,*
>   *My soul might ever feel!*

or on $a_4 b_3 a_4 b_5$ in Milton, *Psalm V* (vol. iii, p. 24):

>   *Jehovah, to my words give ear,*
>   *My meditation weigh;*
>   *The voice of my complaining hear,*
>   *My king and God, for unto thee I pray.*

Stanzas like these are very much in vogue, and may be composed of the most varied forms of verse (cf. *Metrik*, ii, § 330).

§ 259. Among the **five-lined stanzas** the first place must be given to those in which the arrangement of rhymes is parallel, as these are found in Middle English as well as in Modern English poetry. A stanza of form $a a a_4 b_3 b_6$ occurs in Wright's *Spec. of Lyr. Poetry*, p. 60:

> *Wynter wakeneþ al my care,*
> *nou þis leues waxeþ bare;*
> *ofte y sike ant mourne sare,*
>   *when hit cómeþ ín my þóht,*
> *óf this wórldes ióie, hóu hit geþ ál to nóht.*

A similar structure ($a a a_4 b_3 b_5$) is shown in a stanza of a poem quoted by Ritson, *Ancient Songs*, i. 129; the poem belongs to the fifteenth century.

Still more numerous are these stanzas in Modern English;

e. g. the form $a\,a\,a_3\,b\,b_5$ occurs in Herbert, *Sinne* (p. 58), $a\,a\,a_3\,b_4\,b_3$ in Shelley (iii. 244), $a\,a\,a\,b_4\,b_5$ in Suckling (*Poets*, iii. 734); a still more irregular structure $(a_4\,a_5\,b\,b_4\,b_5)$ is in Cowley, *All for love* (Poets, v. 263):

> *'Tis well, 'tis well with them, say I.*
> *Whose short liv'd passions with themselves can die;*
> *For none can be unhappy who,*
> *'Midst all his ills, a time does know*
> (*Though ne'er so long*) *when he shall not be so.*

Here again we meet with the stanzas mentioned above, which are partially characterized by enclosing rhymes, e. g. corresponding to the formula $a\,b\,b\,a$, as in M. Arnold, *On the Rhine* (p. 223), or on the scheme $a\,a\,b\,b_4\,a_5$, as in Byron, *Oh! snatch'd away*, &c. (p. 123):

> *Oh! snatch'd away in beauty's bloom,*
> *On thee shall press no ponderous tomb;*
> *But on thy turf shall roses rear*
> *Their leaves, the earliest of the year;*
> *And the wild cypress wave in tender gloom.*

For other stanzas on the formulas $a\,a_5\,b\,b_4\,A_3$, $a_5\,b\,b_4\,a_5\,a_4$, $a_3\,b\,b_2\,a\,a_3$, &c., see *Metrik* (ii, §§ 332, 333).

In others the chief part of the stanza shows crossed rhyme, as e. g. on the scheme $a\,b\,a\,b_4\,b_3$ in Poe, *To Helen* (p. 205):

> *Helen, thy beauty is to me*
> *Like those Nicean barks of yore*
> *That gently, o'er a perfumed sea,*
> *The weary way-worn wanderer bore*
> *To his own native shore.*

Other stanzas take the forms $a_5\,b_4\,a_5\,b_4\,b_5$, $a_5\,b_2\,a_4\,b_3\,b_5$, $a_4\,b_3\,a_4\,b_3\,b_2$, &c. More uncommon are such forms as $a_3\,b\,b_5\,a_4\,b_5$, $a\,b_5\,b_3\,a\,b_5$, &c. (For specimens see *Metrik*, ii, § 334.)

Stanzas with crossed rhymes throughout, on the other hand, are very frequent, as e. g. type $a\,b\,a\,b_4\,a_3$ in R. Browning's *By the Fireside* (iii. 170):

> *How well I know what I mean to do*
> *When the long dark autumn evenings come;*
> *And where, my soul, is thy pleasant hue?*
> *With the music of all thy voices, dumb*
> *In life's November too!*

There are many other forms, sometimes very complicated, as e.g. $a\,b\,a\,b_5\,a_3$, $a\,b_5\,a_2\,b\,a_6$, $a_3\,b\,a_4\,b_3\,a_5$, &c. (For examples see *Metrik*, ii, § 335.)

§ **260.** The tail-rhyme stanzas shortened by one verse occupy an important position among the five-lined stanzas.

These curtailed forms occur as early as the Middle English period, e.g. in an envoi on the model $a\,a_4\,b_2\,a_4\,b_2$, forming the conclusion of a poem in six-lined stanzas $(a\,a\,a_4\,b_2\,a_4\,b_2)$, printed in Wright's *Spec. of Lyr. Poetry*, p. 38.

> *Ich wolde ich were a þrestelcok,*
> *A bountyng oþer a lauerok.*
> > *Swete bryd !*
> *Bituene hire curtel ant hire smok*
> > *Y wolde ben hyd.*

In Modern English the common form of stanza is much employed, consisting of four- and three-foot verses, $a\,a_4\,b_3\,a_4\,b_3$; there are many varieties of this scheme, as $a\,a\,b\,a_4\,b_3$, $a_5\,a\,b_4\,a_5\,b_3$, $a\,a_2\,b\,a_4\,b_3$, &c. (cf. *Metrik*, ii, § 336).

A similar form, with shortening in the first half-stanza, also occurs in Middle English poetry, though only as an envoi of another form of stanza, viz, in the *Towneley Mysteries* (pp. 34-3²3):

> *Vnwunne haueþ myn wonges wet,*
> > *Þat makeþ me rouþes rede ;*
> *Ne sem i nout þer y am set,*
> > *Þer me calleþ me fule flet*
> > *And waynoun ! wayteglede.*

This stanza is also frequently used in Modern English, e.g. by Thomas Moore, *Nay, do not weep.*

A similar stanza on the model $a_4\,b_2\,a\,a_4\,b_2$ is used by Moore in *Echo* (ii. 211):

> *How sweet the answer Echo makes*
> > *To music at night,*
> *When, roused by lute or horn, she wakes,*
> *And far away, o'er lawns and lakes,*
> > *Goes answering light.*

We find specimens of this stanza consisting of other metres and of different structure (isometrical in the first half-stanza),

e. g. on the schemes $a_5 b_3 a a_5 b_3$, $a b a a_4 b_3$, &c. (For specimens see *Metrik*, ii, § 337.)

Stanzas of this kind are also formed with three rhymes, e. g. $a b_3 c c_2 b_4$, $a b_3 c c_2 b_3$, $a \sim b_4 c \sim c \sim_2 b_4$, &c. (For specimens cf. *Metrik*, ii, § 338.)

Another class of shortened tail-rhyme stanzas, which is deficient not in one of the rhyming couplets, but in one of the tail-verses, comes in here. Omission of the first tail-verse, producing a stanza on the scheme $a a b b c$, occurs in Wordsworth, *The Blind Highland Boy* (ii. 368):

> *Now we are tired of boisterous joy,*
> *Have romped enough, my little Boy !*
> *Jane hangs her head upon my breast,*
> *And you shall bring your stool and rest ;*
> *This corner is your own.*

Another stanza, which is used in Carew's *Love's Courtship* (Poets, iii. 707), is formed on the scheme $a a_4 b_2 c c_4$, where the tail-verse of the second half-stanza is wanting. As to the other varieties, arising from the use of other metres, cf. *Metrik*, ii, § 338.

Sometimes stanzas of three rhymes occur, rhyming crosswise throughout, and of various forms, e. g. $a b a c_4 b_3$ in Longfellow, *The Saga of King Olaf* (p. 565); $a b_4 c_3 a_4 c_2$ in Coleridge; $a b a b_5 C_3$ in Mrs. Hemans (iv. 119); $a b a b_4 C_3$ in Moore, *Weep, Children of Israel*:

> *Weep, weep for him, the Man of God—*
> *In yonder vale he sunk to rest ;*
> *But none of earth can point the sod*
> *That flowers above his sacred breast.*
> *Weep, children of Israel, weep !*

For other varieties see *Metrik*, ii, § 339.

§ **261**. Unequal-membered anisometrical **stanzas of six lines** are only rarely met with in Middle English, as e. g. $a a_4 b b b a_2$ in Dunbar's poem, *Aganis Treason*.

They occur, on the other hand, very frequently in Modern English, especially with parallel rhymes on the scheme $a a a a_4 B C_2$ in *The Old and Young Courtier* (Percy's *Rel.* II. iii. 8):

An old song made by an aged old pate,
Of an old worshipful gentleman, who had a greate estate,
That kept a brave old house at a bountiful rate,
And an old porter to relieve the poor at his gate ;
  Like an old courtier of the queen's,
  And the queen's old courtier.

For specimens of other stanzas, the rhymes of which are arranged in a similar way (according to $a_5 a a b b_4 b_5$, or with partly enclosing rhymes, as $a_5 b b b b_3 a_5$, $a a b b b_4 a_2$, $a a_4 b b b a_2$, &c.), see *Metrik*, ii, § 340.

Forms based upon the tail-rhyme stanza are very popular; of great importance is the entwined form on a Provençal model (cf. Bartsch, *Provenzalisches Lesebuch*, p. 46) which was imitated in Middle English poetry. It corresponds to the scheme $a a a_4 b_3 a_4 b_3$ and gives the impression, according to Wolf in his book, *Über die Lais*, &c., p. 230, note 67, that the second part of a common tail-rhyme stanza is inserted into the first, though it is also possible that it may have been formed from the extended tail-rhyme stanza $a a a_4 b_3 a a a_4 b_3$ by shortening the second part by two chief verses. The first stanza of a poem in Wright's *Spec. of Lyr. Poetry*, p. 94, may serve as a specimen:

  Ase y me rod þis ender day,
  By grene wode to seche play,
  Mid herte y þohte al on a may,
    Suetest of alle þinge ;
  Lyþe, and ich ou telle may
  Al of þat suete þinge.

This stanza occurs frequently in the *Towneley Mysteries*, pp. 120–34, 254–69, &c. In Modern English, however, we find it very seldom; as an example (iambic-anapaestic verses of four and three measures) we may refer to Campbell's *Stanzas on the battle of Navarino* (p. 176).

More frequent in Modern English, on the other hand, is a variety of this stanza with two-foot tail-verses on the scheme $a a a_4 b_2 a_4 b_2$; it is especially common in Ramsay and Fergusson, and occurs in several poems of Burns, e.g. in his *Scotch Drink* (p. 6):

  Let other Poets raise a fracas
  'Bout vines, an' wines, an' drunken Bacchus,
  An' crabbit names an' stories wrack us,
    An' grate our lug,
  I sing the juice Scotch bear can mak us,
    In glass or jug.

The same form of stanza is used by Wordsworth and by M. Arnold in his poem *Kaiser Dead* (p. 495).

The same stanza sometimes occurs with the order of the parts inverted like $a_4 b_3 a a a_4 b_3$, e.g. in Longfellow's *Voices of the Night* (p. 40).

Other unequal-membered varieties of the anisometrical tail-rhyme stanza correspond to $a a_3 b_5 a a_5 b_6$ (cf. the chapter on the Spenserian stanza and its imitations), $a a b c c_4 b_3$ (M. Arnold, *Horatian Echo*, p. 47), $a a b c c_3 b_5$, $a_5 a_3 b_5 c c b_5$, $a_4 a_2 b_4 c_2 c_5 b_4$, $a_4 b_3 a c c_4 b_3$ (entwined *frons*), $a a_4 b_3 c_3 b_4 c_5$ (entwined *cauda*). For examples see *Metrik*, ii, § 343.

Here again we must mention stanzas which in their structure are influenced by the tail-rhyme stanza and are formed on the scheme $a b c a b c$; of these we have several examples in G. Herbert, on the scheme $a b c_5 a b_4 c_5$, e.g. in *Magdalena* (p. 183):

> When blessed Marie wip'd her Saviour's feet,
> (Whose precepts she had trampled on before)
> And wore them for a jewell on her head,
> Shewing his steps should be the street,
> Wherein she thenceforth evermore
> With pensive humblenesse would live and tread.

Other stanzas of his correspond to $a_5 b_4 c_3 c_4 b_3 a_5$, $a_3 b_5 c_4 c_4 b_5 a_3$, &c. In Moore we have a similar stanza: $a b_4 c_2 b a_4 c_2$ which is unequal-membered on account of the arrangement of rhyme (cf. *Metrik*, ii, § 344). An unusual form of stanza, which may also be classed under this head, occurs in M. Arnold's *Human Life* (p. 40), its formula being $a_3 b_4 c a c b_5$.

§ 262. A **stanza of seven lines** is used in Dunbar's poem *The Merchantis of Edinborough*, formed on the scheme $a a a b_4 B_2 a_4 B_4$; it is very interesting on account of the duplication of the refrain-verses (B_2, B_4). Apart from the first short refrain-verse the arrangement of rhymes is the same as it is in the entwined tail-rhyme stanza:

> Quhy will ȝe, merchantis of renoun,
> Lat Edinburgh, ȝour nobill toun,
> For laik of reformatioun
> The commone proffeitt tyne and fame?
>   Think ȝe noht schame,
> That onie other regioun
>   Sall with dishonour hurt ȝour name!

The Modern English stanzas also mostly bear a greater or less resemblance to the tail-rhyme stanza. This relationship is evident in a stanza like $a\, a_4\, b_3\, c\, c\, c_4\, b_3$, used in Wordsworth, *To the Daisy* (iii. 42):

> Sweet flower! belike one day to have
> A place upon thy Poet's grave,
>   I welcome thee once more:
> But He, who was on land, at sea,
> My Brother, too, in loving thee,
> Although he loved more silently,
>   , Sleeps by his native shore.

A peculiar form of stanza occurring in M. Arnold's *In Utrumque Paratus* (p. 45) with the formula $a_5\, b_3\, a\, c\, b\, c_5\, b_3$ likewise belongs to this group.

In other instances the longer part comes first on the model $a\, a\, a_4\, b_3\, c\, c_4\, b_3$, e.g. in Mrs. Hemans, *The Sun* (iv. 251).

Other stanzas correspond to $a\, a_3\, b_2\, c\, c\, c_3\, B_2$ and $a\, a\, a\, b\, c\, c_2\, b_3$.

In other cases the equal-membered tail-rhyme stanza becomes unequal-membered by adding to the second tail-verse another verse rhyming with it, the formula being then $a\, a_4\, B_2\, a\, a_4\, b\, B_2$ (e.g. in Longfellow, *Victor Galbraith*, p. 503) or $a\, a_2\, b_4\, c\, c_2\, b_4\, B_3$ (in Moore, *Little man*), or $a\, a_3\, b_2\, c \sim c \sim b\, b_3$ (id., *The Pilgrim*).

Less closely allied to the tail-rhyme stanza are the forms which are similar to it only in one half-strophe, e.g. those on the model $a_4\, b_2\, a\, b\, c\, c_4\, b_2$ (Shelley, *To Night*, iii. 62), $a\, b_3\, c\, c_2\, a\, a_4\, b_3$ (id. *Lines*, iii. 86), $a\, b\, b_4\, r_2\, a\, R_4\, r_2$ (Tennyson, *A Dirge*, p. 16). For other examples see *Metrik*, ii, § 347.

§ 263. There are also some eight-, nine-, and ten-lined stanzas similar to the tail-rhyme stanza. An **eight-lined stanza** of the form $a_4\, b\, a_5\, c_2,\; b_4\, d\, d_5\, c_2$ occurs in Herbert, *The Glance* (p. 18), and one of the form $a \sim a \sim_4 B\, c \sim d\, c \sim d_4\, B_3$ in Moore's *Thee, thee, only thee*:

> The dawning of morn, the daylight's sinking,
> The night's long hours still find me thinking
>   Of thee, thee, only thee.
> When friends are met, and goblets crown'd,
>   And smiles are near, that once enchanted,
> Unreach'd by all that sunshine round,
>   My soul, like some dark spot, is haunted
>   By thee, thee, only thee.

A stanza used by Wordsworth in *Stray Pleasures* (iv. 12) corresponds to $a\,a_2\,b_3\,c\,c\,d\,d_2\,b_3$.

Two stanzas used by M. Arnold correspond to the formulas $a\,a_2\,b_2\,c_5\,d_4\,c_3\,d_4\,b_2$ (*a a* printed as one line) in *A Question* (p. 44), and $a\,a_3\,b_5\,c\,c_3\,d\,b\,d_3$ in *The World and the Quietist* (p. 46).

A **stanza of nine lines** is found in Tennyson's *Lady of Shalott* (p. 28); it is on the scheme $a\,a\,a\,a\,b\,c\,c\,c_4\,b$; one of ten lines in his *Greeting to the Duchess of Edinburgh* (p. 261) on the model $a\,b\,b\,a_5\,C_2\,d\,e\,e\,d_5\,C_3$ (cf. *Metrik*, ii, § 349).

Other stanzas of this kind are related to the Septenary or the *Poulter's Measure*, e. g. those on the schemes $a_4\,b_3\,a\,b\,c\,d\,c_4\,d_3$, $a\,b\,a_4\,b_3\,c\,d_3\,c_4\,d_3$, and $a\,b_2\,a_4\,b_2\,c_3\,d_2\,c_4\,d_2$, examples of which, from Moore, are given in *Metrik*, ii, § 348.

Stanzas of eleven and **twelve lines** are rare. For examples see *Metrik*, ii, § 350.

§ 264. The bob-wheel stanzas. This important class of bipartite unequal-membered anisometrical stanzas was very much in vogue in the Middle English period. They consist (see § 222) of a *frons* (longer verses of four stresses, or Septenary and Alexandrine verses) and a *cauda*, which is formed of shorter verses and is joined to the *frons* by one or several 'bob-verses', belonging generally to the first part or 'upsong' (in German *Aufgesang*).

Sometimes it is doubtful whether these stanzas belong to the bipartite or to the tripartite class, on account of the variety of rhymes in the *frons*. But as they mostly consist of two quite unequal parts, they certainly stand in a closer relationship to the bipartite stanzas.

A simple stanza of this kind on the scheme $A\,A_7\,C_1\,B_7$ occurs in William of Shoreham (printed in short lines on the model $A_4\,B_3\,C_4\,B_3\,d_1\,E_4\,D_3$):

> *Nou here we mote in this sermon of ordre maky saȝe,*
> *Then was bytokned suithe wel wylom by the ealde lawe*
> > *To aginne,*
> *Tho me made Godes hous and ministres therinne.*

A six-lined stanza of Alexandrines and Septenaries on the scheme $A\,A\,B\,B_6\,c_1C_6$ is found in the poem *On the evil Times of Edward II* (Wright's *Polit. Songs*, p. 323). Another variety originated by the breaking up of the longer verses into short ones by inserted rhyme, as in the closing stanzas of a poem by Minot (ed. Hall, p. 17) according to the formula $A\,B\,A\,B\,A\,B\,A\,B_3\,c_1\,A\,C_3$; cf. the last stanza:

Y

> *King Edward, frely fode,*
> > *In Fraunce he will noght blin*
> *To make his famen wode*
> > *That er wonand tharein.*
> *God, that rest on rode,*
> > *For sake of Adams syn,*
> *Strenkith him maine and mode,*
> > *His reght in France to win,*
> > > *And have.*
> *God grante him graces gode,*
> > *And fro all sins us save.*

A similar form of stanza $(A\ B\ A\ B\ A\ B\ A\ B_3\ c_1\ B\ C_3)$ is used in the Romance of *Sir Tristrem*; that of the Scottish poem *Christ's Kirk on the Green*, however, is formed on the model $A_4\ B_3\ A_4\ B_3\ A_4\ B_3\ b_1\ B_4$.

§ **265.** Still more common than stanzas of this kind composed of even-beat verses, are those of four-stressed rhyming verses with or without alliteration.

Under this head comes a poem in Wright's *Polit. Songs*, p. 69 (cf. § 60), on the scheme $A\ A\ A\ A_4\ B_3\ c_1\ C_3\ B_4$, or rather $A\ A\ A\ A_4\ b_2\ c_1\ c_2\ B_4$, the bob-verse being thus inserted in the *cauda*. The common form comes out more clearly in another poem, ibid., p. 212 (st. 1, quoted pp. 100–1), corresponding to $A\ A\ A\ A_4\ b_1\ c\ c_2\ b_2$, where $A\ A\ A\ A_4$ are verses of four stresses, b a one-stressed bob-verse or the half-verse of a long line, $c\ c_2\ b_2$ half-verses of two stresses.

The Tournament of Tottenham (Ritson's *Anc. Songs*, i. 85–9) is written in a similar form of stanza with the formula $A\ A\ A\ A_4\ b\ c\ c\ c\ b_2$; the cauda consisting of five verses with two stresses only.

This form of stanza is further developed by connecting the halves of the long lines with each other by the insertion of rhymes in the same way as in the stanzas of isometrical verses. An example may be seen in Wright's *Polit. Songs*, p. 153, the scheme being $A\ A\ A\ A_4\ b\ b_1\ b_2$ or $A\ A\ A\ A_4\ b_1\ b_2\ b_4$ (or, with the longer lines broken up, $A\ B\ A\ B\ A\ B\ A\ B_2\ c\ c_1\ c_2$, or $A\ B\ A\ B\ A\ B\ A\ B_2\ c_1\ c_2\ C_4$, &c.).

Similar stanzas, especially those on the model

$$A\ A\ A\ A_4\ b_1\ c\ c\ c_2\ b_2\ (A\ B\ A\ B\ A\ B\ A\ B_2\ c_1\ d\ d\ d_2\ c_2)$$

were much used in the mystery plays, as e. g. in the *Towneley Mysteries* (pp. 20–34), even when in the dialogue the single lines are divided between different speakers (cf. *Metrik*, i, pp. 390–1).

The four-stressed long lines sometimes alternate with Alexandrine and Septenary verses. In these plays stanzas of an eight-lined *frons* consisting of long verses, rhyming crosswise and corresponding to $A B A B A B A B_4 c_1 d d d_2 c_2$ are also common:

> *Peasse at my bydyng, ye wyghtys in wold!*
> *Looke none be so hardy to speke a word bot I,*
> *Or by Mahwne most myghty, maker on mold,*
> *With this brande that I bere ye shalle bytterly aby ;*
> *Say, wote ye not that I am Pylate, perles to behold?*
> *Most doughty in dedes of dukys of the Jury,*
> *In bradyng of batels I am the most bold,*
> *Therefor my name to you wille I descry,*
> > *No mys.*
> > *I am fulle of sotelty,*
> > *Falshod, gylt, and trechery ;*
> > *Therefor am I namyd by clergy*
> > *As mali actoris.*

Other stanzas, the first *cauda*-verse of which has four beats (on the scheme $A B A B A B A B C_4 d d d c_2$), were also very much in vogue. Stanzas of this kind occur in the poems *Golagros and Gawane*, *The Buke of the Howlat*, *Rauf Coilzear*, and *The Awntyrs of Arthure at the Terne Wathelyne* (S. T. S. vol. 28; cf. § 61). An interesting variety of the common form (with a five-lined *cauda*) we have in the poem *Of sayne John the Euangelist* (E. E. T. S., 26, p. 87). The stanza consists of an eight-lined *frons* of crossed rhymes and a *cauda* formed by a six-lined tail-rhyme stanza[1] of two-beat verses, on the scheme $A B A B A B A B_4 c c d c c d_2$.

As to the rhythmical structure of the half-verses used in the *cauda* of the stanza cf. the explanations given in § 64.

§ 266. The bob-wheel stanzas[2] were preserved in the North in Scottish poetry (e.g. Alex. Montgomerie) up to the Modern English period.[3] It is not unlikely that they found their way from this source into Modern English poetry, where they are also met with, though they have not attained any marked popularity.

---

[1] This form of stanza is of great importance in the anisometrical 'lays', which cannot be discussed in this place (cf. *Metrik*, i, § 168). In these poems the strophic arrangement is not strictly followed throughout, but only in certain parts ; a general conformity only is observed in these cases.

[2] As to this form cf. *Huchown's Pistel of Swete Susan*, herausgeg. von Dr. H. Köster, Strassburg, 1895 (*Quellen und Forschungen*, 76), pp. 15–36.

[3] Cf. R. Brotanek, *Alexander Montgomerie*, Vienna, 1896.

It must, however, be kept in mind that the Modern English bob-wheel stanzas are not a direct imitation of the Middle English. Sometimes they were influenced probably by the odes, as there is a marked likeness between these two forms, e. g. in two stanzas of Donne (*Poets*, iv. 24 and 39) on the schemes $A\,B\,A\,B\,C\,C_4\,d\,d_1\,D_4$ and $A_2\,A_5\,B_4\,C\,C_5\,B_4\,d_1\,D\,E\,E_5$; or in a stanza of Ben Jonson in an ode to Wm. Sidney (*Poets*, iv. 558) on the model $A_5\,B_4\,c\,c_1\,B_3\,a\,d\,d\,e_2\,E_5$, and in another in *The Dream* (iv. 566), $A\,A_4\,B_3\,C\,C_4\,A_5\,A_4\,B_3\,b_1\,D\,D_3\,E\,E_4\,B_5$.

In this and other cases they consist of even-measured, seldom of four-stressed verses, as e.g. in Suckling, who seems to have been very fond of these forms of stanza; cf. the following stanza on the model $A\,A_4\,B_3\,c\,c_1\,b_2$ (*Poets*, iii. 736):

> *That none beguiled be by time's quick flowing,*
> *Lovers have in their hearts a clock still going;*
> *For though time be nimble, his motions*
> > *Are quicker*
> > *And thicker*
> *Where love hath its notions.*

Other bob-wheel stanzas in Suckling show the schemes $A\,A_4\,a_2\,b\,b_3$ (ib. iii. 740), $A\,A\,A_4\,B\,B_5\,c_2\,c_1\,C\,D_4\,d_2$ (ib. iii. 729), $A\,A\,B\,B_4\,c_1\,c\,d_2\,D_5$ (ib. 739).

More similar to the older forms is a stanza of a song in Dryden formed after $A\,A\,B\,B\,C\,C_4\,d\,d\,e\,e_2\,e_3$ (p. 339).

In Modern poetry such stanzas are used especially by Burns, Scott, and sometimes by Moore. So we have in Burns a fine simple stanza on the model $A_4\,B_3\,A_4\,B_3\,c_1\,B_3$, similar to the Shoreham stanza (cf. § 264):

> *It was a' for our rightfu' king*
> *We left fair Scotland's strand,*
> *It was a' for our rightfu' king*
> *We e'er saw Irish land,*
> > *My dear;*
> *We e'er saw Irish land.*

Similar stanzas occur in Moore on the formula $A_4\,B_3\,A_4\,B_3\,a_1\,B_3$ in *Then fare thee well*, on $A_4\,B\,\sim_3\,A_4\,B\,\sim_3\,c_1\,B\,\sim_3$ in *Dear Fanny*. Other stanzas by the same poet have a somewhat longer *cauda*, as $A_4\,B\,\sim_3\,A_4\,B\,\sim_3\,c\,\sim\,c\,\sim\,d\,\sim\,d\,\sim_1\,A_4\,C\,\sim_3$

or $A\,B\,\sim\,A\,B\,\sim\,C\,\sim\,C\,\sim_4\,d\,d_2\,E\,F\,\sim\,E\,F\,\sim_4$.

A stanza used by Sir Walter Scott in *To the Sub-Prior* (p. 461) is formed on the model $A\,A\,B\,B_4\,c_1\,c_2\,C_4$, the *frons* consisting of four-stressed verses:

> *Good evening, Sir Priest, and so late as you ride,*
> *With your mule so fair, and your mantle so wide;*
> *But ride you through valley, or ride you o'er hill,*
> *There is one that has warrant to wait on you still.*
> > *Back, back,*
> > *The volume black!*
> *I have a warrant to carry it back.*

Most of these stanzas admit of being looked upon as tripartite on account of the bipartite structure of the *frons*.

Other stanzas may be viewed as consisting of three unequal parts (if not regarded as bipartite); such, for instance, is the stanza on the scheme $(a) \sim A \sim (b) \sim B \sim_4 c_1 (d) D_4 b\sim_1 e\, e\, e\, c\, c_2\, C_4$ occurring in Shelley's *Autumn, A Dirge* (iii. 65), where the symbols (a) and (b) denote middle rhymes.

Stanzas of this kind are met with also in modern poetry, as e.g. in Thackeray, Mrs. Browning, and Rossetti (cf. *Metrik*, ii, §§ 353, 354).

CHAPTER V

TRIPARTITE STANZAS

I. *Isometrical stanzas.*

§ 267. In the anisometrical stanzas (which might, as being the older species, have been treated of first) the distinction between the first and the last part of the stanza (*frons* and *cauda*) is marked as a rule by a difference of metre in them; in isometrical stanzas, on the other hand, the distinction between the two parts depends solely on the arrangement of the rhyme. For this reason certain **six-lined stanzas** consisting of two equal parts and a third of the same structure (the formula being $a\ a\ b\ b\ c\ c_4$ or the like), which now and then occur in the *Surtees Psalter* (e. g. Ps. xliv, st. 5), cannot strictly be called tripartite.

Stanzas like these are, however, not unfrequent in Modern English poetry, as e.g. in a song of Carew's (*Poets*, iii. 292):

> *Cease, thou afflicted soul, to mourn,*
> *Whose love and faith are paid with scorn;*
> *For I am starv'd that feel the blisses*
> *Of dear embraces, smiles and kisses,*
> *From my soul's idol, yet complain*
> *Of equal love more than disdain.*

For an account of many other stanzas of the same or similar structure (consisting of trochaic four-foot lines, iambic-anapaestic lines of four stresses, or lines of five, six, and seven measures), see *Metrik*, ii, §§ 355, 356.

It is only rarely that we find stanzas formed on the scheme $a\ a\ a\ a\ b\ b$ (e. g. in the *Surtees Psalter*, xlix. 21; in Ben Jonson, *Poets*, iv. 574); or on the formula $a\ a\ b\ b\ a\ b_4$, as in Swinburne, *Poems*, i. 248.

One form, analogous to the stanza first mentioned in this section and used pretty often in Modern English, has crossed rhymes $a\ b\ a\ b\ a\ b$. It occurs with four-foot verses in Byron, *She walks in Beauty*:

> *She walks in beauty, like the night*
> *Of cloudless climes and starry skies :*
> *And all that's best of dark and bright*
> *Meet in her aspect and her eyes ;*
> *Thus mellow'd to that tender light*
> *Which Heaven to gaudy day denies.*

The same stanza of trochaic or iambic-anapaestic metres of three or five measures is also frequently met with (cf. *Metrik*, ii, § 358).

The tripartite character of a strophe appears somewhat more distinctly in stanzas formed on the scheme *a b a b b b*, or *a b a b b x* (cf. *Metrik*, ii, § 359).

The only stanzas, however, that are in the strictest sense to be regarded as tripartite are those in which the first and the last part are clearly distinguished by the arrangement of rhymes, as e. g. in the type *a b a b c c*. This stanza is very popular in Modern English poetry ; in the Middle English period, however, we find it very rarely used, as e. g. in the *Coventry Mysteries*, p. 315.

In Modern English it occurs e. g. in Surrey, *A Prayse of his Love* (p. 31):

> *Give place, ye lovers, here before*
> *That spend your boasts and brags in vain ;*
> *My Lady's beauty passeth more*
> *The best of yours, I dare well sayen,*
> *Than doth the sun the candle light,*
> *Or brightest day the darkest night.*

This form of stanza is used with lines of the same metres by many other poets, e. g. by M. Arnold, pp. 195, 197, 256, 318. Similar stanzas of four-foot trochaic (cf. p. 285), or of four-stressed verses, and especially of five-foot verses, are very popular. They are found e. g. in Shakespeare's *Venus and Adonis*, M. Arnold's *Mycerinus* (first part, p. 8), &c. (cf. *Metrik*, ii, §§ 360, 361).

Similar stanzas, however, in which the *frons* precedes the *versus*, according to the formula *a a b c b c* (cf. p. 285), do not occur frequently; a rare form, also, is that in which the *cauda* is placed between the two *pedes* (cf. p. 285 and *Metrik*, ii, § 362).

§ 268. Still more popular than the six-lined stanzas, both in the Middle and in the Modern English periods, are those **of seven lines**, which are modelled on Old French lyric poetry, the

prevailing type being that of an Old French ballade-stanza, viz.
$a b a b b c c$. But it is not before the middle of the fifteenth century
that we meet with an example of this stanza consisting of four-
foot verses, viz. in Lydgate's Minor Poems (*Percy Society*, 1840),
p. 129; a specimen of four-stressed verses occurs in the
Chester Plays, pp. 1–7 and pp. 156–8. We may, however, take
it for granted that this form of stanza was known long before
that time, since four-foot verses were used much earlier than
those of five feet, and a six-lined stanza of five-foot verses
occurs (for the first time, so far as we know) as early as in
Chaucer's *Compleynte of the Dethe of Pite*, and subsequently in
many other of his poems (e. g. *Troylus and Cryseyde*, *The
Assembly of Fowles*, *The Clerkes Tale*) and in numerous other
poems of his successors, e. g. in *The Kingis Quair* by King
James I of Scotland. It has been sometimes maintained that
this stanza was called *rhyme royal* stanza because that royal
poet wrote his well-known poem in it; this, however, is not
so. Guest long ago pointed out (ii. 359) that this name is to
be derived from the French term *chant-royal*, applied to certain
poems of similar stanzas which were composed in praise of God
or the Virgin, and used to be recited in the poetical contests at
Rouen on the occasion of the election of a 'king'. Chaucer's
verses to Adam Scrivener are of this form and may be quoted
as a specimen here (after Skeat's text, p. 118):

> *Adam scriveyn, if euer it thee bifalle*
> *Boece or Troylus to writen newe,*
> *Under thy lokkes thou most haue the scalle,*
> *But after my making thou write trewe.*
> *So oft a day I mot thy werk renewe*
> *Hit to correcte and eek to rubbe and scrape,*
> *And al is through thy negligence and rape.*

In Modern English this beautiful stanza was very popular up
to the end of the sixteenth century; Shakespeare, e. g., wrote his
Lucrece in it; afterwards, however, it unfortunately fell almost
entirely out of use (cf. *Metrik*, ii, § 364).

The same form of stanza, composed of two-, three-, or four-
foot verses also occurs almost exclusively in the Early Modern
English period (cf. ib., § 363).

Some varieties of this stanza, mostly formed of three-, four-,
and five-foot verses, correspond to the schemes $a b a b c c b_4$
(e. g. in Akenside, Book I, Ode iii), $a b a b c b c_5$ (Spenser,
Daphnaïda, p. 542), $a b a b c b c_2$ (R. Browning, vi. 41). Other

stanzas of seven lines are $a\,b\,a\,b\,c\,c\,a_4$, $a\,a\,b\,b\,c\,c\,a_4$, $a\,a\,b\,b\,a\,c\,c_4$, $a\,b\,a\,b\,C\,d\,C_3$, $a\,a\,b\,b\,c\,c\,c_4$, $a\,b\,a\,b\,c\,c\,c_4$, $a\,b\,a\,b\,c\,c\,c_5$, $a\,b\,a\,c\,c\,d\,d_6$ (for specimens see *Metrik*, ii, §§ 365, 366).

§ 269. **Eight-lined isometrical stanzas** are also frequently used in the Middle and Modern English period, though not so often as those of six and seven lines.

The scheme $a\,b\,a\,b\,b\,a\,b\,a$, formed from the simple equal-membered stanza of eight lines $a\,b\,a\,b\,a\,b\,a\,b$, it would seem, by inversion of the last two couplets, is rare in Middle English. We find it in the *Digby Plays*, consisting of four-foot verses. In Modern English, too, it is not very common; we have an example in Wyatt, e. g. pp. 118, 135, and another in the same poet, formed of five-foot verses ($a\,b\,a\,b\,b\,a\,b\,a_5$), p. 135.

Much more in favour in the Middle as well as in the Modern English period is the typical form of the eight-lined stanza, corresponding to the scheme $a\,b\,a\,b\,b\,c\,b\,c$. It is formed from the preceding stanza by the introduction of a new rhyme in the sixth and eighth verses, and it had its model likewise in a popular ballade-stanza of Old French lyrical poetry.

In Middle English poetry this stanza is very common, consisting either of four-stressed verses (e. g. in *The Lyfe of Joseph of Arimathia*, E. E. T. S., vol. 44, and *On the death of the Duke of Suffolk*, Wright's *Polit. Poems*, ii. 232) or of four-foot or five-foot verses. As an example of the form consisting of four-foot verses we may quote a stanza from Wright's *Polit. Songs*, p. 246:

> Alle þat beoþ of huerte trewe,
> A stounde herkneþ to my song
> Of duel, þat deþ haþ diht us newe
> Þat makeþ me syke ant sorewe among !
> Of a knyht, þat wes so strong
> Of wham god haþ don ys wille ;
> Me puncheþ þat deþ haþ don vs wrong,
> Þat he so sone shal ligge stille.

Many other examples occur in later poetry, e. g. in Minot, Lydgate, Dunbar, Lyndesay, in Wyatt, p. 119, Burns, p. 59, Walter Scott, p. 160, &c.

Similar stanzas of two-stressed and three-foot verses are only of rare occurrence; we find them e. g. in Percy's *Rel.* II. ii. 3 ; Wyatt, p. 41.

The same stanza, consisting of five-foot verses, was used by

Chaucer in his *A B C*, the first stanza of which may be quoted here:

> *Almyghty and al merciable Quene,*
>   *To whom that al this world fleeth for socour*
> *To have relees of sinne, sorwe, and teene!*
>   *Glorious Virgyne, of alle floures flour,*
>   *To thee I flee, confounded in errour !*
> *Help, and releve, thou mighty debonaire,*
>   *Have mercy of my perilous langour !*
> *Venquysshed m' hath my cruel adversaire.*

Chaucer uses the same stanza in some other minor poems, and also in *The Monkes Tale*; besides this we find it often in Lydgate, Dunbar, Kennedy; more rarely in Modern English poetry; e.g. in Spenser's *Shepheard's Cal., Ecl. XI*, S. Daniel's *Cleopatra*, &c.

Now and then some other eight-lined stanzas occur, e.g. one with the formula $a\,b\,a\,b\,b\,c\,c\,b$ in Chaucer's *Complaynt of Venus*, and in the *Flyting* by Dunbar and Kennedy. The scheme $a\,a\,b\,b\,c\,d\,c\,d$ is used in a love-song (*Rel. Ant.* i. 70–4). In the Modern English period we have stanzas on the schemes $a\sim b\,a\sim b\,c\,c\,d\sim d\sim_4$ (in Sidney, *Psalm XLIII*), $a\,b\,a\,b\,c\,c\,c\,b_4$ (Scott, *Helvellyn*, p. 472), $a\sim b\,a\sim b\,c\sim c\sim d\sim d\sim_2$ (Moore); cf. *Metrik*, ii, §§ 369–71.

There are also eight-lined stanzas formed by combination with tail-rhyme stanzas, as $a\,a\,b\,a\,a\,b\,c\,c_4$, $a\,a\,b\,c\,c\,d\,d\,b_4$, but they are not frequent; a stanza corresponding to the formula $a\,a\,b\,a\,a\,b\,c\,c_4$ we have in Spenser, *Epigram III* (p. 586); and the variety $a\,a\,b\,c\,c\,d\,d\,b_4$ (the *cauda* being enclosed by the *pedes*) occurs in Moore.

The same peculiarity we find in stanzas formed on the scheme $A\,A\,b\,c\,b\,c\,A\,A_4$ (Moore), or $a\,a\,b\,c\,b\,c\,d\,d_4$ (Wordsworth, ii. 267); cf. *Metrik*, ii, §§ 372, 373.

§ 270. Stanzas of a still larger compass are of rare occurrence in Middle English poetry. A **nine-lined stanza** corresponding to the formula $a\,a\,b\,a\,a\,b\,b\,c\,c_5$ we have in Chaucer's *Complaynt of Mars*; it seems to be formed from the *rhyme royal* stanza, by adding one verse to each *pes*; but it might also be looked upon as a combination with the tail-rhyme stanza. Another stanza of this kind, with the formula $a\,a\,b\,a\,a\,b\,b\,a\,b_5$, is used in Chaucer's *Complaynt of Faire Anelyda* and in Dunbar's *Goldin Targe*.

A similar stanza, corresponding to the formula $a\,a\,b\,c\,c\,b\,d\,b\,d_4$,

occurs in Modern English poetry in John Scott, *Ode XII.*
Other stanzas used in the Modern English period are formed
with parallel rhymes, as e. g. on the scheme $a\,a\,a\,b\,b\,b\,c\,c\,c_4$
(Walter Scott, *Lady of the Lake*, p. 187); forms with crossed
rhymes throughout or partly are also used, as e. g. by Wyatt,
p. 121, according to the formula $a\,b\,a\,b\,c\,c\,c\,d\,d_5$:

> *My love is like unto th' eternal fire,*
> > *And I as those which therein do remain;*
> *Whose grievous pains is but their great desire*
> > *To see the sight which they may not attain:*
> *So in hell's heat myself I feel to be,*
> *That am restrain'd by great extremity,*
> *The sight of her which is so dear to me.*
> *O! puissant Love! and power of great avail!*
> *By whom hell may be felt ere death assail!*

As to other schemes ($a\,b\,a\,b\,b\,c\,d\,c\,d_5$, $a\,b\,a\,b\,b\,c\,b\,c\,c_5$, $a\,b\,a\,b\,c\,d\,c\,d\,R_4$,
$a\,b\,a\,b\,c\,d\,c\,d\,d_4$, &c.) cf. *Metrik*, ii, §§ 374–6.

§ **271.** A Middle English **stanza of ten lines**, similar to those
of nine lines, is used by Chaucer in the *Envoy* to his *Complaynt
of Mars and Venus* ($a\,a\,b\,a\,a\,b\,b\,a\,a\,b_5$); another on the model
$a\,b\,a\,b\,b\,c\,c\,b\,b\,b_4$ is found in a poem *Long Life* (E. E. T. S., 49,
p. 156, quoted in *Metrik*, i. p. 421).

Some of the Modern English stanzas again are formed by
combination with different varieties of the tail-rhyme stanza, as
e. g. one according to the formula $a\,a\,b \sim c\,c\,b \sim d\,d\,e\,e_4$ in Prior,
The Parallel (Poets, vii. 507):

> *Prometheus, forming Mr. Day,*
> *Carv'd something like a man in clay.*
> > *The mortal's work might well miscarry;*
> > *He, that does heaven and earth control,*
> > *Alone has power to form a soul,*
> *His hand is evident in Harry.*
> > *Since one is but a moving clod,*
> > *T'other the lively form of God;*
> *'Squire Wallis, you will scarce be able*
> *To prove all poetry but fable.*

A stanza of trochaic verses corresponding to a similar
scheme, viz. $a\,a\,b\,c\,c\,b\,d\,d\,d\,b_4$, is used by Tennyson in *The
Window* (p. 284).
Sometimes the scheme is $a\,b\,a\,b\,c\,c\,d\,e\,e\,d_4$ (where there are
two *pedes* forming a *frons*, and a tail-rhyme stanza equivalent to
two *versus*), as in Akenside, Book I, Ode II (*Poets*, ix. 773).

Some stanzas, on the other hand, have a parallel arrangement of rhymes, $a\,a\,b\,b\,c\,c\,d\,d\,e\,E$ ($e\,E$ being the *cauda*) as in Walter Scott, *Soldier*, *Wake* (p. 465); or more frequently crossed rhymes, $a\,b\,a\,b\,c\,d\,c\,d\,e\,e_5$, $a\,b\,a\,b\,c\,d\,c\,d\,e\,e_4$, the first eight verses forming the upsong (*pedes*); or with a four-lined upsong $a\,a\,b\,b\,c\,d\,c\,d\,e\,e_4$, $a\,a\,b\,b\,c\,d\,d\,e\,d\,e_3$, $a\,b\,a\,b\,b\,c\,c\,d\,c\,D_5$. The last-mentioned form has been used several times by Swinburne, e.g. *Poems*, ii, pp. 126, 215, 219, &c., in his ballads. For specimens see *Metrik*, ii, §§ 379–81.

§ 272. **Stanzas of eleven lines** are very scarce in Middle English poetry, if used there at all, and even in Modern English very few examples occur. A stanza of Swinburne's may be mentioned here, imitated from an Old French ballade- (or rather *chant-royal*) stanza, corresponding to the formula $a\,b\,a\,b\,c\,c\,d\,d\,e\,d\,E_5$ and used in a *Ballad against the Enemies of France* (Poems, ii. 212). Cf. *Metrik*, ii, § 382.

Twelve-lined stanzas are much more frequently used, even in Middle English poetry; one of four-foot verses according to the scheme $a\,b\,a\,b\,a\,b\,a\,b\,b\,c\,b\,C$ (the stanzas being connected into groups by *concatenatio*) occurs in the fine fourteenth-century poem, *The Pearl*. Another of four-stressed verses corresponding to the formula $a\,b\,a\,b\,a\,b\,a\,b\,c\,d\,c\,d$ we have in Wright's *Polit. Songs*, p. 149; one of four-foot verses together with other forms of stanzas ($a\,b\,a\,b\,a\,b\,a\,b\,a\,b\,a\,b$, $a\,b\,a\,b\,c\,d\,c\,d\,e\,f\,e\,f$) we have in the poem on the *Childhood of Christ* (ed. Horstmann, Heilbronn, 1878).

But it is chiefly in Modern English poetry that stanzas of twelve lines are very common, especially stanzas consisting of three equal parts, with crossed rhymes. In some of these there is no difference at all in the structure of the three parts, as e.g. in a stanza by Prior (*Poets*, vii. 402) on the model $a\,b\,a\,b\,c\,d\,c\,d\,e\,f\,e\,f_4$; while in others the refrain (consisting of the four last verses) forms the *cauda*, as e.g. in Moore's *Song on the Birthday of Mrs.* ———— :

> *Of all my happiest hours of joy,*
>   *And even I have had my measure,*
> *When hearts were full, and ev'ry eye*
>   *Hath kindled with the light of pleasure,*
> *An hour like this I ne'er was given,*
>   *So full of friendship's purest blisses;*
> *Young Love himself looks down from heaven,*
>   *To smile on such a day as this is.*

> *Then come, my friends, this hour improve,*
> *Let's feel as if we ne'er could sever;*
> *And may the birth of her we love*
> *Be thus with joy remember'd ever!*

Now and then certain modifications of this form of stanza are met with, especially stanzas the four-lined refrain of which forms not only the end, but also the beginning, of the stanza (but as a rule only in the first stanza, the others having the refrain only at the end); e.g. $A B A B c d c d A B A B_3$ (st. 1), $d e d e f g f g A B A B_3$ (st. 2), $h i h i k l k l A B A B_3$ (st. 3), in Moore, *Drink to her*.

In other poems Moore uses this type of stanza with lines of four stresses, as in *Drink of this cup*, and with lines of two stresses, as in *When the Balaika*. For some rarely occurring stanzas of this kind see *Metrik*, ii, §§ 385, 386.

A **stanza of thirteen lines** corresponding to the formula $a b a b b c b c d e e e d_4$ occurs in the Middle English poem *The Eleven Pains of Hell* (E. E. T. S., 49, p. 210). Another one on the scheme $a \sim a \sim B c \sim c \sim B d \sim d \sim d \sim b e \sim e \sim B_3$ we have in Moore, *Go where glory waits thee*.

As to stanzas of fifteen and eighteen lines see *Metrik*, ii, § 387.

II. *Anisometrical stanzas.*

§ 273. As mentioned before (§ 267) the anisometrical stanzas of the tripartite class, being older, might have been dealt with before the isometrical stanzas. This chronological order of treatment, however, would have been somewhat inconvenient in practice, as it would have involved the necessity of discussing many of the more complicated stanzas before the shorter and simpler ones, most of which do not occur in Middle English, but in Modern poetry only. Moreover, the absence of certain simple and short forms of stanza constructed in accordance with the principles which were generally adopted in the Middle English period is a purely accidental circumstance, which is liable at any moment to be altered by the discovery of new texts.

In the following paragraphs, therefore, the stanzas belonging to this chapter are discussed according to their arrangement of rhymes and to the length of the lines of which they are composed.

We begin with certain **stanzas of six lines**, the first part (the *frons* or 'upsong') of which is isometrical, the arrangement of rhymes being parallel.

A pretty stanza with the scheme $a\,a\,b\,b\,_3c\,c_4$ presents itself in the song *The Fairy Queen* (Percy's *Rel.* III. ii. 26):

> *Come, follow, follow me,*
> *You, fairy elves that be :*
> *Which circle on the greene,*
> *Come, follow Mab, your queene.*
> *Hand in hand let's dance around,*
> *For this place is fairye ground.*

For similar stanzas conforming to the schemes $a\,a\,b\,b_4\,c\,c\,_5$, $a\,a\,b\,b\,c_4\,c_5$, $a\,a\,b\,b\,c \sim c \sim_5$, $a\,a\,b\,b_6\,c \sim c \sim_5$, $a\,a\,b\,b\,c_4\,c_3$ (in Moore, *The Wandering Bard*), &c., see *Metrik*, ii, § 389.

Another group is represented by stanzas of six rhyming couplets of unequal length, as $a_5\,a_4\,b_5\,b_4\,c_5\,c_4$ (Sidney, *Psalm XXXIX*), $a_6\,a_3\,b_6\,b_3\,c_6\,c_3$ (id. *Psalm II*) ; or $a_5\,a_2\,b_5\,b_2\,c\,c_5$, $a_4\,a_5\,b_4\,b_5\,c\,c_4$, frequently used by Herbert and Cowley, or $a_5\,a_4\,b\,b_3\,c_5\,c_4$, $a\,a\,b_4\,b_3\,c\,c_4$ (in Moore, *St. Senanus and the Lady*), the two *pedes* enclosing the *cauda* (cf. *Metrik*, ii, §§ 390–2).

Similar stanzas with crossed rhymes occur pretty often, especially stanzas of three Septenary verses broken up by inserted rhyme, according to the formula $a_4\,b \sim_3 a_4\,b \sim_3 a_4\,b \sim_3$, as in Moore, *The Gazelle*:

> *Dost thou not hear the silver bell,*
> *Thro' yonder lime-trees ringing?*
> *'Tis my lady's light gazelle,*
> *To me her love-thoughts bringing,—*
> *All the while that silver bell*
> *Around his dark neck ringing.*

For other specimens see *Metrik*, ii, § 393.

§ 274. More popular are stanzas of a more distinctly tripartite character, formed on the scheme $a\,b\,a\,b\,c\,c$ (which occurs also in the isometrical group). These stanzas are used in many various forms, as e.g. one in Cowper, *Olney Hymns* (p. 25), like $a\,b\,a\,b_3\,c\,c_4$:

> *By whom was David taught*
> *To aim the deadly blow,*
> *When he Goliath fought,*
> *And laid the Gittite low?*
> *Nor sword nor spear the stripling took,*
> *But chose a pebble from the brook.*

Numerous other examples are quoted in *Metrik*, ii, § 394, together with similar stanzas formed according to the schemes $a\,b \sim a\,b \sim_3 c\,c_4$, $a\,b\,a\,b_3\,C\,C_4$, $a \sim b\,a \sim b_3\,c\,c_5$, $a\,b\,a\,b_4\,c\,c_5$, $a \sim b\,a \sim b_4\,c\,c_6$, &c.

The reverse order with regard to the length of the verses in the *pedes* and the *cauda* is also not uncommon, as e. g. in stanzas on the schemes $a\,b\,a\,b\,c_5\,c_4$, $a\,b\,a\,b\,c_5\,c_3$, $a\,b\,a\,b_5\,c_4\,c_5$, &c.

Stanzas of this kind are met with chiefly in the earlier Modern English poets, e.g. in Cowley and Herbert. Shorter lines also are used, e. g. in stanzas corresponding to the formulas $a\,b\,a\,b_4\,c\,c_3$, $a\,b\,a\,b_4\,c\,c_2$; stanzas like these also occur later, e.g. in Moore. In Cowley, now and then, a stanza is found with a preceding *frons* (on the scheme $a\,a_5\,b\,c\,b\,c_4$). In Moore we find yet another variety (in *Poor broken flower*), the *cauda* of which is enclosed by the *pedes* (according to the formula $a \sim b_5\,c\,c_3\,a \sim b_5$).

Another group of stanzas is to be mentioned here, the verses of which are of different length in the first part, admitting of many various combinations. Especially stanzas of Septenary rhythm in the first part are very popular, as e. g. in Cowper's fine poem *The Castaway* (p. 400), on the scheme $a_4\,b_3\,a_4\,b_3\,c\,c_4$:

> *Obscurest night involved the sky,*
> *The Atlantic billows roared,*
> *When such a destined wretch as I,*
> *Washed headlong from on board,*
> *Of friends, of hope, of all bereft,*
> *His floating home for ever left.*

There are many varieties of this form of stanza, as e. g. $a_4\,b_3\,a_4\,b_3\,c\,c_5$, $a_4\,b_3\,a_4\,b_3\,c_4\,c_5$, $a_3\,b_2\,a_3\,b_2\,c_4\,c_5$, $a_4\,b_2\,a_4\,b_2\,c\,c_4$, $a_5\,b_4\,a_5\,b_4\,c\,c_5$; $a_3\,b_4\,a_3\,b_4\,c\,c_4$, $a_2\,b_4\,a_2\,b_4\,c\,c_5$. All these different schemes were chiefly used by the earlier Modern English poets, as Browne, Carew, Cowley, Waller, and Herbert. (See *Metrik*, ii, § 397.)

There are some other stanzas of allied structure which may be regarded as extensions of the Poulter's Measure by the addition of a second Alexandrine or Septenary verse, their formulas being $a\,b\,c\,b_3\,d_4\,d_3$ or $a\,b_3\,c_4\,b_3\,d_4\,d_3$. For examples see *Metrik*, ii, § 398.

§ 275. **Stanzas of seven lines** are very common, and have many diverse forms. In the first place may be mentioned those which have parallel arrangement of rhymes, and in which the *frons* is isometrical. Some of these forms, used chiefly by the earlier poets, as Cowley, Sheffield, and others, have the scheme $a\,a\,b\,b\,c_4\,c_2\,c_5$ or $a\,a\,b\,b\,c_4\,c\,a_5$. Another variety, with alternate four- and two-foot iambic-anapaestic lines according to the formula $a\,a\,b\,b_4\,r\,r_2\,R_4$, occurs in Moore, *The Legend of Puck the Fairy*:

> *Would'st know what tricks, by the pale moonlight,*
> *Are play'd by me, the merry little Sprite,*
> *Who wing through air from the camp to the court,*
> *From king to clown, and of all make sport;*
> > *Singing, I am the Sprite*
> > *Of the merry midnight,*
> *Who laugh at weak mortals, and love the moonlight.*

Stanzas with an anisometrical first part, e. g. on the model $a_4\,a_5\,b_4\,b_5\,c\,c_4\,c_5$ in Donne, *Love's Exchange* (Poets, iv. 30), are of rare occurrence.

Numerous stanzas of this kind have in part crossed rhymes; we find, e. g., stanzas with the same order of rhymes as in the *rhyme royal*, on the model $a\,b\,a\,b\,b\,c_3\,c_5$, as in S. Daniel, *A Description of Beauty*:

> > *O Beauty (beams, nay, flame*
> > *Of that great lamp of light),*
> > *That shines a while with fame,*
> > *But presently makes night!*
> > *Like winter's shortliv'd bright,*
> > *Or summer's sudden gleams;*
> > *How much more dear, so much less lasting beams.*

Similar stanzas have the schemes $a\,b\,a\,b\,b_3\,c\,c_5$, $a\,b\,a\,b\,c\,b_4\,c_2$, $a\,b\,a\,b\,c\,c_4\,R_2$, $a\,b\,a\,b\,c\,c_4\,C_5$, $a\,b\,a\,b\,c\,c_4\,b_3$, $a\,b\,a\,b_4\,c\,c_2\,a_4$, &c. For examples see *Metrik*, ii, §§ 401–3.

In many stanzas the first and the last part (*frons* and *cauda*) are anisometrical. Thus Donne, Cowley, and Congreve furnish many examples of the formulas $a_5\,b_4\,a_5\,b_4\,c\,c_4\,b_5$, $a \sim_4 b_5\,a \sim_4 b_5\,c\,c_3\,c_4$, $a_4\,b_5\,a_4\,b_5\,c\,c_2\,b_4$, and later poets make frequent use of similar stanzas composed of shorter lines after the model of the following by Congreve, *Poets*, vii. 546 ($a_4\,b \sim_3 a_4\,b \sim_3 c\,c_4\,b \sim_3$):

> > *Tell me no more I am deceived,*
> > *That Cloe's false and common;*
> > *I always knew (at least believ'd)*
> > *She was a very woman;*
> > *As such I lik'd, as such caress'd,*
> > *She still was constant when possess'd,*
> > *She could do more for no man.*

For examples of other similar stanzas $(a_4\,b_3\,a_4\,b_3\,c\,c\,b_3,$ $a_4\,b_3\,a_4\,b_3\,C\,C_3\,C_5,\ a_3\,b_4\,a_3\,b_4\,c\,c\,c_4,\ a_4\,b\sim_2\,a_4\,b\sim_2\,c\,c\,a_4,$ &c.) see *Metrik*, ii, §§ 404–6.

§ 276. **Eight-lined stanzas** of various kinds are also very popular. They rarely occur, however, with an isometrical *frons*, composed of rhyming couplets $(a\,a\,b\,b\,c\,c\,d_5\,d_3,$ $a\sim a\sim b\sim b\sim_4\,C\sim C\sim_2\,d\sim d\sim_4,\ a\,a\,b\,b\,c\,c\,d_4\,d_5;$ cf. *Metrik*, ii, §§ 408, 410); or with enclosing rhymes in the *cauda* $(a\,a\,b\,b\,c\,d\,d_4\,c_5,\ a\,a\,b\,b_4\,c\,d\,d_2\,c_4,$ ib. § 409); or of an anisometrical structure with parallel rhymes in both parts (ib. § 411).

The usual forms show crossed rhymes; either throughout the whole stanza (in which case the first part is isometrical), or in the first part only. The first form is represented by the following elegant stanza $(a\,b\,a\,b_5\,c_4\,d\sim_3\,c_4\,d\sim_3)$ in the second of Drayton's *Eclogues* (Poets, iii. 590):

> Upon a bank with roses set about,
> Where turtles oft sit joining bill to bill,
> And gentle springs steal softly murm'ring out,
> Washing the foot of pleasure's sacred hill;
> There little Love sore wounded lies,
> His bow and arrows broken,
> Bedew'd with tears from Venus' eyes;
> Oh! grievous to be spoken.

Other schemes that occur are: $a\,b\,a\,b\,c_5\,d_3\,c_5\,d_3,\ a\,b\,a\,b\,c\,d\,c_4\,d_3,$ $a\,b\,a\,b\,c\,c\,d_4\,d_3,\ a\,b\,a\,b_4\,c\,c_2\,d\,d_4,\ a\,b\,a_4\,b_3\,c\,c\,d\,d_4,\ a\sim b\,a\sim b_3\,c_4\,d_3\,c_4\,d_3,$ $a\,b\sim a\,b\sim_3\,c_4\,d\sim_3\,c_4\,d\sim_3,\ a\sim b\,c\sim b\,d\sim e_3\,f_4\,e_3,\ a\sim b\,a\sim b_3\,c\,d\,c_4\,d_3,$ $a\sim b\,a\sim b\,c\sim d\,c\sim_4\,d_5$ (M. Arnold, p. 2), &c.; for numerous examples see *Metrik*, ii, §§ 412, 414, 415.

Sometimes stanzas occur, the isometrical part of which forms the *cauda*, as on the scheme $a_4\,b_3\,a_4\,b_3\,c\,c\,d\,d_4$ in Moore, *Sovereign Woman*:

> The dance was o'er, yet still in dreams,
> That fairy scene went on;
> Like clouds still flushed with daylight gleams,
> Though day itself is gone.
> And gracefully to music's sound,
> The same bright nymphs went gliding round;
> While thou, the Queen of all, wert there—
> The fairest still, where all were fair.

For examples of other forms $(a\,b\,a_4\,b_2\,c\,d\,C\,D_4,\ a\sim_3\,b_4\,a\sim_3\,b_4\,c\,b\,c\,b_4,$ $a_4\,b_3\,c_4\,b_3\,d\,e\,d\,e_3,$ &c.) see *Metrik*, ii, §§ 413, 416.

§ **277.** Very frequently stanzas occur which are of an entirely anisometrical structure in both parts. To this group belong the first tripartite anisometrical stanzas of the Middle English period, contained in Wright's *Spec. of Lyr. Poetry*, p. 111 (two songs). Their stanzaic form $(a_4\,b_3\,a_4\,b_3\,b\,b_5\,c_7\,c_5)$ is also of great importance, on account of the fact that the first five-foot verses as yet known in English poetry occur in the *cauda* of these stanzas. The first strophe may serve as an example :

> Lutel wot hit anymon,
>> Hou loue hym haueþ ybounde,
> Þat for us oþe rode ron,
>> Ant bohte vs wiþ is wounde.
>> Þe loue of hym vs haueþ ymaked sounde,
>> Ant ycast þe grimly gost to grounde.
> Euer ant oo, nyht ant day, he haueþ vs in is þohte,
> He nul nout leose þat he so deore bohte.

This stanza is also interesting on account of its regular use of masculine rhymes in the first and in the third line, and of feminine rhymes in the others. The structure of the five-measured verses employed in this stanza has been referred to before (§ 153).

Very often both main parts, the *upsong* and the *downsong*, have crossed rhymes in Modern English, e. g. in a form of stanza with the scheme $a_5\,b_3\,a_5\,b_3\,c\,d_5\,c_3\,d_2$ in Southey, *To a Spider* (ii. 180) :

> Spider ! thou need'st not run in fear about
>> To shun my curious eyes ;
> I won't humanely crush thy bowels out,
>> Lest thou should'st eat the flies ;
> Nor will I roast thee with a damn'd delight
>> Thy strange instinctive fortitude to see,
>> For there is One who might
>> One day roast me.

A structure analogous to that of the two last-quoted specimens is exhibited in many stanzas occurring in earlier Modern English poetry, as in Cowley, Herbert, Browne, Carew $(a_5\,b_4\,a_5\,b_4\,c_4\,c_5\,d_4\,d_5,$ $a_5\,b_2\,a_5\,b_2\,c_4\,c_3\,d_5\,d_2,\ a_3\,b_2\,a_3\,b_2\,c\,c_4\,d\,d_5,\ a_4\,b_2\,a_4\,b_2\,c_3\,c_2\,d\,d_3)$; other forms, corresponding only in the upsong or downsong to the Middle English stanza quoted above, are $a\sim_4 b_2\,a\sim_3 b_2\,c\sim_4 d_3\,c\sim_4 d_3,$ $a_4\,b\sim_3 a_4\,b\sim_3 b\sim_2 b\sim_3 c_4\,b\sim_3,\ a_4\,b_3\,a_4\,b_3\,c\,d_3\,c_4\,d_3,$ &c., used by Burns, Moore, and Mrs. Hemans. For examples see *Metrik*, ii, §§ 417, 418.

§ **278.** The next group consists of stanzas, one main part of which consists of a half or of a whole tail-rhyme stanza. The first of these two forms is used e. g. by Burns in the song *She's Fair and Fause* (p. 204), where the stanza consists of four- and three-foot verses on the model $a_4 b_3 a_4 b_3 c c c_4 d_3$:

> She's fair and fause that causes my smart,
>   I lo'ed her meikle and lang :
> She's broken her vow, she's broken my heart,
>   And I may e'en gae hang.
>   A coof cam in wi' rowth o' gear,
>   And I hae tint my dearest dear,
>   But woman is but warld's gear,
>   Sae let the bonie lass gang.

Other stanzas of this class correspond to the formulas $a_4 b_3 a_4 b_3 a a a_4 b_3$, $a \sim_4 b_2 a \sim_4 b_3 c \sim c \sim c \sim_4 b_2$, $a_3 b_2 a_3 b_2 c c c_3 b_2$. For examples see *Metrik*, ii, § 419.

There is another form of stanza the first part of which according to the Middle English usage consists of a complete tail-rhyme stanza (cf. the ten-lined stanzas of this group), while the *cauda* is formed by a rhyming couplet, so that its structure corresponds to the scheme $a a_4 b_3 a a_4 b_3 c c_4$; it occurs in Spenser, *Epigrams*, ii (p. 586):

> As Diane hunted on a day,
> She chaunst to come where Cupid lay,
>   His quiver by his head :
> One of his shafts she stole away,
> And one of hers did close convay
>   Into the other's stead :
> With that Love wounded my Love's hart
> But Diane beasts with Cupid's dart.

Similar stanzas of other metres are very frequently met with, as e. g. stanzas corresponding to the formulas $a a_4 b_3 c c_4 b_3 d d_5$, $a a_3 b_2 c c_3 b_2 d d_6$, $a a_2 b_3 c c_2 b_3 b b_7$, and $a \sim a \sim_4 b_5 c \sim c \sim_4 b_5 d d_5$. The reverse order (i. e. *frons* + two *versus*) we have in $a a_3 b b_2 c_3 b b_2 c_3$ and $a a_5 b b_3 c_5 d d_3 e_5$. For examples see *Metrik*, ii, § 420.

A stanza corresponding to the formula $a b_4 c_3 a b_4 c_3 a_4 D_3$ occurs in M. Arnold's *The Church of Brou* (p. 17).

§ **279.** Among **stanzas of nine lines**, those with parallel rhymes must again be mentioned first; as e. g. a strophe on the scheme $a a b b c c d d_4 d_5$, in Akenside, Book I, Ode X, *To the Muse* (Poets, ix. 780). Other stanzas occurring also in more recent poetry (Wordsworth, W. Scott) are on the schemes $a\,a\,b\,b_4\,c\,c_2\,c\,d\,d_4$, $a\,a\,b\,b\,c_4\,d_3\,c\,c_4\,d_3$, $a_4\,b_3\,a\,a_4\,b_3\,c\,c\,d\,D_4$. For examples see *Metrik*, ii, § 421.

Similar stanzas, also with an isometrical first part, but with crossed rhymes, are not very often met with. The schemes are $a\,b\,a\,b_4\,c\,c_2\,c\,d\,d_4$, $a\,b\,a\,b\,c\,c\,d\,d_4\,d_5$, $a\,b\,a\,b\,b\,c\,b_4\,c_3$, $a\,b\,a\,b\,c\,d\,c\,d_4\,e_2$, $a_4\,b_3\,a\,a_4\,b_3\,c\sim d\,c\sim d_4$, &c. Specimens of them are also found in modern poets, as in Moore, Burns, Walter Scott, &c. For examples see *Metrik*, ii, § 422.

More frequently stanzas occur with an anisometrical first and last part and crossed rhymes in each of them; the schemes are $a_4\,b_5\,a_4\,b_5\,c_4\,d_3\,c_5\,d\,d_4$, $a_5\,b_2\,a_5\,b_2\,c\,c_5\,d\,d_2\,c_4$, $a_4\,b_2\,a_4\,b_2\,c_4\,d\,d_2\,c\,c_4$. The most popular, however, are those stanzas in which one or other of the two main parts consists of Septenary verses; they are of frequent occurrence in Burns and other modern poets; a stanza on the scheme $a_4\,b_3\,a_4\,b_3\,c_4\,d\sim_3 c_4\,d\sim_3 r_2$, e. g., is found in Burns, *The Holy Fair* (p. 14):

> *Upon a simmer Sunday morn,*
> *When Nature's face is fair,*
> *I walked forth to view the corn,*
> *An' snuff the caller air.*
> *The risin' sun, owre Galston muirs,*
> *Wi' glorious light was glintin;*
> *The hares were hirplin down the furrs,*
> *The lav'rocks they were chantin*
> *Fu' sweet that day.*

For similar examples see *Metrik*, ii, § 424.

Other stanzas are formed by combination with a complete or a shortened tail-rhyme stanza; so that we have schemes like $a\,a_4\,b_3\,c\,c_4\,b_3\,d\,d\,d_4$, $a\sim a\sim b\,c\sim c\sim b_4\,d\sim d\sim_2 b_4$, $a\,a_2\,b_4\,c\,c_2\,b_4\,d\,d_2\,b_4$. They occur in Carew (*Poets*, iii. 709), Dryden (p. 368), and Thackeray (p. 237). The formula $a_4\,b_3\,a_4\,b_3\,c\,d\,c\,c_4\,d_3$ we find in Campbell (p. 82), $a_4\,b_3\,a_4\,b_3\,c\,c_4\,b_3\,d\,d_4$ in Byron's *Ode to Napoleon* (p. 273):

> *'Tis done—but yesterday a King!*
> *And arm'd with Kings to strive—*
> *And now thou art a nameless thing;*
> *So abject—yet alive!*
> *Is this the man of thousand thrones,*
> *Who strew'd our earth with hostile bones,*
> *And can he thus survive?*
> *Since he, miscall'd the Morning Star,*
> *Nor man nor fiend hath fallen so far.*

For other specimens see *Metrik*, ii, §§ 424, 425.

§ **280.** Among the **stanzas of ten lines**, those with an isometrical first part and parallel rhymes may first be mentioned;
they correspond to the schemes $a a b b c d d e e_4 c_5$, $a a b b c d c d_4 f_3 f_4$,
$a a b b c_4 d_3 c c c_4 d_3$, $a a b b_4 c d c d_2 e e_4$, and are found in Akenside,
Wordsworth, and Moore. Next come stanzas with an aniso-
metrical first part according to the formulas $a_5 a_4 b_5 b_4 c c_5 d d e_4 e_5$,
$a_4 a_5 b_4 b_5 c d c_4 d_3 e e_5$, $a \sim a \sim_3 b b_4 c \sim c \sim_3 d d_4 e \sim e \sim_3$, occurring
in Cowley and Campbell (cf. *Metrik*, ii, §§ 427, 428).

In other stanzas, crossed rhymes are used in the isometrical
first part; they correspond to the formulas $a b a b_5 c_4 d_3 c_4 d_3 e_6 e_7$,
$a b a b c c d e d_5 E_2$, $a b a b c d e_5 c_3 d e_5$, $a b a b c_3 c_2 d_3 d_2 e_3 e_4$, and
are found in Browne, G. Herbert, and Ben Jonson (ib. § 429).

In modern poetry simpler stanzas of this kind are used; one
e. g. on the scheme $a \sim b \sim a \sim b \sim_3 c c_4 d \sim e \sim d \sim e \sim_3$ (the *cauda*
being thus enclosed by the two *pedes*) in Moore's song *Bring the
bright Garlands hither*:

> Bring the bright garlands hither,
>   Ere yet a leaf is dying;
> If so soon they must wither,
>   Ours be their last sweet sighing.
> Hark, that low dismal chime!
> 'Tis the dreary voice of Time.
> Oh, bring beauty, bring roses,
>   Bring all that yet is ours;
> Let life's day, as it closes,
>   Shine to the last through flowers.

Similar stanzas corresponding to the formulas $a \sim b a \sim b_2$
$c c_4 d \sim e d \sim e_2$, $a \sim b \sim a \sim b c \sim d c \sim d_2 e e_4$, $a b a b c d c d_4 e_3 e_4$, and
$a \sim b a \sim b_4 c \sim_4 d_3 c \sim_4 d_3 c \sim_4 d_3$, are used by the same poet in *With
Moonlight Beaming*, *The Young Indian Maid*, *Guess, guess*, and
From this Hour.

Many stanzas of this group with an isometrical first part are
formed by combination with a tail-rhyme stanza, which then
generally forms the *cauda*, as in one of Cunningham's stanzas,
viz. in *Newcastle Beer* (Poets, x. 729), the stanza consisting of
four- and two-stressed verses on the scheme $a b a b_4 c c_2 d_4 e e_2 d_4$:

> When fame brought the news of Great-Britain's success,
>   And told at Olympus each Gallic defeat;
> Glad Mars sent by Mercury orders express,
>   To summon the deities all to a treat:
>   Blithe Comus was plac'd
>   To guide the gay feast,

> *And freely declar'd there was choice of good cheer;*
> *Yet vow'd to his thinking,*
> *For exquisite drinking,*
> *Their nectar was nothing to Newcastle beer.*

For examples of many similar forms, e.g. $a\,b\,a\,b\,c\,c\,d\,e\,e_4\,d_3$, $a_5\,b\,b_4\,a_5\,c\,c\,d\,e\,e\,d_3$, $a\,b\,a\,b_4\,c\,c_2\,d_4\,e\sim e\sim_2 d_4$, $a\,b\,a\,b_4\,c\,c_2\,d_3\,e\,e_2\,d_3$, $a\,b\,a\,b_3\,c\sim c\sim_1 d_3\,e\sim e\sim_1 d_3$, see *Metrik*, ii, § 431.

§ 281. Stanzas of this kind with an anisometrical first part occur in the Middle English period; e.g. in Wright's *Spec. of Lyr. Poetry*, p. 83, on the scheme $a_4\,b\sim_3 a_4\,b\sim_3 c\,c_4\,d\sim_3 e\,e_4\,d\sim_3$:

> *Jesu, for þi muchele miht*
> *Þou ȝef vs of þi grace,*
> *Þat we mowe dai and nyht*
> *Þenken o þi face.*
> *In myn herte hit doþ me god,*
> *When y þenke on iesu blod,*
> *Þat ran doun bi ys syde,*
> *From is herte doun to is fot,*
> *For ous he spradde is herte blod,*
> *His woundes were so wyde.*

The shorter, Septenary part of the stanza represents the *frons*, the tail-rhyme stanza, the *versus*. Of a similar form $(a_4\,b_3\,a_4\,b_3\,a\,a_4\,b_3\,a\,b_3\,a_2)$ is the stanza of the poem *An Orison of our Lady* (E. E. T. S., vol. xlix, p. 158). In Modern English also allied forms occur; one especially with the scheme $a_4\,b_3\,a_4\,b_3\,c\,c\,d\,e\,e_4\,d_3$ in Gray, *Ode on the Spring* (Poets, x. 215); other forms are $a_4\,b_3\,a_4\,b_3\,c\,c_2\,d_3\,e\,e_2\,d_4$, $a_4\,b_3\,a_4\,b_3\,c\,c\,d\,e\,e_4\,d_5$, $a\,b_3\,a_4\,b_3\,d\,d_4\,e_3\,f\,f_4\,e_3$. (For examples see *Metrik*, ii, § 432.)

The reverse combination, viz. tail-rhyme stanza and Septenary (on the scheme $a\,a_4\,b_3\,c\,c_4\,b_3\,d_4\,b_3\,d_4\,b_3$), also occurs in Middle English times[1], e.g. in Wright's *Spec. of Lyr. Poetry*, p. 87:

---

[1] It is worth noticing that there are also tripartite stanzas in Middle English, either allied to the bob-wheel stanza or belonging to it, both in lyric and dramatic poetry; e.g. the ten-lined stanza of a poem in Wright's *Songs and Carols* (Percy Soc., 1847), p. 15, on the scheme $A\,B\,A\,B\,C\,C\,C_4\,d_1\,D\,D_4$ (quoted in *Metrik*, i, p. 406); one of eleven lines according to the formula $A\,A\,A_4\,B_3\,C\,C\,C_4\,B_3\,d_1\,B\,D_3$ in the *Towneley Mysteries*, p. 224 (quoted in *Metrik*, i, p. 407), and one of thirteen lines, used in a dialogue, corresponding to the scheme $A\,B\,A\,B\,A\,A\,B\,A\,A\,B_3\,c_1\,B_3\,C_2$, ibid., pp. 135-9 (quoted in *Metrik*, i, p. 408).

> *Nou skrinkeþ rose and lylie flour,*
> *þat whilen ber þat suete sauour,*
> *in somer, þat suete tyde;*
> *ne is no quene so stark ne stour,*
> *ne no leuedy so bryht in bour,*
> *þat ded ne shal by glyde.*
> *Whose wol fleyshlust forgon,*
> *and heuene blis abyde,*
> *on iesu be is þoht anon,*
> *þat perled was ys syde.*

Similar stanzas occur also in Modern English; e. g. one on the formula $a\,a_2\,b_3\,c\,c_2\,b_3\,d_4\,e_3\,d_4\,e_3$ in Burns (p. 255), another on the scheme $a\,a_2\,b_3\,c\,c_2\,b_3\,d\,e_3\,d_4\,e_3$ ($=$*Poulter's Measure* in the *cauda*), ib. p. 189.

Other ten-line stanzas consisting chiefly of Septenary verses or of *Poulter's Measure* correspond to the formulas $a_4\,b_3\,a_4\,b_3\,c_4\,d_3\,c_4\,d_3\,e\,e_4$, $a\,b_3\,a_4\,b_3\,c\,d_3\,c_4\,d_3\,e\,e_4$, $a\,b\,a_4\,b_3\,c\,d\,c_4\,d_3\,e\,e_3$. For examples, partly taken from Moore, see *Metrik*, ii, § 435.

Stanzas of this kind consisting of five-foot verses are rarely met with, e. g. $a_5\,b_3\,a_5\,b_3\,c_5\,d_3\,c_5\,d_3\,e\,e_4$, $a\,b_4\,a_5\,b_4\,c\,c\,d\,d\,e\,e_5$, $a_5\,b_3\,a_5\,b_3\,c\,c_4\,d_2\,d_5\,e_2\,e_5$; as in Spenser and Browne (cf. *Metrik*, ii, § 434).

§ **282. Stanzas of eleven lines** are also rare. There is one with an isometrical first part (on the scheme $a\,b\,a\,b_5\,c\,c_2\,c_3\,d_2\,d_5\,x_2\,d_6$) in Ben Jonson, *Cynthia's Revels* (Poets, iv. 610); another in Campbell's *Gertrude of Wyoming* (st. xxxv-xxxix), corresponding to the scheme $a\,b\,a\,b_4\,c_3\,d\,d\,d_4\,c_3\,e\,e_4$.

Other stanzas of an almost entirely anisometrical structure consist of a combination with a tail-rhyme stanza, as e. g. a Middle English stanza on the scheme $a\,a_4\,b_3\,a\,a_4\,b_3\,a_4\,b_3\,a\,a_4\,b_3$, with a regular tail-rhyme stanza representing the *pedes*, and a shortened tail-rhyme stanza representing the *cauda*; it occurs in the *Towneley Mysteries*, pp. 221-3. A similar one we have in Phineas Fletcher (*Poets*, iv. 460) on the formula

$$a \sim_2 a \sim_3 b_2\, e \sim_2 e \sim_3 b_2\, d \sim_4 e \sim e \sim_2 d\, d_5,$$

and another one in Leigh Hunt, *Coronation Soliloquy* (p. 225) which corresponds to the formula $a\,a_2\,b \sim_3 c\,c_2\,b \sim_3 d\,d_2\,e \sim_3 f_4\,e \sim_3$.

In other stanzas parts only of tail-rhyme stanzas occur, as in a strophe of the form $a_4\,b \sim_3 c_4\,b \sim_3 d\,e\,d\,d_4\,e_3\,r\,R_4$, used by Wordsworth in *The Seven Sisters* (iii. 15):

> *Seven Daughters had Lord Archibald,*
>   *All children of one mother :*
> *You could not say in one short day*
>   *What love they bore each other.*
> *A garland of seven lilies wrought !*
> *Seven Sisters that together dwell ;*
> *But he, bold Knight as ever fought,*
> *Their Father, took of them no thought,*
> *He loved the wars so well.*
> *Sing mournfully, oh ! mournfully,*
>   *The solitude of Binnorie !*

Other stanzas of this kind are formed on the schemes $a_4 b_2 a_4 b_2 c c_2 d_3 e_4 d_2 e_4 d_2$ (Moore, *Love's Young Dream*), $a b b a c c d e e d_5 e_3$ (Swinburne, *Ave atque Vale*, Poems, ii. 71). Cf. *Metrik*, ii, §§ 436, 437.

§ **283. Stanzas of twelve lines** are very numerous. One of the Middle English period we have in Wright's *Spec. of Lyr. Poetry*, p. 27; it is formed on the scheme $a_4 b_3 a_4 b_3 b b b c_3 D D D_4 C_3$ and is similar to those ten-lined stanzas mentioned above, which consist of two Septenary verses and a tail-rhyme stanza; the second part of which, being the refrain, thus becomes the *cauda* of the stanza. In the Modern English period some simple stanzas with an isometrical first part and parallel rhymes may be mentioned in the first place. These are constructed on the schemes $a a b b c c d d_4 e_4 f_2 e_4 f_2$, $a a b b c c d d e e f_4 f_3$ and occur in Mrs. Hemans (iv. 171; vii. 155); stanzas of this kind with crossed rhymes are likewise met with, e.g. $a \sim b a \sim b_4 c c_3 d_5 e e f f_3 d_5$ in Burns, p. 188.

Pretty often we find stanzas for singing, the *cauda* of which is enclosed by the *pedes*; in the first stanza the two *pedes* together form the refrain, in the others, however, only the last one, e.g. in stanzas on the schemes $A \sim B A \sim B_4 c_4 d_3 c_4 d_3 A \sim B A \sim B_4$, $e \sim f e \sim f_4 g_4 h_3 g_4 h_3 A \sim B A \sim B_4$ in *Hymns Ancient and Mod.*, No. 138, consisting of trochaic verses:

> *Christ is risen ! Christ is risen !*
>   *He hath burst His bonds in twain ;*
> *Christ is risen ! Christ is risen !*
>   *Alleluia ! swell the strain !*
>   *For our gain He suffered loss*
>   *By Divine decree ;*
>   *He hath died upon the Cross,*
>   *But our God is He.*

> *Christ is risen! Christ is risen!*
> *He hath burst His bonds in twain ;*
> *Christ is risen! Christ is risen!*
> *Alleluia! swell the strain.*
>
> *See the chains of death are broken ;*
> *Earth below and heaven above*, &c. &c.

Similar stanzas frequently occur in Moore, e.g. stanzas on the models $A \sim B A \sim B_4 c c d_3 d_2 E \sim B E \sim B_4$, and $f \sim g f \sim g_4 h h i_3 i_2 E \sim B E \sim B_4$ (in *Love's light summer-cloud*), $A B \sim A B \sim_3 c d \sim_3 c_4 d \sim_3 A B \sim A B \sim_3$, $e f \sim e f \sim_3 g h \sim_3 g_4 h \sim_3 A B \sim A B \sim_3$ (in *All that's bright must fade*). For other examples see *Metrik*, ii, § 441.

Similar stanzas of Septenary metres, also common in Moore, have the formulas $a_4 b_3 a_4 b_3 c_4 d_3 c_4 d_3 E_4 F_3 E_4 F_3$ (in *When Time*), $A_4 B_3 A_4 B_3 c_4 d_3 c_4 d_3 A_4 B_3 A_4 B_3$ (st. i), $d_4 e_3 d_4 e_3 f_4 g_3 f_4 g_3 A_4 B_3 A_4 B_3$ (st. ii); only in st. i the *cauda* is in the middle; in the others it closes the stanza (*Nets and Cages*).

Other stanzas have the reverse order of verses, as e. g. stanzas on the schemes $a \sim_3 b_4 a \sim_3 b_4 c \sim_3 d_4 c \sim_3 d_4 E \sim_3 F_4 E \sim_3 F_4$ (*To Ladies' Eyes*), $A \sim_3 B_4 A \sim_3 B_4 c d c d_4 A \sim_3 B_4 A \sim_3 B_4$ (*Oh! Doubt me not*). This sort of stanza also occurs in Moore with other metres, e.g. according to the formulas $A_4 B_2 A_4 B_2 c_3 d_2 c_3 d_2 A_4 B_2 A_4 B_2$, $e_4 b_2 e_4 b_2 f_3 g_2 f_3 g_3 e_4 b_2 e_4 b_2$ (*Not from thee*); and there are still other varieties in Moore and in some of the more recent poets. Cf. *Metrik*, ii, §§ 443–5.

§ **284.** Among the **stanzas of thirteen lines**, one belonging to the Middle English period has been mentioned above (p. 342, note), which is formed by combination with a tail-rhyme stanza.

In the few Modern English stanzas of this length we generally find also a part of a tail-rhyme stanza, as e. g. in the *cauda* of a stanza constructed on the formula $a b \sim a b \sim c d \sim c d \sim_4 E F \sim_4 g g_2 F \sim_4$ (Moore, *Lesbia hath*, &c.); or in a stanza like $a \sim b a \sim b_4 c c c_2 b_4 d d_2 e f e f_4$, deficient in one four-stressed tail-verse as in Moore, *The Prince's Day*:

> *Tho' dark are our sorrows to-day we'll forget them,*
>   *And smile through our tears, like a sunbeam in showers ;*
> *There never were hearts, if our rulers would let them,*
>   *More form'd to be grateful and blest than ours.*
>   *But just when the chain*
>   *Has ceas'd to pain,*

> *And hope has enwreath'd it round with flowers,*
>   *There comes a new link*
>   *Our spirits to sink—*
> *Oh ! the joy that we taste, like the light of the poles,*
>   *Is a flash amid darkness, too brilliant to stay ;*
> *But, though 't were the last little spark in our souls,*
>   *We must light it up now, on our Prince's Day.*

For other forms of stanzas belonging to this group see *Metrik*, ii, § 447.

§ **285.** More numerous are **stanzas of fourteen lines.** Judging by the examples which have come to our knowledge, they are also, as a rule, formed by combination with a tail-rhyme stanza ; as e. g. in a stanza by Browne (*Poets*, iv. 276) on the scheme $a\,b\,a\,b\,c\,a\,c\,a\,a_5\,a\,a_2\,b_3\,c\,c_2\,b_3$; another stanza, frequently used by Burns, corresponds to the formula

$$a\,a_4\,b_3\,c\,c_4\,b_3\,d_4\,e_3\,d_4\,e_3\,f\sim_2 g_3\,h\sim_2 g_3$$

and occurs, e. g., in his *Epistle to Davie* (p. 57) :

> *While winds frae aff Ben-Lomond blaw,*
> *And bar the doors wi' driving snaw,*
>   *And hing us owre the ingle,*
> *I set me down, to pass the time,*
> *And spin a verse or twa o' rhyme,*
>   *In hamely, westlin jingle.*
> *While frosty winds blaw in the drift,*
>   *Ben to the chimla lug,*
> *I grudge a wee the Great-folk's gift,*
>   *That live sae bien an' snug :*
>   *I tent less, and want less*
>   *Their roomy fire-side ;*
>   *But hanker and canker,*
>   *To see their cursèd pride.*

A similar stanza is found in Moore, *The Sale of Loves,* $a_4\,b\sim_3\,a_4\,b\sim_3\,c_4\,d\sim_3\,c_4\,d\sim_3\,E\,E_2\,F\sim_3\,G\,G_2\,F\sim_3.$ In other stanzas used by this poet, the tail-rhyme stanza forms the *cauda* enclosed by two *pedes* (see § 283); e. g. in *Nay, tell me not, dear,* on the scheme $a\,b\,a\,b_4\,c\,c_2\,d_4\,e\,e_2\,d_4\,F\,G\,F\,G_4.$ Another stanza of the form $A\,B\sim A\,B\sim_3 c\,c_2\,d_3\,e\,e_2\,d_3\,A\,B\sim A\,B\sim_3,$ $f\,g\sim f\,g\sim_3\,h\,h_2\,i_3\,k\,k_2\,i_3\,A\,B\sim A\,B\sim_3,$ is used in *Oft, in the stilly night.*

As to other forms cf. *Metrik*, ii, § 448. Stanzas, the enclosing *pedes* of which are formed by two tail-rhyme stanzas, are discussed ib. § 449 (schemes: $a\,a_2\,b\,\sim_3\,C\,C_2\,b\,\sim_3\,d\sim d\sim_3\,e\,\acute{e}_2\,f\,\sim_3\,C\,C_2\,f\,\sim_3,$ $g\,g_2\,h\sim_3\,i\,i_2\,h\sim_3\,k\sim k\sim_3\,l\,l_2\,m\sim_3\,C\,C_2\,m\sim_3$).

§ 286. Some stanzas of still greater extent (not very common) are also formed by combination with tail-rhyme stanzas. There are a few **stanzas of fifteen lines**, e. g. one on the model $a\,a_2\,b_3\,c\,c_2\,b_3\,d\,d_2\,e_3\,ff_2\,e_3\,g\,G_3\,G_4$ in Moore, *Song and Trio*; one on

$$a\sim a\sim b\sim b\sim_2 c_1\,d\sim d\sim e\sim e\sim_2 c_1\,f\sim f\sim g\sim g\sim_2 c_1$$

in Shelley, *The Fugitives* (iii. 55); and one on

$$a\sim a\sim a\sim b\,c\sim c\sim c\sim b\,d\sim d\sim d\sim e\,f\sim f\sim_2 e_4$$

in Swinburne, *Four Songs in Four Seasons* (Poems, ii. 163–76).

Two **stanzas of sixteen lines** occur in Moore on the schemes $a\,a_2\,b\sim_3 c\,c_2\,b\sim_3\,d\,e\,d\,e_3\,ff_2\,g\sim_3\,h\,h_2\,g\sim_3$ (*The Indian Boat*), and $a\,a_2\,b\sim_3\,c\,c_2\,b\sim_3\,d\,d_2\,e\sim_3\,ff_2\,e\sim_3\,G\sim_4\,H\,H_2\,G\sim_3$ (*Oh, the Shamrock*).

A **stanza of seventeen lines**

$$(a\,a_4\,b_3\,a\,a_4\,b_3\,c\,c_4\,b_3\,c\,c_4\,b_3\,d_4\,e_3\,d\,d_4\,e_3)$$

is found in a Middle English poem in Wright's *Spec. of Lyr. Poetry*, p. 47; it consists of two six-lined, common tail-rhyme stanzas (the *pedes*), and a shortened one (forming the *cauda*).

A **stanza of eighteen lines** on the formula

$$a\,a_4\,b_3\,c\,c_4\,b_3\,d\,d_4\,b_3\,e\,e_4\,b_3\,ff\,g\,g\,g\,f_2$$

occurs in Wright's *Pol. Songs*, p. 155 (cf. *Metrik*, i, p. 411); the scheme might also be given as $a\,a_4\,b_2$, &c., if the tail-rhyme verses be looked upon as two-stressed lines. A simpler stanza according to the scheme $a\,a_2\,b_3\,c\,c_2\,b_3\,d\,d_2\,b_3\,e\,e_2\,b_3\,ff_2\,g_3\,h\,h_2\,g_3$ is used in *The Nut-Brown Mayd* (Percy's *Rel.* ii. i. 6). Cf. § 244, also *Metrik*, i, p. 367, and ii, p. 715.

Similar stanzas are used by Shelley (in *Arethusa*, i. 374) and by Moore (in *Wreath the Bowl*). Cf. *Metrik*, ii, § 453.

Lastly, a **stanza of twenty lines** with the scheme $a\,b\sim a\,c\,d\,b\sim d\,c\,e\,e_3\,f_4\,g\,g_3\,f_4\,h\,h_3\,i_4\,k\sim k\sim_3\,i_4$, occurs in *The King of France's Daughter* (Percy's *Rel.* iii. ii. 17); cf. *Metrik*, ii, § 454.

PART III

MODERN STANZAS AND METRES OF FIXED FORM ORIGINATING UNDER THE INFLUENCE OF THE RENASCENCE, OR INTRODUCED LATER

CHAPTER VI

STANZAS OF THREE AND MORE PARTS CONSISTING OF UNEQUAL PARTS ONLY

§ 287. **Introductory remark.** At the very beginning of the Modern English period the poetry of England was strongly influenced by that of Italy. Among the strophic forms used by the Italian poets, two especially have had an important share in the development of English metre: the sonnet and the canzone. Apart from those direct imitations which we shall have to notice later, the sonnet form tended to make more popular the use of enclosing rhymes, which had until then been only sparingly employed in English poetry; while the canzone with its varied combinations of anisometrical verses, mostly of eleven and seven syllables, gave rise to a variety of similar loosely constructed stanzas, as a rule, of three- and five-foot verses.

At the same time, however, these Modern English stanzas of a somewhat loose structure were also affected by the stricter rules for the formation of stanzas which had come down from the Middle English period. Hence their structure frequently reminds us of the older forms, two adjoining parts being often closely related, either by order of rhymes, or by the structure of the verse, or by both together, though the old law of the equality of the two *pedes* or of the two *versus* is not quite strictly observed.

This explains the fact that some stanzas (especially the shorter ones) have a structure similar to that of the old tripartite stanzas; while others (chiefly the longer ones) not unfrequently consist of four or even more parts.

In the first group the chief interest centres round those which have enclosing rhymes in their first or last part. Although the transposition of the order of rhymes thus effected in the *pedes*

or in the *versus* was common both in Northern French and
Provençal poets,[1] the teachers of the Middle English poets, we
find scarcely a single example of it in Middle English, and it
seems to have become popular in Modern English only through
the influence of the Italian sonnet.

In accordance with the analogy of the isometrical stanzas or
parts of stanzas this arrangement of rhymes is found also in the
anisometrical ones; so that we have first parts (*pedes*) both
on the scheme $abba_4$, $a b b a_5$ or $a_4 b b_3 a_4$, $a_5 b_4 b_4 a_5$. From
the arrangement of rhymes this order was transferred to the
lines themselves; thus a stanza with enclosing rhymes consisting of two longer lines with a couplet of short lines between
them, as in the last example, is transformed into a similar stanza
with crossed rhymes according to the formula $a_5 b_4 a_4 b_5$, the
shorter lines being, as before, placed between the longer ones
(or vice versa $a_4 b_5 a_5 b_4$). It is evident that here too in spite
of the regular arrangement of rhymes the two *pedes* are not
alike, but only similar to each other.

§ 288. Six-lined stanzas of this kind, with an isometrical
first part or isometrical throughout, occur pretty often; one
e. g. on the scheme $a b b a c c_4$ is met with in John Scott, *Ode*
XIX (*Poets*, xi. 757):

> *Pastoral, and elegy, and ode!*
> *Who hopes, by these, applause to gain,*
> *Believe me, friend, may hope in vain—*
> *These classic things are not the mode;*
> *Our taste polite, so much refin'd,*
> *Demands a strain of different kind.*

For similar stanzas according to the formulas $a b b a a b_4$,
$a b b a c c_5$, $a b b a c_3 c_5$ (Milton, *Psalm* IV), $a b b a_5 c_4 c_5$, and
$a b b a c_5 c_3$, see *Metrik*, ii, § 456.

Other stanzas have anisometrical first and last parts; as e. g.
one on the model $a_5 b b_4 a_5 c_4 c_3$ which was used by Cowley,
Upon the shortness of Man's Life (Poets, v. 227):

> *Mark that swift arrow, how it cuts the air,*
> *How it outruns thy following eye!*
> *Use all persuasions now, and try*
> *If thou canst call it back, or stay it there.*
> *That way it went, but thou shalt find*
> *No track is left behind.*

---

[1] Cf. Karl Bartsch, 'Der Strophenbau in der deutschen Lyrik' (*Germania*,
ii, p. 290).

Similar stanzas are found in later poets, as e.g. Mrs. Hemans, D. G. Rossetti, Mrs. Browning, corresponding to $a_5\, b\, b_4\, a_5\, c_4\, c_5$, $a_3\, b\, b_5\, a_3\, c\, c_5$, $a_5\, b\, b_3\, a_4\, c_5\, c_3$, $a_3\, b_4\, b_5\, a_4\, b_5\, a_3$, $a\, b_3\, b_4\, a_3\, c\, c_4$, &c. (For specimen see *Metrik*, ii, § 458.)

Even more frequently we have stanzas of three quite heterogeneous parts; the lines rhyming crosswise, parallel, or crosswise and parallel. They occur both in the earlier poets (Cowley, Herbert, &c.) and in those of recent times (Southey, Wordsworth, Shelley, the Brownings, Swinburne, &c.). A song by Suckling (*Poets*, iii. 730) on the scheme $a_3\, a\, b\, b_2\, c\, c_4$ may serve as an example:

> *If when Don Cupid's dart*
> *Doth wound a heart,*
>> *We hide our grief*
>> *And shun relief;*
> *The smart increaseth on that score;*
> *For wounds unsearcht but rankle more.*

For an account of other stanzas of a similar structure (e.g. $a\, a_5\, b\, b_4\, c\, c_3$, $a\, a_4\, b\, b\, c_3\, c_5$, $a_5\, a_3\, b\, b\, c_4\, c_5$, $a_2\, a\, b\, b\, c_4\, c_1$, &c.) see *Metrik*, ii, § 459.

Very often we find stanzas of combined crossed and parallel rhymes; one e.g. on the model $a\, b\, a_5\, b_6\, c\, c_5$ in Shelley, *A Summer-Evening Churchyard* (i. 160):

> *The wind has swept from the wide atmosphere*
> *Each vapour that obscured the sunset's ray;*
> *And pallid Evening twines its beaming hair*
> *In duskier braids around the languid eyes of day:*
> *Silence and Twilight, unbeloved of men,*
> *Creep hand in hand from yon obscurest glen.*

Many stanzas of a similar kind correspond to the schemes $a\, a_4\, b\, c_2\, b_4\, c_3$, $a_4\, b_3\, a\, b\, c\, c_4$, $a_3\, b_5\, a\, b_4\, c_5\, c_4$, $a\, b\, a_5\, b\, c\, c_4$, $a_5\, a\, b\, c\, c\, b_4\, c_5$, $a_4\, b \sim_2 a\, a_4\, b \sim a_4$, $a_5\, b_3\, a\, b\, c_5\, c_3$, and $a\, b\, c\, c\, a_4\, b_3$; for specimens see *Metrik*, ii, §§ 460–3.

Stanzas consisting of shorter lines are not so often met with; we have an example (on the model $a\, b\, a_2\, b\, c_4\, c_3$) consisting of iambic-anapaestic verses in R. Browning, *On the Cliff* (vi. 48):

> *I leaned on the turf,*
> *I looked at a rock*
> *Left dry by the surf;*
>> *For the turf, to call it grass were to mock;*
> *Dead to the roots, so deep was done*
> *The work of the summer sun.*

For stanzas on the schemes $a_4 b_1 a_4 b_2 C D_2$, $a b a_4 c_3 c b_2$ see ibid. § 464.

§ 289. Among **seven-line** stanzas, both in earlier (Ph. Fletcher, S. Daniel, &c.) and more recent poets (Mrs. Browning, Swinburne, R. Browning, D. G. Rossetti), those which are entirely isometrical occur often. One on the model $a b b a b b a_5$ is met with in S. Daniel's *Epistle to the Angel Spirit of the most excellent Sir Philip Sidney* (Poets, iii. 228):

> To thee, pure spir't, to thee alone addrest
> Is this joint work, by double int'rest thine:
> Thine by thine own, and what is done of mine
> Inspir'd by thee, thy secret pow'r imprest:
> My muse with thine itself dar'd to combine,
> As mortal stuff with that which is divine:
> Let thy fair beams give lustre to the rest.

Specimens of stanzas on the schemes $a b b a c c c_4$, $a b b a b b a_4$, $a b b a a c c_3$, $a b b a a c c_5$, $a b b a c c a_5$, and $a b c c d d d_4$, are given in *Metrik*, ii, § 456.

Anisometrical stanzas on the model $a b b a$ in the first part occur only in single examples, one corresponding to the scheme $a b b a_4 b_2 c c_4$ is found in Milton, *Arcades*, Song I; and another of the form $a_3 b b_5 a_3 c c a_5$ in Mrs. Hemans, *The Festal Hour* (iii. 247); cf. *Metrik*, ii, § 466.

Sometimes quite anisometrical stanzas with parallel rhymes occur, especially in the earlier poets, as e. g. in Wyatt, Suckling, Cowley; a stanza of Cowley's poem, *The Thief* (Poets, v. 263), has the formula $a_5 a b b c c_4 c_5$:

> What do I seek, alas! or why do I
> Attempt in vain from thee to fly?
> For, making thee my deity,
> I give thee then ubiquity,
> My pains resemble hell in this,
> The Divine Presence there, too, is,
> But to torment men, not to give them bliss.

Other forms of a similar structure are $a a_3 b b_2 a a_3 B_4$, $a_4 a b b_3 c c_4 x_3$, $a_4 a b_5 b c c_4 c_5$, $a_5 a a b b_4 c c_3$; for examples see *Metrik*, ii, § 467.

Stanzas which have crossed rhymes either in part or throughout are still commoner. Thus a stanza on the model of the *rhyme royal* stanza ($a_3 b a b_5 b_3 c c_5$) which occurs in Mrs. Hemans, *Elysium* (iii. 236) :

> *Fair wert thou in the dreams*
> *Of elder time, thou land of glorious flowers*
> *And summer winds and low-toned silvery streams,*
> *Dim with the shadows of thy laurel bowers,*
> *Where, as they pass'd, bright hours*
> *Left no faint sense of parting, such as clings*
> *To earthly love, and joy in loveliest things!*

Other similar stanzas correspond to $a_4 b a_5 b_4 c_3 c_4 c_5$, $a_3 b a_4 b_2 c c c_5$, $a_5 b a_4 b_5 c_4 c c_5$, $a_5 b c c b a_4 a_5$, $a b a_4 b_3 b_5 a_4 b_3$, and $a b a_3 b_4 c_3 c_2 c_4$; for examples taken from older poets (Donne, Carew, Cowley) and from later literature (Longfellow, D. G. Rossetti) cf. *Metrik*, ii, § 468.

Several other stanza-forms remind us by their structure and arrangement of rhymes of certain shortened forms of the tail-rhyme stanza, e. g. one in *A Parting Song* by Mrs. Hemans (vi. 189), on the scheme $A_4 B_3 c c d d_4 B_2$:

> *When will ye think of me, my friends ?*
> *When will ye think of me ?*
> *When the last red light, the farewell of day,*
> *From the rock and the river is passing away—*
> *When the air with a deep'ning hush is fraught*
> *And the heart grows burden'd with tender thought—*
> *Then let it be.*

Similar stanzas corresponding to the formulas $a b_4 a a_3 b a_4 a_3$, $a_4 b_3 a a_4 b_3 c c_4$, $a a b a_5 b a a_2$ are quoted in *Metrik*, ii, § 469.

§ 290. Most of the **eight-lined stanzas,** which on the whole are rare, are similar to the tail-rhyme stanza, the scheme of which is carried out in both parts, to which a third part is then added as the *cauda* (last part).

Stanzas of this kind, used especially by Cowley, correspond to $a a_5 b_3 c c_4 b_3 d d_4$, $a_5 a_4 b_4 c_5 c_5 b_4 d_4 d_5$, $a_5 a b c c b_4 d d_5$, and $a a_5 b_4 c c b_5 d_4 d_5$ (cf. *Metrik*, ii, § 470).

The half-stanzas (*pedes*) are separated by the *cauda* in a stanza on the scheme $a a_4 b_5 c c d d_4 b_5$, which occurs in Wordsworth, *The Pilgrim's Dream* (vi. 153) :

> *A Pilgrim, when the summer day*
> *Had closed upon his weary way,*
>   *A lodging begged beneath a castle's roof;*
> *But him the haughty Warder spurned;*
> *And from the gate the Pilgrim turned,*
> *To seek such covert as the field*
> *Or heath-besprinkled copse might yield,*
>   *Or lofty wood, shower-proof.*

In other stanzas on the models
$a_4 b_2 a b c c c_4 b_2$, $a \sim b a \sim_4 b_3 c \sim c \sim c \sim_4 b_2$, $a_4 b_2 a_4 c c_2 d d_4 b_2$, and
$a_4 B \sim_2 a a_4 C \sim_2 D_3 D_4$, only a half-stanza of the tail-rhyme form
can be recognized (cf. *Metrik*, ii, § 475).

Sometimes an unequal part is inserted between two parts of
a somewhat similar structure, as in a stanza with the formula
$a a b c b c d_4 d_5$ in Byron, *Translation from Horace* (p. 89):

> *The man of firm and noble soul*
> *No factious clamours can control;*
> *No threat'ning tyrant's darkling brow*
>   *Can swerve him from his just intent;*
> *Gales the warring waves which plough,*
>   *By Auster on the billows spent,*
> *To curb the Adriatic main,*
> *Would awe his fix'd, determined mind in vain.*

Other stanzas correspond to the schemes $a a_5 . b b c c_3 . d \sim d \sim_4$,
$a_5 a_3 a_4 . b b_4 . c c_4 c_5$, $a b_5 b_3 . a_4 a . c c c_5$, $a_3 a . b c b c . d d_5$,
$a a_4 . b_4 c \sim c \sim_2 . d d_2 b_4$, and $a_5 a_2 . b b_5 . c c c_5 c_2$. All these forms
are met with in earlier poets, as e. g. Donne, Drayton, and
Cowley; for specimen see *Metrik*, ii, § 471.

§ 291. A quadripartite structure is sometimes observable in
stanzas with four rhymes, especially with a parallel or crossed
order, or both combined, as e. g. in a poem by Donne, *The
Damp* (Poets, iv. 37), the scheme being $a_5 a_4 b b_5 c c_4 d d_5$:

> *When I am dead, and doctors know not why,*
> *And my friends' curiosity*
>   *Will have me cut up, to survey each part,*
>   *And they shall find your picture in mine heart;*
> *You think a sudden Damp of love*
> *Will through all their senses move,*
>   *And work on them as me, and so prefer*
>   *Your murder to the name of massacre.*

For stanzas of different structure on similar models cf. *Metrik*, ii, § 472 ($a_5 a b_3 b c_5 d_3 c_2 d_4$, $a_5 a b_2 b c_5 c_2 d_4 d_5$, $a_5 a_3 b b_5 c c_4 d d_5$, $a b a_4 b_5 c c_4 d d_5$, $a a_5 b b c d c_4 d_5$, and $a_4 b_5 a_4 b_3 c d_4 c_2 d_4$).

There are other stanzas of this kind which occur in earlier poets, as e. g. Donne, Cowley, and Dryden, or in some of those of later date, as Southey, R. Browning, and Rossetti, one half-stanza having enclosing rhymes and the whole stanza partaking of a tripartite structure. We find, e. g. the form $A b b a c d c_4 d_3$ in D. G. Rossetti, *A Little While* (i. 245):

> *A little while a little love*
> > *The hour yet bears for thee and me*
> > *Who have not drawn the veil to see,*
> *If still our heaven be lit above.*
> *Thou merely, at the day's last sigh,*
> > *Hast felt thy soul prolong the tone;*
> *And I have heard the night-wind cry*
> *And deemed its speech mine own.*

Other similar stanzas correspond to the formulas $a a b_5 b_4 c_5 d d_4 c_5$, $a_5 b b_4 a_5 c c_4 d d_5$, $a_4 b b_2 a c_4 d d_2 c_3$, and $a_5 b_3 a b_5 c_3 d d_5 c_3$; for examples see *Metrik*, ii, § 474. Stanzas on the model $a \sim b c a \sim c_4 B_2 d_4 D_2$, or on $a b c \sim_2 d d a b c \sim_4$, are found only in single examples (cf. *Metrik*, ii, § 476).

§ 292. The most important of the Modern English eight-lined stanzas, however, is an isometrical one on a foreign model, viz. a stanza of hendecasyllabic or rather five-foot verses corresponding to the Italian *ottava rima*, on the scheme $a b a b a b c c$. This stanza, which has always been very popular in Italian poetry, was introduced into English by Wyatt and Surrey; in Surrey we have only an isolated specimen, in *To his Mistress* (p. 32):

> *If he that erst the form so lively drew*
> > *Of Venus' face, triumph'd in painter's art;*
> *Thy Father then what glory did ensue,*
> > *By whose pencil a Goddess made thou art,*
> *Touched with flame that figure made some rue,*
> > *And with her love surprised many a heart.*
> *There lackt yet that should cure their hot desire:*
> *Thou canst inflame and quench the kindled fire.*

The stanza was often used by Wyatt, Sidney, and Spenser for reflective poems, and by Drayton and Daniel for epic poems of some length. In modern literature it has been used by Frere, Byron (*Beppo, Don Juan*), Shelley, Keats, Wordsworth, Longfellow, and others (cf. *Metrik*, ii, § 579).

§ 293. **Stanzas of nine lines** either show a combination of parallel with crossed or enclosing rhymes, as in the forms $a\,a\,b\,c\,b\,c\,d\,d\,d_4$, $a_5\,b\,a_4\,b_5\,b_5\,c_4\,c_5\,d\,d_5$ (Rhyme-Royal+ rhyming couplet), $a\,b_5\,b\,a_4\,c_3\,c\,c\,d\,d_5$, $a_4\,a\,b\,b_5\,c_4\,c_5\,d_4\,d\,d_5$, $a_4\,b\,a_3\,c_4\,b_3\,d\,b\,c_4\,D_1$, &c. (for specimens see *Metrik*, ii, §§ 477 and 479), or, in some of the later poets, they consist of parts of modified tail-rhyme stanzas combined with other forms, as in the following stanza $(a\sim_3 b_4\,a\sim b_3\,c\,c_2\,d_3\,a\sim d_3)$ of a song by Moore:

> *Love thee, dearest? love thee?*
> *Yes, by yonder star I swear,*
> *Which thro' tears above thee*
> *Shines so sadly fair;*
> *Though often dim,*
> *With tears, like him,*
> *Like him my truth will shine,*
> *And — love thee, dearest? love thee?*
> *Yes, till death I'm thine.*

Other stanzas of Moore and others have the formulas $a\,a\,b\,a\,b\,c\,c\,c_4\,d_3$ (Burns, p. 216), $a\,b\sim a\,a_4\,b\sim_3 c\,d\,d_4\,c_3$, $a\,a\,b_4\,c_2\,b_4\,c_2\,d\,d_4\,c_2$, $a_4\,b_3\,a\,a_4\,c\sim_3 c\sim d\sim d\sim_2 b_3$, &c. (cf. *Metrik*, ii, § 478).

§ 294. The **ten-line stanzas** are also based mostly on a combination of earlier strophic systems. Thus in Campbell's well-known poem, *Ye Mariners of England* (p. 71), the *Poulter's Measure* rhythm is observable, the scheme being $a\sim b_3\,c_4\,d_3\,.\,e_4\,f_3\,.\,e_2\,F_3\,G_4\,F_3$:

> *Ye Mariners of England!*
> *That guard our native seas;*
> *Whose flag has braved, a thousand years,*
> *The battle and the breeze!*
> *Your glorious standard launch again*
> *To match another foe!*
> *And sweep through the deep,*
> *While the stormy winds do blow;*
> *While the battle rages loud and long,*
> *And the stormy winds do blow.*

Similar stanzas occurring in the works of earlier poets, as
Sidney and Spenser, correspond to the schemes

$$a_6\,b\,a\,b\,b_5\,c\,c_4\,d_2\,b_5\,d_2,\ a_5\,a_2\,b \sim c\,b \sim c\,D \sim D \sim E\,E_3,\ \&c.$$

But generally speaking most of the earlier poets, as e.g.
Donne, Cowley, and Suckling, prefer a simpler order of rhymes,
the schemes being $a\,a_3\,b\,b\,.\,c_5\,c\,c_4\,.\,d\,d\,d_5,\ a_4\,a\,b\,b_5\,c\,c_4\,d\,d\,e\,e_5,$
$a_5\,a\,a_2\,b\,b\,c\,d\,d_3\,e\,e_5,$ &c.; the more modern poets (Moore,
Wordsworth, Swinburne), on the other hand, are fond of some-
what more complicated forms, as $a_4\,b \sim b \sim_2 a\,a_4\,c \sim c \sim_2 d\,a\,d_4,$
$a\,b\,a_4\,b_3\,c\,c_5\,d\,e_3\,d_4\,e_3,\ a\,b\,b_4\,a_3\,c\,d\,d\,e\,d_4\,d_3,$ &c. (For specimens
cf. *Metrik*, ii, §§ 480, 481.) A fine form of stanza correspond-
ing to the formula $a\,b\,c\,b\,c_5\,a_3\,d\,e\,e\,d_5$ is used by M. Arnold in
his poem *The Scholar Gipsy*, and another on the scheme
$a\,a_3\,b\,c\,c\,b_5\,d_3\,e\,d\,e_5$ in *Westminster Abbey*, p. 479.

§ 295. **Stanzas of eleven lines** do not frequently occur
in earlier poetry, and for the most part simple forms are
employed, e.g. $a\,b_4\,a\,b\,c\,d_5\,c\,d_4\,e\,e_5\,e_4,\ a_5\,a\,b_4\,b_5\,c_4\,d_3\,c_4\,d_3\,e\,e_4\,e_5,$
$a\,a\,b\,b_4\,c_3\,d_5\,d_3\,c\,e\,e\,e_5,$ &c.; the more recent poets, however,
as Moore, Wordsworth, and R. Browning, have usually preferred
a more intricate arrangement, as $a \sim b\,c \sim d\,d\,a \sim b\,c \sim_2 e\,e\,e_4,$
$a\,b\,c_4\,b_3\,d\,e\,f\,f_4\,e_3\,g\,g_4,\ a_4\,b_3\,a\,b\,c_4\,d_3\,c_4\,d_3\,e_2\,e_3\,e_4.$ The last scheme
occurs in a song by Moore:

> *How happy once, tho' wing'd with sighs,*
>   *My moments flew along,*
> *While looking on those smiling eyes,*
>   *And list'ning to thy magic song!*
> *But vanish'd now, like summer dreams,*
>   *Those moments smile no more;*
> *For me that eye no longer beams,*
>   *That song for me is o'er.*
> *Mine the cold brow,*
> *That speaks thy alter'd vow,*
> *While others feel thy sunshine now.*

§ 296. **Stanzas of twelve lines** are more frequent, possibly
on account of the symmetrical arrangement of the stanza in
equal parts, twelve being divisible by three. They are con-
structed on different models, e.g. $a\,a_5\,b_3\,b\,a_5\,c_3\,d_5\,d\,c_4\,c_5\,e\,e_5,$
$a\,a_4\,b \sim b \sim c_3\,c_2\,d_3\,d_2\,e\,f_3\,f_1\,e_3,\ a_4\,b_2\,b_1\,a_3\,c \sim_4 d \sim_3\,d \sim_4\,c \sim_2 e \sim e \sim f \sim f \sim_3$
(*bob-verse* stanzas), $a\,b_4\,c \sim c \sim_2 a_4\,b_3\,d\,d\,e_4\,f_2\,f_4\,e_5,$ &c., occurring
in earlier poets, such as Donne, Browne, Dryden, &c. Similar
stanzas, partly of a simpler structure ($a\,b\,b\,a_5\,a_6\,c\,c_4\,b_5\,d\,d\,e_4\,e_5,$

$a \sim b\, a \sim b_3\, c\, c_4\, d\, d_3\, e \sim f_3\, e \sim f_2$, and $a\, a_4 b_2 c\, c_4 b_1 b_4 a_2 D E \sim F E_4 \sim$),
are found in modern poetry; the last scheme, resembling the
tail-rhyme stanza, occurring in Tennyson (p. 12):

> *A spirit haunts the year's last hours*
> *Dwelling amid these yellowing bowers:*
> > *To himself he talks ;*
> *For at eventide, listening earnestly,*
> *At his work you may hear him sob and sigh*
> > *In the walks ;*
> > *Earthward he boweth the heavy stalks*
> *Of the mouldering flowers :*
> > *Heavily hangs the broad sunflower*
> > > *Over its grave i' the earth so chilly ;*
> > *Heavily hangs the hollyhock,*
> > > *Heavily hangs the tiger-lily.*

Many other examples are quoted in *Metrik*, ii, §§ 484–6.
For several stanzas of a still greater extent, but of rare occurrence, which need not be mentioned in this handbook, see ibid.,
§§ 487–90.

CHAPTER VII

THE SPENSERIAN STANZA AND FORMS DERIVED FROM IT

§ **297.** ONE of the most important Modern English stanzas is the Spenserian, so called after its inventor. This stanza, like the forms discussed in the last chapter, but in a still greater degree, is based on an older type. For it is not, as is some-times said, derived from the Italian *ottava rima* (cf. § 292), but, as was pointed out by Guest (ii. 389), from a Middle English eight-lined popular stanza of five-foot verses with rhymes on the formula *a b a b b c b c*, which was modelled in its turn on a well-known Old French ballade-stanza (cf. § 269). To this stanza Spenser added a ninth verse of six feet rhyming with the eighth line, an addition which was evidently meant to give a very distinct and impressive conclusion to the stanza.

As a specimen the first stanza of the first book of the *Faerie Queene*, where it was used for the first time, may be quoted here :

> *A gentle Knight was pricking on the plaine,*
> *Ycladd in mightie armes and silver shielde,*
> *Wherein old dints of deepe woundes did remaine,*
> *The cruell markes of many a bloody fielde ;*
> *Yet armes till that time did he never wield.*
> *His angry steede did chide his foming bitt,*
> *As much disdayning to the curbe to yield:*
> *Full jolly knight he seemd, and faire did sitt,*
> *As one for knightly giusts and fierce encounters fitt.*

This euphonious stanza became very popular and has been used by many of the chief Modern English poets, as e.g. by Thomson, *The Castle of Indolence*; Shenstone, *The School-Mistress* ; Burns, *The Cotter's Saturday Night*; Byron, *Childe Harold's Pilgrimage*; Shelley, *The Revolt of Islam*.

The great influence it had on the development of the different forms of stanza, especially in the earlier Modern English period, is proved by the numerous imitations and analogous formations which arose from it.

§ **298.** All the imitations have this in common that they consist of a series of two to ten five-foot lines followed by a concluding line of six (or rarely seven) feet.

John Donne, Phineas Fletcher, and Giles Fletcher were, it seems, the inventors of those varieties of stanza, the shortest of which consist of three or four lines on the schemes $a\,a_5\,a_6$, $a\,b\,a_5\,b_6$, and were used by Rochester, *Upon Nothing* (Poets, iv. 413), and Cowper (p. 406). A stanza of five lines, however, on the model $a\,b\,a\,b_5\,b_6$ occurs in Phineas Fletcher's *Eclogue II.*

The favourite six-lined stanza with the formula $a\,b\,a\,b\,c\,c_5$ (cf. § 267, p. 327) was often transformed into a quasi-Spenserian stanza $a\,b\,a\,b\,c_5\,c_6$ by adding one foot to the last line, as e. g. by Dodsley in *On the Death of Mr. Pope* (Poets, xi. 103), Southey, *The Chapel Bell* (ii. 143), and others; cf. *Metrik*, ii, § 493.

It was changed into a stanza of seven lines on the scheme $a\,b\,a\,b\,c\,c_5\,c_6$ by Donne, *The Good Morrow* (Poets, iv. 24) by the addition of a seventh line rhyming with the two preceding lines.

Much more artistic taste is shown by the transformation of the seven-lined *rhyme royal* stanza $a\,b\,a\,b\,b\,c\,c_5$ (cf. § 268) into a quasi-Spenserian stanza $a\,b\,a\,b\,b\,c_5\,c_6$ in Milton's *On the Death of a Fair Infant.*

By the addition of a new line rhyming with the last couplet this form was developed into the eight-lined stanza $a\,b\,a\,b\,b\,c\,c_5\,c_6$ employed in Giles Fletcher's *Christ's Victory and Triumph.*

Omitting some rarer forms (cf. *Metrik*, ii, § 495) we may mention that Phineas Fletcher transformed the *ottava rima* $a\,b\,a\,b\,a\,b\,c\,c_5$ into a quasi-Spenserian stanza of the form $a\,b\,a\,b\,a\,b\,c_5\,c_6$, and that he also extended the same stanza to one of nine lines $(a\,b\,a\,b\,a\,b\,c\,c_5\,c_6)$ by adding one verse more. Other nine-line quasi-Spenserian stanzas occurring occasionally in modern poets, e. g. Mrs. Hemans, Shelley, and Wordsworth, correspond to $a\,b\,a\,a\,b\,b\,c\,c_5\,c_6$, $a\,b\,a\,b\,c\,d\,c\,d_5\,d_6$, $a\,b\,a\,b\,c\,c\,b\,d_5\,d_6$, $a\,a\,b\,b\,c\,c\,d\,d_5\,d_6$. (For specimens see *Metrik*, ii, § 496.)

A stanza of ten lines on the scheme $a\,b\,a\,b\,c\,d\,c\,d\,e_5\,e_6$ was invented by Prior for his *Ode to the Queen* (Poets, vii. 440); but it is not, as he thought, an improved, but only a simplified form of the old Spenserian scheme:

> When great *Augustus* govern'd ancient *Rome*,
>   And sent his conquering bands to foreign wars;
> Abroad when dreaded, and belov'd at home,
>   He saw his fame increasing with his years;

Horace, great bard! (so fate ordain'd) arose,
And, bold as were his countrymen in fight,
Snatch'd their fair actions from degrading prose,
And set their battles in eternal light :
High as their trumpets' tune his lyre he strung,
And with his prince's arms he moraliz'd his song.

This stanza has been used by some subsequent poets, e. g. by Chatterton, who himself invented a similar imitation of the old Spenserian form, viz. $a\,b\,a\,b\,b\,a\,b\,a\,c_5\,c_6$. Other stanzas of ten lines are $a\,b\,a\,b\,b\,c\,d\,c\,d_5\,d_6$, $a\,b\,b\,a\,c\,d\,d\,c\,e_5\,e_6$, $a\,b\,a\,b\,c\,c\,d\,e\,e_5\,d_6$. (For specimens see *Metrik*, ii, § 497.)

A stanza of eleven lines on the scheme $a\,b\,a\,b\,c\,d\,c\,d\,c\,d_5\,d_6$ occurs in Wordsworth in the *Cuckoo-clock* (viii. 161).

§ 299. Amongst the stanzaic formations analogous to the Spenserian stanza, which for the most part were invented by the poets just mentioned, two different groups are to be distinguished ; firstly, stanzas the body of which consists of four-foot (seldom three-foot) verses, a six-foot final verse being added to them either immediately or preceded by a five-foot verse ; secondly, stanzas of anisometrical structure in the principal part, the end-verse being of six or sometimes of seven feet.

The stanzas of the first group consist of four to ten lines, and have the following formulas : four-lined stanzas, $a\,b\,c_4\,b_6$ (Wordsworth); five lines, $a\,b\,a\,b_3\,b_6$ (Shelley); six lines, $a\,b\,a\,a\,b_3\,b_6$ (Ben Jonson), $a\,b\,a\,b_4\,c_5\,c_6$ (Wordsworth, Coleridge), $a\,a_3\,b_5\,c\,c_3\,b_6$ (R. Browning); seven lines, $a\sim b\,b\,a\sim c\,c_4\,c_7$ (Mrs. Browning); eight lines, $a\,b\,a\,b\,c\,c\,d_4\,d_6$ (Gray, Wordsworth), $a\,a\,b\,b\,c\,c\,d_4\,d_6$ (John Scott), $a\,a\,b\,b\,c\,c_4\,d_5\,d_6$ (Coleridge); nine lines, $a\,b\,a\,b\,c\,d\,c_4\,d_5\,c_6$ and $a\,b\,a\,b\,c\,c\,d\,d_4\,d_6$ (Akenside), $a\,b\,a\,b\,b\,c\,b\,c_4\,c_6$ (Shelley, *Stanzas written in Dejection*, i. 370); ten lines, $a\,b\,a\,b\,c\,d\,c\,d_4\,e_5\,e_6$ (Whitehead).

As an example we quote a stanza of nine lines from Shelley's poem mentioned above :

I see the Deep's untrampled floor
With green and purple seaweeds strown ;
I see the waves upon the shore,
Like light dissolved in star-showers, thrown :
I sit upon the sands alone,
The lightning of the noon-tide ocean
Is flashing round me, and a tone
Arises from its measured motion,
How sweet! did any heart now share in my emotion.

For other examples see *Metrik*, ii, §§ 499–503.

§ **300.** Greater variety is found in the second group; they have an extent of four up to sixteen lines and mostly occur in poets of the sixteenth to eighteenth centuries (Donne, Ben Jonson, Cowley, Rowe, Akenside, &c.), rarely in the nineteenth century. Stanzas of four lines are, $a_5 a b_4 b_6$ (Poets, v. 236), $a a_4 b_5 b_6$ (ib. xi. 1207); of five lines, $a_5 a b_3 b_4 a_6$ (ib. v. 281), $a b a_5 b_4 b_6$ (ib. ix. 312), &c.; of six lines, $a_4 b_5 a_4 b c_5 c_6$ (ib. xi. 130), $a_4 b_3 a_4 b_3 c_5 c_6$ (ib. x. 722), $a a_4 b_3 c c_4 b_6$ (ib. xi. 1070; tail-rhyme stanza), $a b_5 a_4 b c_5 c_6$ (Tennyson, *The Third of February*); of seven lines, $a_3 b_5 b_3 a_4 c c_3 c_6$ (Poets, v. 413), $a b a b_5 b_3 c_5 c_6$ (Mrs. Hemans, *Easter Day*, vii. 165, with rhymes in the *rhyme royal* order; of eight lines, $a a_3 b_5 c c_3 b_5 d_4 d_6$ (Milton, *Hymn on the Nativity*, ii. 400; tail-rhyme $+ d_4 d_6$), $a_5 b_2 a b_5 c_3 d_5 c_3 d_7$ (Poets, iv. 36), $a_5 a_4 b b_5 c d c_4 d_6$ (ib. v. 432), $a b_4 b c a_5 d d_4 c_6$ (ib. ix. 794), $a b a b c_5 c_3 d_5 d_6$, and $a b_5 a_4 b_3 c_5 d_4 d_3 c_6$ (Wordsworth, *Artegal and Elidure*, vi. 47, and *'Tis said that some have died for love*, ii. 184, beginning with the second stanza).

The following stanza from the last-mentioned poem may serve as a specimen:

> *Oh move, thou Cottage, from behind that oak!*
> *   Or let the aged tree uprooted lie,*
> *That in some other way yon smoke*
> *   May mount into the sky:*
> *The clouds pass on; they from the heavens depart.*
> *   I look—the sky is empty space;*
> *   I know not what I trace;*
> *But when I cease to look, my hand is on my heart.*

Stanzas of nine lines, especially occurring in Donne, have the formulas $a b b_5 a_3 c c c_4 d_5 d_6$ (Poets, iv. 29), $a a b b c_5 c d_4 d_5 d_7$ (ib. 36), $a_2 b b a_5 c c_2 d d_5 d_7$ (ib. 31), $a a b b b_5 c d d_4 c_6$ (ib. vii. 142), &c.; of ten lines, $a a_4 b b c c_5 d_4 d d_5 d_6$ (ib. iv. 28), $a a b c c_4 b_2 d e d_5 e_6$ (ib. ix. 788), $a b a b_5 c c d d_4 e_5 e_6$ (Shelley, *Phantasm of Jupiter* in *Prometheus Unbound*); of twelve lines, $a b a b_5 c c d d e e_4 f_5 f_6$ (Poets, xi. 588); of thirteen lines, $a b \sim_4 a_5 b \sim_3 c_4 c_5 d d_2 e_5 e_2 f_5 e_2 f_6$ (Ben Jonson, *Ode to James, Earl of Desmond*, ib. iv. 572); of fifteen lines, $a b a b c_5 d d_4 d_6 c e c e d f_5 f_6$ (Shelley, *Ode to Liberty*, i. 360-9); of sixteen lines, $a b a b a b a b_5 c c_3 b_5 d d_3 b_5 e_4 e_6$ (Swinburne, *New-Year Ode to Victor Hugo* (*Midsummer Holiday*, pp. 39-63).

This last stanza has an exceedingly fine structure, consisting of an isometrical first part and an anisometrical tail-rhyme stanza + an anisometrical rhyming couplet, forming the last part :

> *Twice twelve times have the springs of years refilled*
> *Their fountains from the river-head of time,*
> *Since by the green sea's marge, ere autumn chilled*
> *Waters and woods with sense of changing clime,*
> *A great light rose upon my soul, and thrilled*
> *My spirit of sense with sense of spheres in chime,*
> *Sound as of song wherewith a God would build*
> *Towers that no force of conquering war might climb.*
> *Wind shook the glimmering sea*
> *Even as my soul in me*
> *Was stirred with breath of mastery more sublime,*
> *Uplift and borne along*
> *More thunderous tides of song,*
> *Where wave rang back to wave more rapturous rhyme*
> *And world on world flashed lordlier light*
> *Than ever lit the wandering ways of ships by night.*

The three stanzas last quoted, as well as some of the shorter ones occurring in Akenside, Rowe, &c., were also used for odes, and in this way the affinity of formations like these with the odic stanzas to be discussed in the next chapter becomes apparent.

CHAPTER VIII

THE EPITHALAMIUM STANZA AND OTHER ODIC STANZAS

§ 301. THE Spenserian stanza stands in unmistakable connexion with Spenser's highly artistic and elaborate **Epithalamium stanza** (Globe Ed. 587–91) inasmuch as the last line, *That all the woods may answer and their echo ring*, repeated in each stanza as a burden together with the word *sing* which ends the preceding verse, has six measures, the rest of the stanza consisting of three- and five-foot lines.

Like the Spenserian stanza, the Epithalamium stanza has given rise to numerous imitations.

It cannot be said that one fixed form of stanza is employed throughout the whole extent of Spenser's Epithalamium. It rather consists of two main forms of stanza, viz. one of eighteen lines (st. i, ii, iv, v, vi, x, xvi, xxi, xxiii), and one of nineteen lines (st. iii, vii, viii, ix, xi, xii, xiii, xiv, xvii, xviii, xix, xx, xxii), whereas one stanza, the fifteenth, has only seventeen lines. In the arrangement of rhymes there are also sporadic varieties: cf. e. g. iv and ix.

The arrangement of verse, however, is always similar in both groups. The main part of the stanza consists of five-foot verses, the succession of which is interrupted three times by three-foot ones, the final verse of the stanza having six measures. In the stanza of eighteen lines the usual arrangement is $a\,b\,a\,b\,c_5\,c_3\,d\,c\,d\,e_5\,e_3\,f\,g\,g\,f_5\,g_3\,r_5\,R_6$. In those of nineteen lines it is $a\,b\,a\,b\,c_5\,c_3\,d\,c\,d\,e_5\,e_3\,f\,g\,g\,f\,h_5\,h_3\,r_5\,R_6$. The scheme of the stanza of seventeen lines is $a\,b\,a\,b\,c_5\,c_3\,d\,c\,d\,e\,f\,f\,g\,h_5\,h_3\,r_5\,R_6$.

The two following stanzas (ii, iii) may be quoted as specimens of the two chief forms:

> *Early, before the worlds light-giving lampe*
> *His golden beame upon the hils doth spred,*
> *Having disperst the nights unchearefull dampe,*
> *Doe ye awake; and, with fresh lustyhed,*

Go to the bowre of my beloved love,
My truest turtle dove;
Bid her awake; for Hymen is awake,
And long since ready forth his maske to move,
With his bright Tead that flames with many a flake,
And many a bachelor to waite on him,
In theyr fresh garments trim.
Bid her awake therefore, and soone her dight,
For lo! the wished day is come at last,
That shall, for all the paynes and sorrowes past,
Pay to her usury of long delight:
And, whylest she doth her dight,
Doe ye to her of joy and solace sing,
That all the woods may answer, and your eccho ring.

Bring with you all the Nymphes that you can heare
Both of the rivers and the forrests greene,
And of the sea that neighbours to her neare;
Al with gay girlands goodly wel beseene.
And let them also with them bring in hand
Another gay girland,
For my fayre love, of lillyes and of roses,
Bound truelove wize, with a blue silke riband.
And let them make great store of bridal poses,
And let them eeke bring store of other flowers
To deck the bridale bowers.
And let the ground whereas her foot shall tread,
For feare the stones her tender foot should wrong,
Be strewed with fragrant flowers all along,
And diapred lyke the discoloured mead.
Which done, doe at her chamber dore awayt,
For she will waken strayt;
The whiles doe ye this song unto her sing,
The woods shall to you answer, and your Eccho ring.

These stanzas evidently consist of three or four unequal parts,
the two first parts (ll. 1–6, 7–11) being connected by rhyme.
There is a certain similarity between them, the chief difference
being that the second *pes*, as we may call it, is shortened by one
verse. With the third part, a new system of verses rhyming
together commences, forming a kind of last part (*downsong* or
cauda); and as the final couplet of the stanza is generally
closely connected in sense with this, the assumption of a tri-

partite division of the stanza is preferable to that of a quadripartite division.

§ 302. Stanzas of this kind have also been used by later poets
in similar poems. But all these imitations of the Epithalamium
stanza are shorter than their model. As to their structure, some
of them might also be ranked among the irregular Spenserian
stanzas, as they agree with those in having a longer final verse of
six or seven measures. But as a rule, they have—not to speak
of the similarity of theme—the combination of three- and five-foot
verses in the principal part, on the model, it seems, of Spenser's
Epithalamium stanza.

Stanzas of this kind (eight lines up to fourteen) occur in
Donne and Ben Jonson; the schemes being—

> of eight lines : $a\,b\,a\,b_5\,c_3\,c_2\,d_3\,d_6$ (Poets, iv. 588);
> of eleven lines : $a_5\,a\,b_4\,b_5\,c_3\,c\,d\,d\,e\,e_5\,E_7$ (ib. iv. 19);
> of twelve lines : $a_4\,a\,b\,c\,c\,b\,d\,e_5\,e_3\,d\,f_5\,F_6$ (ib. 16);
> of fourteen lines : $a_5\,a\,b_4\,b_5\,c_3\,d\,d\,c_5\,e_4\,e\,f\,f\,g_5\,G_6$ (ib. 15).

For specimens see *Metrik*, ii, § 512.

Stanzas similar in subject and structure, but without the longer
end-verse, may be treated here, as well as some odic stanzas
similar in structure (9–18 lines) and in theme, occurring in
earlier poets, as e.g. Sidney, Spenser, John Donne, Samuel Daniel,
Ben Jonson, Drummond, and Milton. In Modern English poetry
there are only some few examples of such stanzas to be met with
in translations of Italian canzones; e.g. in Leigh Hunt. The
schemes are as follows. Stanzas of nine lines, $a\,b\,a\,b_5\,b\,c_3\,c_5\,d_3\,D_5$
(Sidney, *Arcadia*, p. 388); of ten lines, $a\,a_3\,b_5\,b_3\,c_5\,c\,d\,d_3\,e\,e_5$
(Ben Jonson, *Ode to himself*, Poets, iv. 607); of eleven
lines, $a\,a_4\,b_3\,b_4\,c_3\,c_5\,D_3\,D_2\,E_3\,E_2\,d_5$ (ib. 611); of twelve lines,
$a_2\,b_5\,b_2\,a\,c\,c_5\,d\,d_3\,e_5\,f_3\,f_5\,e_2$ (ib. 572), $a_3\,a\,b_5\,b_3\,c\,c_5\,d_3\,d\,e_5\,e_3\,f\,f_5$
(Drummond, ib. 664); of thirteen lines,

> $a\,b_3\,a_5\,c\,b_3\,c_5\,c\,d\,e\,e_3\,d_5\,f_3\,f_5$ (Sidney, *Arcadia*, p. 394),

$a\,b_3\,c_5\,a\,b_3\,c_5\,c\,d\,e\,e_3\,d_5\,f_3\,f_5$ (S. Daniel, *The Pastoral*, Poets, iv.
225), agreeing in form with the eleventh of Petrarch's canzones,
Chiare, fresche e dolci acque, translated by Leigh Hunt (p. 394)
on the scheme, $a\,a_3\,b_5\,c\,c_3\,b_5\,b\,d\,d_3\,e_4\,e_5\,f_4\,f_5$; of fourteen lines,
$a\,b\,c\,b\,a\,c\,c_5\,d\,d_3\,c\,e_5\,f_3\,f_2\,e_3$ (Milton, *Upon the Circumcision*, ii.
408); of eighteen lines, $a\,b\,b\,a_5\,a_3\,c\,d\,c\,d_5\,d_3\,e\,e\,f\,e_5\,f\,f_3\,G\,G_5$
(Spenser, *Prothalamium*, p. 605). For examples of these
stanzas, partly formed on the model of the Italian canzones,
see *Metrik*, ii, §§ 512–15.

§ **303.** The English odic stanzas have been influenced too, although only in a general way, by the anisometrical structure of the Greek odes. This, however, was only to a slight extent the case in the so-called **Pindaric Odes**, as the metres usually employed in them were essentially the same, and retained in their composition the same anisometrical character exhibited by the odic stanzas considered in the preceding paragraphs.

There are, however, two groups of Pindaric Odes, viz. Regular and Irregular, and it is chiefly the latter group to which the preceding remark refers.

The irregular odes were possibly modelled on certain non-strophical poems or hymns, consisting of anisometrical verses throughout, with an entirely irregular system of rhymes. We have an example of them already in the poems of Donne, the inventor or imitator of some odic stanzas mentioned in the previous paragraph; it is in his poem *The Dissolution* (Poets, iv. 38) consisting of twenty-two rhyming verses of two to seven measures on the model

$$a_3\,b_4\,c_5\,d \sim_3 b_4\,a\,c_5\,d \sim_3 e_4\,e_5\,f_3\,f_5\,e_5\,g_4\,g_5\,h_3\,h_4\,i\,i_5\,k_3\,l_2\,l\,k_5\,k_7.$$

A similar form is found in Milton's poems *On Time* (ii. 411) and *At a Solemn Music* (ii. 412). Other examples taken from later poets are quoted in *Metrik*, ii, § 523. M. Arnold's poems *The Voice* (second half) (p. 36) and *Stagirius* (p. 38) likewise fall under this head.

To the combined influence of the earlier somewhat lengthy unstrophical odes on the one hand, and of the shorter, strophical ones also composed of anisometrical verses on the other, we have possibly to trace the particular odic form which was used by Cowley when he translated, or rather paraphrased, the Odes of Pindar. Owing to Cowley's popularity, this form came much into fashion afterwards through his numerous imitators, and it is much in vogue even at the present day.

The characteristic features of Cowley's free renderings and imitations of Pindar's odes are, in the first place, that he dealt very freely with the matter of his Greek original, giving only the general sense with arbitrary omissions and additions ; and, in the second place, he paid no attention to the characteristic strophic structure of the original, which is a system of stanzas recurring in the same order till the end of the poem, and consisting of two stanzas of identical form, the strophe and antistrophe, followed by a third, the epode, entirely differing from the two others in structure. In this respect Cowley did not even attempt to imitate the original poems, the metres of which were very imperfectly understood till long after his time.

Hence there is a very great difference between the originals and the English translations of Cowley, a difference which is clear even to the eye from the inequality of the number of stanzas and the number of verses in them.

§ 304. The first Nemean ode, e. g. consists of four equal parts, each one being formed of a strophe and antistrophe of seven lines, and of a four-lined epode; twelve stanzas in all. Cowley's translation, on the other hand, has only nine stanzas, each of an entirely different structure, their schemes being as follows:

  I. $a\,a_5\,b\,b_4\,c_3\,c\,d_6\,d_4\,e\,e_3\,e\,f_4\,f_5\,g_4\,g_5,$ 15 l.
  II. $a\,a_4\,b_3\,b_4\,b_5\,c_4\,c_3\,c_5\,d_4\,d_5\,e\,e_4\,f_3\,f_3\,e_5,$ 15 l.
  III. $a_5\,b_3\,b_4\,a\,a_5\,c_3\,c_4\,d\,e\,e_3\,d\,f{\sim}_4\,f{\sim}_6\,g_4\,g_5\,g_7,$ 16 l.
  IV. $a_5\,a\,b\,b_4\,b\,c\,c\,c_5\,d_3\,d_5\,e\,e_4\,e_6,$ 13 l.
  V. $a\,a\,b\,b\,c_5\,c_4\,c_5\,d_4\,e\,d_5\,e\,f\,f_4\,g_5\,g_6,$ 15 l.
  VI. $a\,a_5\,b_4\,b_5\,c_6\,d_5\,d_4\,c\,e\,f_5\,f_4\,f_5\,g_4\,g\,e\,h_5\,h_7,$ 17 l.
  VII. $a_5\,a_3\,b_5\,b_4\,b_5\,c_3\,c_6\,d_4\,e_3\,e_6\,d_5\,f\,f\,g_4\,g_7,$ 15 l.
  VIII. $a_2\,a\,b_5\,b_3\,c_4\,c_6\,d_5\,d\,e_4\,e_3\,f\,f_4\,g_6\,g\,h_4\,h_6,$ 16 l.
  IX. $a_4\,a_5\,b_4\,b\,c_6\,c\,d_4\,d_5\,d\,e_3\,e_6,$ 11 l.

Cowley's own original stanzas and those of his numerous imitators are of a similar irregular and arbitrary structure; cf. Cowley's ode *Brutus* (Poets, v. 303), which has the following stanzaic forms:

  I. $a_4\,a\,b_5\,b_4\,c\,c_5\,c_4\,c_5\,d_6\,d\,d_5\,d_4\,d_5\,d_6,$ 14 l.
  II. $a\,b\,a\,a\,b_5\,b_4\,c\,c\,d\,d_5\,d_3\,e_4\,e_5\,f_3\,g_3\,g_4\,f_6,$ 17 l.
  III. $a_3\,a_5\,b_4\,b_6\,c_5\,c\,d_4\,d\,d\,e\,e_5\,f\,f_4\,g{\sim}_5\,g{\sim}_6,$ 15 l.
  IV. $a\,a\,a_5\,b_3\,b_4\,a_5\,a\,a_4\,b_5\,c_4\,c\,d_5\,d_4\,e_6\,e_5\,f_4\,f_6,$ 17 l.
  V. $a\,b_5\,b_4\,a_6\,c_2\,c_5\,c_4\,a\,c_5\,c_6\,d\,d\,e_4\,e_5\,f_3\,f\,g\,g_5\,h\,h_4\,i\,i_5\,i_4,$ 23 l.

Waller's ode *Upon modern Critics* (Poets, v. 650) has the following stanzaic forms:

  I. $a\,b\,b_4\,a\,c_5\,c\,d_4\,d_5\,d_4\,e\,f_5\,f\,f_4\,e_5\,f_4\,g\,g\,h_5\,i_3\,i\,h\,k_5\,k_6,$ 23 l.
  II. $a\,a_4\,b_3\,b\,c\,c\,d_4\,d_5\,e\,f\,f\,g_4\,g_5\,e_3\,h\,i_4\,i_5\,h\,k\,k_4\,l\,l_5,$ 23 l.
  III. $a\,a\,b\,b\,c_4\,c_5\,d\,d\,e\,e\,f\,f_4\,e_3\,f\,e\,g_4\,h_5\,h\,g\,i_4\,i_6,$ 21 l.
  IV. $a\,b\,b\,a_4\,c\,c_5\,d_3\,d_4\,e_5\,d_4\,d\,f_5\,f_4\,g\,g_5\,h_4\,h_5\,i_4\,i_5,$ 19 l.
  V. $a\,a\,b\,b\,c_4\,d_5\,c_3\,d\,e_5\,e_6\,f_5\,f_4\,g_5\,g\,h\,h_4\,i_3\,i_6,$ 18 l.
  VI. $a_4\,b_3\,a\,b\,a\,c\,c\,d_4\,d_6\,e\,e_4\,f\,f\,g_5\,g_4\,g\,h_5\,h\,i_4\,i_6,$ 20 l.

All the stanzas are of unequal length and consist of the most

various verses (of three, four, mostly five, even six and seven
measures) and arrangements of rhymes. Parallel rhymes are
very common; but sometimes we have crossed, enclosing, and
other kinds of rhyme, as e. g. the system of the Italian *terzina*.
A characteristic feature is that at the end of the stanza very
often three parallel rhymes occur, and that, as a rule, the stanza
winds up with a somewhat longer line of six or seven measures,
as in the Spenserian and the Epithalamium stanza; but sometimes we also find a short final verse.

To these Irregular Pindaric Odes, besides, belong Dryden's
celebrated odes *Threnodia Augustalis* and *Alexander's Feast*, the
latter having a more lyrical form, with a short choral strophe
after each main stanza; and Pope's *Ode on St. Cecilia's Day*.
A long list of references to similar poems from Cowley to
Tennyson is given in *Metrik*, ii, §§ 516–22; amongst these
different forms the rhymeless odic stanzas occurring in Dr. Sayers
(*Dramatic Sketches*), Southey (e. g. *Thalaba*) and Shelley (*Queen
Mab*) are noticeable.

§ 305. To these Irregular Pindaric Odes strong opposition
was raised by the dramatist Congreve, who in a special *Discourse
on the Pindaric Ode* (Poets, vii. 509) proved that Pindar's odes
were by no means formed on the model of such an arbitrary
strophic structure as that of the so-called Pindaric Odes which
had hitherto been popular in English poetry. To refute this
false view he explained and emphasized their actual structure
(see § 303), which he imitated himself in his Pindaric Ode
addressed to the Queen, written soon after May 20, 1706, and
composed in anisometrical rhyming verses. He was mistaken,
however, in thinking that he was the first to make this attempt
in English. Nearly a hundred years before him, Ben Jonson
had imitated Pindar's odic form on exactly the same principles;
in his *Ode Pindaric* to the memory of Sir Lucius Carey and
Sir H. Morison (*Poets*, iv. 585) we have the strophe (*turn*),
antistrophe (*counter-turn*), and the epode (*stand*), recurring four
times (cf. *Metrik*, ii, § 525). Ben Jonson, however, found no
followers; so that his attempt had remained unknown even to
Congreve. The regular Pindaric Odes by this poet, on the
other hand, called forth a great many imitations of a similar
kind and structure. For this reason the first three stanzas of
Congreve's *Pindaric Ode* (Poets, vii. 570) may be quoted here
as an example, the scheme of the strophe and antistrophe being
$a\,a_5\,b_3\,c\,c_4\,b_5\,b_6$, that of the epode $a\,b\,a\,b_4\,c_5\,d_4\,c_3\,d_4\,e_4\,e\,f\,g_3\,g_4\,f_5$:

The Strophe.

Daughter of memory, immortal muse,
Calliope; what poet wilt thou choose,
   Of Anna's name to sing?
To whom wilt thou thy fire impart,
   Thy lyre, thy voice, and tuneful art;
Whom raise sublime on thy aethereal wing,
And consecrate with dews of thy Castalian spring?

The Antistrophe.

Without thy aid, the most aspiring mind
Must flag beneath, to narrow flights confin'd,
   Striving to rise in vain:
   Nor e'er can hope with equal lays
   To celebrate bright virtue's praise.
Thy aid obtain'd, ev'n I, the humblest swain,
May climb Pierian heights, and quit the lowly plain.

The Epode.

High in the starry orb is hung,
   And next Alcides' guardian arm,
That harp to which thy Orpheus sung
   Who woods, and rocks, and winds could charm;
That harp which on Cyllene's shady hill,
When first the vocal shell was found,
   With more than mortal skill
   Inventor Hermes taught to sound:
Hermes on bright Latona's son,
   By sweet persuasion won,
   The wondrous work bestow'd;
   Latona's son, to thine
   Indulgent, gave the gift divine;
A god the gift, a god th'invention show'd.

The most celebrated among the later Pindaric Odes formed on similar principles are Gray's odes *The Progress of Poesy* (Poets, x. 218) and *The Bard* (ib. 220). References to other odes are given in *Metrik*, ii, § 527.

In dramatic poetry M. Arnold attempted to imitate the structure of the different parts of the Chorus of Greek tragedy in his fragment *Antigone* (p. 211), and more strictly in his tragedy

Merope (p. 350). It would lead us too far, however, to give a detailed description of the strophic forms occurring there.

With regard to other lyrical pieces in masques and operas (also of an unequal-membered strophic structure) and with regard to cantata-stanzas and other stanzas differing among themselves, in other poems which cannot be further discussed here, we must refer the reader to §§ 528–31 of our larger work.

CHAPTER IX

THE SONNET

§ 306. **Origin of the English Sonnet.** In early Provençal and French poetry certain lyric poems are found which were called *Son*, sometimes *Sonet*, although they had neither a fixed extent, nor a regulated form. But the Sonnet[1] in its exact structure was introduced into French, Spanish, and English poetry from Italian, and as a rule on the model, or at least under the influence, of Petrarch's sonnets. In English literature, however, the sonnet in part had a more independent development than it had in other countries, and followed its Italian model at first only in the number and nature of the verses used in it. Generally speaking, the Italian and the English sonnet can be defined as a short poem, complete in itself, consisting of fourteen five-foot (or eleven-syllabled) iambic lines, in which a single theme, a thought or series of thoughts, is treated and brought to a conclusion. In the rhyme-arrangement and the structure of the poem, however, the English sonnet, as a rule, deviates greatly from its Italian model, and the examples in which its strict form is followed are comparatively rare.

§ 307. The Italian Sonnet consists of two parts distinguished from each other by difference of rhymes, each of the parts having its own continuous system of rhymes. The first part is formed of two quatrains (*basi*), i. e. stanzas of four lines; the second of two terzetti (*volte*), stanzas of three lines. The two quatrains have only two, the terzetti two or three rhymes.

The usual rhyme-arrangement in the quatrains is *a b b a a b b a*, more rarely *a b b a b a a b* (*rima chiusa*). There are, however, also sonnets with alternate rhymes, *a b a b a b a b* or *a b a b b a b a* (*rima alternata*); but the combination of the two kinds of rhyme, *a b a b b a a b* or *a b b a a b a b* (*rima mista*), was unusual. In the second part, consisting of six lines, the order of rhymes is not so definitely fixed. When only two rhymes are used, which the old metrists, as Quadrio (1695–1756), the Italian

---

[1] For titles of books and essays on the sonnet see *Englische Metrik*, ii, pp. 836–7 note; cf. also L. Bladene, 'Morfologia del Sonetto nei secoli XIII e XIV' (*Studi di Filologia Romanza*, fasc. 10).

critic and historian of literature, regarded as the only legitimate method, the usual sequence is *c d c d c d* (crossed rhymes, *rima alternata*). This form occurs 112 times in those of Petrarch's [1] sonnets which have only two rhymes in the last part, their number being 124; in the remaining twelve sonnets the rhyme-system is either *c d d c d c* or *c d d d c c*. In the second part of Petrarch's sonnets three rhymes are commoner than two. In most cases we have the formula *c d e c d e*, which occurs in 123 sonnets, while the scheme *c d e d c e* is met with only in 78 sonnets. The three chief forms, then, of Petrarch's sonnet may be given with Tomlinson [2] as built on the following models:

abba abba c d e c d e, abba abba c d c d c d,
abba abba c d e d c e.

In the seventy-second and seventy-fourth sonnet we have the unusual schemes *c d e e d c* and *c d e d e c*. The worst form, according to the Italian critics, was that which ended in a rhyming couplet. This kind of ending, as we shall see later on, is one of the chief characteristics of the specifically English form of the sonnet.

The original and oldest form of the sonnet, however, as recent inquiries seem to show, was that with crossed rhymes both in the quatrains and in the terzetti, on the scheme *a b a b a b a b c d c d c d*. But this variety had no direct influence on the true English form, in which a system of crossed rhymes took a different arrangement.

An essential point, then, in the Italian sonnet is the bipartition, the division of it into two chief parts; and this rule is so strictly observed that a carrying on of the sense, or the admission of *enjambement* between the two main parts, connecting the eighth and ninth verse of the poem by a run-on line, would be looked upon as a gross offence against the true structure and meaning of this poetic form. Nor would a run-on line be allowed between the first and the second stanza; indeed some poets, who follow the strict form of the sonnet, do not even admit *enjambement* between the first and the second terzetto, although for the second main part of the poem this has never become a fixed rule.

The logical import of the structure of the sonnet, as understood by the earlier theorists, especially Quadrio, is this: The

---

[1] Cf. *Étude sur Joachim du Bellay et son rôle dans la réforme de Ronsard*, par G. Plötz. Berlin, Herbig, 1874, p. 24.

[2] *The Sonnet: Its Origin, Structure and Place in Poetry*, London, 1874, 8°, p. 4.

first quatrain makes a statement; the second proves it; the first terzetto has to confirm it, and the second draws the conclusion of the whole.

§ **308.** The structure of this originally Italian poetic form may be illustrated by the following sonnet, equally correct in form and poetical in substance, in which Theodore Watts-Dunton sets forth the essence of this form of poetry itself:

THE SONNET'S VOICE.

A metrical lesson by the sea-shore.

Yon silvery billows breaking on the beach
   Fall back in foam beneath the star-shine clear,
   The while my rhymes are murmuring in your ear
   A restless lore like that the billows teach;
For on these sonnet-waves my soul would reach
   From its own depths, and rest within you, dear,
   As, through the billowy voices yearning here,
   Great nature strives to find a human speech.

A sonnet is a wave of melody:
   From heaving waters of the impassioned soul
   A billow of tidal music one and whole
Flows in the 'octave'; then, returning free,
   Its ebbing surges in the 'sestet' roll
   Back to the deeps of Life's tumultuous sea.

Although the run-on line between the terzetti is perhaps open to a slight objection, the rhyme-arrangement is absolutely correct, the inadmissible rhyming couplet at the end of the poem being of course avoided. Other sonnets on the sonnet written in English, German, or French, are quoted in *Metrik*, ii, § 534.

§ **309.** The first English sonnet-writers, Wyatt and Surrey, departed considerably from this strict Italian form, although they both translated sonnets written by Petrarch into English. Their chief deviation from this model is that, while retaining the two quatrains, they break up the second chief part of the sonnet, viz. the terzetti, into a third quatrain (with separate rhymes) and a rhyming couplet. Surrey went still further in the alteration of the original sonnet by changing the arrangement and the number of rhymes in the quatrains also, whereas Wyatt, as a rule, in this respect only exceptionally deviated from the structure of the Italian sonnet. The greater part of Wyatt's sonnets (as well as Donne's, cf. *Metrik*, ii, § 541) have therefore

the scheme *a b b a a b b a c d d c e e*, whereas other forms, as e. g.
a b b a a b b a c d c d e e, occur only occasionally (cf. *Metrik*, ii,
§ 535).

This order of rhymes, on the other hand, was frequently used
by Sir Philip Sidney, who on the whole followed the Italian
model, and sometimes employed even more accurate Italian
forms, avoiding the final rhyming couplet (cf. ib. § 538). He
also invented certain extended and curtailed sonnets which are
discussed in *Metrik*, ii, §§ 539, 540.

§ 310. Of greater importance is Surrey's transformation of the
Italian sonnet, according to the formula *a b a b c d c d e f e f g g*.
This variety of the sonnet—which, we may note in passing,
Surrey also extended into a special poetic form consisting of
several such quatrains together with a final rhyming couplet
(cf. *Metrik*, ii, § 537)—was very much in favour in the sixteenth
and at the beginning of the seventeenth century. Samuel
Daniel, and above all Shakespeare, wrote their sonnets mainly[1]
in this form, sometimes combining a series of them in a closely
connected cycle. As a specimen of this most important form
we quote the eighteenth of Shakespeare's sonnets:

> *Shall I compare thee to a summer's day ?*
> *Thou art more lovely and more temperate :*
> *Rough winds do shake the darling buds of May,*
> *And summer's lease hath all too short a date :*
> *Sometime too hot the eye of heaven shines,*
> *And often is his gold complexion dimm'd ;*
> *And every fair from fair sometime declines,*
> *By chance or nature's changing course untrimm'd ;*
> *But thy eternal summer shall not fade*
> *Nor lose possession of that fair thou ow'st ;*
> *Nor shall Death brag thou wander'st in his shade,*
> *When in eternal lines to time thou grow'st :*
> *So long as men can breathe or eyes can see,*
> *So long lives this, and this gives life to thee.*

Commonly the concluding couplet contains an independent
thought which gives a conclusion to the poem. In certain
cases, however, the thought of the previous stanza is carried on
in the closing couplet by means of a run-on line, as is the case
in Nos. 71, 72, 108, 154, &c. Sometimes, of course, a run-

---

[1] For certain other varieties occasionally used by these poets see
Metrik, §§ 536 and 544-5.

on line connects different portions of the sonnet also, as e. g. Nos. 114, 129, 154, &c. The rhymes, as a rule, are masculine, but not exclusively so.

§ 311. Meanwhile, another interesting form had been introduced, perhaps by the Scottish poet, Alex. Montgomerie,[1] which was subsequently chiefly used by Spenser. When about seventeen Spenser had translated the sonnets of the French poet, Du Bellay, in blank verse, and thereby created the rhymeless form of the sonnet, which, however, although not unknown in French poetry, was not further cultivated. About twenty years later he re-wrote the same sonnets in the form introduced by Surrey. Some years after he wrote a series of sonnets, called *Amoretti*, in that peculiar and very fine form which, although perhaps invented by Montgomerie, now bears Spenser's name. The three quatrains in this form of the sonnet are connected by *concatenatio*, the final verse of each quatrain rhyming with the first line of the next, while the closing couplet stands separate. The scheme of this form, then, is *abab bcbc cdcd ee*; it found, however, but few imitators (cf. *Metrik*, ii, §§ 542, 543, 559, note 1).

The various forms of Drummond of Hawthornden's sonnets had also no influence on the further development of this kind of poetry and therefore need not be discussed here. It may suffice to say that he partly imitated the strict Italian form, partly modified it ; and that he also used earlier English transformations and invented some new forms (cf. *Metrik*, ii, §§ 547, 548).

§ 312. A new and important period in the history of sonnet writing, although it was only of short duration, began with Milton. Not a single one of his eighteen English and five Italian sonnets is composed on the model of those by Surrey and Shakespeare or in any other genuine English form. He invariably used the Italian rhyme-arrangement *abba abba* in the quatrains, combined with the strict Italian order in the terzetti: *cdcdcd, cddcdc, cdecde, cdceed, cdedce*; only in one English and in three Italian sonnets we find the less correct Italian form with the final rhyming couplet on the schemes *cddcee, cdcdee.*

One chief rule, however, of the Italian sonnet, viz. the logical

---

[1] Cf. *Studien über A. M.*, von Oscar Hoffmann (Breslau Dissertation), Altenburg, 1894, p. 32 ; *Engl. Studien*, xx. 49 ff. ; and Rud. Brotanek, *Wiener Beiträge*, vol. iii, pp. 122-3.

separation of the two main parts by a break in the sense, is observed by Milton only in about half the number of his sonnets; and the above-mentioned relationship of the single parts of the sonnet to each other according to the strict Italian rule (cf. pp. 372–3 and *Metrik*, ii, § 533, pp. 839–40) is hardly ever met with in Milton. He therefore imitated the Italian sonnet only in its form, and paid no regard to the relationship of its single parts or to the distribution of the contents through the quatrains and terzets. In this respect he kept to the mono-strophic structure of the specifically English form of the sonnet, consisting, as a rule, of one continuous train of thought.

Milton also introduced into English poetry the playful variety of the so-called tail-sonnet on the Italian model (*Sonetti codati*), a sonnet, extended by six anisometrical verses, with the scheme $abba\ abba\ cdedec_5\ c_3ff_5f_3gg_5$ (cf. *Metrik*, ii, § 549), which, however, did not attract many imitators (Milton, ii. 481–2).

After Milton sonnet-writing was discontinued for about a century. The poets of the Restoration period and of the first half of the eighteenth century (Cowley, Waller, Dryden, Pope, Gay, Akenside, Young, Thomson, Goldsmith, Johnson, and others) did not write a single sonnet, and seem to have despised this form of poetry (cf. *Metrik*, ii, § 550).

§ 313. When sonnet-writing was revived in the second half of the eighteenth century by T. Edwards, who composed some fifty sonnets, by Gray, by Benjamin Stillingfleet, T. Warton, and others of less importance, as well as by Charlotte Smith, Helen M. Williams, Anna Seward, the male poets preferred the strict Italian form, while the poetesses, with the exception of Miss Seward, adopted that of Surrey and Shakespeare (cf. *Metrik*, ii, § 551).

Not long afterwards another very popular and prolific sonnet-writer, William Lisle Bowles, followed in some of his sonnets the strict Italian model (cf. *Metrik*, ii, § 552), but also wrote sonnets (towards the end of the eighteenth century) on a scheme that had previously been used by Drummond, viz. $abba\ cddc\ effegg$, this formula representing a transition form from the Italian to Surrey's sonnet, with enclosing rhymes in the quatrains instead of crossed rhymes (cf. *Metrik*, ii, § 546, p. 860).

Bowles's example induced S. T. Coleridge to write his sonnets, which in part combined in the quatrains enclosing and crossed rhyme ($abba\ cdcd\ efefgg$ or $abab\ cddc\ effe\ fe$; cf. *Metrik*, ii, § 553).

Similar, even more arbitrary forms and rhyme-arrangements,

the terzetti being sometimes placed at the beginning (e.g. No. 13, *a a b c c b d e d e f e f e*) of the poem, occur in Southey's sonnets, which, fine as they sometimes are in thought, have in their form hardly any resemblance to the original Italian model except that they contain fourteen lines. They had, however, like those of Drummond, no further influence, and therefore need not be discussed here (cf. *Metrik*, ii, § 554).

§ 314. A powerful impulse was given to sonnet-writing by Wordsworth, who wrote about 500 sonnets, and who, not least on account of his copiousness, has been called the English Petrarch. He, indeed, followed his Italian model more closely than his predecessors with regard to the form and the relationship of the different parts to each other.

The usual scheme of his quatrains is *a b b a, a b b a*, but there is also a form with a third rhyme *a b b a, a c c a*, which frequently occurs. The rhyme-arrangement of the terzetti is exceedingly various, and there are also a great many sub-species with regard to the structure of the first part. Very often the first quatrain has enclosing rhymes and the second crossed rhymes, or vice versa; these being either formed by two or three rhymes. As the main types of the Wordsworth sonnet the following, which, however, admit of many variations in the terzetti, may be mentioned: *a b b a b a b a c d e c e d* (ii. 303), *a b b a a b a b c d e e d c* (viii. 57), *a b a b b a a b c d c d c d* (vi. 113), *a b a b a b b a c d d c d c* (viii. 29), *a b b a a c a c d e e d e d* (vii. 82), *a b b a c a c a d e d e e d* (viii. 109) or *a b b a c a c a d e d e f f* (viii. 77), &c., *a b a b b c c b d e f e f d* (vii. 29). There are of this type also forms in which the terzetti have the structure *d d f e e f* (vii. 334), or *d e f d e f* (viii. 68), &c., and *a b a b a c a c d e d e d e* (viii. 28). Cf. *Metrik*, ii, § 555.

Very often Wordsworth's sonnets differ from those of the Italian poets and agree with the Miltonic type in that the two chief parts are not separated from each other by a pause[1]; and even if there is no run-on line the train of thought is continuous. For this reason his sonnets give us rather the impression of a picture or of a description than of a reflective poem following the Italian requirements, according to which the sonnet should consist of: assertion (quatrain i), proof (quatrain ii), confirmation (terzet i), conclusion (terzet ii) (cf. p. 373). The following sonnet by Wordsworth, strictly

[1] Cf. Wordsworth, *Prose Works*, ed. Grosart, 1876, vol. iii, p. 323, where he praises Milton for this peculiarity, showing thereby that he was influenced in his sonnet-writing by Milton.

on the Italian model in its rhyme-arrangement, may serve as an example:

> With Ships the sea was sprinkled far and nigh,
>   Like stars in heaven, and joyously it showed;
>   Some lying fast at anchor in the road,
>   Some veering up and down, one knew not why.
> A goodly Vessel did I then espy
>   Come like a giant from a haven broad;
>   And lustily along the bay she strode,
>   Her tackling rich, and of apparel high.
> This Ship was nought to me, nor I to her,
>   Yet I pursued her with a Lover's look;
>   This ship to all the rest did I prefer:
> When will she turn, and whither? She will brook
>   No tarrying; where She comes the winds must stir:
>   On went She, and due north her journey took.

Sonnets, however, like the following, entitled *A Parsonage in Oxfordshire* (vi. 292), give to a still greater extent the impression of monostrophic poems on account of the want of distinct separation between the component parts:

> Where holy ground begins, unhallowed ends,
>   Is marked by no distinguishable line;
>   The turf unites, the pathways intertwine;
>   And, wheresoe'er the stealing footstep tends,
> Garden, and that Domain where kindreds, friends,
>   And neighbours rest together, here confound
>   Their several features, mingled like the sound
>   Of many waters, or as evening blends
> With shady night. Soft airs, from shrub and flower,
>   Waft fragrant greetings to each silent grave;
>   And while those lofty poplars gently wave
> Their tops, between them comes and goes a sky
>   Bright as the glimpses of eternity,
>   To saints accorded in their mortal hour.

The strophic character of many sonnets is still more visible both in Wordsworth and some earlier poets (as e. g. Sidney or Shakespeare) when several consecutive sonnets on the same subject are so closely connected as to begin with the words *But* or *Nor*, as e. g. in Wordsworth's *Ecclesiastical Sonnets* (XI, XV, XVIII, XXIII); or when sonnets (cf. the same collection, No. XXXII) end like the Spenserian stanza in an Alexandrine. This peculiarity, which, of course, does not conform to the strict and harmonious structure of the sonnet, and is found as early as in a sonnet by Burns (p. 119), sometimes occurs in later poets also.[1]

Wordsworth has had an undoubtedly great influence on the further development of sonnet-writing, which is still extensively practised both in England and America.

§ 315. None of the numerous sonnet-writers of the nineteenth century, however, brought about a new epoch in this kind of poetry. They, as a rule, confined themselves to either one or other of the four chief forms noted above, viz. :

1. The specifically English form of Surrey and Shakespeare, used e. g. by Keats, S. T. Coleridge, Mrs. Hemans, C. Tennyson Turner, Mrs. Browning, M. Arnold (pp. 37, 38) (cf. *Metrik*, ii, § 566).

2. The Wordsworth sonnet, approaching to the Italian sonnet in its form or rather variety of forms; it occurs in S. T. Coleridge, Hartley Coleridge, Sara Coleridge, Byron, Mrs. Hemans, Lamb, Tennyson, D. G. Rossetti, M. Arnold (pp. 1–8) (cf. ib. §§ 561–2).

3. The Miltonic form, correct in its rhymes but not in the relationship of its different parts to one another, used by Keats, Byron, Aubrey de Vere, Lord Houghton, Mrs. Browning, Rossetti, Swinburne, and others (cf. ib. § 563).

4. The strict Italian form, as we find it in Keats, Byron, Leigh Hunt, Aubrey de Vere, Tennyson, Browning, Mrs. Browning, Austin Dobson, Rossetti, Swinburne, M. Arnold (pp. 179–85), and most poets of the modern school (cf. ib. §§ 564–5).

[1] On Wordsworth's Sonnets see the Note on the Wordsworthian Sonnet by Mr. T. Hutchinson, in his edition of *Poems in two volumes by William Wordsworth* (1807), London, 1897, vol. i, p. 208.

CHAPTER X

OTHER ITALIAN AND FRENCH POETICAL FORMS OF A FIXED CHARACTER

§ 316. THE **madrigal**, an Italian form (It. *mandriale, madrigale*, from *mandra* flock), is a pastoral song, a rural idyl. The Italian madrigals of Petrarch, &c., are short, isometrical poems of eleven-syllable verses, consisting of two or three terzetti with different rhymes and two or four other rhyming verses, mostly couplets: *a b c a b c d d, a b a b c b c c, a b b a c c d d, a b b c d d e e, a b b a c c c d d, a b a c b c d e d e, a b b c d d e e f f, a b b c d d e f f g g.*

The English madrigals found in Sidney and especially in Drummond resemble the Italian madrigals only in subject; in their form they differ widely from their models, as they consist of from fifteen to five lines and have the structure of canzone-stanzas of three- and five-foot verses. The stanzas run on an average from eight to twelve lines. As a specimen the twelfth madrigal of Drummond (*Poets*, iv. 644), according to the formula $a_3 a_5 b_3 a_5 b_3 b_5 c_5 c_3 d d_5$, may be quoted here:

> Trees happier far than I,
> Which have the grace to heave your heads so high,
> And overlook those plains :
> Grow till your branches kiss that lofty sky,
> Which her sweet self contains.
> There make her know mine endless love and pains,
> And how these tears which from mine eyes do fall,
> Help you to rise so tall :
> Tell her, as once I for her sake lov'd breath,
> So for her sake I now court ling'ring death.

Other madrigals have the following schemes (the first occurring twice in Sidney and once in Drummond, while the rest are found in Drummond only):
fifteen lines, $a_3 a_5 b_3 c_5 c_3 b_5 b_3 d_5 d_3 e e_5 d_3 e f f_5$; fourteen lines, $a a_3 a_5 b_3 c_5 b_3 c d_5 e e_3 d f_5 d_3 f_5$; thirteen lines, $a a_3 b_5 c c_3 b_5 c_3 d d_5 e_3 f e f_5$; twelve lines,

$a_2 b_5 b_3 a_5 c d_3 d c_5 c e_3 f f_5$; eleven lines, $a_3 b c a_5 b d_3 d e e f f_5$; ten lines, $a b_3 b a_5 a c b_3 c d d_5$; nine lines, $a_3 a_5 b c b_3 c c d d_5$; eight lines, $a_3 a_5 b b c_3 c d d_5$; seven lines, $a b a_3 c c_5 a_3 b_5$; six lines, $a b b a c_3 c_5$; five lines, $a b b_3 a b_5$. For specimens of these and other madrigals in Drummond cf. *Metrik*, ii, § 508.

§ **317.** Some poems in Drummond's and Sidney's works entitled epigrams consist, as a rule, of two or more five-foot verses, rhyming in couplets. In Sidney there are also short poems resembling these in subject, but consisting of one-rhymed Alexandrines. We have also one in R. Browning (iii. 146) of seven one-rhymed Septenary verses; several others occur in D. G. Rossetti (ii. 137–40) of eight lines on the schemes $a a_4 b b_4 a a_4 b b_4$ styled Chimes (cf. *Metrik*, ii, §§ 570, 571).

§ **318.** The **terza-rima.** Of much greater importance is another Italian form, viz. a continuous stanza of eleven-syllable verses, the terza-rima, the metre in which Dante wrote his *Divina Commedia*. It first appears in English poetry in Chaucer's *Complaint to his Lady*, second and third part,[1] but may be said to have been introduced into English literature by Wyatt, who wrote satires and penitential psalms in this form (Ald. ed. pp. 186–7, 209–34), and by Surrey in his *Description of the restless state of a Lover* (Ald. ed. p. 1). The rhyme-system of the terza-rima is $a b a b c b c d c$, &c. That is to say, the first and third lines of the first triplet rhyme together, while the middle line has a different rhyme which recurs in the first and third line of the second triplet; and in the same manner the first and third lines of each successive triplet rhyme with the middle line of the preceding one, so as to form a continuous chain of three-line stanzas of iambic five-foot verses till the end of the poem, which is formed by a single line added to the last stanza and rhyming with its second line.

The first stanzas of Surrey's poem may be quoted here:

> *The sun hath twice brought forth his tender green,*
> *Twice clad the earth in lively lustiness;*
> *Once have the winds the trees despoiled clean,*
>   *And once again begins their cruelness;*
> *Since I have hid under my breast the harm*
> *That never shall recover healthfulness.*

---

[1] See Chaucer's Works, edited by W. W. Skeat, *Minor Poems*, pp. 75–6, 310–11.

> *The winter's hurt recovers with the warm;*
> *The parched green restored is with shade;*
> *What warmth, alas! may serve for to disarm*
> *The frozen heart, that mine in flame hath made?*
> *What cold again is able to restore*
> *My fresh green years, &c., &c.*

The terza-rima has not the compact structure of the sonnet, as in each of its stanzas a rhyme is wanting which is only supplied in the following stanza. For this reason it seems to be especially adapted for epic or reflective poetry.

Comparatively few examples of this form are met with in English poetry, as e.g. in Sidney, S. Daniel, Drummond, Milton, and Shelley (cf. *Metrik*, ii, § 572).

In Sidney and R. Browning (iii. 102) we also find a variety of the terza-rima consisting of four-foot verses, and in Browning some others formed of four-stressed verses (iv. 288).

Some similar rhyme-systems of three lines, occurring in Sidney and Drummond, are of less importance (cf. ib., § 573).

§ 319. Certain other varieties of the terza-rima, although found in recent poets, need only be briefly noticed here.

One of four lines on the model $a\,a\,b\,a_5\ b\,b\,c\,b_5\ c\,c\,d\,c_5$, &c., occurs in Swinburne, *Poems*, ii. 32, 34, 239; another on the scheme $a\,a\,b\,a_5,\ c\,c\,b\,c_5,\ d\,d\,e\,d_5$, &c., ib. i. 13; a third one, following the formula $a\,b\,c_3\,b_2,\ a\,b\,c_3\,b_2,\ a\,b\,c_3\,b_2$, called *Triads*, ib. ii. 159 (cf. *Metrik*, ii, § 564).

Five-lined forms, similar to the terza-rima, occur in Sidney, e.g. $a\,b\,c\,d\,d,\ e\,f\,g\,h\,h,\ i\,k\,l\,m\,m$, the rhymeless lines being connected by sectional rhyme, the stanzas themselves likewise by sectional rhyme; another on the model $a_5\,b_3\,c_5\,c_3\,B_5,\ B_5\,d_3\,e_5\,e_3\,D_5,\ D_5\,f_3\,g_5\,g_3\,F_5$; and a third on the scheme $a_3\,a_5\,b\,c_3\,b_5,\ c_3\,c_5\,d\,e_3\,d_5,\ e_3\,e_5\,f\,g_3\,f_5$, &c. A related form, $a\,b\,a\,b\,c_4,\ c\,d\,c\,d\,e_4,\ldots y\,z\,y\,z\,z_4$, is found in Mrs. Browning (iv. 44). For specimen cf. *Metrik*, ii, § 575.

A terza-rima system of six lines may be better mentioned in this section than together with the sub-varieties of the sextain, as was done in *Metrik*, ii, § 578; they pretty often occur in Sidney, e.g. *Pansies*, ix (Grosart, i. 202), on the schemes $a\,b\,a\,b\,c\,b,\ c\,d\,c\,d\,e\,d,\ e\,f\,e\,f\,g\,f,\ v\,w\,v\,w\,x\,w,\ldots x\,y\,x\,y\,z\,y\,y$.

In Spenser's *Pastoral Aeglogue* on Sidney (pp. 506–7) a rhyme-system according to $a\,b\,c\,a\,b\,c_5,\ d\,b\,e\,d\,f\,e_5,\ g\,f\,h\,g\,i\,h_5$, $k\,i\,l\,k\,m\,l_5$, &c. is met with; in Mrs. Browning (iii. 236) a much

simpler system, constructed of five-foot lines on the formula
a b a b a b c d c d c d e f e f e f, &c., is used.

A system of ten lines, consisting of five-foot verses
(*a b a b b c a e d D, D e d e e f d f g G, G h g h h i g i k K*, &c., ending
in a stanza of four lines, *X y x y*) occurs in Sidney, pp. 218–
20 (221–4, xxxi); cf. *Metrik*, ii, § 580.

§ 320. Still less popular was another Italian poetical form,
the **sextain**, originally invented by the Provençal poet, Arnaut
Daniel, and for the first time reproduced in English poetry by
Sidney in his *Arcadia*.

The sextain consists of eleven-syllabled or rather five-foot
verses and has six stanzas of six lines each, and an envoy of
three lines in addition. Each of the six stanzas, considered
individually, is rhymeless, and so is the envoy. But the end-
words of the lines of each stanza from the second to the sixth
are identical with those of the lines in the preceding stanza,
but in a different order, viz. six, one, five, two, four, three. In
the envoy, the six end-words of the first stanza recur, in the same
order, alternately in the middle and at the end of the line.
Hence the whole system of rhymes (or rather of recurrence of end-
words) is as follows : *a b c d e f . f a e b d c . c f d a b e . e c b f a d .
d e a c f b . b d f e c a* + (*a*) *b* (*c*) *d* (*e*) *f*.

The first two stanzas of Sidney's *Agelastus Sestine*, pp. 438–9
(426–7, lxxiv), together with the envoy and with the end-words
of the other stanzas, may serve to make this clear :

> *Since wayling is a bud of causefull sorrow,*
> *Since sorrow is the follower of evill fortune,*
> *Since no evill fortune equals publike damage ;*
> *Now Prince's losse hath made our damage publike*
> *Sorrow, pay we to thee the rights of Nature,*
> *And inward griefe seale up with outward wayling.*

> *Why should we spare our voice from endlesse wayling*
> *Who iustly make our hearts the seate of sorrow,*
> *In such a case, where it appears that Nature*
> *Doth adde her force unto the sting of Fortune !*
> *Choosing, alas, this our theatre publike,*
> *Where they would leave trophees of cruell damage.*

The other stanzas have the corresponding rhyme-words in
this order :

III	IV	V	VI
damage	*Nature*	*publike*	*fortune*
wayling	*damage*	*nature*	*publike*
publike	*Fortune*	*sorrow*	*wayling*
sorrowe	*wayling*	*damage*	*nature*
fortune	*sorrowe*	*wayling*	*damage*
Nature	*publike*	*fortune*	*sorrow*

The envoy is:

> *Since sorrow, then, concludeth all our fortune,*
> *With all our deaths shew we this damage publique :*
> *His nature feares to dye, who lives still wayling.*

This strict form of the sextain, which in Sidney, pp. 216–17 (219–21, xxx), occurs even with a twofold rhyming system, but, of course, with only one envoy, has, as far as we know, only once been imitated in modern poetry, viz. by E. W. Gosse (*New Poems*). Cf. *Metrik*, ii, § 576.

§ 321. Besides this original form of the sextain several other varieties are met with in English poetry. Thus Spenser, in the eighth eclogue of his *Shepherd's Calendar* (pp. 471–2), has a sextain of a somewhat different structure, the rhymeless end-words being arranged in this order : $a\,b\,c\,d\,e\,f\,.\,f\,a\,b\,c\,d\,e\,.\,e\,f\,a\,b\,c\,d\,.\,d\,e\,f\,a\,b\,c\,.\,c\,d\,e\,f\,a\,b\,.\,b\,c\,d\,e\,f\,a + (a)\,b\,(c)\,d\,(e)\,f.$ Here the final word of the last verse of the first stanza, it is true, is also used as final word in the first verse of the second stanza, but the order of the final words of the other verses of the first stanza remains unchanged in the second. The same relation of the end-words exists between st. ii to st. iii, between st. iii to st. iv, &c., and lastly between st. vi and the envoy ; the envoy, again, has the end-words of the first stanza ; those which have their place in the interior of the verse occur at the end of the third measure.

Some other sub-varieties of the sextain have rhyming final words in each stanza.

In Sidney's *Arcadia*, p. 443 (430–1, lxxvi), e. g. one sextain has the following end-words : *light, treasure, might, pleasure, direction, affection.* These end-words recur in the following stanzas in the order of the regular sextain ; hence st. ii has *affection, light, direction, treasure, pleasure, might,* &c. In this variety, also, the rhyme-words of the envoy occur at a fixed place, viz. at the end of the second measure. Drummond wrote two sextains of the same elegant form.

In Swinburne also (*Poems*, ii. 46) we have a sextain of rhymed stanzas, the first stanza rhyming *day, night, way, light, may, delight.* All these recur in the following stanzas in a similar order, though not so strictly observed as in the sextain by Spenser, mentioned above (cf. *Metrik,* ii, § 577).

One example (probably unique in English poetry) of what is known as the *Double Sextain* is found in Swinburne's *The Complaint of Lisa* (Poems, ii. 60–8), a poem in which he has given one of the most brilliant specimens of his skill in rhyming. It consists of twelve twelve-lined stanzas and a six-lined envoy. The first two stanzas rhyme *a b c A B d C e f E D F, F a f D A C b e c E d B*; the envoy on the scheme

$$(F)\ E\ (e)\ f\ (C)\ A\ (c)\ d\ (b)\ a\ (D)\ B\ ;$$

where the corresponding capital and small letters denote different words rhyming with each other. Cf. *Metrik,* ii, § 581.

§ **322.** Side by side with these well-known poems of fixed form, mostly constructed on Italian models, there are some others influenced by French poetry which have been introduced into English for the most part by contemporary modern poets, as e. g. Swinburne, Austin Dobson, Robert Bridges, D. G. Rossetti, A. Lang, and E. W. Gosse[1]. These are the virelay, roundel, rondeau, triolet, villanelle, ballade, and chant royal. The **virelay** seems to have been in vogue in earlier English poetry. Chaucer, e.g. in his *Legende of good Women,* v. 423, says of himself that he had written *balades, roundels,* and *virelayes.* But only isolated specimens of it have been preserved; in more recent times it has not been imitated at all.

According to Lubarsch[2] the virelay consists of verses of unequal length, joined by *concatenatio* so as to form stanzas of nine lines on the scheme: *a a b a a b a a b, b b c b b c b b c, c c d c c d c c d,* &c.

Apart from this, however, there were undoubtedly other forms in existence (cf. Bartsch, *Chrestomathie de l'ancien français,* p. 413). Morris, in the Aldine edition of Chaucer's Works, vol. vi, p. 305, gives a virelay of two-foot iambic verses in six-lined stanzas on the model

a a a b a a a b, b b b c b b b c c c c d c c c d, &c.

(quoted *Metrik,* i, § 155).

§ **323.** The **roundel,** used by Eustache Deschamps, Charles d'Orléans, and others, was introduced into English poetry, it seems, by Chaucer. But there are only a few roundels of his in existence; one of these occurs in *The Assembly of Fowles*

---

[1] Cf. the essay by Gosse in *The Cornhill Magazine,* No. 211, July, 1877, pp. 53–71.

[2] *Französische Verslehre,* Berlin, 1879, p. 388.

(ll. 681–8); if the verses of the burden are repeated, as printed in the Globe Edition, pp. 638–9, it has thirteen lines (**a b b** *a b a b a b a b b* **a b b**, the thick types showing the refrain-verses):

> *Now welcom, somer, with thy sonne softe,*
> *That hast this wintres weders overshake*
> *And driven awey the longe nyghtes blake;*
>
> *Seynt Valentyn, that art ful hy on lofte,*
> *Thus syngen smale foules for thy sake:*
> *Now welcom, somer, with thy sonne softe,*
> *That hast this wintres weders overshake.*
>
> *Wel han they cause for to gladen ofte,*
> *Sith ech of hem recovered hath his make;*
> *Ful blisful mowe they ben when they awake.*
> *Now welcom, somer, with thy sonne softe,*
> *That hast this wintres weders overshake*
> *And driven awey the longe nyghtes blake.*

Three other roundels of Chaucer on the scheme last mentioned have been published lately by Skeat in *Chaucer's Minor Poems*, pp. 386–7; some other Middle English roundels were written by Hoccleve and Lydgate.

In French the roundel was not always confined to one particular metre, nor did it always consist of a fixed number of verses; the same may be said of the English roundels.

The essential condition of this form, as used by the French poets, was that two, three, or four verses forming a refrain must recur three times at fixed positions in a tripartite iso-metrical poem consisting mostly of thirteen or fourteen four- or five-foot verses. A common form of the French roundel consisted of fourteen octosyllabic verses on the model

a b b a a b a b a b b a a b.

Conforming to this scheme is a roundel by Lydgate [1]:

> *Rejoice ye reames of England and of Fraunce!*
> *A braunche that sprange oute of the floure de lys,*
> *Blode of seint Edward and [of] seint Lowys,*
> *God hath this day sent in governaunce.*

---

[1] Ritson's *Ancient Songs*, i. 128, written, it is true, in five-foot verses; the repetition of the two refrain-verses in the proper place, however, is not indicated in the edition, and a slight emendation of the text is also required by the sense, viz. *hath sprung* instead of *that sprang* in the last line.

> *God of nature hath yoven him suffisaunce*
> *Likly to atteyne to grete honure and pris.*
> *Rejoice ye reames of England and of Fraunce!*
> *A braunche hath sprung oute of the floure de lys.*
>
> *O hevenly blossome, o budde of all plesaunce,*
> *God graunt the grace for to ben als wise*
> *As was thi fader, by circumspect advise,*
> *Stable in vertue withoute variaunce.*
> *Rejoice ye reames of England and of Fraunce,*
> *A braunche hath sprung oute of the floure de lys.*

Another roundel of four-foot verses, by Lydgate (Ritson, i. 129), corresponds to **a b** *a b a b* **a b** *a b a b* **a b** (cf. *Metrik*, i, § 180); some other roundels, of a looser structure, consisting, seemingly, of ten lines, are quoted in the same place (cf. *Metrik*, ii, § 583).

A Modern English roundel of fourteen lines, constructed of three-foot verses, by Austin Dobson, has the scheme **a b** *a b b* **a a b** *a b a b* **a b** (quoted ib. § 583). The French roundel of thirteen lines may be looked upon as a preliminary form to the rondeau, which was developed from the roundel at the end of the fifteenth and the beginning of the sixteenth century.

§ 324. The **rondeau** is a poem consisting of thirteen lines of eight or ten syllables, or four or five measures. It has three stanzas of five, three, and five lines, rhyming on the scheme *a a b b a   a a b   a a b b a*. It has, moreover, a refrain which is formed by the first words of the first line, and recurs twice, viz. after the eighth and thirteenth verses, with which it is syntactically connected. Strictly speaking it therefore has fifteen lines, corresponding to the scheme *a a b b a   a a b + r   a a b b a + r*. The rondeau was much cultivated by the French poet, Clément Marot. It was introduced into English by Wyatt, from whom the rondeau *Complaint for True Love unrequited* (p. 23) may be quoted here:

> *What 'vaileth truth, or by it to take pain?*
> *To strive by steadfastness for to attain*
> *How to be just, and flee from doubleness?*
> *. Since all alike, where ruleth craftiness,*
> *Rewarded is both crafty, false, and plain.*

Soonest he speeds that most can lie and feign:
True meaning heart is had in high disdain,
Against deceit and cloaked doubleness,
                                    What 'vaileth truth?

Deceived is he by false and crafty train,
That means no guile, and faithful doth remain
Within the trap, without help or redress:
But for to love, lo, such a stern mistress,
Where cruelty dwells, alas, it were in vain.
                                    What 'vaileth truth?

This is the proper form of the rondeau. Other forms deviating from it are modelled on the schemes:

$$a\,a\,b\,b\,a\ \ b\,b\,a + r\ \ b\,b\,a\,a\,b + r\ \text{(Wyatt, p. 24)},$$
$$a\,a\,b\,b\,a + r\ \ c\,c\,b + r\ \ a\,a\,b\,b\,a + r\ \text{(ib. p. 26)},$$
$$a\,b\,b\,a\,a\,b + r\ \ a\,b\,b\,a + r\ \text{(D. G. Rossetti, i. 179)}.$$

Austin Dobson, Robert Bridges, and Theo. Marzials strictly follow the form quoted above.

Another form of the rondeau entirely deviating from the above is found in Swinburne, *A Century of Roundels*,[1] where he combines verses of the most varied length and rhythm on the scheme $A\,B\,A + b\ B\,A\,B\ A\,B\,A + b$, where b denotes part of a verse, rhyming with the second, but repeated from the beginning of the first verse and consisting of one or several words (cf. *Metrik*, ii, §§ 584, 585).

§ 325. The triolet and the villanelle are unusual forms occurring only in modern poets, e. g. Dobson and Gosse.

The **triolet**, found as early as in Adenet-le-Roi at the beginning of the thirteenth century, is a short poem of eight mostly octosyllabic verses, rhyming according to the formula **a** b *a a a b* **a b**, the first verse recurring as a refrain in the fourth, the first and second together in the seventh and eighth place. Two specimens have been quoted, *Metrik*, ii, § 586.

§ 326. The **villanelle** (a peasant song, rustic ditty, from *villanus*) was cultivated by Jean Passerat (1534–1602); in modern poetry by Th. de Banville, L. Baulmier, &c. It mostly consists of octosyllabic verses divided into five stanzas (sometimes a larger or smaller number) of three lines plus a final stanza of four lines, the whole corresponding to the scheme

---

[1] London, Chatto & Windus, 1833.

$a^1 b a^2 + a b a^1 + a b a^2 + a b a^1 + a b a^2 + a b a^1 a^2$. Hence the first and the third verses of the first stanza are used alternately as a refrain to form the last verse of the following stanzas, while in the last stanza both verses are used in this way. A villanelle by Gosse on this model consisting of eight stanzas, perhaps the only specimen in English literature, has been quoted, *Metrik*, ii, § 587.

§ 327. The **ballade** is a poetical form consisting of somewhat longer stanzas all having the same rhymes. Several varieties of it existed in Old French poetry. The two most usual forms are that with octosyllabic and that with decasyllabic lines. The first form is composed of three stanzas of eight lines on the model *a b a b b c b C* (cf. § 269). The rhymes in each stanza agree with those of the corresponding lines in the two others, the last line, which is identical in all the three, forming the refrain; this refrain-verse recurs also at the end of the *envoi*, which corresponds in its structure to the second half of the main stanza, according to the formula *b c b C*. The decasyllabic form has three stanzas of ten verses on the scheme *a b a b b c c d c D* (cf. § 271), and an *envoi* of five verses on the scheme *c c d c D*; the same rules holding good in all other respects as in the eight-lined form. It is further to be observed that the *envoi* began, as a rule, with one of the words *Prince*, *Princesse*, *Reine*, *Roi*, *Sire*, either because the poem was addressed to some personage of royal or princely rank, or because, originally, this address referred to the poet who had been crowned as 'king' in the last poetical contest.

In England also the ballade had become known as early as in the fourteenth century. We have a collection of ballades composed in the French language by Gower,[1] consisting of stanzas of either eight or seven (*rhyme royal*) decasyllabic verses with the same rhyme throughout the poem. Similar to the French are Chaucer's English ballades in his Minor Poems, which, however, in so far differ from the regular form, that the *envoi* consists of five, six, or seven lines; in some of the poems even there is no *envoi* at all. Accurate reproductions of the Old French ballade are not found again until recent times. There are examples by Austin Dobson and especially by Swinburne (*A Midsummer Holiday*, London, 1884). They occur in both forms, constructed as well of four- and five-foot iambic, as of

---

[1] *The Works of John Gower*, ed. G. C. Macaulay, Oxford, 1899, vol. i, pp. 335 ff.

six-, seven-, or eight-foot trochaic or of five- and seven-foot
iambic-anapaestic verses. (For specimens cf. *Metrik*, ii, § 588.)

§ 328. The **Chant Royal** is an extended ballade of five
ten-lined ballade-stanzas (of the second form mentioned above),
instead of three, together with an *envoi*. In Clément Marot we
meet with another form of five eleven-line stanzas of decasyllabic verses also with the same rhymes throughout; the
envoi having five lines. The scheme is *a b a b c c d d e d E* in
the stanzas and *d d e d E* in the *envoi*.

A Chant Royal by Gosse, composed on this difficult model
(perhaps the only specimen to be found in English poetry), is
quoted *Metrik*, ii, § 589.

A more detailed discussion of these French poetical forms
of a fixed character and of others not imitated in English
poetry may be found in Kastner's *History of French Versification* (Oxford, at the Clarendon Press, 1903), chapter x. Cf.
also Edmund Stengel, *Romanische Verslehre*, in Gröber's *Grundriss der Romanischen Philologie* (Strassburg, 1893), vol. ii,
pp. 87 ff.

OXFORD : HORACE HART M.A.
PRINTER TO THE UNIVERSITY